Money Laundering
A New International Law En

C000126695

This book gives a broad analysi
tional fight against money laur
tive research of the criminal and preventive law aspects from an
international perspective. Guy Stessens portrays money laundering as a
new criminal trend threatening both national and international societies which must be addressed multilaterally through banking practice,
international conventions, and human rights.

Most of this volume is devoted to specific legal problems that spring
from the international nature of the money laundering phenomenon.
It contains the most detailed overview yet published on the rules and
practices of international co-operation in the fight against money laundering. The publication gives a thorough examination of the exchange
of information, lifting banking secrecy, and seizing and confiscating
assets, as well as the jurisdictional questions that inevitably arise in
this context. The result is a rich and detailed study of international and
comparative law.

Dr Guy Stessens has been working at the Law Department of the
University of Antwerp (www.uia.ua.ac.be) from October 1992. His
research is focused on international and national criminal law and he
also teaches international and European human rights protection. He
has published widely in these fields in international legal periodicals
such as the *International and Comparative Law Quarterly* and the *European
Law Review*, especially on topics of economic criminal law and of international co-operation in criminal matters. He is also the co-editor of
*International Criminal Law: A Collection of International and European
Instruments*. Guy Stessens has given papers at many international con-
gresses and universities. He is also counsel with the law firm of
Dauginet & Co in Antwerp (www.dauginet.com).

CAMBRIDGE STUDIES IN INTERNATIONAL AND COMPARATIVE LAW

This series (established in 1946 by Professors Gutteridge, Hersch Lauterpacht and McNair) is a forum for studies of high quality in the fields of public and private international law and comparative law. Although these are distinct sub-disciplines, developments since 1946 confirm their interrelation. Comparative law is increasingly used as a tool in the making of law at national, regional and international levels. Private international law is now often affected by international conventions, and the issues faced by classical conflicts rules are frequently dealt with by substantive harmonisation of law under international auspices. Mixed international arbitrations, especially those involving state economic activity, raise mixed questions of public and private international law, while in many fields (such as the protection of human rights and democratic standards, investment guarantees, and international criminal law) international and national systems interact. National constitutional arrangements relating to 'foreign affairs', and to the implementation of international norms, are a focus of attention.

Professor Sir Robert Jennings edited the series from 1981. Following his retirement as General Editor, an editorial board has been created and Cambridge University Press has recommitted itself to the series, affirming its broad scope.

The Board welcomes works of a theoretical or interdisciplinary character, and those focusing on new approaches to international or comparative law or conflicts of law. Studies of particular institutions or problems are equally welcome, as are translations of the best work published in other languages.

A list of books in the series can be found at the end of this volume

Money Laundering
A New International Law Enforcement Model

Guy Stessens
University of Antwerp

CAMBRIDGE
UNIVERSITY PRESS

CAMBRIDGE UNIVERSITY PRESS
Cambridge, New York, Melbourne, Madrid, Cape Town, Singapore, São Paulo

Cambridge University Press
The Edinburgh Building, Cambridge CB2 8RU, UK

Published in the United States of America by Cambridge University Press, New York

www.cambridge.org
Information on this title: www.cambridge.org/9780521781046

First published 2000
Third printing 2002
This digitally printed version 2008

A catalogue record for this publication is available from the British Library

Library of Congress Cataloguing in Publication data

Stessens, Guy.
  Money laundering: a new international law enforcement model / Guy
Stessens.
      p.   cm. – (Cambridge studies in international and comparative law)
      ISBN 0 521 78104 3 (hb)
   1. Money laundering.   2. Money – Law and legislation – Criminal provisions.
3. International cooperation.   I. Title.   II. Series.

K1089.S74 2000 341.7′7–dc21   99-056427

ISBN 978-0-521-78104-6 hardback
ISBN 978-0-521-05074-6 paperback

To my parents

Contents

Preface

At the beginning of the millennium, the fight against money laundering features very high on the international, and in many countries, also on the domestic, political agenda. The speed with which norm-makers have put in place a set of legal rules designed to fight the laundering of the proceeds, first from drug trafficking, and, later on, of the proceeds from many other criminal activities as well, is impressive. There is of course more than one explanation for the high level of attention the subject of money laundering is receiving. The vigorousness with which authorities beat the drum of the fight against money laundering should of course be set against the backdrop of the widespread concern about the phenomenon of organized crime, and in particular organized drug trafficking, and may in part also be attributable to international pressure. At the same time, however, the eagerness of legislators to adopt rules to combat money laundering also betrays an implicit, though (apparently very) strong, belief in the effectiveness of these rules. The anti-money laundering regulations are apparently looked upon as a very powerful instrument against various forms of acquisitive crime.

It is the burden of this book to investigate whether the set of legal rules that have been put in place on an international and domestic level to curb money laundering can indeed make an effective contribution to the fight against money laundering and, if these rules prove to be unsatisfactory, how deficiencies can be remedied. The book aims to provide an extensive discussion of the legal framework for money laundering and the main legal problems that may arise in the implementation of these rules. The chief aim of this book is therefore to probe into, on the one hand, the legal impediments that may hinder the fight against money laundering and, on the other hand, the legal adaptations that are required to make the fight against money laundering effective. Although the emphasis is thus clearly put on the goal of fighting crime, the due process perspective also receives attention. The exceptional procedures that have been elaborated to make the profit-oriented approach to criminal justice effective in this context inevitably evoke questions about the protection of individual rights. This study has been undertaken from an international and comparative viewpoint. Given the international nature of the phenomenon of money laundering, any effective solution has necessarily to be devised and implemented on an international level. The international approach is apparent in two ways: first, the various legal rules designed to fight money laundering are studied from an international and comparative angle and, second, an important part of the book is devoted to the legal measures that may further curb international money laundering operations. Both strands of this international approach also necessitate a comparative law perspective. For it is impracticable to study the international set of rules that have been created to fight money laundering without studying domestic implementation legislations as well. Also, the study of legal mechanisms to fight international money laundering operations – be they unilateral extra-territorial measures, or be they international co-operative mechanisms – by essence implies a comparative perspective: these mechanisms do not operate in an 'international legal vacuum', but take effect through domestic legal systems. For practical reasons, the number of legal systems that could be studied in this comparative approach was of course limited. Apart from that of the author's own country, Belgium, the following countries' legal systems were taken into account: The Netherlands, Luxembourg, Switzerland, the United Kingdom and the United States of America. The United States and Switzerland's approach to money laundering were studied in detail because many of the rules on money laundering originated in either of both of these countries. Switzerland and Luxembourg were also selected because of their stringent rules on banking secrecy. England and Wales and The Netherlands were selected in view of their detailed legislation, both substantive and procedural, on confiscation and on the repression and prevention of money laundering.

The book starts by describing the wider context which spawned the fight against money laundering. Notwithstanding the high 'popularity' of anti-money laundering regulation, there is often little clarity about the social, economic and legal background of the fight against money laundering and even less about the goals of this fight. An essential knowledge of these contextual elements is, however, an absolute prerequisite to a thorough understanding of the problem of money laundering and its legal aspects. Thus, a grasp of the profit-oriented criminal justice model, which is aimed at depriving offenders of their ill-gotten gains rather than at depriving them of their liberty, is essential to a full understanding of the goal of anti-money laundering rules. Part I further contains an analysis of the two main instruments of the criminal law in the curbing of acquisitive crime: the confiscation of illegally derived proceeds and the criminalisation of money laundering.

Part II charts the preventive legislation on money laundering. The discussion of these rules is centred on the three principal activators in the implementation of money laundering. First, the obligations of financial and other institutions that are prone to be misused for the purposes of money laundering are set out in detail. Second, the role of the financial intelligence authorities, that is the authorities that receive information from financial institutions on suspicious transactions and that are in general responsible for combating money laundering, is explained. Third, attention is paid to the role of the authorities that supervise financial institutions.

Parts III and IV are both devoted to a study of the problems that are posed by the need to combat money laundering on an international level. The third part deals with jurisdictional problems that are likely to arise in the context of the international fight against money laundering. It contains a theoretical analysis, based on comparative research, of the jurisdictional questions that are bound to arise in the context of many prosecutions of international money laundering operations.

Part IV aims to give a comprehensive coverage of the international measures that can be taken to tackle money laundering schemes that take place in the territory of more than one state and therefore by their very nature defy the territorial limitations of the range of actions available to governmental authorities. This problem of the territorially limited range of national law enforcement authorities can in essence be solved in two ways: either by resorting to unilateral measures which are intended to have an extra-territorial effect or by having recourse to co-operative mechanisms whereby the territorially competent state is asked to take certain measures on behalf of another state. In the context of the international fight against money laundering, this problem presents itself mainly in three different forms. The first problem with which law enforcement authorities are confronted is that of getting access to information located in foreign countries where they have, as a matter of principle, no authority to act. In the context of the fight against money laundering, this international law problem is compounded by the fact that the information sought after is often covered by domestic banking secrecy rules. The various legal mechanisms that are deployed to obtain access to this information are therefore scrutinised. Another major problem is that of taking provisional measures relating to property located abroad. The third stumbling block for an effective international approach to the phenomenon of money laundering is the confiscation of property located abroad and, related to that, the problem of asset sharing, that is the sharing of assets between states or authorities that have collaborated in depriving the offender of his illegally derived proceeds.

This book is the English-language version of my Ph.D. thesis, which I defended at the University of Antwerp in 1997. I undertook myself the daunting task of translating my Dutch-language dissertation into English. This gave me an opportunity at the same time to adapt a doctoral dissertation into a book aimed at a wide international audience from diverse legal cultures and from equally diverse professional backgrounds. It is my sincere hope that the reader who comes to this book will in it find what he is looking for. It was, however, not my purpose – and, given the wide variety of national legal rules on the topic, it would at any rate have been impossible – to provide the reader with detailed information on domestic law. On the contrary, the book is intended to provide the reader with a breadth of perspective that he would not have if he were to confine his attention to his own legal system or to the professional sector in which he is active. Of course, this does not alter the fact that the study which I undertook is inherently limited to a number of countries and that interesting legal mechanisms that exist in other legal systems have not been analysed. I am equally well aware of the fact the all the legal systems that have been studied, save that of the United States, are European. This does not spring from some form of Eurocentric attitude, but from the simple fact that it is very difficult for linguistic, logistical and many other reasons, to study non-Western legal systems. In addition, it is a simple matter of fact that most international legal instruments relating to money laundering have largely been inspired by legal rules incepted in the Western legal culture, especially in the United States and Switzerland.

In adapting and translating my dissertation, I have also been able to incorporate into the text recent developments relating to the international combat of money laundering. The effective date of completion of my study is therefore 30 June 1999.

In writing this book, I have enjoyed the support of many people. I will not venture to thank them all individually here, lest I forget some. I would nevertheless like to express my gratitude to those to whom I owe special thanks. In the first place, I would like to express my deepest gratitude to

Professor Christine Van den Wyngaert who was the supervisor of my thesis and with whom I have been working at the University of Antwerp, for over six years now. I have been truly privileged, not only to have had the benefit of her enormous expertise in the field of international criminal law, but also to have had her constant encouragement and support. Furthermore, I also wish to thank the other members of my doctoral jury: Professor Herman Braeckmans of the University of Antwerp, Professor Alain De Nauw of the Free University of Brussels, Professor Luc Huybrechts, Judge in the Belgian Supreme Court, Professor Julian Schutte, Director at the European Council and Professor Bert Swart of the University of Amsterdam (formerly of the University of Utrecht).

Last, but not least, I wish to express my profound gratitude to my parents, without whose constant encouragement this book would never have been finished.

Table of treaties and agreements

Abbreviations

CCE	Continued Criminal Enterprise
CDB	Convention relative à l'obligation de diligence des banques (1992 version, unless specified otherwise)
CJA	Criminal Justice Act
CJ(IC)A	Criminal Justice (International Co-operation) Act (C(IC)A)
CMLR	*Common Market Law Review*
Co.L	*The Company Lawyer*
Col.LRev.	*Columbia Law Review*
Colum.JTransnat'l L	*Columbia Journal of Transnational Law*
Crim.App.R	*Criminal Appeal Reports*
Crim.LRev.	*Criminal Law Review*
DD	*Delikt en Delinkwent*
DEA	Drug Enforcement Agency
Denv.JInt'l L & Pol'y	*Denver Journal of International Law and Policy*
Dick.J.Int'l.L	*Dickinson Journal of International Law*
DPCI	*Droit et Pratique du Commerce International*
DTA	Drug Trafficking Act
DTOA	Drug Trafficking Offences Act
Duke LJ	*Duke Law Journal*
ECCP	European Committee on Crime Problems (Council of Europe)
ECHR	European Convention on Human Rights
ECLR	*European Competition Law Review*
ELR	*European Law Review*
Emory Int'l LRev.	*Emory International Law Review*
ETS	*European Treaty Series*
EuGRZ	*Europäische Grundrechte Zeitschrift*
Eur.JCr., Cr.L & Cr.J	*European Journal of Crime, Criminal Law and Criminal Justice*
FATF	Financial Action Task Force on Money Laundering
FATF-I	First report of the Financial Action Task Force on Money Laundering, containing 40 recommendations (1990)
FATF-II	Second report of the Financial Action Task Force on Money Laundering (1991)
FATF-III	Third report of the Financial Action Task Force on Money Laundering (1992)

FATF-IV	Fourth report of the Financial Action Task Force on Money Laundering (1993)
FATF-V	Fifth report of the Financial Action Task Force on Money Laundering (1994)
FATF-VI	Sixth report of the Financial Action Task Force on Money Laundering (1995)
FATF-VII	Seventh report of the Financial Action Task Force on Money Laundering (1996)
FATF-VIII	Eighth report of the Financial Action Task Force on Money Laundering (1997)
FATF-IX	Ninth report of the Financial Action Task Force on Money Laundering (1998)
FATF-X	Tenth report of the Financial Action Task Force on Money Laundering (1999)
Fordham L.Rev.	*Fordham Law Review*
FRD	*Federal Rules Decisions*
Geo.Wash.JInt'l L & Econ.	*The George Washington Journal of International Law and Economics*
Harv.Int'l LJ	*Harvard International Law Journal*
Harv.LRev.	*Harvard Law Review*
HKLR	*Hong Kong Law Review*
Houston JIL	*Houston Journal of International Law*
HRLJ	*Human Rights Law Journal*
ICCPR	International Covenant on Civil and Political Rights
ICLQ	*International and Comparative Law Quarterly*
ILM	*International Legal Materials*
IML	Institut Monétair Luxembourgeois
Int'l L Enf. R	*International Law Enforcement Reporter*
Int'l Law.	*The International Lawyer*
IRS	Internal Revenue Service
J.Bus.L	*Journal of Comparative Business and Capital Market Law*
JCr.L	*Journal of Criminal Law*
JCr.L&Crim.	*The Journal of Criminal Law and Criminology*
J.Comp.Bus. & Cap. Market L	*Journal of Business Law*
JDF	*Journal de droit fiscal*
JDI	*Journal de droit international*
JIBL	*Journal of International Banking Law*

Journ.Proc.	Journal de Procès
JT	Journal des Tribunaux (Belgium)
JT(suisse)	Journal des Tribunaux IV (Switzerland)
Law QRev.	Law Quarterly Review
Lloyd's Mar. & Com.LQ	Lloyd's Maritime and Commercial Law Quarterly
MLAT	Mutual Legal Assistance Treaty
MLR	Modern Law Review
NJ	Nederlandse Jurisprudentie
NJB	Nederlands Juristenblad
NJW	Neue Juristen Wochenschrift
NLJ	New Law Journal
Nova LRev.	Nova Law Review
Nw.JInt'l.L & Bus.	Northwestern Journal of International Law & Business
Nw.ULRev.	Northwestern University Law Review
NYLSch.JInt'l & Comp.L	New York Law School Journal of International and Comparative Law
NYUJ Int'l L. & Comp.L.	New York University Journal of International and Comparative Law
NYUJInt'l L & Pol.	New York University Journal of International Law and Politics
Ohio NUL Rev.	Ohio Northern University Law Review
OJ	Official Journal of the European Communities
PACE	Police and Criminal Evidence Act 1984
Pan.	Panopticon
Parl. St.	Parlementaire Stukken
Pas.	Pasicrisie
PCA	Proceeds of Crime Act
Publ. ECHR	Publications of the European Court on Human Rights
RDP	Revue de Droit Pénal et de Criminologie
Rec.Cours	Receuil des Cours de l'Académie de droit international
Report US Delegation	Report of the United States Delegation to the United Nations Conference for the adoption of a Convention Against Illicit Traffic in Narcotic Drugs and Psychotropic Substances, reprinted in W. C. Gilmore, International Efforts To Combat Money Laundering (Cambridge: Grotius Publications Limited, 1992), p. 98.
Restatement (Second)	Restatement of The Law (Second). The Foreign Relations Law of the United States. As Adopted and Promulgated by The American Law Institute

	at Washington D.C., St. Paul., Minn., American Law Institute Publishers, 1962.
Restatement (Third)	Restatement of The Law (Third). The Foreign Relations Law of the United States. As Adopted and Promulgated by The American Law Institute at Washington D.C., May 14, 1986, St. Paul., Minn., American Law Institute Publishers.
Rev.Crit.DIP	Revue critique de droit international privé
Rev.int. de crim. et de pol.techn.	Revue internationale de criminologie et de police technique
Rev.sc.crim	Revue des sciences criminelles
RICO	Racketeer Influenced and Corrupt Organisations Act
RIDP	Revue Internationale de Droit Pénal
RIPC	Revue Internationale de Police Criminelle
RMC	Revue du Marché Commun et de l'Union européenne
RPS	Revue pénale suisse
RSC	Revue des Sciences Criminelles et de Droit Comparé
RSDA	Revue Suisse de Droit des Affaires
RTDH	Revue Trimestrielle des Droits de l'Homme
RW	Rechtskundig Weekblad
SEC	Securities and Exchange Commission
SFO	Serious Fraud Office
SJ	Solicitor's Journal
Stanford JInt'l L	Stanford Journal of International Law
Tex.Int'l LJ	Texas International Law Journal
TVVS	Tijdschrift voor venootschappen, verenigingen en stichtingen
UNTS	United Nations Treaties Series
U.Pa.J.Int.Bus.L.	University of Pennsylvania Journal of International Business Law
Va.L.Rev.	Virginia Law Review
Vand.J.Transnat'l L.	Vanderbilt Journal of Transnational Law
WLR	Weekly Law Reports
Yale LJ	Yale Law Journal
Z.St.W.	Zeitschrift für die gesammte Strafrechtswissenschaften

PART I · NEW INSTRUMENTS IN THE FIGHT AGAINST ACQUISITIVE CRIME: CONFISCATION OF PROCEEDS FROM CRIME AND CRIMINALISATION OF MONEY LAUNDERING

1 The background of the fight against money laundering

The fight against money laundering aims at a more effective enforcement of the criminal law in relation to profit-oriented crime. This chapter seeks to clarify the background of this fight. It will be shown that the introduction of the two main legal devices that are used in the fight against money laundering, the confiscation of the proceeds from crime and the incrimination of money laundering, are closely linked to changes that occurred on a legal and a socio-economic level. These criminal law instruments have, however, created a momentum of their own. The most important example of how the fight against money laundering has separated itself from the background that gave rise to it is the drastic expansion of the application field of the confiscation of the proceeds from crime and the incrimination of money laundering itself. Whereas the scope of these instruments was originally limited to drug offences or offences related to organised crime, it has now been drastically expanded to cover other, if not all, types of offences. In addition, the international fight against money laundering also signifies an evolution of the norm-making process in the field of law enforcement law.

Legal background

Pecunia non olet,[1] money does not stink. For a long time this seems to have been the prevailing attitude of most criminal justice systems and, in a sense, of most societies in general, towards proceeds from crime. Until quite recently, most criminal justice systems – implicitly if not explicitly – allowed offenders to enjoy the fruits of their crimes. This attitude should be set against the backdrop of the type of offences that criminal courts

---

[1] Statement attributed to Emperor Vespasianus on raising taxes on public toilets (*Concise Oxford Dictionary of Quotations*, Oxford, 1986, 262).

traditionally had to deal with. When an offence had resulted in damages of any kind, the victim of the offence would most probably institute civil proceedings which would normally result in the restitution of any ill-gotten gains. Some criminal justice systems (e.g. those of Belgium and France) even allow the victim (the *partie civile*) to institute civil claims in the course of the criminal proceedings.

In the post-Second World War era, however, legislators increasingly started to make criminal acts which often did not cause any direct harm to an identifiable victim. A great number of commercial, fiscal or environmental offences are crimes without a victim. Even though this type of offence normally does not result in any direct damage to a victim, this does not mean that offenders do not reap any benefits from these crimes. On the contrary, this type of offence often generates huge profits for whose removal the law generally fails to provide adequate legal mechanisms.

Given the absence of identifiable victims, the only legal instrument which could ensure that offenders were deprived of their illegal profits was the confiscation of the proceeds of crime. Whereas the majority of criminal justice systems were familiar with the more traditional forms of confiscation, namely, the confiscation – often known as forfeiture – of the instruments (*instrumentum sceleris*) or the subject of crime (*objectum sceleris*), most of these systems did not provide for the confiscation of proceeds from crime (*producta/fructa sceleris*). This gap in the law often became painfully clear in the course of criminal proceedings against drug traffickers, for example in the English case of *R. v. Cuthbertson* (1981),[2] where criminal courts had to acknowledge their lack of competence to take away the profits from crime.

In other countries, such as Belgium,[3] where the confiscation of proceeds from crime was provided for in respect of drug offences, this possibility did not extend to other offences. In those countries whose legislation provided for the confiscation of proceeds from crime (e.g. Switzerland and The Netherlands), it was perceived that the provisions concerned did not in practice result in an effective deprivation of the proceeds from crime.[4]

---

[2] [1981] AC 470. In this case the court had to acknowledge that section 27(1) of the Misuse of Drugs Act 1971 only allowed for instruments of crime to be forfeited, and did not extend to profits from drug trafficking.

[3] See the decision of the Belgian Supreme Court of 4 July 1986 (*RDP* (1986), 910) based on Article 4, para. 6 of the Belgian Drug Offences Act of 24 February 1921.

[4] For The Netherlands see L. F. Keyser-Rignalda, *Boef en buit. De ontneming van wederrechtelijk verkregen vermogen* (Arnhem: Gouda Quint, 1994), p. 10. As far as Switzerland is concerned, see C. K. Graber, *Geldwäscherei. Ein Kommentar zu Art.305bis und 305ter StGB* (Berne: Verlag Stämpfli, 1990), p. 95.

One of the first countries to take legislative action in order to fill this gap, was England. Following one of the main recommendations of the *Hodgson Committee*,[5] Parliament empowered courts to confiscate the proceeds of drug trafficking through the Drug Trafficking Offences Act 1986 (DTOA 1986) later replaced by the Drug Trafficking Act 1994 (DTA 1994).

Urged on by the international initiatives that were taken in this respect at the end of the 1980s (the 1988 UN Convention against Illicit Traffic in Narcotic and Psychotropic Substances[6] and the 1990 Council of Europe Convention on Laundering, Search, Seizure and Confiscation of the Proceeds from Crime[7]), other countries soon followed suit. Thus the Belgian law of confiscation was changed in 1990,[8] Dutch law in 1992[9] while the Luxembourg[10] and Swiss parliaments amended their legislation in respect of confiscation in 1994.[11]

Criminals who, through their criminal activities, dispose of huge amounts of money, need to give this money a legitimate appearance: they need to 'launder' it. The phenomenon of money laundering is essentially aimed at two goals: preventing 'dirty money' from serving the crimes that generated it, and ensuring that the money can be used without any danger of confiscation. The interest of law enforcement authorities in detecting the link between an offender and the proceeds of the crimes he has allegedly committed, is consequently also twofold: detecting the crimes that were committed in order to bring the alleged perpetrators to trial, and identifying the proceeds from crime so that they can be confiscated.[12]

It is useful to point out that most forms of money laundering eventually

---

[5] On the establishment and the functioning of this committee, named after its president, Justice Hodgson, and on its recommendations see A. R. Mitchell, M. G. Hinton and S. M. E. Taylor, *Confiscation* (London: Sweet & Maxwell, 1992), p. xii and D. McClean, *International Judicial Assistance* (Oxford: Clarendon Press, 1992), p. 203 *et seq.*

[6] Vienna, 20 December 1988, *ILM* (1989), 493.

[7] Strasbourg, 8 November 1990, *ETS*, No. 141.

[8] Act of 17 July 1990, amending Articles 42, 43 and 505 of the Belgian Criminal Code. See G. Stessens, *De nationale en internationale bestrijding van het witwassen van geld. Onderzoek naar een meer effectieve bestrijding van de profijtgerichte criminaliteit* (Antwerp: Intersentia, 1997), p. 5.

[9] Act of 10 December 1992, amending Article 36e of the Dutch Criminal Code. See Keyser-Rignalda, *Boef en Buit*, p. 83.

[10] Act of 13 June 1994, amending Articles 31 and 32 of the Luxembourg Criminal Code. See D. Spielmann, 'La confiscation en droit luxembourgeois à l'aube de la réforme du Code pénal', *Ann.Dr.Louv.* (1995), 202–207.

[11] See Act of 14 March 1994, amending Articles 58 and 59 of the Swiss Criminal Code. See N. Schmid, 'Das neue Einziehungsrecht nach StGB Art.58ff.', *RPS* (1995), 322.

[12] See E. Nadelmann, 'Unlaundering Dirty Money Abroad: US Foreign Policy and Financial Secrecy Jurisdictions', *Inter-American L R* (1986), 34.

result in the injection of 'dirty money' into the legal economy. To attain this goal, the co-operation of third persons is necessary. Irrespective of the specificities of the various domestic legislations in this field, the criminalisation of money laundering – which will be discussed later[13] – can be generally defined as a criminalisation aimed at disrupting the co-operation provided by third persons in hiding the proceeds from crime and giving those proceeds a legitimate appearance.

Social-economic background: organised crime and drug offences

The need to confiscate the proceeds from crime and to fight money laundering has nowhere been more prominent than in the context of organised crime, and even more specifically, of organised drug trafficking. As was stated in the Note of the Secretary-General of the United Nations on organised crime: 'The connection between organized crime and illicit drug trafficking has changed both the panorama of organised crime and the way criminal justice seems to react to this phenomenon'.[14]

Organised crime

Though already known in the United States in the 1920s (and maybe even earlier), organised crime has developed enormously in the second half of the twentieth century, and especially in later decades. There have been numerous attempts to define organised crime, but most definitions are criminological. Given the complex and varied nature of the phenomenon of organised crime, it has proved very difficult to elaborate a precise legal definition.[15] Legal definitions of organised crime often function as a kind of password for the use of far-reaching investigative powers or, on an international level, for relaxing the conditions for international co-operation in criminal matters. Thus the American–Swiss Mutual Assistance Treaty

---

[13] See *infra* pp. 82–129.

[14] Secretary-General of the UN, *Note: Strengthening Existing International Co-operation in Crime Prevention and Criminal Justice, including Technical Co-operation in Developing Countries, with Special Emphasis on Combating Organized Crime. Addendum: Money Laundering and Associated Issues: the Need for International Co-operation* (Vienna: UN, 1992), E/CN.15/1992/4/ Add.5, p. 3. On the link between organised crime, drug trafficking and money laundering, see also L. Krauskopf, 'Geldwäscherei und organisiertes Verbrechen als europäische Herausforderung', *RPS* (1991), 386–7.

[15] See in general on this problem: C. L. Blakesley, 'The Criminal Justice System Facing The Challenge of Organised Crime. Section II: The Special Part', *RIDP* (1998), 73–6.

(1973)[16] and the EU Convention on Extradition (1996)[17] remove some of the obstacles (notably the requirement of double incrimination) if the request for co-operation concerns organised crime.

Whereas legal definitions often comprise an enumeration of criteria for organised crime,[18] criminological definitions tend to underline the danger for society emanating from organised crime. It is impossible to give an overview of all definitions that have been given, but most of them have a number of common denominators. Many definitions emphasise the fact that organised crime activities essentially take place in the context of a group. A good example is the definition given by the United Nations in 1992 of an organised crime group as 'a relatively large group of continuous and controlled criminal entities that carry out crimes for profit and seek to create a system of protection against social control by illegal means such as violence, intimidation, corruption and large-scale theft'.[19] The organised character of this type of crime is also prominent in other definitions.[20]

Another discerning feature of organised crime is the generation of huge profits. The definition of organised crime given by Interpol's first symposium on the subject, correctly pinpoints this as the main objective of organised crime.[21] The enormous turnover realised by organised crime can be explained by various factors, but two of the most important aspects are the following. First, organised crime groups are involved in a crime in

[16] Article 6 of the Treaty on Mutual Assistance in Criminal Matters Between the United States and Switzerland, 25 May 1973, *ILM* (1973), 916 (entered into force on 23 January 1977). See A. Ellis and R. L. Pisani, 'The United States Treaties on Mutual Assistance in Criminal Matters', in *International Criminal Law*, ed. M. C. Bassiouni (New York: Transnational Publishers, 1986), pp. 168–9.

[17] See Article 3 of the Convention relating to extradition between the Member States of the European Union, drawn up by the Council Act of 27 September 1996 (*OJ* C 313, 23.10.1996, p. 11).

[18] See P. Bernasconi, 'La criminalité organisée et d'affaires internationale', in *Changes in Society, Crime and Criminal Justice in Europe: A Challenge for Criminological Education and Research, Volume II: International Organized and Corporate Crime*, C. Fijnaut, J. Goethals, T. Peters and L. Walgrave (Antwerp: Kluwer, 1995), p. 6; M. Pieth, '"Das zweite Paket gegen das Organisierte Verbrechen", die Überlegungen des Gesetzgebers', *RPS* (1995), 228; H. Vest, '"Organisiertes Kriminalität" – Überlegungen zur Kriminalpolitischen Instrumentalisierung eines Begriffs', *RPS* (1994), 125 *et seq.*

[19] *Practical Measures Against Organized Crime, Formulated by the International Seminar on Organized Crime*, held at Suzdal, Russian Federation, From 21 to 25 October 1991, Annex II to Ecosoc Resolution 1992/23 of 30 July 1992 concerning organised crime. For a very similar definition, see resolution 1 of the International Association of Penal Law (*AIDP*), Section I of the XVIth Congress (Budapest, 1999), *RIDP* (1999), 895.

[20] See, e.g., the definition given by Bernasconi, 'La criminalité organisée', 2–5.

[21] Cited by Blakesley, 'The Criminal Justice System', 73.

a structural way in order to make profits. Second, the thrust of their activities is in providing illegal goods and services. Illegal goods and services are often much more expensive than legal goods, especially because the monopoly position of providers of illegal goods and services allows them to make predatory profits. This is not only the case for drug trafficking, but also for arms trafficking, the illegal trade of human organs, child prostitution, etc.

The enormous financial profits from organised crime explain some of the most striking features of organised crime. The egregiously corruptive power of these profits provides organised crime groups with political and economic leverage.[22] The influence organised crime may yield on politicians, civil servants and law enforcement authorities can eventually result in a declining belief in two of the most fundamental pillars of modern society: the rule of law and democratic government. The economic consequences of organised crime can scarcely be gauged. Some of the calculations that have been made regarding the turnover of organised crime will be discussed later,[23] but the economic consequences of organised crime go much further than the profits of organised crime. Given the fact that organised crime does not operate along the rules that apply to the market, organised criminals are often able to outpace their legal competitors. Because of their illegal character, the economic activities of organised criminals tend to escape any kind of government control (tax law, administrative law, etc.).

Apart from its political and economic effects,[24] the sheer amount of profits made by organised crime also accounts for the pressing need to launder these profits. The relatively small profits realised by traditional crime could in most cases easily be consumed or invested in the legal economy without attracting any attention from law enforcement, fiscal or other authorities. This is not possible any more with regard to the enormous gains from organised crime. Without sophisticated money laundering operations, which give these gains an apparently legitimate origin, the amount of profits of organised crime would in itself be an indication of their illegal origin. As was stated by the former American Attorney-General Edwin A. Meese in 1985 in the House of Representatives: 'Money laundering is the life blood of the drug syndicate and traditional organised crime'.[25]

---

[22] Bernasconi, 'La Criminalité organisée', 2.   [23] See *infra* pp. 87–9.

[24] See in general V. Tanzi, *Money laundering and the international financial system*, IMF Working Paper No 96/55, 14p. and P. J. Quirk, *Macroeconomic implications of money laundering*, IMF Working Paper No 96/66, 33p.

[25] Cited by P. Bernasconi, 'Geldwäscherei und organisierte Kriminalität', in *Finanzunterwelt. Gegen Wirtschaftskriminalität und organisiertes Verbrechen* (Zürich: Verlag Orell-Füssli, 1988), p. 26.

In addition, the increasing globalisation and diversification of organised crime makes it necessary for organised crime groups, just as for legal enterprises, to engage in active financial management. The ability to use legal savings and investing instruments (often through financial institutions) inevitably requires money laundering operations. The need for organised crime groups to manage their cash flow becomes especially pressing from the moment organised crime groups start to make profits which they do not need to reinvest in their criminal activities.

Given the intrinsic link between organised crime and money laundering, the incrimination of money laundering itself should be considered as a new tool, or even a new strategy in the fight against organised crime. As the classic criminal law concepts of complicity and of *association de malfaiteurs*[26] were often inadequate to fight organised crime groups, some jurisdictions chose to establish membership of an organised crime group[27] as an offence, or as an aggravating circumstance, in addition to the common law offence of conspiracy which was already in existence.[28] Irrespective of the practical effects of this type of legislation, it can only result in convictions of members of organised crime groups. In most cases it does not fundamentally affect the structure and the illegal activities of these groups as such, as the activities of imprisoned members are carried on by others. Taking into account the low conviction rate and the lucrative nature of organised crime, the deterrent effect of classic sanctions consisting of deprivation of liberty was generally estimated as being very low, although some have argued that this thesis has never been proven with regard to mafia-type organisations because American law enforcement authorities have never consistently targeted them.[29]

Because the classic tools of the criminal law were perceived to have failed in the fight against organised crime, legislators – with those from the United States in the front rank – considered the confiscation of the proceeds of crime and the incrimination of money laundering as new, more effective tools for tackling the problem of organised crime. These instruments are part of a new strategy against organised crime which is aimed at the structures of organised crime, rather than at deterring individuals from taking part in organised crime. This strategy is directed

[26] Illegal association, see, e.g., Article 322 of the Belgian Criminal Code and Article 450 of the New French Criminal Code.

[27] See, e.g., Article 416bis of the Italian Criminal Code (*associazione per delinquere e di tipo mafioso*), Article 260ter of the Swiss Penal Code and Article 324bis of the Belgian Criminal Code.

[28] On these different legislative approaches towards organised crime, see Blakesley, 'The Criminal Justice System', 73–80.

[29] D. J. Fried, 'Rationalizing Criminal Forfeiture', *J.Cr.L & Crim.* (1988), 367–72.

at the crucial function of organised crime: making money. By taking away the proceeds from crime and by making it more difficult to launder its proceeds, law enforcement authorities not only take away the incentive for organised crime, but, more importantly, seek to disrupt the functioning of organised crime itself. Organised crime groups depend on cash and assets to function just as much as their legitimate counterparts do.

Drug offences

The production, trafficking and consumption of narcotic and psychotropic drugs are one of the biggest problems faced by contemporary society, both on a domestic and an international level. Already at the beginning of the twentieth century, international initiatives were being taken to control the use of drugs. Between 1912 and 1972 no less than 12 multilateral conventions were adopted with regard to the regulation of drugs,[30] submitting the production and selling of drugs to state control and restricting its use to certain, mostly medical, purposes. The 1961 UN Single Drug Convention, supplemented by the 1972 Protocol, consolidated most of the preceding conventions. The 1971 UN Convention on Psychotropic Substances[31] complemented this by establishing an international regulation of chemical and pharmaceutical drugs.[32]

The main purpose behind this international regulation system of drugs was to limit the supply of drugs, and thereby to limit the use of drugs and the drug problem in general. The enormous social dimensions of the drug problem in many countries have, however, undermined this strategy. Whereas drugs were originally seen as an almost exclusively medical problem of drug users, the scope of the production, use and trafficking of drugs is nowadays of such a nature that drugs have come to be seen as a problem for society as a whole. Various factors account for this. In drug producing countries, it is sometimes hard to underestimate the economic and political clout of drug traffickers. In this respect, the terms 'narco-democracies' and 'narco-cracies' have even been coined to denote the

---

[30] For an overview of these conventions, see M. C. Bassiouni, 'Critical Reflections on International and National Control of Drugs', *Denv.JInt'l L & Pol'y* (1990), 312–3, footnote 3. See also S. Glaser, *Droit Pénal International Conventionnel* (Brussels: Bruylant, 1970), pp. 133–39 and P. Stewart, 'Internationalising The War on Drugs: The UN Convention Against Illicit Traffic in Narcotic Drugs and Psychotropic Substances', *Denv.JInt'l L & Pol'y* (1990), 388–90.   [31] Vienna, 21 February 1971, *ILM* (1971), 261.

[32] For an explanation as to the lack of an international regulation system regarding chemical and pharmaceutical drugs up till that date see Bassiouni, 'Critical Reflections on Control of Drugs', 314.

influence of drug trafficking.[33] In addition, drug trafficking is often connected to other criminal phenomena, such as corruption and terrorism.
All these factors resulted in an increasing awareness for policy makers
that drugs cannot be curbed simply by attacking the supply and demand
side but also in a third way, by attacking drug trafficking. It was hoped
that by attacking drug trafficking, law enforcement authorities would be
able to cut the link between the supply and the demand side. Given the
huge scale of organised drug trafficking, this fight was directed against
the profits of drug trafficking. The legal tools used in this respect are the
confiscation of proceeds from crime and the criminalisation of money
laundering. The introduction of these two instruments in the legislation
of the United States and that of many other countries was initially closely
linked to the fight against drug trafficking. The fight against money
laundering was not just a new strategy in the fight against crime, but also
in the fight against drug trafficking.

This changing awareness with respect to the drug problem was also
reflected in the nature of the relevant international conventions. The
early drug conventions were basically concerned with the administrative
regulation of the production and transport of drugs, but there were no
enforcement conventions. The penal provisions featuring in those early
conventions were aimed at supporting the administrative regulation
established by these conventions. The 1988 UN Convention Against Illicit
Traffic In Narcotic Drugs and Psychotropic Substances was in effect the
first convention to emphasise the law enforcement aspects of the fight
against drugs.[34]

Expansion of the application field to other offences

Although the introduction of the confiscation of the proceeds of crime
and the criminalisation of money laundering was part of a new criminal
justice strategy aimed at fighting organised crime and, even more specifically, drug trafficking, in many domestic laws the application field of
these legal tools has now been drastically expanded. Whereas the criminalisation of money laundering was originally often limited to proceeds
from drug trafficking, many legislators have now broadened its application field to the proceeds from many offences (not limited to organised
crime), or even all offences. This means that the group of 'predicate

---

[33] E. A. Nadelmann, *Cops Across Borders. The Internationalization of US Criminal Law Enforcement*
(Pennsylvania: The Pennsylvania State University Press, 1993), pp. 251–312, especially p.
271.   [34] McClean, *International Judicial Assistance*, pp. 172–4.

offences' (*infraction principale, Katalogstraftat, hoofdmisdrijf*), that is, the original offence that generated the proceeds in the first place, is not limited any more to drug offences. The confiscation of the proceeds of crime and the criminalisation of money laundering have undergone a profound evolution in this respect: from instruments designed to fight organised crime, they have now become general law enforcement tools that can be used in almost any case. They have in a sense inaugurated a new criminal justice policy, which is oriented towards the financial profits from crime. This new policy strives to curb crime by taking away the profits of crime, rather than by punishing the individuals who have allegedly committed the crimes. Various factors contribute to an explanation of this evolution.

A first factor relates to the phenomenon of organised crime. Although drug trafficking is the best known type of organised crime, it is not the only activity of organised crime groups. On the contrary, it has become increasingly clear that organised crime has diversified its activities, so that its profits are not exclusively derived from drug offences. Legislators, and for that matter lawyers in general, have grappled for a long time with the concept of organised crime without being able to come up with a precise definition capable of encompassing any form of organised crime. Lest any type of organised crime should fall outside the scope of the criminalisation of money laundering, many legislators have broadened the application field of this criminalisation to all serious offences or even to all offences.

This broadening is also a consequence of the fact that many profitable forms of crime – such as arms trafficking, environmental crime, illegal trade in cultural property etc.– are now high on the international political agenda.[35] This is connected to the geo-political argument: whereas the fight against drug trafficking is especially promoted by the western world, notably by the United States, many African and Asian countries are more interested in fighting the laundering of flight capital. This helps to explain why the provisions of the Commonwealth Scheme on Mutual Assistance in Criminal Matters regarding mutual assistance in the field of proceeds of crime also extend to offences other than drug offences.[36]

A third impulse for this evolution has come from the phenomenon of money laundering itself. Bernasconi has astutely pointed out that money

[35] W. C. Gilmore, 'International Initiatives', in *Butterworths International Guide to Money Laundering Law and Practice*, ed. R. Parlour (London: Butterworths, 1995), p. 15.
[36] Harare, July 1986, amended at the Commonwealth Law Ministers Meeting, Christchurch, New Zealand, 23–27 April 1990. See B. Rider, 'Launderers and Whistle-Blowers', *Co.L.* (1992), 202.

laundering constitutes the Achilles' heel of organised crime, as it forces organised crime groups to co-operate with the institutions from the legal economy.[37] Because money laundering operations often require a highly technical know-how and access to legal businesses and institutions such as banks, members of organised crime sometimes call on established businessmen to launder their ill-gotten gains. In this way the money laundering phenomenon is able to spread from organised crime to the legitimate business world and may provoke other economic crimes on behalf of certain businessmen.[38] This constitutes an example of the corruptive influence of organised crime. It would therefore be contradictory if only the laundering of proceeds from organised crime were punishable and the laundering of the proceeds from related criminal activities (e.g. corruption or swindling) were not punishable. In order to take away not only the proceeds from the organised crime groups, but also from the businessmen – the launderers, who have become accomplices of the criminals – it is sometimes necessary to expand the application field of the confiscation of proceeds from crime and the criminalisation of money laundering. In this context it is also interesting to learn that the investigation of criminal groups and of the laundering of their ill-gotten gains are often two quite distinct investigation targets.[39]

A fourth argument in favour of an expansion of the range of predicate offences touches on the efficacy of the fight against money laundering. The original limitation of the application field of the incrimination of money laundering to drug offences, or to the most serious predicate offences, was often justified by an economic argument, namely that law enforcement authorities and the courts have neither the time nor the means to investigate all types of money laundering with regard to the proceeds of any kind of predicate offence. Regardless of the veracity of this statement, it is not certain whether this should automatically lead to a limited application field. Even if one conceives the criminalisation of money laundering as a tool to be used exclusively for the purpose of fighting organised crime, a limitation of the application field to predicate offences connected with drug trafficking could give rise to practical difficulties. Not only would the laundering of the proceeds of some organised

---

[37] Bernasconi, 'La Criminalité organisée', 7–8 and 'Geldwäscherei und organisierte Kriminalität', 28–9.

[38] See L. Paoli, 'The Banco Ambrosiano Case: an Investigation Into the Underestimation of the Relations between Organised and Economic Crime', *Crime, Law & Social Change* (1995), 345–65 and especially 349–51.

[39] United Nations Office for Drug Control and Crime Prevention, *Financial Havens, Banking Secrecy and Money-Laundering* (New York: United Nations, 1998), 12.

crime activities obviously stay immune, but the limitation could also create problems of an evidential nature. Often the proceeds of various activities of organised crime groups are intermingled, with the result that the proceeds from drug trafficking cannot be separated from other proceeds, or cannot even be calculated.[40] In order to avoid this, the application field of the incrimination of money laundering should include as many predicate offences as possible. Here we come to the heart of the matter: regardless of the criminal policy that law enforcement authorities choose to adopt with respect to money laundering, legislation should sanction any kind of money laundering and permit confiscation of the proceeds of any kind of crime. The limitation of confiscation and money laundering legislation is likely to hamper the efficacy of law enforcement actions. A limitation of the application field of a money laundering incrimination to some predicate offences is prone to cause technical legal difficulties which may impede the fight against money laundering.[41] Thus defendants may argue that, although they suspected that the proceeds were criminally sourced, they thought that the proceeds were derived from an offence falling outside the scope of predicate offences covered by the incrimination. On an international level, the variety of the domestic money laundering laws relating to the range of predicate offences may hamper international co-operation for lack of double criminality.[42]

Finally, it may be pointed out that a limitation of the application field of the incrimination of money laundering to drug related predicate offences also runs into a moral objection: from an ethical point of view it is hard to understand why the laundering of drug proceeds should be criminalised and not the laundering of, say the proceeds of environmental offences. On a macro-political level, as long as some criminal funds (notably those stemming from tax evasion) may be 'laundered' legally, some (offshore) financial centres will be able to argue that their financial infrastructure which allows them to hide funds, has a legitimate purpose.[43]

Transformations of the norm-making process

The development of a set of norms designed to tackle money laundering and, more generally, to result in a more effective punishment of acquisi-

---

[40] See Recommendation 18 of the Aruba Report of FATF and Secretary-General of the UN, *Note: Strengthening Existing International Co-operation*, 18.

[41] See *infra* pp. 117–21.   [42] See *infra* pp. 289–92.

[43] United Nations Office for Drug Control and Crime Prevention, *Financial Havens, Banking Secrecy and Money Laundering*, 66.

tive crime, has brought about a number of transformations that pertain to the way the law itself is shaped. The thesis which will be expounded in the following pages is that the fight against money laundering is significative of two very important evolutions in the norm-making process, namely the influence of soft law and the international impetus for the creation of anti-money laundering law. Some of the effects of these transformations of the legislative process will be illustrated with respect to the European Money Laundering Directive. These evolutions are especially notable as they take place in field of law enforcement, traditionally considered the exclusive 'playground' of national courts and parliaments.

The influence of soft law

Notwithstanding the prerogatives of parliaments to criminalise acts of money laundering, the fight against money laundering has been deeply influenced by a number of so-called 'soft' law instruments. The term 'soft law' refers to the lack of justiciability of the instruments in which the rules are enshrined (instrumentum), rather than to the content of the rules themselves (negotium).[44]

An important factor which explains the role of soft law in the fight against money laundering, is the aversion to government interference financial institutions have often displayed. In some countries, money laundering was initially fought, not through legislative measures, but via codes of conduct (see, e.g., Switzerland[45]) or by regulatory measures issued by banking supervisors. The content of a number of initiatives to curb money laundering was thus highly influenced by the financial sector itself. Although this did not prevent parliament from taking action, as was in effect done in many countries later on, the influence of these initiatives on subsequent legislation has in some cases been very clear. Although the practice of involving financial institutions themselves in the drafting of the regulations with which they have to comply has been subjected to criticism by some,[46] others look upon it as a useful practice, because the persuasive force of a rule is often more important than its binding nature.[47] This view has also been espoused by the UN Commission on Crime Prevention and Criminal Justice:

---

[44] G. Abi-Saab, 'Eloge du "droit assourdi". Quelques réflexions sur le rôle de la *soft law* en droit international contemporain', in *Nouveaux itinéraires en droit. Hommage à François Rigaux* (Brussels: Bruylant, 1993) pp. 62–3.   [45] See *infra* pp. 101–3.

[46] See, e.g., B. Rider, 'Cosmetics or Surgery – Fraud in the City', Co.L (1992), 162.

[47] M. Elvinger, 'Libres propos sur l'utilité d'un code de bonne conduite en matière bancaire', in *Droit Bancaire et financier au Grand-Duché de Luxembourg* (Brussels: Larcier, 1994), I, p. 598.

It could be said that policies and strategies against the laundering of the proceeds of crime should have as one of their prime objectives the creation of an atmosphere of consensus regarding the measures to be devised and implemented. The financial institutions should be parties to that process and consensus. It remains the prerogative of Governments to adopt and implement measures of a legislative and regulatory nature. Financial institutions should be consulted, however, in view of their immediate involvement, and should share the burden of efforts against the laundering of proceeds of crime.[48]

Given the absence of a formal international legislator, it is not surprising that the influence of soft law has been especially notable on the international level.[49] The contribution of international soft law instruments to the fight against money laundering is impressive. One of the earliest international initiatives undertaken in the field of money laundering was the Recommendation No.R(80)10 adopted by the Committee of Ministers of the Council of Europe on 27 June 1980 entitled 'Measures against the transfer and safeguarding of the funds of criminal origin'.

The first international instrument to address the issue of money laundering specifically was the Basle Statement of Principles of 12 December 1988, issued by the Basle Committee on Banking Regulations and Supervisory Practices.[50] The Basle Committee, which comprises the authorities charged with banking supervision of twelve western countries,[51] thought it necessary to take action against money laundering lest public confidence, and hence the stability of banks, should be undermined by adverse publicity as a result of inadvertent association by banks with criminals. Regardless of the fact that the primary function of banking supervision is to maintain overall the financial stability of the banking system rather than to ensure that individual financial transactions are legitimate, the supervisors thought that they could not stay indifferent to the use made of banks by criminals.

The Statement contains a number of ethical principles and good banking practices, such as the know-your-customer rule, but, as the pre-

[48] UN Economic and Social Council, Commission on Crime Prevention and Criminal Justice, *Review of Priority Themes, Control of Proceeds of Crime–Report of the Secretary-General* (Vienna, 13–23 April 1993, E/CN.15/1993) p. 14.

[49] See also O. R. Young, 'International Regimes: Problems of Concept Formation', *World Politics* (1980), 333.

[50] 'Statement on the Prevention of Criminal Use of the Banking System for the Purpose of Money Laundering (hereinafter referred to as the Basle Statement of Principles)', reproduced in W. C. Gilmore (ed.), *International Efforts To Combat Money Laundering* (Cambridge: Grotius Publications, 1992), p. 273.

[51] Belgium, Canada, France, Germany, Italy, Japan, Luxembourg, the Netherlands, Sweden, Switzerland, the UK and the USA.

amble explicitly states: '[it] is not a legal document, and its implementation will depend on national practice and law'. Notwithstanding its non-binding character, the Statement was made indirectly binding upon the financial institutions in various countries.[52] Different legal techniques were used to this end: sometimes the legislator referred to the Statement (Luxembourg) or financial institutions committed themselves to respect the principles laid down in the statement (Switzerland and Austria), or supervisory authorities indicated that they would punish infringements of the said principles (Belgium,[53] France, the UK[54]). It is thus clear that, although soft law, the Basle Statement of Principles had a very marked influence on the fight against money laundering. In most countries it has now been superseded by legislation on the prevention of the misuse of financial institutions for the purposes of money laundering, but the Statement, however, played a pioneer role: as often with soft law, it provided a framework of rules in an area where formal legislation was still lacking.[55]

The crown jewel of soft law, however, is the set of forty recommendations issued by the Financial Action Task Force on money laundering (FATF) in 1990. At the 1989 Paris summit of the seven most industrialised nations in the world (G7), and in the presence of the President of the European Commission, this working party was established. Its remit was ' . . . to assess the results of co-operation already undertaken in order to prevent the utilisation of the banking system and financial institutions for the purpose of money laundering, and to consider additional preventive efforts in this field, including the adaptation of the legal and regulatory systems as to enhance multilateral judicial assistance.[56]

The first report of the FATF was issued in 1990 and contained an analysis of the extent and nature of the money laundering process and an overview of the programmes already in place to combat money laundering. Its most extensive and influential part, however, is the 40 recommendations

---

[52] FATF-I, 11.

[53] See A. De Nauw, *Les métamorphoses administratives du droit pénal de l'entreprise* (Ghent: Mys & Breesch, 1994), p. 132.

[54] As far as the UK is concerned, the Bank of England controls the respect for the Basle Statement when deciding on the extension of bank licences: J. Drage, 'Countering Money Laundering: The Response of the Financial Sector', in *Money Laundering*, ed. The David Hume Institute (Edinburgh: Edinburgh University Press, 1993), p. 62.

[55] Abi-Saab, 'Eloge du "droit assourdi"', 65 and J. Pardon, 'Déontologie des opérations bancaires et financières', *Revue de l'économie financière* (1993) 51–2.

[56] 'Group of Seven Economic Declaration of 16 July 1989', reproduced in W. C. Gilmore (ed.), *International Efforts To Combat Money Laundering* (Cambridge: Grotius Publications, 1992), p. 3.

which embrace both the repressive fight against money laundering and the enhancement of the role of the financial system in fighting money laundering.

Originally only fifteen countries participated, but membership was enlarged to twenty-six countries and two international institutions (the European Commission and the Gulf Co-operation Council).[57] The recommendations are no more and no less than recommendations: non-binding soft law. It was a deliberate choice not to cast the recommendations into the mould of a treaty. This was to avoid elaborate ratification procedures and to allow flexible adaptation of the recommendations, as was done in 1996. Flexibility was also the motive behind the loose structure of the FATF, which is merely a working party, supported by the OECD Secretariat in Paris. Since 1991, the FATF has issued annual reports which contain mutual evaluations, carried out by other member states of the FATF, of the legislative and regulatory measures member states have put in place to fight money laundering.

The FATF recommendations often functioned as *droit vert*,[58] provisions which help shape domestic legislation, with regard to money laundering. The recommendations also yield their unifying influence through the EC Council Directive of 10 June 1991 on Prevention of the Use of the Financial System for the Purpose of Money Laundering: no less than fifteen FATF recommendations found their way to the EC Directive, which made them into binding law for EC Member States.[59]

The internationalisation of law enforcement

Given the inherent transnational nature of the money laundering phenomenon, an international response was required. Various international organisations have engaged in the fight against money laundering, sometimes issuing recommendations, directives, or drafting international conventions. Some authors have referred to an international regime in this respect[60] (a term which seems to have been coined by Robert Keohane and

---

[57] On the origin, the membership, structure and functioning of FATF, see W. C. Gilmore, *Dirty Money. The Evolution of Money Laundering Counter-Measures* (Strasbourg: The Council of Europe Press, 1995) pp. 93–8.

[58] According to Abi-Saab, 'Eloge du "droit assourdi"', 65, this term was coined by Professor René-Jean Dupuy.   [59] See FATF-II, 38.

[60] B. Zagaris and E. Kingma, 'Asset Forfeiture Under International and Foreign Law: An Emerging Regime', *Emory Int'l LRev.* (1991), 446 *et seq.* and S. B. McDonald, 'Frontiers for International Money Regulation After BCCI: International Co-operation or Fragmentation', contribution in *Am.Soc'y Int'l L.Proc.* (1992), 191.

Joseph Nye[61]). Although the concept is derived from international economics and political science, it can also be applied in the sphere of international law enforcement. An international law enforcement regime can
be defined as: 'a global arrangement among governments to co-operate
against particular transnational crimes'.[62] The term 'international law
enforcement regime' should, however, not be confused with the enforcement of international law. The predicate 'international' only pertains to
the international co-operation in the enforcement of municipal criminal
law. Sometimes, as is the case with money laundering, the relevant
domestic provisions will have been inspired by international conventions,
but this does not alter the principal fact that it is still domestic criminal
law that is being enforced.

The fact that a domestic criminal offence is rooted in, or at least has a
counterpart in, an international convention, of course makes international co-operation much easier. When a government of one state wants
to enforce internationally a transnational crime, it will try to make this
offence illegal under international law. Making a type of (transnational)
behaviour illegal under international law is only one part of international
law enforcement regime. One can distinguish between the substantive
and procedural dimensions of an international law enforcement regime,
which, to a large extent, coincide, with the substantive and procedural
dimensions of international criminal law. That certain conduct is considered an international offence mostly follows from an international convention, but can also follow from customary practices amongst states
(customary law). Sometimes an international law enforcement regime
also includes the creation of extraterritorial jurisdiction (another aspect
of substantive international criminal law).[63] The procedural dimension of
international criminal law relates to international co-operation amongst
municipal police and judicial authorities, to combat transnational
crime. International conventions establishing an international offence
will often also provide the legal foundation required for international

---

[61] See R. O. Keohane and J. Nye, *Transnational Relations and World Politics* (1972); R. O.
Keohane and J. Nye, *Power and Interdependence: World Politics in Transition* (Boston: Little,
Brown & Co., 1977) and R. O. Keohane and J. Nye, *After Hegemony: Co-operation and Discord
in the World Political Economy* (1984).

[62] E. Nadelmann, *Cops Across Borders. The Internationalization of U.S. Criminal Law Enforcement*,
PhD thesis, University of Pennsylvania, p. 22.

[63] The link between an international offence and the establishment of extraterritorial
jurisdiction is often surrounded by confusion. See C. Van den Wyngaert, 'Double
Criminality as a Requirement to Jurisdiction', in *Double Criminality, Studies in International
Criminal law* (Uppsala: Iustus Förlag, 1989), pp. 47–8.

co-operation to fight this type of crime, as is the case, for example, in the context of money laundering.[64]

The influence of an international anti-money laundering regime in shaping domestic money laundering law should not be underestimated and has indeed been instrumental. The international anti-money laundering regime is, however, not a universal, homogeneous bloc but is instead composed of different layers, some of them universal, others regional. The most universal layer is provided by the 1988 UN Convention Against Illicit Traffic in Narcotic Drugs and Psychotropic Substances, the influence of which is difficult to overestimate. In making the laundering of drug proceeds an international offence under this convention, the role of the United States, the first country to incriminate money laundering,[65] was instrumental.[66] Although the 1998 UN Convention is the most global instrument, the United Nations expressly call on states to establish or strengthen regional or subregional instruments and mechanisms.[67] Other instruments have been forged in the context of regional co-operation mechanisms.

The most prominent example is that of the FATF which was started as a 'regional' initiative, but whose influence has been extended to non-FATF members and which now has world-wide influence. The FATF is effectively striving to set up a world-wide anti-money laundering network. Not only is the FATF, presently made up of 26 mainly 'western' countries, studying the possibility of extending its membership, it has also been actively engaged in the development of FATF-style regional bodies, thus aiming to extend the reach of its recommendations against money laundering beyond its membership. Thus a Caribbean Financial Action Task Force (CFATF) as well as an Asia/Pacific Group on Money Laundering have been set up with support of the FATF.[68] Moreover, the FATF also closely works together with other relevant international organisations, such as the United Nations Office for Drug Control and Crime Prevention.[69] Likewise,

---

[64] The jurisdictional questions surrounding money laundering will be discussed in Part III and the international co-operation in criminal matters regarding money laundering in Part IV.   [65] See *infra* pp. 99–100.

[66] See E. Nadelmann, *Cops Across Borders. The Internationalization of US Criminal Law Enforcement*, PhD thesis, University of Pennsylvania, p. 13.

[67] See Point 8 of the Political Declaration against Money Laundering, adopted at the Twentieth Special Session of the United Nations General Assembly devoted to 'countering the world drug problem together', New York, 10 June 1998.

[68] See, amongst others, Report of the Caribbean Drug Money Laundering Conference published at W. C. Gilmore, *International Efforts To Combat Money Laundering*, p. 25 and FATF-VIII, pp. 22–3. See in general the annual reports published by the CFATF.

[69] See FATF-IX, p. 4.

the European Union has been making considerable efforts to export the *acquis* of the European Money Laundering Directive to other parts of the world. The spatial application field of the Directive has been extended to Iceland, Norway and Liechtenstein under the European Economic Area Agreement.[70] In addition, all of the Association Agreements contain an article committing the signatories to combating money laundering in line with the Directive and other international instruments. The European Union also provides assistance in the field of anti-money laundering measures to central and eastern European countries and to 'new independent states', as well as to other countries (e.g. the Andean Community).[71]

Other regional efforts to combat money laundering have been undertaken by the Organisation of American States (OAS) and the Commonwealth. In 1992, the Inter-American Drug Abuse Control Commission (CICAD) of the OAS issued the 'Model Regulations Concerning Laundering Offences Connected to Illicit Drug Trafficking, Related and Other Serious Offenses' (amended in 1997 and hereinafter referred to as the CICAD Model Regulations[72]). The 1986 Commonwealth Scheme Relating to Mutual Assistance in Criminal Matters makes, amongst others, explicit provision for international co-operation in the field of seizure and confiscation.[73] The Commonwealth Secretariat also drafted a Money Laundering Model Law.

As will already be clear from the above, apart from conventions and other binding international legal instruments, soft law plays an important role in this international anti-money laundering regime. Sometimes

---

[70] See, e.g., Article 36 of the Agreement on the European Economic Area (Decision of the Council and the Commission of 13 December 1993 on the conclusion of the Agreement on the European Economic Area between the European Communities, their Member States and the Republic of Austria, the Republic of Finland, the Republic of Iceland, the Principality of Liechtenstein, the Kingdom of Norway, the Kingdom of Sweden and the Swiss Confederation, *OJ*, L 001, p. 1, 3.01.1994), the appendixes of which explicitly refer to the Money Laundering Directive as an example of the *acquis communautaire*. See also the *Report of the EFTA Surveillance Authority on the implementation of the Money Laundering Directive by Iceland, Liechtenstein and Norway* (Brussels, 1998), p. 69.

[71] *Second Commission report to the European Parliament and to the Council on the Implementation of the Money Laundering Directive*, (Luxembourg: Office for Official Publications of the European Communities, 1998), COM(1998) 401 final, pp. 5–7.

[72] X., 'OAS Strengthens Anti-Money Laundering Efforts', *Int'l L Enf. R* (1998), pp. 260–4.

[73] Scheme Relating to Mutual Assistance in Criminal Matters within the Commonwealth including Amendments made by Law Ministers in April 1990, reproduced in C. Van den Wyngaert and G. Stessens (eds.), *International Criminal Law. A Collection of International and European Instruments* (The Hague: Kluwer Law International, 1996), p. 345. See D. McLean, 'Mutual Assistance in Criminal Matters: The Commonwealth Initiative', *ICLQ* (1988), 177–88.

an organisation may wish to pursue both strands. Thus, the travails carried out under the aegis of the United Nations have not only spawned the 1988 Convention, but also the Optional Protocol to the UN Model Treaty on Mutual Assistance in Criminal Matters concerning the Proceeds of Crime[74] and the Model Law on Money Laundering, Confiscation and International Co-operation in Relation to Drugs.[75] Both instruments contain a number of provisions regarding international co-operation on identification, seizure and confiscation of proceeds from crime. The latter instrument also deals with purely domestic issues in the context of confiscation and money laundering, but is, unlike the former, restricted to proceeds from drug trafficking. Other than the Vienna Convention, the Protocol and the Model Law is only model legislation (i.e. soft law) and cannot function as a basis for international co-operation between states.

Likewise, the activities of the European Union in the field of anti-money laundering policies have not only resulted in the Money Laundering Directive, which is directly binding on all fifteen Member States, but also in the Joint Action of 3 December 1998 concerning arrangments for co-operation between Member States in respect of identification, tracing, freezing or seizing and confiscation of instrumentalities and the proceeds from crime,[76] which has a much less binding legal status.

Some of the most important legal instruments of the international anti-money laundering regime will be often referred to throughout this book. For the sake of clarity, they will now be discussed briefly.

The 1988 UN Convention against Illicit Traffic in Narcotic Drugs and Psychotropic Substances

Following a call from the UN Secretary-General, the UN General Assembly decided to convene a world conference at the ministerial level to deal with all aspects of drug abuse. The conference was held in Vienna from 17 through 26 June 1987 and resulted in the adoption of a Comprehensive Outline of Future Activities in Drug Abuse Control.[77] The Outline is an ambitious document, which sets out the various efforts the United Nations plan to undertake in order to curb the world-wide drug problem. The four chapters of the outline cover the main aspects of the fight against drug abuse and illicit trafficking: the prevention and reduction of illicit

---

[74] *ILM*, 1991, 1432. See also Van den Wyngaert and Stessens (eds.), *International Criminal Law. A Collection of International and European Instruments*, p. 319.

[75] United Nations International Drug Control Programme (UNDCP), Legal Advisory Programme, November 1995.   [76] *OJ* No. L 333, 09.12.1998, p. 1.

[77] *ILM* (1987), 1637–724.

demand, the control of supply, action against illicit trafficking and treat-ment and rehabilitation. The convention, which was already being pre-pared at the time of the 1987 conference, obviously relates to a third aspect. From 25 November to 20 December 1988 the United Nations Conference for the Adoption of a Convention against Illicit Traffic in Narcotic Drugs and Psychotropic Substances took place in Vienna.[78] The convention will hereinafter be referred to as the Vienna Convention. By the end of 1999, it had been signed by 154 states.

Given its ambit, the relevant provisions of the convention only pertain to the confiscation and the laundering of drug proceeds, not of the pro-ceeds of other crimes. The convention contains a number of substantive criminal law provisions, as well as mechanisms for international co-oper-ation in criminal matters. Unlike the 1990 Council of Europe Convention, the Vienna Convention is a comprehensive co-operation instrument, encompassing all forms of international judicial co-operation in criminal matters (including extradition, which is not provided for in the Council of Europe Convention).

The 1990 Council of Europe Convention on Laundering, Search, Seizure and Confiscation of the Proceeds of Crime

The text of this convention was drafted by a limited committee within the European Committee for Crime Problems (ECCP) of the Council of Europe. It constitutes the first international binding legal instrument that focuses exclusively on money laundering. Like the Vienna Convention, it deals only with the repressive fight against money laundering and it contains a number of substantive criminal law provisions, as well as mechanisms for international co-operation in criminal matters. The Council of Europe Convention, however, differs from the Vienna Convention in that its scope is not limited to drug proceeds, but in principle encompasses the proceeds from any offence. The drafters of the Council of Europe Convention nev-ertheless attempted to use, as far as possible the same terminology as the Vienna Convention.

The convention was opened for signature on 8 November 1990 and is open to all states, including states who are not members of the Council of Europe. Therefore it is not bestowed with the epithet 'European Convention' and will hereinafter also be referred to as the Money

---

[78] On the background of this conference, see B. Zagaris, 'Developments in International Judicial Assistance and Related Matters', *Den. J Int'l L & Pol'y* (1990), 340–1 and *Official Records of the United Nations Conference for the Adoption of a Convention against Illicit Traffic in Narcotic Drugs and Psychotropic Substances*, Volume II, E/CONF.82/16/Add.1.

Laundering Convention. At the end of 1999, the Money Laundering Convention had been ratified by 28 states.

The forty recommendations of the Financial Action Task Force on Money Laundering (FATF)

The background and importance of these recommendations have already been highlighted.

The EC Council Directive of 10 June 1991 on the Prevention of the Use of the Financial System for the Purpose of Money Laundering[79]

The relevant provisions of the EC Directive and their influence on the domestic law systems of Member States will be discussed in detail in the second part of this book. It is useful, however, to investigate the background and to trace the history of this directive, because of its wider significance as to the transformations that have been taking place in the shaping of law enforcement law. The genesis of the European Money Laundering Directive effectively illustrates the effects of the two movements that were outlined: the influence of other legal norms than criminal law and the internationalisation of the legislative process.

Although the directive, as its name suggests, relates only to the prevention of money laundering and not to the repression of money laundering, its legal basis has nevertheless been fiercely disputed. The preamble of the directive cites two provisions of the EC Treaty: Article 57(2) on the co-ordination of provisions concerning the taking-up and pursuit of activities as self-employed persons; and Article 100a allowing for measures for the approximation of the legislative, regulatory and administrative provisions pertaining to the establishment and functioning of the single market. If such preventive measures were not adopted, it was feared that money launderers could try to take advantage of the freedom of movement of capital and of the freedom to supply financial services which follow from the introduction of the integrated financial area.[80] Case law of the European Court of Justice has made it clear that the powers of national authorities to restrict the movement of capital in order to fight money laundering are indeed quasi non-existent. On at least two occa-

---

[79] *OJ* No. L 166, 28.6.1991, p. 77.

[80] Second paragraph of the preamble of the Money Laundering Directive. See also G. W. Smith, 'Competition in the European Financial Services Industry: The Free Movement of Capital versus the Regulation of Money Laundering', *UPa.JInt.Bus.L* (1992) 101–40.

sions, the Court of Justice held that national authorities could not submit the export of monies within the European Union to a preliminary authorisation.[81] Because almost any type of legislative measures designed to prevent the use of the financial system for the purpose of money laundering imposes burdens on financial institutions, it was also important to take appropriate measures at Community level in order to 'level the playing field' and to avoid possible competition distortion.

The directive has given rise to ardent discussions as to its legal basis, not only on a political level (see e.g. the attitude of the British government[82]), but also on a doctrinal level.[83] There is no point in denying that the context in which the directive was drafted and adopted, was one of fighting (organised) crime and, more particularly, fighting money laundering. The preamble of the directive explicitly refers to other international instruments designed to fight money laundering, such as the Vienna Convention and the Money Laundering Convention. On 22 October 1990 the Council of the European Communities had also decided to accede to the Vienna Convention.[84] Also, the directive was part of a number of regulations and directives that had been adopted or were being

---

[81] Court of Justice, 23 February 1995, *Bordessa*, ECR (1995), 361; see annotations by M. Dassesse, 'La lutte contre le blanchiment et la fraude fiscale ne donne pas aux autorités tous les droits', *JDF* (1995), 242 and by F. Castillo de la Torre, *CMLR* (1995), 1025. The Court of Justice did accept that the Spanish authorities could impose a preliminary notice for the export of cash money, but a preliminary authorisation was found to contravene Articles 1 and 4 of Council Directive 88/361/EEC of 24 June 1988 for the implementation of Article 67 of the Treaty, OJ No. L178, 08.07.1988, p. 5. In the context of Article 73B EC Treaty, introduced by the European Union Treaty, the Court of Justice ruled in the same sense: Court of Justice, 14 December 1995, *LE Sanz de Lera e.a.*, ECR (1995), 4821; see also the annotation by F. Castillo de la Torre, *CMLR* (1996), 1065.

[82] See P. J. Cullen, 'Money Laundering: The European Community Directive', in *Money Laundering*, The David Hume Institute (Edinburgh: Edinburgh University Press, 1993), p. 37.

[83] See the discussions with P. J. Cullen,'Money Laundering', 34–8; M. Dassesse, 'Les rapports entre la proposition de directive blanchiment et la seconde directive bancaire de décembre 1989. Incohérences et Contradictoires', *Banque et Droit-Numéro Spécial* (1990), 14; A. Ewing, 'The Draft EEC Money Laundering Directive: An Overview', *JIBL* (1991), 140; K. D. Magliveras, 'Defeating the Money Launderers – the International and European Framework', *J Bus. L* (1992), 171–2; J. Pardon, 'Le blanchiment de l'argent et la lutte contre la criminalité axée sur le profit', *RDP* (1992), 741–57; J. Pardon, 'Le blanchiment de l'argent. Aspects internationaux et européens', *Banque et Droit-Numéro Spécial* (1990), 11; J. J. E. Schutte, 'Strafrecht in Europees verband', *Justitiële Verkenningen* (1990, No.9), 15 and J. P. Van Soest, 'Europees witwassen', in *Misdaadgeld*, P. C. Van Duyne, J. M. Reijntjes and C. D. Schaap (Arnhem: Gouda Quint, 1993), p. 149.

[84] Council Decision of 22 October 1990 concerning the conclusion, on behalf of the European Economic Community, of the United Nations Convention against Illicit Traffic in Narcotic Drugs and Psychotropic Substances, OJ No. L 326, 24.11.1990, p. 56.

drafted, in the field of fighting organised (drug) criminality,[85] in view of the opening of the internal borders on 1 January 1993. Especially, the European Parliament displayed a remarkable activity in the field of fighting drug criminality and the laundering of (drug) money.[86]

The original proposal of the Commission on prevention of the use of the financial system for the purpose of money laundering[87] also contained an obligation for Member States to provide criminal sanctions for money laundering. On protest from various Member States, this obligation was watered down to an obligation to prohibit money laundering (by whatever means). As the Community lacks (legislative) jurisdiction to lay down criminal sanctions, Article 2 of the directive requires only that money laundering shall be prohibited and Article 14 does not specify what kind of sanctions should be applied for infringements of measures to be adopted pursuant to this directive.

When adopting the directive, the representatives of the governments of the Member States, however, issued a statement in which they refer to Vienna Convention and the Money Laundering Convention. They explicitly state that the description of money laundering contained in Article 1 of the directive derives its wording from the relevant provisions of these conventions and 'undertake to take all necessary steps by 31 December 1993 at the latest to enact criminal legislation enabling them to comply with their obligations under [these] instruments'. The impossibility of laying down criminal sanctions or an incrimination in the directive was thus circumvented by an intergovernmental statement attached to the directive.[88]

All these factors lead to the conclusion that, notwithstanding its seemingly preventive outlook, the directive is an integral part of the international law enforcement regime concerning money laundering. This was recognised as such in the Cooney Report of the European Parliament.[89]

---

[85] See Council Regulation (EEC) No. 3677/90 of 13 December 1990 laying down measures to be taken to discourage the diversion of certain substances to the illicit manufacture of narcotic drugs and psychotropic substances, OJ No. L357, 20.12.1990, p. 1; as modified by Council Regulation No. 900/92 of 31 March 1992 amending Regulation (EEC) No 3677/90 laying down measures to be taken to discourage the diversion of certain substances to the illicit manufacture of narcotic drugs and psychotropic substances, OJ No. L96, 20.04.1992, p. 1. See also Council Directive 92/109/EEC of 14 December 1992 on the manufacture and the placing on the market of certain substances used in illicit manufacture of narcotic drugs and psychotropic substances, OJ, No. L370, 19.12.1992, p. 76.   [86] See K. D. Magliveras, 'Defeating the Money Launderers', 167–8.

[87] OJ No. C 106, 28.4.1990, p. 6.   [88] OJ No. L 166, 28.6.1991, p. 83.

[89] Mr Patrick Cooney, the Rapporteur of the *Report drawn up by the Committee of Enquiry on*

Likewise, the first report of the Commission on the implementation of the Money Laundering Directive warrants this conclusion.[90] The Commission explicitly acknowledges that the directive has influenced domestic criminal law, as all Member States have chosen to implement the prohibition of money laundering which follows from Article 3 of the directive, through criminal law.[91]

Apart from the institutional context of the Community, the dispute regarding the legal basis for the directive is an excellent example of the transformations that are taking place in the domain of law enforcement. It reveals the erosion of power of national legislators, even in the field of criminal law, which most of them still regard as their *chasse gardée*. Given the fact that the territorial range of domestic criminal law is by definition limited, the clout of municipal legislators is also limited. An effective response to transnational crime phenomena such as money laundering therefore requires that legislation regarding law enforcement is, at least in part, taken over on a higher, international level. The traditional approach to this is by the negotiation of bilateral or multilateral treaties. This is, however, a cumbersome way of working which often involves lengthy negotiations and difficult ratification procedures. Its effectiveness is especially doubtful in view of the fact that the actual implementation of what states agree on an international level still depends on the willingness of those states to implement it domestically. It is not surprising therefore that international law enforcement is increasingly based on other types of international instruments such as non-binding recommendations (e.g. the FATF recommendations) or by supranational binding instruments (e.g. the European Money Laundering Directive). Although resorting to this type of international instrument sometimes obfuscates the penal aspects of the law, these aspects are nevertheless present, as the analysis of the European Money Laundering Directive has shown.

It is to be expected that the future development of international law enforcement will move increasingly away from the traditional intergovernmental type of conventions and will use other types of

---

the spread of organised crime linked to drug trafficking in the Member States of the European Community, A3–0358/91, 23.04.1992, p. 61), refers to the possible danger of distortion of competition between financial institutions as a consequence of diverging rules on the prevention of money laundering, as a suitable pretext for the Community to lay down rules in this field.   [90] COM/98/0401 final.

[91] *First Commission's report on the implementation of the Money Laundering Directive (91/308/EEC) to be submitted to the European Parliament and to the Council* (Luxembourg: Office for Official Publications of the European Communities, 1995), p. 4.

international instruments. The recent changes to the institutional structure of the European Union, brought about by the Treaty of Amsterdam,[92] notably the transfer of certain policies from the intergovernmental third pillar to the community first pillar,[93] bear witness of this evolution.

[92] Treaty of Amsterdam amending the Treaty on European Union, the treaties establishing the European Communities and certain related acts, *OJ* C 340, 10.11.1997, p. 1.
[93] See H. Bribosia, 'Liberté, sécurité et justice: l'imbroglio d'un nouvel espace', *RMC* (1998), 27–54.

2   The confiscation

The first and most important legal tool for depriving offenders of illegal profits is confiscation of proceeds from crime. In studying the various concepts of confiscation, it is necessary to distinguish this modern type of confiscation which relates to the fruits of crime (*fructum sceleris*) from more traditional concepts of confiscation that relate to the instrumentalities of crime (*instrumentum sceleris*) or even to the subject of crime (*objectum sceleris*). Other relevant legal distinctions in respect of confiscation will be analysed in this part, both from the point of view of effective law enforcement and from the standpoint of the rights of the concerned parties. This analysis will, amongst others, show that, as a model of confiscation, value confiscation is to be preferred to object confiscation. It will be argued that, although confiscation of proceeds from crime is often looked upon as a civil, reparatory measure, this new type of confiscation has an inherently punitive character. The extensive use of confiscation as a source of funding for law enforcement further illustrates its non-reparatory nature. This conclusion will in turn make it necessary to investigate a number of far-reaching features of this type of confiscation. In many jurisdictions the legislation regarding confiscation of proceeds from crime can be questioned in light of human rights limitations. One very sensitive and highly debated question in this area concerns the room for reversal of the burden of proof in relation to the criminal origin of alleged proceeds from crime. It will also be argued that *in rem* procedures, which are popular in some jurisdictions, cannot be reconciled with the fundamental right to a fair trial. Other debatable issues concern the risk of double jeopardy which is endemic with this type of confiscation and the protection of *bona fide* third parties.

General concepts of confiscation

Most criminal justice systems are traditionally familiar with the possibility of confiscating property as a result of its relation to an offence. Confiscation can be generally defined as a governmental decision through which property rights can be affected as a consequence of a criminal offence.[1] Article 1(f) of the Vienna Convention refers to confiscation as the 'permanent deprivation of property by order of a court or other competent authority' and Article 1(d) of the Money Laundering Convention speaks of 'a penalty or a measure, ordered by a court following proceedings in relation to a criminal offence or criminal offences resulting in the final deprivation of property'.

According to both definitions, confiscation amounts to the final deprivation of property. Whereas the Vienna Convention allows any competent authority to issue a confiscation order, the Money Laundering Convention limits this power to courts. The concept of court also comprises non-judicial tribunals, but is clearly intended to exclude administrative confiscations, ordered by administrative authorities,[2] for example Customs and Excise authorities.

Types of confiscation

Three types of confiscation can be distinguished according to the relation between the property at stake and the acts for which confiscation is being pronounced. Confiscation of the instrumentalities of crime (*instrumentum sceleris*) relates to the instruments that were used in the perpetration of the crime (e.g. the knife used for a murder). Confiscation of the *objectum sceleris* concerns the subject of crime, that is, the goods subjected to the criminal behaviour (e.g. a falsified passport). The most recent type of confiscation relates to the proceeds from crime, that is the financial gains obtained through criminal activities, sometimes referred to as the *fructum sceleris* or the *productum sceleris*.

Some legal systems classify different types of confiscation, according to either preventive or punitive goal. Thus, Dutch law makes a distinction between the confiscation of the instrumentalities of crime, which is con-

---

[1] See J. Schutte, *Ter vergroting van de afpakkans, een inleiding op de ontwikkeling van de interstatelijke samenwerking gericht op het ontnemen van wederrechtelijk verkregen voordeel* (Arnhem: Gouda Quint, 1990), p. 8.

[2] *Explanatory Report with the Convention on Laundering, Search, Seizure and Confiscation of the Proceeds from Crime* (Strasbourg: Publications of the Council of Europe, 1991), pp. 15–16.

sidered to constitute a criminal sanction, and confiscation of the subject of crime, which is looked on as a merely preventive measure.[3] Other legal systems distinguish between criminal confiscations, which serve a repressive purpose, and confiscations which have a preventive goal. This distinction is, for example, known in Belgian, Luxembourg[4] and Swiss law (which distinguishes between *Abschöpfungseinziehung* and *Sicherungseinziehung*).[5] In some cases, a criminal confiscation can also have a reparative function, as, for example, is the case when confiscated property is used to compensate victims of the offence.[6]

Although it may be useful for domestic purposes to classify these confiscation types according to their purposes, this nominal classification is not decisive from a human rights point of view. As will be shown, many confiscation sanctions which seemingly only serve a preventive purpose are in fact punitive sanctions. The imposition of this type of confiscation should therefore be conditioned by the fundamental guarantees of a fair trial (as laid down in Article 6 ECHR and Article 14 ICCPR).

Object confiscation v. value confiscation

Apart from the various types of confiscation, two models of confiscation can be distinguished: object confiscation and value confiscation.[7] The distinction in the first place concerns the mode in which property rights are affected: either through the imposition of an obligation to pay a certain amount of money or through transfer of property. It will be argued, however, that this distinction also concerns the *in rem* or *in personam* character of confiscation. Both the Vienna Convention and the Money Laundering Convention provide for both models. Recommendation 8 of the Aruba Report of the FATF urges states to use both models and a 1997 comparative FATF study showed that all but two FATF members have legal

[3] For a critical approach of this distinction, see L. F. Keyser-Rignalda, *Boef en buit*, pp. 104–9 and D. R. Doorenbos, *Over witwassen en voordeelsontneming* (Deventer: Tjeenk Willink, 1997), pp. 70–2.

[4] See Stessens, *De nationale en internationale bestrijding van het witwassen*, pp. 39–40.

[5] See Pieth, 'Das zweite Paket gegen das Organisierte Verbrechen', 237 and Schmid, 'Das neue Einziehungsrecht', 328–329.

[6] See, e.g., for Belgian law: M. De Swaef, 'De bijzondere verbeurdverklaring van de vermogensvoordelen uit misdrijven', *RW* (1990–91), 493 and E. Dirix, 'De verbeurdverklaring met toewijzing aan de benadeelde', in *Om deze redenen. Liber Amicorum Armand Vandeplas* (Ghent: Mys & Breesch, 1994), p. 195; and for Luxembourg law: Spielmann, 'La confiscation en droit luxembourgeois à l'aube de la réforme du Code pénal', 202.

[7] Schutte, *Ter vergroting van de afpakkans*, pp. 9–10.

systems that allow for both models.[8] An in-depth study of both models, will show, however, that value confiscation is to be preferred to property confiscation, with a view to both effective law enforcement and legal protection.

Object confiscation is a powerful criminal sanction: it results in the transfer of property title to the state. The moment of transfer of property title usually coincides with the moment at which the decision ordering the confiscation becomes final. The United States, however, adhere to the so-called relation-back doctrine, according to which the transfer of property title is deemed to take place at the moment the offence at issue is committed. The judicial decision ordering the confiscation has only declaratory power, in contrast to most other jurisdictions where this decision has constitutive power. This doctrine already existed under common law, but was statutorily entrenched in 1984 through the Comprehensive Forfeiture Act and is now applicable to almost any confiscation in the United States.[9] This legal fiction under which the state is deemed to have been owner of the property involved in the offence from the moment the offence was committed, has important consequences: proceeds from crime which can be confiscated under the relation-back doctrine in principle remain always 'untouchable' as any transfer of property title is in principle void, given the fact that the state has become owner at the moment the offence at issue was committed. The Supreme Court, however, has considered that fictional and retroactive vesting of title is not self-executing, but occurs only when the government has obtained a judgment of forfeiture. Until the government has won such a judgment, someone else owns the property and that person may invoke an innocent-owner defence.[10] This presupposes, however, that such an innocent-owner defence is available under the applicable statute, as there is no constitutionally mandated innocent-owner defence.[11]

In most jurisdictions, object confiscation operates blindly as it is ordered without paying heed to who is the actual possessor of the property. In principle, only the relation with the offence is material. In addition, this type of confiscation is usually enforced in rem.[12] Rights of third parties established after the offence has been committed are only guaran-

---

[8] FATF, *Report of the Caribbean Drug Money Laundering Conference*, Oranjestad, Aruba, 8–10 June 1990 and FATF, *Evaluation of laws and systems in FATF members dealing with asset confiscation and provisional measures*, p. 2.

[9] 18 USC. § 841(h). See N. Kohler, 'The Confiscation of Criminal Assets in the United States and Switzerland', *Houston JIL* (1990–91), 18.

[10] *US v. 92 Buena Vista Avenue, Rumson, NJ*, 507 US 111, 125–9 (1993).   [11] See *infra* pp. 41–2.

[12] See McClean, *International Judicial Assistance*, p. 215.

teed if they can be established. Neither the Vienna Convention, nor the Money Laundering Convention prohibit goods in the hands of third persons from being confiscated,[13] although they both contain provisos concerning the rights of bona fide third parties.[14] Most FATF members have in place laws that allow the confiscation of criminally derived proceeds from third parties.[15]

Object confiscation, often known as forfeiture, functions in many criminal justice systems in relation to the instrumentalities of crime. The application field of this type of confiscation, when extended to the proceeds from crime, creates a number of sometimes insurmountable problems. A definite drawback of object confiscation, especially in relation to proceeds from crime, is its aleatory character; property which at the time of the judicial decision has been consumed or which can not be traced any more, escapes confiscation. That this may cause inherently unjust consequences, needs little explanation. As an American judge once put it succinctly: 'A racketeer who dissipates the profits . . . on wine, women and song has profited from organised crime to the same extent as if he had put the money in his bank account'.[16] This is all the more so as many of the proceeds are often spent before the arrest of the alleged criminals.[17] The goal of an effective deprivation of the fruits of crime may thus suffer from the fact that (some of) the property constituting the fruits of crime can not be traced any more.

A possibly more harmful disadvantage of object confiscation relates to the right of bona fide third parties, whose rights may suffer because of the 'blind' application of object confiscation. In relation to proceeds from crime, this type of confiscation normally functions independently of any property rights that may be established in relation to the proceeds. As far as the person who committed the crime is concerned, this is only logical; he can indeed not have any bona fide rights with regard to property he obtained through an offence. This conclusion can not be broadened, however, to third parties who have established rights with respect to the property representing proceeds from crime, after the offence has been committed. Nevertheless, in those systems where a type of object confiscation exists in relation to proceeds from crime (e.g. the United States), no

---

[13] See *Explanatory Report with the Convention on Laundering, Search, Seizure and Confiscation of the Proceeds from Crime*, p. 14.

[14] See Article 5(8) of the Vienna Convention and Article 5 of the Money Laundering Convention.   [15] FATF, *Evaluation of laws and systems in FATF members*, p. 5.

[16] *United States v. Ginsberg*, 773 F.2d, 789, 802 (7th Cir. 1985).

[17] M. Levi, 'Taking the Profit Out of Crime: The UK Experience', *Eur.JCr, Cr.L & Cr.J* (1997), 228.

attention is often paid to these rights, just as is the case with forfeiture of instruments of crime. Once it is established that property constitutes the proceeds from crime, it can often be confiscated, irrespective of the ownership at that time. Typically, this line of reasoning is valid, both at the stage of the judgment and of the enforcement of the confiscation. When it is said that forfeiture (i.e. object confiscation) operates *in rem*, this pertains both to the judgment and to its enforcement. The rights of bona fide third parties will be more extensively discussed later,[18] but it is typical of forfeiture that these rights can be guaranteed only through separate procedures instituted by the third parties themselves, either at the stage of the judgment ordering the forfeiture, or at the stage of enforcement.

In some legal systems that operate object confiscation in relation to proceeds from crime, the sharp edges of this forfeiture type of confiscation have been removed, either by legislation or by case law. Thus, Swiss legislation provides that property constituting proceeds from crime cannot be confiscated if a third party has acquired the property, unaware of the criminal acts allowing its confiscation (Article 59(1) of the Swiss Criminal Code). A similar requirement exists under Dutch law in respect of traditional forfeiture (Article 33(2) of the Dutch Criminal Code). An analogous provision is contained in the UN Model Law on Money Laundering in respect of confiscation of instrumentalities of offences (Article 29). In respect of the confiscation of the instrumentalities of crime, the blind application of object confiscation is sometimes also softened by the requirement that the property involved in the perpetration of the offence was owned by the perpetrator(s). This requirement, which is, for example, posed by Belgian law (Article 42, 1° and 2° Belgian Criminal Code), needs to be assessed at the moment the offence is committed;[19] otherwise, it would suffice to change ownership after the perpetration of the offence in order to escape confiscation of the instrumentalities of the offence. In respect of the object confiscation of proceeds from crime, Belgian case law has established that it is not possible to confiscate proceeds from crime which are possessed by third parties.[20]

These adjustments of the concept of object confiscation do not provide a satisfactory solution, however. For one thing, they will often make it impossible to deprive the offender of his ill-gotten gains, when he has succeeded in stashing them away in an off-shore or other construction so that

---

[18] See *infra* pp. 76–9.   [19] See Belgian Supreme Court, 13 June 1955, *Pasicrisie* (1955, I), 1114.

[20] See on the controversy surrounding Belgian law in this respect: Belgian Supreme Court, judgment of 18 March 1997, *Tijdschrift voor milieurecht* (1997), 270 and judgment of 10 February 1999, *Recente Arresten van het Hof van Cassatie* (1999), 341.

they are technically no longer in his possession. More generally, confiscation will always be impossible when proceeds from crime are technically owned by juristic persons in those criminal justice systems that do not know corporate criminal liability (e.g. Switzerland).

In many respects value confiscation represents a more attractive alternative. This type of confiscation, also known as a pecuniary penalty order (Australia), does not consist of the deprivation of property (representing proceeds from crime), but of a judicial order to pay a certain amount of money, corresponding to the value of the proceeds from crime.[21] This entails that value confiscation can in principle only be envisaged in relation with proceeds from crime (although Article 31(2) of the Luxembourg Criminal Code also foresees value confiscation as a subsidiary alternative to forfeiture of the instruments of crime). Whereas some jurisdictions, such as those of England and Wales[22] and the Netherlands,[23] have opted for value confiscation as the main model for depriving offenders of the fruits of their crimes, many jurisdictions such as Belgium[24] and Switzerland,[25] for example, at least theoretically only allow value confiscation as a subsidiary alternative for object confiscation, namely when the property constituting the proceeds can not be traced any more, although in practice, value confiscation may be applied as frequently as object confiscation. In these cases value confiscation is often referred to as the confiscation of an equivalent sum of money.

Once a value confiscation has been ordered, the state can in principle use the remedies available to a private creditor to ensure payment (attachment of property, etc.). This will generally be the case in respect of object confiscation as well. Unlike object confiscation, a value confiscation can normally also be enforced on property which has been legally acquired and has no connection with the offence for which the confiscation was ordered (although it is not clear whether this is accepted in all legal systems).[26] This follows, for example, from the definition of realisable property in English law (s.6(2)DTA 1994)[27] and from Dutch confiscation

---

[21] See Schutte, *Ter vergroting van de afpakkans*, p. 10.

[22] See ss. 2–7 of the Drug Trafficking Act 1994 for proceeds from drug offences and ss.71 and 72 of the Criminal Justice Act (CJA) 1988, as far as proceeds from other offences are concerned.

[23] See Article 36e of the Dutch Criminal Code (F. C. V. De Groot, 'De ontneming van wederrechtelijk verkregen voordeel', in *Maatregelen tegen witwassen in het koninkrijk*, G. J. M. Corstens, E. J. Joubert, S. C. J. J. Kortmann (Arnhem: Gouda Quint, 1995), pp. 67–73.

[24] See Article 43bis of the Belgian Criminal Code and Stessens, *De nationale en internationale bestrijding van het witwassen*, p. 50.   [25] See Article 59(2) of the Swiss Criminal Code.

[26] FATF, *Evaluation of laws and systems in FATF members*, p. 5.

[27] *R v. Chrastny (No.2)* [1992] 1 All ER 193, 202; *R v Walbrook and Glasgow* [1994] Crim.LR 613.

legislation.[28] In this respect there is a clear analogy between a value confiscation and a criminal fine, the latter in most cases also being judicially enforceable. At the same time value confiscation is fundamentally different from object confiscation, the scope of which is restricted to property that can be traced to the offence. Some systems of object confiscation, however, go some way towards value confiscation by enabling the confiscation of property with which proceeds have been intermingled, up to the assessed value of the intermingled proceeds (see also Article 5(6)(b) of the Vienna Convention).

A marked difference between criminal fines and value confiscations concerns the judicial determination of the amount of money by the court. In the case of value confiscations, this is in principle solely determined by evaluating the proceeds derived by the criminal offence at issue, whereas the amount of a fine may be influenced by the gravity of the offence and the personal circumstances relating to the convicted person, such as his criminal record, his personality, his financial means, etc. When it is not possible to determine the exact amount of money corresponding to the value of the proceeds from crime, the sum will often be assessed.[29] The legal concept of this crime-fighting tool is deeply influenced by the meritocratic idea that crime should not pay.

Some legislation nevertheless allows the judge to take into account other factors than a mere evaluation of the value of the proceeds from crime when ordering a confiscation of proceeds from crime. Not surprisingly, this seems especially to be the case in those criminal justice systems that in the first place operate a system of object confiscation of proceeds from crime. Because of the blind operation of this type of confiscation, the need for judicial discretion is more acute. A first method of allowing courts to take into account other factors (besides deciding the question whether property constitutes proceeds from crime or not) is to make confiscation optional. The Belgian Parliament opted for an optional confiscation system in order to allow judges to forgo confiscation if the detrimental social effects a confiscation may have would outweigh its advantages.[30] Swiss law explicitly allows the judge to pay heed to personal

---

[28] See Article 36e of the Dutch Criminal Code and Articles 577b(1) j° Article of the 573 Dutch Code of Criminal Procedure. See L. F. Keyser-Rignalda, *Boef en buit*, pp. 44–5 and 73–6.

[29] See, e.g., Article 59(4) of the Swiss Criminal Code and the judgment of the Belgian Supreme Court of December 14, 1994, *Recente Arresten van het Hof van Cassatie* (1995), 99.

[30] See the discussion in Belgian Parliament: *Parl.St.*, Senaat, 890/2, 1989–90, p. 9 and also the critique by A. Vandeplas, 'De verbeurdverklaring van vermogensvoordelen', in *Liber Amicorum Marc Châtel* (Antwerp: Kluwer, 1991), pp. 390–1.

factors by desisting from confiscation of (part of) the proceeds if this would hamper the social reintegration of the offender (Article 59(2) of the Swiss Criminal Code).

The clearest advantage of value confiscation lies in the fact that, unlike object confiscation, it operates *in personam*, meaning that confiscation can in principle be pronounced only with regard to the proceeds enjoyed by the offender and can also be enforced only on property owned by the offender. The rights of bona fide third parties established after the offence has been committed can in principle not be affected by value confiscation. Nevertheless, this feature at the same time reveals a major drawback of this type of confiscation, namely that it can be circumvented by transferring property to third parties (e.g. family members, associates or juristic persons). Because of the fact that value confiscation can also be enforced on legally acquired property, this 'escape route' functions only when there is no more (or not enough) property left to enforce the confiscation on.

This loophole can moreover be plugged by incriminating money laundering; persons who aid criminals in hiding their proceeds from crime will thus risk criminal prosecutions. Although prosecuting persons on a charge of money laundering burdens the prosecution with proof of the offence, it is preferable to the blind operation of object confiscation with a view to the protection of the rights of bona fide third parties. In some cases, a prosecution for money laundering can even lead to a more effective deprivation of proceeds from crime. In order to escape object confiscation, it will often suffice for third parties that they demonstrate that they acted in good faith when they acquired the property (see, however, the stringent requirements laid down in Article 6 of the CICAD Model Regulations).[31] If third parties are prosecuted for money laundering, however, a good faith defence will not normally suffice to escape conviction. To invoke good faith when being prosecuted on a count of money laundering will in most cases boil down to invoking error of fact. In many criminal justice systems error of fact exonerates a suspect only under certain requirements, which are usually substantially more stringent than mere good faith.

Another way to plug the loophole is to extend the reach of value confiscation to property held by third parties.[32] This is, however, a legal technique to be applied with great caution and one which will often introduce the externalities of object confiscation. If legislators choose to provide for this type of technique, they should make sure to safeguard the legitimate

---

[31] See website address http://www.cicad.cas.org/en/legal_development/legal-regulations-money.pdf   [32] Cf. McClean, *International Judicial Assistance*, p. 215.

rights of third parties. A good example of this is provided by Dutch legislation which has created a revocatory action under criminal law which allows the prosecution to confiscate property held by third parties if it can establish that these third parties acted in connivance with the offender(s). Article 94d of the Dutch Code of Criminal Procedure gives the prosecution the power to declare any legal transaction entered into by the offender invalid, provided the prosecution can establish that he was not obliged to do so and acted in bad faith. In addition, it must also establish that the third party acted in bad faith (except if it concerns a gift). Once the legal transactions are declared invalid, the property is deemed to belong to the offender again, so that it can be seized and subsequently confiscated.[33] The rights of third parties are safeguarded in two ways. Firstly, this revocatory action under criminal law is subjected to a number of conditions; and secondly, third parties can call on a court of law to judge whether the conditions for applying the revocatory action under criminal law are met (Article 552c of the Dutch Code of Criminal Procedure).

The revocatory action under criminal law does not solve all problems, however. It does not allow for the deprivation of an offender of proceeds that were never in his possession but went straight into the 'pocket' of a third person, e.g. a company.[34] In such cases, deprivation of proceeds can take place only if the third person can be successfully charged either with the predicate offence or the offence of money laundering. In the case of a company, this requires the acknowledgment of corporate criminal liability.

Notwithstanding the fact that the Vienna Convention and the Money Laundering Convention foresee both models of confiscation, it is clear that value confiscation is to be preferred. It provides a better legal model for depriving offenders of their ill-gotten gains in that it is not restricted to the property which constitutes the proceeds from crime, but rather departs from an evaluation of these proceeds. Because its reach is in principle confined to property held by the offender, the risk for an infringement of the legitimate rights of third parties is in principle very low. Another distinct advantage of value confiscation over object confiscation, which will be discussed later on, is that it makes it possible to avoid the same proceeds being confiscated more than once (*non bis in idem* protection).

---

[33] See J. T. K. Bos, 'Plukze-wet', *AA* (1993), 822 and L. F. Keyser-Rignalda, *Boef en buit*, p. 117. See also R. M. Hermans, 'Het ontmantelen van verhaalsconstructies. Enkele civielrechtelijke problemen bij de toepassing van de "plukze-wet"', *NJB* (1995), 774.

[34] See Hermans, 'Het ontmantelen van verhaalsconstructies', 779–82.

Confiscation procedures

Confiscations are often imposed at the end of criminal proceeding conducted against a suspect. Confiscation, can, however, also be imposed through *in rem* procedures. These are procedures that are not conducted against a person (*in personam*), but against a thing. The American Supreme Court referred to *in rem* procedures as follows: 'It is the property which is proceeded against and, by resort to a legal fiction, held guilty and condemned as though it were conscious instead of inanimate and insentient'.[35]

A sharp distinction should be drawn between, on the one hand *in personam versus in rem* procedures, and on the other hand, the *enforcement* of confiscations *in rem* (object confiscation) or *in personam* (value confiscation). Whereas an *in rem* procedure can give rise only to object confiscation, because the procedure is conducted against a thing, an object, *in personam* procedures can result in both object and value confiscation.

Although *in rem* procedures are especially popular with American legislators, examples of this type of procedure can also be found in other legal systems. Swiss law, for example, allows for the confiscation of instrumentalities and proceeds from crime both in the course of an *in personam* procedure and an *in rem* procedure.[36] Belgian[37] and Dutch law[38] are also familiar with *in rem* procedures, but only when confiscation has a protective function.

Whereas in most systems, *in rem* procedures are exceptional, American law is rife with them. American law distinguishes between three types of confiscation – administrative, civil and criminal confiscations – of which only criminal confiscations are imposed in *in personam* procedures.

Administrative forfeitures take place through seizures by the investigating law enforcement authority. This type of forfeiture is limited to objects with a value below US$500,000 and requires that interested parties are notified. If an interested party reacts within twenty days, the case can be dealt with by a court. Interested parties may, however, also prefer to have their objections dealt with by the law enforcement authority.[39]

The concept of civil forfeitures logically follows from the relation-back doctrine; given the fact that the state is, by legal fiction, deemed to be the

---

[35] *United States v. Various Items of Personal Property*, 82 US 577, 581
[36] Schmid, 'Das neue Einziehungsrecht', 324 and 360–1.
[37] See Stessens, *De nationale en internationale bestrijding van het witwassen*, p. 51.
[38] Keyser-Rignalda, *Boef en buit*, pp. 45–6.
[39] L. K. Osofsky, 'Comparing the US Law of "Forfeiture" with the Law of "Confiscation" in England and Wales', *JIBL* (1994), 301.

owner of the property from the moment the offence was committed, American law enforcement authorities can avail themselves of all civil remedies available to an owner in order to trace, seize and confiscate 'their' property. Civil forfeitures are imposed through procedures against the property, not against the owner or possessor. It is the property which is accused and which can also be held guilty. Although the practical consequences of civil and criminal forfeitures are very similar, the case law adheres to the legal distinction. Even though some constitutional guarantees surrounding a criminal procedure may attach to civil forfeitures as well (such as the Fourth Amendment right against unreasonable search and seizure and the Fifth Amendment privilege against self-incrimination),[40] legal rights are generally much better safeguarded in respect of criminal forfeitures than with regard to civil forfeitures.[41] The Supreme Court has repeatedly held that civil forfeiture proceedings do not violate the constitutional due process requirements as these procedures are aimed at preventing crimes by requiring the owners of property to take precautions.[42] The Court has, however, applied the prohibition of excessive fines from the Eighth Amendment to the US Constitution.[43] In the leading case *United States v. Bajakajian*,[44] the Supreme Court stated that a punitive forfeiture violates the Excessive Fines Clause if it is grossly disproportionate to the gravity of the offence that it is designed to punish. Bearing in mind that judgments about the appropriate punishment belong in the first instance to the legislature and that any judicial determination regarding the gravity of an offence will be inherently precise, the Supreme Court adopted a gross disproportionality standard.

The prosecution has to show probable cause, that is, reasonable ground to believe that the assets were acquired with illegally obtained proceeds.[45] The onus of proof is located somewhere between a mere

---

[40] *Boyd v. United States*, 116 US 616, 634–5 (1886); *One 1958 Plymouth Sedan v. Pennsylvania* 380 US 693, 696 (1965). Cf. *United States v. Ward* 448 US 242, 254–5 (1980).

[41] See M. B. Stahl, 'Asset Forfeiture, Burdens of Proof and the War on Drugs', *J Cr. & Cr. L*, 1992, 298–299 and J. A. E. Vervaele, 'La saisie et la confiscation à la suite d'atteintes punissables au droit aux Etats-Unis', *RDP* (1998), 987–93.

[42] *J. W. Goldsmith-Grant Co. v. US* 254 US 505, 510–11 (1921). See also *Calero-Toledo v. Pearson Yacht Leasing Co.*, 416 US 663, 685–8 (1974).

[43] *Austin v. US*, 113 S.Ct. 2801 (1993). This prohibition is applicable to both civil and criminal forfeitures (*Alexander v. US*, 113 S.Ct. 2766 (1993)). See L. Larose, '*Austin v. United States*; applicability of the Eighth Amendment to Civil *in rem* forfeitures', *New. Eng. L Rev.* (1995), 729–61.   [44] 524 US 321 (1988).

[45] Cf. N. Kohler, 'The Confiscation of Criminal Assets', 20. See also J. E. Gordon, 'Prosecutors Who Seize too Much and the Theories They Love: Money Laundering, Facilitation, and Forfeiture', *Duke LJ* (1995), 749–50.

suspicion and a prima facie case and therefore much lower than in criminal proceedings, where the guilt of the accused has to be established beyond reasonable doubt. When this initial requirement has been successfully established by the prosecution, the burden of proof shifts to the claimant of the property. This reversal of the burden of proof passed the constitutional muster of the Supreme Court.[46] Once the probable cause is established, the owner has to demonstrate by a preponderance of evidence either that the property does not qualify for confiscation, or that he has done all he reasonably could be expected to prevent the proscribed use of his property, or that the property had been taken from the defendant without his consent. These stringent requirements were for the first time set out by the US Supreme Court in *Calero-Toledo v. Pearson Yacht Leasing Co.*[47] In this case, a yacht had been forfeited because drugs had been found on it while it was being used by lessees. Although the lessor of the yacht, Pearson Yacht Leasing Co., was not involved in the wrongdoing, it could not establish that it had done all it reasonably could to prevent the unlawful use of the yacht and therefore did not succeed in claiming its property back. The Supreme Court emphasised the preventive and remedial purpose of civil forfeitures. Confiscating property of innocent owners supposedly forces them to take greater precaution in transferring goods to third parties. According to the Supreme Court, the American Constitution does not offer any autonomous protection (i.e. other than the protection that may be provided by the applicable statute) for an innocent owner who has temporarily transferred property to a third party and was not aware of the unlawful use of the property.[48] In a 1993 decision, *Austin v. United States*,[49] the Supreme Court stated it never accepted forfeiture of property if the owner had done everything in his power to prevent unlawful use of it. This also explains why an owner whose property has been stolen, is entitled to compensation when that property is confiscated.[50]

Although there is thus no provision for constitutionally mandated innocent-owner protection, numerous forfeiture statutes – both at federal and at state level – nowadays contain an explicit innocent-owner protection.[51] The ways in which these innocent-owner defences have been

[46] *United States v. One Assortment of 89 Firearms*, 465 US 354, 362 (1984).
[47] 416 US 663, 689 (1974).
[48] *Calero-Toledo v. Pearson Yacht Leasing Co*, 416 US 663, 688 (1974). This line of case law was confirmed in *Bennis v. Michigan* (116 S.Ct. 994 (1996)). See also A. Nicgorski, 'The Continuing Saga of Civil Forfeiture', 385–7.   [49] 113 S.Ct. 2801, 2809 (1993).
[50] Gordon, 'Prosecutors Who Seize too Much', 751 and 759–60.
[51] See e.g. 18 USC 981(a)(2).

drafted vary considerably as does their judicial interpretation.[52] There seems nevertheless to have evolved a rule in American case law to the effect that financial institutions that have carried out financial transactions that did not make sense from an economic point of view cannot claim the 'innocent owner status'.[53]

From a law enforcement point of view, civil or administrative *in rem* procedures offer many advantages over traditional *in personam* procedures. *In rem* procedures do not require the conviction of a suspect and the onus of proof is much lower than in criminal cases. More generally speaking, the prosecution will be less hampered by constitutional safeguards which accrue to criminal prosecutions. Another major advantage is that confiscation of proceeds from crime or of instrumentalities of crime remains possible, even when the alleged offender has absconded or is deceased. In the latter case an *in personam* confiscation procedure is obviously excluded, but at the same time in the former case it will be impossible for American prosecution authorities to obtain confiscation through an *in personam* procedure as American and other common law systems are not familiar with *in absentia* procedures.

The combination of these factors allows to explain why, at least in the context of drug offences, the vast majority of confiscations in the United States take place through *in rem* procedures.[54]

Some European countries have introduced separate confiscation procedures, which, though not *in rem* procedures, are conducted separately from, or rather subsequent to, the procedure against the suspect. The confiscation procedure is a sequel, or an extension of the *in personam* procedure, which takes place after the suspect has been found guilty and convicted. Procedures against suspects are often conducted under severe time pressure, notably because the suspect is in custody. By instituting a separate confiscation procedure, more time becomes available for investigating the whereabouts of the financial gains of the offences without infringing on the suspect's right to a speedy trial. Thus English law allows the confiscation procedure to be postponed till six months after conviction[55] and under Dutch law this is even possible up till two years after the

---

[52] M. F. Zeldin and R. G. Weiner, 'Innocent Third Parties and Their Rights in Forfeiture Proceedings', *Am.J.Cr.L.* (1991), 846–53.

[53] *US v. 15603 85th Avenue North* 933 F.2d 976 (11th Cir. 1991), 979–980 and *United States v. 6960 Miraflores Ave.*, 731 F. Supp. 1563 (SD Fla. 1990). See also W. Adams, 'Effective Strategies for Banks in Avoiding Criminal, Civil, and Forfeiture Liability in Money Laundering Cases', *Ala.L.Rev.* (1993), 694–5.

[54] See the figures cited by N. Kohler, 'The Confiscation of Criminal Assets', 17.

[55] S.3(3) Drug Trafficking Act (DTA) 1994 and s.72A(3) Criminal Justice Act (CJA) 1988.

conviction.[56] Immediately upon conviction courts will often lack the necessary information to assess the proceeds from crime and the availability of assets; deferring the decision on confiscation to a separate procedure in this sense serves a useful purpose. In addition, separating the decision on the confiscation from the decision on the guilt of the accused, clearly establishes that the former decision is in principle independent from the second one, and may even be taken by a different judge, as is possible in the Netherlands.[57] This should not be taken as a fair-trial requirement, however. The argument that a judge who took part in the conviction of the accused, is, by virtue of the requirement of an impartial tribunal, foreclosed from taking part in the confiscation procedure, has rightly been rejected by the Dutch Supreme Court.[58] The determination of the confiscation is only the logical sequel of the determination of the criminal charge – which is in itself a *conditio sine qua non* for confiscation – and as such part of the same procedure. Maybe the most important argument for the establishment of a separate confiscation procedure lies in the fact that it allows to confine clearly a (partial) reversal of the burden of proof to the criminal origin of alleged proceeds from crime, in that it erects a procedural wall between the determination of guilt (according to the general standard of proof) and the determination of the confiscation of proceeds from criminal conduct.

No matter how obvious the advantages of postponing the decision on the confiscation of proceeds from crime may in some cases be, it requires a legal basis in the absence of which judges are usually not allowed to postpone the decision on confiscation, but have to decide on confiscation at the same time as deciding on the guilt of the accused.[59]

Confiscation of the instrumentalities or the subject of crime

Confiscation of the instrumentalities of crime rests on the assumption that the convicted person has shown himself unworthy to use property by using it for criminal purposes. Confiscation of instrumentalities of crime, or forfeiture as it is often called, is sometimes physically associated with the offence in which the instruments were used, even to the extent that the property itself is considered to be 'contaminated' or 'guilty'.[60] This type of confiscation is therefore often compulsory.

---

[56] Article 511b of the Dutch Code of Criminal Procedure.

[57] F. Keyser-Rignalda, 'De buitgerichte benadering van de Pluk ze-wetgeving', *NJB* (1993), 338.   [58] Dutch Supreme Court, judgment of 9 September 1997, *NJ* (1998), No. 90.

[59] This is, e.g., the case in Belgium: Stessens, *De nationale en internationale bestrijding van het witwassen*, p. 55.   [60] Fried, 'Rationalising Criminal Forfeiture', 380–8.

The rationale of confiscation of the subject of crime, on the other hand, is of a protective nature: to protect society against the uncontrolled use of dangerous property. Thus, the interest of society in depriving offenders from drugs or falsified passports is undeniable. Forfeiture of the *objectum sceleris* is the clearest example of object confiscation: it operates *in rem*, because it concerns the property, not so much the person who possesses it. Even in jurisdictions that generally do not adhere to *in rem* confiscation procedures, this type of confiscation can sometimes be imposed through *in rem* procedures because of its clearly preventive goal.

In accordance with Article 37 of the 1961 Single Convention on Narcotic Drugs and Article 22(3) of the 1971 Convention on Psychotropic Substances, most domestic legal systems have already elaborated the required legal provisions to confiscate the tools and devices used in committing drug offences.[61] Article 5(1)(b) of the 1988 Vienna Convention nevertheless stipulates that it should also be possible to confiscate 'materials and equipment or other instrumentalities used in or intended for use in any manner in offences established in accordance with Article 3, paragraph 1' (i.e. drug trafficking). Article 2 of the Money Laundering Convention requires that parties are able to confiscate instrumentalities, meaning 'any property used or intended to be used, in any manner, wholly or in part, to commit a criminal offence or criminal offences' (Article 1(c)). Both definitions were clearly drafted with the intent to encompass any kind of property used, or even merely intended to be used, in connection with a (drug trafficking) offence.[62] A wide definition is likely to smooth international co-operation, even though it is the requested state which will eventually determine whether property is considered to be 'instrumentality' or not.[63]

Neither of the multilateral conventions contain provisions on the confiscation of the *objectum sceleris*. According to the Explanatory Report to the Money Laundering Convention, the drafters considered that, if necessary, the confiscation of the *objectum sceleris* could fall into the category of 'instrumentalities'.[64] The Convention of Vienna contains an obligation to enable the confiscation of narcotic drugs and psychotropic substances

---

[61] See UN *Outline*, 71.

[62] See *Report of the US Delegation to the UN Conference for the adoption of a Convention Against Illicit Traffic in Narcotic Drugs and Psychotropic Substances,* 101st Congress, 1st Session, SENATE, Exec. Rept. 101–15, (hereinafter cited as *Report US Delegation*), reproduced in W. C. Gilmore, *International Efforts To Combat Money Laundering,* p. 112.

[63] *Explanatory Report with the Convention on Laundering,* p. 15.

[64] *Explanatory Report with the Convention on Laundering,* p. 15.

(Article 5(1)(b)), but the drafters seemed to consider these as instrumentalities, rather than the subject of crime.[65]

The lack of any explicit treaty provision on the confiscation of the *objectum sceleris* can also be explained by the fact that, in principle, this type of confiscation does not require any international provision. Because of their inherent dangerousness, all domestic legal systems in principle allow to confiscate this type of property, irrespective of the *locus delicti*.

Both the confiscation of instrumentalities of crime and of the subject of crime are sometimes described as 'preventive' or 'remedial'. In the following paragraphs it will be argued that this preventive epithet rarely corresponds to reality as these types of confiscation almost always have a punitive overtone. Only if property is indispensable to the perpetration of criminal activities and if it is irreplaceable – or difficult to replace – can its confiscation be called truly preventive. Often these two conditions will not be met, however, and the confiscation of instruments or the subject of crime does not significantly prevent future crimes. In this respect, it has correctly been pointed out that a distinction should be drawn between contraband per se and derivative contraband.[66]

Some property is considered so dangerous that it is illegal to possess it under any circumstances. This may, for example, be the case with certain drugs or weapons, where there is the clear interest of society that this property be confiscated in order to prevent future crimes. This type of property can be called contraband per se. Often when property is confiscated because it has been used to facilitate a crime, it is not contraband per se, but derivative contraband, that is, otherwise legally held property which is used for illegal purposes. The confiscation of derivative contraband does not serve a preventive goal. Thus it cannot be said that the confiscation of a truck that was used to transport drugs will prevent future drug trafficking offences; confiscation undoubtedly imposes hardship on the owner of the truck, but does not prevent him from committing future offences. Because the confiscation of instrumentalities of crime in the vast majority of cases concerns derivative rather than per se contraband, this type of confiscation serves a punitive instead of preventive purpose.[67] The same will often be true in respect of the confiscation of the subject of a crime. Admittedly, it will often be in society's interest that the subject of a crime (e.g. a falsified passport) is confiscated, but examples of derivative contraband can also be found in this category.

---

[65] *Report US Delegation*, p. 112 and Stewart, 'Internationalising The War on Drugs', 395.
[66] See Stahl, 'Asset Forfeiture', 306–7.
[67] See also Stahl, 'Asset Forfeiture', 318 et seq.

The punitive nature of confiscation of instrumentalities of crime also appears from the sometimes disproportionate sanctioning which takes place under the veil of 'preventive' confiscations of instruments of crime. The case (already cited) of the yacht that was confiscated because the lessees had used drugs on it, is an excellent example of this.[68] More generally, reference may be made to 21 USC § 881(a) which provides for forfeiture of property which 'facilitated' a drug crime, under which American authorities have, for example, sought to forfeit a house in which the owner's son sold drugs.[69] Not only is the (value of the) property that is confiscated blatantly disproportionate to the offence for which it is imposed; the degree of sanctioning of an offence is also made dependent on fortuitous circumstances surrounding the offence. In principle, it does not matter whether drug consumption or selling takes place on a yacht, in a house or on a bicycle. Not surprisingly, American courts have sometimes held such draconian applications of the concept of forfeiture to be violative of the Eighth Amendment's Excessive Fines Clause.[70]

The punitive nature is sometimes disguised by invoking its so-called remedial effect. Confiscations are thus deemed to compensate for the costs of law enforcement. The concept of confiscation itself, however, flouts the idea of compensation. Confiscation of instrumentalities and also of proceeds from crime in no way relates to the costs that have been incurred by law enforcement authorities in the course of investigating and prosecuting the offence. In some cases this cost will be much higher than the value of the confiscated property, in other cases the amount confiscated may exceed the costs incurred by the government.[71] Reimbursement of the government's cost in investigating the offence is not the goal, but at the most, a fortuitous side-effect of confiscation. Hence the remedial purpose of confiscation can therefore only be linked to the general costs of law enforcement. Such a wide concept of damage, however, cannot be reconciled any more with a remedial goal:

A suit can be viewed as compensatory only if property is transmitted to an identifiable individual or group of individuals and the value of that property is actually determined by estimating the value of the interests lost by the recipient as a result of the actions by the defendant. Any less rigorous standard permits the government to obfuscate, to its own benefit, the distinction between compensatory and punitive actions.[72]

---

[68] *Calero-Toledo v. Pearson Yacht Leasing Co.*, 416 US 663 (1974).
[69] *US v. Real Property Located at 6625 Zumirez Drive*, 845 F Supp 725 (CDCal.1994).
[70] *US v. Real Property Located at 6625 Zumirez Drive*, 845 F Supp 725 (CDCal.1994).
[71] Stahl, 'Asset Forfeiture', 331–7.
[72] J. Charney, 'The Need for Constitutional Protections for Defendants in Civil Penalty Cases', *Cornell L. Rev.* (1974), 499–500.

In any case, the value of instrumentalities that are confiscated, has no relation at all to the 'costs of law enforcement', as this value is purely coincidental. In essence, confiscation of instrumentalities is not designed to compensate costs or losses occurred as a consequence of crimes. Individual losses should be compensated through civil proceedings and the costs to society (in law enforcement) through fines.

The conclusion that the confiscation of instrumentalities of crime is a punitive sanction which in general lacks any preventive or remedial function, makes it necessary to reconsider some of the features of this type of confiscation. Thus, confiscation of instrumentalities is usually compulsory. It is submitted that compulsory confiscation is justified in the case of per se contraband, where the uncontrolled possession in itself is dangerous. It is, however, problematic in respect of derivative contraband, the confiscation of which is a punitive sanction for which, as with any other punitive sanction, judges should have a margin of discretion. The punitive character of this type of confiscation also results in a number of limitations – amongst others those derived from human rights – on the confiscation power of courts. These limitations will be dealt with later, together with those of the confiscation of proceeds from crime.

Confiscation of the proceeds of crime

The confiscation of proceeds from crime is of relatively recent vintage and aims to enhance the effectiveness of criminal justice in its fight against any type of profit-driven crime. Although in many jurisdictions legislators only started to introduce this type of confiscation in the 1980s, some jurisdictions were already familiar with a similar type of confiscation, namely the confiscation of what was physically produced by a criminal offence such as forged bank notes, for example. These 'fruits' or 'products' of crime were, however, very narrowly defined so that this type of confiscation did not encompass the proceeds from crime, that is, the financial gains from an offence, but only items that were physically produced by an offence. This limited possibility was totally insufficient to deprive offenders of their ill-gotten gains, as it did not even allow the offender to be deprived of goods that were stolen.

Some legal systems (Belgium's,[73] but also Switzerland's[74]) thus draw a

---

[73] See G. Jakhian, 'L'infraction de blanchiment et la peine de confiscation en droit belge', *RDP* (1991), 772 and Vandeplas, 'De verbeurdverklaring van vermogensvoordelen', pp. 388–9.
[74] See Kohler, 'The Confiscation of Criminal Assets', 8–9 and Pieth, 'Das zweite Paket gegen das Organisierte Verbrechen', 237.

distinction between goods that are produced as a result of an offence and the financial profits gained through an offence. We will not dwell on this distinction any longer, however, as it is not material to our purpose and many legal systems are not familiar with it. When the term *fructum sceleris* is henceforth used, it will be deemed to refer principally to the financial proceeds from an offence, but it may occasionally also encompass goods produced by an offence.

The concept of confiscation of proceeds of crime

Although both the Convention of Vienna (Article 5(1)(a)) and the Money Laundering Convention (Article 2(1)) require states to make the confiscation of proceeds from crime possible, the conventions nevertheless differ in scope on some points.

A merely terminological difference is to be found in the definition of property that can be confiscated. Article 1 of the Vienna Convention defines property as follows: 'assets of every kind, whether corporeal or incorporeal, movable or immovable, tangible or intangible, and legal documents or instruments evidencing title to, or interest in such assets'. The definition in the Money Laundering Convention differs only slightly: 'property of any description, whether corporeal or incorporeal, movable or immovable, and legal documents or instruments evidencing title to, or interest in such property'. The only difference is that the Convention of Vienna explicitly provides that both tangible and intangible property can be confiscated, a provision which is absent in he definition of the Money Laundering Convention. The drafters of the latter convention thought this was clear from the definition itself.[75]

Another possible difference between the two conventions concerns the causal link that has to be established between the offence and the property whose confiscation is sought. It is beyond debate that the primary proceeds, that is the proceeds which have been 'immediately' generated by the offence, such as a work of art which has been stolen, or the cash that is received by the drug dealer, can be confiscated. As far as object confiscation is concerned, the question may arise whether confiscation is still possible if proceeds have been transformed or converted into other property. The relevance of this question is obvious: criminals will part as soon as possible with the property which constitutes the primary proceeds from their crimes in order to obstruct any efforts to trace the property.

---

[75] *Explanatory Report with the Convention on Laundering*, pp. 14–15.

Article 5(6)(a) of the Vienna Convention answers this question in the affir-
mative, whereas the Money Laundering Convention remains silent on the
subject. Under the Vienna Convention, confiscation of property with
which proceeds have been intermingled, is also possible (Article 5(6)(b)).
When a legal system operates a value confiscation system, neither of these
aspects is likely to pose a problem as a value confiscation can be enforced
on every kind of property held by the convicted person, even if legally
acquired.

What might, however, pose a problem even under a value confiscation
system, is the question as to whether secondary proceeds from crime, that
is indirect proceeds from crime generated by the primary proceeds themselves, can also be confiscated. When this is the case, all property
purchased with and traceable to criminal profits can be confiscated,
including any appreciation in their value which is not attributable to any
criminal activity, but rather to the criminal's investor skills or to his luck.
Again, the Vienna Convention is more articulate in this respect than its
European counterpart. Article 5(6)(c) of the former convention allows the
confiscation of income or other benefits derived from proceeds, property
into which proceeds have been transformed or converted, or property
with which proceeds have been intermingled, a possibility which also
exists under the Money Laundering Convention's broad definition of 'proceeds' ('any economic advantage from criminal offences').

Undoubtedly the most important difference between the Vienna
Convention and the Money Laundering Convention relates to the offences
for which confiscation of the proceeds is possible. In accordance with its
goal, the Convention of Vienna (Article 5(1)(a)) limits the scope of the obligation to enable confiscation in drug offences. Article 2 of the Money
Laundering Convention calls on states to enable confiscation of the proceeds in respect of any offence, although its second paragraph allows for
declarations to be made in order to limit the application field of confiscation of proceeds from crime, to certain offences or categories of offence.
While this possibility was inserted with a view to a rapid ratification and
hence entry into force of the convention,[76] the European Union has called
upon its Member States not to avail themselves of this possibility.[77] Only

---

[76] *Explanatory Report with the Convention on Laundering*, pp. 17–18 and H. G. Nilsson, 'The
Council of Europe Laundering Convention: A Recent Example of a Developing
International Criminal Law', in *Principles and Procedures For A Transnational Criminal Law*,
A. Eser and O. Lagodny, (Freiburg: Max-Planck Institut, 1992), pp. 467–8.

[77] See Article 1 of the EU Joint Action concerning arrangements for co-operation between
Member States in respect of identification, tracing, freezing or seizing and confiscation
of instrumentalities and the proceeds from crime.

those parties to the Money Laundering Convention that have not made a declaration in this respect allow confiscation of proceeds in respect of every type of offence. This is the case in Belgium,[78] England[79] and Switzerland,[80] for example. The Netherlands is one of the states to have made a declaration in this respect.[81] It has excluded fiscal offences from the application field of confiscation,[82] as fiscal law offers enough remedies to recover money which has unduly been obtained from, or not paid to the fiscal authorities. Other states which are not party to the Money Laundering Convention sometimes also have a limited application field. Thus, Luxembourg has limited confiscation of proceeds from crime for certain offences, notably drug offences.[83] United States legislation does not contain a general confiscation provision but is replete with statutory provisions, enabling confiscation of the proceeds from specific offences.

Punitive nature of confiscation of the proceeds of crime

Confiscation of the proceeds of crime is – even more than confiscation of the instrumentalities from crime – often portrayed as a remedial, reparative sanction. In some jurisdictions such as England, this so-called reparative nature has been invoked to justify a number of deviations from the traditional rules of criminal procedure:[84] the appropriate court for making a confiscation order is a civil court (the High Court of Justice), the use of a civil standard of proof, the fact that a confiscation order is not a 'sentence' for the purposes of an appeal to the Court of Appeal (Criminal

---

[78] Article 42, 3° of the Belgian Criminal Code. This possibility also extends to fiscal offences: see Stessens, *De nationale en internationale bestrijding van het witwassen*, pp. 67–8.

[79] Before 1 November 1995 the scope of confiscation under English law was limited to drug offences (s.1 DTA 1994) and indictable offences and a number of summary offences (s.72(9)(b) CJA 1988). The scope of confiscation was, however, expanded to all offences by ss.1 and 2 of the Proceeds of Crime Act 1995.

[80] Article 59 of the Swiss Criminal Code.

[81] Other states to have made a reservation in respect of Article 2 of the Money Laundering Convention, include Cyprus, Ireland, Lithuania, Norway, Sweden and the United Kingdom.

[82] See Article 74 of the Dutch General Tax Law (*Algemene Wet inzake Rijksbelastingen*). See also Dutch Supreme Court, judgment of May 2, 1995, NJ (1995), 613 and Doorenbos, *Over witwassen en voordeelsontneming*, p. 78.

[83] See Article 8–2 of the Luxembourg Drug Act (*Loi du 19 février 1973 concernant la vente de substances médicamenteuses et la lutte contre la toxicomanie*, 29 October 1992). For other examples, see Spielmann, 'La confiscation en droit luxembourgeois', 207.

[84] See R. Fortson, 'Annotations with the Criminal Justice Act 1993', *Current Law*, 1993, c.36., 22–3.

Division)[85] and the fact that a court is not obliged to resolve an ambiguity in favour of the defendant.[86]

At first sight, the characterisation of confiscation as a reparative, even civil sanction seems borne out by the concept of this type of confiscation, which in principle gives courts the possibility to take away from the offender what he has illegally obtained and thus to restore the *status quo ante*. In the following paragraphs it will nevertheless become apparent that, both in concept and in its practical ramifications, this type of confiscation has a punitive nature and has to be treated as a criminal sanction.

Confiscation of the proceeds of crime springs from a fundamental idea of justice, holding that 'crime should not pay'. A similar idea lies at the basis of the law of tort and of contract and of the doctrine of unjust enrichment.[87] The point has already been made that this restorative function was previously almost exclusively fulfilled by compensation and other civil remedies. Confiscation of proceeds from crime now allows the exercise of the same function in respect of 'crimes without a victim'. This analogy is in part false, however. The reparative nature of this type of confiscation is in many cases illusory rather than real. Although in principle it restores the *status quo ante*, confiscation of the proceeds of crime, unlike compensation, does not always repair the damages that have occurred as a result of the offence. The confiscation of the proceeds from drug trafficking will often have no relation at all to the social and economic damage that has been caused by the drug trafficking. This is all the more so when a court confiscates proceeds which have been obtained by saving costs in an illegal way, that is, in violation of criminal law (e.g. in the context of environmental crime).

More fundamentally, it is questionable whether it is at all appropriate to start from a concept of damage in the context of confiscation. When an offence has resulted in individual damage, this can and should be compensated through civil remedies. With respect to those cases in which an offence has not made any identifiable individual victims, but has only resulted in general costs that have to be borne by society as a whole (especially through law enforcement), it has already been argued that these general costs cannot be considered as costs that have to be compensated. Many 'crimes without a victim' do not actually deprive society of property, but 'only' result in additional costs, although this assertion does not always hold water as, for example, in the case of subvention fraud.

[85] This assertion was not accepted by the Court of Appeal: *R v. Johnson* [1991] 2 QB 249.
[86] This was held in *R v. Chapman*, *The Times*, 18 November 1991.
[87] Mitchell, Hinton and Taylor, *Confiscation*, p. 3.

Even though the confiscation of the proceeds of crime does not in most cases serve a reparative purpose, it aims to restore the situation to what it was before the offence was committed. It thus aims to attain a fundamental goal of justice, namely to make sure that no one benefits from his own wrong-doing. The very idea that the deprivation of proceeds from crime will effectively result in a reduction of (profitable) crime starts from the concept of a *homo economicus*, who carefully balances the pros and cons before engaging in any activity, whether legal or illegal (the rational choice theory).[88] The thrust of the new criminal justice policy is precisely that offenders, if convicted, will not be able to benefit from the crimes they have committed. In this way, the confiscation of the proceeds of crime is characteristic of a meritocratic vision which prevails in contemporary society: it is aimed at ensuring that no one gets what they do not deserve. This makes clear that the new criminal justice policy is of a retributive, and not of a preventive, nature. It could therefore be viewed as the ideal minimum penalty for any crime committed for the sake of economic gain,[89] were it not for the fact that the actual implementation of this type of confiscation often exceeds the boundaries of this restorative goal and has distinctly punitive features.

An important factor which often enhances the punitive nature of the confiscation of the proceeds of crime is the way in which confiscation is fixed by the courts. It has already been pointed out that the relevant multilateral treaties allow them to confiscate the secondary as well as the primary proceeds of crime. The conventions however, are silent, on the question of how the exact economic advantage which has been obtained through criminal activity should be calculated. Consequently, this matter is governed solely by domestic law. Many countries have opted for a very wide definition of the concept of 'proceeds of crime' whereby it is impossible for criminals to deduct their expenses.

When enacting RICO (the Racketeer Influenced and Corrupt Organisations Act), the American Congress chose the term 'proceeds', which is thought to encompass all property purchased with and traceable to criminal profits, including any appreciation in value not attributable to a criminal activity. Congress did not make clear, however, whether the choice of this term was also intended to exclude the possibility of accused persons deducting costs incurred in carrying out their criminal activities or any taxes they may have paid. American case law has been equivocal on

---

[88] J. M. Nelen, 'Ontnemingswetgeving; uitgangspunten en praktische uitwerking', *Justitiële Verkenningen* (1996, No.9), 46–7.   [89] Fried, 'Rationalising Criminal Forfeiture', 410–12.

the question of whether 'proceeds' equate to gross receipts or to net profits.[90]

English courts, on the contrary, have been very clear in this respect and have stated that the gross receipts should be confiscated, thereby excluding any possibility of deducting costs.[91] This broad character of confiscation under English law was one of the elements that induced the European Court of Human Rights, in the case of *Welch v. UK*, to consider confiscation as a criminal sanction, the imposition of which was governed by Article 7 of the European Convention on Human Rights.[92]

In continental Europe some other jurisdictions have also opted for a broad concept of 'proceeds'. The Belgian Parliament[93] has clearly opted for such a broad concept, as has the Swiss Supreme Court.[94] Dutch case law, on the contrary, allows convicts to deduct their expenses in order to calculate the exact amount of money to be confiscated.[95]

Arguments can be invoked both in favour of a broad and a narrow definition of the proceeds of crime. The broad concept is in the first place supported by an intuitive feeling that criminals should not be allowed to deduct the expenses they have incurred in committing criminal activities with a view to obtaining illicit profits. Moreover, a confiscation, being a criminal sanction designed to punish criminal behaviour, is different from a fiscal measure which is imposed to tax (legal) activities. One could therefore argue that it is only logical to allow for the deduction of expenses in respect of the latter and to exclude the former. However, this line of reasoning is not completely convincing for two reasons. First, in

---

[90] See in general on the American position: Fried, 'Rationalising Criminal Forfeiture', 375–80.

[91] *R v. Smith (Ian)* [1989] 1 WLR 765 (CA). Section 2(3) DTA 1994 (previously s.1(3) DTOA 1986) refers to 'any payment or other reward in connection with drug trafficking'.

[92] European Court of Human Rights judgment of 9 February 1995, *Welch v. UK, Publ. ECHR*, Series A, vol. 307-A, para. 33.

[93] *Doc.Parl.*, Chambre, 1989–90, 987/1, 5; Belgian Supreme Court, judgment of 18 February, *Proces & Bewijs* (1998), 75. See also Stessens, *De nationale en internationale bestrijding van het witwassen*, pp. 61–2.

[94] See the following cases decided by the Swiss Supreme Court: ATF 97 IV 252; ATF 100 IV 264; ATF 101 IV 363 and ATF 103 IV 143. Courts at lower instance have, however, sometimes allowed criminals to deduct their expenses. See J. Gauthier, 'Quelques aspects de la confiscation selon l'article 58 du Code pénal suisse', in *Lebendiges Strafrecht. Festgabe zum 65. Geburtstag Hans Schultz*, H. Walder and S. Trechsel, (Berne: Revue Pénal Suisse/Verlag Stämpfli, 1977), p. 375; Graber, *Geldwäscherei*, pp. 159–60 and S. Trechsel, *Schweizerisches Strafgesetzbuch, Kurzkommentar* (Zürich: Schulthess Polygraphisher Verlag, 1989), p. 212.

[95] Doorenbos, *Over witwassen en voordeelsontneming*, pp. 92–93. See, however, R. Persoon, 'Geplukt of aangeslagen? De fiscaalrechtelijke implicaties van de strafrechtelijke maatregel ter ontneming van wederrechtelijk verkregen voordeel', *DD* (1996), 750–1.

some jurisdictions taxes are also imposed in respect of illegal activities. Second, some taxes (e.g. environmental taxes) are in part also aimed at restoring the *status ante quo* (e.g. of the environment). In those cases the difference between legal, taxed activities and criminal activities resides in the degree of harm that is done, or perceived to be done, to society. Whereas the detrimental consequences of the former activities do not outweigh their benefits, the reverse is clearly the case with the latter, criminal, activities though there will of course often be other reasons to criminalise certain behaviour. In addition, it is sometimes argued that allowing criminals to deduct their expenses can result in insurmountable problems of proof if the proceeds are from crimes committed abroad.[96] This argument can easily be countered, as in practice, the defence will always be at pains to point out to the court the expenses that were incurred in calculating the proceeds at risk from confiscation. The main argument against a broad concept of proceeds lies, however, in the nature and purpose of the confiscation of proceeds from crime itself. This type of confiscation aims to ensure that criminals will reap no economic benefits from their crime by restoring the *status quo ante*. It is submitted that the attainment of this goal does not require the confiscation of gross receipts, but that it suffices to take away the economic profits. Using this type of confiscation to obtain more than the net proceeds from crime is somehow at odds with the very concept of this type of confiscation. That is not to say that criminals should not face punitive financial sanctions, only that this should be done not by confiscation, but through fines. The detrimental effects which confiscation of gross receipts may have can be shown in the following way. For example, the broad concept of proceeds from crime prohibits a company which, in the course of its legal activities, has violated a criminal statute and thus committed a criminal offence, from deducting its legal expenses. However, the confiscation of gross receipts in the case of white collar crime may be regarded as unseemly in that it usually involves the performance of illegal activities by illegal means, in the operation of a legitimate business. To apply a broad concept of proceeds under these circumstances would mean that a white collar criminal who pays taxes will ultimately be worse off than a (professional) criminal who does not, as the former will not be able to deduct his taxes.[97]

Notwithstanding the conclusion that only the net proceeds should be confiscated, it has been shown that actual practice in many jurisdictions

---

[96] See Trechsel, *Schweizerisches Strafgesetzbuch*, p. 213.

[97] This seems to have happened on at least one occasion: *United States v. Lizza Industries, Inc.*, 775 F.2d 499 (2nd Circ. 1985), *cert. den.* 475 US 1082 (1986).

tends towards a broader concept and thereby adds an unmistakably punitive side to the confiscation of the proceeds of crime.

This punitive nature is sometimes even enhanced by other aspects of
confiscation law such as the facilitation theory, which has been adopted
as part of American case law. According to this theory, property which has
facilitated the laundering of proceeds from crime should be confiscated
as well as the actual proceeds. This theory is based on a broad interpretation of 18 USC § 981(a)(1)(A) which holds that all property 'involved in'
money laundering should be forfeited. Some courts have used this provision to order forfeiture of all money held at a certain bank account
through which criminal proceeds have been laundered.[98]

It is, however, not only the punitive nature of confiscation which leads
to the conclusion that confiscation of the proceeds of crime is a criminal
sanction. Leaving aside *in rem* procedures, these sanctions are always
imposed in the course of a criminal procedure, precisely as a sanction for
a criminal offence. The confiscation of proceeds from the offence can be
ordered when a person is found guilty of an offence, and only then. This
is perceived to be a weak point of *in personam* confiscation procedures *vis-
à-vis in rem* confiscation procedures which allow, even after a person has
died or absconded, the confiscation of the proceeds of crime independently of the outcome of a criminal procedure. If one accepts that the
imposition of a confiscation of criminally derived proceeds amounts to a
'criminal charge' under Article 6 of the European Convention on Human
Rights,[99] the presumption of innocence (Article 6(2)) prevents the confiscation of proceeds from being ordered after the owner is deceased. As was
explicitly stated by the European Court of Human Rights in respect of
punitive fiscal sanctions, 'inheritance of the guilt of the dead is not compatible with the standards of criminal justice in a society governed by the
rule of law'.[100] It may be noted in passing that this case law also casts a
doubt over the legitimacy of a number of international recommendations
which aim to introduce confiscation rules in respect of deceased offenders (Action point 26(c) of the EU Action Plan to combat organised crime[101]
and Article 30 of the UN Model Law on Money Laundering).

Moreover, the confiscation of the proceeds of crime is often optional
while some legal systems even allow judges to take into account personal
circumstances when determining the amount to be confiscated. Such
discretion would surely not be appropriate if confiscation were not a

---

[98] Gordon, 'Prosecutors who Seize too Much', 744–66.   [99] See also *infra* pp. 60–6.
[100] European Court of Human Rights, 29 August 1997, *AP, MP and TP v. Switzerland*, *Reports of judgments and decisions* (1997–V), 1447, para. 48.   [101] *OJ* No. C 251, 15.08.1997, p. 1.

criminal, but a civil, reparative sanction. In addition, one can also point to the fact that under some confiscation statutes (e.g. in England and The Netherlands), confiscation orders can carry severe terms of imprisonment in default, a possibility which is excluded for civil judgments.

A number of these arguments were expressly taken into account by the European Court of Human Rights to determine the criminal nature of confiscation orders imposed under the DTOA 1986.[102] Although the case centred on the applicability of Article 7 of the European Convention on Human Rights (the prohibition of retroactive application of penal sanctions) to the confiscation of proceeds from drug trafficking, the Court was forced to ascertain whether confiscation was a criminal sanction or, as the British government alleged, a civil, reparative measure. Now that it is clearly established that confiscation of proceeds from crime is a punitive, criminal 'penalty' in the sense of Article 7, it is time to establish the confines within which law enforcement authorities can seek to exercise their confiscation powers.

The dangerous attractiveness of confiscation: policing and prosecuting for profit

Confiscation of the proceeds of crime, and of the *instrumentum* or *objectum sceleris*, can be very profitable for the government and is sometimes, especially in the United States, considered a source of funding of the costs of law enforcement. As a criminal or civil sanction confiscation is therefore much more attractive to government as a sanction than costly imprisonment. The disadvantages of this profit-oriented approach to criminal justice arise particularly from two practices: the need for the retention of confiscated assets by law enforcement agencies and the need to use out-of-court settlements to deprive offenders of alleged proceeds from crime. Whereas the former practice is especially known in the United States, the latter is also used in other countries.

Confiscation to fund law enforcement agencies

Since the 1984 Comprehensive Crime Control Act, US federal law enforcement agencies are allowed to retain and use the proceeds obtained through asset forfeitures, rather than having to deposit them in the Treasury's General Fund. A specific Assets Forfeiture Fund was set up into

---

[102] European Court of Human Rights judgment of 9 February 1995, *Welch v. UK, Publ. ECHR*, Series A, No. 307-A, para. 33.

which money seized by purely federal agencies must normally be transferred, after deduction of expenses. At the same time a so-called federal equitable sharing programme was established, providing state and local police agencies with the lion's share of seized or forfeited property, even if federal agencies were involved in the operation,[103] including a federal 'adoption' procedure whereby state police agencies who hand over seized property to the federal Justice Department for federal forfeiture are 'rewarded' with up to 80% of the value, which should be used exclusively for law enforcement purposes.[104]

Notwithstanding a very powerful incentive for law enforcement which is provided by the sharing of confiscated assets with state and local police agencies, this technique has been rightly subjected to sharp criticism.[105] In the following paragraphs, a number of arguments will be presented which ineluctably suggest that this technique should be rejected.

A first line of criticism holds that it is fundamentally wrong to investigate and prosecute criminal activities with a view to the financial profits arising from them that will accrue to government. Law enforcement may serve several goals (e.g. prevention and deterrence) and confiscation as a tool of law enforcement can subsequently serve various purposes (reparative, punitive function), but the view that law enforcement authorities have a legitimate interest in striving for confiscation as a means of funding law enforcement operations is difficult to accept. This view was nevertheless endorsed by the US Supreme Court which held that the 'Government has a pecuniary interest in forfeiture that goes beyond merely separating a criminal from his ill-gotten gains . . . The sums of money . . . are substantial, and the Government's interest in using profits of crime to fund these [law enforcement] activities should not be discounted'.[106]

A second line of criticism is closely related to the first and concerns the influence of this personal pecuniary interest in the functioning of criminal justice, that is, its influence on the way police officers, prosecutors and judges carry out their tasks. The risk cannot be totally excluded that this personal interest may also influence the way these persons perform their duties. Even if this risk were never to materialise, this personal interest

---

[103] 21 USC § 881(e)(1) and 19 USC § 1616(a).

[104] E. Blumenson and E. Nilsen, 'Policing for Profit: The Drug War's Hidden Economic Agenda', *University of Chicago Law Review* (1998), 51.

[105] For this criticism, see Blumenson and Nilsen, 'Policing for Profit', 56–83; Fried, 'Rationalizing Criminal Forfeiture', 360–6; Nadelmann, 'Unlaundering Dirty Money', 34; T. M. Schalken, 'Rechtshandhaving en het nieuwe premiejagen', *DD* (1992), 543–6.

[106] *Caplin & Drysdale v. United States*, 491 US 617, 629 (1989).

may have a perceived influence on the functioning of criminal justice. From a due process point of view it is not only required that courts be impartial, but also that they be perceived as impartial. According to the Supreme Court even a possible temptation suffices to disqualify a judge under the Fourteenth Amendment.[107] The well-known maxim that justice must not only be done, but must also be seen to be done, however, only applies to courts and not to police and prosecutorial agencies.

Irrespective of possible due process objections, the technique of funding law enforcement authorities by means of funds which have been confiscated as a result of their operations is bound to run into a number of policy objections. Its influence on law enforcement strategies in the United States has been very strong. Many police and other law enforcement agencies have become dependent on the 'income' derived from drug law enforcement (i.e. asset forfeitures) to meet their budgetary requirements. At least in the United States, the quest for funding derived from forfeitures has on occasions led to illegal police action in some states.[108] The techniques of retention of confiscated assets by and of sharing confiscated assets with law enforcement agencies involved in the investigation and the prosecution has undeniably had a very marked influence on the strategies of law enforcement. As far as drug crimes are concerned, it has led to an increasingly assertive style of law enforcement, annihilating the legislative debate on alternative methods to deal with the drug problem. Moreover, the considerable financial benefits that can be reaped from drug law enforcement may lead police and prosecutors to pay excessive attention to drug crimes (cf. the 'war on drugs') and to neglect other equally or even more pressing crime problems.

Out-of-court settlements

The goal of depriving offenders of their ill-gotten gains cannot be attained only through confiscation, but also through out-of-court settlements by which an accused agrees to pay a sum of money or to hand over property to the state's treasury, supposedly equivalent to the proceeds of his criminal activities.

US prosecutors have often used plea bargaining techniques to get hold of the proceeds of crime, reducing the charge in return for the handing over of criminal proceeds. Similar techniques can, however, also be used

---

[107] *Tumey v. Ohio*, 273 US 510, 523, 532 (1927).
[108] For a vivid account of the egregious consequences of this, see Blumenson and Nilsen, 'Policing for Profit', 67–72.

in other countries. Some continental legislations, however, are only familiar with out-of-court settlements which make it impossible to institute
criminal proceedings after an out-of-court settlement has been reached.
This is, for example, the case under Belgian law which allows the
Prosecutor's Office to enter into an out-of-court settlement with the
suspect under certain conditions, one of the possible conditions being
that the suspect waives his rights to property liable to confiscation.[109]
After such an agreement the prosecution will not be able to prosecute the
suspect with regard to the facts underlying the settlement.

The Dutch legislature has sought to circumvent this inconvenience by
instituting a special type of out-of-court settlement, which allows entry
into an agreement with the accused for the payment of his proceeds.[110]
This special type of out-of-court settlement excludes a further confiscation
procedure but as such has no bearing upon the actual criminal proceedings. Such an agreement can even be entered into after the offender has
already been convicted as the confiscation procedure is separate from the
actual criminal proceedings under Dutch law.[111]

The use of plea bargaining, or, more generally, of out-of-court settlements, is open to criticism in various ways. Deprivation of the proceeds of
crime by way of out-of-court settlements offers an attractive avenue to
prosecutors as it avoids the necessity for lengthy and often delicate trials
and enables courts to get their hands on the 'loot' immediately. The attractiveness of these techniques only increases when the property constituting the proceeds is located abroad and the prospect of a successful
enforcement of an eventual confiscation order is unsure.

These techniques carry with them an undeniable risk of class justice as
suspects who dispose of assets liable to confiscation are prone to get a
better treatment than poor offenders, in that they can reduce the charges
they will have to face, or even escape trial through out-of-court settlements, by handing over these assets to government.

On the other hand, it must be acknowledged that it may be hard for
innocent suspects to resist the pressure which comes from the possibility
of evading trial through out-of-court settlements. This is especially true in
the case of financial institutions or other economic operators who have an

---

[109] Article 216ter Belgian Code of Criminal Procedure.
[110] Article 511c Dutch Code of Criminal Procedure.
[111] On this type of out-of-court settlement, see C. P. M. Cleiren and J. F. Nijboer (eds.),
    Strafvordering. Tekst & Commentaar (Deventer: Kluwer, 1995), p. 933; L. F. Keyser-Ringnalda,
    Boef en buit, p. 58 and J. J. E. Schutte, 'Het wetsvoorstel inzake ontneming van
    wederrechtelijk verkregen voordeel', in *Hercodificatie Wetboek van Strafvordering.*, ed. D. R.
    Doorenbos and R. J. Verweij (Nijmegen: Ars Aequi Libri, 1991), pp. 168–9.

economic reputation to uphold and may be willing to pay considerable sums in order to eschew the damage to their economic reputation which comes from a criminal trial. The prosecution should therefore refrain from cajoling suspects into accepting out-of-court settlements. It follows from the case law both of the European Court of Human Rights[112] and the Court of Justice of the European Communities[113] that there should be a balance between the two alternatives facing the defendant, that is, between entering into the out-of-court settlement and defending himself in court. Such is the requirement that flows from the right to access to court.

Human rights limitations to the confiscation sanctions

The imposition of a punitive, criminal 'penalty', needs to be accompanied by a number of fundamental guarantees. Reference has already been made to the disparate American case law.[114] The most important guarantees are those laid down in domestic or international human rights provisions. A first crucial question to be answered in this respect is whether *in rem* confiscation procedures can be reconciled with Article 6 of the European Convention on Human Rights. The applicability of Article 6 also raises further questions, for example, regarding the compatibility of a number of techniques that have been used by domestic legislators to shift the onus of proof regarding the criminal origin of alleged proceeds from crime. In addition, these techniques of reversal of the burden of proof and the multiplication of legal possibilities for confiscation enhance the risk of double jeopardy. Confiscation procedures sometimes also risk endangering the legitimate rights of third parties who have vested property rights in the assets that are confiscated.

Compatibility of in rem procedures with Article 6 of the European Convention on Human Rights

In rem procedures obviously do not afford the same degree of procedural protection for the owner of the property at stake as do *in personam* proceedings. Even though *in rem* proceedings are not formally concerned with the

---

[112] European Court of Human Rights, judgment of 27 February 1980, *Deweer v. Belgium*, Publ. ECHR, Series A, No.35, para. 51. See also B. De Smet, 'De versnelling van de strafrechtspleging met instemming van de verdachte. Is de invoering van een "guilty plea" naar Angelsaksisch model wenselijk?', *Panopticon* (1994), p. 442.

[113] Court of Justice, 23 January 1997, *Trans-Cap GmbH*, ECR (1997), 285.

[114] See *supra* pp. 40–1.

guilt of the owner of the property, the punitive nature of confiscation of both proceeds and instrumentalities of crime makes it necessary to investigate the procedural guarantees afforded to everyone facing a criminal charge. These procedural rights – in the first place the right to a fair and public hearing within a reasonable time by an independent and impartial tribunal established by law – are laid down both in Article 14 of the International Covenant on Civil and Political Rights and in Article 6 of the European Convention on Human Rights. In view of the interesting case law of the European Court of Human Rights in this field, the latter provision will in particular be studied.

In *AGOSI v. United Kingdom* the Court was faced with the question whether the imposition of a confiscation necessarily implies that the owners of the confiscated property should have been afforded the same rights as those granted to everyone in the determination of a criminal charge. The German company AGOSI had suffered a considerable economic loss when the UK's Customs & Excise department had seized and eventually forfeited golden Krugerrands to a value of £120,000 that had been illegally imported into the United Kingdom. Defendants X and Y were caught by UK Customs & Excise officers as they attempted to smuggle into the United Kingdom on 2 August 1975 the golden Krugerrands they had bought on the same day from AGOSI in Germany. Because the cheque presented by them for payment had been drawn without provision, the sale contract was *ab initio* null and void and AGOSI had retained ownership of the Krugerrands. AGOSI initiated several procedures in the United Kingdom for restitution of the confiscated Krugerrands but was unsuccessful. AGOSI therefore took the case to the European Court of Human Rights, complaining that the confiscation amounted to a procedure for the determination of a criminal charge in which it had been denied the fair trial rights laid down in Article 6 of the European Convention. The Court responded that: 'The fact that measures consequential upon an act for which third parties were prosecuted affected in adverse manner the property rights of AGOSI cannot itself lead to the conclusion that, during the course of the procedures complained of, any "criminal charge", for the purposes of Article 6, could be considered as having been brought against the applicant company.'[115]

As a general statement this is undoubtedly true. The mere fact that persons own property that is being confiscated does in itself not necessarily imply that a criminal charge is being brought against them. When, for

[115] European Court of Human Rights, judgment of 24 October 1986, *AGOSI v. United Kingdom*, *Publ. ECHR*, Series A, No.108, para. 65.

example, instrumentalities of an offence are being confiscated, that does not necessarily imply that a criminal charge should be brought against the owners who may very well have not been implicated in the offence in any way. Confiscation of proceeds from crime as a matter of fact often implies that the person who is being prosecuted is not the real owner.

Nine years after *AGOSI*, the European Court of Human Rights arrived at a similar decision in *Air Canada v. United Kingdom*, which again involved a seizure by the UK Customs & Excise, this time of an aircraft on board which drugs had been found on several occasions, including a few days earlier. The aircraft was only seized temporarily for a few hours until Air Canada paid a sum of £50,000.[116] The European Court agreed with the English Court of Appeal that the case did not concern an *in personam* procedure but an *in rem* procedure and therefore did not require that *mens rea* of the owner or the possessor was established.[117] This, as well as the fact that non-payment of the sum could not give rise to criminal prosecutions, unlike some out-of-court settlements (transactions) and that the procedure did not involve the intervention of criminal courts at any stage, induced the Court to reach the conclusion that the action of the UK's Customs & Excise department did not amount to a criminal charge in the sense of Article 6 of the European Convention on Human Rights.

It is submitted that this decision is flawed. The case law of the European Court of Human Rights regarding the applicability of Article 6 to confiscation procedures should be seen in close connection to its case law regarding the right to property, entrenched in Article 1 of the First Protocol to the European Convention on Human Rights. In *AGOSI* the Court held that an import prohibition on golden coins constituted a law 'necessary to control the use of property' and that the seizure and confiscation of the Krugerrands were consequently measures taken in accordance with this prohibition and were therefore governed by the second paragraph of Article 1 of the First Protocol.[118] The Court ruled in the same

---

[116] On the factual background, see *Customs and Excise Commissioners v. Air Canada* [1989] 2 All ER 22; European Court of Human Rights, judgment of 5 May 1995, *Air Canada v. United Kingdom, Publ. ECHR*, Series A, No.316–A, paras.6–10. See also J. A. E. Vervaele, 'Les sanctions de confiscation en droit pénal: un intrus issu du droit civil? Une analyse de la jurisprudence de la CEDH et de la signification qu'elle revêt pour le droit (procédural) pénal néerlandais', *Rev.sc.crim.* (1998), 41–4.

[117] See *Customs and Excise Commissioners v. Air Canada* [1991] 1 All ER 570, 586–7 per Lord Purchas; European Court of Human Rights judgment of 5 May 1995, *Air Canada v. United Kingdom, Publ. ECHR*, Series A, No.316–A, para. 52.

[118] European Court of Human Rights, judgment of 24 October 1986, *AGOSI v. United Kingdom, Publ. ECHR*, Series A, No.108, para. 51.

sense in *Air Canada*.[119] The text of Article 1, however, prompts the question whether confiscation of proceeds from crime should not be considered a deprivation of property under the first paragraph of this provision:

1 Every natural or legal person is entitled to the peaceful enjoyment of his possessions. No one shall be deprived of his possessions except in the public interest and subject to the conditions provided by law and by general principles of international law.

2 The preceding provisions shall not, however, in any way impair the right of a State to enforce such laws as it deems necessary to control the use of property in accordance with the general interest or to secure the payment of taxes or other contributions or penalties.

This question was answered in the negative in *Raimondo v. Italy*, which concerned seizure and confiscation of real estate that was derived from mafia practices. It was held that '[a]lthough it involves deprivation of possessions, confiscation of property does not necessarily come within the scope of the second sentence of the first paragraph of Article 1 of Protocol No.1'.[120] The Court referred to its prior judgments in *AGOSI* and *Handyside*, in which the Court seemed to have considered confiscation as a preventive measure. This was undoubtedly the case in *Handyside* where the Court held that the seizure, confiscation and destruction of obscene publications constitute a law 'necessary to control the use of property' and were thus governed by the second paragraph of Article 1 of the First Protocol.[121] These measures effectively prevented further distribution of the publication.

It is, however, submitted that the confiscation of the illegally imported Krugerrands in *AGOSI* did not constitute a preventive measure as it did not pertain to the use of the property but only to certain economic-political goals that were set by the British Parliament.[122] The (possession of) property was not unlawful *per se*; at most, the confiscation dealt with derivative contraband, but not with *per se* contraband. An even more flagrant example is that of *M v. Italy*, a case decided by the European Commission of Human Rights, in which it was accepted that the confiscation of proceeds from crime under the Italian anti-mafia laws pursuant to a reversal

---

[119] European Court of Human Rights, judgment of 5 May 1995, *Air Canada v. United Kingdom*, Publ. ECHR, Series A, No.316-A, paras.31–34.

[120] European Court of Human Rights, judgment of 22 February 1994, *Raimondo v. Italy*, Publ. ECHR, Series A, No.281-A, para. 29.

[121] European Court of Human Rights, judgment of 7 December 1976, *Handyside v. United Kingdom*, Publ. ECHR, Series A, No.24, para. 63.

[122] W. Peukert, 'Die Rechtsprechung des EGMR zur Verhältnismässigkeit einer Eigentumsentziehung nach zollrechtlichen Vorschriften', *EuGRZ* (1988), 510.

of burden of proof did not fall foul of Article 6 of the Convention nor of Article 1 of Protocol No.1 as these confiscation measures were 'preventive' and hence did not amount to a criminal penalty.[123]

Although all these cases differed from the earlier mentioned case of *Welch v. UK* (in which the Court did accept the criminal nature of the confiscation of drug trafficking proceeds)[124] in that the imposition of these confiscations did not require that the person was found guilty of a criminal offence, it is submitted that the punitive character of these confiscations could and should have been deduced from the possibility that the owner might avoid confiscation by demonstrating his innocence – a possibility which was explicitly acknowledged by the European Commission and the Court of Human Rights.[125] In this perspective, it is useful to refer to the line of reasoning adopted by the American Supreme Court which explicitly deduced the punitive nature of *in rem* confiscations from the fact that confiscation is excluded in case owners can demonstrate 'exceptional innocence'.[126] It inevitably follows from this line of reasoning that the confiscation in *AGOSI* amounted to a penalty, as it was at least in part based on guilt of the owner.[127] In *Air Canada* the punitive nature of the seizure of the aircraft as an instrument of crime was even more blatant, as it was not the aircraft as such that constituted the contraband, but the drugs that had been found on it on earlier occasions. It should be equally clear that the confiscation of assets belonging to a mafia member and presumedly derived from an illegal origin, though termed preventive, is in fact nothing else but a criminal penalty.

The European Court of Human Rights seems to take the view that confiscation is a measure designed to prevent the use of dangerous property. It is submitted this is a flawed conception of confiscation, given the often punitive nature of confiscation. In their joint dissenting opinion in *Air Canada*, Judges Martens and Russo correctly point out that confiscation of the *objectum sceleris* and *instrumentum sceleris* are penalties in the sense of Article 1(2) and can therefore not be considered to fall under the 'control [of] the use of property in accordance with the general interest'.[128]

As it has been established that confiscation almost always amounts to a punitive sanction,[129] it is submitted that the holding of the European

[123] Application No.12386/86, *Decisions and Reports* (1991), 59.   [124] See *supra* p. 56.
[125] European Court of Human Rights, judgment of 24 October 1986, *AGOSI v. United Kingdom*, Publ. ECHR, Series A, No.108, paras. 53–5.   [126] *Austin v. US* 509 US 602 (1993).
[127] Peukert, 'Die Rechtsprechung des EGMR', 510.
[128] See the joint *dissenting opinion* of judges Martens and Russo with the judgment of the European Court of Human Rights of 5 May 1995, *Air Canada v. United Kingdom*, Publ. ECHR, Series A, No.316–A.   [129] See *supra* pp. 50–6.

Court of Human Rights in *AGOSI* and *Air Canada* that confiscation procedure can take place outside a procedure governed by Article 6 of the
Convention is incorrect.

As far as confiscation of the proceeds of crime is concerned, the Court
itself has explicitly held that this type of confiscation amounts to a
'penalty'. This was established by the Court in *Welch v. United Kingdom*,[130] a
case regarding the application of Article 7 of the European Convention on
Human Rights (laying down a prohibition on retroactive penal sanctions),
in which the Court investigated the real nature of confiscation of proceeds
from drug offences, not limiting its research to the denomination given
by the English legislator.

Although it does not follow directly from the European Convention on
Human Rights that the criteria for defining a 'penalty' under Article 7
coincide with the definition of a 'criminal charge' under Article 6, there
are no valid reasons for distinguishing between the two.[131] In respect of
the term 'law' referred to in Article 7, the European Court of Human
Rights has already explicitly held that this is the same concept as referred
to in other provisions of the Convention, e.g. Articles 8(2) and 10(2).[132] In
his dissenting opinion in *Air Canada*, Judge Martens also comes to the conclusion that the seizure and its remittal upon payment of £50,000 were
intended to penalise Air Canada and that the procedure therefore
amounted to a criminal charge under Article 6.[133] In a more general
context not concerned with confiscations, the European Court of Human
Rights has repeatedly held that the punitive nature of sanctions imposed
is a sufficient criterion to decide that a procedure leading to the imposition of this sanction pertains to the determination of a criminal charge
and should therefore be governed by Article 6.[134]

[130] European Court of Human Rights, judgment of 9 February 1995, *Welch v. United
Kingdom*, Publ. ECHR, Series A, No.307-A, para. 35.
[131] See also Vervaele, 'Les sanctions de confiscation en droit pénal', 49.
[132] European Court of Human Rights, *SW v. United Kingdom*, judgment of 22 November
1995, Publ.ECHR, Series A, No.335-B, para. 35; *CR v. United Kingdom*, judgment of
22 November 1995, Publ.ECHR, Series A, No.335-C, para. 33.
[133] Dissenting opinion of Judge Walsh with the judgment of the European Court of
Human Rights of 5 May 1995, *Air Canada v. United Kingdom*, Publ. ECHR, Series A,
No.316-A.
[134] The Court has established three criteria to determine whether a procedure amounts to
a 'criminal charge': (i) the municipal denomination of the sanction (criminal or not)
and (ii) the general character of the violated rule and the question whether the
sanction has a repressive and preventive nature and (iii) the nature and gravity of the
sanction. See, e.g., the following decisions of European Court of Human Rights: the
judgment of 8 June 1976, *Engel v. The Netherlands*; of 21 February 1984, *Öztürk v. Germany*;
of 25 August 1987, *Lutz v. Germany* and of 24 February 1994, *Bendenoun v. France*,

The conclusion that procedures leading to the imposition of a confiscation must be compatible with the requirements of Article 6 is thus inevitable. These requirements can only be guaranteed in *in personam*
proceedings, in which the owner/defendant can defend himself. Article 6
does not prohibit, however, that a confiscation is imposed by an administrative authority if there is a possibility to bring the case before a court
which may decide upon facts and law and which meets the criteria of
Article 6.[135]

From a fair-trial point of view, *in rem* proceedings can be allowed only
insofar as they concern truly preventive measures, designed to prevent the
use of contraband *per se* and are thus not concerned with a criminal
charge.

Reversal of the burden of proof regarding the criminal origin of proceeds

Various domestic legislators have introduced legal techniques that are
intended to make it easier to demonstrate the criminal origin of proceeds
and consequently to order their confiscation.[136] These reversals of the
burden of proof should be distinguished from other ways of 'tinkering'
with the standard of proof, which are related either to the proof of the
offence or the evaluation of the amount of proceeds. Thus, the American
in rem procedures allow the civil standard of proof ('probable cause')
instead of the criminal standard of proof ('beyond reasonable doubt').
Alternatively, the case law of some countries, while requiring the criminal standard of proof in respect of the offence, allows the civil standard as
far as the evaluation of the value of the proceeds is concerned.[137]

Here, we are, however, concerned only with the reversal of the burden
of proof regarding the criminal origin of proceeds from crime. Article 5(7)

Publ.ECHR, Series A, Nos.22, 73, 123 and 284). See also M. Delmas-Marty, 'La "matière
pénale" au sens de la Convention européenne des droits de l'homme, flou du droit
pénal', *Rev.sc.crim. et dr.pén.comp.* (1987), 819–62 and A. Den Hartog, *Artikel 6 E.V.R.M.:
grenzen aan het streven de straf eerder op de daad te doen volgen* (Antwerp: Maklu, 1992), pp.
107–11.

[135] European Court of Human Rights, judgment of 24 February 1994, *Bendenoun v. France*,
Publ. ECHR, Series A, No.284, para. 46. See also the joint *dissenting opinion* of judges
Martens and Russo in European Court of Human Rights judgment of 5 May 1995, *Air
Canada v. United Kingdom*, *Publ. ECHR*, Series A, No.316–A.

[136] According to the FATF (*Evaluation of Laws and Systems in FATF Members*, p. 4) ten of its
members have introduced some kind of reversal of the burden of proof.

[137] FATF, *Evaluation of Laws and Systems in FATF Members*, p. 4. See, e.g., the decision of the
Belgian Supreme Court of 14 December 1994, *Recente Arresten van het Hof van Cassatie*
(1995), 99.

of the Convention of Vienna allows states to 'consider ensuring that the onus of proof be reversed regarding the lawful origin of alleged proceeds or other property liable to confiscation, to the extent that such action is consistent with the principles of its domestic law and with the nature of the judicial and other proceedings'.[138] This reversal of the burden of proof is partly dictated by the international nature of the phenomenon of money laundering; in the case of proceeds with a foreign origin, it will be often very difficult for the prosecution to demonstrate that these proceeds have been generated in violation of foreign criminal law. In its *Draft Report* the informal Money Laundering Experts Group of the EU Multidisciplinary Working Group on Organised Crime reached the conclusion that it was in practice almost impossible to prove, beyond reasonable doubt, the criminal origin of assets if these were owned by (legal) persons domiciled in offshore centres.[139]

The departure from the international standard of proof is in part also dictated by the nature of many predicate offences, namely offences without a victim. Because there is no victim to give evidence on the nature of the offences and the extent of the proceeds, the classic modes of evidence are deficient. Moreover, when offenders are caught *flagrante delicto* – as may often be the case with the use of proactive police techniques – there will be no proceeds (as the offender is caught before he is able to receive the proceeds of his crime).

With a view to achieving a more effective deprivation of ill-gotten gains, several legislators have opted to introduce a (partial) reversal of the burden of proof regarding the criminal origin of proceeds of which the confiscation is sought. Sometimes domestic legislators not only provide for a reversal of the onus of proof regarding the criminal origin of proceeds, but also sever the link between the offences for which the offender was convicted and the confiscation order by allowing confiscation of proceeds that were generated by offences other than the one for which the offender stood trial.

It is to be stressed that this reversal of the burden of proof relates only to the criminal origin of the proceeds for the purposes of their confiscation and does not pertain to the guilt of the accused. Mostly this reversal of the burden of proof has been procedurally embedded in special confiscation procedures which take place after the decision on the guilt of the accused. These special techniques that provide for a reversal of the onus

---

[138] See also Article 30 of the UN Model Law on Money Laundering.
[139] *Draft Report of the informal Money Laundering Experts Group*, 12706/98, CRIMORG 173, Brussels, 6 November 1998, p. 37.

of proof are, however, in opposition to two fundamental aspects of fair trial rights which, it has been demonstrated, apply to confiscation procedures, namely the presumption of innocence and the right to silence.

The presumption of innocence is entrenched in Article 6(2) of the European Convention on Human Rights and Article 14(2) of the ICCPR, which both state that 'everyone charged with a criminal offence shall have the right to be presumed innocent until proved guilty according to law'.

Although it has been established that Article 6 applies to confiscation procedures, it might be argued that the presumption of innocence as such is not applicable to confiscation procedures as they concern only the sanctioning and not the determination of guilt. This argument should be rejected, however, as the European Commission of Human Rights has decided that Article 6 *in toto* applies to procedures (e.g. an appeal procedure) that are solely concerned with the determination of the penalty.[140] Even though earlier case law of the European Court of Human Rights seemed to suggest the contrary,[141] the Court clearly stated in *Minelli v. Switzerland*: 'Article 6(2) governs criminal proceedings in their entirety, irrespective of the outcome of the prosecution, and not solely the examination of the merits of the charge'.[142] In *AP, MP and TP v. Switzerland*, the European Court of Human Rights even read an obligation into Article 6(2) not to pass punitive sanctions on to the heirs of the (alleged) offender.[143]

It would indeed be contradictory to accept the punitive nature of the sanction as one of the main arguments for deciding on the applicability of Article 6, but to exclude one of the most fundamental guarantees laid down in this provision from the stage during which this punitive sanction is imposed. If it can be accepted that some of the evidential requirements may be relaxed at the stage during which the sanction is imposed (as opposed to the stage during which the merits of the charge are examined), the guarantees of Article 6, including the presumption of innocence, can not be circumvented by excluding its applicability to the stage during which the exact scope of confiscation is determined. Whereas some

---

[140] European Commission of Human Rights, report of 5 March 1980, *X. v. Austria*, No.8289/78, *DR* (18), p. 160. See Den Hartog, *Artikel 6 EVRM*, p. 82.

[141] European Court of Human Rights, judgment of 8 June 1976, *Engel v. The Netherlands*, Publ. ECHR, Series A, No.22, para. 90.

[142] European Court of Human Rights, judgment of 25 March 1983, *Minelli v. Switzerland*, Publ. ECHR, Series A, No.62, para. 30.

[143] European Court of Human Rights, *AP, MP and TP v. Switzerland*, judgment of 29 August 1997, *Reports of judgments and decisions* (1997–V), 1447, para. 48.

domestic courts have acknowledged the applicability of Article 6(2) to confiscation procedures,[144] others have starkly denied it.[145]

The precise requirements flowing from the presumption of innocence
were clarified by the European Court of Human Rights in *Salabiaku v.
France*. Apart from the self-evident condition that the conduct the accused
is charged with constituted a criminal offence at the time it was committed, the term 'according to law' (Article 6(2)) also contains a number of
qualitative requirements. The Court rightly emphasised that the mere fact
that certain presumptions are laid down in the municipal legislation is
not enough to make them compatible with the presumption of innocence.
Such a holding would give *carte blanche* to municipal legislators to do away
with the presumption of innocence. As was stated by the Court:

Presumptions of fact or law operate in every legal system. Clearly the Convention
does not prohibit such presumptions in principle. It does, however, require the
Contracting States to remain within certain limits in this respect as regards criminal law. If, as the Commission, would appear to consider ... paragraph 2 of Article
6 merely laid down a guarantee to be respected by the courts in the conduct of
legal proceedings, its requirements would in practice overlap with the duty of
impartiality imposed in paragraph 1. Above all, the national legislature would be
free to strip the trial court of any genuine power of assessment and deprive the
presumption of innocence of its substance, if the words 'according to law' were
construed exclusively with reference to domestic law. Such a situation could not
be reconciled with the object of and purpose of Article 6, which by, protecting the
right to a fair trial and in particular the right to be presumed innocent, is intended
to enshrine the fundamental principle of law ... Article 6(2) does not therefore
regard presumptions of fact or law provided for in criminal law with indifference.
It requires states to confine them within reasonable limits which take into account
the importance of what is at stake and maintain the rights of the defence ...[146]

Although the Court is not in principle opposed to presumptions of law
or fact, in order to be compatible with Article 6(2), those presumptions
should leave the accused with the procedural possibility of demonstrating
his innocence.[147] Moreover, the 'importance of what is at stake' needs to

144 See the judgment of the Dutch Supreme Court of 5 December 1995, *NJ* (1996), No.411.
145 See the judgment of the Geneva Supreme Court of 22 November 1996, *La Semaine
judiciaire* (1997), 186.
146 European Court of Human Rights, judgment of 7 October 1988, *Salabiaku v. France*, *Publ.
ECHR*, Series A, No.141, para. 28.
147 European Court of Human Rights, judgment of 7 October 1988, *Salabiaku v. France*, *Publ.
ECHR*, Series A, No.141, paras. 29–30. This was even more clearly articulated by the
Court in *Phoam Hang v. France*, judgment of 25 September 1992, *Publ. ECHR*, Series A,
No.243, para. 34.

be taken into account. It seems to follow from the judgment of the Court in *Phoam Hang v. France*, as compared to *Salabiaku*, that presumptions can only be allowed in relation to relatively minor offences in respect of which no grave sanctions can be imposed. In *Phoam Hang* the Court explicitly held that: 'the considerable importance of what was at stake called for greater vigilance in respecting the rights of the defence . . .'[148]

This line of reasoning, although attractive, is open to criticism in three respects. The most fundamental of which is that the Court has in this way introduced a proportionality test in respect of Article 6. The presumption of innocence is, however, an 'absolute right' in respect of which, unlike the rights laid down in Articles 8, 9 and 10 of the European Convention on Human Rights, no limitations are possible, even if proportionate. Even the implied limitations theory is not accepted in respect of the presumption of innocence.[149] This means that, in assessing whether a presumption of law or fact is compatible with the presumption of innocence, courts should not look to the interests in respect of which this presumption has been called into being, but should only investigate whether the law reasonably allows the accused to rebut this presumption.

A second objection is that, if a proportionality test is to be applied anyway, it is far from clear why presumptions should only be allowed in respect of minor offences. Surely, if a balancing exercise is to take place between the presumption of innocence (i.e. an aspect of the right to a fair trial) and the interest of society in fighting crime, the need for presumptions is more pressing in respect of serious offences, such as organised crime, than in respect of minor offences. This was accepted by the Privy Council in *Attorney-General of Hong Kong v. Lee*, a case which was concerned with presumptions in respect of drug trafficking offences. The Privy Council used a proportionality test to assess whether the Hong Kong legislation, which provided for a reversal of the onus of proof, was compatible with the presumption of innocence, as entrenched in Section 11(1) of the Hong Kong Bill of Rights Ordinance 1991 (the text of which is analogous to the one of Article 6(2) of the European Convention on Human Rights and of Article 14(2) of the ICCPR).[150] It is therefore submitted that

---

[148] European Court of Human Rights, judgment of 25 September 1992, *Phoam Hang v. France*, Publ. ECHR, Series A, No.243, para. 32.

[149] P. Van Dijk and G. J. H. Van Hoof, *Theory and Practice of the European Convention on Human Rights*, (Boston: Kluwer, 1990), p. 574.

[150] [1993] 3 All ER 939. See G. Nardell, 'Presumed Innocence, Proportionality and the Privy Council', *LQR* (1994), 223–8. See also the decision of the South African Supreme Court in *S v. Coetzee* 1997 (4) BCLR 437 (CC), which balances the infringement of the presumption of innocence with the expected advantage for the prosecution.

in essence two factors need to be taken into account in assessing the compatibility of domestic presumptions of criminal origin of proceeds with Article 6(2), namely whether these presumptions operate automatically and whether it is open to the defence to rebut these presumptions. In the following three domestic examples (The Netherlands, England and Wales and Switzerland) reversal of the onus of proof in respect of the criminal origin of alleged proceeds will be analysed with special attention to these two factors. It should be emphasised that with respect to the latter factor, courts need to show some flexibility concerning the evidential requirements for the rebuttal of the presumption, given the fact that it is always much more arduous to deliver proof that something did not happen than that it did and in view of the limited investigating powers of private individuals.

A third objection to the limitation of a reversal of burden of proof with regard to the criminal origin of proceeds to a number of specified offences is that this may in practice actually result in stronger infringements of the presumption of innocence than a general reversal. To establish a specific regime in respect of a limited number of offences may eventually create the (judicially acknowledged) perception that these offences are so heinous that the basic rights of the defence can be infringed for someone convicted of – or, even worse, only charged with – these offences.

Dutch law has introduced a partial reversal of the burden of proof when new legislation allowing the confiscation of the proceeds of offences was introduced. For not only can the proceeds of offences for which the accused has been convicted be confiscated, but also the proceeds obtained from similar offences or from offences for which it is also possible to impose a fine of the fifth (i.e. the highest) category, even if the accused has not been charged with these offences.[151] These already far-reaching possibilities laid down in the second paragraph of Article 36 of the Dutch Criminal Code are further extended in its third paragraph, which allows for the confiscation of all proceeds which are probably derived from other criminal activities. This requires, however, that the accused has been convicted of an offence punishable with a fine of the fifth category and that the probability that the convicted person has profited from offences other than that for which he has been convicted has been demonstrated in the course of a specific criminal financial investigation. There are no restrictions as to the modes of proving this requirement, even though the

---

[151] Keyser-Rignalda, 'De buitgerichte benadering', 336 and J. Wöretshofer, '"Pluk ze" – Nieuwe mogelijkheden tot ontneming van crimineel vermogen', in Misdaadgeld, ed. P. C. Van Duyne, J. M. Reyntjes and C. D. Schaap (Arnhem: Gouda Quint, 1993), pp. 36–9.

burden of proof seems relatively heavy in relation to Article 36(2) which requires that indications exist that the proceeds spring from offences committed by the convicted person.

Notwithstanding the fact that Dutch confiscation legislation obviously deviates from the normal burden of proof in criminal matters, it seems reconcilable with Article 6(2) of the European Convention on Human Rights. This was also explicitly held by the Dutch Supreme Court.[152] The most important factor which induces this conclusion is the fact that, once a presumption of criminal origin of proceeds has been established by the prosecution, the defence can always reverse this presumption. A mere denial will not be sufficient, however. Once the criminal origin of the proceeds has been made probable, the burden to rebut – not simply to deny – this presumption lies with the defence. The presumptions do not, however, operate automatically but have to be established by the prosecution by demonstrating that the criminal origin of proceeds, though not proven, is probable. In this respect it is probably more apposite to refer to a partial sharing, rather than a reversal of the burden of proof.[153]

English law offers drastic powers to order the confiscation of proceeds of crime. Although the law was initially developed in relation with drug offences under the Drug Trafficking Offences Act 1986 (now the Drug Trafficking Act 1994 (DTA 1994)), confiscation powers are equally available under the Criminal Justice Act 1988 (CJA 1988) in respect of other offences and, since the Proceeds of Crime Act 1995 (PCA 1995), in respect of all offences.

The court will confiscate the proceeds of crime if it considers appropriate to do so or if the prosecution has given written notice to this effect (see s.2(1) DTA 1994 and s.71(1)CJA 1995): confiscation is not ordered automatically in order to avoid costly confiscation procedures resulting in meagre confiscations. The first issue for the court to determine is whether the person has obtained any proceeds from drug trafficking, or, under the CJA 1988, from any relevant criminal conduct. The concept of proceeds of crime is thus not linked to the offences for which the person has stood trial, but is extended to other criminal activities from which he may have benefited even though they may not have been proven in court. In the case of drug trafficking this may even extend to payment or other rewards

---

[152] See the judgment of the Dutch Supreme Court of 5 December 1995, *NJ* (1996), No.411.
[153] This point of view was also defended by the Dutch Minister of Justice. See L. F. Keyser-Ringnalda, 'De "Pluk ze-wetgeving" in het licht van de rechtsbeginselen', *DD* (1991), 1095 and L. Wemes, 'Over het ontnemen van voordeel en het omkeren of (redelijk) verdelen van de bewijslast', *NJB* (1988), 419.

received by that person in connection with drug trafficking carried on by another person (s.2(3) DTA 1994).

Although the burden of proof technically lies with the prosecution, the standard of proof to determine whether someone has benefited from offences and to determine the amount to be recovered is the one applicable in civil proceedings: the balance of probabilities (s.2(8) DTA 1994 and s.71(7A) CJA 1988). In addition, the court can make presumptions provided for in statute law. In the case of drug trafficking the court is obliged to make the presumptions, whereas it may do so in respect of other offences, but only if there is a pattern of offending. This requirement is laid down in the CJA 1988 under two forms: the offender must either have been convicted of at least two offences in the present proceedings or must already have been convicted since the beginning of a period of six years ending when the proceedings were instituted against him. The presumption is that any property appearing to the court to have been held by the defendant at any time since his conviction, or to have been transferred to him at any time since the beginning of the period of six years ending when the proceedings were instituted against him (s.4(3) DTA 1994 and s.72AA(4) CJA 1988), is deemed to have been received by him as payment or reward in connection with drug offences or, under the CJA 1988, relevant criminal conduct. It has correctly been pointed out in this respect that the 'burden of proof has . . . been assumed away'.[154] These statutory presumptions seem to open the gate for purely speculative case law with regard to the criminal origin of proceeds held by the defendant.

In contrast to Dutch confiscation legislation, it is not even required under English law that the prosecution establish the probability that the proceeds are derived from criminal activities. Although the court is not obliged to make the presumptions in respect of non-drug trafficking offences, there are no guarantees for the defendant. Both s.72AA(5) CJA 1988 and s.4(4) DTA 1994 provide for two exceptions to these presumptions, namely: when 'that assumption is shown to be incorrect in the defendant's case'; or when 'the Court is satisfied that there would be a serious risk of injustice in this case if the assumption were to be made'. In respect of non-drug trafficking offences, there is also a third exception when the benefit has already been the subject of a previous confiscating order.[155] Although in principle the court can apply these exceptions *ex officio*, in practice it will often be upon the defendant to invoke them.

---

[154] C. Sallon and D. Bedingfield, 'Drugs, Money and the Law', *Crim.LRev.* (1993), 168.
[155] See *infra* pp. 80–1.

Notwithstanding the fact that it is open to the defendant to rebut the presumptions made by the court, the prosecution is not obliged to establish a balance of probabilities before the presumptions can be made as this is entirely at the discretion of the court. Whether or not these presumptions can be reconciled with the presumption of innocence therefore depends very much upon the practical application that is made of these presumptions. There is, however, a risk that automatic use of these presumptions by the courts will often constitute an infringement of the presumption of innocence, given the great weight that is attached by the European Court of Human Rights to the question whether or not there was 'automatic reliance on the presumptions'.[156]

Although confiscation of the proceeds of crime in Switzerland can in principle be ordered only in respect of offences for which the offender was convicted, the Swiss legislation has chosen to introduce a reversal of the burden of proof in respect of organised crime. If a person supports or participates in a criminal organisation, as defined by Article 260ter Swiss Criminal Code, the Court is under a duty to order the confiscation of all assets belonging to that person. Article 59(3) Swiss Criminal Code lays down a legal presumption holding that the criminal organisation yields power over all assets belonging to anyone convicted for the offence laid down in Article 260ter Swiss Criminal Code. The application of this presumption does not even presume that the person has been convicted for membership of a criminal organisation or any other offence, although that will very often be the case.[157] Defendants can, however, always rebut the presumption, either by demonstrating that the assets are not controlled by the criminal organisation, or – at least in the case of subordinate members of the organisation – by demonstrating the legal origin of the assets.[158] The presumption seems compatible with the presumption of innocence in that the presumption is not triggered automatically upon conviction of any offence, but requires that it is somehow established that the person belongs to a criminal organisation and that it is open to the defendant to rebut the presumption.

As pointed out, techniques of reversing the onus of proof may not only collide with the presumption of innocence, but also with another human

---

[156] European Court of Human Rights, judgment of 25 September 1992, *Phoam Hang v. France, Publ. ECHR*, Series A, No.243, paras.35–36

[157] Schmid, 'Das neue Einziehungsrecht', 349–50. See also the judgment of the Swiss Supreme Court of 27 August 1996, *La Semaine Judiciaire* (1997), 1.

[158] Schmid, 'Das neue Einziehungsrecht', 356 and J. Natterer, 'Money-Laundering and Forfeiture Legislation in Switzerland', *Eur.JCr., Cr.L & Cr.J* (1997), 224–5.

right: the privilege against self-incrimination. Often, these techniques in one way or another boil down to the drawing of adverse inferences from the accused's silence at trial. In some legal systems this is held incompatible with the right to silence. The prohibition to draw such inferences is often looked upon as a derivative application of the privilege,[159] which is laid down in Article 14(3)(g) of the ICCPR and has been recognised by the European Court of Human Rights as forming part of the right to a fair trial enshrined in Article 6(1) of the European Convention on Human Rights.[160] For example under Dutch legislation, once the prosecution has made it probable – but not proven – that the proceeds at issue have a criminal origin, the silence of the offender effectively results in the application of a presumption that the proceeds have a criminal origin. Reversed, the onus is on the accused/convicted person to prove that the proceeds have a legal origin. The silence of the accused will thus often lead to the confiscation of the proceeds at stake.

Nevertheless, the privilege against self-incrimination does not embody an absolute prohibition on the drawing of adverse inferences from the accused's silence. The European Court of Human Rights has correctly pointed out that while 'evidence against the accused' calls for an 'explanation which the accused ought to be able to give' a failure to give any explanation 'may as a matter of common sense allow [the Court] to draw the inference that there is no explanation and that the accused is guilty'.[161] It should be emphasised that it is not the silence of the accused as such which is taken as proof of his guilt, but, more generally, his failure to provide a reasonable explanation in connection with a fact which calls for an explanation.[162] It is this fact, rather than the silence which should be considered the proof. When, however, presumptions can also be made

---

[159] See on the status of the privilege against self-incrimination: G. Stessens, 'The Obligation to Produce Documents Versus the Privilege Against Self-incrimination: Human Rights Protection Extended Too Far?', ELR, Human Rights Survey 1997, 47–54 and on the notion of derivative application of the privilege: I. Dennis, 'Instrumental Protection, Human Right or Functional Necessity: Reassessing the Privilege Against Self-Incrimination', Cambr.LJ (1995), 345–7.

[160] See European Court of Human Rights, judgment of 25 February 1993, Funke v. France, Publ. ECHR, Series A, No.256–A, para. 44 and European Court of Human Rights, judgment of 8 February 1996, Murray v. United Kingdom, (1996) HRLJ 39, para. 45.

[161] European Court of Human Rights, judgment of 8 February 1996, Murray v. United Kingdom, (1996) HRLJ 39, para. 51. See also with regard to pre-trial detention (Article 5(3) of European Convention on Human Rights): judgment of 26 January 1993, W v. Switzerland, Publ.ECHR, Series A, No.254, para. 42.

[162] See in this respect the opinion of Advocate General Fokkens with the judgment of the Dutch Supreme Court of 12 March 1996, NJ (1996), No.539.

in respect of a situation which does not call for an explanation, as may be the case under English confiscation law, this also seems to imply that in these circumstances adverse inferences can be drawn from the silence of the accused. It is submitted that this is not compatible with the right to silence. As was already stressed with respect to the presumption of innocence, courts should not rely automatically on presumptions, but only when the prosecution has made it probable that the proceeds are derived from criminal activities, that is when there is at least a beginning of evidence which 'calls for an explanation which the accused ought to able to give'.

In the past, domestic courts have also accepted that adverse inferences can be drawn from the accused's silence under some circumstances, namely in respect of the criminal origin of property in handling stolen goods.[163] This also illustrates another interesting point, namely, that in a number of jurisdictions there was already a *de facto* reversal of the burden of proof in respect of offences of handling stolen goods, where it was often sufficient that the prosecution demonstrated that it was probable the goods found in the possession of the defendant were stolen goods without having to prove their exact origin.

Protection of bona fide third parties

The dire consequences confiscation sanctions may have on the rights of third parties have already been illustrated in the context of the discussion of American civil forfeitures.[164] It was shown that, according to the case law of the US Supreme Court, the US Constitution offers no protection for innocent owners. Effective protection of the legitimate rights of third parties therefore depends on the applicable confiscation legislation.

On an international level, such protection is imposed by Article 5 of the Money Laundering Convention, which requires that '[e]ach Party shall adopt such legislative and other measures as may be necessary to ensure that interested parties affected by measures under Article 2 and 3 shall have effective legal remedies in order to preserve their rights'. This requirement goes further than the one flowing from Article 5 of the Vienna Convention, which states that nothing in that provision shall be construed as prejudicing the rights of bona fide third parties. It flows from the wording of Article 5 of the Money Laundering Convention that the obligation to provide effective legal remedies, not only pertains to confis-

---

[163] See the judgment of 20 October 1992 of the Belgian Supreme Court, *Arr.Cass.* (1991–92), No.675.   [164] See *supra* pp. 40–2.

cation measures, but also to investigative and preventive measures (i.e. the measures referred to in Article 3). As far as the latter measures are concerned, the protection should in principle not only extend to third parties, but also to the accused as he fully enjoys the presumption of innocence at that stage.

It is a remarkable fact that the requirements flowing from these international provisions are limited to procedural rights. Thus the protection afforded under Article 5 of the Money Laundering Convention encompasses the right for these parties, if known, to be duly informed by the authorities that they may challenge decisions or other measures. They have the right to a hearing in court, in the course of which they have the right to legal representation.[165] The most adequate way of protecting the rights of bona fide third parties is at the trial stage, that is, by allowing them to intervene in the procedure through which the possible confiscation order will be determined. If third parties have not been able to safeguard their rights during the trial stage, however, the law should also allow them to protect their rights after a confiscation has been ordered, or even after the confiscation has become enforceable.

The Money Laundering Convention thus does not impose any substantive requirements or standards as to the protection that should be afforded to third parties. It is even more remarkable that the same conclusion can be drawn with respect to the case law of the European Court of Human Rights. The Court has essentially approached the matter from the angle of Article 6 of the Convention. Even though the Court has held that confiscation measures which affect the rights of third parties in adverse manner do not necessarily amount to a 'criminal charge' for the purposes of Article 6,[166] the civil rights of third parties should be guaranteed in a procedure governed by Article 6(1).

Article 6(1) amongst others requires that, in the determination of his civil rights, everyone is entitled to a fair and public hearing. Without an effective access to court, bona fide third parties risk being treated less well than the actual offenders, who are – or at least in principle should be – always afforded the safeguards of fair criminal proceeding. The issue of the applicability of Article 6(1) under its civil heading was not raised in *AGOSI*, but in *Air Canada* the parties accepted that the seizure of the

---

[165] *Explanatory Report with the Convention on Laundering, Search, Seizure and Confiscation of the Proceeds from Crime*, pp. 19–20.
[166] European Court of Human Rights, judgment of 24 October 1986, *AGOSI v. United Kingdom*, Publ. ECHR, Series A, No.108, para. 65. See the discussion of this case, *supra* pp. 61–4.

aircraft and the subsequent payment of £50,000 for its release concerned the civil rights of Air Canada.

The Court was, however, of the opinion that English law met the requirements of Article 6(1). As far as the seizure was concerned, the law obliged the UK Customs & Excise department to bring its case before a court in order to obtain the forfeiture of the aircraft. Regarding the customs' decision to request a payment for the release of the aircraft, the Court pointed to the fact that this decision could have been subjected to judicial review.[167] The reference to the possibility of judicial review was rightly criticised however, especially in view of the rule that an application before the European Commission and European Court of Human Rights is possible only if all domestic remedies have been exhausted (Article 35 of European Convention on Human Rights).[168]

The Court seemed to content itself with checking whether third parties had access to court and did not impose any substantive conditions as to how the rights of bona fide third parties should be safeguarded. Both in *AGOSI* and in *Air Canada* the European Court of Human Rights accepted that third parties had to suffer the consequences of seizures or confiscations which were imposed because of the illegal conduct of others (i.e. the smugglers of the Krugerrands and the traffickers who put the drugs on board the Air Canada aircraft). This judicial lack of consideration for the position of third parties came under trenchant attack in the dissenting opinions in both decisions. Already in *AGOSI*, Judge Pettiti arrived at the conclusion that Article 1 of Protocol No.1 implies that 'an innocent owner, acting in good faith, must be able to recover his property'.[169] Although this issue was notably dealt with under the heading of Article 1 of Protocol No.1, the compatibility with Article 6(1) is inherently linked to it. Thus it was rightly emphasised in the dissenting opinion of Judge Martens joined by Judge Russo in *Air Canada* that the absence of defence of innocent ownership is incompatible with Article 1 of Protocol No.1 and that every system should permit an owner to have a dispute about a confiscation (e.g.

---

[167] European Court of Human Rights, judgment of 5 May 1995, *Air Canada v. United Kingdom*, Publ. ECHR, Series A, No.316-A, paras.43–8. See also Vervaele, 'Les sanctions de confiscation en droit pénal', 43–44.

[168] See the dissenting opinion of Judge Pettiti in European Court of Human Rights, judgment of 24 October 1986, *AGOSI v. UK*, Publ. ECHR, Series A, No.108, and the dissenting opinions of Judges Walsh, Martens and Russo, and Pekkanen in European Court of Human Rights, judgment of 5 May 1995, *Air Canada v. UK*, Publ. ECHR, Series A, No.316-A and Peukert, 'Die Rechtsprechung des EGMR', 510–13 and G. Cohen-Jonathan, *La convention européenne des droits de l'homme* (Paris: Economica, 1989), pp. 536–7.

[169] Dissenting opinion of Judge Pettiti in European Court of Human Rights, judgment of 24 October 1986, *AGOSI v. UK*, Publ. ECHR, Series A, No.108.

regarding the question whether the owner is 'guilty' or not) settled by an independent and impartial tribunal which meets the requirements of Article 6(1), that is, a court with full jurisdiction as to the facts and the law.[170] It was correctly enunciated that 'the right of the owner to get back his property which has been confiscated "illegally" . . . is a civil right also'.[171] Although it seems preferable that civil rights of third parties could be judged within the context of the criminal proceedings against the offenders (e.g. by allowing third parties to intervene in these proceedings), their civil rights can also be safeguarded in separate, subsequent civil proceedings.

Protection against double jeopardy: non bis in idem

Both domestic and international law provide protection against double jeopardy by prohibiting the same person from being tried or punished twice for the same offence (see Article 14 (7) ICCPR and Article 4 (1) of Protocol No.7 of the European Convention on Human Rights). These *non bis in idem* rules do not, however, necessarily prevent the same proceeds from the same offence from being confiscated more than once. Some domestic courts exclude the *non bis in idem* protection in respect of confiscations because, for example, these are not deemed criminal sanctions, as is the opinion of the American Supreme Court. The Supreme Court repeatedly held that civil *in rem* forfeitures – though considered punishment under the Eighth Amendment's Excessive Fines Clause – were not 'punishment' for purposes of the Fifth Amendment's Double Jeopardy Clause.[172] To this end, the Court applied a two-part test asking first, whether Congress intended the forfeiture at hand to be a remedial civil sanction or a criminal sanction and second, whether the forfeiture proceedings are *de facto* so punitive that they can only be legitimately considered as criminal in nature, in spite of congressional intent to the

---

[170] Dissenting opinion of Judge Martens joined by Judge Russo in European Court of Human Rights, judgment of 5 May 1995, *Air Canada v. UK, Publ. ECHR*, Series A, No.316-A, para. 8.
[171] Dissenting opinion of Judge Martens joined by Judge Russo in European Court of Human Rights, judgment of 5 May 1995, *Air Canada v. UK, Publ. ECHR*, Series A, No.316-A, para. 8.
[172] *Various Items of Property v. United States* 282 US 577, 581 (1931); *One Lot Emerald Cut Stones v. United States* 409 US 232, 235–6 (1972); *United States v. One Assortment of 89 Firearms* 465 US 354 (1984); *United States v. Ursery* 116 S.Ct. 2135 (1996). See also L. J. Candler, 'Tracing and Recovering Proceeds of Crime in Fraud Cases: A Comparison of US and UK Legislation', *The International Lawyer* (1997), 7–10 and Vervaele, 'La saisie et la confiscation', 993–6.

contrary.[173] But even when confiscation procedures formally fall under the *non bis in idem* rules, the real protection against double jeopardy may be shaky. There are several reasons for this. First, under some legislation the same proceeds may be confiscated as direct proceeds from the offence from which they are derived (e.g. arms trafficking) and as *objectum sceleris* of a money laundering offence as well. In some instances it may even be possible that the perpetrator of the predicate offence is subsequently tried and punished for laundering the proceeds of the predicate offence he committed himself and that the confiscation of same proceeds is therefore ordered a second time. In neither of these situations will the *res iudicata* effect of a previous conviction prohibit double confiscation, as this only excludes a second trial in as far as it relates to the same person and to the same offence. The risk of double confiscation is exacerbated by the fact that some jurisdictions allow the confiscation of proceeds of crime for offences – or, more generally, for criminal activities – for which the defendant has not been convicted or even charged. In addition, a defendant may also have to comply with compensation orders which will also result in the deprivation of the same proceeds.

Given the lack of an adequate international system that protects against double confiscation, domestic legislators should take it upon themselves to create such a system. It is therefore submitted that, apart from the existing domestic *non bis in idem* rules, which normally erect a bar to new proceedings for the same offence after a first proceeding (*Erledigungsprinzip*), an additional protection should be conceived in the form of a duty to impute previously imposed payment obligations (*Anrechnungsprinzip*) in respect of the same proceeds. Inspiration for the introduction of a well-functioning system of protection against 'double deprivation' of the same proceeds can be drawn, for example, from Dutch, English or Swiss law.

Such a system should oblige a judge, in the determination of the amount of money to be confiscated, to take into account any kind of payment obligations (e.g. a compensation order or an out-of-court settlement) that have been previously imposed with respect to the proceeds from the same fact.[174] The concept of the 'same fact' should be sufficiently broad for this purpose to encompass both the predicate offence and the money laundering offence. Admittedly, courts will not always be aware of, nor have the means to check, whether there are such previously imposed payment obligations, but it may be safely assumed that the defence will be astute to bring such previously imposed payment obligations to the

---

[173] This test was developed in: *United States v. One Assortment of 89 Firearms* 465 US 354, 362–6 (1984).   [174] See, e.g., Article 36e(6)(7) Dutch Criminal Code.

attention of the court. The imputation of previously imposed payment obligations can, however, function only in the framework of value confiscation, where the court has the option, or even the obligation, to assess the total value of the proceeds of the defendant.[175] It is impossible to envisage such an obligation under a system of object confiscation. It can be held to the advantage of an object value system that, no matter how many times the confiscation of an object (i.e. the property constituting the proceeds of an offence) is ordered, it can only be 'physically' taken away once. This advantage only avails, however, in a 'pure' object confiscation system, but not in mixed systems, such as those of Belgium and Switzerland, where a value confiscation can be ordered if the property constituting the proceeds can not be traced.

The imputation of previously imposed payment obligations should not be confined to previous confiscations, but should extend to compensation which has been ordered or voluntarily paid out (e.g. in result of an out-of-court settlement).[176] It is unacceptable that – as is the case in Belgium, for example – proceeds of an offence can still be confiscated after an offender has already restituted them to the victim from whom they were illegally taken. Legislators need also to take care to avoid that victims are left in the cold because the proceeds have already been subjected to a confiscation order. Thus English law stipulates that if the court is satisfied that 'a victim ... has instituted or intends to institute civil proceeding against the defendant in respect of loss, injury or damage' (s.71(1C) CJA 1988), the court is not obliged to order confiscation.[177] A perhaps even more effective means of protecting the victim's right is provided by Swiss law, which allows victims to file a motion for the recovery of property the confiscation of which was already ordered and enforced.[178] A similar possibility exists under Dutch law.[179] Swiss judges can also order confiscation with a proviso to the compensation of the victim.[180]

---

[175] See ss.71 and 72AA CJA 1988, s.4 DTA 1994.
[176] See Article 36e(6) of the Dutch Criminal Code and Article 59(1) of the Swiss Criminal Code.
[177] See also s.72(7) CJA 1988 and Candler, 'Tracing and Recovering Proceeds', 18–19.
[178] Articles 59(1) and 60(1)(b) Swiss Criminal Code. See Schmid, 'Das neue Einziehungsrecht', 341–2 and also ATF 117 IV 107, judgment of 8 March 1991, JT (suisse), IV (1993), 70.   [179] Article 577(2) Dutch Code of Criminal Procedure.
[180] Articles 59(1) and 60(2) Swiss Criminal Code and Schmid, 'Das neue Einziehungsrecht', 333–4 and 357–60. See also ATF 117 IV 107, judgment of 8 March 1991, JT (suisse), IV (1993), 70.

3   The fight against money laundering: genesis of a new crime

In this chapter, the contours of the phenomenon of money laundering will be outlined as will the reasons which have been advanced for fighting this phenomenon. In doing so, two jurisdictions, the United States of America and Switzerland, deserve special attention, because of their influence in the shaping of the international money laundering regime. Whereas the influence of US legislation is especially visible with respect to the incrimination of money laundering as laid down by international conventions, Swiss anti-money laundering measures have left their mark on the preventive legislation prescribed by international instruments. The international anti-money laundering regime which has subsequently developed, is characterised by a twin track approach in the fight against money laundering. The criminal strand of this money laundering regime will be discussed in this chapter while the preventive strategy will be analysed later.[1]

Money laundering: the phenomenon and the reasons for fighting it

Concept of money laundering

The term 'money laundering' arose in the United States in the 1920s. It was apparently used by American police officers with reference to the ownership and use of launderettes by mafia groups. These groups showed an active interest in acquiring these launderettes, many of which were already owned by criminal groups, as they gave them a means of giving a legitimate appearance to money derived from criminal activities. These illicit proceeds were declared to be profits gained through launderettes

---

[1] See *infra* Part II.

and were thus 'laundered'.[2] The term 'money laundering' was apparently first used with a legal meaning in an American judgment of 1982 concerning the confiscation of laundered Columbian drug proceeds.[3]

Before attempting to give a juridical definition of money laundering, it is necessary to investigate the phenomenon of money laundering itself. Many descriptions of money laundering draw on the definition that was given in 1985 by the American *President's Commission on Organized Crime* in its interim report *The Cash Connection: Organized Crime, Financial Institutions, and Money Laundering*: 'Money laundering is the process by which one conceals the existence, illegal source, or illegal application of income, and then disguises that income to make it appear legitimate'[4].

The ultimate goal of any money laundering operation is twofold: to conceal the predicate offences from which these proceeds are derived and to ensure that the criminals can 'enjoy' their proceeds, by consuming or investing them in the legal economy.[5] It is to be noted that some forms of crime, especially financial crimes such as insider trading, for example, almost automatically and immediately imply money laundering operations as the offenders will obviously try to conceal the benefits they have reaped from their criminal activities.

In order to fulfil these ultimate goals, a number of intermediate goals have to be attained. Money laundering operations generally boil down to 'a . . . complex process often using the latest technology, of sanitising money in such a manner that its true nature, source or use is concealed, thereby creating an apparent justification for controlling or possessing the laundered money'.[6] This is sometimes called money laundering in the first degree, as opposed to the actual integration of criminal proceeds into the legitimate economy, sometimes referred to as 'recycling'.[7] The recycling element is not required when the proceeds are reinvested in (organised) crime activities.

---

[2] D. A. Chaikin, 'Money Laundering as a Supra-national Crime: An Investigatory Perspective', in *Principles and Procedures For A Transnational Criminal Law*, A. Eser and O. Lagodny (Freiburg: Max-Planck Institut, 1992), pp. 415–16; G. Picca, 'Le "blanchiment" des produits du crime: vers de nouvelles stratégies internationales?', *Rev.int.de crim.et de pol.techn.* (1992), 483–5; Secretary-General of the UN, *Note Strengthening Existing International Cooperation*, p. 4 and United Nations Office for Drug Control and Crime Prevention, *Financial Havens, Banking Secrecy and Money-Laundering*, pp. 5–6.

[3] *US v. $4,255,625.39*, *Federal Supplement*, vol.551, South District of Florida (1982), 314, cited by Secretary-General of the UN, *Note Strengthening Existing International Cooperation*, p. 5.

[4] (Washington, DC: U.S., Government Printing Office 1985), p. 7.

[5] Secretary-General of the UN, *Note Strengthening Existing International Cooperation*, p. 7.

[6] Secretary-General of the UN, *Note Strengthening Existing International Cooperation*, p. 4.

[7] Graber, *Geldwäscherei*, pp. 56–8.

By a definition given in a 1990 report of the Canadian Ministry of the Solicitor-General, three elements are material to most money laundering operations: '. . . the conversion of illicit cash into another asset, the concealment of the true ownership or source of the illegally acquired proceeds, and the creation of the perception of legitimacy of source and ownership'.[8] These three elements can also be found in a widely accepted analysis, according to which most money laundering operations – especially those related to drug money[9] – can be split into three stages. The first stage is the placement stage, when money is placed, often, but not necessarily, in a financial institution. During the second stage, attempts are made to hide the paper trail, that is, to obscure the criminal origin of the proceeds, usually by carrying out various transactions, subsequently (layering) or sometimes at the same time.[10] The last stage is the integration into the legitimate economy of proceeds which have thus been given a legitimate appearance.[11] Both from a repressive and a preventive point of view, the placement stage is crucial for the detection of money laundering operations.[12]

Reasons for combating money laundering

Even more than the confiscation of the proceeds of crime, money laundering has been the subject of sustained interest among police officers, prosecutors, politicians and academics alike. The explanation for this remarkable interest should be sought in the socio-economic consequences of this phenomenon. Money laundering is rightly considered as a derivative from predicate (often organised) crime activities and as such it is able to spread the detrimental consequences of these criminal activities to many parts of society. The impetuses for attempting to tackle money laundering operations are numerous, but they all have in common that

---

[8] M. Beare and S. Schneider, *Tracing of Illicit Funds: Money Laundering in Canada* (Ottawa: Ministry of the Solicitor General of Canada, 1990), p. 304.
[9] See M. Pieth, 'Zur Einfuhrung: Geldwäscherei und ihre Bekämpfung in der Schweiz', in *Bekämpfung der Geldwäscherei. Modellfall Schweiz?*, M. Pieth (ed.) (Basle: Helbing & Lichtenhahn, 1992), p. 12.
[10] B. A. K. Rider, 'Taking The Profit out of Crime' in *Money Laundering Control*, B. A. K. Rider and M. Ashe (Dublin: Round Hall Sweet & Maxwell, 1995), p. 10.
[11] See F. Bernard, 'Les banques contre le blanchiment de l'argent', *Eurépargne* (1990, No.49), 18–19; Gilmore, *Dirty Money*, pp. 37–8; A. Taymans and P. Nihoul, 'Money Laundering: An Analysis of European and International Legal Instruments', *Bank.Fin.* (1992), 58 and Secretary-General of the UN, *Note Strengthening Existing International Co-operation*, p. 4.
[12] See e.g. FATF-I, p. 9 and Secretary-General of the UN, *Note Strengthening Existing International Co-operation*, p. 9.

they view money laundering not as a reprehensible activity in itself, but as part of a larger criminal activity which is harmful to society. Three reasons for fighting money laundering will now be set out; the first is a general one but the others relate to organised crime.

The primary reason for fighting money laundering is to enable law enforcement authorities to confiscate the proceeds of predicate criminal activities in those situations where confiscation might otherwise not be possible. Object confiscation of proceeds of crime can be circumvented through laundering operations which make it difficult to trace the property constituting the proceeds by, for example, giving the property a different appearance or by 'selling' to third parties the property constituting the proceeds of crime. The latter 'escape route' can be blocked by extending the scope of confiscation to property held by third parties. This legal technique may, however, have negative consequences for the rights of third parties. In addition, it can be applied only in the context of object confiscation and not with respect to value confiscation, which can likewise be circumvented by selling or giving property to third parties, thereby ensuring one is insolvent. Criminalising the laundering techniques whereby property or its source is hidden or given a legitimate appearance is therefore a more attractive legal means of blocking this escape route. Under many laws this criminalisation has as its primary purpose the punishment of third parties who impede the course of justice, that is, the confiscation of these proceeds (see e.g. in Switzerland[13] and Belgium[14]), by making it a crime to give *post factum* aid to conceal and launder proceeds from an offence. The criminalisation of money laundering – which is often conceived as an offence against the administration of justice[15] – and also the legislation designed to prevent money laundering, are therefore part of a larger shift in criminal justice from an offender-oriented towards a proceeds-oriented system. Consequently the reasons for incriminating money laundering to a great extent coincide with those for confiscating proceeds from crime or, more fundamentally, for criminalising the predicate offence as such. As with the confiscation of proceeds from crime, the criminalisation of money laundering aims to undermine crime and especially organised crime by taking away the incentive for these crime activities, that is, the financial gains. As Bernasconi put it,

13 See *infra* p. 104.
14 See F. Verbruggen, 'Proceeds-oriented Criminal Justice in Belgium: Backbone or Wishbone of a Modern Approach to Criminal Justice', *Eur.JCr., Cr.L & Cr.J* (1997) 318–19, especially footnote 21.
15 See in general J. Vogel, 'Geldwäsche – ein europaweit harmonisierter Straftatbestand?', *Z.St.W.* (1997), 350–1.

money laundering is the Achilles' heel of organised crime[16] as most money laundering operations imply contact with the legitimate economy and therefore expose criminals to the chance of being caught. This statement can be broadened to other types of crime as well, however. Unfortunately, as with the confiscation of the proceeds from crime, the broader fight against money laundering is sometimes seen as a way of making law enforcement pay for itself.[17]

A second rationale for the fight against money laundering stems from the evidential difficulties prosecutors have run into when they tried to have top – or, at any rate, high level – criminals convicted. While the high-level criminals mostly stay aloof from criminal activities as such and avoid coming into contact with the illicit goods from which they benefit, they do come into contact with the proceeds of these activities, thereby creating a 'paper trail' of records which track the movement of money. This paper trail may constitute evidence of their implication in these criminal activities.[18] The fight against money laundering is thus looked on as a means of gathering evidence against the top criminals of organised crime groups.

The most powerful impetus for devising strategies against money laundering, however, has undoubtedly come from the recognition of the prejudicial influence the flows of 'dirty money' may have on the financial sector, and more generally, on the economy as a whole. The much feared influence of organised crime on the legitimate economy is likely to manifest itself through money laundering operations as these necessarily imply, at one stage or another, contact with persons or institutions from the legitimate economy. This may entail corruption, and more generally a warped functioning of some institutions such as banks. In an extreme version of this argument, the influence of organised crime may even result in the establishment of control by organised crime over institutions from the legitimate economy. The action which has been taken – sometimes on the highest political level – with a view to combating money laundering is therefore inspired by a *cordon sanitaire* idea, that is, the idea that organised crime has to be ostracised from the rest of society and especially from the legitimate economy. It is to be noted that this idea has also been advanced with respect to drastic RICO (Racketeer Influenced and Corrupt Organisations Act) forfeitures in the United States.[19]

Apart from the general corruptive influence of organised crime and

---

[16] Bernasconi, 'La criminalité organisée', p. 12.
[17] Nadelmann, 'Unlaundering Dirty Money', 34.
[18] Nadelmann, 'Unlaundering Dirty Money', 34.
[19] Fried, 'Rationalising Criminal Forfeiture', 336.

money laundering,[20] the externalities of the money laundering phenomenon for the world economy may be illustrated as follows. Its harmful
effects on the effective allocation of resources and capital are two-fold: not
only are labour and capital used in illegal, socially disruptive activities
instead of legal activities, world capital also tends to be less optimally
invested than would be the case in the absence of money laundering.
Because money launderers primarily look to jurisdictions that allow them
to invest their criminally derived proceeds safely and to recycle them, even
when this involves a lower rate of return, money may be moved from countries with sound economies to countries with poorer economic policies.[21]
Because of its corruptive influence on financial markets and the reduction
of the public's confidence in the international financial system it may
entail, money laundering creates a certain risk of inherent instability for
the world economy and even a potential for organised crime groups to
destabilize a national economy. Volatility in exchange rates and interest
rates, and asset price 'bubbles' resulting from the disposition of 'illegal'
money, may also be counted among the possible externalities of money
laundering. Taken together, the externalities of money laundering are
likely to impact the growth rate of the world economies.[22]

The extent of the money laundering phenomenon

The risks to which legitimate businesses and the legal economy as a whole
are exposed because of money laundering is often illustrated by reference
to data relating to the economic volume of the flows of 'dirty money' that
are being laundered. In its first report (1990), the FATF used three methods
to assess the scale of financial flows arising from drug trafficking: an estimation of world drug production, an estimation of the consumption
needs of drug abusers and a calculation based on the actual seizures of
illicit drugs (to which a multiplier is applied). In 1990 the FATF thus established that the sale of cocaine, heroin and cannabis amounted to approx-
imately US$122 billion per year in the United States and in Europe, 50 per
cent to 70 per cent of which was thought to be available for laundering.
In 1987, the United Nations estimated the turnover of global drug trafficking at US$300 billion, but in 1990 this figure had already increased to
US$500 billion,[23] and in 1994 the United Nations estimated the combined

---

[20] See *supra* p. 8.   [21] Tanzi, *Money Laundering and the International Financial System*, pp. 6–7.
[22] See, in general, Tanzi, *Money Laundering and the International Financial System*, specifically
p. 4. See also Quirk, *Macroeconomic Implications of Money Laundering*, pp. 27–9.
[23] Smith, 'Competition in the European Financial Services Industry', 123.

turnover of drug trafficking, weapons trafficking and prostitution at US$750 billion.[24] All these estimations seem to have been made by micro-based methodologies, such as data from prosecutions and/or police investigations. Other attempts to assess the extent of the money laundering problem use macroeconomic methodologies, drawing on varying, indirect macroeconomic indicators, such as monetary and tax compliance data. Most of the econometric estimations of the extent of money laundering, and, more generally, of the underground economy, seem to have focused on displacements in the demand for currency and near-currency due to money laundering.[25]

All these guesstimates are, however, by definition very uncertain. It is simply impossible to determine the size of illicit traffic or of the financial benefits reaped from it. It is therefore useful to keep in mind the warning contained in the 1990 report of the Canadian Solicitor-General: 'There is no verifiable method for determining the size of the illicit economy. Estimated figures in this area of illicit proceeds, however carefully calculated, are only guesses. Once stated, they take on a reality they do not deserve'.[26]

Moreover, a number of reasons warrant particular caution with respect to any estimation of money laundering.[27] Before any estimation can even be described as scientific (which does not necessarily say anything about its veracity), a number of conditions have to be fulfilled. First, in estimating the extent of financial flows from crime, it should be clear as to the proceeds from which criminal activities the estimations relate; many estimations are confined to drug trafficking, but there are other very profitable forms of criminality, such as weapons trafficking. Second, a sharp distinction should be drawn between the proceeds (i.e. gross receipts) and the profits (i.e. proceeds after deduction of expenses). From an economic point of view, the illegal transactions turnover, rather than the value added in illegal activity, seems most relevant to an assessment of the extent of money laundering.[28] A distinction should moreover be made

---

[24] C. D. Schaap, 'Witwassen als verschijnsel', in *Maatregelen tegen witwassen in het koninkrijk*, G. J. M. Corstens, E. J. Joubert and S. C. J. J. Kortmann (Arnhem: Gouda Quint, 1995), p. 37.
[25] For a good overview of the econometric analysis carried out in this field: Quirk, *Macroeconomic Implications of Money Laundering*, pp. 7–14.
[26] Beare and Schneider, *Tracing of Illicit Funds*, p. 2.
[27] See in this respect P. C. Van Duyne, 'Geld witwassen: omvangschattingen in nevelslierten', in *Misdaadgeld*, ed. P. C. Van Duyne, J. M. Reijntjes and C. D. Schaap (Arnhem: Gouda Quint, 1993), pp. 14–18 and M. Levi, 'Taking financial services to the cleaners', *NLJ* (1995), 26.
[28] Quirk, *Macroeconomic Implications of Money Laundering*, p. 14.

between the illegal proceeds that are obtained and the part of these sums that are laundered; some proceeds are never laundered or integrated into the legal economy. It seems safe, therefore, to assume that the value of the total stock of laundered money must be larger than the yearly amount of money that is laundered.[29] For the purposes of estimating the extent of the money laundering phenomenon, it is also necessary to define the moment at which a sum is counted if the same sums are not to be counted more than once as, for example, at the placement and at the layering stage. Fourth, any estimation of financial flows should make clear the geographical and temporal area to which it relates. As far as the third and fourth factors are concerned, it is probably preferable only to take into account the placement of proceeds from crime, certainly in view of the fact that most reports with respect to suspicious transactions concern the placement stage.

Given the impossibility of giving any accurate assessment of the extent of the phenomenon of money laundering,[30] it is also impossible to assess mathematically the impact of anti-money laundering legislation. The only truly reliable figures are probably those which relate to the actual amounts of contraband and proceeds of crime that have been seized and confiscated by police and judicial authorities. It has correctly been noted that there is a dire need for better micro-data which must be specifically created for the purpose of assessing the extent of the money laundering phenomenon.[31] If the above-mentioned conditions are heeded, estimates can be made, but even then there are no guarantees as to their veracity. In addition, the possibility that the size of the problem may be exaggerated in order to mobilise the necessary force for the fight against money laundering cannot be excluded.[32] Many combatants in the field of money laundering – politicians, law enforcers, etc. – have an interest in increasing the estimations of 'dirty money' flows, whereas others – bankers or lawyers – have an interest in decreasing these estimations for example, for the purpose of whittling down proposed measures against money laundering.[33]

---

[29] Tanzi, *Money Laundering and the International Financial System*, p. 4.
[30] See e.g. M. Levi, 'Réglementation sur le blanchiment de l'argent au Royaume-Uni: une évaluation', *Déviance et société* (1995), 380 and 382; Tanzi, *Money Laundering and the International Financial System*, p. 3 and L. Van Outrive, 'La lutte contre le blanchiment de l'argent: un emplâtre sur une jambe de bois?', *Déviance et société* (1995), 372.
[31] Quirk, *Macroeconomic Implications of Money Laundering*, p. 16.
[32] Van Duyne, 'Geld witwassen', p. 20 *et seq.*
[33] A. Haynes, 'Money Laundering and Changes in International Banking Regulation', *JIBL* (1993), 454.

The internationalisation of the money laundering phenomenon

Empirical evidence suggests that the overall majority of money laundering operations have an international dimension. In Canada 80% of the
money laundering operations detected by the police are said to contain an
extraneous element[34] and in a small country such as Belgium this figure
rises to 90%.[35]

This internationalisation is the exponent of various factors. Most forms
of illicit trafficking are carried out on an international scale because the
producer and the buyer are usually not located within the same jurisdiction. This internationalisation has in part been brought about by the
larger phenomenon of the increasing internationalisation of the legitimate economy. One could even look upon the internationalisation of
crime as a mere illegal spin-off of the globalisation of the legal economy.[36]
Whilst organised crime in general has undoubtedly been the subject of a
growing internationalisation, this process should not be exaggerated: all
organised crime groups are still firmly rooted in their home territory,
where they often dominate certain criminal activities and where their
social and economical influence is very disruptive.[37] At the same time,
however, they undoubtedly take advantage of the facilities of the global
economy, sometimes by colluding with other criminal groups, but also by
laundering their criminal proceeds on an international scale. The internationalisation of money laundering is influenced by a number of specific
circumstances. It is a relatively safe assumption that the authorities of at
least some countries are less zealous in investigating the laundering of
foreign money than would be the authorities of the state in which the
predicate crime activities took place. Another important factor is that the
proceeds of crime are not evenly distributed among countries. With
respect to drug money laundering, it should be emphasised that the economies of the drug producing countries, notably those of Latin America,
are often not powerful enough to absorb the huge profits that are made

---

[34] Beare and Schneider, *Tracing of Illicit Funds*, p. 304.

[35] Centrale Dienst ter bestrijding van de georganiseerde economische en financiële
delinquentie, *2e Activiteitenverslag Jaren 1994–96* (Brussels, 1997), p. 49.

[36] Nadelmann, *Cops Across Borders*, pp. 104–5. See also P. Wilkitzki, 'Development of an
Effective International Crime and Justice Programme – A European View', in *Principles
and Procedures For A Transnational Criminal Law*, ed. A. Eser and O. Lagodny (Freiburg: Max-
Planck Institut, 1992), p. 270.

[37] See in this respect the very interesting comments by E. Savona and M. A. De Feo,
'International Money Laundering Trends and Prevention/Control Policies', in *Responding
to Money Laundering. International Perspectives*, ed. E. Savona (Amsterdam: Harwood
Academic Publishers, 1997), pp. 52–4.

through international drug trafficking.[38] The economies of many drug-producing countries are economically unstable and the uncontrolled injection of huge amounts of money from abroad makes it more difficult to control the rocketing inflation with which some of these countries are faced. Contrary to what is sometimes asserted,[39] drug trafficking is on the whole not beneficial to the economies of drug producing countries. Given these factors, it is not surprising that many drug barons have therefore often geographically diversified the investment of the proceeds of their drug trafficking.

The internationalisation of money laundering has been facilitated by a number of factors. A first, economic, factor is that there are a number of elements and conditions in the late twentieth century world economy which have created both a strong demand for foreign financial capital and the conditions that facilitate the anonymous investment of this capital. Amongst these developments can be cited: the growth of stock markets in developing countries, the large-scale privatisation of public enterprises in many countries and the diversification of financial instruments.[40] A number of these factors merit specific attention.

One of the most important factors in facilitating international money laundering is undoubtedly the globalisation of the world's economy, sometimes even referred to as a 'speculative global economy'.[41] This globalisation has in part been caused by a technological evolution that has created possibilities for international communication and transport hitherto unknown. One of the results of this evolution is the creation of an instantaneous payment system,[42] which has opened unparalleled opportunities for laundering money. Another important development which has greatly contributed to the globalisation of the world economy and of the world capital markets in particular is the liberalisation of exchange controls. It is clear, however, that this evolution, while undoubtedly beneficial to the growth of the world economy, also creates considerable difficulties for law enforcement authorities who seek to monitor transnational financial flows. This does not, however, mean that these economic

---

[38] Smith, 'Competition in the European Financial Services Industry', 123.

[39] See M. Sauloy and Y. Le Bonniec, *A qui profite la cocaïne* (Paris: Calman-Lévy, 1992), 408p.

[40] Tanzi, *Money Laundering and the International Financial System*, p. 4. See also L. Dini, 'The Problem and its Diverse Dimensions', in *Responding to Money Laundering. International Perspectives*, E. Savona (Amsterdam: Harwood Academic Publishers, 1997), pp. 5–6.

[41] United Nations Office for Drug Control and Crime Prevention, *Financial Havens, Banking Secrecy and Money Laundering*, p. 19.

[42] B. Zagaris and S. B. McDonald, 'Financial Fraud and Technology: The Perils of an Instantaneous Economy', *Geo.Wash.JInt'l L & Econ.* (1992), 62–72.

and financial reforms should be reversed or that the freedom of capital movements should be restricted,[43] but rather that measures against money laundering should be adopted. Thus, it has astutely been pointed out, the main externality of exchange control deregulation in the field of money control is not the lack of information – the information provided by exchange controls tends to be largely irrelevant for these purposes anyway – but is in fact the same as that of economic growth: the increase of the overall volume of international transactions provides more opportunity to disguise illegal funds.[44]

The liberalising effects of this mainly technological evolution have been reinforced by another, ideological evolution which took place during the 1980s and 1990s. Because of the collapse of a number of communist regimes, the capitalist economic model has now been adopted by most states, which has led to the development of wholly new financial sectors in formerly communist states. This not only allows legitimate businesses to flourish but also provides new avenues for money laundering. These states are attractive to money launderers because of their lack of a fully functioning regulatory system and are therefore sometimes called regulatory havens. This is especially the case in those states that have recently converted to capitalism in that the supervisory and regulatory authorities whose task it is to supervise and control the proper functioning of financial institutions are often inexperienced and under-equipped and have to work against a background of a new resistance to state interference of any kind.[45]

Moreover, a number of countries are so eager for an inflow of foreign capital that their authorities are not likely to scrutinise the origin of the monies invested. This is especially the case in respect of a number of secrecy havens and regulatory havens, some of which have even advertised their willingness to accept criminally derived proceeds. Thus it was only under heavy diplomatic pressure that the Seychelles withdrew its Economic Development Act (EDA), which would have guaranteed immunity from criminal proceedings to foreign investors who placed more than US$10 million (unless the investor had committed acts of violence or drug trafficking in the Seychelles itself).[46] These jurisdictions have often established a reputation for their stringent secrecy laws mostly, but not exclu-

---

[43] See FATF recommendation 22. Cf. M. Camdessus, 'Money Laundering: the Importance of International Countermeasures', Address by the Managing Director of the IMF at the Plenary Meeting of the FATF in Paris, 10 February 1998, p. 2.

[44] Quirk, *Macroeconomic Implications of Money Laundering*, pp. 22–3.   [45] FATF-III, p. 35.

[46] See the press statement issued by the FATF on 1 February 1996 and FATF-VII, p. 17.

sively, related to banking secrecy which make it difficult for police and judicial authorities to trace the origin or even the location of sums of money deposited in these secrecy jurisdictions. The attractiveness of these arrangements is often heightened by lenient tax rules which make it possible for non-residents to escape taxation on their capital. A number of Caribbean jurisdictions are often cited as secrecy and tax havens, a description which might equally apply to the Channel Islands, Liechtenstein, Monaco, Andorra, Malta, Madeira, Gibraltar, Switzerland and Luxembourg.[47] They are often also referred to as offshore financial centres. In the context of financial transactions the term 'offshore' refers to transactions which take place between non-residents. An offshore bank can be defined as a financial institution which is legally domiciled in one jurisdiction, but conducts business solely with non-residents.[48] By this definition 'offshore transactions' can take place in any jurisdiction, but as a result of their fiscal and secrecy rules, some jurisdictions attract a very high number of offshore transactions and offshore banks and have thereby become known as offshore financial centres. It is of course evident that money launderers often use offshore financial centres to stash away the proceeds of criminal activities or legitimate earnings to dodge taxes on their capital. In both instances they are likely to benefit from the secrecy rules and from the inertia of local law enforcement or fiscal authorities or their refusal to reply to requests for information.

The internationalisation of money laundering has drastic consequences with regard to the effectiveness of anti-money laundering measures. Purely national measures are likely to result only in a geographical shift of the phenomenon. Because of the increasing globalisation of the financial world, the proceeds of crime which have been deposited within one jurisdiction where the rules on the prevention of money laundering are less strict can penetrate into the financial system of other countries as

---

[47] For a more comprehensive list, see United Nations Office for Drug Control and Crime Prevention, *Financial Havens, Banking Secrecy and Money-Laundering*, p. 29; P. Bernasconi, 'The Fight against Money Laundering in the Prevention of the Drug Supply', in *Toward Scientifically Based Prevention*, ed. F. Bruno, M. E. Andreotti and M. Brunetti (Rome: UNICRI, 1990), p. 132; J. Antenen, 'Problématique nouvelle relative à la poursuite pénale du blanchissage d'argent, à la confiscation et au sort des avoirs confisqués', RPS (1996), 45. These jurisdictions are also listed as fiscal havens by the American Internal Revenue Service: Internal Revenue Manual 4233, Exhibit 500–8 (30 June 1989), cited by J. V. Ivsan, 'Informational Liability and International Law: A Post-*Ratzlaf* Comparative Analysis of the Effect of Treasury Reporting Requirements on International Funds Transfers', *Ohio Northern University LR* (1994), 263, footnote 2.

[48] United Nations Office for Drug Control and Crime Prevention, *Financial Havens, Banking Secrecy and Money Laundering*, p. 15.

well: 'These jurisdictions are part of the world payments system without any restriction. So long as this is the case, cash exports will tend to go to these countries for integration into the financial system there and return by means of wire transfers. This means that detection of the outflow of cash becomes especially important when internal avenues have been blocked'.[49]

This leads to several conclusions. On a legislative level, international harmonisation of anti-money laundering legislation is an absolute prerequisite for success in the fight against money laundering. This holds not only for criminal legislation, but also in the context of preventive legislation, where the argument for effectiveness is reinforced by an economic argument, namely the desirability of imposing the same type of anti-money laundering measures on financial institutions in different countries with a view to an international levelling of the playing field.[50] On an operational level, the globalisation of money laundering makes it necessary to establish effective international co-operation mechanisms which allow national authorities to co-operate in the prevention and prosecution of money laundering and in international 'proceeds-hunting'.[51] In terms of global economics, offshore havens are in effect free-loaders who profit from their membership of a globalised economy and seek the benefit from the fact that most other countries have introduced rules that discourage the inflow of illegal capital. In order to exclude this type of activity that undermines the viability of the international financial system, the proposition has been made that the international community establish a set of rules which would form the basis for full participation by any country in the international financial market. This presupposes that offshore havens radically change their legislation and practice.[52] The establishment of such a set of rules would be accompanied by punitive measures for those countries that do not play by these rules. Examples of such punitive measures could be the denial of international legal recog-

---

[49] FATF-I, p. 8. See also *Second Commission Report to the European Parliament and the Council on the Implementation of the Money Laundering Directive*, p. 4.

[50] United Nations Economic and Social Council, Commission on Crime Prevention and Criminal Justice, *Review of Priority Themes, Control of Proceeds of Crime-Report of the Secretary-General*, Vienna, 13–23 April 1993, E/CN.15/1993, p. 18.

[51] See M. C. Bassiouni and D. S. Gualtieri, 'International and National Responses to the Globalisation of Money Laundering', in *Responding to Money Laundering. International Perspectives*, ed. E. Savona (Amsterdam: Harwood Academic Publishers, 1997), pp. 109 *et seq.* These international co-operation mechanisms will be discussed in Part IV.

[52] P. Bernasconi, 'Obstacles in Controlling Money Laundering Crimes', in *Responding to Money Laundering. International Perspectives*, ed. E. Savona (Amsterdam: Harwood Academic Publishers, 1997), pp. 255–6.

nition to financial operations transacted within those countries or the imposition of punitive withholding taxes on capital flows from or to these countries.[53] At the heart of the matter lies the issue of sovereignty. While this concept undeniably allows every state to draft its legislation according to its own will, it might also be argued that a corollary of this concept is that no state should assist citizens of another state in the violation of the laws of their home countries. There is no denying that this is precisely what a number of offshore jurisdictions do: some of the financial facilities they offer or the advantages attached to them, are often only available to non-residents. This is the case with so-called IBCs (international business corporations), for example, which typically are incorporated in offshore jurisdictions, but do not do business there.[54]

A truly global anti-money laundering regime is still far from reality, however. At the moment, one of the few timid steps that has been taken by regional anti-money laundering regimes, such as the FATF, is the issuance of a public statement that one of its members is insufficiently in compliance with regard to anti-money laundering measures.[55] Yet, there are signs that political pressure on offshore havens to change their legislation is mounting as is evidenced by the call for better financial regulation made by the UK Foreign Secretary to the Dependent Territories Association in 1998.[56] On a multilateral level, initiatives have also been taken to curb abuse of offshore banks, such as the 29 recommendations of the Basle Committee designed to strengthen the effectiveness of the supervision of banks operating outside their national boundaries (1996),[57] the establishment of an *ad hoc* FATF group to study which steps could be taken in respect of non co-operative jurisdictions[58] and the co-operation between the Offshore Group of Banking Supervisors (OGBS) with the FATF on evaluating the effectiveness of the money laundering laws and policies of their members.

---

[53] See the interesting proposals made by Tanzi, *Money Laundering and the International Financial System*, pp. 12–13.

[54] See United Nations Office for Drug Control and Crime Prevention, *Financial Havens, Banking Secrecy and Money Laundering*, 59–60.

[55] See, e.g., FATF-VII, p. 15 and FATF-VIII, p. 7.

[56] See speech delivered by the UK's Foreign Secretary, Mr Robin Cook, to the Dependent Territories Association, Queen Elizabeth II Conference Centre, London, 4 February 1998.

[57] www.bis.org/publ   [58] See FATF-X, p. 35.

The fight against money laundering in the United States of America

In this section the contours of the American fight against money laundering are delineated, whereas the following section aims to give an overview of the efforts that have been undertaken in Switzerland to tackle the money laundering phenomenon. Both serve as a prelude to the fourth section, which will set out the twin track approach of the international anti-money laundering environment that has developed out of these differing national approaches.

First generation American anti-money laundering measures

A study of American anti-money laundering legislation should be set against the background of failing fiscal control by the American federal government. Until the 1960s, the annual income return was the only source of information for American authorities about the incomes of American citizens. This forced American authorities to have recourse to a number of legal techniques and theories to determine the real income of citizens. One theory is especially worth mentioning: the *Klein conspiracy* – named after the principal defendant in the case in which the theory was first successfully utilized[59] – was developed into a powerful legal concept which allowed the US government to sanction persons who conspired to defraud it. The facts of the Klein case were that Canadian whisky was bought by a New York distributor, through a Cuban subsidiary which falsified the records, returning excess profits to Klein and his employees through secret bank accounts. The scheme made it effectively impossible to prove how much income was unreported or on which tax returns it should technically have been reported. This loophole was plugged, however, by charging Klein and his associates with participation in a conspiracy to defraud the Internal Revenue Service (IRS) in its task to determine the real income and to levy taxes. This concept of conspiracy was successfully used to fight money laundering practices because they often involve an illegal agreement intended to impair the functions of the government (e.g. hindering forfeiture of proceeds). Conspiracy can there-

---

[59] *United States v. Klein*, 247 F.2d 908 (1957), *cert.denied*, 355 US 924 (1957). See M. De Feo, 'Depriving International Narcotics Traffickers and Other Organised Criminals of Illegal Proceeds and Combating Money Laundering', *Denv.J.Int'l L.& Pol'y* (1990), 407–8 and Goldstein, 'Conspiracy to Defraud the United States', *Yale LJ* (1959), 405. Conspiracy to Commit Offense or to Defraud the United States is now laid down in 18 USC § 371 (1988).

fore be described as one of the first generation of American anti-money laundering measures, later complemented by second and third generation measures. Conspiracy, however, continues to be an important tool in the fight against money laundering. The Anti-Money Laundering Act 1992 even introduced a specific provision which made it a criminal offence to conspire to launder the proceeds of crime.[60]

Second generation American anti-money laundering measures

In 1970, the Bank Secrecy Act (BSA) was enacted which, in spite of its name, is a disclosure law defining the circumstances that allow the lifting of banking secrecy rules.[61] Title I of the BSA provided for a number of record-keeping duties and for an obligation to ask for the customer's fiscal identification number (usually his social security number). The most important feature of the BSA is, however, contained in Title II, which authorises the Secretary of Treasury to lay down reporting duties. Three types of reporting duty have been imposed on financial institutions. American financial institutions should file Currency Transaction Reports, or CTRs (31 USC § 5313), every time they carry out a transaction above US$10,000. The US Treasury Department may lower this threshold in specific geographic locations that are especially prone to attracting money launderers by issuing Geographic Targeting Orders. The Money Laundering and Financial Crimes Strategy Act 1998 authorises the Secretary of the Treasury, in consultation with the Attorney General, to designate regions as high risk money laundering areas.[62]

These threshold-based reports should be filed with the Financial Crimes Enforcement Network (FinCEN). Second, every person who physically transports, mails or ships currency or other monetary instruments in excess of US$10,000 to a place outside the United States, or into the United States from anywhere outside, is required to file a Currency and Monetary Instruments Report (CMIR) with the US Customs Services (31 USC § 5316).

---

[60] 18 USC § 1956(g) allows for the punishment of the offence of conspiracy to launder with an imprisonment sentence up to 20 years and make it equally possible to forfeit the underlying assets: L. K. Osofsky, 'Fighting Money Laundering, American Style', *JIBL* (1993), 362.

[61] P. W. Schroth, 'Bank Confidentiality and the War on Money Laundering in the United States', in *Blanchiment d'argent et secret bancaire*, Rapport général du XIVe Congrès international de droit comparé, P. Bernasconi (The Hague: Kluwer Law International, 1996), pp. 291–5 and E. A. Stultz, 'Swiss Bank Secrecy and United States Efforts to Obtain Information from Swiss Banks', *Vand.J.Transnat.L.* (1988), 91–6.

[62] See 31 USC § 5342. See also B. Zagaris, 'US Enacts Anti-Money Laundering Act', *International Enforcement Law Reporter* (1998), 485–7.

A third reporting requirement concerns all persons subject to American jurisdiction and with a financial interest in, or with signatory or other authority over, bank accounts, securities, or other financial accounts in foreign jurisdiction with an aggregate value greater than US$10,000 who are required to file an annual report with Department of Treasury.

The Comprehensive Crime Control Act 1984 re-enacted these duties and made it possible to extend the obligation to report and record transactions in excess of US$10,000 to other trades and businesses (26 USC § 60501(a)). Other statutes (the Money Laundering Control Act 1986, the Anti-Drug Abuse Act 1988; the Anti-Money Laundering Act 1992 and the Money Laundering Suppressing Act 1994) brought further changes to the reporting regime.

The enactment and re-enactment in 1984 of these reporting duties was inspired by the desire to counter the laundering of money, both from the proceeds of crime and from tax evasion. The offence of conspiracy fell short here as persons or corporations (financial institutions) who accept funds without asking about their origin, cannot be charged with conspiracy. These legislative measures focused not only on internal money laundering, but also on international money laundering, in view of the considerable difficulties American authorities had run into when they tried to obtain information about the assets held by American citizens abroad. By subjecting American citizens to a reporting obligation in this respect, American legislators hoped to circumvent these difficulties.

However, this hope was not borne out by the facts, as these reporting duties remained largely unenforced throughout the 1970s as a result of financial institutions' ignorance of them. It was only in the 1980s that the amended Bank Secrecy Act was increasingly used to prosecute financial institutions by the IRS, the Treasury Department and the US Customs.[63]

It is to be emphasised that, although non-compliance with the duties imposed under the BSA can be criminally and civilly enforced (31 USC §§ 5321 and 5322), merely transacting or transporting monies is not incriminated as such. The record-keeping and reporting duties are nevertheless of a paramount interest to the repression of money laundering as they provide law enforcement authorities with indispensable information.[64] This is obviously the case for the reporting requirements: 12 USC § 1829(b)

---

[63] See Nadelmann, 'Unlaundering Dirty Money', 38–42. On the role of these institutions in enforcing anti-money laundering measures, see W. Adams, 'Effective Strategies for Banks in Avoiding Criminal, Civil, and Forfeiture Liability in Money Laundering Cases', Ala.L.Rev. (1993), 674–6.

[64] See Levi, 'Pecunia non olet', 252–4 and J. J. Byrne, 'The Bank Secrecy Act: Do Reporting Requirements Really Assist the Government?', Ala.L.Rev. (1993), 819–21.

– the statutory authorisation for the imposition of reporting duties – expressly states that 'the maintenance of appropriate types of records and other evidence by insured depository institutions has a high degree of usefulness in criminal, tax, or regulatory investigations or proceedings'. It is equally true of record-keeping duties: they provide the government with a paper trail, which later may used as evidence against an accused in a criminal trial. The preventive function of these duties, on the other hand, is minimal. Because the reporting duties are threshold-based, they are often circumvented by so-called 'smurfing' practices, which consist of splitting up one transaction into smaller transactions which fall below the threshold. The usefulness of these reporting duties for the government as such is at any rate doubtful as FinCEN is currently overwhelmed by the sheer volume of reports that are made (over 12 million in 1997),[65] which causes a permanent backlog in investigations and puts a considerable strain on the effectiveness of anti-money laundering law enforcement. This has caused a shift in the US law enforcement policy towards the reporting of suspicious transactions.[66] Under the Money Laundering Suppressing Act 1994 financial institutions may be obliged to file reports for suspicious transactions (12 USC § 5314(g)), and in 1995 FinCEN and the financial regulators issued rules defining the circumstances under which banks should report financial transactions.

Third generation American anti-money laundering measures

Money laundering was only criminalised in the United States in 1986 as a result of the travails of the President's Commission on Organised Crime, which considered the fight against money laundering as a prime tool in the fight against organised crime.[67] The Money Laundering Control Act of 1986 not only envisages persons who launder the proceeds from their crimes but also third parties, notably financial institutions, who launder those proceeds. It enacted two federal crimes, the crime of money laundering (18 USC § 1956) and the crime of monetary transactions (18 USC § 1957).

Enactment 18 USC § 1956 prohibits domestic money laundering, in

---

[65] FinCEN Information Leaflet: 'FinCEN Further Streamlines Exemption Process' (21 September 1998). In 1992, the figure was 9.2 million reports a year: Byrne, 'The Bank Secrecy Act', 803.

[66] GAO, *Money Laundering: Needed Improvements for Reporting Suspicious Transactions are Planned* (GA/GGD-95-156, 30 May 1995), p. 2 *et seq.*

[67] See J. D. Harmon, 'United States Money Laundering Laws: International Implications', *NYUJ Int'l L. & Comp.L.* (1988), 2–3.

essence by incriminating financial transactions concerning criminally derived proceeds, when these are carried out (i) with the intent of promoting certain kinds of criminal activity; or (ii) with the intent to avoid paying taxes on the proceeds involved. Persons who conduct financial transactions with criminally derived proceeds are also criminally liable when (iii) they know that the transaction is designed to 'conceal or disguise the nature, the location, the source, the ownership, or control of the proceeds'; or to avoid a transaction reporting requirement under State or Federal law. The definition of a 'financial transaction' (18 USC § 1956(c)(4)) is so wide as to encompass almost any exchange of money between two persons.[68] This concept has sometimes even been construed to apply to the mere receipt and transportation of criminally derived property or even payment for drugs.[69]

18 USC § 1957 incriminates engaging in a monetary transaction in property derived from specified unlawful activity of a value in excess of US$10,000. This provision has a very wide application field as it concerns not only financial transactions but also any transaction involving monetary instruments and thereby may reach out to cover seemingly innocent acts or commercial transactions.[70] This broad application field illustrates Congress's will to isolate persons engaged in (organised) crime from the rest of society.[71] The provision's broad character is accentuated by the absence of a specific intent requirement: it is sufficient that the accused was aware of the criminal origin of the property. But even this qualifier is very liberal: unlike § 1956, § 1957 does not even require that the defendant knew that the money was derived from a felony; a general knowledge of its criminal origin (or even wilful blindness) will suffice.[72]

The fight against money laundering in Switzerland

Swiss anti-money laundering legislation, both in origin and in content, is characterised by a strong input from the private sector. The self-imposed

---

[68] E. Chang and A. M. Herscowitz, 'Money Laundering', Am.J.Cr.L. (1995), 511–2.

[69] For an in-depth criticism of this case law, see J. Gurulé, 'The Money Laundering Control Act of 1986: Creating a New Federal Offence or Merely Affording Federal Prosecutors an Alternative Means of Punishing Specified Unlawful Activity?', Am.Cr.LR (1995), 829–37.

[70] Chang and Herscowitz, 'Money Laundering', 504 and Harmon, 'United States Money Laundering Laws', 12–13.

[71] See C. T. Plombeck, 'Confidentiality and Disclosure: The Money Laundering Control Act of 1986 and Banking Secrecy', Int'l Law. (1988), 80 and Chang and Herscowitz, 'Money Laundering', 504.

[72] Chang and Herscowitz, 'Money Laundering', 507. But see Ratzlaf v. United States, 510 US 135.

regulatory regime of Swiss financial institutions can be considered as the legal womb that has spawned Swiss anti-money laundering legislation.

Self-regulation: the Swiss Code of Conduct

The first reaction to the (alleged) misuse of Swiss financial institutions for the purposes of laundering money of dubious origins, and of capital flight,[73] was seen in 1977 when Swiss banks, the Swiss Union of Banks and the Swiss National Bank signed a Code of Conduct on the acceptance of funds and the use of banking secrecy, the *Convention relative à l'obligation de diligence des banques lors de l'acceptation de fonds et à l'usage du secret bancaire*, or CDB. Under the 1977 version of the CDB, Swiss banks were obliged to refrain from carrying out a transaction if it would frustrate the goals of the CDB as, for example, when it was clear that the funds were criminally derived. This anti-money laundering measure was, however, left out of the subsequent versions of 1982, 1987 and 1992. The argument invoked to justify this amendment was that Swiss criminal law already allowed for the penalisation of money laundering, a statement which was, however, at least debatable before 1990.[74] Additionally, whereas the original version of the CDB also contained an obligation on financial institutions to investigate the origin of funds, in 1982 this was watered down into an obligation to identify them. Consequently, it is only through the identification duties it imposes that the CDB may potentially prevent money laundering. These obligations have at least had the effect of outlawing anonymous bank accounts, but not numbered bank accounts, of which the identity of the account holder is only known to a number of staff members of the bank.[75] This exclusive emphasis on the identification of the customer should be set against the background of the stringent Swiss banking secrecy rules (Article 47 of the Swiss Banking Secrecy Act),[76] which – before the Swiss Money Laundering Act of 10 October 1997 – in principle

---

[73] See on the background of the CDB: M. Giovanoli, 'Switzerland. Some Recent Developments in Banking Law', in *European Banking Law: The Banker–Customer Relationship*, R. Cranston (London: LLP, 1993), p. 189; P. Nobel, 'Die neuen Standesregeln zur Sorgfaltspflicht der Banken', *Wirtschaft und Recht* (1987), 150; P. Nobel, 'Bankgeschäft und Ethik – Freiheit und Strafrecht', *RSDA* (1996), 99 and R. G. Peters, 'Money Laundering and Its Current Status In Switzerland: New Disincentives For Financial Tourism', *Nw. J. of Int'l L. & Bus.* (1990), 105–6.

[74] See Peters, 'Money Laundering', 112 and D. Zuberbühler, 'Das Verhältnis zwischen der Bankenaufsicht, insbesondere der Überwachung der einwandfreien Geschäftstätigkeit und der neuen Sorgfaltspflichtvereinbarung der Banken', *Wirtschaft und Recht* (1987), 181.

[75] Giovanoli, 'Switzerland. Some Recent Developments in Banking Law', p. 190.

[76] Loi fédérale sur les banques et les caisses d'épargne du 8 novembre 1934.

prohibited banks from disclosing on their own initiative any information relating to their customers.[77]

The ambitious design of the CDB – a detailed text comprising 15 articles and 58 explanatory notes – was thus effectively curtailed in its subsequent versions of 1982, 1987 and 1992. Since September 1987, the Swiss National Bank has ceased to be a party to the Code of Conduct. Notwithstanding its private law character,[78] the objectives of the CDB, as stated in its preamble, are of a mixed nature:

> En vue de préserver le renom du système bancaire suisse sur les plans national et international, - en vue d'établir des règles assurant, lors de l'acceptation de fonds et dans le domaine du secret bancaire, une gestion irréprochable, les banques s'obligent . . . à: a) vérifier l'identité de leurs cocontractants et à se faire remettre, en cas de doute, une déclaration du cocontractant relative à l'ayant droit économique des valeurs confiées à la banque; b) ne prêter aucune assistance active à la fuite de capitaux; c) ne prêter aucune assistance active à la fraude fiscale ou des actes analogues, en délivrant des attestations incomplètes ou trompeuses.

> In order to preserve the reputation of the Swiss banking system, both on a domestic and international level, in order to establish a set of rules, guaranteeing an irreproachable management in the acceptance of funds and the field of banking secrecy, the banks commit themselves . . . to: a) verifying the identity of their contracting parties and to request, in case of doubt, a declaration of the contracting party regarding the beneficial owner of the funds handed over to the bank; b) to providing no active assistance to capital flight; c) to providing no active assistance to financial fraud or analogous acts, by giving incomplete or false attestations.

Administrative supervision of the Swiss banks

Some of the requirements laid down in the private Code of Conduct (CDB) of the Swiss bankers have, albeit indirectly, been elevated into a form of binding Swiss law by the supervisory practice of the Swiss Banking Commission (*Commission fédérale des banques*). Article 3(2)(c) of the Swiss Banking Act requires that the management of a bank provide the necessary guarantees for an irreproachable activity (*garantie d'une activité irréprochable*). Although this requirement was originally designed as a con-

---

[77] See e.g. F. Taisch, 'Swiss Statutes Concerning Money Laundering', *Int'l Law.* (1992), 711–13.

[78] See the decision of the Swiss Supreme Court ATF 109 Ib 146 (1982). See also C. Graber, 'Zum Verhältnis der Sorgfaltsplichtvereinbarung der Banken zu Art.305ter Abs1 StGB', *R.S.D.A.* (1995), 162 and M. Kistler, *La vigilance requise en matière d'opérations financières. Etude de l'article 305ter du Code pénal suisse* (Zurich: 1994), p. 112.

dition for a banking licence, it has now developed into the legal foundation for the supervision function carried out by the Swiss Banking Commission.[79] This provision does not state, however, which conditions have to be met for an irreproachable activity. Given that the Swiss Banking Act does not only aim to protect the interest of creditors but also purports to safeguard the trust in the Swiss financial system as a whole,[80] the Swiss Banking Commission has used Article 3(2)(c) of the Swiss Banking Act to require that banks investigate the economic background of financial transactions they are asked to carry out. The Swiss Supreme Court has construed this provision as aiming to prevent illegal transactions and did not refrain from stating that, by obliging banks to investigate the economic background of financial transactions, the identification requirement had implicitly become part of Swiss law.[81] Given the stringent Swiss banking secrecy rules, the supervision practice of the Swiss Banking Commission – like the CDB – did not, however, seek to impose a reporting obligation.

The Swiss criminalisation of money laundering

Notwithstanding the requirements flowing from the CDB and the supervision practice of the Swiss Banking Commission, Swiss legislation lacked adequate (criminal) legislation to fight money laundering. This had become painfully clear in an international money laundering case involving Swiss banks, the *Pizza-connection*.[82] Paolo Bernasconi, who had prosecuted this case, was subsequently asked by the Swiss Department of Justice to produce a draft statute on the incrimination of money laundering. Although his draft was finished in 1986, it would take till 23 March 1990 before the bill, which eventually entered into force on 1 July 1990, was voted. As well as the actual money laundering offence itself (Article 305bis Swiss Criminal Code), failure to identify a customer was also criminalised (Article 305ter Swiss Criminal Code). These criminalisations do not stand on their own, however. As follows, it will be shown that the practical application of both laws is heavily influenced by the CDB's rules and by the supervision practice of the Swiss Banking Commission in effect

---

[79] See C.-A. Junod, 'La garantie d'une activité irréprochable. De la surveillance à la tutelle des banques?', in *Beiträge zum Schweizerischen Bankenrecht*, R. v. Grafenfried, (Bern: Verlag Stämpfli, 1989), p. 91.

[80] Giovanoli, 'Switzerland. Some Recent Developments in Banking Law', 192 and Junod, 'La garantie d'une activité irréprochable', 93–4.

[81] ATF 111 1b 126. See also Graber, *Geldwäscherei*, p. 188.

[82] See on this case: Graber, *Geldwäscherei*, pp. 36–8 and Bernasconi, 'Geldwäscherei und organisierte Kriminalität', 31 and 57.

giving rise to a form of legal cross-pollination between money laundering criminalisations and these civil law developments.

Article 305bis of the Swiss Criminal Code holds everyone criminally liable who has committed an act which impedes the identification of the origin, the discovery or the confiscation of proceeds which he knew or should know were derived from a crime (i.e. an offence liable to a term of imprisonment of one to twenty years). The general nature of the criminalisation and the criminalisation of money laundering as an offence against the administration of justice (*délit contre la justice*) has been criticised[83] because it is not confined to money laundering related to organised crime.[84] Initially, this legislation had the paradoxical effect that a Swiss banker who refused to carry out a suspicious transaction could also be seen as perverting the course of justice as he *de facto* interrupted the paper trail.[85] Given the stringency of Swiss banking secrecy rules, a banker was not allowed to disclose his suspicions or even knowledge regarding the criminal origin of proceeds to police, judicial or any other authorities. Although the criminalisation of money laundering obliged a banker to refrain from carrying out transactions which he knew involved criminally derived funds and thus contributed to the prevention of the misuse of the financial system, its input in terms of information flows to the government was almost zero.

This conundrum was solved by the Swiss Money Laundering Act of 14 March 1994, which, for the first time, allowed Swiss bankers to disclose at their own initiative information covered by Swiss banking secrecy laws. The Swiss Money Laundering Act of 10 October 1997[86] subsequently established a legal obligation for Swiss financial intermediaries to disclose any knowledge or reasonable suspicion (*soupçon fondé*) they may have regarding proceeds that are derived from a crime or subject to the power of a criminal organisation. Reports must be made to the competent federal office (*Centrale de communication en matière de blanchissage d'argent* – Article 9 of the Swiss Money Laundering Act of 10 October 1997). The whistle-

---

[83] G. Stratenwerth, 'Geldwäscherei-ein Lehrstuck der Gesetzgebung', in *Bekämpfung der Geldwäscherei. Modellfall Schweiz?*, ed. M. Pieth (Basle: Helbing & Lichtenhahn, 1992), p. 102.

[84] This was confirmed by the Swiss Supreme Court, judgment of 20 January 1993, *La Semaine Judiciaire* (1993), 610.

[85] See Kistler, *La vigilance requise*, p. 102; D. Zuberbühler, 'Banken als Hilfspolizisten zur Verhinderung der Geldwäscherei? Sicht eines Bankaufsehers', in *Bekämpfung der Geldwäscherei. Modellfall Schweiz?*, M. Pieth (Basle: Helbing & Lichtenhahn, 1992), p. 59 and Stratenwerth, 'Geldwäscherei-ein Lehrstuck der Gesetzgebung', p. 110.

[86] Loi fédérale du 10 octobre 1997 concernant la lutte contre le blanchissement d'argent dans le secteur financier.

blowing protection provided for by this article ensures that diligent disclosure cannot give rise to any criminal or civil liability for violating banking secrecy, for example (Article 11 of the Swiss Money Laundering Act of 10 October 1997).

Article 305ter Swiss Criminal Code states that any financial intermediary who omits to verify the identity of the beneficial owner with the due diligence required by the circumstances is guilty of a crime of omission and so liable for punishment. It is not even necessary for criminally derived proceeds to be involved for an offence to be committed:[87] Article 305ter punishes the mere non-observance of the identification obligation. This provision is subsidiary to Article 305bis in that it only applies if Article 305bis does not. In addition, it has a much more narrow application field *rationae personae* as the Swiss legislator has chosen to limit its application field to the 'risk-group' of financial intermediaries, that is, everyone who professionally accepts, holds, helps to deposit or transfers proceeds from a third person. The law targets only persons who work in the financial sector, not other professionals who may also carry out these tasks as a by-product of their main professional activities.[88] Although the wording of Article 305ter – contrary to Article 2 of the Swiss Money Laundering Act of 10 October 1997 – does not clearly enumerate the institutions and professions to which it applies, it is deemed to apply to any kind of financial institution, investment adviser, *bureau de change* or dealer in precious metals. Even lawyers are covered by this law, insofar as they are engaged in activities which fall outside the scope of their traditional tasks and are concerned rather with asset management.[89] This distinction between activities specific to the profession of lawyers and other activities is one which is well known in Swiss law.[90]

The criminal enforcement of the obligation to verify the identity of the beneficial owner with the due diligence required by the circumstances is the clearest example of the legal cross-pollination that has taken place in

[87] H. Dietzi, 'Der Bankangestellte als eidgenössisch konzessionierter Sherlock Holmes? Der Kampf gegen die Geldwäscherei aus der Optik des Ersten Rechtskonsulenten einer Grossbank', in *Bekämpfung der Geldwäscherei. Modellfall Schweiz?*, M. Pieth (Basle: Helbing & Lichtenhahn, 1992), p. 76; Graber, *Geldwäscherei*, pp. 185–6; Friedli, 'Der gebotene Sorgfalt nach Art.305ter Strafgesetzbuch für Banken, Anwälte und Notäre', in *Bekämpfung der Geldwäscherei. Modellfall Schweiz?*, M. Pieth (Basle: Helbing & Lichtenhahn, 1992), p. 132 and Kistler, *La vigilance requise*, pp. 167–8.

[88] Graber, *Geldwäscherei*, p. 183 and Stratenwerth, 'Geldwäscherei-ein Lehrstuck der Gesetzgebung', p. 117.

[89] Kistler, *La vigilance requise*, pp. 149–151; Graber, *Geldwäscherei*, pp. 183–4 and Friedli, 'Der gebotene Sorgfalt', p. 141.

[90] Swiss Supreme Court, judgment of 29 December 1986 (ATF 112 Ib 606).

Switzerland between criminal law and rules such as the CDB's private Code of Conduct and the supervision practice of the Swiss Banking Commission. Neither the concept of the beneficial owner, nor that of due diligence required by the circumstances are defined in Article 305ter or in any other provision of the Swiss Criminal Code. It would not be until the Money Laundering Act of 10 October 1997 was introduced that the concept of the beneficial owner would be further defined by Swiss law. These definitions, as well as the meanings that were attached to these concepts in the meantime, were heavily influenced by the CDB's rules and the supervision practice of the Swiss Banking Commission.

By criminalising failure to identify the beneficial owner, Swiss law in effect criminalised the non-observance of existing duties. It illustrates how soft law, even privately drafted regulations (i.e. the CDB rules), can shape hard law. The criminal enforcement of a concept derived from a soft law instrument, did, however, create a difficulty from the point of view of the legality principle.[91] More specifically, the fact that the criteria that establish whether the identification of the beneficial owner had been accomplished were not defined in the criminal law could create problems. Although these criteria are now laid down in Article 4 of the Swiss Money Laundering Act of 10 October 1997, they were originally introduced by Article 3 of the CDB 1977. This provision requires identification of the beneficial owner in two circumstances: in case of doubt about the real identity of the contracting party or in case of a cash transaction of a value of more than 25,000 Swiss francs. The CDB rules also enumerate a number of unusual circumstances in which the financial institution should require a written declaration as to who is beneficial owner through a so-called Form A (explanatory note 18). Article 4 of the CDB rules further imposed identification of the beneficial owner of a so-called domiciliary company, that is, a company which does not carry out any commercial or industrial activity in its home state. These three criteria have been copied by Article 4 of the Money Laundering Act of 10 October 1997 except that in respect of the second criterion, it refers to 'an important amount'.

The concept of due diligence required by the circumstances is derived from the CDB rules (explanatory note 18), according to which the general rule that a financial institution is entitled to presume that the contracting party is the beneficial owner, is set aside under a number of unusual circumstances. In these exceptional circumstances the financial institu-

---

[91] See also Graber, *Geldwäscherei*, pp. 192 and 198; Friedli, 'Der gebotene Sorgfalt', p. 128; Kistler, *La vigilance requise*, pp. 149–51 and Stratenwerth, 'Geldwäscherei – ein Lehrstuck der Gesetzgebung', 116.

tion should require a written declaration as to who is beneficial owner. Should serious doubts which cannot be lifted through further enquiries remain as to the veracity of the written declaration, the bank should refrain from the transaction (explanatory note 21).

The Swiss Supreme Court has, in its judicial review of the administrative supervision practice of the Swiss Banking Commission, elaborated case law to the effect that a bank is obliged to investigate the economic background of a transaction whenever there are concrete indications that the transaction could be part of an illegal or immoral construction, or when complicated, unusual or important business is involved.[92] As under the CDB rules, a simple identification is not as such deemed sufficient when further investigations into the economic background of a transaction are required.[93] It is striking that both the Swiss Banking Commission and the Supreme Court referred to the CDB rules as the minimum standard for an irreproachable banking activity.[94]

Notwithstanding the fact that Swiss law in this way indirectly contained a number of criteria for defining the circumstances in which a beneficial owner had to be identified, the lack of clearly defined statutory criteria made Article 305ter Swiss Criminal Code problematic with respect to the legality principle.[95] In a clear attempt to fill this gap, the Swiss Banking Commission issued a directive on 18 December 1991 on the prevention and the fight against money laundering.[96] The directive defines a number of circumstances in which banks should make further inquiries into the identity of the beneficial owner, including an appendix laying down indices of money laundering. If doubts remain as to the real identity of the beneficial owner, the bank should refrain from opening a bank account or stop the existing business relationship. The Banking

---

[92] Swiss Supreme Court, ATF 108 Ib 190. See also A. Hirsch, '"Dirty Money" and Swiss Banking Regulations', *J.Comp.Bus. & Cap.M.* (1986), 375–7; Junod, 'La garantie d'une activité irréprochable', pp. 96–115 and Taisch, 'Swiss Statutes Concerning Money Laundering', 705.

[93] Taisch, 'Swiss Statutes Concerning Money Laundering', 706–7 and Zuberbühler, 'Banken als Hilfspolizisten', pp. 53–4.

[94] See, e.g., ATF 111 1b 126 and ATF 109 1b 146; *Eidgenössisches Bankenkommission-Jahresbericht 1988*, 24, cited by Peters, 'Money Laundering', 126 and Zuberbühler, 'Das Verhaltnis zwischen der Bankenaufsicht', p. 180.

[95] Although the Swiss Supreme Court ruled that this provision was reconcilable with the legality principle: non-published judgment of 22 September 1993, cited by M. Aubert, P.-A. Béguin, P. Bernasconi, J. Graziono-Von Burg, R. Schwob and R. Treuillaud, *Le secret bancaire suisse. Droit privé, pénal, administratif, fiscal, procédure, entraide et conventions internationales* (Bern: Ed.Staempfli et Cie, 1995), p. 294.

[96] Circulaire de la Commission fédérale des banques: Directives relatives à la prévention et à la lutte contre le blanchiment de capitaux du 18 décembre 1991, CBF 91/3.

Commission made it explicitly clear that the directive was meant to provide elements to allow banks to avoid criminal liability under Article 305ter as well as to put into writing its supervision practice regarding the requirements flowing from Article 3(2)(b) and (c) of the Swiss Banking Act. These are, again, undeniable signs of a legal cross-pollination between criminal law and banking law: the directive has even been described as the main weapon in the fight against money laundering.[97] Even though it is in itself laudable that the Swiss Banking Commission provided a 'hard' law text defining the circumstances in which a financial institution should make inquiries into the identity of the beneficial owner, it is regrettable that the Swiss legislator waited until 1997 before intervening with the Money Laundering Act of 10 October of that year. As a matter of principle, it is questionable that a supervisory authority should be forced or at least permitted to fill gaps left in criminal legislation by parliament.

The twin-track fight against money laundering: the preventive and the repressive approach

A twin track policy has gradually evolved in the fight against money laundering, consisting of a preventive approach, founded in banking law, and a repressive approach founded in criminal law. To portray the distinction between the preventive and the repressive approach to money laundering as a dichotomy between criminal and financial law is, however, an oversimplification. The discussion of American and especially of Swiss law has shown that both approaches cannot be seen as operating completely separately from each other, but that they should rather be seen as connected. Many of the rules of financial law on the prevention of money laundering eventually serve a repressive goal and the prevention of money laundering is often backed up by the threat of criminal sanctions. Both the Swiss and the American anti-money-laundering regimes contain elements of what has sometimes generally been described as *droit administratif pénal* and *droit pénal administratif*, terms which have been coined to designate respectively a type of administrative law enforcement through punitive sanctions imposed by an administrative body and a type of criminal law enforcement in which administrative bodies wield important powers.[98]

---

[97] Dietzi, 'Der Bankangestellte', p. 83 and P. Gasser, 'Von der vermuteten Unschuld des Geldes-Die Einziehung von Vermögenswerten krimineller Herkunft', in *Bekämpfung der Geldwäscherei. Modellfall Schweiz?*, M. Pieth (Basle: Helbing & Lichtenhahn, 1992), p. 169.

[98] On these concepts see A. De Nauw, *Les métamorphoses du droit pénal de l'entreprise* (Ghent: Mys & Breesch, 1994), p. 48 and H.-D. Bosly, 'Du droit pénal d'affaires', in *Punir mon beau souci* (Brussels: Ed. de l'Université de Bruxelles, 1984), p. 191.

Notwithstanding the close entwinement of the repressive and preventive approach, both can and should indeed be distinguished. Overall, the American model can be described as predominantly repressive, whereas the Swiss model is predominantly preventive. The American anti-money-laundering regime emphasises the criminal enforcement of the money laundering prohibition: even though money laundering was only criminalised in 1986, the first legislative measures against money laundering, the disclosure rules contained in the Banking Secrecy Act 1970, were designed to provide the law enforcement authorities with information. The Swiss model on the other hand, is characterised by a strong emphasis on financial anti-money-laundering rules. Although the Swiss law criminalised money laundering, it has been shown that this was in part no more than the criminal enforcement of existing rules on the identification of the beneficial owner (Article 305ter Swiss Criminal Code) and that, before the introduction of the right for a banker to disclose suspicions, the actual incrimination of money laundering (Article 305bis Swiss Criminal Code) only had a very limited input in terms of criminal law enforcement.

The difference in orientation is also reflected in the different purposes that are served by financial anti-money laundering measures in both countries. The American Banking Secrecy Act 1970 is aimed at creating and conserving documentary evidence and especially at establishing a financial information flow from financial institutions to law enforcement authorities. Until the Swiss Money Laundering Act of 10 October 1997, this goal was almost completely lacking under Swiss law. The main purpose of the Swiss Code of Conduct (CDB) as well as of the supervision practice of the Swiss Banking Commission was – at least initially – to protect the reputation of the Swiss financial system and to prevent financial institutions from being used for the purposes of money laundering.

Although this difference can perhaps in part be explained by differences in legal culture between the two countries, it is mainly the reflection of a different policy on money laundering. Whereas the United States has clearly opted for a repressive approach to money laundering, combined with an active engagement in proceeds-hunting (most notably the proceeds from drug trafficking), Switzerland puts more emphasis on the prevention of money laundering. The Swiss fondness for preventive rules seems related to the important role that financial institutions play in the Swiss economy and their concurrently privileged role under Swiss law, reflecting very stringent banking secrecy rules. Swiss financial institutions themselves took the initiative in 1977 by elaborating the Code of Conduct (CDB), an initiative that would eventually strongly influence the legislation that was to follow – and international instruments in the field of the prevention of money laundering. Although in principle a matter for speculation, it is doubtful whether the Swiss legislator could have waited till the Money Laundering Act of 10 October 1997 to put in place truly preventive legislation had the Swiss banks not acted as they did by elaborating a set of private rules, which, albeit indirectly, served to prevent money laundering. The role of self-regulation in the American anti-money laundering style is, to the regret of some American commentators,[99] very limited in Swiss law.

Another part of the explanation for the difference in approach is to be found in the geographical origin of the proceeds that are laundered. Most of the proceeds of crime that are laundered in the United States probably stem from offences committed within the United States, even though the money laundering operations involved may have international ramifications. On the other hand, most of the funds that are deposited in Switzerland, including criminally derived proceeds, are derived from foreign activities. In this perspective, the preference of Swiss authorities for preventive action against money laundering rather than active engagement in the criminal enforcement of the law against money laundering is not surprising as the overall majority of funds that are laundered in Switzerland are derived from predicate offences that took place outside Switzerland and which consequently in most cases have little relevance to Switzerland. Swiss authorities and Swiss banks were therefore more interested in safeguarding their own interests, the reputation of the Swiss financial industry, than in preventing the financial spin-off of criminal activities that occurred outside Switzerland. Criminal law and criminal law enforcement are looked upon as tools for defending society – tools of last resort, even: the criminal law is sometimes referred to as an *ultimum remedium* and is therefore primarily used by the Swiss in defence of their own nation, rather than others. The criminalisation of money laundering, including of the proceeds derived from a foreign offence,[100] is an important deviation from this traditional approach to the criminal law.

On a more general level, the repressive and preventive model differ both in goals and in investigative methods. The preventive approach has as its primary purpose the prevention of money laundering and, more specifically, the misuse of financial institutions for these purposes. The prevention of money laundering in this sense serves the larger goal of preventing financial institutions from being misused. In this sense preventive rules

---

[99] T. D. Grant, 'Towards a Swiss Solution for an American Problem: An Alternative Approach for Banks in the War on Drugs', *Ann.Rev.Bank.L.* (1995), pp. 231–53.
[100] See *infra* pp. 226–9.

have to be distinguished from protective rules which aim to protect individual depositors and financial markets when financial institutions get into trouble.[101] This goal also explains the self-regulatory nature of some of the first initiatives in the fight against money laundering, such as the Swiss Code of Conduct (CDB), but also, on an international level, the Declaration of Principles of the Basle Committee. In the United States and other countries, where the rules on the prevention of money laundering serve broader purposes than merely preventing financial institutions from getting into trouble, these preventive rules are laid down in statutory legislation. In Switzerland, the rules on the prevention of money laundering have only provided a significant advantage to the law enforcement authorities when cast in statutory legislation and notably when Swiss legislation allowed Swiss bankers to disclose their suspicions.

The criminalisation of money laundering should have as its primary purpose the repression of activities which are deemed to be socially reprehensible. Nevertheless, it should be noted that the criminalisation of money laundering can only substantially fulfil this role when the legislative framework allows banks and other institutions and professions to disclose any suspicions they may harbour. This is not to say that if this option is absent, the criminalisation of money laundering is useless but instead that, rather than playing a repressive function, it will have a predominantly preventive function, preventing third parties from aiding and abetting the laundering of the proceeds of crime.

Moreover, the repressive and preventive approach has a different 'investigative method', that is a different approach as how to investigate money laundering.[102] In a repressive approach to money laundering, the criminalisation of money laundering is the logical corollary of the confiscation of proceeds from crime. The criminalisation of money laundering is essentially aimed at third persons who launder proceeds, that is who 'render proceeds of crime unrecognisable as such'[103] and therefore frustrate the law enforcement goal of proceeds-hunting. In this repressive perspective, the paper trail leads from the predicate offence to the laundered proceeds. The knowledge of the predicate offence is the logical starting point and its purpose is to unveil the laundering operation in order to be able to

---

101 R. Dale, 'Reflections on the BCCI Affair: A United Kingdom Perspective', *Int'l Law* (1991), 949.

102 See in this respect G. Arzt, 'Das schweizerischen Geldwäschereiverbot im Lichte amerikanische Erfahrungen', *RPS* (1989), 163–7.

103 This concise definition of money laundering was given by S. Gleason, 'The Involuntary Launderer: The Banker's Liability for Deposits of the Proceeds of Crime', in *Laundering and Tracing*, ed. P. Birks (Oxford: Clarendon Press, 1995), p. 115.

hunt down the proceeds. If the launderers had initially instigated the predicate offence (as may often be the case in the context of organised crime), then the paper trail will in addition lead to the principals of the crime.

The preventive approach, with its stress on the reporting obligation as first laid down in the American legislation, follows the paper trail from the other end: from the laundering of money to the predicate offence. By subjecting financial institutions to a number of financial law duties, a greater transparency of financial transactions is envisaged, which should make it possible to detect 'dirty money flows'. Reporting duties are intended to provide the competent authorities with information on suspicious or unusual transactions (or information which allows them to filter such transactions), thus allowing those authorities to reconstitute the paper trail towards the predicate offence and its perpetrators. The effectiveness of the preventive rules approach, which will be examined in Part 2, is difficult to assess but it is useful at this stage to point out that authoritative commentators have argued that, in view of the limitations of rules as a means of preventing money laundering and of artificial intelligence models in tracing and unveiling criminal money, not too many resources should be shifted away from traditional policing (i.e. the repressive approach to money laundering control) and into the use of artificial intelligence models (i.e. the repressive approach to money laundering).[104]

Both the repressive and the preventive approach to money laundering have their roots in American and Swiss law but were subsequently developed in other countries. The American repressive approach, notably its incrimination of money laundering, has been internationalised by the Vienna Convention and the Money Laundering Convention. The prevention of money laundering, drawing on the American and the Swiss experience, was internationalised through the FATF Recommendations and the European Money Laundering Directive, as well as other international instruments. The influence of this international law on the criminalisation of money laundering will be studied in the fifth section of this chapter. The content of these preventive rules as well as their implementation into domestic law and their possible effect on criminal law enforcement will be scrutinised in Part 2.

---

[104] United Nations Office for Drug Control and Crime Prevention, *Financial Havens, Banking Secrecy and Money Laundering*, p. 14.

The international treaty obligation to criminalise money laundering: a drastic expansion of criminal liability?

The obligation to incriminate money laundering that flowed from the Vienna Convention and the Money Laundering Convention has led to a plethora of domestic criminal legislation. The criticism which has often been levelled at these domestic anti-money laundering instruments is that their broad character has led to a drastic inflation of criminal liability. Although it is true that the definition of *actus reus* is under many domestic money laundering incriminations very wide, both in regard of type of activities that fall under the incriminations and in regard of the range of predicate offences covered by these incriminations, it will be argued that in most cases this wide application field can be kept in balance by the requirement to prove *mens rea*. Finally, the question of the liability of the perpetrator of the predicate offence for laundering the proceeds which flow from it will be studied.

Actus reus: three types of money laundering activity

Article 3(1) of the Vienna Convention calls on states to incriminate three types of money laundering activities:

(b) (i) The conversion or transfer of property, knowing that such property is derived from any offence or offences established in accordance with subparagraph (a) of this paragraph, or from an act of participation in such offence or offences, for the purpose of concealing or disguising the illicit origin of the property or of assisting any person who is involved in the commission of such an offence or offences to evade the legal consequences of his actions.

(ii) The concealment or disguise of the true nature, source, location, disposition, movement, rights with respect to, or ownership of property, knowing that such property is derived from an offence or offences established in accordance with subparagraph (a) of this paragraph or from an act of participation in such an offence or offences.

(c) Subject to its constitutional principles and the basic concepts of its legal system:

(i) The acquisition, possession or use of property, knowing, at the time of the receipt, that such property was derived from an offence or offences established in accordance with subparagraph (a) of this paragraph or from an act of participation in such an offence or offences.

The definition of these three types of activity was copied almost verbatim into Article 6(1) of the Money Laundering Convention and into Article 2 of the European Money Laundering Directive, although the reference to the predicate offence differs. These three types of criminal conduct differ as to the extent to which the nexus with the predicate offence can be established. Although all three types of criminalisation require that the alleged offender be aware of the criminal origin of the proceeds (termed 'property' under the Vienna Convention), it is clear that the first type of conduct constitutes a more active type of money laundering than either the second or the third type, in that the first type of conduct implies a kind of active engagement in the predicate offence (one could even think of it as a type of complicity after the fact) which is completely absent in respect of the third type of money laundering conduct. In this sense, one could metaphorically refer to three concentric circles that widen from the centre, that is, the predicate offence,[105] although the second type of conduct is probably the most typical money laundering offence. Notwithstanding the international law obligation to criminalise the various money laundering offences, it will be shown that there are large differences as to how and which of the three types of conduct have been criminalised in various countries.[106]

Although much of the language used to criminalise this first type of conduct seems derived from the American model,[107] this type of conduct is, perhaps surprisingly, only implicitly subject to that model. Following the treaty obligations established by the Vienna Convention and the Money Laundering Convention, money laundering has been criminalised in Belgium[108] and Luxembourg.[109] In England and Wales this type of conduct was in part already punishable under s.50 DTA 1994 and s.93A CJA 1988 ('assisting another to retain the benefit of drug trafficking/of criminal conduct'), but the English legislation introduced a new money laundering offence, 'transferring proceeds of drug-trafficking/criminal conduct' (s.49(1)(b) and (2)(b) DTA 1994 and s.93C(1)(b) and (2)(b) CJA 1988),

---

[105] D. Flore, 'Quelle répression pour le blanchiment des bénéfices tirés des fraudes? Le droit international et comparé', in *De juridische bescherming van de financiële belangen van de Europese gemeenschappen*, ed. F. Tulkens, C. Van den Wyngaert and Y. Verougstraete (Antwerp: Maklu, 1992), p. 168.   [106] Vogel, 'Geldwäsche', 342–7.

[107] Notably 18 USC § 1956(a)(i)(B)(I). See *Report US Delegation*, p. 102.

[108] Article 505, 3° Belgian Criminal Code, as amended by the Act of 7 April 1995.

[109] Article 8-1 of the Luxembourg Act of 17 February 1973 and Article 506-1 of the Luxembourg Criminal Code. See the Luxembourg Money Laundering Act of 11 August 1998.

in part to meet fully the requirements of the Vienna Convention.[110] This type of conduct has not been incriminated, however, in Switzerland or in the Netherlands.

This type of money laundering offence in principle requires proof of an ulterior intent, namely the design to conceal or disguise the illicit origin of the proceeds or to assist any person who is involved in the commission of such an offence or offences to evade the legal consequences of his actions. But many countries such as Luxembourg, for example, have done away with this requirement.[111]

The second type of conduct described by Article 3(b) of the Vienna Convention, namely the concealment or disguise of criminally derived proceeds *as such*, lies at the heart of the offence of money laundering in that it is, from a criminological viewpoint, the most typical money laundering conduct.[112] The treaty description clearly draws from the American criminalisation model (18 USC § 1956(a)(i)(B)(I)) and its provisions have been incorporated into the legal systems of all the countries that are studied for the purposes of this book bar The Netherlands. Thus, this type of conduct has been criminalised in Belgium (Article 505, 4° Belgian Criminal Code, as amended by the Act of 7 April 1995), Luxembourg (Article 8–1 of the Luxembourg Act of 17 February 1973 and Article 506–1 of the Luxembourg Criminal Code) and in England and Wales ('concealing proceeds of drug-trafficking/criminal conduct' (s.49(1)(a) and (2)(a) DTA 1994 and s.93C(1)(a) and (2)(a) CJA 1988)). As Swiss money laundering law was drafted before any treaty obligations to incriminate money laundering existed, Article 305bis Swiss Criminal Code eschews a formal classification according to the categories of conduct set out in the relevant conventions, but actions can nevertheless be brought under the heading of the second type of money laundering conduct.

The third type of conduct is the most passive form of co-operation with the perpetrator of the predicate offence as it requires proof not of any kind of active engagement in illegal constructions of whatever kind, but merely the acquisition, possession or use of proceeds, and the knowledge, at the time of their receipt, that those proceeds were criminally derived. It is clear that these criminalised activities may encompass a broad array of

---

[110] A. Dickson, 'Taking Dealers to the Cleaners', *NLJ* (1991), 1069 and R. Fortson, 'Annotations with the Drug Trafficking Act 1994', *Current Law* (1994), c.37, 77.

[111] See for Luxembourg: A. Jonckheere, M. Capus-Leclerc, V. Willems and D. Spielmann, *Le blanchiment du produit des infractions en Belgique et au Grand-Duché de Luxembourg* (Brussels: Larcier, 1995), pp. 110–11. See in general: Vogel, 'Geldwäsche', 345.

[112] Vogel, 'Geldwäsche', 340.

'normal' economic activities. Because of its far-reaching character, both the Vienna Convention and the Money Laundering Convention have qualified the treaty's obligations in respect of the criminalisation of this type of conduct (subject to the constitutional principles and the basic concepts of the legal system of the concerned state). It had become clear during the negotiations which eventually resulted in the Vienna Convention, that it was difficult to devise a form of words that would be acceptable to every state. It was particularly necessary, therefore, in respect of countries whose prosecuting systems operate according to the so-called legality principle, that is the obligation for prosecutors to prosecute every offence, to provide some leeway so as not to force them to prosecute innocent people.[113]

Nevertheless this type of conduct has been criminalised in all the countries that are studied for the purposes of this book, except Switzerland. This offence can be likened to handling of stolen goods, except that the subject to which it pertains is wider: criminally derived proceeds in whatever form. It is not surprising that in a number of countries this type of money laundering conduct has been criminalised as a wider form of handling of stolen goods (*recel, Hehlerei, heling*). This is the case in Belgium, for example,[114] and The Netherlands,[115] where the existing offences of handling stolen goods were broadened. In England and Wales this conduct was incriminated as 'acquisition, possession or use of proceeds of drug trafficking/of proceeds of criminal conduct' (s.51 DTA 1994 and s.93B CJA 1988). The English legislation can be used as an example because it provides an apposite excuse for the defendant who had no intent to launder money: if the defendant can prove that he acquired the property 'for adequate consideration', he is not liable. Thus under English law it is not criminal, for example, to buy a yacht from a drug trafficker, originally purchased with drug money, as long as one pays an adequate amount of money for it.[116]

In Luxembourg, this conduct is also criminalised as part of the wider offence of money laundering.[117] In the United States, it appears that this conduct is punishable under the Monetary Transactions Crime,[118] but it is noteworthy that knowingly engaging in a monetary transaction involving

---

[113] *Report US Delegation*, p. 103 and Stewart, 'Internationalizing The War on Drugs', 393.
[114] Article 505, 2° of the Belgian Criminal Code.
[115] Article 416a of the Dutch Criminal Code.
[116] R. Fortson, 'Annotations with the Criminal Justice Act 1993', *Current Law* (1993), c.36., 61.
[117] Article 8-1 of the Luxembourg Act of 17 February 1973 and Article 506-1 of the Luxembourg Criminal Code.   [118] 18 USC § 1957.

criminally derived property is only punishable if the value of the property involved exceeds US$10,000.

A broad range of predicate offences

While the money laundering activities that should be criminalised are the same under the Vienna Convention and the Money Laundering Convention, the predicate offence is not. The former convention only applies to proceeds from drug trafficking offences (as defined by Article 3(a) of the Vienna Convention), whereas the latter in principle applies to the proceeds from any predicate offence, even though it allows contracting parties to make a declaration – as many have done[119] – to the effect that money laundering will only be criminalised with respect to certain categories of predicate offence. These may, for example, be the most serious offences or only intentional offences. The Money Laundering Convention is nevertheless clearly part of the trend to open up the fight against money laundering to other predicate offences than drug-related offences. This trend is also notable, for example, in the 1998 amendments to the CICAD Model Regulations Concerning Laundering Offences[120] and in the 1998 United Nations Political Declaration and Action Plan against Money Laundering.[121] As was pointed out above,[122] this trend has led to the criminalisation of money laundering being seen as an instrument that can be used against any type of acquisitive crime. This is especially the case of legislation where the operation of the confiscation of proceeds operates *in personam* and hence does not allow the removal of proceeds which have been channelled to third parties. Once the criminalisation of money laundering is seen as an alternative, rather than a complement, to the *in rem* confiscation of criminally derived proceeds,[123] it is only logical to have a wide application field of predicate offences, as a conviction on a charge of money laundering may often be the only way, save value confiscation, to ensure deprivation of proceeds that can no longer be traced in the estate of the person who has committed the predicate offence.

---

[119] See the declarations made by Austria, Cyprus, Denmark, Italy, The Netherlands, Norway, Sweden and Switzerland.

[120] See X., 'OAS Strengthens Anti-Money Laundering Efforts', *Int'l Enf. L.Rep.* (1998), 260. For an updated version of the CICAD Model Regulations, see website http://www.cicad.oas.org/en/legal_development/legal-regulations-money.pdf

[121] Adopted at the Twentieth Special Session of the United Nations General Assembly devoted to 'countering the world drug problem together', New York, 10 June 1998. See specifically Resolution S-20/4D (Countering Money Laundering).

[122] See *supra* pp. 11–14.   [123] See *supra* pp. 31 et seq., especially p. 37.

The 1991 European Money Laundering Directive, which asked states only to prohibit money laundering, was in principle limited to dealing with the proceeds from drug trafficking offences (i.e. crimes defined in Article 3(a) of the Vienna Convention), but allowed states to extend the application field to other types of criminal activity as well. In its 1999 proposal to amend the Money Laundering Directive, the European Commission sponsored the extension of the directive's application field to the proceeds from participation in activities linked to organised crime and of fraud, corruption or any other illegal activities damaging or likely to damage the European Communities' financial interests.[124] It is to be emphasised that the application field of the Money Laundering Directive as such is not concerned with the incrimination of money laundering, but rather with the duty to report suspicious transactions, as the directive itself does not imply any obligation to incriminate money laundering. The Member States of the European Community consequently have the option of introducing an administrative rather than a criminal definition of money laundering, which may even result in the coexistence of two money laundering definitions in one country, both criminal and administrative.[125]

The latitude available to individual states arising from the flexibility of these international instruments has resulted in a patchwork of predicate offences, centred on drug trafficking offences, which are recognised by every state as predicate offences in relation to the offence of money laundering. States that confine the application field of their domestic anti-money laundering legislation to proceeds from drug offences are, however, increasingly rare. At the end of 1994, only four of the twelve Member States of the European Community limited their predicate offence to drug trafficking[126] and by mid-1998 these had all changed their legislation. At the end of 1998, the EU Member States adopted a Joint Action in which they pledged not to make or confirm any reservation for predicate offences punishable with a deprivation of liberty of more than one year as a maximum penalty or of more than six months as a minimum penalty.[127] The last

---

[124] European Commission, *Proposal for a European Parliament and Council Directive Amending Council Directive 91/308/EEC of 10 June 1991 on Prevention of the Use of the Financial System for the Purpose of Money Laundering*, Brussels, 14.7.1999, COM(1999) 352 final, 99/152 (COD), pp. 6–7 and 18. See on the background of this proposal *infra* pp. 167–8.

[125] See *infra* pp. 141–2 and 164.

[126] *First Commission's Report on the Implementation of the Money Laundering Directive (91/308/EEC) to be Submitted to the European Parliament and to the Council*, pp. 5, 28.

[127] See Article 1 of the EU Joint Action of 3 December concerning arrangements for cooperation between Member States in respect of identification, tracing, freezing or seizing and confiscation of instrumentalities and the proceeds from crime, *OJ* No. L 333, 09.12.1998, p. 1.

country to extend its legislation beyond the proceeds from drug offences was Luxembourg, whose money laundering legislation now also encompasses proceeds from organised crime, certain offences against public morals, corruption and infringements of the arms trading legislation.[128] In the broader context of the FATF, only two countries (Japan and Singapore) out of twenty-six had not yet extended the scope of their anti-money laundering legislation beyond the criminalisation of the proceeds of drug trafficking by mid-1999.[129]

It is difficult to devise a solution which would somehow create some harmony in this patchwork of domestic money laundering incriminations in respect of the predicate offences that are covered. Although it would be conceivable to create an international obligation for states to extend their domestic incrimination of drug money laundering to one based on serious offences, this would not necessarily result in substantially greater harmony between domestic legislation. This is illustrated by the non-binding FATF Recommendations in this respect. The 1990 version of recommendation 5, which was centred on drug money laundering (although it called on states to consider extending the offence of drug money laundering to include any other crimes linked to narcotics, or to some or even all serious crimes[130]) was replaced in 1996, after the revision of the FATF Recommendations, by recommendation 4, which requests that states extend their definition of the offence of drug money laundering to one based on serious offences. The recommendation goes on to say, however, that every state should decide for itself which serious crimes to designate as money laundering predicate offences. This is only logical as it is an essential attribute of every state's sovereignty that it should be able to decide what type of conduct to criminalise and what sanctions to provide for that criminalisation in its domestic criminal legislation.

Whereas some legislations, for example 18 USC § 1956 and Article 506-1 of the Luxembourg Criminal Code, enumerate the predicate offences, other domestic anti-money laundering legislation refers to categories of offences as, for example, Article 416 of the Dutch Criminal Code or Article 305bis of the Swiss Criminal Code, which both refer to the category of most severe offences. This does not, however, mean that the list of predicate offences covered by Dutch and Swiss money laundering law is

---

[128] See Article 506-1 of the Luxembourg Criminal Code, inserted by the Luxembourg Act of 11 August 1998.   [129] FATF-X, p. 7.

[130] According to the sixth annual FATF Report, nineteen out of twenty-eight member states of FATF had extended their money laundering offence to include proceeds from serious offences: FATF-VI, p. 6.

identical. Not only is the definition of the category of 'severest offences' (i.e. the threshold of offences) different under Dutch law from Swiss law, but the Dutch and Swiss legislators may also have diverging opinions on the blameworthiness of certain types of conduct and hence on the sanctions that certain crimes should carry, assuming that they are criminal offences in both countries.

Even if one were to establish an international obligation to criminalise money laundering with regard to the proceeds from any offence – an approach which has been adopted, for example, in Belgium (Article 505, 2°, 3° and 4° of the Belgian Criminal Code) – this would not result in a full harmonisation of domestic money laundering legislation, as every state retains the freedom to decide which type of conduct should be criminalised. Although the case for an extension of the field of predicate offences of money laundering to all offences is a strong one – particularly in the field of mutual assistance in criminal matters where the disparity of predicate offences may stand in the way of international co-operation[131] – an international obligation to this end would therefore not result in complete harmonisation.

The fundamental freedom of every state to decide what conduct to criminalise even presents itself with respect to the expansion of the application field of the Money Laundering Directive to types of criminal activity other than drug trafficking offences. Although the directive as such does not require that states criminalise money laundering, it is always required that the predicate activities be criminalised under the domestic legislation of every Member State. For drug trafficking this did not pose a problem as there existed an international obligation to criminalise this type of behaviour under the Vienna Convention, in respect of which it was clear that this obligation was or would be accepted by all Member States of the European Union. Once one decides to expand the application field of the directive to predicate offences other than drug trafficking, it is not easy to come up with a list of offences for which there is a generally accepted obligation under international law to criminalise. In its 1999 proposal to amend the Money Laundering Directive, the European Commission circumvented this problem by couching the extended application field in very general terms, referring to organised crime rather than to specific offences. Furthermore it referred to a number of crimes affecting the financial interests of members of the European Community,

---

[131] See *infra* pp. 289–92. See also the *Second Commission Report to the European Parliament and to the Council on the Implementation of the Money Laundering Directive*, p. 8.

where there exists an obligation to criminalise the laundering of the proceeds of EU-based fraud and corruption in the context of the institutional framework of the Third Pillar of the European Union.[132]

Application of the anti-money laundering legislation to persons who committed the predicate offence

Originally, the criminalisation of money laundering was primarily seen as a law enforcement tool for punishing third parties who assisted offenders to retain the benefits of their crimes. It was, in other words, the proverbial stick wielded by government to ensure that the gatekeepers of the legitimate economy (financial institutions, various economic operators, attorneys, etc.) did not allow the proceeds of a number of criminal activities to enter the legal economy. This was reflected in a number of domestic anti-money laundering laws, the application of which excluded the perpetrators of the predicate offence, as was expressly allowed by Article 6(2)(b) of the Money Laundering Convention. This was the case, for example, in respect of anti-money laundering laws that were modelled on the traditional offence of handling stolen goods. Given the fact that, under most jurisdictions, this offence could traditionally not be applied to the perpetrators of the predicate offence, this rule was expanded to cover the new offence of money laundering in, for example, The Netherlands[133] and in part also in Belgium (Article 505, 2° Belgian Criminal Code).[134] The *ratio iuris* of this limitation stemmed from the belief that, just as no offender could be expected to surrender himself to the police or judicial authorities out of his free will, neither could it be expected that he would not try to render the proceeds of his own crimes unrecognisable.[135] In the same vein, it could be argued that to punish an offender for laundering the proceeds from the predicate offence he committed himself would amount to punishment for being an accomplice to his own offence.

Gradually, however, the criminalisation of money laundering came to be seen, not only as a stick with which to beat the gatekeepers, but also

---

[132] See Article 2 of the Second Protocol, drawn up on the basis of Article K.3. of the treaty on European Union to the Convention on the protection of the European Communities' financial interests, *OJ* No. C 221, 19.07.1997, p. 12.

[133] See Doorenbos, *Over witwassen en voordeelsontneming*, pp. 18–19 and M. S. Groenhuijsen and D. Van der Landen, 'De financiële aanpak van de georganiseerde criminaliteit', *NJB* (1995), 615.

[134] Stessens, *De nationale en internationale bestrijding van het witwassen*, pp. 162–3.

[135] See Graber, *Geldwäscherei*, pp. 110–11 and Arzt, 'Das schweizerischen Geldwäschereiverbot', 191.

those who needed to be kept out: the predicate offenders. Although the rationale behind the restriction of the application field *ratione personae* of anti-money laundering legislation was clear, it was thought unfair that banks or businessmen who accepted the proceeds of crime from criminals could successfully be prosecuted for money laundering if they were aware of the criminal origin of the proceeds they accepted, but that the criminals themselves should be immune from prosecution for money laundering. This unfairness could even result in impunity for criminals who were able to transport their criminally derived proceeds out of the 'country of origin'. If they then tried to launder their proceeds in another country, they could effectively stay immune as that country would in most cases lack jurisdiction with regard to the foreign predicate offence and could not prosecute the offenders for money laundering as they were the perpetrators of the predicate offence. Although this type of circumstance can also be addressed through a combination of extensive jurisdiction and mutual assistance in criminal matters, the defects of a limited application field of the *ratione personae* of anti-money laundering legislation in this respect should clearly not be underestimated. Thus, the low number of convictions for money laundering offences in some countries (e.g. The Netherlands) is often attributed to the fact that the predicate offender cannot be convicted for money laundering.

It is not surprising therefore that the legislation of some countries allows the conviction for money laundering of the persons who have committed the predicate offences. Thus, the Swiss Supreme Court has ruled that Article 305bis of the Swiss Criminal Code also applies to persons who have committed the predicate offence.[136] The United States money laundering offence under 18 USC § 1956, as well as the English offences of 'concealing or transferring proceeds of drug trafficking/criminal conduct' (s.49 DTA 1994 and s.93C CJA 1988) also apply to persons who have committed the predicate offences. The English incriminations were even specifically introduced with a view to allowing the punishment of the predicate offender for laundering the proceeds of his own crimes.[137]

In other countries, the legislation has been amended with a view to allowing the punishment of money laundering offences committed by those who have committed a predicate offence. Similar legislative developments took place along these lines in Belgium[138] and Luxembourg.[139]

---

[136] ATF 120 IV 323, 21.   [137] Dickson, 'Taking Dealers to the Cleaners', 1068–9.

[138] Article 505, 3° and 4° Belgian Criminal Code, as inserted by the Act of 7 April 1995. See Stessens, *De nationale en internationale bestrijding van het witwassen*, pp. 162–3.

[139] See Article 506-4 of the Luxembourg Criminal Code.

Mens rea required for a conviction on a money laundering charge

The sometimes very broad application field of anti-money laundering legislation arising from the wide definition of the *actus reus* can be kept in balance by the requirement for the prosecution to establish *mens rea*. This moral element is twofold: the required knowledge of the criminal origin of the proceeds and the required (specific) intent. The first element, the scienter element, has undoubtedly caused most discussion. At the heart of almost every money laundering trial is a dispute about the knowledge of the defendant. As it is often very difficult for the prosecution to establish that the defendant actually knew that proceeds were criminally derived (and even less that he knew from which offences they were derived), in most cases the prosecution will try to infer knowledge from factual circumstances. This way of proving the knowledge requirement is sanctioned on an international level by Article 3(3) of the Vienna Convention and Article 6(2)(c) of the Money Laundering Convention and has been endorsed by the courts and/or the legislators in many jurisdictions (see e.g. Belgium,[140] the United States[141]).

What has given rise to heated legal debate in various countries, however, is the question of whether a defendant can also be convicted on charges of money laundering if he was not aware of the criminal origin of the property involved – or when his knowledge cannot be established – but when he was merely negligent. In many countries (such as Belgium, Luxembourg, Switzerland, the United Kingdom and the United States), money laundering is a criminal offence only when carried out knowingly. Article 6(3)(a) of the Money Laundering Convention, however, allows prosecution for an offence of negligent money laundering, namely in cases where the offender ought to have assumed that the property was proceeds derived from criminal conduct. Such a drastic move away from the requirement of intent seems more inspired by the desire to make convictions for money laundering easier than by motives regarding the blameworthiness of this type of negligent conduct.[142] Nevertheless, some countries such as The Netherlands (Article 417 Dutch Criminal Code), for example, have opted to make negligent money laundering an offence.

Unlike the inference of knowledge from factual circumstances, negligence does not presuppose that the offender actually knew that the

---

[140] See Stessens, *De nationale en internationale bestrijding van het witwassen*, pp. 157–8.

[141] Gurulé, 'The Money Laundering Control Act of 1986', 837–8.

[142] See G. Stessens, 'La négligence et les infractions du droit pénal économique: un mal nécessaire?', *RDP* (1994), 537–40. Cf. Vogel, 'Geldwäsche', 347.

proceeds were criminally derived. Although in both cases, courts will rely on circumstantial facts to infer *mens rea*, in the former case these circumstantial facts must be sufficient as such to infer actual knowledge, whereas in the latter case the facts will be used in conjunction with general, abstract rules of conduct to infer negligence. The gist of the difference is that in the former case circumstantial facts are used to demonstrate that the defendant in fact knew that the proceeds were criminally derived, whereas in the latter case they will be used in conjunction with abstract rules of conduct to show that, although the defendant may not have known that the proceeds were derived from criminal conduct, every prudent person in those circumstances ought to have known. This was, for example, clearly the case under the (now abridged) provision of the Luxembourg legislation according to which there was criminal liability for money laundering, if certain activities were carried out in contravention of the professional duties of the person concerned ('*méconnaissance de leurs obligations professionnelles*').[143]

Although most legislators have shrunk from criminalising mere negligent money laundering, abstract rules of conduct may nevertheless also come into play with respect to the assessment of criminal liability for intentional money laundering offences. In particular, the refutation of one common line of defence in respect of money laundering charges, namely error of fact, will often involve a reference to abstract rules of conduct. Error of fact will often be invoked regarding the criminal origin of the proceeds, especially under those laws that recognise only a limited number of predicate offences (which is precisely one of the arguments against limiting the application field of anti-money laundering legislation to a number of predicate offences). In principle 'money laundering' activities will not be criminal if the alleged offender honestly believed that the proceeds involved were derived from an activity – whether criminal or not – that does not constitute a predicate offence for the purposes of the anti-money laundering legislation. In view of the detailed statutory, regulatory or deontological rules on the prevention of money laundering that nowadays exist in many jurisdictions, it will, however, be increasingly difficult for defendants to avail themselves of an error of fact defence

---

[143] See the former version of Article 8-1 of the Luxembourg Act of 19 February 1973, as amended by the Act of 7 July 1989. On the background to that legislation, see J. Guill, 'Législation internationale et luxembourgeoise sur le blanchiment d'argent', in *Droit bancaire et financier au Grand-Duché de Luxembourg*, 10e anniversaire de l'association luxembourgeoise des juristes de banque (Brussels: Larcier, 1994), p. 584. See also Jonckheere, Capus-Leclerc, Willems and Spielmann, *Le blanchiment*, pp. 112–15.

against a charge of money laundering if they have not abided by these rules. Thus, for example, it is doubtful whether a Swiss banker can successfully argue that he presumed the proceeds which he may have been accused of handling were derived from a non-criminal source (e.g. capital flight), if, notwithstanding the fact there was an indication that money laundering may have taken place if, as he is obliged to do under Swiss law, he has failed to ascertain the identity of his customer and that of the beneficial owner.[144]

It has correctly been argued that taking into account abstract rules for the purpose of inferring *mens rea*, boils down to holding defendants liable for intentional offences in cases of mere negligence.[145] One might, however, also try to justify the exclusion of error of fact as an excuse in these circumstances by reference to the concept of wilful blindness. However, the mere fact that a defendant in, for example, conducting a financial transaction did not abide by the rules on the prevention of money laundering is not sufficient to impute to him knowledge of the criminal origin of the proceeds. Only if a defendant effectively harboured a suspicion that the proceeds were derived from an illegal source and paid no further attention to those suspicions by, for example, asking questions about their origin, may his actions be construed as wilful blindness, a common law concept, which corresponds to the concept of *dolus eventualis*. The possibility of convicting a defendant on a money laundering charge in the case of *dolus eventualis* is accepted by courts in the United States,[146] Switzerland[147] and The Netherlands[148] and has also been endorsed by the Belgian parliament.[149] Although it will obviously be easier to use this concept successfully when a defendant has not complied with the rules on the prevention of money laundering, the concept of *dolus eventualis* nevertheless requires that the defendant has at least acknowledged the

---

[144] See Zuberbühler, 'Banken als Hilfspolizisten', p. 43 and P. Bernasconi, 'Achtung Briefkastenfirmen! Warnzeichen für Unternehmer, Treuhänder und Revisoren sowie für Staatsanwälte und Steuerfahnder', *RPS* (1996), 299. Cf. Graber, *Geldwäscherei*, pp. 142, 146–7.

[145] See H. Schultz, 'Remarques sur l'élément moral dans l'Avant-projet de Code pénal', *Ann.Dr.Louv.* (1986), 137–8 and J. Verhaegen, 'L'erreur non invincible de fait et ses effets en droit pénal belge', *RDP* (1989), 24–7.

[146] *United States v. Antzoulatos*, 962 F.2d, 720 (7th Cir.), *cert.denied*, 113 S.Ct. 331 (1992). See also Chang and Herscowitz, 'Money Laundering', 507; Gurulé, 'The Money Laundering Control Act of 1986', 838–39 and Harmon, 'United States Money Laundering Laws', 14–16.   [147] Swiss Supreme Court: ATF 119 IV 242.

[148] Dutch Supreme Court, judgment of 19 January 1993, *NJ* (1993), No.491.

[149] *Parl.St.*, Senaat, 1989–90, 890/2, p. 28. See also Stessens, *De nationale en internationale bestrijding van het witwassen*, p. 157.

possibility that the proceeds were criminally derived. It is not sufficient that he was merely negligent in not playing by the rules on the prevention of money laundering.

Even though the mere fact that a defendant may have harboured suspicions about the origin of the proceeds is technically not sufficient to convict him in respect of an intentional money laundering offence,[150] it is fair to say that this information, where it exists, may sometimes be used as circumstantial evidence to infer either actual knowledge or wilful blindness. In some jurisdictions – as with the English offence of 'assisting another to retain the benefit of drug trafficking/criminal conduct' (s.50 DTA 1994 and s.93A CJA 1988), for example, – it is even explicitly stipulated that reasonable suspicion is enough to fulfil the *mens rea* requirement.

It is to be emphasised that the preceding only pertains to the scienter element of *mens rea*. Some money laundering offences, however, also require a specific intent. This is in principle required in respect of money laundering offences that criminalise the first type of conduct envisaged by Article 3(b) of the Vienna Convention[151] and also, for example, by the American federal money laundering incrimination (18 USC § 1956(a)(1)). Under the first part (A) of this legislation, an intent to promote criminal activity or to avoid paying taxes must be established. Under the second, it is necessary to establish that the defendant knew that the transaction was designed to launder proceeds from crime.

Broad application field of anti-money laundering legislation versus the legality principle

It follows from the preceding overview of domestic money laundering legislation that most legislators have opted for what could be described as the legal equivalent of carpet bombing: (almost) every activity that may be construed as being for the purpose of money laundering has been criminalised. The broad character of American money laundering legislation, for example, was demonstrated in a 1998 case in which two interior designers who had worked for and been paid by a member of the Cali cartel, one of the leading cartels in drug trafficking, were convicted of money laundering.[152] This broad character of domestic anti-money laundering

---

[150] See, e.g., in respect of the United States: Gurulé, 'The Money Laundering Control Act of 1986', 837–8.   [151] See, however, *supra* p. 115.

[152] See X., 'Two US Interior Designers Convicted of Laundering for Cali Cartel Member', *Int'l. Enf. L. Rep.* (1998), 93–4.

legislation has sometimes been challenged,[153] although few commentators seem to take note of the fact that these circumstances are in great part the result of the treaty's requirement that money laundering be criminalised. From a law enforcement point of view, the broad character of anti-money laundering legislation is necessary in order to be able to respond to the varied and shifting nature of the phenomenon of money laundering.[154] From the defendant's viewpoint, however, the broad character of the legislation may be viewed as problematic in that the type of conduct that is prohibited may be unclear or vague. This allegedly vague character could be invoked to challenge anti-money laundering legislation as violating the legality principle. The *nullum crimen sine lege* principle not only imposes a ban on the retroactive introduction of legislation but also implies a qualitative requirement: the law should be sufficiently clear and precise (*Bestimmtheitsgebot*) that citizens can know beforehand what type of conduct is considered criminal. This requirement of foreseeability[155] can be found in the case law of the European Court of Human Rights relating to Article 7 of the European Convention on Human Rights.[156] Although any judgment in this matter always depends of course on the wording of the domestic law, it is questionable whether the anti-money laundering legislation can be held to violate the legality principle on the ground that it does not 'provide effective safeguards against arbitrary prosecution, conviction and punishment'.[157] At least the Swiss Supreme Court has ruled that Swiss anti-money laundering legislation does not violate the legality principle, as it allows citizens to assess the consequences of their actions.[158] The mere fact that a very substantial number of economic activities may be construed as transgressing the law does in itself not constitute a breach of the legality principle: the clarity of a definition of an offence should not be confused with its narrowness. The same can be said in respect of the fact that – at least under some domestic

---

[153] See, e.g., Vogel, 'Geldwäsche' 355–6 and (as far as Belgium is concerned): J. P. Buyle, 'Le blanchiment: status quaestionis', in *Financieel recht tussen oud en nieuw*, E. Wymeersch (Antwerp: Maklu, 1996), p. 489 and F. Grosjean, 'Le blanchiment de l'argent: l'esprit des loi à l'épreuve du quotidien', *Journ.Proc.* (1996, No.301), 15.

[154] Guill, 'Législation internationale', p. 558.

[155] On the requirement of foreseeability see M. S. Groenhuijsen, 'Legaliteit als probleem', *NJ* (1982), 279 and A. Heijder, 'Nullum crimen sine lege', in *Non sine causa. Opstellen aangeboden aan Prof. Mr. G. J. Scholten ter gelegenheid van zijn afscheid als hoogleraar aan de Universiteit van Amsterdam* (Zwolle: Tjeenk Willink, 1979), p. 144.

[156] European Court of Human Rights, judgment of 22 November 1995, *SW v. United Kingdom*, Series-A, No.335-A, paras. 34–6.

[157] European Court of Human Rights, judgment of 22 November 1995, *SW v. United Kingdom*, Series-A, No.335-A, para. 34.   [158] ATF 119 IV 242.

legislation – the laundering of the proceeds of any criminal activity is regarded as criminal, which considerably widens the application field of a law which is in the first place directed towards third persons not involved in the predicate offence.

In addition, it should be emphasised that the extent to which a law is compatible with the legality principle cannot be assessed solely with regard to the *actus reus*, but also with the *mens rea* requirement. The requirement that it always needs to be proven that the defendant knew or should have known that the proceeds were criminally derived, constitutes an essential safeguard against violations of the legality principle.

Nevertheless, it may be necessary to limit the application field of the anti-money laundering legislation in two respects.

The first relates to the *actus reus* of the money laundering offence. It cannot be denied that the broad range of activities falling under the heading of money laundering, together with the widening range of predicate offences, exposes many who participate in economic life, particularly those who have stewardship of other persons' finances, to an increased risk of criminal liability. From a policy point of view, it might be preferable to limit this risk by providing defendants with statutory defences such as that provided by English law in respect of the 'acquisition, possession or use of proceeds of drug trafficking/of proceeds of criminal conduct', where the defendant can escape conviction by proving that he acquired the property 'for adequate consideration'.[159]

The second aspect concerns a specific problem of *mens rea*, namely knowledge of the criminal origin of proceeds which arises after the defendant has already acquired the proceeds. This problem is especially likely to arise with respect to the third type of money laundering incrimination, which will often involve a continuing offence. In relation to the traditional offence of handling stolen goods, the maxim *mala fides superveniens non nocet* embodied the rule that a person could not be punished if he found out only after he had handled them that the goods he had handled were stolen. In respect of some domestic anti-money laundering legislation – e.g. Belgian law[160] – this principle no longer holds water, however. This can obviously lead to grave injustices and it may indeed be one circumstance where the application of an anti-money laundering law may

---

[159] See *supra* p. 116.

[160] Stessens, *De nationale en internationale bestrijding van het witwassen*, p. 157 and A. De Nauw, 'De verschillende luiken van het wettelijk systeem tot bestraffing en tot voorkoming van het witwassen van gelden en de fiscale fraude', in *Fiscaal strafrecht en strafprocesrecht*, ed. M. Rozie (Ghent: Mys & Breesch, 1996), p. 234 and R. Verstraeten en D. Dewandeleer, 'Witwassen na de Wet van 7 april 1995: kan het nog witter?', *RW* (1995–96), 699.

violate the legality principle, precisely because the incrimination will not 'provide effective safeguards against arbitrary prosecution, conviction and punishment'. As the legality principle requires that it should always be possible for a defendant to avoid committing a crime, domestic legislations that have done away with the maxim *mala fides superveniens non nocet* should provide the person who becomes aware of the criminal origin of the proceeds only after he has taken them into possession, with a legal 'escape route'. If domestic anti-money laundering legislation fails to provide such 'escape route',[161] it can be held to contravene the legality principle, most notably in relation to the issue of foreseeability. Probably the best legal technique for providing for such an 'escape route' is to allow timely (i.e. as soon as is reasonably possible after knowledge intervenes) disclosure to an appropriate authority of knowledge (or suspicion) of the possible criminal origin of the proceeds as a defence against criminal liability. Again, English law provides an excellent example here by explicitly stipulating in respect of some of its anti-money laundering legislation that disclosure to a police officer of suspicion or belief regarding the possible criminal origin of proceeds excludes criminal liability if the disclosure, made after the offence took place, was made on the initiative of the defendant as soon as it was reasonable for him to make it.[162]

---

[161] See, e.g., in respect of Belgian law: Stessens, *De nationale en internationale bestrijding van het witwassen*, pp. 149–50 and Verstraeten and Dewandeleer, 'Witwassen na de Wet van 7 april 1995', 694–6.

[162] See s.50(3)(b) DTA 1994; s.93A(3)(b) CJA 1988; s.51(5)(b) DTA 1994 and s.93B(5)(b) CJA 1988.

PART II · THE PREVENTION OF MONEY LAUNDERING

Preventive measures, though often intrinsically connected with the repressive fight against money laundering, have a distinctly different purpose from that of penal measures. It has already been shown that financial measures which centre on the role of financial institutions in the fight against money laundering can have two functions. On the one hand, there is the type of financial anti-money laundering measure that was developed in the United States, the importance of which lies in the information that is provided to the government, both in terms of an instant intelligence flow through the imposition of reporting obligations and in terms of a database that financial institutions are forced to keep through record-keeping obligations. The Swiss-type of financial anti-money laundering measures, on the other hand, are more directed towards the prevention of the misuse of financial institutions. The international financial anti-money laundering measures, and accordingly the preventive legislations of most countries that have implemented these international measures, integrate both functions. They are nevertheless referred to as 'preventive legislation' as the emphasis of the aforementioned international instruments is clearly on the preventive side.

The term 'financial legislation' can moreover be confusing as the application field of some domestic preventive legislation has been expanded to other than financial institutions and professions. The application field will be studied not only in *ratione personae* but also in *ratione materiae*, that is, with regard to the range of predicate offences. Subsequently, the role that has been attributed to financial institutions, financial intelligence units and to the supervisory authorities will be scrutinised.

4 The application field of legislation on the prevention of money laundering

The application field of ratione personae

Other than the criminal anti-money laundering legislation that in principle applies to every citizen,[1] the legislation on the prevention of money laundering has often a limited application field in that it applies only to specified categories of institution and professions. Whereas the criminal law focuses on money launderers (*blanchisseurs*), the preventive legislation is geared towards 'money launderettes' (*blanchisseries*), that is, institutions and professions that are prone to being misused for the purpose of money laundering. The distinction is by no means watertight as any 'money launderette' may become a money launderer – and hence be guilty of a money laundering offence – the moment it knowingly engages in a money laundering operation. In the following, the rationales for focusing on financial institutions and the arguments with respect to an expansion of the application field will be discussed.

Rationales for focusing on financial institutions

All preventive anti-money laundering measures adopted at an international level, are focused on the role of financial institutions. Thus the very first international instrument which tentatively attempted to deal with the problem, the Council of Europe Measures Against the Transfer and Safekeeping of Funds of Criminal Origin,[2] comprised four preventive measures, three of which centred on the role of financial institutions:

[1] See, however, Article 305ter Swiss Criminal Code, which applies only to financial intermediaries. See *supra* pp. 105–8.
[2] Recommendation No.R(80)10 adopted by the Committee of Ministers of the Council of Europe on 27 June 1980 and Explanatory Memorandum, reproduced at Gilmore, *International Efforts To Combat Money Laundering*, p. 169.

customer identification, limitation of the use of safes and the training of personnel. In 1988 the Committee on Banking Regulations and Supervisory Authorities, made up of the representatives of twelve supervisory authorities charged with the supervision and control of financial institutions, took it upon itself to warn financial institutions of the risks of money laundering and issued a Statement of Principles. These principles were reaffirmed in 1997 in the Basle Core Principles for Effective Banking Supervision.[3]

Twenty-one out of the forty FATF Recommendations issued in 1990 focus on the enhancement of the role of the financial system. A year later, fifteen of these recommendations were incorporated into the European Money Laundering Directive of 10 June 1991. Because the Directive, unlike the FATF Recommendations, is a binding instrument, its application field is precisely demarcated. The Directive covers credit and financial institutions in the sense that this term is defined in Community banking legislation (see Article 1 of the Directive). References made hereinafter to financial institutions in the context of the European Money Laundering Directive include both credit and financial institutions.

This focusing of preventive anti-money laundering measures on financial institutions is only the logical response to the nature of the money laundering phenomenon itself. In its first report, FATF found that both formal and informal financial institutions play an important role in money laundering operations as they are the main transmitters of money. Already in 1984 the American President's Commission on Organised Crime pointed out that every financial institution should consider itself a potential target of money laundering operations. Several features of financial institutions make them particularly attractive to money launderers. In the first place, the magnitude of the proceeds of organised crime – often in the form of cash – explains in part why money launderers have a preference for financial institutions in laundering money: the cash-intensity of financial institutions makes it possible to channel huge amounts of money through financial institutions without arousing their suspicion. Moreover, the financial system is highly internationalised which makes it very easy to transfer proceeds from one jurisdiction to another, often in a very short period of time. A third explanation for the attractiveness of financial institutions relates to the cloak of secrecy with which they are often surrounded. The problems posed by secrecy laws to the fight against money laundering will be discussed in detail later on, but

[3] 22 September 1997, *ILM* (1998), 405.

suffice it to mention here that the protection afforded by secrecy laws is undoubtedly an alluring factor for any money launderer as they make it much more difficult for law enforcement authorities to trace proceeds and their origin. In addition, in some jurisdictions customers can even remain anonymous to the financial institutions, a possibility which is of course relished by money launderers and also explains the attractiveness of other types of economic activity, such as the art trade, for the purpose of money laundering.

Arguments against an expansion of the application field of preventive legislation to professions and institutions other than financial institutions

Although the reasons adduced above warranted the focus on financial institutions – especially in the light of the fact that even proceeds that are laundered through other sectors of the economy are eventually chan-nelled through financial institutions – this focus logically results in the exclusion of other professions and institutions from the application field. There are undeniably drawbacks to this exclusive attention on the role of financial institutions in the fight against money laundering. Not only may it create the impression for financial institutions that they are the only economic operators saddled with responsibility for preventing money laundering, more importantly, an increased compliance by financial insti-tutions with anti-money laundering measures is likely to bring about a shift in the money laundering phenomenon to other sectors of the economy.[4]

In an attempt to pre-empt this shift, international instruments aimed at preventing money laundering allowed and even urged national author-ities to broaden the application field of their domestic preventive legisla-tion to professions and institutions other than financial institutions. According to recommendation 9 of the FATF (1990), recommendations 12 to 29 (i.e. all the FATF recommendations that were aimed at enhancing the role of the financial system in combating money laundering) should not only apply to banks, but also to non-bank financial institutions. With regard to other professions that deal with cash, recommendation 10 was more ambiguous: it asked that the recommendations be implemented 'on as broad a front as is practically possible'. Already one year later, the FATF noted in its annual report that 'money launderers have increasingly turned to non-traditional financial institutions or other businesses or

---

[4] FATF-VIII, p. 4.

professions to convert the proceeds of their illegal activities into legitimate funds – as countries have tightened their control on traditional financial institutions or professions'.[5] It was nevertheless clear to the FATF that, in order to address this problem, it should not try to make an exhaustive, single list of all non-traditional financial institutions or professions that might used for money laundering practices, but should rather concentrate on some 'high-risk professions' that were likely to be targeted for the placement of criminally derived cash. With a view to the drafting of a common, minimum list of non-bank financial institutions and other professions dealing with cash to which the recommendations should also be applied (the drafting of such a list was required by recommendation 11 (1990)), four types of professions were singled out by the FATF: organisations whose prime function is to provide a form of financial service, but are not regulated; organisations that specialise in gambling activities; organisations that buy and sell high value items (e.g. auction houses, real estate dealers), and professionals who in the course of providing their professional services, offer client account facilities (e.g. lawyers, notaries).

At the European Community level, Article 12 of the 1991 European Money Laundering Directive required Member States to extend the application field of the Directive 'in whole or in part to professions and to categories of undertakings . . . which engage in activities which are particularly likely to be used for money laundering purposes'. Its open-ended nature, however, left the Member States with a wide margin of discretion as how to implement the obligation of Article 12. At the end of 1994 only six Member States had broadened the application field of their preventive legislation to non-financial professions or categories of undertakings.[6] Calls were increasingly made to expand the application field of the Money Laundering Directive: by the Contact Committee (set up under the aegis of the European Commission with a purely advisory task),[7] by the Ecofin Council (20 March 1995) and by the European

---

[5] FATF-II, p. 38. See also FATF-IV, p. 17, FATF-V, p. 24, FATF-VI, pp. 3 and 15, FATF-VII, p. 7 and T. Sherman, 'International Efforts to Combat Money Laundering: the Role of the Financial Action Task Force', in *Money Laundering*, The David Hume Institute (Edinburgh University Press, 1993), p. 14.

[6] *First Commission's Report on the Implementation of the Money Laundering Directive*, p. 8 and annex 6.

[7] *Professions and Undertakings Beyond the Financial System: Conclusions from the Contributions Provided by the Member States*, Directorate-General XV/1172/94, EN, 25 November 1994, p. 5, cited by T. M. C. Asser Instituut, *De strijd tegen het witwassen van geld en de fraudemelding in Europa: wetgeving en gedragscodes voor de vrije beroepen* (The Hague: T. M. C. Asser Instituut, 1995), p. 14. See also *First Commission's Report on the Implementation of the Money Laundering Directive*, p. 9.

Parliament in its Resolution on the First Commission's report on the implementation of the Money Laundering Directive.[8]

It is, however, at least debatable whether an extension of the application field of preventive legislation will automatically result in a heightened effectiveness. A major problem almost any attempt to broaden the application field of preventive legislation to other institutions and professions is likely to run into is the lack of control and supervision on a prudential basis of these institutions and professions. The problem was even present with regard to some of the institutions covered by the 1991 version of the Directive. Given the very wide definition under Community legislation of 'credit and financial institutions', the list of institutions to which the Directive applies includes a number of financial intermediaries, for example *bureaux de change*, that are not, or were not, subject to supervision on a prudential basis. Empirical evidence indicated that these bureaux were frequently misused for money laundering operations,[9] and it was therefore very important that *bureaux de change* were included in the application field of the Directive. The 1999 proposal for amending the Directive brought further clarification in this respect.[10]

Although FATF issued a recommendation (27), asking that countries designate competent administrative and regulatory authorities to ensure the effective implementation of the recommendations with regard to other than financial business dealing with cash, the FATF quickly came to the conclusion that it would be too expensive and burdensome for national governments to introduce a system of prudential supervision with regard to all non-bank financial institutions solely for the purpose of fighting money laundering.[11] The problem of effectively controlling how professions and institutions observe anti-laundering measures is a serious one and will be discussed more in detail later.[12] Suffice it to say here that the authorities that are charged with responsibility for the administrative supervision of the implementation of anti-money laundering measures by non-financial businesses or professions should not necessarily be charged with responsibility for supervision on a prudential basis.

In general, the lack of supervision in respect of some institutions and

---

[8] *OJ*, 8 July 1996, No. C198, p. 245.

[9] See e.g. FATF-VII, p. 8, FATF-VIII, p. 4; FINPOL, *What's the Colour of Money?* 1995, pp. 20–1 and CFI (Belgian financial intelligence unit), *Activiteitenverslag 1993/1994*, p. 21 and *3e Activiteitenverslag 1995/1996*, p. 38.

[10] See Article 1 (1) of the *Proposal for a European Parliament and Council Directive, Amending Council Directive 91/308/EEC of 10 June 1991 on Prevention of the Use of the Financial System for the Purpose of Money Laundering*, Brussels, 14.7.1999, COM(1999) 352 final, 99/152 (COD).

[11] FATF-III, p. 31.   [12] See *infra* pp. 199–205.

categories of professions has not prevented international norm-makers from making calls to extend (some aspects of) the preventive legislation to them. In the course of the 1996 stocktaking review of the 40 FATF recommendations, the FATF asked that governments ensure an effective implementation of the FATF recommendations regarding the role of the financial system in combating money laundering through non-bank financial institutions, even if those institutions are not subject to a formal prudential supervisory regime in all countries (recommendation 8 (1996)). The FATF also decided that countries should consider applying the appropriate recommendations (10 to 21 and 23) regarding the role of the financial system in combating money laundering to the conduct of financial activities by non-financial businesses or professions. The recommendation leaves it to individual countries to decide which financial activities and which situations should be covered by the recommended anti-money laundering measures, but lists a number of relevant financial activities in an annex.

On a European level, the Commission, while acknowledging that in most Member States the necessary supervision on a prudential basis is lacking with regard to a number of the professions and categories of undertakings to which the Directive's application field might be expanded, nevertheless supported such expansion if these professional activities involved a comparable risk of money laundering. Undertakings to this effect were made in the Action Plan to combat organised crime (action point 26 (e)),[13] approved at the 1997 Amsterdam European Council and in the Second Commission Report on the implementation of the Money Laundering Directive[14] (approved by the European Parliament in its resolution on this report).[15] On 14 July 1999 the Commission disclosed a proposal to amend the Money Laundering Directive, in which it proposed to extend its application field of *ratione personae* to the following professions: external accountants and auditors; real estate agents; dealers in high-value goods such as precious stones or metals; transporters of funds; operators, owners and managers of casinos; and notaries and independent legal professions, albeit under limited circumstances.[16]

A specific problem regarding the extension of the application field of the preventive legislation concerns the legal profession. Although in

---

[13] *OJ* No. C 251, 15.08.1997, p. 1.   [14] *Second Commission Report*, pp. 9–12 and 24.
[15] Resolution of 9 March 1999 on the 'Second Commission Report to the European Parliament and the Council on the implementation of the Money Laundering Directive'.
[16] See Article 1 (2) of the *Proposal for a European Parliament and Council Directive Amending Council Directive 91/308/EEC of 10 June 1991 on Prevention of the Use of the Financial System for the Purpose of Money Laundering*, Brussels, 14.7.1999, COM(1999) 352 final, 99/152 (COD).

many jurisdictions practising lawyers, including attorneys and notaries, are subject to deontological supervision so that the problem of lack of control does not arise in this respect, it is difficult to impose the same type of preventive anti-money laundering measures on them, because of their professional function and, more specifically, their duty of confidentiality to clients. Notwithstanding the outspoken reluctance of some jurisdictions[17] to include the legal professions, especially attorneys, in the application field of preventive legislation, various countries have subjected them to their preventive anti-money laundering measures, albeit often to a more limited extent.[18] The obligations which are imposed on them often apply only in respect of professional activities which are not covered by their legal privilege. This is the case in England and Wales, for example, where the obligation to report suspicious transactions under s.52 DTA 1994 does not apply to a legal adviser in respect of 'any information or other matter which has come to him in privileged circumstances'. Likewise, Article 9(2) of the Swiss Money Laundering Act of 10 October 1997, exempts advocates and notaries from reporting well-founded suspicions when they are bound by their duty of professional secrecy under Article 321 of Swiss Criminal Code.[19] On the other hand, no such exemption is provided for in the Luxembourg legislation obliging notaries to report suspicions of money laundering.[20]

The 1999 proposal of the European Commission to amend the 1991 Money Laundering Directive likewise exempts lawyers from any identification or reporting requirement in any situation connected with the representation or defence of a client in legal proceedings, for it confines the obligations of notaries and other independent legal professions under the Directive to assistance or representation of clients in respect of the '(a) buying and selling of real property or business entities, (b) handling of client money, securities or other assets, (c) opening or managing bank, saving or securities accounts, (d) creation, operation or management of

---

[17] See, in general: *Second Commission Report*, p. 11; and in particular with regard to Belgium: G. Stessens, 'Beroepsgeheim versus (economisch-financieel) strafrecht', in *CBR Jaarboek 1996–97* (Antwerp: Maklu, 1997), pp. 442–4. For The Netherlands, see D. R. Doorenbos, 'Bestrijding van witwassen door vrije beroepsbeoefenaars', in *Maatregelen tegen witwassen in het koninkrijk*, ed. GJM Corstens, E. J. Joubert, S. C. J. J. Kortmann (Arnhem: Gouda Quint, 1995), pp. 137–8.

[18] For a general overview, see: T. M. C. Asser Instituut, *De strijd tegen het witwassen van geld en de fraudemelding in Europa: wetgeving en gedragscodes voor de vrije beroepen* (The Hague: T. M. C. Asser Instituut, 1995), 112p and FATF, *Evaluation of Measures Taken by FATF Members Dealing with Customer Identification*, p. 15.   [19] See also *infra* p. 315.

[20] Article 12–1 of the Luxembourg Act of 9 December 1976, inserted by Article 16 of the Money Laundering Act of 11 August 1998.

companies, trusts or similar structures, (e) execution of any other financial transactions'.[21] Moreover, the proposal makes full allowance for the
professional secrecy duty by permitting Member States to allow lawyers to
make suspicious transactions reports to their professional associations
rather than to the financial intelligence units to which financial institutions make their reports.

The application field of ratione materiae

Preventive anti-money laundering legislation imposes a number of rules
on certain professions and categories of organisation (the application
field of *ratione personae*) in respect of the prevention of money laundering.
With a view to legal certainty, the concept of money laundering, that is,
the application field of *ratione materiae*, naturally needs to be defined as
precisely as possible. Two questions merit specific attention in this
respect: with respect to which money laundering acts do the preventive
measures attach and with respect to which predicate offences do these
measures apply.

The former question does not give rise to much discussion. As was indicated earlier,[22] the European Money Laundering Directive has copied the
definition of money laundering acts from the Vienna Convention.
Although the FATF recommendations urge states to incriminate the
money laundering acts set forth in the Vienna Convention, they do not
contain any specification as to what needs to be understood by 'money
laundering' for the purposes of implementing the preventive anti-money
laundering measures.

Far more important, however, is the latter question, namely which
predicate offences are covered by the money laundering definition for
the purposes of preventive anti-money laundering measures. Although
the scope of the FATF recommendations is confined to the incrimination
of laundering of proceeds from drug offences and serious offences
(Recommendation 4 (1996)), recommendation 15 states that financial
institutions should be required to report suspicions that funds stem from
'a criminal activity', without any qualification. The scope of the
European Money Laundering Directive is as such limited to the laundering of drug proceeds, but the Directive allows Member States to extend

---

[21] European Commission, *Proposal for a European Parliament and Council Directive Amending
Council Directive 91/308/EEC of 10 June 1991 on Prevention of the Use of the Financial System for
the Purpose of Money Laundering*, Brussels, 14.7.1999, COM(1999) 352 final, 99/152 (COD),
p. 10.   [22] See *supra* pp. 113–14.

the application field of their implementation legislation to other predicate offences.

There are, broadly speaking, two avenues for the implementation of the Directive and, more specifically, the prohibition (Article 2 of the Directive) – and concurrently the definition – of money laundering and its predicate offences for the purpose of the preventive measures which the Directive imposes. As with any Community obligation to prohibit certain types of conduct, Member States are free to choose whether they prohibit the conduct through criminal law (i.e. by incriminating it), or through other legal techniques (mostly an administrative prohibition). Even if the intergovernmental Statement joined to the Directive obliges Member States to incriminate drug money laundering,[23] this does technically not alter their obligations under Community law, that, is under the Directive. A minority of Member States (the UK, Ireland and Denmark) have opted for a partial criminal implementation of the Directive and their definition of money laundering concomitantly coincides with the incriminated money laundering conduct. This is the case in England and Wales, for example, as far as the obligation to report suspicious transactions is concerned. In Member States which have opted for an administrative implementation of the Directive, the definition may refer to the incrimination of money laundering. This technique has, for example, been applied in the Luxembourg Act of 5 April 1993, which refers to the incrimination of money laundering.[24] Other Member States that have also opted for an administrative implementation of the Directive have created a proper administrative definition of money laundering which can be either more narrow than the criminal definition (Belgium) or broader (Denmark, Spain and France).[25]

It is obviously preferable that the concept of money laundering in the preventive legislation coincides with the incrimination of money laundering, as, at least at the end of 1995, was the case in the majority of the Member States (Germany, Ireland, Italy, Luxembourg, the Netherlands, Portugal, Ireland and the United Kingdom).[26] Nevertheless, some states may wish to confine the application field of the *ratione materiae* of their preventive legislation to a number of predicate offences. This need will be

---

[23] See *supra* p. 26.

[24] J. Kauffman, 'Le secret bancaire en droit luxembourgeois – aspects actuels et perspectives', in *Droit bancaire et financier au Grand-Duché de Luxembourg*, 10e anniversaire de l'association luxembourgeoise des juristes de banque (Brussels: Larcier, 1994), I, pp. 531–2 and 540–1.

[25] *First Commission's Report on the Implementation of the Money Laundering Directive*, p. 6.

[26] See, however, the incrimination of 'failure to disclose knowledge or suspicion of money laundering', which is confined to proceeds from drug offences and terrorism.

especially felt in those countries, whose money laundering incrimination covers a very broad – or unlimited, as is the case in Belgium – range of predicate offences. The Belgian legislator opted for a limitation of the application field of the preventive legislation[27] because it was thought that an unlimited application field, that is, an application field covering proceeds from any kind of predicate offence, would impose a burden too heavy on financial institutions and the legislator clearly wanted to exclude proceeds from fiscal offences from the application field.[28]

From an international and comparative point of view, there is a tendency to favour an expansion of the predicate offence of money laundering: in its 1999 proposal for amending the Money Laundering Directive, the Commission argued for an expansion of the definition of the predicate offences of money laundering to activities related to organised crime and a number of offences damaging the European Communities' financial interests. As the arguments surrounding the discussion of the extension of the application field of the *rationae materiae* of the preventive legislation, however, primarily concern the reporting obligations of financial institutions, these arguments will be set out under that heading.[29]

---

[27] Article 3 of the Belgian Money Laundering Act of 11 January 1993.

[28] See Stessens, *De nationale en internationale bestrijding van het witwassen*, pp. 180–2 and De Nauw, 'De verschillende luiken van het wettelijk systeem tot bestraffing en tot voorkoming van het witwassen van gelden en fiscale fraude', p. 241.

[29] See *infra* pp. 164–9.

5 The role of financial institutions in the prevention of money laundering

Preventive anti-money laundering measures impose a number of obligations on financial institutions. Before discussing these obligations in detail, we will first investigate how these obligations derogate from traditional banking principles. Subsequently the obligation to identify customers and the record-keeping obligation will be analysed. Whereas the former obligations derogate from the principle of non-interference in a customer's business, the obligation to report suspicious transactions constitutes a severe inroad into banking secrecy. A last aspect of the preventive legislation concerns the issue of compliance. Finally, the extent to which these preventive anti-money laundering measures have cajoled financial institutions into a policing role will be discussed.

Preventive obligations derogating from traditional banking principles

Banking is in almost any jurisdiction surrounded with – some would say cloaked in – a certain degree of secrecy. The preventive anti-money laundering measures that have been imposed on financial institutions deviate from this tradition of secrecy. To be able to assess the precise impact of these measures, it is therefore necessary to know the exact legal nature of this tradition of secrecy in the banking industry. Although this depends to a large extent upon domestic law, some general principles can nevertheless be outlined. A contractual relationship between a bank and its customer (sometimes referred to in German as the *Bankvertrag*) generally entitles the customer to a two-pronged discretion. First, there is a general prohibition on a banker – leaving aside a number of exceptions – disclosing any information on his customers to third parties, including government authorities. This first aspect of a banker's discretion, banking secrecy, which is undoubtedly the best known, will be further discussed in Part 4 in the context of measures designed to lift foreign banking secrecy.[1] There is, however, also a second aspect of a banker's contractual discretion obligation which is not covered by banking secrecy, namely the obligation to refrain from interference in the customer's private and business affairs. This is the banker's principle of non-interference (*non-ingérence du banquier*).[2] Sometimes customers may esteem their privacy to such a degree that they want to remain anonymous *vis-à-vis* their banker. It is important to underline that anonymity is not tantamount to and should indeed not be confused with banking secrecy. The former relates to the relationship between a banker and his customer, whereas the latter concerns the relation between a banker and third parties. An anonymous bank account is therefore a bank account the identity of the holder of which is not known even to the bank holding the account.

As both aspects of the banker's discretion can be linked to the customer's right to privacy, the question arises whether the measures imposed by the anti-money laundering legislation do not transgress the strictures of the right to privacy (which is not only guaranteed by muncipal constitutions, but also by Article 8 of the 1950 European Convention on Human Rights and Article 17 of the 1966 International Covenant on Civil and Political Rights). As far as the identification obligations are concerned, it is submitted that the right to privacy is not at stake as these obligations merely concern the communication of the identity of a customer which is not as such covered by the right to privacy.[3] As far as the reporting obligations are concerned, the question is more intricate. In *California Bankers Ass'n v. Schultz* (1974),[4] the US Supreme Court found that the reporting obligations that were issued on the basis of the Bank Secrecy Act 1970 did not violate the US Constitution's Fourth Amendment's 'right of the people to be secure in their persons, houses, papers and effects, against unreasonable searches and seizures'. It was held that 'neither incorporated nor unincorporated associations can plead an unqualified right to conduct their affairs in secret'[5] and that the information sought was suf-

---

[1] See *infra* pp. 314–18.

[2] See M. Vasseur, 'La loi du 12 juillet 1990 relative à la participation des organismes financiers à la lutte contre le blanchiment de capitaux provenant du trafic des stupéfiants', *Banque et Droit-Numéro spécial* (1990), 24 and F. J. Crédot, 'Le principe de non-ingérence et le devoir de vigilance', *Banque et Droit-Numéro spécial* (1990), 17–22.

[3] This was, for example, argued by G. J. Wiarda, Emeritus President of the European Court of Human Rights, reported in X., 'Identificatieplicht', *NJB* (1987), 836–7. See also J. De Boer, 'Art.8 EVRM Algemeen', in *Handelingen der Nederlandse Juristenvereniging* (Zwolle: Tjeenk Willink, 1990), pp. 39–40.   [4] 416 US 21, 63.   [5] 416 US 21, 67.

ficiently described and limited in nature so as not to fall foul of a Fourth Amendment right. Two years later, in 1976, the Supreme Court even fended off Fourth Amendment challenges against the seizure of cheques and deposits slips voluntarily conveyed to a bank on the ground that an individual has no legitimate expectation of privacy in this respect: 'the depositor takes the risk, in revealing his affairs to another, that the information will be conveyed by that person to the government'.[6]

This limitation of the sphere of privacy is difficult to square with the European view of the right to privacy, or with the Canadian view[7] for that matter. Although the type of information reported by financial institutions usually tends to be more of a business or professional than of a private nature, this does not allow the question of compatibility with the right to privacy under Article 8 of the European Convention on Human Rights to be ignored. In respect of telephone-tapping and search of premises, the European Court of Human Rights has held that there is no reason why the notion of private life should be taken to exclude activities of a professional or business nature which in practice may moreover be very difficult to separate from private activities.[8] These reporting obligations are, it is submitted, nevertheless compatible with Article 8 of the European Convention on Human Rights as they are stipulated by law with a view to combating (serious forms of) criminality and can be considered necessary in a democratic society.[9] This is certainly the case for the suspicion-based type of reporting obligation which obliges banks to disclose information only if they suspect money laundering,[10] but also for other, threshold-type of reporting obligations, in respect of which the US Supreme Court correctly held that they were sufficiently circumscribed.[11]

---

[6] *US v. Miller* 425 US 425, 443.

[7] Canadian Supreme Court, *Schreiber v. Canada (Attorney General)*, 1 [1998] SCR 841.

[8] European Court on Human Rights, *Niemetz v. Germany*, judgment of 16 December 1992, *Publications of the European Court on Human Rights*, Series A, No.251-B, paras.29–31. Cf. *Huvig v. France*, judgment of 24 April 1990, *Publications of the European Court on Human Rights*, Series A, No.176-B, paras.8 and 25; *Chappell v. United Kingdom*, judgment of 30 March 1989, *Publications of the European Court on Human Rights*, Series A, No.152-A, paras.26 and 51 and *Kopp v. Switzerland*, judgment of 25 March 1998, *Reports of Judgments and Decisions* (1998), para. 50.

[9] Article 8(2) of the European Convention on Human Rights allows interferences with the exercise of the right to privacy if this is 'in accordance with the law and is necessary in a democratic society . . . for the prevention of disorder or crime . . .'.

[10] On the suspicion-based type of reporting obligation, see *infra* pp. 159–78.

[11] *California Bankers Ass'n v. Schultz* 416 US 21, 67 (1974). See, however, the dissenting opinions of Justice Douglas (416 US 21, 90) and Brennan (416 US 21, 93).

Customer identification

Relevance and criteria for customer identification

Compulsory customer identification and the broader 'know-your-customer' principle obviously run counter to the traditional banking principle of non-interference in a customer's affairs. It also automatically excludes customer anonymity, notably anonymous bank accounts, that is, bank accounts of which the identity of the account holder is unknown to the bank. Absolute anonymity, much sought after by money launderers, is therefore made impossible by this obligation. Numbered bank accounts, however, are still permitted (e.g. in Belgium and Switzerland).[12] The fact that a customer needs to be identified does not mean that his identity is known to everyone within a financial institution. It is possible to know the identity of the holder of a numbered account, but to restrict that knowledge to a limited number of employees in a financial institution.

The primary purpose of compulsory customer identification is undoubtedly of a preventive nature, that is, to deter possible money launderers from attempting to enter criminally derived proceeds in the financial system and thereby to uphold the reputation of financial institutions. This goal was explicitly embraced by the 1977 Swiss Code of Conduct (CDB), which introduced an obligation to identify customers. By making identification mandatory, regulators warn money launderers that they will have to give up their anonymity. It is hoped that they will therefore think twice before they try to misuse a financial institution for money laundering purposes. In addition, such an obligation can, together with other preventive measures (such as the mandatory reporting of suspicious transactions), contribute significantly towards the repression of money laundering. By obliging banks to identify customers and to keep records of the identification pieces, a paper trail is created which may eventually be useful for law enforcement purposes.

The most vulnerable moment for a money launderer is when he enters into a business relation with a financial institution or other institution or person chosen as 'launderette'. The chance of detection of a money laundering operation is at its highest during the stage when the (alleged) proceeds are entering the financial system, not in the least because vigilance is then at its highest and there is usually physical contact with the customer. This assertion is borne out by statistical evidence on reports

---

[12] FATF, *Evaluation of Measures*, p. 9.

made by financial institutions, which show that most reports relate to transactions in the placement stage.[13] The fact there is scant evidence of money laundering in financial sectors – for example the securities sector[14] – which do not lend themselves to placing, but only to layering or injecting criminally derived proceeds, also lends credibility to this thesis.

Most international and municipal anti-money laundering measures therefore contain an obligation to identify every customer at the moment of entering into a business relation. Thus Article 3 of the European Money Laundering Directive requires that financial institutions identify their customers 'when entering into business relations, particularly when opening an account or savings accounts, or when offering safe custody facilities'. This hypothesis was also envisaged by the Statement of Principles of the Basle Committee and was in fact already retained by the 1980 Recommendation of the Council of Europe (Measures Against the Transfer of Funds of Criminal Origin). Both instruments also mentioned the case of transactions of an important amount. Analogous criteria are contained in FATF recommendation 10 (1996). Apart from the moment of entering into business, Article 3 of the European Money Laundering Directive mentions two other criteria for compulsory customer identification. Every non-identified customer requesting a transaction (i.e. a one-off transaction), involving a sum amounting to ECU15,000 or more needs to be identified, also when the transaction is carried out in several operations which seem to be linked. In the event the sum is not known at the time the transaction is undertaken, identification needs to take place as soon as the financial institution establishes that the threshold has been reached. Second, the Directive also requires that financial institutions identify a customer wherever there is a suspicion of money laundering, even if the amount involved is lower than the threshold. It is to be emphasised that this criterion should not be construed as indicative of any criminal intent on behalf of the customer, but is merely an objective criterion for due diligence.[15]

Of course, the precise nature of the identification requirements will ultimately depend on domestic law. Thus the concept of 'suspicion of

---

13 See, e.g., the reports filed with the Belgian financial intelligence unit: C.F.I. *3e Activiteitenverslag 1995/1996*, p. 51 and *4e Activiteitenverslag 1996/1997*, p. 64.
14 International Organisation of Securities Commissions, *Report on Money Laundering* (1992), p. 4.
15 See Dietzi, 'Der Bankangestellte als eidgenössisch konzessionierter Sherlock Holmes? Der Kampf gegen die Geldwäscherei aus der Optik des Ersten Rechtskonsulenten einer Grossbank', in *Bekämpfung der Geldwäscherei. Modellfall Schweiz?*, ed. M. Pieth (Basle: Helbing & Lichtenhahn, 1992), pp. 73–4.

money laundering' featuring in Article 3(6) of the Directive needs to be construed with reference to the concept of money laundering laid down in the implementation legislation concerned. As indicated, this concept of money laundering may differ from the one defined in the incrimination of money laundering. Moreover, the threshold of ECU15,000 can be lowered in the implementation legislation as, in 1994, was the case for seven EU Member States.[16] In the future, a lower threshold of Euro1,000 will apply in respect of all customers of casinos purchasing or exchanging gambling chips.[17]

Identification of the beneficial owner

Customer identification can evidently contribute to the fight against money laundering only if it is in practice not reduced to a mere formality. FATF recommendation 10 not only prohibits anonymous accounts (i.e. accounts of which the holder has not been identified) but also accounts in obviously fictitious names. Often money launderers will take recourse to devices to disguise their real identity from the financial institutions (and hence from any investigating agency that might carry out an investigation at the financial institution). Men of straw, shell corporations (often incorporated offshore) and even the professional secrecy provided by some members of professions who are willing to serve as middlemen, are sometimes used to shield the identity of the beneficial owner of funds, whether criminally derived or not.[18]

Many anti-money laundering rules therefore require that the beneficial owner (ayant droit économique) be identified. Although the beneficial owner concept is of common law origin, it was apparently first introduced in the context of anti-money laundering measures in the Swiss Code of Conduct (CDB) in 1977 and thus found its way into international anti-money laundering instruments.[19] On an international level, the need to identify

[16] First Commission's report on the implementation of the Money Laundering Directive, p. 9.
[17] See Article 3a of the Money Laundering Directive, as presented in the Proposal for a European Parliament and Council Directive amending Council Directive 91/308/EEC of 10 June 1991 on Prevention of the Use of the Financial System for the Purpose of Money Laundering, Brussels, 14.7.1999, COM(1999) 352 final, 99/152 (COD), p. 19.
[18] See P. Bernasconi, 'Achtung Briefkastenfirmen! Warnzeichen für Unternehmer, Treuhänder und Revisoren sowie für Staatsanwälte und Steuerfahnder', RSC (1996), 289–312.
[19] See P. Bernasconi, 'Modèle internationale d'ordonnance judiciaire de saisie et de production des documents. Un nouvel instrument de l'enquête internationale concernant le blanchiment de l'argent', in Bulletin de la Societé internationale de défense sociale, Cahiers de défense sociale (1990/91), 174 and H. Dietzi, 'Der Bankangestellte', p. 80. On the CDB, see supra pp. 101–2.

the beneficial owner of funds (i.e. to determine the true identity of all customers) was already acknowledged in the Explanatory Memorandum with
the 1980 Council of Europe Recommendation and in the 1988 Statement
of Principles of the Basle Committee. FATF Recommendation 11 (1996)
further specified the exact nature of the obligation on financial institutions, namely to 'take reasonable measures to obtain information about
the true identity of the persons on whose behalf an account is opened or
transaction conducted if there are any doubts as to whether these clients
or customers are acting on their own behalf'. An almost identically
worded obligation was laid down in Article 3(5) of the European Money
Laundering Directive. The term 'reasonable measures' is not specified and
both the Commission and the Council, probably mindful of the fact that
a Directive under Community law is binding only as to the result and not
to the means, refused to give a list of circumstances requiring identification of the beneficial owner.[20] Such a list was, for example, drawn up by
the Swiss Banking Commission.[21]

In practice, the identification of the true owners of accounts opened in
the name of customers who are not natural persons is especially likely to
pose problems. Although this is especially true in the case of domiciliary
companies (defined by FATF recommendation 11 as 'institutions, corporations, foundations, trusts, etc. that do not conduct any commercial or
manufacturing business or any other form of commercial operation in
the country where their registered office is located'), legitimate corporations with a conventional economic background can also be misused to
launder criminally derived proceeds. In its interpretative note on the
subject,[22] the FATF stated that – in the absence of other reliable sources –
financial institutions should ask the customer if this is necessary in order
to ensure that the corporate structure is not being misused for money
laundering purposes, who the principal owners and beneficiaries are, or,
if the customer is unable to provide such information, who has the actual
control.

It is important to stress that the international instruments do not
impose an absolute obligation on the financial institution to obtain the
identification of the beneficial owner. On the contrary both the Directive
and the FATF recommendations refer to 'reasonable measures', thereby
indicating that there may indeed be circumstances in which it is

---

[20] Ewing, 'The Draft EEC Money Laundering Directive', 142.   [21] See *supra* pp. 107–8.
[22] Interpretative Note to recommendations 12, 13, 16 through 19 concerning the
utilisation in money laundering schemes of accounts in the names of customers who
are not natural persons, FATF-V, p. 31.

effectively impossible to ascertain the true identity of the true owners of an account. In respect of legal entities, the FATF Interpretative Note set out the line of action financial institutions need to take if they cannot identify the beneficial owner. The Note provides that, where adequate information is not available, the financial institution should pay special attention to business relations and transactions with the customer. Only when the financial institution has reason to believe that the customer's account is being utilised in money laundering transactions should the financial institution report its suspicion to the appropriate authority or terminate business with that customer. Although the Note does not explicitly so provide, it must be presumed that the latter alternative is applicable only when domestic legislation does not allow a financial institution to report its suspicions. In general, the mere fact that identification of the beneficial owner is impossible does in itself not oblige financial institutions to terminate an account or even to file a report.

Identification of the beneficial owner in the case of accounts held by financial institutions

Sometimes so-called sub-accounts (sometimes referred to as omnibus accounts, trust accounts, *comptes nostro* or *Sammelkonti*) are opened by trusts or other financial institutions. These trusts or financial institutions accept deposits of individual clients so that the sub-accounts they open are in fact joint accounts which group the deposits of a number of clients. The financial institution where the sub-account is opened, knows the identity only of the customer (i.e. the financial institution or the trust) but is in the dark as to the identity of the beneficial owners. This situation undeniably creates a risk for misuse for money laundering purposes.[23] One way to tackle the problem is to require from the customer institution a list detailing all the beneficial owners. This requirement is, for example, laid down in Article 4(2) of the Swiss Money Laundering Act of 10 October 1997, which also requires that any modification of this list be immediately communicated to the financial institution. The weak point in this system is indeed that such lists are likely to become out of date very quickly.[24]

The problem is in reality closely linked to the application field of the *ratione personae* of the preventive legislation. If the customer institutions

---

[23] On this problem see: United Nations Economic and Social Council, Commission on Crime Prevention and Criminal Justice, *Review of Priority Themes, Control of Proceeds of Crime-Report of the Secretary-General* (Vienna: 13–23 April 1993, E/CN.15/1993), pp. 12–13 and FATF-III, p. 31.   [24] Friedli, 'Die gebotene Sorgfalt', pp. 151–2.

also fall under this application field, they will be obliged to identify the beneficial owner. The European Money Laundering Directive exempts credit and financial institutions from the identification requirements where the customer is also a credit or financial institution covered by the Directive (Article 3(7)). The rationale for this exemption is obvious: financial institutions subject to the same regime do not need to identify each other.

This does not mean, however, that the identification requirement does not apply to a customer whose one-off payment for a financial transaction is to be debited from an account opened with a credit institution subject to this Directive. Such an exemption was, in spite of a broader proposal of the European Commission, introduced in the Directive only with respect to payments for insurance operations (Article 3(8)).[25] This problem is especially material with regard to the increasing number of so-called remote (i.e. non-face-to-face) financial transactions.[26] In its 1999 proposal to amend the Directive, the Commission set out a number of principles to be applied by credit and financial institutions in the case of non-face-to-face transactions.[27] Notwithstanding the limited exemption in Article 3(8) of the Directive, at least two Member States have introduced a wider exemption. In The Netherlands, exemption was extended to include financial services related securities trading while in the United Kingdom there is a general exemption for one-off transactions and business relationships other than the opening of bank and building society accounts when it is reasonable that the operation be carried out on a remote basis. Although there may indeed be circumstances in which it would be unreasonable to impose burdensome identification procedures for one-off remote transactions if that customer has already been identified by another financial institution covered by the Directive, such a solution should be devised at a European level.

The general exemption for customers who are themselves a credit or financial institution covered by the Directive obviously only applies in so far as the customer-institution is located within the European Union. There is no exemption in respect of financial institutions that are located

---

[25] *First Commission's report on the implementation of the Money Laundering Directive*, p. 11. Payments to insurance companies are in some cases even exempted as such: Article 3(3) and (4).   [26] FATF, *Evaluation of Measures*, pp. 16–22.

[27] These principles would be specified in an annex to the Money Laundering Directive: European Commission, *Proposal for a European Parliament and Council Directive amending Council Directive 91/308/EEC of 10 June 1991 on Prevention of the Use of the Financial System for the Purpose of Money Laundering*, Brussels, 14.7.1999, COM(1999) 352 final, 99/152 (COD), pp. 10 and 23–4.

outside the European Union and maybe are not subject to equivalent anti-money laundering measures but which wish to open an account with a financial institution located within the European Union. Notwithstanding this geographically restrictive exemption, three Member States' legislation allows the exoneration of non-EU financial institutions as well. Luxembourg[28] and the United Kingdom[29] require that these institutions are subjected to anti-money laundering measures equivalent to those required by the Directive, whereas in the Netherlands the Minister of Finance has the statutory power to exempt the identification duty for transactions with financial institutions from those non-EU countries he lists.[30] It would of course be preferable that a list of countries whose money laundering legislation could be considered equivalent to the Directive was drafted on a European level, but negotiations in the Contact Committee set up under Article 13 of the Directive have indicated that it would be very hard to find agreement on such a list. In the absence of a truly global levelled playing field as far as anti-money laundering measures are concerned, it is indeed very difficult to work out a satisfactory set of criteria of equivalence, given the fact that it is not only the legislation on the statute books but also its practical day-to-day implementation that needs to be scrutinised.[31]

The problem can be especially delicate in respect of financial institutions located in jurisdictions that contain what is known as secrecy havens. The inability to obtain relevant information on the beneficial owner of foreign legal entities was identified by the FATF as one of the major impediments to the successful fight against international money laundering operations.[32] American banking regulators overseeing the activities of the overseas branches of American banks have run into similar problems.[33] Particularly when the customer-institution is subject

---

[28] Article 39(5) of the Luxembourg Act of 5 April 1993. See also circular letter IML 94/112 (*Lutte contre le blanchiment et prévention de l'utilisation du secteur financier à des fins de blanchiment*, p. 15) of the *Institut monétaire luxembourgeois* (IML).

[29] Section 9(5) of the Money Laundering Regulations 1993. See L. Jason-Lloyd, 'Money laundering–the complete guide', *NLJ* (1995), 279. For criticism, see W. C. Gilmore, 'International and Regional Initiatives', in *International Tracing of Assets*, M. Ashe and B. Rider (eds.) (London: FT Law & Tax, 1997), Vol.1, pp. R1/16–17.

[30] Articles 2(4), 4,(4) and 5,(5) Wet identificatie financiële dienstverlening (Wif).

[31] *First Commission's report on the implementation of the Money Laundering Directive*, pp. 10–11.

[32] FATF-X, p. 31.

[33] See US General Accounting Office, *Money Laundering. Regulatory Oversight of Offshore Private Banking Activities*, Report to the Chairman, Subcommittee on General Oversight and Investigations, Committee on Banking and Financial Services, House of Representatives, GAO/GGD-98-154, Washington D.C., June 1998, p. 9 *et seq.*

to banking secrecy and will hence not be able to disclose the identity of the beneficial owners to another financial institution, it will be often very difficult to identify the beneficial owners of the deposits held on sub-accounts opened by these foreign institutions. Again, as with accounts opened by offshore companies, the impossibility of obtaining the identification of the beneficial owners of a sub-account opened by a foreign financial institution or trust as such does not impose an obligation to report the transaction, let alone to terminate business with the customer. FATF recommendation 21 does, however, require that special attention be paid to business relations and transactions with persons, including companies and financial institutions, from countries which do not, or insufficiently, apply the FATF recommendations. This recommendation is reflected in the thirteenth 'whereas' of the European Money Laundering Directive, but not in the text of the Directive as such. Article 5 of the Directive enshrines only the general due diligence principle that financial institutions 'examine with special attention any transaction which they regard as particularly likely, by its nature, to be related to money laundering'. The 'whereas' is the watered-down result of an amendment which was introduced by the European Parliament to prohibit financial transactions with third countries which do not apply comparable standards against money laundering to those established by the Community or to other equivalent standards. The amendment was in part rejected because it was rightly thought impossible to find agreement on such a list of countries.[34] In the same vein, the FATF rejected the idea of establishing a 'black list' of non-cooperative countries.[35] Also now, the fact that a financial transaction originated in a jurisdiction known as a secrecy jurisdiction does not make this a suspicious transaction *per se*, even though there are often considerable difficulties in obtaining the identity of the originating parties in international transfers, especially international electronic funds transfers.[36] Only where 'these transactions have no apparent or visible lawful purpose, should their background and purpose, as far as possible, be examined' and the findings established in writing (FATF recommendation 21). This obligation to record the operation in writing and to keep this record does not as such exist under Community law, but has nevertheless been introduced in the domestic preventive legislation of some Member

---

[34] On this amendment, see Ewing, 'The Draft EEC Money Laundering Directive', 142 and L. Van Outrive, 'De intergouvernementele communautaire behandeling van drughandel en georganiseerde misdaad in de Europese Gemeenschap', *Panopticon* (1992), 596.

[35] FATF-II, pp. 48–49.

[36] FATF-VIII, p. 5 and FATF, *1998–1999 Report on Money Laundering Typologies*, p. 6.

States (namely, Belgium, France and Portugal).[37] The absence of strong measures against transactions with offshore bank centres has spawned proposals to deal with this problem by, for example, excluding offshore banking centres from the international payment system or by imposing punitive taxes on funds coming from those jurisdictions.[38]

Identification of the beneficial owner in the case of accounts held by legal professionals

In discussing the application field of the *ratione personae* of the preventive legislation, we have already emphasised that some legal professions cannot be subjected to the same anti-money laundering measures as financial institutions. It is not surprising therefore that many national bar associations – as urged by the International Bar Association moreover[39] – have taken it on themselves to issue guidelines on the prevention of money laundering, as the Belgian,[40] Dutch,[41] Luxembourg[42] and Swiss Bar Associations,[43] for example, have already done.

Although these measures require attorneys under some circumstances to identify their customers, they are not as elaborate as the preventive legislation with which financial institutions must comply. Given professional secrecy obligations, these guidelines do not impose an obligation to report transactions under any circumstances. This legal impossibility of disclosing information of any kind, combined with the obligation of financial institutions to identify the beneficial owners of accounts, creates a conundrum in the case of professional accounts held by members of the legal profession. These accounts often hold funds which belong to third parties, mainly clients. Supervisory authorities in different countries have

---

[37] *First Commission's report on the implementation of the Money Laundering Directive*, p. 12.

[38] See *supra* pp. 94–5.

[39] See M. Raphael, 'Money laundering and the legal profession', *NLJ* (1995), 1377–1378 and X., 'IBA Adopts Anti-Laundering Resolution', *Int'l Enf.L.R.* (1996), 45–6.

[40] Aanbeveling van de Nationale Orde van Advocaten inzake witwassen van geld, entered into force on 1 April 1996.

[41] Richtlijnen ter voorkoming van de betrokkenheid van de advocaat bij criminele handelingen, *Advocatenblad* (1995), 809. See Doorenbos, 'Bestrijding van witwassen door vrije beroepsbeoefenaars', pp. 140–4.

[42] *Circulaire n° 13/1989–90 de l'Ordre des Avocats concernant la répression des opérations dites de blanchiment des gains réalisés par le trafic illicite de stupéfiants*, 25 May 1990; *Circulaire n° 14/1992–93*, 24 June 1993 and *Règlement d'Ordre Intérieur sur certaines obligations professionnelles*, 24 June 1993. See Jonckheere et al., *Le blanchiment du produit des infractions*, pp. 116–18.

[43] Guidelines issued by the *Schweizerische Anwaltsverband* in March 1992, cited by Friedli, 'Die gebotene Sorgfalt', p. 129.

sought to resolve this conundrum and the Contact Committee set up under Article 13 of the European Money Laundering Directive has agreed that in case of an intermediary bound by a duty of professional secrecy, a statement can be accepted in which the intermediary declares that the transaction is not related to money laundering.[44]

Notwithstanding the apparent endorsement of this practice by the Contact Committee, it is necessary to investigate whether this practice can be unconditionally approved. It is instructive to look at the evolution of the Swiss practice in this respect. Under Article 5 of the 1987 version of the Swiss Code of Conduct (CDB), a Swiss legal professional bound by a duty of professional secrecy could fill out a 'Form B' in which he declares that he knew the beneficial owner and that, all due diligence taken into account, he was not aware of any fact that could indicate an improper use of banking secrecy, or, in particular, that the funds were criminally derived. In addition, the intermediary is obliged to warrant that he was acting within his professional capacity as an attorney and that his mandate was not provisional and did not have as its principal goal the shielding of the identity of the beneficial owner from the bank. This deontological rule was set aside, however, through the circular letter of 25 April 1991 from the Swiss Banking Commission, according to which Form B needed to be replaced, at the latest by 1 May 1992, by a written declaration stating the identity of the beneficial owner. The move of the Swiss Banking Commission was inspired by its conviction that the use of Form B was at odds with Article 305ter of the Swiss Penal Code, which obliged financial intermediaries to identify the beneficial owner.[45] This initiative also demonstrated, however, that compliance with the private Code of Conduct (CDB) did not provide a watertight guarantee that the criminal liability of the financial institution would not be engaged. The Swiss banks reacted promptly and revised the CDB to the effect that in the 1992 version the obligation to identify the beneficial owner extends to accounts held by intermediaries bound by a duty of professional secrecy. In a number of precisely delineated circumstances, attorneys and notaries admitted to the Swiss bar retain the right not to disclose the identity of their clients if they warrant in writing – through a Form R – that the account is only used for a limited number of goals specific to their legal profession. Article 5 CDB 1992 enumerates a number of circumstances corresponding to the exceptions laid down in the aforementioned circular

[44] See T. M. C. Asser Instituut, *De strijd tegen het witwassen van geld*, p. 15.
[45] On Article 305ter see *supra* pp. 105–8.

letter of the Swiss Banking Commission.[46] Should the bank come to the conclusion that a Form R has been improperly used (i.e. in a situation not covered by one of the exceptions), it may require the identification of the beneficial owner through a Form A. In case the beneficial owner is not identified or the bank has reason to believe it has been misled regarding the identity of the beneficial owner, it should as a rule terminate business (Article 6 CDB 1992).

This new Swiss set of rules regarding the identification of the beneficial owner of funds deposited in a professional account held by an attorney or notary constitutes an important improvement in comparison with the previously existing situation in Switzerland and the practice endorsed by the Contact Committee and still existing in some countries, such as Belgium, for example.[47] The major improvement in the new Swiss rule, and at the same time the most difficult point in its practical implementation, is the distinction between activities that are specific to the legal profession of attorney and activities that are not. In Switzerland this distinction was explicitly made by the Swiss Supreme Court in a leading case in 1986[48] and the distinction has been judicially acknowledged by the supreme courts of other jurisdictions (e.g., Belgium[49] and the Netherlands[50]) as well. The leading criterion used by the Swiss Supreme Court to distinguish activities that are specific to the profession of attorney from activities that are not, is the commercial nature of the transaction.[51] The delicate nature of the distinction also flows from the fact that activities which are covered by professional secrecy in one jurisdiction (e.g. trustee in bankruptcy in Switzerland) fall outside the scope of professional secrecy in other countries (e.g. Belgium[52]). To refuse to make such a distinction, however, opens the gate to the misuse of professional secrecy for money laundering purposes, for example. It cannot be accepted that the identity of the beneficial owner of any kind of financial transaction channelled through the professional account of an attorney is therefore protected by professional secrecy. In two highly publicised

---

[46] Taisch, 'Swiss Statutes Concerning Money Laundering', 707.

[47] Stessens, De nationale en internationale bestrijding van het witwassen, pp. 194–6.

[48] ATF 112 Ib 606.

[49] Belgian Supreme Court, judgment of 13 June 1963, Pasicrisie (1963), I, 1079.

[50] Dutch Supreme Court, judgment of 29 March 1994, NJ (1994), 537. See also D. R. Doorenbos, 'Witwassen en (misbruik) van verschoningsrecht', Advocatenblad (1996), 113.

[51] Swiss Supreme Court, ATF 112 Ib 606 and judgment of 11 April 1996, La semaine judiciaire (1996), 454 and B. Corboz, 'Le secret professionnel de l'avocat selon l'article 321 CP', La Semaine Judiciaire (1993), 86–88.

[52] P. Lambert, Règles et usages de la profession d'avocat du barreau de Bruxelles (Brussels: Bruylant, 1994), p. 468.

cases (which, however, did not involve money laundering) concerning two partners in the same law firm in the Netherlands, it was correctly pointed out that this protection attaches only when the transaction was linked to an activity proper to the profession of attorney, such as payment of a fee for a criminal defence,[53] but not in relation to other activities, such as payment to a trustee in a bankruptcy.[54] Recommendation 6 of the Caribbean Drug Money Laundering Conference therefore rightly stated that the fact 'that a person acting as a financial advisor or nominee is an attorney, should not in and of itself be sufficient reason for such person to invoke an attorney-client privilege'. The goal of identifying the beneficial owner of funds deposited in an account can consequently not be frustrated by the mere fact that it concerns a professional account belonging to an attorney.

The identification and record-keeping obligations method

Relevance of record-keeping obligations

The methods used for identification of customers and of beneficial owners and the record-keeping obligations have a greater use in view of possible investigations into money laundering practices than with respect to the prevention of money laundering. By keeping customer identification records and records of financial transactions, financial institutions are in fact keeping a database of information which can be tapped by law enforcement authorities in their investigations into money laundering. In their efforts to trace the proceeds of crime, law enforcement authorities need to reconstruct the paper trail left by the movement of those proceeds. This task is often frustrated by various factors, the first of which is that the information sought is often kept by institutions or professionals bound by a duty of secrecy which can be lifted only after cumbersome judicial proceedings have been successfully instituted.[55] A second, often neglected, problem is that, even if the secrecy duty is lifted, there may be no, or insufficient, information available. To ensure that the paper trail is not broken, it is necessary to impose an obligation on financial institutions not only to identify customers, but also to keep identification

---

[53] Court of Appeal in economic cases (College van Beroep voor het bedrijfsleven), judgment of 23 April 1996, *Advocatenblad* (1996), 573.

[54] Court of Appeal in economic cases (College van Beroep voor het bedrijfsleven), judgment of 23 April 1996, *Advocatenblad* (1996), 575.

[55] On the appropriate judicial procedure for lifting banking secrecy, see *infra* pp. 315–17.

records as well as records of financial transactions. This was also the main goal behind the American Bank Secrecy Act which imposed a number of record-keeping obligations on banks. The identification of the beneficial owner serves a particularly useful purpose in this respect; if carried out effectively, it will allow investigators to pierce corporate or other structures used to conceal the true source of funds.[56]

Identification methods and record-keeping

The European Money Laundering Directive scarcely gives any indication as to how identification should take place: Article 3 refers only to 'supporting evidence'. As far as the record-keeping duty is concerned, Article 4 requires that a copy or a reference of the evidence required should be kept for five years. In respect of the records of transactions, the Directive further stipulates that the supporting evidence and records should consist of the original documents or copies admissible in court proceedings under the applicable domestic legislation. This record-keeping duty is inspired by FATF recommendation 12, which also underlines that these documents should be available to domestic competent authorities in the context of relevant criminal prosecutions and investigations. It is also important that financial institutions store their documents in such a way that swift information retrieval at the request of investigating authorities is possible. Although this does not necessarily follow from the international instruments, specific requirements to this end have been inserted in some domestic legislation.[57]

It is noteworthy that the FATF recommendations – which, other than the Directive, are not strictly binding – are more specific in this respect: they require that identification takes place on the basis of an official or other reliable identifying document (recommendation 10) and that the financial institutions keep copies or records of these identification documents, such as identity cards, passports or driving licences. In various Member States of the European Union (e.g. Belgium,[58] Luxembourg,[59] The Netherlands[60]) identification takes place on the basis of this type of docu-

---

[56] See in this respect P. Bernasconi, 'Bankbeziehungen und internationale Rechtshilfe in Strafsachen: Neuere Entwicklungen', *RSDA* (1995), 67.

[57] FATF, *Evaluation of Measures*, p. 10.

[58] Circular letter 93/4 from the Belgian Banking Commission.

[59] Circular letter IML 94/112 (*Lutte contre le blanchiment et prévention de l'utilisation du secteur financier à des fins de blanchiment*, pp. 11–12) of the *Institut monétaire luxembourgeois* (IML). See A. Schmitt and F. Thoma, 'Droit financier luxembourgeois en 1994', *Bank.Fin.* (1995), pp. 170–1.   [60] Article 3 of the Wet identificatie bij financiële dienstverlening.

ment. This identification method has, however, one drawback, namely that it relies solely on information sources provided by the customer. This may be solved by cross-checking this information by independent sources (e.g. a voters' register), as is, for example, required by the UK Guidance Notes.

FATF Recommendation 10 further specifies what measures financial institutions should take concerning the identification of legal identities: verification of the legal existence and structure of the customer by obtaining proof of incorporation (from a public register or from the customer), including information concerning the customer's name, legal form, address, directors and provisions regulating the power to bind the entity; and verification of the acting person and his power to represent the customer.

Obligations to report (suspicious) transactions

The reporting of certain transactions that are likely to be connected to money laundering operations is one of the pillars of the preventive anti-money laundering system. It is a necessary condition for an effective fight against money laundering. As the history of the Swiss anti-money laundering regulation shows,[61] a set of rules designed to prevent money laundering without an obligation to report suspicious transactions may succeed in closing the doors of the financial institutions to a number of dubious financial transactions, but is unlikely to have much impact on the repression of money laundering as these dubious transactions will not be reported to any government authority. In the following, it will be argued that a reporting obligation is an essential prerequisite for an effective money laundering regime. Various models of due diligence and reporting obligations will be compared with a view to their effectiveness. Resistance against (mandatory) reporting obligations especially stemmed from the traditional principle of banking secrecy.[62] The question that will be studied, therefore, is the extent to which financial institutions that co-operate by reporting transactions should benefit from exoneration of civil and/or criminal liability they might otherwise incur by disclosing information or by carrying out suspicious transactions.

---

[61] See *supra* pp. 101–4   [62] On banking secrecy, see *infra* pp. 314–18.

Need for a reporting obligation

Effective criminal law enforcement almost invariably depends upon information on offences that have been committed. Law enforcement authorities rarely take action *proprio motu*, but in most cases rely instead on information provided by third parties. It has correctly been pointed out that the extent to which offences are traceable through in statistics depends on two factors, namely the visibility of those statistics and the reporting of the offences.[63] Money laundering, however, often takes place through systems which are not easily accessible to law enforcement authorities (e.g. in financial institutions or through black market operations of all sorts).[64] Maybe the most important factor is that many of the proceeds of crime derive from 'crimes without a victim', which means that there is no victim who can provide the government with information on the fact that proceeds have been obtained illegally, let alone on the magnitude of those proceeds. In addition, money laundering itself is a consensual crime without direct victims. Therefore, alternative ways to provide law enforcement with information on money laundering operations had to be devised. The function of providing law enforcement agencies with intelligence can be fulfilled either by private institutions through which money laundering operations are channelled (especially financial institutions), or by administrative authorities which routinely have access to such information (authorities charged with prudential supervision of financial institutions). The reporting of suspicious transactions will be examined in the following paragraphs and the input of financial intelligence from supervisory authorities will be discussed in Chapter 7. Both new methods of gathering information should be seen as part of a larger trend of establishing new ways of information gathering designed to deal with the information deficit of law enforcement authorities. The rapid rise of proactive investigation techniques, which have been foremostly deployed in the fight against organised crime, is also part of this trend.[65] This is not the place to elaborate on this new trend, but it is clear that it stems from new patterns in criminality, such as the rise of organised crime and the internationalisation of crime. It seems that one very important, underlying factor is the growth of crimes without a direct,

---

[63] Ph. Robert and Cl. Faugeron, *Les forces cachées de la justice. La crise de la justice pénale* (Paris: Le Centurion, 1980), pp. 32–3.

[64] H.-J. Albrecht, 'The Money-Trail, Developments in Criminal Law, and Research Needs: An Introduction', *Eur.JCr., Cr.L & Cr.J* (1997), 194.

[65] Albrecht, 'The Money-Trail', 194 and P. J. Van Koppen, 'Financieel rechercheren in de opsporing', *Justitiële Verkenningen* (1996, No.9), p. 61 *et seq.*

identifiable victim which makes it essential for law enforcement to rely on other ways of gathering information than reporting by the victim.

Different models of due diligence and of reporting

Two reporting models can be distinguished overall.[66] According to the first which was, for example, introduced in the United States in 1970,[67] all transactions involving an amount above a certain threshold (in the US, $10,000) have to be reported. Under the second model, only transactions that appear to be linked to a money laundering operation need be reported. This model is not threshold-based but suspicion-based. The American experience has shown that the first model generates an enormous number of reports which are difficult to process adequately – the Financial Crimes Enforcement Network (FinCEN) received over 12 million reports in 1997.[68] This very high number of reports is the logical consequence of the fact that the reporting obligation operates 'blindly', on the basis of an objective threshold criterion and not more selectively on the basis of suspicions harboured by the reporting financial institutions. Under the former model, suspicious transactions are detected only after the financial intelligence unit has sifted through all the data collected. The latter model, on the contrary, departs from a concrete assessment of the nature of financial transactions made by the financial institution and requires only the reporting of transactions deemed suspicious by the financial institutions themselves. It is obvious that the second model is much more cost-efficient and it is not surprising that even the United States have started to rely increasingly on suspicion-based reports.[69] In addition, it has the distinct advantage – at least from the banker's point of view – that financial institutions have to disclose less information and that consequently fewer customers are exposed to the scrutiny of law enforcement authorities. Given these advantages, most international instruments have opted to adopt this model. The FATF recommendations, however, while requiring countries to set up a suspicion-based reporting system (recommendation 15), still urge countries to consider the feasibility and utility of a system under which financial systems would report all domestic and international currency transactions to a national agency

---

[66] See also J. F. Thony, 'Processing Financial Information in Money Laundering Matters: The Financial Intelligence Units', *Eur.JCr., Cr.L & Cr.J* (1996), 258–61.   [67] See *supra* pp. 97–9.

[68] FinCEN Information Leaflet: 'FinCEN Further Streamlines Exemption Process' (21 September 1998). In 1992, the figure was at 9.2 million reports a year: Byrne, 'The Bank Secrecy Act', 803.   [69] See *supra* p. 99.

with a computer database accessible to law enforcement agencies. This model seems feasible only in those countries such as Australia and South Africa, for example, that have in place an electronic system of threshold-based reporting of large currency transactions. Nevertheless, the more automated banking systems become, the greater may be the potential for the control of automatically transmitted data (also known as 'cyber-watch').

The obligation to report suspicious transactions is part of a larger requirement of due diligence of financial institutions. The obligation of enhanced diligence in fact takes precedence over the obligation to report suspicious transactions in that it may already be operative in circumstances when there is as yet no suspicion of money laundering. In its Statement of Principles, the Basle Committee on Banking Regulations and Supervisory Practices indicated that banks 'should not set out to offer services or provide active assistance in transactions which they have good reason to suppose are associated with money laundering activities', nor to provide assistance 'to customers seeking to deceive law enforcement agencies through the provision of altered, incomplete or misleading information'. In the same vein, FATF recommendation 14 requires that financial institutions pay special attention to 'all complex, unusual, large transactions, and all unusual patterns of transactions, which have no apparent economic or visible lawful purpose'. This FATF recommendation differs from the Directive in different ways. Whereas FATF recommendation 14 refers to unusual transactions, the European Money Laundering Directive operates a more limited concept of suspicious transactions, namely 'any transaction which they regard as particularly likely, by its nature, to be related to money laundering' (Article 5 of the Directive). FATF recommendation 14 moreover contains an additional requirement that is not present in the Directive, namely that the background and purpose of unusual transactions be as far as possible examined and that the findings be established in writing. Given the fact that the obligation to record the result of an examination in writing was not inserted in the Directive, only three Member States of the EU (Belgium, France and Portugal[70]) have incorporated such a requirement into their preventive legislation.

The reporting obligation: the pivotal issues

In studying the various concepts of obligations to report suspicious transactions, two essential distinctions should be made. First, a distinction

---

[70] *First Commission's report on the implementation of the Money Laundering Directive*, p. 12.

should be made between an obligation to report information and the right or the liberty to disclose information or, alternatively, between an active and a passive co-operation obligation. Thus, the Swiss model evolved from a right for a banker to disclose information on suspicious transactions (introduced in 1994) to an obligation to report founded suspicions on financial transactions (introduced in 1997).[71] A second, material distinction is between *proactive* reporting of information (i.e. on the initiative of the reporting institution) and *reactive* reporting of information, upon a request from an authority.[72]

As far as the proper reporting obligation is concerned, FATF recommendation 15 requires financial institutions to report promptly to the competent national authorities their suspicions that funds stem from a criminal activity. Whilst originally leaving the FATF member countries the choice whether to institute a reporting obligation or merely a right to disclose information, the FATF in 1996 clearly opted for a mandatory reporting system, lest there be competition distortion between countries that have and countries that do not have a mandatory reporting system in place.[73] During the drafting process of the European Money Laundering Directive a clear choice was made in favour of a suspicion-based reporting obligation, even though the European Parliament favoured the threshold-based reporting system. This model was considered too expensive and the Commission opined that financial institutions themselves were best placed to assess which transactions might be linked to money laundering.[74] Article 6 of the Directive contains both a proactive and a reactive reporting obligation. As far as the proactive reporting obligation is concerned, the compliance officers of the financial institutions shall inform the authorities 'of any fact which might be an indication of money laundering'.

Under no circumstances are financial institutions and their directors and employees allowed to disclose to the customer nor to any third person that information has been transmitted to the authorities or that a money laundering investigation is being carried out. This prohibition, which was already contained in FATF recommendation 17, was inserted in the Directive (Article 8) subsequent to an amendment proposed by the European Parliament.

It is obviously impossible within the scope of this book to give an in-depth

---

[71] See *supra* pp. 104–8.
[72] M. Levi, *Consumer Confidentiality, Money-Laundering, and Police Bank Relationships: English Law and Practice in a Global Environment*, p. 9 and 'Pecunia non olet', 225–6.
[73] FATF-VII, p. 7.   [74] Magliveras, 'Defeating the Money Launderers', 172.

analysis of the various ways in which the reporting obligation has been inserted into domestic law but it is nevertheless useful to outline some general differences in the ways in which these reporting obligations have been implemented on a domestic level. Three distinctions are especially important in this respect: the choice between administrative and criminal implementation of the reporting obligation; the extent of the reporting obligation as far as the predicate offence is concerned; and the (lack of) criteria for determining the suspicious nature of a transaction.

The first distinction relates to the administrative versus the criminal implementation of this Community obligation. While England and Wales (as well as Ireland and Denmark) have criminalised the failure to report a suspicious transaction, other Member States have opted for an administrative obligation to report suspicious transactions. Under the administrative model, as exemplified by Article 12 of the Belgian Money Laundering Act of 11 January 1993 or Article 40 of the Luxembourg Money Laundering Act of 5 April 1993, financial institutions have an obligation under administrative law to report suspicious transactions, which can be administratively enforced, but non-observance of which does not constitute a criminal offence. Under English law, s.52 DTA 1994 makes it an offence for anyone who knows, or suspects, that another person is engaged in drug money laundering, not to disclose that information to a constable as soon as is reasonably practicable after it comes to his attention, when 'the information, or other matter on which that knowledge or suspicion is based came to his attention in the course of his trade, profession, business or employment'.[75]

Another striking feature of English legislation is that its application field is limited to drug money laundering. This limited concept of the obligation to report suspicious transactions needs to be set, however, against the larger liberty to disclose information. Both s.93A (assisting another to retain the benefit of criminal conduct) and 93B (acquisition, possession or use of proceeds of criminal conduct) CJA 1988 allow timely disclosure as an excuse to criminal liability for money laundering offences.[76] The limitation of the application field of the *ratione materiae* (i.e. concerning the predicate offence) of the English reporting obligation should of course also be seen in connection with its broad application field *ratione personae*, which is not limited to financial institutions but covers all citizens. In addition, it is worthwhile to point out that also in another respect the reporting obligation or liberty under English law is broader than under

---

[75] See A. Brown, 'Money Laundering: A European and U.K. Perspective', *JIBL* (1997), 308–309.
[76] See *infra* p. 176.

many other law systems, namely in that it relates to proceeds not only derived from offences, but also connected to a criminal activity (e.g. a payment with legitimate income for illegal, criminal services).

The limitation of the application field of the *ratione materiae* of the reporting obligation under English law leads to the more general question of whether the obligation to report suspicious financial transactions should cover proceeds from any kind of offence or should be limited to a number of serious offences, as is the case in England and Wales. On the international level, there is a tendency in favour of an expansion of the predicate offence of money laundering. There is, however, divergence of opinion on the question of whether a drastic expansion of the application field of the *ratione materiae* of the reporting obligation will automatically result in a greater effectiveness of anti-money laundering legislation. Even if it is probably not difficult to find common agreement on the necessity of imposing preventive anti-money laundering measures with respect to all serious crimes, it is at least debatable whether the due diligence obligation, and in particular the obligation to report suspicious transactions – whether on a domestic or international level – should be extended to all offences. A number of arguments can be marshalled against such an extension.

A first argument against such an expansion is that it will increase the administrative burden on financial institutions as well as the workload of the financial intelligence units responsible for processing the reports made by financial institutions. This purely economic argument should not be allowed to outweigh any expected benefits from introducing a wide reporting obligation in the fight against money laundering. It is moreover doubtful whether an expansion of the application field will result in a drastic increase of the number of reports made. The criterion for reporting a transaction is its suspicious nature and very often banks will not be able to pinpoint the exact criminal source of the proceeds or even to distinguish between a genuine tax crime and other forms of serious criminality.[77] This is also evident from practice in English law where financial institutions, notwithstanding the limited nature of the reporting obligation under s.52 DTA 1994, often report their suspicions of non-drug money laundering to the National Criminal Intelligence Service (the British financial intelligence unit responsible for combating money laundering), not least with the intention of avoiding criminal liability for money laundering.

---

[77] See in this respect also the finding of the Multidisciplinary Group on Organized Crime, *Draft Report of the informal Money Laundering Experts Group*, 12706/98, CRIMORG 173, Brussels, 6 November 1998, p. 39.

Many of the reports made by financial institutions in the UK about suspected drug money laundering in fact relate to proceeds from other types
of offences. One could of course very well argue that, if financial institutions are often not able to distinguish drug money laundering from the
laundering of proceeds from other crimes or from fiscal fraud, the logical
action to take is to broaden the application field of the reporting obligation to all kinds of criminally derived proceeds. Even though this is, admittedly, a strong argument in favour of such an expansion, it is important
to make a distinction between acknowledging that reports that are made
by financial institutions may well relate to lesser offences or to fiscal fraud
than those for which they were made, and obliging financial institutions
to report these transactions even if they know perfectly well that they
relate to fiscal fraud and not to a more serious crime.

As some of the obligations which are imposed on financial institutions
in the context of the prevention of money laundering constitute severe
inroads into traditional banking principles such as maintaining banking
secrecy, it has sometimes also been argued that an expansion of the application field of *ratione materiae* will result in even more serious derogations
from these traditional banking principles. Again, this argument wrongly
presupposes that an expansion will automatically lead to a drastic
increase of the number of reports.

A further argument against plans for expansion is that it is much more
difficult for financial institutions to 'detect' money laundering transactions involving the proceeds from economic, fiscal, or other forms of
white-collar crime than to 'detect' laundering operations involving the
proceeds from serious crimes, such as drug trafficking or organised
crime.[78] Regardless of the veracity of this argument, the mere fact that it
is more difficult to 'detect' money laundering operations involving other
types of proceeds does not mean that they should be excluded from the
application field. The reporting obligations relate to any suspicions financial institutions may harbour and do not impose an obligation to achieve
a given result, but only oblige financial institutions to make reasonable
efforts to distinguish suspicious transactions from others.

The only arguments that, in the author's view, may truly justify a limitation of the application field of the *ratione materiae* are based on practical
politics towards financial institutions. First, on a policy level an expansion
of the application field of the *ratione materiae* to all crimes is only justified

[78] See, e.g., A. Lutgen, 'Les moyens de lutte internationaux contre le blanchiment de
l'argent et la protection du budget des Communautés européennes', *Agon* (May 1994),
11–12.

in one respect. The preventive anti-money laundering measures seek to protect financial institutions and other economic operators against the scourge of organised crime. It is not immediately clear why financial institutions need special protection from laundering the proceeds of other crimes (i.e. crimes which have not been committed in the context of organised crime). While it is of course necessary to avoid banks acting as accomplices to criminals, the danger of the 'corruption' of financial institutions seems to be limited to the context of organised crime. In reality, the expansion of the application field of preventive anti-money laundering measures only serves a repressive purpose, that is to supply law enforcement authorities with information on the widest possible range of offences.

A second argument relates to the co-operation of financial institutions on which the effective prevention of money laundering and especially the reporting of suspicious transactions hinges. Although observance of these measures can be enforced through supervision on a prudential basis,[79] it will in practice often be very difficult to detect non-observance, especially of the obligation to report suspicious transactions. The fulfilment of these obligations to a certain degree always depends on a subjective assessment of the concrete situation. Financial institutions have been asked to co-operate in the prevention of laundering of proceeds from serious crimes and are obliged to report their suspicions in this respect. It is doubtful whether they will allow themselves to be cajoled into reporting transactions which might involve the proceeds of offences less serious or even from fiscal fraud. This position has also been adopted by the European Commission in its 1999 proposal for amending the Money Laundering Directive. In defiance of other international instruments, such as FATF recommendation 4 (1996) and the EU Joint Action of 3 December 1998 concerning arrangements for co-operation between Member States in respect of identification, tracing, freezing or seizing and confiscation of instrumentalities and the proceeds from crime, the Commission did not propose to extend the reporting duty to all other serious offences, but only participation in combating activities related to organised crime and to a number of offences damaging the financial interests of the European Community. This restricted approach towards the extension of the reporting duty was expressly motivated by the perceived need to ensure the sustained goodwill and co-operation of the financial sector, which had expressed considerable reluctance to comply with any reporting

[79] See *infra* pp. 202–3.

requirement that would extend to cover an excessively wide range of offences.[80]

The question as how far the reporting duty should be extended is especially vexed in respect of fiscal offences. From a point of view of realpolitik, one has to acknowledge that in many societies fiscal fraud is a widespread phenomenon whose effects touch many citizens and hence many customers, and is certainly not one that is restricted to a number of dubious individuals who want to misuse financial institutions. Although no reliable statistics exist as to the number of financial transactions that involve 'black money' (i.e. money on which no taxes have been paid), it is likely to represent a significant part of the turnover of financial institutions. It is questionable whether it is realistic under these circumstances to expect financial institutions to report a type of transaction which involves a substantial percentage of their customers. The position of the European Commission which, in its 1999 proposal for amending the Money Laundering Directive, at least implicitly excluded fiscal offences from the extended reporting duty, therefore seems a realistic one. Nevertheless, the G7 countries and the FATF have formally adopted the position that the obligation to report suspicious transactions continues to apply even where such transactions are thought to involve tax offences. This position was adopted at the meeting of G7 Finance Ministers in May 1998 and in 1999 the FATF adopted a specific Interpretative Note to Recommendation 15 to this end. This Interpretative Note closed the so-called fiscal excuse by stipulating that financial institutions are required to report suspicious transactions, and transactions stated by clients to relate to tax matters.[81]

Some fear that preventive anti-money laundering measures will be a Trojan horse, used not only to trace proceeds from criminal offences, but also from fiscal fraud. The fear that (preventive) anti-money laundering measures will not be used just for fighting serious crime but also for the purposes of fighting tax-dodging[82] is, certainly in view of the position adopted by the G7 and the FATF, a realistic one. In this respect reference

---

[80] European Commission, *Proposal for a European Parliament and Council Directive amending Council Directive 91/308/EEC of 10 June 1991 on Prevention of the Use of the Financial System for the Purpose of Money Laundering*, Brussels, 14.7.1999, COM(1999) 352 final, 99/152 (COD), pp. 6–7 and 18.

[81] See the conclusions of G7 Finance Ministers, London, 9 May 1998, point 16, rendered at FATF-X, p. 33.

[82] See the remarks made in *Proceedings of the American Society of International Law* (1992), 202 and 208 and by Pieth, 'Einführung', p. 27 and Dassesse 'Les rapports entre la proposition de directive blanchiment', 13.

should also be made to the calls for enabling or facilitating co-operation between the money laundering authorities and fiscal/customs authorities which have been made, not only by the G7 countries,[83] but also within the European Union.[84] The fear of fiscal use of information obtained through anti-money laundering measures (especially through the reporting of suspicious transactions) can, however, be allayed through the introduction of a so-called specialty principle which limits the use of the information obtained. Whether or not this is the case depends on the domestic legislation of the state concerned which will be discussed later on.[85]

A third field in which the implementation of the reporting obligation considerably varies from one jurisdiction to another is the determination of the suspicious nature of transactions. In the Directive, the obligation to co-operate actively with the authorities responsible for combating money laundering is sketchily defined as an obligation to inform the authorities of 'any fact which might be an indication of money laundering'. Most domestic implementation legislation refers to an obligation to report 'suspicious' transactions. This begs of course the question as to which transactions should be considered as suspicious. In many jurisdictions, financial institutions are left to themselves to determine which transactions are considered suspicious and which are not. In other jurisdictions, however, a government authority is authorised by the legislator to issue guidelines on which transactions need to be considered as suspicious. The Swiss Banking Commission was probably one of the first institutions to issue such guidelines on 18 December 1991, albeit not strictly speaking in connection with the obligation to report suspicious transactions – which at that time did not exist under Swiss law – but in relation to the due diligence obligation to identify the beneficial owner.[86] The possibility of issuing guidelines has now been laid down in respect of all financial intermediaries subject to the Swiss Money Laundering Act of 10 October 1997 (Article 16). In Luxembourg, the supervisory authority, the *Institut monétaire luxembourgeois*, has issued a circular letter – modelled on the Swiss example – containing a number of indices for determining whether a transaction is suspicious.[87] Both the Swiss and the Luxembourg circular letters contain a number of indices for determining whether money

---

[83] Conclusions of G7 Finance Ministers, London, 9 May 1998, point 16, rendered at FATF-X, p. 33.   [84] See the *Draft Report of the informal Money Laundering Experts Group*, p. 39.
[85] See *infra* pp. 193–9.   [86] See on this circular letter, *supra* pp. 107–8.
[87] Circular letter of the IML 94/112 (*Lutte contre le blanchiment et prévention de l'utilisation du secteur financier à des fins de blanchiment*).

laundering may be taking place, without pretending to constitute an exhaustive list of suspicious circumstances.

They therefore differ significantly in outlook from the system that was adopted in The Netherlands. Dutch legislation does not refer to 'suspicious transactions' but to 'unusual transactions', a concept which is derived from the FATF recommendations rather than from the Directive. Under Article 8 of the Dutch Act on the Disclosure of Unusual Transactions of 16 December 1993, an unusual transaction is defined as a transaction deemed unusual according to the indicators laid down by Departmental Order. The Dutch model reflects a vision that the sifting of suspicious transactions is a law enforcement task which should be carried out by the government and not by private (financial) institutions.[88] The Departmental Order therefore not only contains subjective criteria which concern subjective facts (e.g. nervous behaviour by a customer), but especially objective criteria. The latter are obviously much favoured by the financial institutions[89] as they concern objective facts (such as exchange operations in certain currencies, though not threshold criteria as in the United States), the application of which requires less time and which are therefore much easier and cheaper to operate. As soon as a transaction meets a number of objective criteria or a subjective criterion, a financial intermediary is obliged to report the transaction to the Dutch financial intelligence unit. The content of the objective criteria as well as their number are defined by Departmental Order, which allows the government to change objective criteria with a view to preventing too high a volume of report flows.[90] The fact that the number of criteria as well as the criteria themselves, may be modified by Departmental Order, however, also introduces an element of legal insecurity.[91] The effectiveness of this mechanism can nevertheless still be questioned as it has so far generated

---

[88] A. F. M. Dorresteijn, 'Aansprakelijkheid van banken bij weigering of melding van ongebruikelijke transacties', in *Misdaadgeld*, ed. P. C. Van Duyne, J. M. Reijntjes and C. D. Schaap (Arnhem: Gouda Quint, 1993), p. 162; Groenhuijsen and Van der Landen, 'De financiële aanpak', 616 and Doorenbos, *Over witwassen en voordeelsontneming*, p. 36.

[89] G. J. Terlouw and U. Aron, *Twee jaar MOT. Een evaluatie van de uitvoering van de Wet melding ongebruikelijke transacties* (Arnhem: Gouda Quint, 1996), pp. 48–50 and A. A. Franken and D. Van der Landen, 'Het zwarte gat van de MOT', *NJB* (1997), 60.

[90] T. Peeman, 'Het MOT-meldpunt: een (te) moeizaam compromis?', in *Financiële integriteit. Normafwijkend gedrag en (zelf)regulering binnen het financiële stelsel*, ed. A. B. Hoogenboom, V. Mul en A. Wielinga (Arnhem: Gouda Quint, 1995), p. 99. For an example, see Meldpunt Ongebruikelijke Transacties, *Jaarlijks Verslag 1998*, p. 10.

[91] S. C. J. J. Kortmann, 'De (ontwerp) landsverordeningen MOT; civielrechtelijke aspecten', in *Maatregelen tegen witwassen in het koninkrijk*, ed. G. J. M. Corstens, E. J. Joubert and S. C. J. J. Kortmann (Arnhem: Gouda Quint, 1995), p. 162.

a huge amount of financial data. In its first year of operations (1994), the Dutch financial intelligence unit received 14,756 reports, a figure which has gone up to 16,974 in 1997.[92] In addition, the analysis of the data collected by the reports of the financial institutions shows that the reports made on the basis of subjective criteria lead to a far higher result in terms of newly started investigations than reports made on the basis of objective criteria.[93] It may be noted in passing that the same conclusion has also been arrived at in Australia, which likewise has both suspicion- and threshold-based reporting requirements.[94]

Notions such as 'effectiveness' are very difficult to measure with regard to reporting of suspicious transactions, especially given the 'statistical black hole' in this respect: few reliable figures are available on the extent of the money laundering phenomenon and on the extent of proceeds of crime. Comparing different countries' preventive legislation from a viewpoint of effectiveness is even more difficult, especially since non-legal factors related to the cultural and economic environment in which financial institutions operate are also likely to influence the reporting rate. It seems nevertheless possible to assert that a reporting system that provides some leeway to financial institutions to determine whether transactions are suspicious or not is likely to be more effective – that is to provide more useful intelligence to the law enforcement authorities. From a legalistic point of view, a system based on objective criteria is, admittedly, more attractive in that it is much easier to control whether a financial institutions complies with its obligation to report or not, but this benefit does not outweigh its disadvantages. Besides its lower effectiveness in terms of usefulness to the law enforcement authorities, the latter system is also much less efficient in that it generates a huge amount of financial data which can barely – and in any case only at high cost – be processed, as is demonstrated by the American model.

Exonerations for financial institutions that report a suspicious transaction

In order to obtain co-operation from financial institutions, it may be necessary to reassure financial institutions that they will not be held

92 Meldpunt Ongebruikelijke Transacties, *Jaarlijks Verslag 1998*, p. 10.
93 M. S. Groenhuijsen and D. Van der Landen, *Financiële instellingen en de strafrechtelijke bestrijding van het witwassen van geld* (Amsterdam: Nederlands Instituut voor het Bank- en Effectenbedrijf, 1995), p. 67.
94 M. Levi, 'Evaluating the "New Policing": Attacking the Money Trail of Organised Crime', *The Australian and New Zealand Journal of Criminology* (1997), 9.

responsible, either civilly or criminally, if they inform the authorities responsible for combating money laundering of facts which are covered by banking secrecy, or because they carried out a transaction which they suspected might be linked to money laundering. Theoretically, a third hypothesis could be envisaged in which a financial institution could be faced with a claim for damages, when it refuses to carry out a transaction because it suspects that it is linked to money laundering. It is hard to see, however, how financial institutions could incur liability in this way as they are obviously entitled to refuse to carry out transactions when they fear that, by carrying out the transaction, they would incur criminal liability for money laundering.

By virtue of banking secrecy rules, which – under one form or another – are embedded in many jurisdictions, banks are prohibited from disclosing any information about their customers, or funds they hold, to government authorities. Before the introduction of reporting duties in the context of the fight against money laundering, banking secrecy was normally lifted only when judicial authorities requested information in the course of an ongoing investigation. The present reporting duties are different in that they require banks to disclose information spontaneously, which puts banks in a much more delicate position vis-à-vis their clients, especially in view of their possible civil liability. Nevertheless, in most countries, both in common law[95] and in civil law,[96] the general legal framework of banking secrecy made a general allowance for any type of disclosure to be compulsory by law, even in those jurisdictions such as Switzerland,[97] where banking secrecy was protected by the criminal law.

Without an entrenched statutory obligation to report suspicious transactions, banks that become aware of, or harbour suspicions about, the criminal origin of proceeds deposited with the bank or involved in transactions, can, however, only take a limited number of steps: denying assistance, severing relations with customers or closing/freezing accounts. These were the steps set out in 1988 for banks by the Basle Committee in

---

[95] *Tournier v. National Provincial and Union Bank of England*, [1924] 1 K. B. 461, 472 per Bankes L. J.

[96] See generally Stessens, *De nationale en internationale bestrijding van het witwassen*, pp. 268–9.

[97] See Article 47(4) Swiss Banking Law. See M. Aubert and others, *Le secret bancaire suisse*, p. 148; H. Bollman, 'Switzerland', in *International Bank Secrecy*, ed. D. Campbell (London: Sweet & Maxwell, 1992), pp. 674–9; K. Mueller, 'The Swiss Banking Secret From a Legal View', *ICLQ* (1969), 366–73; E. A. Stultz, 'Swiss Bank Secrecy and United States Efforts To Obtain Information From Swiss Banks', *Vand.J.Transnat.L.* (1988), 73–76 and 79–81 and Taisch, 'Swiss Statutes', 711.

its Statement of Principles. In order to avoid any friction with domestic banking secrecy rules, FATF recommendation 16 requires that financial institutions and their personnel be protected by the law from criminal or civil liability for breach of any restriction on disclosure of information, even if they did not precisely know what the underlying criminal activity was, and regardless of whether the activity had actually occurred. A similar whistle-blowing protection can be found in Article 9 of the European Money Laundering Directive which requires Member States to exonerate the employee who, or director of a financial institution which, in good faith discloses information under his obligations to co-operate with the authorities responsible for money laundering. Such disclosure 'shall not constitute a breach of any restriction on disclosure of information imposed by contract or by any legislative, regulatory or administrative provision, and shall not involve the credit or financial institution, its directors or employees in liability of any kind'. Both the FATF recommendation and the Directive have worded the exemption broadly so as to cover the variety of legal techniques that are used to protect banking secrecy and hence to repress any infringement of banking secrecy.[98] In most legal systems, the mere introduction of a number of statutory reporting obligations should in principle suffice to protect bankers from liability claims. It was, however, thought wise to afford the financial institutions an explicit whistle-blowing protection. This can be seen as part of the 'carrot and stick' approach that has been adopted towards financial institutions: faced with possible criminal prosecution for money laundering, banks can secure themselves against civil liability when they co-operate with the authorities responsible for combating money laundering. For instance, customers who incur substantial losses as a result of a report that was made through, for example, a delay in the execution of a transaction may want to sue for damages. French legislation provides that any damages a customer might incur as a result of a report made by a financial institution and which he cannot claim back from the financial institution by virtue of the whistle-blowing protection, will be recoverable from the state.[99] Although proposals to introduce a similar rule have also been put forward in other countries (e.g. Belgium[100] and The Netherlands[101]), there

[98] See *infra* pp. 314–18.

[99] Article 8 of the Act of 12 July 1990 (*Loi Nº 90–614 du 12 juillet 1990 relative à la participation des organismes financiers à la lutte contre le blanchiment des capitaux provenant du trafic des stupéfiants*). See Vasseur, 'La loi du 12 juillet 1990', 26.

[100] See the proposal made in the Belgian Senate: Verslag van de Commissie voor de Financiën van de Senaat, *Parl. St.*, Senaat, B. Z. 1991–1992, 468–2, pp. 35–6.

[101] Kortmann, 'De (ontwerp) landsverordeningen MOT', p. 168.

seems to be no compelling reason to burden the state with any costs that might be incurred by the execution in good faith of obligations that have been imposed by a democratic legislator because they were deemed to be in the general interest.

All EU Member States have inserted a whistle-blowing protection in their domestic legislation, but two Member States are more stringent than the Directive in that the fact that the report was made in good faith is not always exonerating. In Germany the exoneration does not apply if the report has been made in a deliberately or gross negligently false manner[102] and in the Netherlands Article 13 of the Dutch Act on the Disclosure of Unusual Transactions of 16 December 1993 excludes the exoneration if, considering all facts and circumstances, it is plausible that no disclosure should have been made. Thus a financial institution which reports a transaction which it thinks is, for the customer in question, unusual might possibly be held civilly liable for any losses incurred by the customer if it turns out that the transaction was not in fact unusual at all.[103] Although these stringent provisions seem to run counter to the protection provided by Article 9 of the Directive, banks cannot directly avail themselves of this provision. While a state is estopped from invoking its failure to implement a directive, that does not give a non-implemented directive horizontal effect between private persons.[104]

Also, in Switzerland – which is not a Member State of the European Union – the exemption from civil and criminal liability for disclosing information on suspicious transactions only applies if the financial intermediary has acted with due diligence, that is, with the diligence required by the circumstances (Article 11 of the Swiss Money Laundering Act of 10 October 1997). Under Swiss law, the same exemption applies to the civil and/or criminal liability that could be incurred by the financial intermediary who has frozen – as he is legally obliged to do – the funds to which his disclosure relates.

---

[102] *First Commission's report on the implementation of the Money Laundering Directive*, p. 14.

[103] Dorresteijn, 'Aansprakelijkheid van banken', p. 171 and V. Mul, 'Vrijwaringsbepalingen: vrijheid of gebondenheid?', in *Financiële integriteit. Normafwijkend gedrag en (zelf)regulering binnen het financiële stelsel*, ed. A. B. Hoogenboom, V. Mul and A. Wielinga, pp. 112–13. See also D. R. Doorenbos, 'Money Laundering. De rol van de financiële sector', *DD* (1993), 775 and Kortmann, 'De (ontwerp) landsverordeningen MOT', p. 165.

[104] See P. Craig, 'Directives: Direct Effect, Indirect Effect and the Construction of National Legislation', *ELR* (1997), 519.

Exonerations for financial institutions that carry out a suspicious transaction

In principle, financial institutions should refrain from carrying out transactions which they know or suspect are related to money laundering until they have apprised the authority responsible for combating money laundering which may then instruct them not to execute the transaction. This rule has been laid down expressly in Article 7 of the Directive and can also be read in FATF recommendation 18 which requires that financial institutions reporting their suspicions comply with instructions from the competent authorities. Under Belgian law, for example, the Belgian Financial Information Processing Unit can suspend a suspicious transaction for a maximum period of twenty-four hours. As already indicated, in Switzerland, financial institutions are even required to freeze the funds to which the report they have made relates. The financial intermediary must freeze the funds which it controls until the competent prosecuting authority has taken a decision, but for a maximum period of five working days after the report has been filed. This obligation of financial intermediaries to freeze 'suspicious' funds on their own initiative is a very far-reaching, but potentially very effective, measure which does not feature in the European Directive. In practice it seems, however, that, in those jurisdictions where the financial intelligence unit has the power to order a freeze, this power is seldom used. A variety of reasons may account for this: funds may already have been moved to financial institutions in other jurisdictions by the time the financial intelligence unit has been apprised or the institution's suspicions at that initial stage may not be strong enough to warrant a freeze.

Article 7 of the Directive, however, allows financial institutions to carry out the suspicious transaction concerned before apprising the authority if it is impossible to refrain from carrying out the transaction or where doing so is 'likely to frustrate efforts to pursue the beneficiaries of a suspected money laundering operation'. In that case the financial institution should apprise the authority immediately after completing the transaction. This practice is sometimes referred to as 'controlled money laundering', after an analogy with the controlled delivery of drugs. Just as the controlled delivery of drugs can obviously exonerate only participating (i.e. infiltrating) police officers and not the drug traffickers, from criminal liability, so 'controlled' money laundering exonerates only the financial institution from criminal liability, not the transaction principals, that is the persons who sought to launder the proceeds. Given the fact that the

Directive is not concerned with law enforcement as such, it is not surprising that such exemption was not foreseen by the Directive itself. An exoneration is nevertheless very necessary if financial institutions are expected to carry out suspicious transactions rather than deny assistance to the transaction principals which would simply force the funds to flow through other channels, thereby frustrating the efforts of law enforcement authorities to trace the proceeds and clamp down on money laundering. To its credit, the UN Model Law on Money Laundering has provided for an explicit exoneration in this respect (Article 18).

The most sensible attitude in this respect has probably been taken by the British legislator who has provided that, where a person who has timely disclosed his suspicion or belief that any funds or investments are derived from or connected to a criminal activity, his acts shall not be considered as assisting another to retain the benefit of criminal conduct (s.93A(3)(b)) or acquisition, possession or use of proceeds of criminal conduct (s.93B(3)(b) CJA 1988). Timely disclosure means that the disclosure takes place either before the person carries out the act concerned (e.g. acquisition of property) and does so act with the consent of a constable (police officer) or takes place after the act, on his own initiative, as soon as it is reasonable for him to make the disclosure.

Other jurisdictions have been less successful in elaborating a satisfactory exemption from criminal liability in this type of situation. Although 'controlled money laundering' has been made possible in most EU Member States under the influence of Article 7 of the Directive, legislators have often omitted to stipulate an explicit exemption from criminal liability. This is the case in Belgium, for example, where the legal position of financial institutions that have carried out transactions after or immediately before apprising the Belgian financial intelligence unit is surrounded by insecurity. Notwithstanding divergence of opinion on this point, the only possibility for defendants to be exempted from criminal liability under these circumstances is to avail themselves of the general exonerating force of the Money Laundering Act of 11 January 1993, which allows them to carry out a transaction under certain circumstances.[105]

In The Netherlands, Article 7 of the Directive has not been implemented which makes it necessary for Dutch financial institutions to refuse to carry out suspicious financial transactions if it is impossible for them to apprise the Dutch financial intelligence unit of their suspicions beforehand.[106] Even after a report has been made, there is no watertight guaran-

---

[105] Stessens, *De nationale en internationale bestrijding van het witwassen*, pp. 211–13.
[106] H. E. M. Velthuyse, 'Money Laundering in the Netherlands', *JIBL* (1994), 375.

tee that the financial institution will not be prosecuted. The problem has been only partially solved by a statutory use immunity for financial institutions that report suspicious transactions (Article 12 of the Dutch Act on the Disclosure of Unusual Transactions of 16 December 1993). This statutory provision, primarily intended to safeguard a defendant's right not to incriminate himself,[107] guarantees that financial data that are reported by financial institutions cannot be used as evidence against the reporting institution accused of having committed a money laundering offence under Dutch law. The precise extent of this statutory use immunity is disputed: whereas some authors limit its reach to the actual reports that were made,[108] others argue that it should be extended to evidence found as a result of the report (derivative use immunity).[109] In any case, the financial institution can still be prosecuted if the transaction involves offences other than money laundering. The Public Prosecutor's Office does, however, have the power to guarantee in writing that a financial institution will not be prosecuted for carrying out a transaction, although this solution rests on the assumption that the financial institution has the time to apprise the Public Prosecutor's Office of its suspicions.

The fact that so few legislators have succeeded in providing a satisfactory solution to the risk of criminal liability for financial institutions that carry out a suspicious transaction in co-operation with the government can be explained by various factors. It may very well be that some legislators have not fully grasped the problem. But even if they did take stock of it, they may have shrunk from providing a full immunity from criminal prosecution for money laundering (as seems to have been the case in The Netherlands). There is, however, little reason for such fear as the immunity extends only to the reporting institution, not to its customers (i.e., those who try to launder their money). The risk that a bank would first knowingly lend its assistance to a money laundering operation and then report it in order to provide itself with criminal immunity is hypothetical and could occur only in a preventive anti-money laundering system with a specialty principle which limits the use of information that was disclosed to the prosecution of some offences (as is e.g. the case in Belgium[110]), thereby providing immunity to customers as well as to the institution. Only under such a legal regime, may a financial institution

---

[107] Groenhuijsen and Van der Landen, 'De financiële aanpak', 617.

[108] B. F. Keulen, 'MOT met de strafrechter', *TVVS* (1993), 285 and Velthuyse, 'Money Laundering in the Netherlands', 375.

[109] Mul, 'Vrijwaringsbepalingen', 105 and Doorenbos, *Over witwassen en voordeelsontneming*, p. 41. [110] See *infra* pp. 195–6.

decide to file a suspicious transactions report, for it knows that the information it discloses cannot be used to prosecute for the offences concerned.

Internal control procedures and training programmes for employees

FATF recommendation 19 requires financial institutions to develop programmes against money laundering, which should include: the establishment of internal policies, procedures and controls (including the designation of compliance officers and adequate screening procedures for personnel recruitment); an ongoing employee training programme; and an audit function to test the system. The first two of these points are also laid down in Article 11 of the European Money Laundering Directive.

Adequate internal control procedures and training programmes for employees are useful both for financial institutions and for law enforcement authorities. They are useful for financial institutions in that they allow them to detect more suspicious transactions and decrease the possibility of money laundering transactions passing through unnoticed. Moreover, the level of internal control procedures and compliance will often be very material when a money laundering operation does take place through a financial institution and criminal charges are laid against the financial institution. Especially under a system of corporate criminal liability where a financial institution itself – not just its personnel – can be held criminally liable, adequate internal control procedures and training programmes can be used by financial institutions to demonstrate that they did all they possibly could to prevent money laundering and that the financial institutions should not therefore be held criminally liable for the money laundering operation that took place. Compliance programmes are particularly important to avoid liability for wilful blindness.[111] Especially in the United States, compliance programmes have become very important because they are seen more as a means of avoiding criminal liability than as a means of co-operating with the government in combating money laundering.[112] Every American bank is also required to develop its own 'know-your-customer' programme.[113] On the other hand, law enforcement authorities can reap the benefits of training

---

[111] W. Adams, 'Effective Strategies for Banks in Avoiding Criminal, Civil, and Forfeiture Liability in Money Laundering Cases', *Ala.LRev.* (1993), 699–701.

[112] Adams, 'Effective Strategies', 690.

[113] See B. Zagaris, 'Proposed US Know Your Customer Rule Will Formalise Internal Control Procedures', *International Enforcement Law Reporter* (1998), 488–91.

and compliance programmes developed by financial institutions because they will receive more, and especially more relevant, information from financial institutions.[114] Lack of appropriate training can have two kinds of negative effect on the reporting of suspicious transactions: either too few or too many reports may be made.

Financial institutions as policemen?

Preventive anti-money laundering measures are characteristic of a trend by which financial institutions are cajoled into carrying out police-like functions. This privatisation of law enforcement is not novel. In many jurisdictions, for example, the victim is allowed to play a role in the prosecution of the alleged offender. In the past, the actions of private citizens in the field of law enforcement were, however, directed towards financial compensation so that the privatisation of law enforcement could therefore be described as reward-driven. Coercion-driven privatisation of law enforcement on the other hand, is of more recent vintage,[115] though not limited to the context of money laundering. The legal provisions on whistle-blowing in many legal systems bear witness of this trend.[116] Most whistle-blowing provisions, admittedly, differ from the suspicion-based reporting system imposed in the context of money laundering in that they impose a reporting obligation only in case of knowledge of certain facts as, for example, Article 5 of the so-called anti-BCCI Directive, which imposes an obligation on accountants to report irregularities.[117]

It cannot therefore be said that the obligations imposed on financial institutions for the purpose of combating money laundering are a legal innovation without precedent. But their negative economic impact should not be overrated, given the fact that they are imposed on an

---

[114] M. Levi, 'Taking Financial Services to the Cleaners', *NLJ* (1995), 26–7 and 'Regulating Money Laundering. The Death of Bank Secrecy in the UK', *Br.JCr.* (1991), 118–19.

[115] See on this distinction P. H. Bucy, 'Epilogue: The Fight Against Money Laundering: A New Jurisprudential Direction', *Ala.LRev.* (1993), 850–5.

[116] See S. M. Froomkin, 'The Reluctant Policemen', in *The Regulation of Financial and Capital Markets*, pp. 84–93; and Public Concern at Work, *Whistleblowing, Fraud and the European Union* (London: Public Concern at Work, 1996), 40p.

[117] European Parliament and Council Directive 95/26/EC of 29 June 1995 amending Directives 77/780/EEC and 89/646/EEC in the field of credit institutions, Directives 73/239/EEC and 92/49/EEC in the field of non-life insurance, Directives 79/267/EEC and 92/96/EEC in the field of life assurance, Directive 02/22/EEC in the field of investment firms and Directive 85/611/EEC in the field of undertakings for collective investment in transferable securities (Ucits), with a view to reinforcing prudential supervision, *OJ*, 18.07.1995, L168, p. 7.

international, or at least supranational, level which has ensured a minimum levelling of the playing field. The costs that are brought about by the implementation of anti-money laundering measures should moreover also be set against the many advantages that financial institutions enjoy because their position is secured by government action (e.g., through economic and financial legislation). Nevertheless, it is legitimate to ask whether these preventive anti-money laundering measures have put an excessive burden on financial institutions in that private institutions have been forced to take on tasks that should be carried out by the government. It will be argued that this is not the case and that, on the contrary, the preventive legislation clarifies and even alleviates the legal situation of financial institutions. It will be shown that this is especially the case in continental European law systems where financial institutions are generally approached on a co-operative basis.

The starting point for any analysis of the preventive legislation should be that financial institutions should not be havens through which criminals can channel their ill-gotten gains. As was shown earlier, the fight against money laundering is the logical corollary of law enforcement efforts to trace proceeds from crime. Any effective strategy against money laundering requires that third parties who launder proceeds be prosecuted and punished for money laundering. Given banking secrecy, the mere fact of creating an offence of money laundering is unlikely to have a very significant impact on the repression of money laundering, as is shown by the history of Swiss anti-money laundering regulation, which was long handicapped by the lack of a proactive reporting obligation. Without a reporting obligation, the fight against money laundering risks resulting solely in a shift of the phenomenon from financial institutions to other economic sectors or to result in some haphazard prosecutions. The co-operation of financial institutions and of economic intermediaries in general is a necessary precondition for an effective war against money laundering. In the same vein, it has been shown that the identification and record-keeping obligations, in particular the obligation to identify the beneficial owner, are very material with regard to an effective enforcement of the prohibition of money laundering.

Moreover, the lack of a reporting obligation and of preventive anti-money laundering measures is not necessarily beneficial to financial institutions. In the period during which there was no preventive anti-money laundering legislation in England and Wales, financial institutions had to take into account only a criminalisation of money laundering which allowed financial institutions to disclose their suspicions, but did not impose on them an obligation to report those suspicions. Evidence suggests that banks chose to file reports on a wide scale even then because they feared criminal liability. Even before the Money Laundering Regulations 1993 came into force, British financial institutions had already assumed responsibility for identifying customers and keeping records by agreeing to comply with a set of Guidance Notes for Banks and Building Societies, drawn up in consultation between representatives of various associations of British financial institutions, the Bank of England and representatives of British law enforcement agencies.[118]

One of the definite advantages of a legal obligation to report suspicious transactions is that legislators can provide not only a whistle-blowing protection, but also an exemption from criminal liability for carrying out suspicious transactions. It is regrettable that so few legislators have availed themselves of the possibility of providing a satisfactory statutory solution to this problem. This in part also explains the emphasis that is put, not just by legislators but also by financial institutions themselves, on compliance and training programmes as means of avoiding criminal liability. Even in the absence of a legal obligation to do so, financial institutions have sometimes obliged themselves to comply with a number of self-regulatory anti-money laundering measures (e.g. the Swiss private Code of Conduct and the British Guidance Notes), in part to uphold their reputation, but also in part to avoid criminal liability. Without detracting from the positive aspects of such self-regulatory initiatives, it is preferable that such measures be laid down by statute. This increases the legal security of financial institutions which are thereby better able to avoid criminal or civil liability. As a matter of principle, deontological rules should be protected from influencing the assessment of criminal liability to the extent that they determine whether a person is guilty of an offence. From that perspective, a statutory set of rules is to be preferred to self-regulation. Furthermore, statutory preventive legislation allows anti-money laundering measures a broader application field of the *ratione personae* than is the case with self-regulation which is by definition limited to the institutions and categories of the professions it regulates. Thus, the Swiss Money Laundering Act of 10 October 1997 extends to a much wider category of professions and institutions than did the Code of Conduct (CDB).

Whereas the jurisdictions of most common law countries have opted for a partially criminal law implementation of preventive legislation, those of continental European countries have generally opted to implement preventive measures through administrative legislation. This flows from a different attitude towards financial institutions. The use of administrative,

---

[118] *Money Laundering Guidance Notes for Banks and Building Societies*, December 1990.

rather than criminal, legislation and the concurrent use of exemptions from civil and even criminal liability reflect a co-operative attitude towards financial institutions which are seen as partners rather than adversaries in the fight against money laundering. The same co-operative stance towards economic operators can be found in other branches of the law such as European competition law, for example.[119] Although it has been argued that the reliance of continental European law systems on administrative rather than on criminal law should be seen in the context of a lack of corporate criminal liability,[120] this argument can only hold water in respect of the few continental law systems such as Belgium's that have no concept of corporate criminal liability and cannot be broadened to all continental law systems. In the United States, and also in England and Wales, a much more repressive approach is taken in which financial institutions are threatened by criminal law instruments, not just for money laundering, but also for not reporting transactions, for example. Here, financial institutions are apparently seen much more as possible offenders who might knowingly engage in money laundering than as private institutions willing to co-operate with the government. Some also attribute this underlying attitude to a criminological factor: certainly until the 1990s, many of the financial institutions in the United States were less 'professional' than those in Europe,[121] so that American law enforcement authorities, rightly or wrongly, came to view financial institutions as their adversaries and not their partners. Thus, the aggressive enforcement of anti-money laundering measures is seen as an essential part of the fight against money laundering, especially by Americans. This stance should, however, also be seen against the general background of the common law, and in particular of American law, which has a tradition of relying more on criminal law than does European continental law (e.g., in respect of competition law which in the United States – in some senses – is also brought under the aegis of criminal law). This more rigid attitude however, is somewhat softened by the fact that common law systems tend, to a much greater extent than continental European law systems, to make use of plea bargaining and other procedures to co-operate with defendants; in that sense, therefore, common law systems also allow co-operation with financial institutions.

[119] See in this respect the opinion of Advocate-General Darmon in *Orkem*, Court of Justice, judgment of 18 October 1989, *ECR* [1989], 3342, para. 155.
[120] See, e.g., De Nauw, *Les métamorphoses*, p. 138.
[121] Cf. Levi, 'Regulating Money Laundering', 112 and M. Levi, 'Money Laundering and Regulatory Policies', in *Responding to Money Laundering. International Perspectives*, ed. E. Savona (Amsterdam: Harwood Academic Publishers, 1997), p. 280.

6   The role of financial intelligence units in combating money laundering

In most jurisdictions, financial institutions report their suspicions to financial intelligence units (FIUs). The status and role of FIUs in combating money laundering will be discussed hereinafter, especially the duty of secrecy and the specialty principle to which the information they process is subject.

The creation of financial intelligence units

Combating money laundering requires the expertise of specialised law enforcement agencies. The setting up of specialised financial intelligence units designed to receive and process financial information from financial institutions (and possibly other institutions) should be seen against the background of the larger phenomenon of an increasing proliferation of specialised law enforcement agencies.

Most international instruments are silent on the nature and the role of FIUs. Only recommendation 1 of the Caribbean Drug Money Laundering Conference asks that there be competent authorities which specialise in money laundering investigations and prosecutions and related forfeiture actions. The FATF recommendations refer only to the 'competent authorities' to which financial institutions should make their reports. The European Money Laundering Directive likewise refers to 'authorities responsible for combating money laundering' and limits itself to obliging the Member States to make sure that these authorities are able to request information from the financial institutions (Article 6). The silence of the Directive on this point is attributable to the lack of competence of the European Community in criminal matters.[1] It follows that no international harmonisation has taken place with respect to the nature of these

---

[1] See also *supra* pp. 25–8.

authorities, their functioning, the conditions in which suspicious trans-actions can be suspended and the procedures to be applied for the process-ing and transmittal of information received from financial institutions.

Under the auspices of the Egmont Group, a loosely-organised group of national FIUs,[2] a general definition of a financial intelligence unit was drawn up which was later also formally inserted into the CICAD Model Regulations (Article 8bis). The following definition is intended to function as the lowest common denominator: 'A central, national agency respon-sible for receiving (and, as permitted, requesting), analysing and dissemi-nating to the competent authorities, disclosures of financial information: (i) concerning suspected proceeds from crime, or (ii) required by national legislation or regulation, in order to counter money laundering'.

The definition contains the three basic functions that can be attributed to almost any type of FIU. First, any FIU has a 'repository function', meaning that the unit is called upon to be the centralised point of infor-mation on money laundering. Not only does it receive disclosed informa-tion on financial transactions, it also yields at least a certain degree of control over what happens to this information. A second function is the 'analysis' function: in processing the information it receives, the unit nor-mally provides added value to it. It is clear that the performance of this processing function is dependent on the information sources to which the financial intelligence unit has access. Processing information may allow a financial intelligence unit to decide whether or not the information war-rants a judicial investigation. The last function for any financial intelli-gence unit is its 'clearing house' function: the unit serves as a conduit for facilitating the exchange of information on unusual or suspicious finan-cial transactions. This exchange can relate to information in many forms (individual or general) and can take place with various partners: with domestic regulatory agencies, with domestic judicial authorities, or with foreign financial intelligence units.

Many EU Member States, as well as other states, have chosen to set up a central reporting unit to receive all the reports made by financial institu-tions.

The choice of setting up a central FIU, rather than having the reports made to (local) law enforcement agencies, is usually grounded in various reasons. A first reason is the need to have specialised expertise pooled in one institution, expertise which is not present within all law enforcement agencies. Second, centralising all reports and their processing in one spe-

---

[2] On the Egmont group see *infra* pp. 269–70.

cialised unit allows the authorities to move quickly. Thus, the period during which suspicious transactions are sometimes suspended can be kept to a minimum while action to freeze assets can be taken swiftly. Third, FIUs have an economic function: on the one hand they allow a much more efficient collection and analysis of information (notably by matching this information with intelligence) while on the other, the processing and analysis task of FIUs alleviates the work of the investigating police and judicial authorities who can then concentrate their attention on files which have already been scrutinised or even documented by an FIU. In countries where there is no centralised reporting unit (e.g. Germany), this poses great difficulties.[3] Fourth, the establishment of an intermediary between financial institutions and law enforcement authorities is in many cases intended to foster a climate of trust between financial institutions and the authorities since those institutions do not have to report their suspicions directly to police or judicial authorities, but can instead report to FIUs that will first analyse the institutions' reports. This significantly decreases the risks that 'innocent' customers will be faced with police or judicial investigations. This fourth reason is also strongly underlined by the UN Model Law on Money Laundering which also advocates the establishment of FIUs, termed national money laundering control services (Articles 14 and 15). Finally, the establishment of an administrative (or police) financial intelligence unit, has also allowed some legislators to subject the use of financial data that have been disclosed by financial institutions to a stringent specialty principle.[4] It would be difficult to establish such a principle if financial institutions had to report their suspicions directly to the judicial authorities.

Financial intelligence units can be classified by their nature: they may be administrative, or run by the police or a judicial authority. In some jurisdictions such as the United Kingdom, for example, a police force is charged with responsibility for receiving and analysing reports made by financial institutions. In 1987 a section was created within the National Drug Intelligence Unit (NDIU) to deal with information concerning the illicit movements of capital derived from drug trafficking offences. This special police unit, which pools its personnel both from police forces and from Customs & Excise, and which also includes civil analysts, was turned into the National Crime Intelligence Service (NCIS) in 1992. In 1998 the NCIS was established on an independent statutory footing by the Police

---

[3] See K. Oswald, 'Money-Laundering Legislation in Germany: Selected Results from a Recent Research Project', *Eur.JCr., Cr.L & Cr.J* (1997), 201–2.   [4] See *infra*, pp. 193–9.

Act 1997. It filters all reports of suspicious transactions and then distributes them to the police force or the customs service with the appropriate territorial responsibility (usually for the region where the suspected person lives). The NCIS is thus not a fully fledged investigation service but an intelligence unit, whose remit also includes supporting the law enforcement authorities in the prevention and detection of serious crimes (Security Service Act 1996). It also advises both the government and the private sector (in particular financial institutions) on the measures that can be taken to prevent money laundering. This police-led option wholly fits into the English criminal justice system which reserves a much more important role for the police than do most continental systems.

In Switzerland financial institutions have to report their suspicions to a central police unit, the *Bureau de Communication en matière de blanchiment d'argent*, which is run by the Central Police Unit Against Organised Crime (*l'Office central de la lutte contre le crime organisé*). By law,[5] this Central Police Unit Against Organised Crime has wide investigative powers and also has extensive access to information. However, once it presumes by well-founded suspicions, that a money laundering offence has been committed or an offence of participation in organised crime is involved, it is obliged to report the case to the competent prosecuting authority.

This option of charging an existing or a newly set up police force with responsibility for receiving and analysing reports made by financial institutions has also been taken up by other countries such as Canada, Germany, Sweden, Austria and Japan, for example.[6] The major advantage of this option is undoubtedly the access it gives to the enormous information sources available to police forces: apart from extensive internal information networks, they also have access to international information exchange channels (Interpol, Europol), sometimes on a very informal basis. The main disadvantage of this approach lies in the sometimes strained relationship between financial institutions and police services that it creates. Police services are in essence law enforcement agencies whose task it is to investigate and gather evidence with a view to bringing criminal charges. Bankers know that, by reporting a suspicion to the police, the financial circumstances of their client may very well become investigated by the police, even if the institution's suspicion eventually appears to be unfounded. It is not unrealistic to assume that banks will therefore be more reluctant to report their suspicions to police forces than to special administrative financial intelligence units, or will do so

---

[5] Swiss Act of 7 October 1994: *Loi fédérale sur les Offices centraux de police criminelle de la Confédération.*   [6] Thony, 'Processing Financial Information', 266–7.

only when their suspicion is very strong. The fact that the NCIS receives a very high number of reports – in 1996 the number of reports reached 16,125 – should be attributed to the exceptionally good relationship between banks and the police,[7] and maybe also to the fact that banks fear criminal liability under s.52 DTA 1994 (failure to report a transaction suspected to be related to drug money laundering is an offence).

Other jurisdictions have opted for a judicial authority to run the FIU. Particularly in a number of continental civil law countries, there is a strong preference for attaching this function to the public prosecutor's office, because of the (quasi-)judicial status of that office and the constitutionally enshrined guarantees of independence that reside within it. Very often the public prosecutor is not only charged with prosecuting but is also in charge – at least in theory – of the investigation and hence controls the investigatory agencies. When it receives reports of suspicious transactions, the public prosecutor's office will decide which reports deserve further investigation by the police (or other investigatory agencies).

This path was chosen in Luxembourg, where all reports have to be made to the *Ministère Public*,[8] and also in Denmark, Iceland and Portugal.[9] The judicial option offers the advantage that the reports are received by an independent office which is likely to inspire more confidence with financial institutions than a police FIU, although this advantage may be illusory in countries such as Portugal, where the function of the receiving judicial authority seems to be limited to that of a postbox through which information is passed to the police. Unlike what is possible with an administrative or a police-led FIU, information transmitted to a judicial FIU can, however, not be subjected to a specialty principle so that any relevant information will almost automatically end up in the judicial information channels. This disadvantage is only partially counterbalanced by the fact that, in most jurisdictions, the prosecutor has the discretionary authority to drop cases so that a report by a financial institution does not automatically result in a criminal prosecution. Nevertheless, it is true that judicial FIUs are – together with fully independent FIUs – the only ones which have control over the full 'life-cycle' of the information that is disclosed unlike administrative FIUs which pass their information on to investigative authorities. Another weak point of the judicial option is that judicial authorities seldom have recourse to the same operational means, nor have they the same access to information channels, as police forces which

---

[7] Levi, 'Incriminating Disclosures', 216 and Thony, 'Processing Financial Information', 267.
[8] Article 40 of the Luxembourg Act of 5 April 1993. See also Kauffman, 'Le secret bancaire en droit luxembourgeois', 533.   [9] Thony, 'Processing Financial Information', 268.

compels them to co-operate with police units which will *de facto* lead the investigation. On an international level, judicial authorities do not have access to the same international channels of information exchange as do the police. In most cases they are able to co-operate only through cumbersome judicial co-operation procedures, governed by treaties and domestic legislation which may contain a number of restrictive conditions and exceptions.[10] In addition, countries often limit judicial co-operation to cases where there is a well-founded suspicion of a defined criminal offence.

Many countries, however, have opted to create an administrative FIU as an interface between financial institutions and the criminal justice system (i.e. the police and the judicial authorities). This choice is especially motivated by the fourth and the fifth of the reasons mentioned above (creation of a climate of trust and imposition of a specialty principle), as the other advantages of a centralised reporting unit can equally be assured through a judicial FIU or a police FIU. Another reason which makes administrative FIUs very suitable for dealing with reports made by financial institutions is that, on an international level, these FIUs are able – as will be further demonstrated[11] – to exchange information in a very flexible way, while at the same time guaranteeing respect for confidentiality and the specialty principles.

Whilst all administrative FIUs enjoy a considerable degree of independence, some are attached to a supervisory authority and hence are not completely independent. The American Financial Crimes Enforcement Network (FinCEN), for example, is a part of the US Department of Treasury and regards itself as a law enforcement service. It is primarily an information analysis centre. Its information gathering and processing task includes the processing of the enormous number of reports (mainly Currency Transaction Reports) that are yearly made by US banks. FinCEN operates its own database and has also links to numerous other databases, including private sector databases. Although it also has investigation powers, FinCEN was not set up to carry out money laundering investigations. It does, however, actively provide assistance to investigating agencies in the form of providing expertise, information and technical knowledge. FinCEN is also unique in that, apart from its executive powers, it also has a regulatory power: it can issue banking regulations necessary for the application of anti-money laundering regulations. In addition, it has supervisory powers in that it monitors how financial institutions apply the Banking Secrecy Act.

[10] On international judicial co-operation in criminal matters, see *infra* pp. 283–307.
[11] See *infra* pp. 258–78.

Other administrative FIUs are found in France, Italy, Spain and Australia.[12] Because of their institutional links to a supervisory authority, central bank or treasury ministry, these FIUs and their personnel are well versed in the intricacies of the financial system. Only a few administrative FIUs, however, enjoy a completely independent status guaranteed by law. Two provide an interesting model: the Belgian and the Dutch FIUs. The Belgian Financial Information Processing Unit (*Cel voor financiële informatieverwerking/Cellule pour le traitement des informations financières*) was established by the Belgian Money Laundering Act of 11 January 1993 and has its own legal personality.[13] Although it reports to the Ministers of Justice and Finance, it has a fully fledged decision-making autonomy and also enjoys a high degree of budgetary independence as it is financed by contributions from the financial institutions. It is chaired by a member of the judiciary seconded from the Public Prosecutor's Office and its board is mainly composed of magistrates (and also by personnel seconded from supervisory authorities), which gives it a quasi-judicial status. The Belgian Financial Information Processing Unit has extensive access to information, not only from financial institutions, but also from all government authorities. Although it has certain investigative powers of its own, in practice it co-operates only with one special police unit. If serious indications of money laundering are established, the Belgian Financial Information Processing Unit reports this information to the Public Prosecutor's Office with territorial jurisdiction (while at the same time forwarding a copy to the central Public Prosecutor's Office). As will be shown further on, the Belgian Financial Information Processing Unit transmits information with regard to only a limited number of predicate offences.[14]

In The Netherlands, the Unusual Transactions Reporting Unit (*Meldpunt Ongebruikelijke Transacties, MOT*) was called into being by the Dutch legislator in 1993 (Disclosure of Unusual Transactions Act of 16 December 1993) with a view to receiving, registering, processing and analysing the disclosed information. Although technically a part of the Ministry of Justice, it enjoys a high degree of autonomy. The reporting unit checks whether the information can potentially be useful for investigating or preventing crime. For this purpose, it can ask for additional information. If the Unusual Transactions Reporting Unit finds that, after analysis, an unusual transaction is indeed suspicious, it will hand over the case to the local police (while at the same time forwarding a copy of its findings to

---

[12] Thony, 'Processing Financial Information', 270 and *Second Commission Report*, p. 14.
[13] On the Belgian Financial Information Processing Unit, see Stessens, *De nationale en internationale bestrijding van het witwassen*, pp. 225-8.   [14] See *infra* pp. 195-6.

the central Public Prosecutor's Office).[15] The prosecutor in turn of course collaborates with police units, in particular FINPOL.

Both the Belgian and the Dutch FIUs enjoy a high degree of independence and are clearly set up in a way that inspires a high degree of trust in financial institutions which do not have to report their suspicions immediately to a judicial or police authority. The main difference between the two FIUs lies in the fact that the information transmitted to the Belgian Financial Information Processing Unit is subjected to a very stringent specialty principle. Before discussing this specialty principle, we will turn to the secrecy duty to which most FIUs are subjected.

Secrecy duty of financial intelligence units

The secrecy obligation imposed on FIUs is very important in several respects. First, it enables FIUs to exercise their function as an intermediary between financial institutions and law enforcement agencies. A special climate of trust between the reporting financial institutions and the reporting unit can be fostered only if the financial institutions are assured that the information which they disclose will not be automatically passed on to other government agencies. Banking secrecy could effectively be emptied of its meaning if this information, which it previously covered, could be passed to third parties (including other government agencies) in this way. Financial institutions and government authorities are in no way natural partners and a special legal arrangement for ensuring secrecy is therefore necessary. The necessity for such arrangements is generally inversely proportionate to the prevailing climate of trust.[16]

Second, the secrecy duty is also intended to protect the personnel of reporting institutions. It is essential that disclosure of the identity of those who have filed a suspicious transactions report and the identity of the compliance officers is avoided at all costs, for this would expose them to a serious risk of retaliation.

Third, in as far as the information disclosed is considered to be protected by the right to privacy,[17] the secrecy duty of course also protects the

---

[15] On the Unusual Transactions Reporting Unit in general see: Meldpunt Ongebruikelijke Transacties, *Verslag '94* (The Hague: Ministerie van Justitie, 1994), p. 11 *et seq.*; Peeman, 'Het MOT-meldpunt', pp. 95–102 and A. C. H. Smid, 'Ervaringen vanuit politie en justitie met het meldpunt MOT', in *Maatregelen tegen witwassen in het koninkrijk*, ed. G. J. M. Corstens, E. J. Joubert, S. C. J. J. Kortmann, (Arnhem: Gouda Quint, 1995), pp. 185–200.

[16] See Conseil de l'Europe, *Secret et transparence: l'individu, l'entreprise et l'administration. Actes du colloque du dix-septième Colloque de droit européen* (Strasbourg: 1988, Editions du Conseil de l'Europe), pp. 43–4.   [17] On this bone of contention see, *supra* pp. 144–5.

right to privacy of the individuals to whom the information disclosed relates.

Finally, the imposition of a secrecy duty also allows the information to be subjected to a specialty principle. While the secrecy duty and the specialty principle are often confused, they are not in fact synonymous. The specialty principle concerns the use of information, whereas the duty to secrecy concerns the disclosure of information. A specialty principle which restricts the purposes for which certain types of information can be used is of course only enforceable when the reporting unit which receives the reports is also bound by a duty to secrecy.

If the reports are made directly to a judicial (Luxembourg) or police-led (Switzerland, the United Kingdom) FIU, there is normally no need for a specific secrecy duty as these law enforcement agencies are mostly already subjected to a general secrecy duty. In those jurisdictions where an administrative FIU has been set up to deal with reports made by financial institutions, these reporting units are explicitly subject to a duty to secrecy. We will limit our analysis to two examples already discussed: Belgium and the Netherlands.

Article 17 of the Belgian Money Laundering Act of 11 January 1993 subjects the Belgian Financial Information Processing Unit to a stringent secrecy duty: any personnel member who discloses professionally received information in violation of his duty of professional secrecy commits a criminal offence. The reporting unit is even exempted from the duty to report any offence to the Public Prosecutor, as any government agency is normally obliged to do under Belgian law. There are, however, a number of exceptions to the duty of professional secrecy. A first exception relates to international administrative assistance: the Belgian Financial Information Processing Unit is allowed to disclose information to its foreign counterparts.[18] A second exception relates to so-called vertical assistance to a supranational authority (as opposed to horizontal assistance between national authorities), namely the fraud-fighting unit of the European Commission (OLAF). Lastly, the Belgian FIU is also allowed and sometimes even obliged to disclose information to the authorities charged with supervision of financial institutions on a prudential basis, thus ensuring a minimum of feedback to the supervision authorities.

All reports made to the Dutch Unusual Transactions Reporting Unit are also protected by the secrecy duty which applies to the police database held by the Unusual Transactions Reporting Unit, access to which is

---

[18] On this co-operation, see *infra* pp. 262–78.

strictly limited to its personnel. The Dutch system, however, allows for greater possibilities in the use of the information as the Unusual Transactions Reporting Unit, apart from transmitting transactions that are deemed suspicious, also discloses information to investigating officers if the information can be useful to the investigation or prosecution of crimes (other than money laundering). Unlike in Belgium, where the FIU is only allowed to disclose information in the case of suspicions of money laundering, a reasonably flexible flow of intelligence takes place in The Netherlands from the FIU to law enforcement agencies outside the context of money laundering.[19] It is not surprising therefore that the very stringent secrecy obligations imposed upon the Belgian FIU – which in principle can only disclose information to the Public Prosecutor's Office in case of serious indications of money laundering – have given rise to practical difficulties in the co-operation with police forces, for the FIU only issues requests for information but is legally prohibited from disclosing any information to the police services.

The secrecy obligations to which FIUs have been subjected in Belgium, but also in other countries, have often given rise to a more general problem, namely the impossibility of providing feedback to financial institutions. This has sometimes resulted in friction with financial institutions, or their representative organisations, which receive very little or even no feedback at all on the outcome of the reports that they have made. This is very regrettable since feedback can be highly beneficial to the co-operation between financial institutions and the authorities responsible for money laundering in that they give financial institutions information on the result of their actions. Other advantages of feedback are that it allows reporting institutions to better educate their staffs as to which transactions are suspicious and in particular provides compliance officers of reporting institutions with information and results that make it possible for them to filter out reports made by staff that are not significant. It also allows a reporting institution to take appropriate action in specific cases, for example by closing an account. In general, it can lead to a more efficient and effective use of procedures by reporting institutions and the FIU.[20]

---

[19] For more detail see Doorenbos, 'Money Laundering', 773–4; Kuus, 'De Wet melding ongebruikelijke transacties en de privacy van klanten van banken', Computerrecht (1994), 165–6 and R. Lamp, 'Financiële informatie de grens over', DD (1999), 42–3.

[20] See Providing Feedback to Reporting Financial Institutions and Other Persons. Best Practice Guidelines (Annex to FATF-IX), para. 6 and, in general: Byrne, 'The Bank Secrecy Act', 813–14; F. Grosjean, 'Le blanchiment de l'argent: l'esprit des loi à l'épreuve du quotidien', Journ. Proc. (1996, No.302), 23 and Terlouw and Aron, Twee jaar MOT, p. 48.

Feedback can take place on a case-to-case basis, but also in a more general way (e.g. by providing financial institutions with general information on the *modi operandi* used by money launderers). Of these, the former is especially problematic, not only because it may violate privacy laws, but also because it may expose a current investigation. Therefore, a reporting institution often receives only an acknowledgment of receipt of the report. However, there is no principle objection against a limited feedback on the result after an investigation or prosecution has been closed.[21]

The specialty principle

Concept of specialty principle

By obliging financial institutions to co-operate in the fight against money laundering, an enormous pool of financial intelligence is tapped. Mostly this intelligence ends up in databases controlled by FIUs. One of the moot points of law surrounding the fight against money laundering is whether this information should also be made available for other purposes than fighting money laundering. Even if one restricts the use of information to the fight against money laundering, the question may arise as to the scope of the money laundering offence (and in particular its predicate offences), especially in those countries where the definition of money laundering in the (administrative) preventive legislation differs from the incrimination of money laundering (e.g. in Belgium).[22] Apart from money laundering prosecutions, the information supplied by financial institutions can of course also prove to be very useful in other prosecutions, notably those regarding the predicate offence. Perhaps even more important, however, is the question as to whether information supplied by financial institutions in the context of the prevention of money laundering can also be used for non-judicial, notably fiscal, purposes. Financial institutions – as well as the many other institutions and categories of profession that are used for money laundering – are not only favoured for the purpose of laundering the proceeds of crime, but are also excellent conduits for committing fiscal fraud and stashing away or even laundering 'black money' (i.e. income on which no taxes have been paid). In some countries (e.g.

---

[21] See *Providing Feedback to Reporting Financial Institutions and Other Persons. Best Practice Guidelines* (Annex to FATF-IX), paras.27–31.

[22] On the differences between the administrative and criminal definition of money laundering, see *supra* pp. 141–2 and 164.

Belgium[23] and Luxembourg[24]) fiscal administrations normally have no, or only very limited, access to information held by financial institutions. If fiscal administrations are allowed to have access to the information databases held by FIUs, fiscal administrations can circumvent the legal impediments to accessing bank files and the legislation on the prevention of money laundering may turn out to be a very powerful device for fighting fiscal fraud. Only in a very limited number of countries – Australia being a prominent example[25] – do anti-money laundering measures have an increased revenue from tax collection as one of their official goals.

This may change in the future, however, if and when one of the conclusions of the meeting of G7 Finance Ministers in May 1998 is implemented at the national level. This conclusion holds that 'money laundering authorities [i.e. financial intelligence units] should be permitted, to the greatest extent possible, to pass information to their tax authorities to support the investigation of tax related crimes, and such information should be communicated to other jurisdictions in ways which would allow its use by their tax authorities'.[26] Although this conclusion is designed to trigger a broad exchange of information between the FIUs and the tax authorities, its wording limits the use of this information to the investigation of tax related crimes, thereby excluding purely administrative use by tax authorities, that is, for the purpose of imposing or collecting taxes.

Even in its limited wording, this conclusion runs foul of the European Money Laundering Directive according to which information supplied by the financial institutions to the FIUs can be used only in connection with the combating of money laundering. Without stating it in so many words, Article 6 of the Directive has thus imposed a specialty principle.

A specialty principle defines and at the same time limits the purposes for which information can be used, often the same as those for which the information was gathered. The use of a number of intrusive and far-reaching investigative and/or information gathering techniques is sometimes legally restricted by a number of conditions. Certain techniques can only be used with a view to a limited number of purposes (e.g. the investigation of specified offences). It is sometimes argued that to allow the use of information or evidence gathered in consequence of these techniques

---

[23] Article 318 of the Belgian Code of Income Tax. See Stessens, *De nationale en internationale bestrijding van het witwassen*, p. 234.

[24] Règlement grand-ducal of 24 March 1989.   [25] FATF-VIII, p. 9.

[26] Conclusions of G7 Finance Ministers, London, 9 May 1998, point 16, rendered at FATF-X, p. 33.

for purposes other than those for which the technique could be used in the first place would empty the restrictions imposed by law of their meaning. This argument is not automatically valid, however, for it confuses restriction of the use of certain investigative techniques with the restrictions of the use of information gathered through these techniques. Nevertheless, the specialty principle may be justified on other grounds. According to some authors, the specialty principle was founded in extradition law (where it limits the offences for which an extradited person can be prosecuted).[27] In the context of the prevention of the misuse of financial institutions for the purpose of money laundering, the specialty principle has both a domestic and an international aspect. The former aspect will now be discussed while the latter will be dealt with in Part 4.[28]

Comparative overview of the (absence of) restrictions on the use of information supplied by financial institutions

As an exception to the specialty principle to which it in principle subjects any information supplied by financial institutions, the Directive allows Member States to provide that this information may nevertheless be used for other purposes. It is clear from what has already been said regarding the reporting duty in England and Wales, that the information collected as a result of the reporting duties (and liberties) contained in the Drug Trafficking Act 1994 and the Criminal Justice Act 1993 can be used in connection with any offence and not just (drug) money laundering.[29] However, information provided by NCIS may not be used for fiscal purposes.

At least one EU Member State has introduced a very stringent specialty principle in its domestic preventive legislation, again – as with the Directive – without stating it in so many words. According to Article 16 of the Belgian Money Laundering Act of 11 January 1993, the Belgian Financial Information Processing Unit can transmit information to the Public Prosecutor's Office only if there are serious indications of money laundering as defined by Article 3(2) of the Act. The administrative statute operates a more restricted definition of money laundering than the criminalisation of money laundering in that it only applies to a limited

---

[27] See e.g. P. Bernasconi, 'Droit pénal européen et droit de l'entraide suisse face au droit pénal fiscal européen', in *Aktuelle Probleme der Kriminalitätsbekämpfung, Festschrift zum 50jährigen bestehen der Schweizerischen Kriminalistischen Gesellschaft*, ed. J. Gauthier, D. F. Marty and N. Schmid (Bern: Verlag Stämpfli, 1992), pp. 480–1. See *in extenso infra* p. 342.
[28] See *infra* pp. 341–7.   [29] See *supra* pp. 164–6.

number of predicate offences. If the Belgian Financial Information Processing Unit suspects or knows that the money laundering operation involves proceeds from predicate offences excluded from the definition of Article 3(2) of the Money Laundering Act, it is not legally entitled to transmit the information to the Public Prosecutor. It should, however, be emphasised that the specialty principle which is imposed on the Belgian Financial Information Processing Unit in this way, is not binding on the Public Prosecutor, or on any other judicial or police authority for that matter. Once information has been lawfully transmitted to the Public Prosecutor's Office, it can use the information to any end, including the prosecution of offences falling outside the scope of Article 3(2) of the Money Laundering Act.

When information has been transmitted to the Public Prosecutor in violation of Articles 16 juncto 3(2) of the Belgian Money Laundering Act of 11 January 1993, however, it will not be possible to use it in court. Should this information be introduced as evidence against a defendant, he will be able to argue successfully for the exclusion of this evidence, although this type of situation does not seem to have occurred so far. This information needs only to be excluded, however, if it is clear that, at the time of the transmittal, the Belgian Financial Information Processing Unit was not aware of serious indications of money laundering as defined by Article 3(2) of the Act. In addition, only the information that was unlawfully transmitted must be excluded, not the derivative evidence gathered in consequence of this information.[30]

Other EU Member States, like The Netherlands and Luxembourg, have introduced only a very limited specialty principle.

In The Netherlands, intelligence supplied by financial institutions can also be used for other purposes than money laundering investigations. Even the Tax Department can, under certain circumstances, have access to the police database held by the Dutch Unusual Transactions Reporting Unit, albeit only for the purpose of instituting criminal proceedings.[31] There is a limited specialty principle in the sense that information cannot be used for purely administrative (e.g. fiscal) purposes.

The Luxembourg legislator originally wanted to subject the use of information supplied by financial institutions to a specialty principle, but the Luxembourg *Conseil d'Etat* objected to this plan on the ground that it

---

[30] On the specialty principle and its consequences under Belgian law of evidence see Stessens, *De nationale en internationale bestrijding van het witwassen*, pp. 235–9.

[31] Nederlands Instituut voor het Bank- en Effectenbedrijf, *Handboek bestrijding money laundering* (Amsterdam), 9.3.-13–14.

would be unacceptable to limit the general power of the Public Prosecutor to investigate and prosecute any offence. Given the judicial nature of the Luxembourg FIU it is indeed almost impossible to keep information supplied by financial institutions outside the 'normal' channels of the criminal justice system. The text of Article 41(5) of the Luxembourg Act of 5 April 1993 still stipulates that information supplied by financial institutions can be used only for the purposes for which the law allows the disclosure of confidential information, without derogating from the principles of criminal law. Thus phrased, this specialty principle prohibits the use of the information only for other purposes than criminal purposes, notably for fiscal purposes. In respect of the reporting duties imposed on notaries, casinos and auditors, it is stipulated that information forwarded to authorities other than judicial authorities, will be used only for the purpose of combating money laundering.[32]

The question of whether and to what extent information supplied by financial information in the context of combating money laundering should be subject to a specialty principle is not an easy one to answer. As has already been indicated, variants of the specialty principle which has its origins in the law of extradition can also be found in other branches of the law. In order to assess the necessity for a specialty principle, it is useful to draw a comparison with another area of Community law where a specialty principle operates in a very analogous way, namely competition law. Under Regulation 17/62[33] economic operators are obliged to inform the European Commission of facts that might be indicative of the existence of cartels, or can do so on their own initiative. This information can be communicated by the Commission to national authorities in order to apprise them of the Commission's action and to allow them to aid the Commission in its investigations. As far as information requested by the Commission on the basis of Article 11 of the Regulation is concerned, it is explicitly stipulated (Article 20(1)) that this information can be used only for the purposes of the Commission's investigation. In *Direccion General de Defensa de la Competencia v. Asociacion Espanola de Banca Privada and others* the Court of Justice of the European Community reached the same conclusion in respect of other information in respect of which the Regulation contains no such provision and held that national authorities hence may not use this information in national cartel procedures. The Court did accept, however, that after communication of this information by the

---

[32] See Articles 16 and 17 of the Luxembourg Money Laundering Act of 11 August 1998.
[33] EEC Council Regulation No. 17: First Regulation implementing Articles 85 and 86 of the Treaty, *OJ*, 21.02.1962, L13, p. 0204.

Commission to national authorities, those authorities may start an investigation though they may not use the information as evidence.[34]

Leaving aside the different legal background, an at least partially common rationale of the specialty principle can be recognised in both instances. The specialty principle is intended to foster and sustain a climate of mutual trust between the reporting economic operators and the reporting units. In his conclusion before the Court of Justice in the above-mentioned case, Advocate-General Jacobs explicitly referred to mutual trust as a requirement for the proper functioning of European competition law and as the prime motive underpinning the specialty principle. This climate of trust is particularly important in view of the fact that the authorities rely not only on information supplied on request, but also on proactive information supplies. Many enforcement systems which rely on and are indeed – at least partially – dependent on information supplied by the economic operators they regulate, seem to recognise some form of specialty principle in order to guarantee swift co-operation from the economic operators.[35]

The fact that – precisely in view of this requirement of trust – the specialty principle is justified, does not answer the question of how widely or narrowly the principle should be defined. As has been shown, domestic practices vary greatly in this respect. The only common denominator seems to be that national tax departments do not have access to information supplied by financial institutions for purely fiscal purposes, although the information may be used in some countries for the purpose of the investigation and prosecution of tax related crimes, as is now also required by the conclusion of the G7 meeting of the Ministers of Finance in May 1998. Suspicion-based reports filed by financial institutions will often not contain indications only of the laundering of proceeds from criminal offences, but also of fiscal fraud. It has already been argued that financial institutions are often not in a position to pinpoint the origin of funds involved in suspicious transactions and will often in fact report transactions which involve proceeds from activities falling outside the scope of the preventive legislation. By imposing a specialty principle, legislators have excluded the possibility that anti-money laundering regulation could be used as a so-called Trojan horse by which fiscal authorities may tap information sources to which they would not otherwise have

---

[34] Court of Justice, judgment of July 16, 1992, *ECR* [1992] 4820. See J. Shaw, 'The use of information in competition proceedings', *ELR* (1993), 154–9.

[35] See R. Guldenmund, C. Harding and A. Sherlock, 'The European Community and Criminal Law', in *Criminal Justice in Europe: A Comparative Study*, C. Harding, P. Fennel, N. Jörg and B. Swart (Oxford: Clarendon, 1995), p. 124.

access. With reference to what was propounded earlier on with respect to the need to ensure the co-operation of financial institutions in the fight against money laundering, it is submitted that this was a wise choice. An unlimited use of the information provided by financial institutions for purely fiscal purposes may impair the co-operation of these institutions, which was apparently also acknowledged by the G7 Ministers of Finance, who stated in their conclusion that the information 'should be used in a way which does not undermine the effectiveness of anti-money laundering systems'.[36]

The differences in form of the specialty principle seem to spring from non-legal factors, such as the existing relationship and degree of trust between the economic operators (in the context of money laundering: financial institutions) and government authorities. Again – as with the duty of secrecy imposed on FIUs – it seems that the less the trust, the more stringent the specialty principle.

Even if one compares jurisdictions that have opted for an administrative FIU, such as those of Belgium and The Netherlands, the differences are striking. Whereas Belgium has a very stringent specialty principle, this is almost completely absent in the Netherlands so that one could argue that financial institutions are much more protected in Belgium than in the Netherlands. It is certainly true that the filtering role of the Belgian FIU is much greater than its Dutch counterpart which has even been called purely 'cosmetic'.[37] This is, however, in part offset by the fact that Dutch legislation provides for a use immunity which excludes the use of information supplied by financial information as evidence against that institution.[38] Additionally, in other countries where there is no, or a much less stringent, specialty principle there seems to be some type of protection for financial institutions. In England and Wales, for example, the legislation has provided explicit exemptions from criminal liability for money laundering for any person, including financial institutions, who reports his suspicions in a timely fashion. All this should be set against the much wider background of the co-operative stance of the government towards financial institutions in Europe, which are – to a certain extent – considered partners and not adversaries in the fight against money laundering. It has already been argued that this co-operative approach is especially embedded in administrative preventive legislation. The creation of administrative FIUs and a concomitant specialty principle are an essential component of this co-operative approach.

---

[36] See FATF-X, p. 33.   [37] Franken en Van der Landen, 'Het zwarte gat van de MOT', 63.
[38] See *supra* p. 177.

7 The role of the supervisory authorities in combating money laundering

Whereas prudential supervision originally was limited to quantitative, economic aspects, it has gradually extended to cover qualitative aspects, such as ensuring that financial institutions, their management and their shareholders, are fit and proper. Various international instruments have emphasised the role financial and credit institutions can play in the fight against money laundering. The Statement of Principles issued by the Basle Committee in 1988 had already warned that supervisors could not remain indifferent to the use made of banks by criminals. The FATF underlined the importance of supervisory authorities in the implementation of money laundering measures and asked for prudential supervision to be extended to cover non-bank financial institutions. The close nexus between the definition of the application field of the *ratione personae* of preventive legislation and prudential supervision has already been under-scored at the beginning of Part 2[1] but it is clear that the effective func-tioning of a suspicion-based reporting system is – to a much greater extent than a threshold-based reporting system – dependent on thorough bank supervision.

Whereas supervisory authorities have a wide range of options to hand with which to fight money laundering (as exemplified by Article 17 of the CICAD Model Regulations), their main tasks in combating money launder-ing are twofold. First, they can inform the authorities responsible for com-bating money laundering (i.e. the FIUs) of any money laundering operations they may detect in the course of their supervision activities. In addition, they have mostly administrative powers to punish financial institutions that have failed to observe anti-money laundering rules.

---

[1] See *supra* pp. 137–9.

The duty of supervisory authorities to report facts of money laundering

In its recommendations 26 and 27 the FATF asks that supervisory authorities co-operate with judicial and police authorities. The European Money
Laundering Directive is more specific in this respect in that it asks that 'if,
in the course of inspections carried out in credit or financial institutions
by competent authorities [ie. the supervisory authorities], or in any other
way, those authorities discover facts that could constitute evidence of
money laundering, they inform the authorities responsible for combating
money laundering' (Article 10). This reporting duty for supervisory
authorities can be a very interesting source of information, especially in
instances where the financial institution fails to provide (enough) information on suspicious transactions because, for example, its personnel is
corrupt or because – as may still be the case in some jurisdictions – it is
legally prohibited from disclosing such information to the government on
its own initiative. The importance of prudential supervision in this
respect is demonstrated by the fact that the investigation into malprac-
tices, including widespread money laundering at the Bank of Credit and
Commerce International (BCCI) initially started in reaction to a criminal
referral by the US Federal Reserve.[2]

It is to be stressed that this reporting duty – which has been implemented in most EU Member States – is triggered only if the supervisory
authorities become aware of facts that could constitute evidence of
money laundering, and not – as is the case with the reporting duty of
financial institutions – by mere suspicion. To require supervisory authorities to report mere suspicion of money laundering would constitute a
severe inroad into the essential climate of trust between financial institutions and their supervisory authorities. Moreover, supervisory authorities
are well placed to distinguish mere criminal transactions from money
laundering practices. Nevertheless, the reporting duty laid down in
Article 10 of the Directive is not revolutionary, but is in fact only part of a
larger Community legal framework for banking supervision; the First
Banking Directive (as amended by the Second Banking Directive), for
example, also contains an exception to the secrecy duty of supervisory
authorities in cases falling under the criminal law.

---

[2] A. Haynes, 'Money Laundering and Changes in International Banking Regulation', *JIBL*
(1993), 460 and Adams, 'Effective Strategies', 675–8.

The administrative sanctioning powers of supervisory authorities in case of non-observance of the legislation to prevent money laundering

The FATF recommendations do not contain any specific references to the sanctioning powers of supervisory authorities, but only broadly refer to the role of supervisory authorities in ensuring that financial institutions have adequate programmes in place to guard against money laundering. But in its report on the Caribbean Drug Money Laundering Conference (1990), the FATF urged countries to apply appropriate administrative, civil or criminal sanctions to financial institutions, but only in respect of one feature of the preventive anti-money laundering system, namely for those institutions which fail to maintain records for the required retention period. Article 14 of the CICAD Model Regulations designates the wilful failure of financial institutions to comply with the prevention of anti-laundering measures as a criminal offence.

Article 14 of the Directive contains the broad requirement that each Member State shall 'determine the penalties to be applied for infringement of the measures adopted pursuant to this Directive'. Reference to the comparative table of penalties for violations of the Member States' preventive legislation, provided in annex to the *First Commission's Report on the Implementation of the Money Laundering Directive*,[3] will show that very severe sanctions can be imposed on financial institutions for such violations. In most Member States such infringements are punished with administrative sanctions,[4] which are often imposed by the supervisory authorities and may go up to more than 1 million ECU (see e.g. Article 22 of the Belgian Money Laundering Act of 11 January 1993).[5] This is especially the case in those jurisdictions that have no concept of corporate criminal liability. In other countries, infringements are sanctioned through the criminal law (Denmark, Ireland, Italy, The Netherlands and the United Kingdom). In principle, only the supervisory authority of the financial institution's home state is legally empowered to impose the most severe sanction, namely the withdrawal of its licence.[6]

This is also the case under US legislation, which provides an excellent example of the distinction between criminal and administrative sanc-

---

[3] pp. 32–4.

[4] *First Commission's Report on the Implementation of the Money Laundering Directive*, pp. 15 and 32–4.   [5] Stessens, *De nationale en internationale bestrijding van het witwassen*, pp. 245–7.

[6] The extraterritorial features of the sanctioning powers in respect of money laundering, both criminal and administrative, will be discussed in Part 3.

tions. The Annunzio-Wylie Anti-Money Laundering Act of 1992[7] gave US bank regulators powerful weapons to enforce anti-money laundering rules. After a financial institution has been convicted of money laundering, bank regulators (the Federal Reserve, or any other primary regulator such as the Office of the Comptroller of the Currency) hold a hearing, which is intended to determine whether the offending bank should lose its licence, deposit insurance or whether a court-appointed conservator should be installed to run the institution.[8] Such a hearing is mandatory for any conviction on money laundering charges, but can also be held after a conviction for violating the Banking Secrecy Act (e.g. for not filing the CTRs).

In the United States the 'administrative' or 'regulatory' sanctioning powers of the supervisory authorities are thus clearly separated from the penal assessment carried out by the courts. This is possible, however, only because US legislation has extensively criminalised non-observance of money laundering legislation, by allowing prosecutions for violations of reporting and recording-keeping duties (Bank Secrecy Act, for example). In Europe, on the other hand, most legislators have confined themselves to criminalising money laundering and have left the punishment of violations of preventive anti-money laundering rules to administrative (supervisory) authorities.

This is liable to cause problems from a human rights point of view, particularly in respect of the *non bis in idem* rule. Many of the sanctions imposed by supervisory authorities, though administrative in name, are in fact penal sanctions, the imposition of which amounts to a criminal charge in the sense of Article 6 of the European Convention on Human Rights. The European Court of Human Rights has elaborated an autonomous concept of 'criminal charge' which allows it to bring the imposition of a number of administrative sanctions under the umbrella of Article 6, notwithstanding the fact that the domestic legislator may have omitted to do so. There is no scope within this book to give an exhaustive overview of the Court's case law in this respect,[9] but one of the criteria used by the Court to determine whether a criminal charge is at stake is the nature and

---

[7] Title XV of the Housing and Community Development Act, signed on 28 October 1992.

[8] S. J. Galli and J. L. Wexton, 'Anti-Money Laundering Initiatives And Compliance – US Perspective', in *Money Laundering Control*, ed. B. Rider and M. Ashe (Dublin: Round Hall Sweet & Maxwell, 1996), pp. 365 and 371–2.

[9] See in particular the following cases: *Engel v. the Netherlands* (judgment of 8 June 1976, *Publ.ECHR*, Series A, No.22), *Öztürk v. Germany* (judgment of 21 February 1984, *Publ.ECHR*, Series A, No.73) and *Lutz v. Germany* (judgment of 25 August 1987, *Publ.ECHR*, Series A, No.123). See *supra* p. 65.

gravity of the sanction imposed. In view of the very severe sanctions that can be imposed for such violations by financial institutions, the imposition of these sanctions, irrespective of their domestic denomination, amounts to a criminal charge in the sense of Article 6 which implies that, as a minimum requirement, the defendant should have the right to lodge an appeal against his administrative sanction with an independent judicial instance.[10] A possibly more far-reaching consequence is the *non bis in idem* effect which consequently attaches to these sanctions. The drastic consequences of the prohibition of double sanctioning, as laid down in Article 4 of the Seventh Additional Protocol to the European Convention on Human Rights,[11] were made clear in the case of *Gradinger v. Austria* before the European Court of Human Rights. In this case an administrative penalty had been inflicted after the defendant had been acquitted in a criminal court for partially the same facts, namely drunken driving.[12] The European Court of Human Rights, after having ascertained that the imposition of the administrative penalty did indeed amount to a 'criminal charge', found that this was violative of the *non bis in idem* clause of the Fourth Protocol, given the fact that a criminal court had already acquitted Mr Gradinger for at least partially the same facts, notwithstanding the differences in nature and purpose between the administrative and criminal sanctioning. This very stringent view of the Court may bode problems for the co-existence of administrative and criminal sanctioning systems in general and in particular with respect to anti-money laundering regimes as non-observance of anti-money laundering rules may also be taken into account in assessing a financial institution's criminal liability for money laundering. If a financial institution has already been administratively sanctioned for non-observance of preventive legislation, the *non bis in idem* principle, as construed by the European Court of Human Rights, may preclude that it be criminally punished for money laundering or *vice versa*, as at least partially the same facts will very often be taken into account in both procedures. Admittedly, this problem may also arise if non-observance of preventive legislation is criminally sanctioned, but in that case the same facts may be charged under the heading of various criminal offences at the same time, or in the course of different procedures. In *Oliveira v. Switzerland* the European Court of Human Rights held that Article 4 of Protocol No. 7 does not preclude separate

---

[10] European Court of Human Rights, judgment of 24 February 1994, *Bendenoun, Publ.ECHR,* Series A, No.284, para. 46.   [11] *ETS,* No.117.

[12] European Court of Human Rights, judgment of 23 October 1995, *Publ. ECHR,* Series A, No.328.

offences, even if they are part of a single criminal act, being tried by different courts.[13]

In practice, however, the *non bis in idem* problem may often not arise at all, for at least two reasons. First, domestic courts may take a less stringent view of the *non bis in idem* principle than the European Court of Human Rights. Second, administrative sanctions will often be applied to financial institutions whereas criminal charges may be laid against individuals operating within financial institutions for the simple reason that corporations cannot be criminally prosecuted under some domestic law systems.

---

[13] European Court of Human Rights, judgment of 30 July 1998, *Reports of Judgments and Decisions*, 1998.

PART III · JURISDICTION OVER MONEY LAUNDERING

8   Various types of jurisdictional problem in the fight against money laundering

The international nature of the money laundering phenomenon requires an international response. International harmonisation efforts in respect of confiscation and of the criminalisation of money laundering were set out in Part 1. In addition to this harmonising of substantive criminal law, an effective fight against money laundering also requires that jurisdictional problems that are likely to arise in an international money laundering context be solved. Often it will be unclear which state has jurisdiction to investigate money laundering offences and to prosecute and try alleged money launderers or to seize and order the confiscation of (alleged) proceeds from crime.

To provide a clear answer to these questions, it is necessary to distinguish between various forms of jurisdiction. The term jurisdiction has more than one meaning. In a domestic context it usually denotes the power, the competence of a (judicial) authority to do certain legal acts. In an international context it refers to 'a State's right under international law to regulate conduct in matters not exclusively of domestic concern'.[1] As this regulation can take place through various types of measures, state jurisdiction has also been described as 'the class of actions by which various individuals or bodies exercise power in the name of the State'.[2] Essentially, one should distinguish between legislative, judicial and executive measures and, consequently, between prescriptive jurisdiction (also known as jurisdiction to prescribe), adjudicative jurisdiction (otherwise known as jurisdiction to adjudicate) and enforcement jurisdiction (also known as jurisdiction to enforce).

Jurisdiction to prescribe concerns the right of a state to establish the

---

[1] F. A. Mann, 'The International Doctrine of Jurisdiction in International Law', in *Rec. Cours* (1964), I, 9–15.

[2] J. E. S. Fawcett, 'General Course on Public International Law', in *Rec.Cours* (1971), I, 373.

content and scope of domestic rules with respect to a certain situation. Jurisdiction to adjudicate concerns the right of courts of a state to give a judgment concerning facts with an extraneous element. It is sometimes also defined as the right to apply established jurisdiction in a particular litigation or proceedings.[3] Problems concerning jurisdiction to adjudicate were often neglected by practitioners of international law who viewed it as an ancillary feature of prescriptive jurisdiction, namely the right under international law to subject persons to the jurisdiction of their judicial or government authorities.[4] Moreover, the need to distinguish questions of jurisdiction to adjudicate from questions of jurisdiction to prescribe is especially present in the field of civil law and, to a much lesser extent, in the context of criminal law. The fact that the legislator of State A has jurisdiction to prescribe a number of criminal law rules in respect of a certain situation, almost invariably means that the courts of State A have jurisdiction to apply those rules in that situation. Whereas questions of prescriptive jurisdiction arise for legislators when determining the scope of the rules they issue, jurisdiction to adjudicate starts from the viewpoint of the courts. In practice the two types of question almost coincide. Thus, the question of whether a state has jurisdiction to provide for the confiscation of criminal proceeds and to incriminate money laundering acts corresponds to the question as to whether the courts of that state can issue confiscation orders and try alleged money laundering acts.

Gardocki is therefore right in pointing out that criminal conflict laws determine both the jurisdiction of a state's courts and the spatial application field of that state's criminal laws: *cuius lex criminalis eius iurisdictio* or *cuius iurisdictio eius lex criminalis*.[5] When a state has jurisdiction with respect to certain facts, its criminal law is applicable to those facts. Unlike in private international law, in international criminal law a judge can apply only the *lex fori*. This unilateral application of domestic criminal law flows from the deeply ingrained national character of criminal law: courts

---

[3] C. L. Blakesley, 'Extraterritorial Jurisdiction', in *International Criminal Law*, Volume II, Procedure, ed. M. C. Bassiouni (New York: Transnational Publishers, Inc., 1986), p. 1; European Committee on Crime Problems, *Extraterritorial Criminal Jurisdiction* (Strasbourg, 1990), p. 18.

[4] F. J. Knecht, 'Extraterritorial Jurisdiction and the Federal Money Laundering Offense', *Stanford J. Int'l L.* (1986), 405; F. A. Mann, 'The Doctrine of International Jurisdiction Revisited After Twenty Years', in *Rec. Cours* (1984), III, 67.

[5] L. Gardocki, 'The Principle of Universality', in *Double Criminality. Studies in International Criminal Law*, ed. A. Agell, R. Boman and N. Jareborg (Uppsala: Iustus Förlag, 1989), p. 57. See also European Committee on Crime Problems, *Extraterritorial Criminal Jurisdiction*, 20.

apply criminal law rules only of the state whose authority they represent.[6]

Related to this is the fact that the territoriality principle is the predominant jurisdiction basis for prescriptive jurisdiction.[7] Territorial jurisdiction stems from and is indeed considered a part of state sovereignty, although it cannot be equated with it.[8] This also gives the territoriality doctrine a universal and reciprocal character: all states are sovereign and can therefore be expected to respect each other's sovereignty and jurisdiction.[9] As sovereignty is still primarily linked to territory, a state's first claim of jurisdiction therefore relates to all conduct on its national territory.

Nevertheless, the territoriality principle should not be seen as the sole basis for jurisdiction. Already in 1927, the exclusive character of the territoriality principle as a basis of jurisdiction was repudiated by the Permanent Court of International Justice in the Lotus case.[10]

A strict application of the territoriality principle is moreover strained by the increasing internationalisation of the contemporary society which sometimes makes it difficult to ascertain the *locus delicti*. Greater mobility, heightened transport and communication possibilities and the paramount role of corporations – which, other than physical persons, can be present in different countries at the same time – provide an important part of the explanation for this evolution.

The internationalisation of the money laundering phenomenon which can be seen as part of this trend has already been highlighted in Part 1; here the jurisdictional consequences of this internationalisation will be scrutinised. Technological evolutions, in particular in the field of international finance, have resulted in a hitherto unknown facility to move money internationally: 'provided that the client feels safe from fraud or expropriation, money will move where the regulation is lightest'.[11]

---

[6] See C. Van den Wyngaert, 'Double Criminality as a Requirement to Jurisdiction', in *Double Criminality. Studies in International Criminal Law*, ed. A. Agell, R. Boman and N. Jareborg (Uppsala: Iustus Förlag, 1989), p. 45.

[7] European Committee on Crime Problems, *Extraterritorial Criminal Jurisdiction*, 20–1.

[8] I. Brownlie, *Principles of Public International Law* (Oxford: Clarendon, 1990), p. 298; Fawcett, 'General Course on Public International Law', 371–80; R. Jennings and A. Watts, *Oppenheim's International Law* (London: Longman, 1992), vol. I, p. 457; C. Lombois, *Droit pénal international*, 1971, p. 250; Mann, 'The Doctrine of International Jurisdiction', 16–17; I. Seidl-Hohenfeldern, *Völkerrecht* (Cologne: Carl Heymanns Verlag, 1975), pp. 236–7.

[9] Mann, 'The Doctrine of International Jurisdiction Revisited', 20; European Committee on Crime Problems, *Extraterritorial Criminal Jurisdiction*, 17–18; L. Sarkar, 'The Proper Law of Crime in International Law', *ICLQ* (1962), 447 and P.-M. Dupuy, *Droit international publique* (Paris: Dalloz, 1995), pp. 23, 78.

[10] Permanent Court of International Justice, *Lotus SS, France v. Turkey, Publ. CPIJ* (1927), Series A., No.10., 19.   [11] Levi, 'Pecunia non olet', 223.

Money laundering operations will therefore often stretch over the territory of different countries. This internationalisation is moreover sometimes deliberately sought out by money launderers in order to frustrate investigations, thereby 'misusing' the effects of State sovereignty for their own good.[12] It will be demonstrated hereafter that this primarily technological evolution has, however, resulted not so much in a greater use of extraterritorial jurisdiction bases, but in an expansion of the concept of territorial jurisdiction. It will thus be shown that, notwithstanding the considerable state freedom in this respect, the territoriality principle still remains the main basis for prescriptive and adjudicative jurisdiction.

An analysis of how money laundering acts have been localised will show that in the vast majority of cases, states can claim jurisdiction on the basis of the territoriality principle. This analysis will lead to the conclusion that the requirement that the predicate offence is also punishable in the state where it took place should not be seen as a requirement for prescriptive jurisdiction, but as an element of the offence of money laundering in an international context.[13]

The third type of jurisdiction is enforcement, or prerogative, jurisdiction which concerns the right under international law to enforce a rule in a concrete situation. It can be defined as the jurisdiction that enables the issuing of enforcement orders or prescriptive rules emanating from the judiciary or the legislature in a situation involving an extraneous element. It is important to emphasise that, when a state has prescriptive jurisdiction with respect to a certain situation, this does not automatically mean that it also has enforcement jurisdiction. When in a given situation a state has jurisdiction to order the confiscation of proceeds derived from an offence, it does not necessarily also have jurisdiction to enforce that confiscation as the proceeds may, for example, be located in another state's territory. Conversely, a state can never have enforcement jurisdiction if it does not have prescriptive jurisdiction regarding the facts at hand: prescriptive jurisdiction is a necessary but not sufficient requirement for enforcement jurisdiction.[14]

---

[12] See J.-B. Ackermann, *Geldwäscherei – Money Laundering. Eine vergleichende Darstellung des Rechts und der Erscheinungsformen in den USA und der Schweiz* (Zurich: Schultess Polygraphischer Verlag AG, 1992), p. 326 and also Law Commission, *Jurisdiction Over Offences of Fraud and Dishonesty*, Report No.180 (London: HMSO, 1989), § 1.2.

[13] See *infra* pp. 226–31.

[14] On the relation between prescriptive and enforcement jurisdiction see Mann, 'The Doctrine of International Jurisdiction Revisited', 34–8 and Mann, 'The Doctrine of International Jurisdiction', 13–14 and § 7 of the *Restatement (Second)* (1962), pp. 21–3.

In the *Lotus* case before the Permanent Court of International Justice[15] it became apparent that the leeway of states to regulate affairs in a situation involving an extraneous element goes much further in respect of prescriptive jurisdiction than in respect of enforcement jurisdiction. Whereas the Court took a very liberal position in respect of the former type of jurisdiction, it was much more stringent in respect of the latter. According to the Court, a state cannot enforce its rules in another state's territory without its permission:

... the first and foremost important restriction imposed by international law upon a State is that – failing the existence of a permissive rule to the contrary – it may not exercise its power in any form in the territory of another State. In this sense jurisdiction is certainly territorial; it cannot be exercised by a State outside its territory except by virtue of a permissive rule derived from international custom or from a convention.[16]

This dictum still adequately represents the current state of international law in respect of enforcement jurisdiction. This does of course not mean that this principle is always respected in state practice. Thus, the law enforcement authorities of some states have, in breach of international law, mounted investigations on the territory of foreign states – directly, or indirectly, through informants – in order to obtain information covered by banking secrecy. In the context of banking secrecy, the American Internal Revenue Service (IRS) in particular has a long 'tradition' of extra-territorial investigations aimed at piercing foreign banking secrecy by, for example, using informants.[17] The introduction of evidence thus collected has been approved of by the American Supreme Court,[18] although American law enforcement agencies may in practice prefer not to use it lest they 'burn' their informant.[19] In 1998 it was made public that, in what was described as the biggest money laundering investigation ever undertaken, American Drug Enforcement Agency (DEA) undercover agents had infiltrated a number of banks in Mexico (allegedly) engaged in large-scale laundering of drug money.[20]

---

[15] Permanent Court of International Justice, *Lotus SS, France v. Turkey*, Publ. CPIJ (1927) Series A., No.10.

[16] Permanent Court of International Justice, *Lotus SS, France v. Turkey*, Publ. CPIJ (1927), Series A., No.10, 18–19.

[17] See in general Mann, 'The Doctrine of Jurisdiction', pp. 139–41. See also the Swiss Mail Watch Programme, which was designed to copy all letters departing from Swiss banks: Stultz, 'Swiss Bank Secrecy', 99.   [18] *United States v. Payner*, 447 US 727, 734–7 (1980).

[19] Nadelmann, 'Unlaundering Dirty Money', 44–5.

[20] See 'Yankee Drug-Busters Head South', *The Economist*, 23 May 1998, 51.

The problem of extraterritorial enforcement of investigative or provisional measures in respect of banking secrecy, both through unilateral and co-operative mechanisms, will be further discussed in Part 4. The rest of this Part is mainly concerned with prescriptive and adjudicative jurisdiction in respect of money laundering offences, both territorial jurisdiction (Chapter 9) and extraterritorial (Chapter 10).

Territorial jurisdiction in respect of money
        laundering offences

Distinction with jurisdiction in respect of the predicate offence

This chapter deals with the question of when a state has jurisdiction over
a money laundering offence. As this problem should sharply be distinguished from the question of when a state has jurisdiction to order confiscation of the proceeds from a predicate offence, attention will be paid
to the latter question first. The question of whether a state has jurisdiction
to order confiscation of the proceeds from a predicate offence coincides
with the question of whether the state has jurisdiction over that offence,
as confiscation is in principle a criminal sanction which is imposed for
that offence. This will be the case when the offence takes place on the
state's territory or when the state concerned can claim extra-territorial
jurisdiction (e.g., on the basis of the nationality principle, when the
offence is committed by one of its nationals abroad). As far as prescriptive
jurisdiction is concerned, it does not in principle matter whether or not
the proceeds can be found in the territory of the state that claims jurisdiction.[1]

In most cases, the state where the proceeds from an offence are located
will lack jurisdiction over the offence which took place abroad and will,
as a consequence, be unable to order the confiscation of those proceeds.
This has been made clear in, for example, the case law of the Swiss
Supreme Court regarding (alleged) proceeds from foreign corruption
offences which have been deposited in Swiss bank accounts.[2] Criminal

---

[1] The question of prescriptive jurisdiction should, however, sharply be distinguished from
the one of enforcement jurisdiction, which will be dealt with in Part 4, at pp. 381–5.
[2] Swiss Supreme Court, judgment of 8 November 1993, *La semaine judiciaire* (1994), 110. See
also M. Harari, 'Corruption à l'étranger: quel sort réserver aux fonds saisis en Suisse',
RPS, 3–4 and the criticism of this case law by Schmid, 'Das neue Einziehungsrecht', pp.
325, 332.

sanctions, as well as procedures in respect of a criminal offence, can in principle only be ordered if a state has jurisdiction in respect of that offence, that is when the offence can be prosecuted in that state. The one exception to this is when the state is requested to take measures (e.g. seizure) by the state which has jurisdiction over the offence. Although it is true that the seizure and/or confiscation of the instrumentalities of an offence can be ordered even if the state concerned has no jurisdiction, this is only because these measures are deemed to be precautionary (safety), rather than punitive, measures. Article 8 of the CICAD Model Regulations runs counter to his rule by demanding that competent authorities be given the power to freeze and forfeit proceeds or instrumentalities located in its territory and which are derived from offences committed against the laws of other countries, though subject to the condition of double crimi-nality. As a rule, the authorities of a given state will be able to order seizure or confiscation of (alleged) proceeds from an offence only if the state has (extra)territorial jurisdiction over the offence in question. Extraterritorial jurisdiction automatically results in a drastic expansion of the sentencing powers.

Thus, while Swiss authorities lacked adjudicative jurisdiction to order the seizure of bribes held in Swiss bank accounts and related to foreign corruption offences, they were entitled to seize proceeds from drug offences that had been committed outside Switzerland, because Swiss law provides universal jurisdiction in respect of drug offences (Articles 19 and 24 of the Swiss Drug Offences Act).[3] This type of jurisdiction gives a state jurisdiction over offences – mostly very severe offences that shock the 'universal' conscience – regardless of where and by whom they are com-mitted. In the same vein, universal jurisdiction also exists under English law in respect of drug offences (see the definition of drug trafficking in s.1 DTA 1994).[4] American law enables civil forfeiture of proceeds from a number of designated offences against a foreign nation, namely drug offences in respect of which it is required that they be punishable both under American law and according to the *lex loci delicti* with at least one year imprisonment (18 USC § 981(a)(1)(B)).[5]

It is against this legal backdrop that the money laundering offence assumes a very important, though often not acknowledged, jurisdictional

---

[3] Swiss Supreme Court, judgment of 23 January 1996, *La semaine judiciaire* (1996), 357.

[4] See A. Harding, 'Treaty-Making in the Field of International Co-operation', in *Principles and Procedures For A Transnational Criminal Law*, ed. A. Eser and O. Lagodny (Freiburg: Max-Planck Institut, 1992), p. 238.

[5] On the background of this provision, see Harmon, 'United States Money Laundering Laws', 22 and Plombeck, 'Confidentiality and Disclosure', 81–2, footnote 94.

function. By criminalising money laundering, a state establishes a legal basis which allows its judicial authorities to take action in respect of the proceeds from a foreign offence. The money laundering offence gives jurisdiction to a state in whose territory the money laundering acts took place and hence allows it to take action in respect of proceeds that are located in its territory but which are derived from an offence which took place abroad, outside its territorial jurisdiction. Even if a state lacks prescriptive jurisdiction in respect of the predicate offence, the criminalisation of money laundering nevertheless allows the judicial authorities of that state to order the seizure or confiscation of the proceeds located in its territory which would otherwise be excluded.

This jurisdictional function is especially important in those countries that – because of their limited geographical contours – are mostly confronted with proceeds from a foreign offence that as such have no connecting point with that state.[6]

In order to ascertain whether a state has jurisdiction over a money laundering offence, two sub-questions need to be answered. The first concerns whether the state has jurisdiction over the money laundering acts. As jurisdiction will almost invariably be claimed on the basis of the territoriality principle, this question will be studied under the exclusive heading of territorial jurisdiction, while extra-territorial jurisdiction bases will be dealt with at a later stage.[7] Second, the question arises whether a state claiming jurisdiction over money laundering conduct can or should also pose requirements regarding the double criminality of the predicate offence.

Localising money laundering acts

A money laundering offence that takes place purely on the territory of one state poses no problem of localisation. As most money laundering operations at one point or another involve transnational transactions, the question is likely to arise as to what degree a money laundering operation may have involved a violation of the legal order of a given state before the courts of that state can apply their criminal law and, more specifically, their domestic anti-money laundering law as to the facts at hand. This question of localisation can be solved in accordance with one of the two prevailing theories: either the ubiquity theory or the effects doctrine.

---

[6] See, e.g., in respect of Switzerland: Bernasconi, 'Modèle internationale', 171; and in general: McClean, *International Judicial Assistance* (Oxford: Clarendon Press, 1992), p. 216.

[7] See *infra* pp. 231–48.

Ubiquity theory

Under this theory, an offence is deemed to have taken place on the territory of a state as soon as a constituent or essential element of this offence has taken place on that territory.[8] This theory, widely adhered to in continental law systems, has now also been adopted in English law, though not formally. Traditionally, English courts claimed jurisdiction on the basis of the so-called 'last act' rule, according to which English courts had jurisdiction if the last relevant act took place in the UK. This often resulted in an unsatisfactory situation in which English courts had to decline to accept jurisdiction. In order to solve this problem, the Criminal Justice Act (CJA) 1993 introduced a new rule under which English courts can try an offence as soon as a relevant act, that is 'any act or omission or other event (including any result of one or more acts or omissions) proof of which is required of the offence' (s.2(1) CJA 1993), has taken place on the territory of the United Kingdom.

Even the American concept of the subjective territoriality principle, which gives a state jurisdiction over offences which were initiated on its territory but which were completed or consummated on the territory of another state,[9] can sometimes be categorised under the heading of the ubiquity doctrine, in that the preparatory acts concerned constitute constituent elements of the crime. A variant of this concept can be found in the section of English law concerning conspiracy: under English law, a conspiracy committed in the UK, even if set up with a view to the perpetration of an offence abroad, is always punishable under English law.[10]

The doctrine of ubiquity is generally considered to be more stringent than the doctrine of effects which allows a state to claim jurisdiction on the basis of a mere effect of an offence on its territory, whereas under the doctrine of ubiquity, a state may only claim jurisdiction if the effect constituted a constituent element of the offence. Money laundering, however, is almost invariably considered to be a conduct offence and not a result offence. The result of money laundering is therefore not considered to be a constituent element of the crime. Moreover, the offence of money

---

[8] Permanent Court of International Justice, *Lotus SS, France v. Turkey, Publ. CPIJ* (1927), Series A., No.10., p. 23; Harvard Research in International Law, 'Jurisdiction with Respect to Crime', *Am.J.Int'l Law, Supplement* (1935), 495; Mann, 'The Doctrine of International Jurisdiction', 85.

[9] Harvard Research in International Law, 'Jurisdiction with Respect to Crime', 484–7; C. Blakesley and O. Lagodny, 'Finding Harmony', 16–17.

[10] *Samchai Liangsiriprasert v. United States* [1990] 2 All ER 866; *R. v. Samson and others* [1991] 2 All ER 145. See also ss.5, 6 Criminal Justice Act 1993.

laundering is often categorised as an 'offence creating a danger' (*abstraktes Gefährdungsdelikt*).[11] This is a category of offence in respect of which it is conceptually illogical to claim jurisdiction on the basis of an effect or of a violation of the protected interest, as the conduct in question is criminalised regardless of whether the protected interests at stake are violated or not.[12] Nevertheless, it will be argued that, even under the ubiquity doctrine, states will often be able to claim jurisdiction over money laundering offences.

Given the broad scope of most money laundering incriminations,[13] many acts can give rise to criminal liability. Whenever one transaction takes place on the territory of a state, even if the broader money laundering scheme is located abroad, that state will be able to try the money laundering offence. The combination of the very wide character of most money laundering incriminations and the ubiquity doctrine is therefore likely to result in a multiplication of jurisdictional claims over the same money laundering scheme. This is the result of a so-called atomization of criminal behaviour (*Handlungsatomisierung*),[14] through which every single act out of a money laundering scheme can in itself give rise to criminal liability.

Often, every single money laundering act will be considered a new money laundering offence, which as consequence can repeat itself numerous times. Whereas in some jurisdictions, courts tend to amalgamate all money laundering offences constituting one money laundering scheme and consider them as one 'collective' offence (e.g. in Belgium: *délit collectif*[15]), in other jurisdictions courts will allow separate indictments of every money laundering act (e.g. the United States).[16] In both instances, courts will have jurisdiction, whenever one money laundering act took place on their territory (see e.g. Switzerland[17]). In Belgium, the legislator even amended the money laundering incrimination through the Act of 7 April 1995 with the deliberate purpose to give courts the power to punish

---

[11] For an explanation of this point, in respect of Swiss law see: Graber, *Geldwäscherei*, pp. 131–6.

[12] H. D. Wolswijk, *Locus delicti en rechtsmacht* (Deventer: Gouda Quint, 1998), pp. 172–5.

[13] See *supra* pp. 113–16.   [14] Ackermann, *Geldwäscherei – Money Laundering*, p. 304.

[15] See, e.g., Belgian Court of Cassation, judgment of 31 October 1995, *TRV* (1996), 635 with annotations by F. Hellemans.

[16] This is possible under *Blockburger v. United States*, 284 US 299 (1932). See specifically in the context of money laundering: *United States v. Kramer*, 73 F.3d 1067, 1072 (11th Cir.1996), cited by Paust and others, *International Criminal Law*, p. 1336; Chang and Herscowitz, 'Money Laundering', 513–14; M. G. Pickholz, *Securities Crimes* (New York: CBC, 1997), § 5.03[6].

[17] Ackermann, *Geldwäscherei – Money Laundering*, pp. 304–5 and Graber, *Geldwäscherei*, p. 166.

money laundering transactions that were carried out in Belgium, but initiated abroad because the funds were accepted abroad. Even before this legislative amendment, however, Belgian courts had accepted that they had jurisdiction over money laundering offences initiated abroad.[18]

In the United States jurisdiction over money laundering acts is even more stretched by the broad concept of 'conduct[ing] a financial transaction' (18 U.S.C. § 1956(a)(1)). Not only are financial transactions broadly defined (§ 1956(c)(2)), but also 'conduct' is defined very extensively as 'initiating, concluding, or participating in initiating, or concluding a transaction' (§ 1956(c)(3)). This broad concept functions as a compensation to the narrow jurisdiction under American law over acts of complicity, which can be punished only if the offence itself took place on American territory. By separately incriminating acts that normally would be punishable under American law only as acts of complicity to a broader offence, the American legislator ensured jurisdiction over these acts even if the rest of the offence was carried out abroad. The 'atomization' of the money laundering offence thus clearly serves a jurisdictional purpose.

Apart from the jurisdictional effects of the 'atomization' of the money laundering offence, some applications of the ubiquity theory may also result in far-reaching jurisdiction claims. It may, for example, suffice that one accomplice has committed a money laundering act on the territory of a state in order for that state to be able to claim jurisdiction over all other acts of money laundering committed abroad, not only by that person but also by all other persons involved in the same offence. Sometimes courts have even accepted extraterritorial jurisdiction over other offences merely connected with the offence over which they had territorial jurisdiction, invoking unity of procedure because of the close connection (l'indivisibilité) among the offences. Thus, the French Supreme Court even accepted jurisdiction over the offence of handling stolen goods on the ground that the offence was connected with a swindling offence which had taken place in France.[19] Although possibly justified by the facts of the case, in general this ground for jurisdiction is too far-reaching as it would allow a state on whose territory the predicate offence took place, to claim jurisdiction over any subsequent money laundering transaction carried out abroad by invoking the 'indivisible connection' between the money laundering transaction and the predicate offence.

---

[18] See Stessens, De nationale en internationale bestrijding van het witwassen, p. 355.
[19] French Court of Cassation, judgment of 9 December 1933, Gazette du Palais (1934), 79. See, however, the criticism by J. Larguier, 'Chronique de jurisprudence. Droit pénal général', RSC (1983), 464–5.

Effects doctrine

Under this doctrine, an effect of offences on a national territory suffices to grant that state jurisdiction over that offence, even if the effect is not a constituent element of the offence. This doctrine, which was especially developed in the context of American competition law, is widely accepted in the United States, but has been the subject of fierce criticism in Europe.[20] In American criminal law, the doctrine has even received acceptance outside the boundaries of competition law. Under the objective territoriality principle, American courts can claim jurisdiction over offences that took place abroad, but which have (and are intended to have) detrimental results on American territory: 'acts done outside a jurisdiction but intended to produce and producing detrimental effects within it, justify a State in punishing the cause of the harm as if he had been present at the effect, if the State should succeed in getting him into its power'.[21]

This doctrine has been statutorily entrenched in respect of the money laundering offence in 18 U.S.C. § 1956(f), which states that: 'There is extra-territorial jurisdiction over the conduct prohibited by this section if (1) the conduct is by a United States citizen or, in the case of a non-United States citizen, the conduct occurs in part in the United States; and (2) the transaction or series of related transactions involves funds or monetary instruments of a value exceeding US Dollar 10,000'.

The first prong of this provision, namely the extraterritorial application of the American money laundering incrimination to acts done by U.S. citizens abroad, falls under the heading of the nationality principle and is as such in keeping with international law. The second prong is liable to be problematic, however, given the broad interpretation that is sometimes given to the expression 'if . . . in the case of a non-United States citizen, the conduct occurs in part in the United States'. The American Departments of Justice and Treasury have indicated that a person who authorizes an American bank to transfer monies to an account held at a foreign

[20] It is impossible even to attempt to give an overview of the doctrine in this respect. See R. Jennings, 'Extraterritorial Jurisdiction and the United States Antitrust Laws', *British Yearbook of International Law* (1959), pp. 146–74; Mann, 'The Doctrine of International Jurisdiction', 86–9 and 95 *et seq.* and M. R. Mok and R. A. A. Duk, 'Toepassing van het Nederlandse strafrecht op buiten Nederland begane delicten', in *Handelingen der Nederlandse Juristenvereniging*, I (Zwolle: Tjeenk-Willink, 1980), 45–86. See also H. G. Maier, 'Extraterritorial Jurisdiction at the Crossroads: an Intersection between Public and Private International Law', *AJIL* (1982), 296–8

[21] *Strassheim v. Dailey*, 221 US 280 (1911). See also Harvard Research in International Law, 'Jurisdiction with Respect to Crime', 488 e.v.; Blakesley and Lagodny, 'Finding Harmony', 19 and Blakesley, 'Extraterritorial Jurisdiction', 17–18.

bank, would fall under the American money laundering incrimination. Likewise, a person in the United States, who telephonically authorizes a foreign bank to transfer money to another foreign bank, can be held guilty of money laundering in the United States.[22] Even when criminally derived funds have only 'passed through' an American bank in the course of a transaction between non-American banks, the United States may claim jurisdiction; in the BCCI case former BCCI employees were convicted by a U.S. court for money laundering activities conducted from outside the United States, but with funds within the United States.[23]

Furthermore, United States courts have also developed the Restatement on Foreign Relations Third's suggestion to expand the objective territoriality theory to include offences intended to have an effect on the U.S. territory (§ 402(d)).[24] American courts have claimed jurisdiction over extraterritorial attempts and conspiracies even in cases when they were intended, but eventually did not have an effect within the United States. The use of the objective territoriality principle to claim jurisdiction over extraterritorial thwarted conspiracies is very debatable given the fact that there is no effect on American territory.[25] On occasions, courts have claimed jurisdiction on the basis of the subjective territoriality doctrine when a constituent part of the crime occurred on American territory. Thus a Cayman Island bank that participated in conspiracy to launder money for American drug dealers was convicted of criminal conspiracy. The court, basing itself on the subjective territoriality principle, did not hesitate to affirm its jurisdiction over a criminal conspiracy that took place both in the United States and a foreign country, even if no overt act was performed within the United States.[26]

Also in England, conspiracies intended to perpetrate an offence on English territory, are liable to punishment by English courts,[27] even if no overt acts were carried out in consequence of the conspiracy in English territory.[28]

[22] Staff of the Departments of Justice and Treasury, *Analysis of Proposed Money Laundering and Related Crimes Act of 1985*, 9, cited by Knecht, 'Extraterritorial Jurisdiction', 396.
[23] *United States v. Awan*, 966 F.2d 1415 (11th Cir. 1992).
[24] *US v. De Weese*, 532 F.2d 1267 (5th Cir. 1986), *cert.denied*, 451 US 902 (1987).
[25] For a recent overview, see R. M. Reynolds, J. Sicilian and P. S. Wellman, 'The Extraterritorial Application of the US Antitrust Laws to Criminal Conspiracies' (1998) *ECLR*, 151–5. See also Wolswijk, *Locus delicti en rechtsmacht*, pp. 50–6 and, critical: Blakesley, 'Extraterritorial Jurisdiction', pp. 33–52.
[26] *United States v. Inco Bank 1 Trust Corp.*, 845 F.2d 919 (11th Cir. 1988). See Blakesley and Lagodny, 'Finding Harmony', 17.   [27] *DPP v. Doot* [1973] 1 All ER 940.
[28] *Samchai Liangsiriprasert v. United States*, [1990] 2 All ER 866. See also *Harv. Int'l LJ*, 1992, 223–232.

Although a number of continental states decline to claim jurisdiction over extraterritorial attempts that, though intended to have an effect within the territory, did not result in an effect on that state's territory,[29] other continental states do.[30] As a rule, legal systems that adhere to the objectivist theory of attempt (i.e. punish attempt because the intent has revealed itself through behaviour) are unable to claim jurisdiction over attempts that did not result in any conduct on their territory, as an attempt is punishable only if supported by outward behaviour. Only in case of a subjectivist theory of attempt (for which the mere intent to commit an offence suffices), could the state on whose territory the offence was planned to be carried out claim jurisdiction.[31]

The question whether these extraterritorial claims for jurisdiction are justified from an international law point of view, is a fiercely debated one. The question whether a state has jurisdiction over an offence, that is whether it can claim such a right under international law, depends on whether there is a sufficiently close connection with the offence. According to the Restatement (Third) of The Foreign Relations Law of the United States (1986) criminal jurisdiction is indeed allowed in those cases.[32] According to other authors, however, an effect on a state's territory can only justify a jurisdictional claim in case of direct or primary effects.[33] Support for this restrictive reasoning is often sought in the following statement in the Lotus case: 'offences, the authors of which at the moment of commission, are in the territory of another State, are nevertheless to be regarded as having been committed in the national territory, if one of the constituent elements of the offence, and more especially its effects have taken place there'.[34] Wolswijk has, however, astutely pointed out that it is difficult to conceive how the requirement that an effect is a constituent element of an offence could be a limiting factor to the right to claim jurisdiction under international law, as every state is free to decide what elements will constitute a constituent element.[35] Neither does it, from an international law point of view, come into play whether

---

[29] See, e.g., Belgium, France and the Netherlands: Wolswijk, *Locus delicti*, pp. 274–6.

[30] See, e.g., Austria, Denmark, Germany and Switzerland: Wolswijk, *Locus delicti*, p. 276.

[31] Wolswijk, *Locus delicti*, pp. 279–81. See also G. A. M. Strijards, *Internationaal strafrecht, strafmachtsrecht. Algemeen deel* (Arnhem: Gouda Quint, 1984), pp. 236–64.

[32] American Law Institute (ALI), *Restatement (Third) of the Law, The Foreign Relations Law of the United States, Volume I* (St. Paul, Minn.: ALI Publishers, 1986), p. 239. See also American Law Institute, *Cumulative Supplement 1992–93*, p. 181.

[33] Jennings, 'Extraterritorial Jurisdiction', p. 160 and Mann, 'The Doctrine of International Jurisdiction', pp. 86–7.

[34] Permanent Court of International Justice, *Lotus SS, France v. Turkey*, Publ. CPIJ (1927), Series A., No.10., p. 23.   [35] Wolswijk, *Locus delicti*, p. 45.

the effect was intended or not.[36] Nevertheless, it seems dubious to accept that any effect on a national territory would justify a jurisdictional claim by that state.

Even if there are no international law objections to jurisdiction claims over crimes that had or were only intended to have an effect on the territory of the state concerned,[37] it is submitted that such claims can be accepted only if they pay due consideration to the requirements flowing from the legality principle. A state should be allowed to claim criminal jurisdiction over conduct that takes place outside its territory only if it is foreseeable for the perpetrator that he risks criminal liability in that state. The requirement that it should be foreseeable and accessible which conduct is incriminated follows from the legality principle, as laid down in Article 7 of the European Convention on Human Rights and in Article 15 of the International Covenant on Civil and Political Rights.[38] This requirement not only holds in a domestic context, but also in an international one.

Paragraph 18 of the Restatement (Second) of The Foreign Relations Law of the United States (1962) (which has been superseded by the Restatement (Third) of The Foreign Relations Law of the United States (1986)) states:

> A state has jurisdiction to prescribe a rule of law attaching legal consequences to conduct that occurs outside its territory and causes an effect within its territory, if either
> (a) the conduct and its effect are generally recognized as constituent elements of a crime or tort under the law of states that have reasonably developed legal systems, or
> (b) (i) the conduct and its effect are constituent elements of activity to which the rule applies; (ii) the effect within the territory is substantial; (iii) it occurs as a direct and foreseeable result of the conduct outside the territory; and (iv) the rule is not inconsistent with the principles of justice generally recognized by states that have reasonably developed legal systems.

This provision distinguishes, for the purposes of claiming jurisdiction, between generally recognised crimes (one could refer to *mala per se*) and

---

[36] Permanent Court of International Justice, *Lotus SS, France v. Turkey, Publ. CPIJ* (1927), Series A., No.10., p. 24. See Jennings, 'Extraterritorial Jurisdiction', pp. 160–1. See, however, the dissenting opinion of Judge Loder in the Lotus case, p. 37, which supports the opposite view (see also Harvard Research in International Law, 'Jurisdiction with Respect to Crime', 501).

[37] Wolswijk, *Locus delicti*, p. 282 and Harvard Research in International Law, 'Jurisdiction with Respect to Crime', 501.

[38] See, e.g., European Court of Human Rights, *SW v. United Kingdom*, judgment of 22 November 1995, *Publ.ECHR*, Series A, No.335–B, para. 35 and *CR v. United Kingdom*, judgment of 22 November 1995, *Publ.ECHR*, Series A, No.335–C, para. 33.

crimes that are not generally recognised (*mala quia prohibita*). In both cases the Restatement (Second) requires that both the conduct and the effect be constituent elements of the offence, but in respect of offences that are not generally recognised, the Restatement imposes a number of additional requirements.

In 1986 Knecht opined that the money laundering offence does not fall within paragraph 18, as money laundering was not a generally recognised crime.[39] This opinion should be reviewed, however, at least as far as drug money laundering is concerned. Given the ratification rate of the Vienna Convention,[40] drug money laundering can be considered a generally recognised crime, although this does not go in respect of money laundering of proceeds from other predicate offences.

This does not automatically mean, however, that states will be able to claim jurisdiction over money laundering offences which in main were carried out in another state but had an effect on the territory of that state. As was already said, the consequence of a money laundering operation is in principle not a constituent element of the crime and the fact that the offence is usually considered an offence creating a danger makes it moreover conceptually difficult to localize on the territory of the state where a consequence of the offence took place.[41]

Jurisdiction conflicts and non bis in idem

Both the ubiquity doctrine and the doctrine of effects can give rise to jurisdiction conflicts in that neither of these theories purports to grant exclusive jurisdiction to a state. This is even exacerbated by the so-called 'atomization' of the money laundering offence, which gives every state on whose territory a money laundering act took place, jurisdiction over the entire money laundering offence. At the present state of international (human rights) law, there is no general international *non bis in idem* principle that is applicable on the transnational level.[42] The only protection for a person who has already been (or is being) prosecuted and/or tried abroad for the same offence, can therefore come from international

---

[39] Knecht, 'Extraterritorial Jurisdiction', 408.
[40] By the end of 1999, 154 states had signed the Vienna Convention.   [41] See *supra* p. 219.
[42] See, however, the resolution B.4. by the Fourth Section of the International Association of Penal Law, drafted at the Preparatory Colloquium in Utrecht, 13–17 May 1998 (1999), 908 and approved at the XVIth International Congress on Penal Law in Budapest, 5–11 September 1999: *RIDP*. See also C. Van den Wyngaert, 'The Transformations of International Criminal Law as a Response to the Challenge of Organised Crime', *RIDP* (1998), 169–78.

co-operation treaties, which in most cases only provide a piecemeal protection in this respect.[43]

Double criminality in respect of the predicate offence

If State A has jurisdiction over money laundering acts that concern the
proceeds from an activity in State B, most legal systems require that these
predicate activities are both incriminated in State A and State B. In the following it will be argued that this condition of double criminality regarding the predicate offence is not a precondition to jurisdiction, but is
rather a logical consequence from the legality principle.

Condition of double criminality of the predicate offence

The Vienna Convention remains silent on this subject, which is only
logical in view of the fact that all parties are obliged under the convention
to incriminate the predicate offence, namely drug trafficking. The question of double criminality of the predicate offence only arises once the
application field *ratione materiae* of the money laundering offence is broadened to other predicate offences. Article 6(2) of the Money Laundering
Convention, which defines the money laundering offence, explicitly
states that 'it shall not matter whether the predicate offence was subject
to the criminal jurisdiction of the Party'. In respect of the prevention of
money laundering an analogous provision is contained in Article 1 of the
European Money Laundering Directive.

It follows from Article 6(2) of the Money Laundering Convention that
money laundering is a criminal offence irrespective of the place where the
predicate offence took place. This is only logical as money laundering is a
separate offence from the predicate offence and can consequently also
independently give rise to jurisdiction claims. The 'jurisdictional' function of the money laundering offence was already underlined earlier.[44]
Obviously, the money laundering offence can fulfil its 'jurisdictional'
function only if it is not required that the state concerned should also
have jurisdiction over the predicate offence.

Although it clearly follows from Article 6(2) of the Money Laundering
Convention that it does not matter where the predicate offence took
place, this does not rule out any requirements that domestic law may pose

---

[43] See, in general, C. Van den Wyngaert and G. Stessens, 'International Non Bis in Idem:
Resolving Some of the Unanswered Questions', *ICLQ* (1999), 788–90.
[44] See *supra*, pp. 216–17.

regarding the double criminality of the predicate offence, that is the requirement that the predicate activities which generated the proceeds constitute an offence under the law of both the state where they were carried out and under the law of the state where the proceeds were eventually laundered. This requirement should not be seen as a condition to jurisdiction, but as a legal consequence from the legality principle. An example will clarify this. If there would be no such requirement, State A could punish the laundering of proceeds from trafficking in endangered species carried out in State B, even if trafficking in endangered species is not a criminal offence in State B. It would obviously be unacceptable for State A to consider activities carried out in State B as criminal, if they are perfectly legitimate in State B. This would in effect amount to a heinous form of *Hineinregieren*: State A would clearly step out of its boundaries by declaring activities outside its jurisdiction as criminal. It would also infringe on the legality principle, as one of the constituent elements of the money laundering offence is that the proceeds should be criminally derived. Whether proceeds are criminally derived or not, should be judged according to the law of the place where the predicate activities were committed. Any other solution would fall foul of the legality principle.

In case the predicate offence was committed within the same state as the money laundering offence, there is of course no problem. When a predicate offence does not fall under the jurisdiction of the state where the money laundering offence took place, then that state should consequently defer to the *lex loci delicti* regarding the question whether the predicate activities constituted a criminal offence or not. Only if the state where the money laundering took place had extraterritorial jurisdiction over the predicate offence, should no heed be paid to the *lex loci delicti* of the foreign predicate offence. If a state has extraterritorial jurisdiction over a foreign predicate offence – for example, because it was committed by one of its nationals (nationality principle) – then that state is in principle entitled to judge the punishability of the predicate offence solely on the ground of its own legislation. Even in this hypothesis, however, a state will often have to take account of the *lex loci delicti*, as the application of extraterritorial jurisdiction bases is in turn often subjected to the principle of double criminality.[45]

In view of the fact that, as a consequence of the legality principle, the criminal origin of proceeds should in principle be judged according to the *lex loci delicti*, one could argue that there is no need for an extra

[45] See Van den Wyngaert, 'Double Criminality as a Requirement to Jurisdiction', pp. 43–56.

requirement, namely that the predicate activities should also constitute a criminal offence according to the law of the state where the money laundering offence took place, had they been committed in that state. Nevertheless, most states impose a condition of double criminality in respect of the predicate offence. This is only logical as it would make little sense for law enforcement authorities to prosecute the laundering of proceeds from activities that are not criminal according to the domestic law of that state.

There is one very important exception in this respect, which relates to capital flight. Combating the laundering of monies that are derived from capital flight may be desirable, even though capital flight is not recognised as an offence in the country where the laundering takes place. This problem has sometimes been circumvented, however, by linking the proceeds with a 'catch-all' offence, for example forgery, which is also known under the domestic law of the country where the laundering takes place.

The condition of double criminality of the predicate offence seems to be adhered to in all of the jurisdictions that were studied for the purpose of this book, even though it is not always explicitly stated in the relevant statute.

In the Netherlands this seems to follow from the parliamentary *travaux préparatoires*,[46] as is the case in Italy.[47] In Belgium it follows from case law that the predicate offence must be a crime both under the *lex loci delicti* and under Belgian law.[48] Both the German,[49] the Luxembourg[50] and the Swiss legislator have explicitly entrenched the condition of double criminality in respect of the predicate offence in the statutory definition of money laundering. Article 305bis(3) of the Swiss Penal Code also requires the predicate offence to have been a *crime* punishable by imprisonment (and not merely by a fine), but this is to be judged solely according to Swiss law.[51] Swiss law in addition explicitly provides that it does not matter

---

[46] M. Pisani, 'Italie: Criminalité organisée et coopération internationale', *RIDP* (1999), 557.

[47] D. R. Doorenbos, *Over witwassen en voordeelsontneming*, p. 16. See also M. Den Boer, A. M. M. Orie, J. M. Sjöcrona, M. I. Veldt and H. van der Wilt, 'The Criminal Justice System facing the Challenge of Organised Crime. International Cooperation', *RIDP* (1999), 579.

[48] See Tribunal of First Instance Antwerp, 14 April 1994, *RW* (1994–95), 508 and in respect of concealment: Belgian Supreme Court, 17 August 1982, *Arr.Cass.* (1981–82), 1407. See F. Verbruggen, 'Proceeds-oriented Criminal Justice in Belgium', 319 and Stessens, *De nationale en internationale bestrijding van het witwassen*, p. 366.

[49] For Germany see: § 261, para. 8 of the German Criminal Code. See J. Vogel, 'Combating International Organised Crime by International Co-operation. The German View', *RIDP* (1999), 337.

[50] Article 506–3 of the Luxembourg Criminal Code and Article 8–1(4) of the Luxembourg Drug Offences Act of 19 February 1973.

[51] Ackermann, *Geldwäscherei – Money Laundering*, pp. 216–17; Chapuis, 'Le droit de

whether money laundering is as such punishable or not according to the law of the state where the predicate offence was committed, as is generally the case under all money laundering legislations.[52]

In principle, the American money laundering offence requires that the predicate offence, that is specified unlawful activity as defined by 18 U.S.C. § 1956(7), has occurred on American territory. This rigid principle is, however, alleviated in two ways. First, there is a number of predicate offences where this principle does not apply, referred to as 'offenses against a foreign nation'. Before 1992 this was limited to a number of drug offences, but the Anti Money Laundering Act 1992 extended this category to a number of other offences, namely kidnapping, robbery, extortion and bank fraud (18 U.S.C. § 1956(7)(B)). Second, in case of international money laundering, there is no requirement that the funds involved have been criminally derived. Section 1956(a)(2)(A) punishes the mere transportation, transmission, or transfer of monetary instruments or funds extraterritorially with the intent to promote the specified unlawful activity. There is thus no requirement that the funds were derived from a criminal activity.[53] Thus a transfer of money that is derived from legitimate activities, but imported into the United States to be used as bribes, falls under this international money laundering offence.

Under the English Drug Trafficking Act 1994 the laundering of drug money is punishable, irrespective of the place where the drug trafficking offence was committed. This flows from the very wide definition of money laundering, which encompasses both drug trafficking in and outside England and Wales. As far as other predicate offences are concerned, s.93A(7) CJA 1988 requires that the predicate offence falls under the application field as defined in the CJA 1988, or would have fallen if it had occurred in England and Wales or Scotland.

Double criminality of the predicate offence in concreto or abstracto

The question whether the condition of double criminality of the predicate offence should be judged in concreto or in abstracto is misleading in that it

---

communication du financier', 268; Graber, Geldwäscherei, p. 164; Harari, 'Corruption à l'étranger', 14–15 and Peters, 'Money Laundering and Its Current Status In Switzerland', 132.

[52] P. Bernasconi, 'Blanchiment d'argent. Les nouvelles solutions légales suisses', RSC (1990), 647; Graber, Geldwäscherei, pp. 108–9 and 163–4 and Kistler, La vigilance requise, pp. 87–8. This supplementary provision has given rise to some criticism: see Graber, Geldwäscherei, p. 164 and Arzt, 'Das schweizerischen Geldwaschereiverbot', 198.

[53] United States v. Piervinanzi, 23 F.3d 670, 679–680 (2d Cir. 1994). See also Paust and others, International Criminal Law, p. 1337.

suggests that it concerns jurisdiction. Double criminality *in abstracto* means that the conduct should constitute a criminal offence under the laws of both countries involved (i.e. the country claiming extraterritorial jurisdiction and the country where the offence took place). Double criminality *in concreto* moreover requires that the conduct could effectively be punished under both laws, taking into account the factual circumstances of the case, including possible grounds of exclusion of criminal liability. In this context, however, double criminality of the predicate offence does not amount to a question of jurisdiction, but is a consequence of the legality principle and as such even a constituent element of the money laundering offence. (Of course, this always depends upon the domestic incrimination of money laundering.)

In most countries, the prosecution is not burdened with the charge to prove the precise origin of the proceeds; it generally suffices that it is proven that the proceeds were somehow criminally derived. Consequently, the prosecution is not under an obligation to prove that the predicate offence was *in concreto* liable to punishment. From this rule of evidence, it should not be inferred that it suffices that the predicate offence was punishable *in abstracto*. When the defendant can successfully argue that, under the concrete circumstances of the case, there was a reason to exclude criminal liability in respect of the predicate offence, then there is no predicate offence. One of the constituent elements of any money laundering offence will hence be lacking, namely the requirement that the proceeds were criminally derived. This is valid both in respect of foreign predicate offences and of domestic predicate offences. If the defendant can, for example, demonstrate that the perpetrator of the predicate offence was excused by mistake of law, then the proceeds from that offence should not be deemed 'criminally derived proceeds' as they could, as a rule, not have been confiscated by the judicial authorities of the state where the predicate offence was committed. One could tentatively speak about a requirement of 'double confiscability' in this respect. This phrase cannot be used as a general model, however, given the fact that in some jurisdictions the proceeds from some offences cannot be confiscated and in other jurisdictions alleged proceeds can be confiscated even if the offence is not punishable under the concrete circumstances of the case. Thus, under Dutch law, proceeds from fiscal offences cannot be confiscated, although the laundering of proceeds from fiscal offences is liable to punishment under Dutch law.[54] In the United States on the other hand,

---

[54] Doorenbos, *Witwassen en voordeelsontneming*, p. 78.

civil forfeiture procedures allow the police to confiscate proceeds from crime in some situations, also in cases where it might not have been possible to convict the perpetrator of the predicate offence. It can therefore not be sustained that the requirement that the proceeds be 'confiscable' (i.e that they would have been liable to confiscation according to the *lex loci delicti* of the predicate offence) is a constituent element of the money laundering offence, nor that the laundering of these proceeds would have constituted a criminal offence under the law of the country where the predicate offence was committed. What is generally required, however, is that the predicate offence which generated the proceeds was *in concreto* punishable under the law of the country where it was committed.

Proof of criminal origin of proceeds

In practice, it will often be very difficult for the prosecution to prove the criminal origin of proceeds that have been imported from abroad. As most domestic money laundering incriminations do not require that the perpetrator of the predicate offence have been convicted,[55] there is equally no requirement that the criminal origin of foreign proceeds should be proven by a foreign judicial conviction. It is highly exceptional that money laundering legislation contain a requirement – as is the case in France (see Article 113(5) of the French Penal Code) – that the criminal origin of the foreign proceeds should be proven by a judgment of the *forum delicti comissi*. It is submitted that such a requirement is far too rigid and may constitute an unjustified impediment in the international combat against money laundering.[56] It makes the effectiveness of domestic procedures against money laundering dependent on the outcome of foreign judicial procedures. Leaving aside the problems that could be caused by plea bargaining procedures and out-of-court-settlements, the value of foreign judgments would often give rise to intricate legal debates.

[55] As far as Belgium is concerned, see Stessens, *De nationale en internationale bestrijding van het witwassen*, p. 369; for Switzerland: Swiss Supreme Court, judgment of 21 September 1994, *La Semaine judiciaire* (1995), 308; Graber, *Geldwäscherei*, pp. 129–30 and B. Messerli, 'Die Geldwäscherei de lege lata et ferenda', *RPS* (1989), 430; and the United States: Adams, 'Effective Strategies for Banks', 681.

[56] P. Bernasconi, 'Rapport général', in *Blanchiment d'argent et secret bancaire*, Rapport général du XIVe Congrès international de droit comparé, P. Bernasconi (The Hague: Kluwer Law International, 1996), p. 12. See also Swiss Supreme Court, judgment of 21 September 1994, *La Semaine judiciaire* (1995), 308.

10   Extra-territorial jurisdiction in respect of money laundering offences

In the first chapter of Part 3, increasing globalisation was marked as a factor which favours increased use of extra-territorial jurisdiction bases. In Chapter 9 it was shown that, in defiance of this globalisation, many states seem to base their anti-money laundering activities primarily on the territoriality principle. In this chapter, the possible use of extra-territorial jurisdiction in respect of money laundering offences will be investigated. The most important jurisdiction basis in this respect is undoubtedly the nationality principle. Finally, an attempt will be made to shed some light on the reasons for the strong emphasis on the territoriality principle compared to other jurisdiction principles.

Jurisdiction on the basis of the nationality principle

The extraterritorial jurisdiction basis that is most likely to play a role of some importance in the international fight against money laundering is the nationality principle. The nationality (or active personality) principle is underpinned by two rationales, the first being that it serves international solidarity and the interest of the individual in that he can better defend himself in his own country and, in the case of a conviction, stands a better chance of rehabilitation. In the context of money laundering, the second rationale is more likely to be the driving force behind the recourse to the nationality principle in the fight against money laundering: it provides a state with a kind of supervision over conduct by its nationals abroad: *rei publicae interest bonos subditos habere*.[1] This concern may hold not

---

[1] European Committee on Crime Problems, *Extraterritorial criminal jurisdiction*, p. 10; Harvard Research in International Law, 'Jurisdiction with Respect to Crime', 519–20; Blakesley, 'Extraterritorial Jurisdiction', p. 23 and Mok and Duk, 'Toepassing van het Nederlandse strafrecht', 112–13.

only in respect of individuals but also in respect of corporations, notably financial institutions. To an even larger extent than physical persons, juridical persons are internationally active. Unlike the former, the latter can be present in more than one country at the same time. Financial institutions may be tempted to use their branches in secrecy havens as channels for money laundering operations. The state on whose territory the head office of a financial institution is located may have an obvious interest in preventing and punishing money laundering through foreign branches in view of the lower chances that these money laundering operations will be punished in those secrecy havens.

The application of the nationality principle to foreign corporate crimes, however, requires the solving of a preliminary question namely, how the nationality of a financial institution, that is, a corporation, should be determined. After that, the influence of the condition of double criminality, which is imposed by many domestic jurisdiction legislations, on the effectiveness of the international fight against money laundering will be critically investigated. A crucial question in this respect is whether this condition presupposes that both countries involved accept corporate criminal liability. It will be argued that, although this is not the case, the condition of double criminality still considerably limits the effectiveness of the nationality principle to the international fight against money laundering.

Nationality of a corporation

This essentially non-criminal question is much more difficult to answer in the case of corporations than of individuals. The legal status of a body corporate (i.e., the essential question as to whether a corporation is recognised as such), is determined by the legal system in which it is incorporated and from which, in principle, it derives its legal personality. The legal status and the nationality of a corporation are therefore intrinsically linked.[2]

From a comparative perspective, one can distinguish two criteria that are used in private international law to determine by which country's legislation a corporation is governed and hence whose nationality it has. According to a first theory widely adhered to in common law countries (but e.g. also in The Netherlands), corporations are deemed to have the nationality of the state under whose law they have been incorporated.

---

[2] See e.g., F. Rigaux, *Droit international privé. Tome I. Théorie générale* (Brussels: Larcier, 1987), p. 135.

Under the second theory, which applies in Belgium, Luxembourg, France and Germany, for example, the principal centre of business (the *siège social*) is taken as the apposite criterion for determining to which legislation a corporation is subjected and hence which nationality it has.[3] Depending on the theory that is adhered to by the *ius fori* principle, the same corporation can therefore have different nationalities.

It is submitted that, at least from a criminal law viewpoint, there is no pressing need for a unification of the criteria that are used to determine the nationality of a corporation. Given the divergence of opinion on this point,[4] this would in any case not be an easy task. One might propose that, as is the case for corporate bodies under public law, corporate bodies under civil law should have the nationality of the state that has granted them their legal status as a body corporate. The question as to the nationality of a corporation would thereby clearly be separated from the question of recognising its legal status.[5] In the context of the nationality principle there is no need to recognise a foreign corporation's legal status as this principle allows a state to claim jurisdiction only over crimes committed by corporations that have its nationality. The legality principle, with its inherent requirement of predictability, however, demands that it is clear which criterion is used for determining the nationality of a corporation for the purposes of claiming jurisdiction over corporate crimes committed abroad.

The obvious drawback of this proposal is that it does not exclude the possibility of jurisdictional conflicts as more than one state may grant its nationality to the same corporation and hence claim jurisdiction over the crimes committed by that corporation on the basis of the nationality principle. Thus, a company incorporated in the United Kingdom, with its principal centre of business in France, for example, will be considered by both the United Kingdom (on the basis of the incorporation criterion) and France (on the basis of the *siège social* criterion) as having both UK and French nationality respectively. This potential for jurisdictional conflicts is, however, inherent in the use of the nationality principle and, for that

---

[3] On these various theories, see P. Vlas, *Rechtspersonen in het internationaal privaatrecht* (Deventer: Kluwer, 1982), pp. 47–53 and F. Rigaux and M. Fallon, *Droit international privé. Tome II. Droit positif belge* (Brussels: Larcier, 1993), pp. 731–5.

[4] Whereas some are staunchly in favour of the *siège social* as the only relevant criterion for nationality for criminal jurisdiction purposes (Mok and Duk, 'Toepassing van het Nederlandse strafrecht', 131; Wolswijk, *Locus delicti*, p. 272 and Van Strien, 'De rechtsmacht van Nederland', 78), others have advocated the incorporation criterion: European Committee on Crime Problems, *Extraterritorial Criminal Jurisdiction*, 28.

[5] Rigaux, *Droit international privé. Tome I. Théorie générale*, 96.

matter, to any criminal jurisdiction principle. Unlike in private international law, the use of an extra-territorial criminal jurisdiction principle does not result in the exclusive use of the criminal law of that country;[6] crimes, including corporate crimes, can of course always be judged by the courts of the state where they were committed on the basis of the principle of the *lex loci delicti*.

Does the condition of double criminality require double corporate criminal liability?

Often, extra-territorial jurisdiction claims made, for example, on the basis of the nationality principle, are subjected to the condition of double criminality. Its function in the context of jurisdiction is different from that in the context of international co-operation in criminal matters. In the former context, the condition of double criminality is a condition for the state that seeks extra-territorial jurisdiction to be able to punish extra-territorial conduct whereas in the latter context, it is a condition for the requested state to be able to pose investigatory or provisional measures that are requested by a foreign state.[7]

When a state seeks to punish foreign corporate crimes on the basis of the nationality principle, the question arises as to whether the condition of double criminality also demands that there be corporate criminal liability according to the *lex loci delicti* principle. The answer to this question in turn depends on the question whether double criminality should be judged *in concreto* or *in abstracto*.[8] Some, holding that the condition of double criminality needs only to be judged *in abstracto*, argue this matter should not be allowed to play a role.[9] Others contend that the lack of corporate criminal liability should be considered a ground of non-liability which precludes the fulfilment of the condition of double criminality judged *in concreto*.[10] They seem to base their view on the legality principle, amongst others which not only concerns criminalisation, but also general questions of criminal liability.

It is submitted, however, that there is no logical nexus between double criminality as a precondition to extra-territorial jurisdiction and the legality principle. The legality principle is not put at issue by extra-territorial

---

[6] See also L. Sarkar, 'The Proper Law of Crime in International Law', 457.

[7] See also *infra* pp. 287–8.

[8] On this distinction see *supra* pp. 229–31 and Van den Wyngaert, 'Double Criminality', 51–2.   [9] Mok and Duk, 'Toepassing van het Nederlandse strafrecht', 102.

[10] Van Strien, 'De rechtsmacht van Nederland', pp. 79–80.

jurisdiction claims, as the punishability of conduct will be judged according to the law of the state that seeks jurisdiction and not according to the *lex loci delicti* principle (which is taken into account for the purposes of checking the condition of double criminality). Claiming extraterritorial jurisdiction in the absence of 'double corporate criminal liability' is not *a fortiori* violative of the legality principle: by incorporating a company in a given state, a deliberate choice is made to subject that corporation to the laws of that state, including its jurisdiction laws.

Double criminality as a precondition for extra-territorial jurisdiction should not be seen as purporting to safeguard the legality principle, but as a mechanism for avoiding conflict of laws. Without the requirement of double criminality, the nationality principle would create the risk that individuals and corporations alike would be confronted with obligations under their national law that would conflict with the territorial law (i.e., the *lex loci delicti* in the case of an offence). It is submitted that it would be unacceptable for a corporation (or an individual for that matter) to be punished on the basis of its 'national' law for conduct that was licit or even mandatory under the law of the country where the conduct took place. Should a possible conflict of laws arise, 'the state of nationality must not require compliance with its laws at the expense of its duty to respect the territorial sovereignty of the state of residence'.[11]

In order to achieve this goal of avoiding conflict of laws as fully as possible, the condition of double criminality needs to be judged *in concreto*. An example may clarify this. Suppose a Dutch bank carries out a financial transaction in Belgium involving criminally derived proceeds. The bank is liable to prosecution and punishment in the Netherlands for money laundering, given that money laundering is an offence under both Dutch and Belgian law. At first sight, there is no conflict of laws. If, however, the Dutch bank had apprised the Belgian financial intelligence unit of its suspicions, in good faith and in a timely manner then, under Belgian law, the bank would be excused from criminal responsibility. Should The Netherlands, where this ground of non-liability is not recognised,[12] decide to prosecute and try the bank under these circumstances, there is – notwithstanding the fulfilment of the condition of double criminality *in abstracto* – a conflict of law.

---

[11] R. Jennings and A. Watts, *Oppenheim's International Law*, p. 464. See also I. Seidl-Hohenfeldern, *Völkerrecht*, p. 237 and on the generally recognised primacy of the territoriality principle in the context of criminal jurisdiction: European Committee on Crime Problems, *Extraterritorial Criminal Jurisdiction*, p. 22.

[12] See on the difference between Dutch and Belgian law in this respect, *supra* pp. 176–7.

Whether corporate criminal liability is accepted under the *lex loci delicti* principle, however, does not seem material to judge the condition of double criminality *in concreto*. The question as to whether corporations can be held criminally liable does not come into play in the assessment of the punishability of conduct as such. Unlike a mistake in law or rules that take precedence, non-liability of corporations is not a ground for exclusion of criminal liability but merely an element which comes into play after the assessment of the criminality of conduct has taken place, namely when imputing criminal conduct to the juridical person deemed responsible for it.

Some of those authors who have defended the view that 'double corporate criminal liability' should be taken into account in the assessment of the condition of double criminality *in concreto* have at the same time proposed to soften this rigid application by taking cognisance, not only of systems of corporate criminal liability, but also of administrative systems of corporate liability that may exist under the principle of *lex loci delicti*.[13] This line of reasoning draws on an autonomous concept of criminal liability, independent of the domestic legislation concerned, as was developed by the European Court of Human Rights, for example, in its case law on what constitutes a 'criminal charge' (in order to determine the applicability of fair trial rights guarantee).[14] However, this founders on one major objection, that is, that administrative sanctioning systems are generally not taken into account in the assessment of the condition of double criminality.[15]

Limited effectiveness of the nationality principle

While it does not require that there be double corporate criminal liability, the condition of double criminality does considerably limit the utility of the nationality principle to the international fight against money laundering. The application of the nationality principle subjected to the

[13] Delmas-Marty, 'Personnes morales étrangères et françaises', 260; B. Swart, 'Human Rights and the Abolition of Traditional Principles', in *Principles and Procedures For A Transnational Criminal Law*, A. Eser and O. Lagodny (Freiburg: Max-Planck Institut, 1992), pp. 524–5 and Van Strien, 'De rechtsmacht van Nederland', p. 80.

[14] See in particular the following cases: *Engel v. the Netherlands* (judgment of 8 June 1976, *Publ.ECHR*, Series A, No.22), *Öztürk v. Germany* (judgment of 21 February 1984, *Publ.ECHR*, Series A, No.73) and *Lutz v. Germany* (judgment of 25 August 1987, *Publ.ECHR*, Series A, No.123). See *supra* p. 65.

[15] K. Cornils, 'The Use of Foreign Law in Domestic Adjudication', in *Double Criminality. Studies in International Criminal Law*, ed. N. Järeborg (Uppsala: Iustus Förlag, 1989), p. 73.

condition of double criminality is rife with potential conflicts of law, given the disparate state of money laundering legislations, particularly in respect of the predicate offence.[16] The money laundering legislation of State A may have a broader application field (i.e., may cover the proceeds of more predicate offences), than that of State B. If State A tends to claim jurisdiction over money laundering operations in State B involving A's own nationals or branches of financial institutions having their head office in State A, the condition of double criminality prevents State A from punishing extra-territorial money laundering operations on the basis of a broader legal concept than the one contained in the legislation of State B (i.e., the territorially applicable law). This takes away the potential for conflict, but at the same time reduces the practical relevance of the nationality principle as it can be used only to punish money laundering offences that were already punishable under the *lex loci delicti* principle. The only type of situation where the nationality principle may be of use is where State B refuses to take action or is legally prevented from taking action (e.g., because of lack of corporate criminal liability under the legislation of State B).

Jurisdiction over foreign corporate conduct under financial preventive law

General context of the globalisation of finance

The increasing globalisation of finance and financial systems creates a need for international co-operation between supervisory authorities and for jurisdiction over conduct of financial institutions abroad as not all states have equally rigid rules for the prevention of money laundering through their financial system. It is therefore necessary to delineate the spatial application field of preventive legislation: is it limited by the territoriality principle, or can preventive legislation extend to the activities of financial institutions outside the territory of their 'home state'? In answering this question, two international regimes will be taken into account: the European Money Laundering Directive and the FATF recommendations.

Only within the European Union has a substantial degree of harmonisation in respect of financial services been agreed. The common market for financial services was part of the broader objective of arriving at a

---

[16] See also *supra* pp. 117–21.

common market within the European Community as from 1 January 1993. After the First Banking Directive of 1977,[17] the Second Banking Directive of 1989 introduced a new philosophy: in lieu of a prior and general harmonisation of all existing rules, the Community decided in favour of a limited harmonisation of the most essential features and the establishment of two fundamental principles: mutual recognition of legislation and home Member State control.[18]

An international bank, that is, a bank having its head office in one state while conducting business activities in other states, can choose to set up a fully-fledged subsidiary with its own corporate legal status or may opt for local branches without separate juridical personality. The principle of mutual recognition allows a financial institution that has been duly set up in compliance with the legislation of one Member State to carry out its activities in another Member State, or States, through local branches and/or cross-border financial services (i.e. without a local branch), without needing the permission of all the Member States concerned: the bank therefore operates under a single banking licence. The principle of mutual recognition implies that, given the harmonisation of the essential features of financial law, each Member State is bound to recognise other Member States' financial legislation and to refrain from applying its own legislation to financial institutions from other Member States that are active on their territory.

The second principle of home Member State control flows logically from the first principle: given the mutual recognition of legislation, there is a need for mutual recognition of the supervisory authorities that control the implementation of that legislation. Allotting the vast majority of tasks of prudential supervision to the home Member State authorities amounts, however, to a radical break with the tradition of host Member State control. The radical nature of this change is clear from Article 15 of the Second Banking Directive, for example, which allows the home state authorities to carry out on-the-spot investigations in local branches of financial institutions in other Member States.

---

[17] First Council Directive 77/780/EEC of 12 December 1977 on the co-ordination of laws, regulations and administrative provisions relating to the taking up and pursuit of the business of credit institutions, *OJ*, L322, p. 30, 17.12.1977.

[18] Second Council Directive 89/646/EEC of 15 December 1989 on the co-ordination of laws, regulations and administrative provisions relating to the taking up and pursuit of the business of credit institutions and amending Directive 77/780/EEC, *OJ*, L386, p. 1, 30.12.1989. See P. Clarotti, 'Un pas décisif vers le marché commun des banques', *RMC* (1989), 454 and W. Van Gerven, 'La deuxième directive bancaire et la jurisprudence de la Cour de Justice', *Bank.Fin.* (1991), 39.

Article 21 concerns the residual powers of the host Member State authorities, the exercise of most of which implies some form of co-opera- tion with the authorities of the home Member State. Article 21(5), however, gives the host state authorities the exclusive power to 'take appropriate measures to prevent or punish irregularities committed within their territories which are contrary to the legal rules they have adopted in the interest of the general good. This shall include the possibil- ity of preventing offending institutions from initiating any further trans- actions within their territory'. The concept of 'measures in the interest of the general good' was not circumscribed by the Council and the Commission.[19] Notwithstanding the lack of definition of the concept of 'measures in the interest of the general good', it will be shown that the domestic legislation for the prevention of the use of the financial system for the purpose of money laundering does fall under this concept and is hence excluded from extraterritorial application by the home state, but should instead be applied territorially by the host state.

Territorial application of the legislation for the prevention of the use of the financial system for the purpose of money laundering

As far as branches of financial or credit institutions having their head offices outside the Community are concerned, the principle of territorial application follows from Article 1 of the Directive. Article 6 of the Directive furthermore specifies that, in respect of the information duties of financial institutions, the information needs to be forwarded to the 'authorities responsible for combating money laundering of the Member State in whose territory the institution forwarding the information is sit- uated'. This territorial application automatically excludes the application of the money laundering prevention legislation of the home state. This is also confirmed in a non-published advice of the Contact Committee set up under Article 13 under the aegis of the European Commission and by the 1999 Commission proposal for amending the Money Laundering Directive.[20] Only when a financial institution is active in another Member State by provision of service without setting up a branch (*libre prestation de services*) need the legislation of the home state be applied. Thus there is no

---

[19] For the reasons for this lack of definition, see Clarotti, 'Un pas décisif', 462 and Van Gerven, 'La deuxième directive bancaire', 43.

[20] European Commission, *Proposal for a European Parliament and Council Directive amending Council Directive 91/308/EEC of 10 June 1991 on Prevention of the Use of the Financial System for the Purpose of Money Laundering*, Brussels, 14.7.1999, COM(1999) 352 final, 99/152 (COD), p. 11.

need for the financial institution to familiarise itself with the legislation on the prevention of money laundering of the Member State where it offers financial services.

As the legislation on the prevention of the use of the financial system for the purpose of money laundering comes under the general application field of the principle of mutual recognition, the conclusion that this legislation nevertheless needs to be applied territorially can be squared with the general framework of the Second Banking Directive only if this legislation is deemed to fall under the heading of 'measures in the interest of the general good' of Article 21(5) of the Second Banking Directive. This conclusion can be justified in the following way.

The case law of the Court of Justice regarding domestic 'measures in the interest of the general good', generally requires a number of conditions to be met before measures of this nature can be allowed. This is not the place to give an exhaustive overview of these measures,[21] but one of the requirements is that the legislation concerned may not yet have been harmonised by the Community or that this harmonisation is deemed insufficient.[22] It is submitted that this is indeed the case in respect of the European Money Laundering Directive. Given the freedom given to Member States to determine in respect of which predicate offences the preventive measures – notably the reporting duties – have to be applied, the mutual recognition of the home state's legislation on the prevention of money laundering would give rise to very complicated problems. It would, for example, be hardly conceivable that an Athens branch of a Belgian bank (i.e., a bank having its head office in Belgium) should need to report its suspicions to the Belgian financial intelligence unit. Leaving aside the practical problems this would entail, the question arises as to the width of the reporting duty: should the Athens branch report according to the Greek or to the Belgian reporting duty? If the local branch obeys a reporting duty as defined in its home legislation, it may contravene the banking secrecy law of the host state if the legislation of the host state operates a more narrow concept of which transactions need to be reported. The application of the territoriality principle avoids this type of conflict of laws.

Alternatively, a branch may risk sanctions from its home state authorities if it does not report all transactions it is required to report under the legislation of the home state. Were the principle of mutual recognition to be applied, this would indeed imply that the prudential authorities of the

---

[21] Clarotti, 'Un pas décisif', 462–3 and Van Gerven, 'La deuxième directive bancaire', 42–6.
[22] See CJEC, judgment of 4 December 1986, *Commission v. Germany, Jur.* [1986], 3633.

home state would be charged with supervising the observance by the foreign bank branches all over the Community of the legislation of the home state on the prevention of money laundering. This might give rise to difficult situations not only for the bank branches but also for the host state authorities which might have to tolerate prudential supervision on their territory in respect of the laundering of proceeds from predicate offences over which they do not exercise supervision themselves, or which may not even be considered as offences in that country.[23] This also demonstrates that the principle of mutual recognition is closely linked to a minimal harmonisation of financial legislation: without such harmonisation, the principle of mutual recognition cannot function. Now, it is the supervisory authority of the host state that exercises prudential supervision of compliance with the anti-money laundering regulations of the host state. But only the competent authorities of the home state can decide on the most severe sanction, the withdrawal of the banking licence, given the principle of mutual recognition of authorization that underlies the Second Banking Directive.

Another objection to the use of the principle of mutual recognition in this context concerns the use of the information gathered through the application of the Money Laundering Directive's implementation legislation. Under the Second Banking Directive, the prudential authorities of the home state that have gathered information at the branches located in other Member States can in principle use this information only for prudential purposes. Only in cases covered by criminal law (i.e., the criminal law of the home Member State), can they transmit this information to other authorities of the home Member State. If the authorities of the home Member State were to exercise control over the implementation of the preventive legislation in branches all over the Community, this would imply that they could also transmit this information to the authorities responsible for combating money laundering, and possibly in cases that might not fall under the criminal law of the host Member State as well. This risk would be all the more pernicious as some Member States have provided for the possibility of using the information for other purposes than the combating of money laundering. In view of the very strong arguments against mutual recognition of the preventive anti-money laundering legislation, it is not surprising that notably the European Money Laundering Directive, but also the United States legislation, avoids extraterritorial application of anti-money laundering rules. The Bank Secrecy

---

[23] Dassesse, 'Les rapports entre la proposition de directive blanchiment', 15 and Ewing, 'The Draft EEC Money Laundering Directive', 143.

Act has indeed no extra-territorial reach so that US financial institutions operating overseas are under no BSA obligation to file reports or keep records.

Possible extra-territorial application of the legislation for the prevention of the use of the financial system for the purpose of money laundering

Notwithstanding the principle of territorial application of the legislation for the prevention of the use of the financial system for the purpose of money laundering, FATF recommendation 20 asks that the first nineteen of its recommendations also be applied 'to branches and to majority owned subsidiaries located abroad, especially in countries which do not or insufficiently apply these Recommendations, to the extent that local applicable laws and regulations permit. When local applicable laws and regulations prohibit this implementation, competent authorities in the country of the mother institution should be informed by the financial institutions that they cannot apply these Recommendations'. This recommendation should not be understood as deviating from the territoriality principle, as it gives priority to local applicable laws and regulations. Within the European Union this recommendation will not give rise to friction as all Member States have adopted the vast majority of the FATF's recommendations.[24] The principles contained in the European Money Laundering Directive have even been extended to countries outside the European Union, through association, partnership or co-operation agreements signed between the European Union and those countries.[25]

Many domestic legislators or regulators have issued rules inspired by FATF recommendation 20, all of which take account of territorially applicable money laundering regulations. Some, like the Belgian circular letter B93/4 of the Banking Commission,[26] or the Luxembourg circular letter 94/112 of the *Institut monétair luxembourgeois*,[27] give priority to the local law

[24] See FATF-IV, 7.

[25] See in general the *First Commission's Report on the Implementation of the Money Laundering Directive*, p. 3. The special provisions in these agreements were greeted with enthusiasm by the European Parliament in its Resolution on the First Commission's report on the implementation of the Money Laundering Directive. Cf. Cullen, 'Money Laundering: The European Community Directive', p. 49 and W. C. Gilmore, 'Money Laundering: The International Aspect', in *Money Laundering*, The David Hume Institute (Edinburgh University Press, 1993), p. 10.

[26] On this circular letter, see Stessens, *De nationale en internationale bestrijding van het witwassen*, pp. 385–6.

[27] Circular letter IML 94/112 of 25 November 1994 of the *Institut Monétaire Luxembourgeois* (*Lutte contre le blanchiment et prévention de l'utilisation du secteur financier à des fins de blanchiment*).

if it contains equivalent regulations. Other instruments, such as the money laundering circular letter of the Swiss Banking Commission,[28] are somewhat stricter in that the only 'safety valve' is where local laws do not allow foreign financial institutions to comply with the rules imposed by the home state. The circular letter explicitly warns that financial institutions should not use their foreign subsidiaries and branches to evade the legal and/or regulatory requirements on the prevention of money laundering.

It is interesting to note that statutory provisions on the prevention of money laundering stand a better chance of being applied extra-territorially if they are contained in criminal law. This allows the home state to apply the nationality principle in order to sanction money laundering operations carried out by nationals abroad, including bank professionals. This is, for example, possible under 18 USC § 1956(f)(1) and under Article 305ter of the Swiss Criminal Code which is, however, only applicable to financial professionals (and not even to corporations as such, given the lack of corporate criminal liability under Swiss law).[29]

The limited utility of other extra-territorial jurisdiction bases

It has been shown that the territoriality principle, notwithstanding the increasing globalisation of the money laundering phenomenon, continues to play a major jurisdictional role in the fight against money laundering.

The prevalence of the territoriality principle is attributable to various factors. First, the incrimination of money laundering fulfils an important jurisdictional function in that it allows states to claim jurisdiction over transactions involving funds derived from an offence over which they have no jurisdiction. This jurisdictional function is promoted by the provision in the Money Laundering Convention which says that it does not matter where the predicate offence took place. Although most domestic states require that the predicate offence be criminal according to both the *lex loci delicti* principle and the law of the 'money laundering' country, it has been demonstrated that this condition should not be seen as a restrictive condition for jurisdiction, but merely as a consequence of the legality principle. In addition, most states have taken a very liberal approach in localising money laundering offences on their territory by considering

---

[28] *Circulaire de la Commission fédérale des banques: Directives relatives à la prévention et à la lutte contre le blanchiment de capitaux (Blanchiment de capitaux)* of 18 December 1991.
[29] See *supra* p. 105.

every transaction to be a separate offence, a process for which the term 'atomisation' was coined. A third factor which is probably also very important is the new, profit-oriented goal of criminal justice: when the state in whose territory criminal proceeds have been located succeeds in claiming jurisdiction over a money laundering offence, it may be able to seize and confiscate the criminally derived funds. The use of an extra-territorial jurisdiction base to punish money laundering, on the other hand, does not allow a state to seize the criminally derived proceeds located in the territory of another state.

The predominant use of the territoriality principle can, however, also be explained through the relatively minor importance of extra-territorial jurisdiction bases. The only extra-territorial jurisdiction which could have played a role of some importance is the nationality principle, but its practical utility is limited by the condition of double criminality.[30]

Other extra-territorial jurisdiction bases are practically of no avail in the international fight against money laundering. Given the fact that money laundering is a so-called crime without a victim, the passive personality principle, which gives jurisdiction to the state of which the victim is a national, is of no use. The protective principle, which allows a state to punish foreign conduct that constitutes an infringement of the essential interests of that state (e.g., counterfeiting or an attack on a head of State), is of no use either in the context of fighting money laundering in that money laundering is not an offence against the interests of a state, even if one adopts a broad concept of the interests of a state, including not only security interests, integrity and sovereignty, but also the interests of treasury or other important governmental functions.[31]

The universality principle is the broadest jurisdiction basis in that it gives every state adjudicatory jurisdiction to hold persons criminally liable for a number of offences that are considered so heinous that they can be punished by any state, regardless of whether there is a connection between that state and the conduct or not. Some international conventions (e.g., on counterfeiting, hijacking and actions endangering the safety of civil aviation) authorise the assertion of universal jurisdiction, others require such jurisdictional action so as not to leave certain offences unpunished.[32] Even though it is not required that there be an explicit

---

[30] See *supra* pp. 236–8.   [31] Blakesley and Lagodny, 'Finding Harmony', 20.

[32] Gardocki, 'The Principle of Universality' 65; J. Meyer 'The Vicarious Administration of Justice: An Overlooked Basis of Jurisdiction', *Harv.Int'l LJ* (1990), 115. For a list of offences for which there exists universal jurisdiction, see C. Blakesley, *Terrorism, Drugs, International Law, and the Protection of Human Liberty. A Comparative Study in International*

treaty provision allowing the universality principle,[33] it cannot be said that there is universal jurisdiction in respect of the offence of money laundering, not even in respect of drug money laundering.[34] The universal jurisdiction that is foreseen in some international conventions in respect of drug trafficking cannot be equated with universal jurisdiction over money laundering offences involving the proceeds from these drug trafficking offences.[35]

The representation principle is often branded as a variant of the universality principle (even called subsidiary universal jurisdiction).[36] It allows states to exercise (judicial) jurisdiction over a given offence if they are deemed to be acting for another state which is more directly involved, provided that certain conditions are met. The state that originally had jurisdiction may, for example, transmit the procedure; or the state on whose territory the alleged suspect resides may have refused an extradition request by the state originally having jurisdiction. In respect of the offences they cover, some treaties explicitly provide for a treaty basis for the representation mechanism, thereby embodying the principle *aut dedere, aut judicare*[37] (see, e.g. in respect of drug trafficking offences and drug money laundering, Article 4(2) of the Vienna Convention). This mechanism is, however, intended to function in the context of a suspect-oriented justice model and as such is of little avail in a profit-oriented perspective. The representation principle generally provides adjudicatory jurisdiction to the state on whose territory the suspect is found, which does not necessarily coincide with the territory where the (alleged) pro-

Law, Its Nature, Role, and Impact in Matters of Terrorism, Drug Trafficking, War, and Extradition (New York: Transnational Publishers, Inc., 1992), pp. 137–49; European Committee on Crime Problems, *Extraterritorial Criminal Jurisdiction*, 15; Harvard Research in International Law, 'Jurisdiction with Respect to Crime', 476–80 and 569–72.

[33] Mann, 'The Doctrine of Jurisdiction in International Law', 95, Blakesley and Lagodny, 'Finding Harmony', 34, Meyer, 'The Vicarious Administration of Justice', 115 and D. Oehler, *Internationales strafrecht: Geltungsbereich des Strafrechts, internationales Rechtshilferecht, Recht der Gemeinschaften, Völkerstrafrecht* (Cologne: Carl Heymann Verlag, 1983), 538. See also European Committee on Crime Problems, *Extraterritorial Criminal Jurisdiction*, 15.   [34] *Contra* Blakesley, *Terrorism, Drugs*, p. 140.

[35] See also P. Bernasconi, *Die Geldwäscherei im Schweizerischen Strafrecht, Bericht mit Vorschlägen einer Gesetzrevision (neuer Artikel 305bis StGB) im Auftrag des Eidgenössisches Justiz- und Polizeidepartement* (1987), cited by Graber, *Geldwäscherei*, p. 164 and Taisch, 'Swiss Statutes Concerning Money Laundering', 697.

[36] See C. Van den Wyngaert, 'De toepassing van de strafwet in de ruimte', in *Liber Amicorum F. Dumon* (Antwerp: Kluwer, 1983), 517 *et seq.*

[37] On the representation mechanism, see the European Committee on Crime Problems, *Extraterritorial criminal jurisdiction*, 14; Meyer, 'The Vicarious Administration of Justice', 115–16; Mok and Duk, 'Toepassing van het Nederlandse strafrecht', 134 and Van den Wyngaert, 'De toepassing van de strafwet in de ruimte', 517.

ceeds from his offence are located. In the context of transfer of criminal proceedings, a distinction is classically made between two forms of jurisdiction to adjudicate: original jurisdiction and subsidiary, or derivative, jurisdiction.[38] In the former case the requested state will already have had jurisdiction over the offence (e.g., on the basis of the personality principle), irrespective of the request for co-operation; whereas in the case of derivative jurisdiction, the requested state only obtains jurisdiction by requesting that it takes over criminal proceedings. In the context of confiscation proceedings, there is, however, another type of original jurisdiction to adjudicate for the requested state that may be much more important: as pointed out earlier, the state on whose territory the criminally derived proceeds are located will often have adjudicatory jurisdiction over a money laundering offence involving the proceeds and will, at least as far as the money laundering offence is concerned, not be dependent on a foreign request for co-operation to obtain adjudicatory jurisdiction. Although requested states may circumvent the need for co-operation by claiming territorial jurisdiction over a money laundering offence involving proceeds derived from a foreign offence, this is only possible in cases where the request concerns an object confiscation order related to the property representing the proceeds from crime, but not in the case of a request for the enforcement of a value confiscation order on legitimately acquired property located on the requested state's territory, for in the latter case there will be no money laundering offence in that state.

In Part 4, we will see that, in respect of assets located abroad, new co-operation mechanisms have been devised that allow the transfer of confiscation proceedings from the state originally having jurisdiction over the predicate offence to the state where the assets are located.[39] Both the Vienna Convention and the Money Laundering Convention contain provisions to this effect, but only the latter provides an explicit basis for adjudicatory jurisdiction by stipulating that the requested state 'shall whenever necessary have competence to institute confiscation proceedings under its own law' (Article 13(2)). According to the Explanatory Report with the Convention on Laundering, such a basis for adjudicatory jurisdiction is required whenever the requested state has no competence under his own law to institute a confiscation procedure.[40] In line with this reasoning, the absence of an explicit basis for adjudicatory jurisdiction in the Vienna Convention would give rise to problems when a state is

[38] See Y. G. M. Baaijens-van Geloven, *Overdracht en overname van strafvervolging* (Arnhem: Gouda Quint, 1996), p. 56.   [39] See *infra* pp. 392–4.

[40] p. 28. See also Harari, 'Corruption à l'étranger', 17.

requested to institute new confiscation proceedings in respect of the (alleged) proceeds from an offence over which that state has no jurisdiction to adjudicate. It is, however, submitted that this should not give rise to problems, as proper jurisdiction to adjudicate is required only for the power of tribunals to hold someone criminally liable, and not for procedural acts – whether it be at the stage of the investigation, the trial, or the enforcement of the sanction – for which a request of a state which has adjudicatory jurisdiction over the offence concerned in principle suffices. The problem with which we are concerned here is particularly intricate, however, as the procedural act that is required, i.e., a new confiscation procedure, though it does not amount to a criminal trial, does result in a criminal sanction. The difference between this and proper criminal procedures for which jurisdiction to adjudicate is required is therefore admittedly very thin. Nevertheless, the institution of a confiscation procedure on request of a foreign authority is not an exercise of adjudicatory jurisdiction, but of enforcement jurisdiction (even though it necessarily involves court proceedings). Co-operation may even be refused if the requesting state has not yet made a judgment regarding the offences at stake.[41] The exercise of enforcement jurisdiction of course requires a legal basis, but a provision in the domestic legislation of the requested state, or even in the relevant treaty[42] allowing for such measures, suffices in this respect. The institution of confiscation proceedings cannot be held to require adjudicatory jurisdiction over the offences which generated the proceeds the confiscation of which is sought.

---

[41] See *infra* pp. 398–9.

[42] *Explanatory Report with the Convention on Laundering*, p. 28. Cf. *Explanatory Report on the European Convention on the Transfer of Proceedings in Criminal Matters*, paras.31(2) and 32.

PART IV · INTERNATIONAL CO-OPERATION IN COMBATING MONEY LAUNDERING

11 The money laundering regime: new objectives of international co-operation in criminal matters

Objectives of domestic and international criminal justice

The general objectives of international co-operation in criminal matters are in principle the same as those of domestic criminal justice. The primary purpose is to immobilize the criminal, which requires the tracing and arrest of the suspect as well as the gathering of evidence with a view to his prosecution. The fight against money laundering and the new, profit-oriented perspective of the fight against crime has given criminal justice a new important objective: the confiscation of the proceeds and instrumentalities from crime.[1] These objectives not only govern the activities of law enforcement authorities in a domestic situation, but also in an international context.

International co-operation is sometimes indeed necessary to attain these goals given the transnational nature of the crime phenomenon, for example money laundering. From a strictly international law point of view, international co-operation is necessitated by the concept of sovereignty, which limits powers of a state to take investigatory, provisional and enforcement measures to its own territory (although this view merits to be attenuated from a common law viewpoint[2]). It follows that, conceptually, international co-operation in criminal matters is mostly intended to deal with a lack of enforcement jurisdiction on the side of the requesting state.[3] In the context of the international fight against money laundering, the lack of enforcement jurisdiction may take two forms. First, information required to prove the money laundering offence and/or the predicate offence will often be located on the territory of another state than the state which intends to prosecute the money laundering offence.

---

[1] Nadelmann, *Cops Across Borders*, pp. 4 and 315. [2] See *infra* pp. 278–81.
[3] On the concept of enforcement jurisdiction, see *supra* pp. 212–13.

Second, criminally derived proceeds may be located on the territory of another state than the one which intends to prosecute the money laundering offence or the predicate offence. International co-operation in criminal matters in the context of money laundering is therefore geared towards two goals: the gathering of information which can be introduced as evidence in the requesting state and the tracing of criminally derived proceeds with a view to their seizure and confiscation.[4] Taking into account these goals, international co-operation in criminal matters in a proceeds-oriented perspective can be divided into three phases: the investigation, the seizure and the enforcement of confiscation sanctions. This division differs from the four-stages division that has sometimes been made with regard to the suspect-oriented international co-operation in criminal matters: the investigation stage without a suspect, the investigation stage geared towards a suspect, trial stage and the enforcement stage.[5] As far as the proceeds-oriented division is concerned, special care needs to be taken with respect to the classification of seizure measures. When a piece of evidence is seized, this is an investigatory measure, but when the seizure concerns alleged proceeds of crime in order to secure a possible future confiscation, this measure falls clearly into the second stage.

The case for a reform of the international co-operation in criminal matters

The effectiveness of the fight against transnational crime is in part dependent upon the effectiveness of international co-operation in criminal matters. In this sense the attainment of the goals of a domestic criminal justice system is often contingent upon international co-operation. The globalisation of the economy and the concurrent internationalisation of crime require international co-operation as a response.[6] In the following paragraphs it will be argued that the need for an effective international co-operation requires both an extension of traditional co-operation mech-

---

[4] American authors sometimes distinguish, without an obvious reason, between gathering and transfer of evidence. See P. B. Heymann, 'Two Models of National Attitudes Toward International Cooperation in Law Enforcement', *Harv. Int'l L. J.* (1990), 99 and Nadelmann, *Cops Across Borders*, pp. 4–5.

[5] See the report by the European Committee on Crime Problems of the Council of Europe: *The European conventions on mutual assistance in criminal matters seen as an instrument of a common criminal policy* (Strasbourg, 1971), p. 3, of which the Dutch scholar Louk Hulsman is the *auctor intellectualis*.   [6] Nadelmann, *Cops Across Borders*, pp. 103–107.

anisms to other mechanisms and a reconsideration of traditional principles of international co-operation in criminal matters. The quest for more
effective ways of international co-operation should, however, not lead to a
deterioration of the human rights protection.

Extension of international co-operation in criminal matters

The movement towards a more effective international co-operation has
resulted in an extension of international co-operation in criminal matters
in two directions.

First, a number of new forms of international co-operation in criminal
matters have seen the light. In the context of money laundering, judicial
assistance in criminal matters is no longer limited to the exchange of
evidence, but also extends to forms of co-operation that fall into the
second and third stage of international co-operation (seizure and
enforcement). These new forms of international co-operation can be
brought under the heading of primary co-operation. The distinction
between primary and secondary forms of international co-operation was
introduced in 1965 by the Dutch scholar Louk Hulsman.[7] Primary co-
operation in criminal matters covers all forms of co-operation that
require one state to 'take over' at least part of the procedure of the other
state, either by instituting criminal proceedings or by enforcing criminal sanctions pronounced in another state. Traditional, secondary forms
of international co-operation in criminal matters are confined to the rendering of assistance by one state to another, but do not involve the transfer of procedural responsibility: the requesting state remains *dominus
litis*. In the latter case, the co-operation of the requested state is limited
to investigatory measures or extradition of the (alleged) offender, in
order to allow the requesting state to continue its proceedings. Although
primary forms of co-operation were heralded as the new avenue of international co-operation in criminal matters as early as the 1970s,[8] they
only seem to have gained a practical importance in the context of the

---

[7] L. H. C. Hulsman, 'Transmision des poursuites pénales à l'état de séjour et exécution des
décisions pénales étrangères', in *Le droit pénal international. Recueil d'études en hommage à
Jacob van Bemmelen* (Leiden: E. J Brill, 1965), p. 113.

[8] See e.g. the statement by Hans Schultz in 1970 over the 'end of extradition' ('Das Ende
der Auslieferung', in *Aktuelle Probleme des Internationalen Strafrechts. Heinrich Grützner zum
65. Geburtstag* (Hamburg: R. v. Decker's Verlag, 1970), pp. 138–145), aiming at the
expected increase of primary forms of co-operation in regard to extradition, the then
most 'popular' form of secondary assistance.

new co-operation forms that were devised for the purpose of fighting money laundering.[9]

Second, apart from the existence of new forms of international judicial co-operation in criminal matters, there is also an increasing trend towards new forms of co-operation between other authorities than judicial authorities, namely administrative and police authorities. This evolution will be expounded further.[10]

Reconsideration of traditional principles of international co-operation in criminal matters

In view of the need for effective international co-operation in criminal matters, some of the traditional cornerstones of international co-operation will be re-examined in this final part of the book. It is submitted that the sovereignty claims that have shaped some of the traditional conditions and exceptions to international co-operation need to be reconsidered. Some of these conditions and exceptions tend to have a chauvinistic or even parochial overtone in that they are exclusively focused on the norms and interests from one jurisdiction in order to assess the admissibility of requests for co-operation from another. It is submitted that this pattern of legal thinking should, as much as possible, be replaced by an internationalist approach which pays due respect to the importance of international co-operation by excluding as much as possible chauvinistic obstacles.

In particular, the condition of double criminality, the *locus regit actum* principle and the exceptions related to banking (and professional) secrecy, fiscal and political offences will be critically analysed in the following chapters. It will be shown that at least some of these mantras of international co-operation in criminal matters are underpinned by rationales that are linked to national sovereignty rather than to the protection of individual rights.

International co-operation in criminal matters and human rights

The pursuit of the above-mentioned goals of international co-operation should not take place to the detriment of the human rights of the persons

---

[9] Before, the practical importance of primary forms of assistance was rather limited: C. Van den Wyngaert and G. Stessens, 'Mutual Legal Assistance in Criminal Matters in the European Union', in *Changes in Society, Crime and Criminal Justice in Europe. Volume II. International Organised and Corporate Crime*, ed. C. Fijnaut, J. Goethals, T. Peters and L. Walgrave (Antwerp: Kluwer, 1995), pp. 142–3.   [10] See pp. 258–86.

involved. These include not only suspects, but also third parties. Some ambitiously argue that international co-operation should never be allowed to result in a lowering of the protection of the rights of the persons concerned.[11] Although it is open to debate whether this ambitious goal is in practice always attainable, international co-operation in criminal matters should never result in an infringement of the human rights of the person concerned. It is beyond dispute that any investigatory or provisional measure that is taken on request of another state, should meet with the same human rights requirement as an investigatory or provisional measure in a purely domestic procedure of the requested state. This position has been adopted by the European Commission of Human Rights,[12] but not by all municipal constitutional courts. In the infamous *Verdugo-Urquidez* case, the American Supreme Court refused to apply the guarantees of the Fourth Amendment to the US Constitution to extraterritorial investigations mounted by DEA agents in Mexico.[13] In other jurisdictions, the situation is often more complicated. Thus, the Canadian Supreme Court has applied some constitutional guarantees to extraterritorial investigations, although this does not automatically result in the exclusion of evidence gathered in violation of these guarantees.[14] In *Schreiber v. Canada (Attorney General)*, the Canadian Supreme Court, however, declined to apply s.8 of the Canadian Charter of Rights and Freedoms, which guarantees the right to privacy, to the procedure by which Canada requested Switzerland to search and seize bank records of a Canadian citizen.[15] At any rate, the procedures in which decisions are taken with respect to the admissibility of requests for co-operation are not governed by the human rights requirement of a fair trial, as they are not

---

[11] European Committee on Crime Problems, *The European Conventions on Mutual Assistance in Criminal Matters seen as an Instrument of a Common Criminal Policy*, 7 and A. H. J. Swart, 'Human Rights and the Abolition of Traditional Principles', in *Principles and Procedures For A Transnational Criminal Law*, A. Eser and O. Lagodny (Freiburg: Max-Planck Institut, 1992), p. 508.

[12] This is confirmed by case law of the European Commission on Human Rights, *X, Y and Z v. Austria*, Decision of 5 February 1973, *Collection of Decisions* (43), p. 38 and *R v. Austria*, Decision of 6 March 1989, *Collection of Decisions* (60), p. 201.

[13] *US v. Verdugo-Urquidez*, 110 S.Ct. 1056 (1990). For comment, see C. Gane and M. Mackarel, 'The Admissibility of Evidence Obtained from Abroad into Criminal Proceedings – The Interpretation of Mutual Legal Assistance Treaties and Use of Evidence Irregularly Obtained', *Eur.JCr., Cr.L & Cr.J* (1996), 111–12; Nadelmann, *Cops Across Borders*, pp. 448–449 and R. Wedgwood, 'International Decisions. *US v Verdugo-Urquidez*', *AJIL* (1990), 747–754.

[14] See the judgment of the Canadian Supreme Court of 1 October 1998 in *R. v. Cook*, *ILM* (1999) 271.

[15] *Schreiber v. Canada (Attorney General)* [1998] 1 S. C. R. 841. See on this judgment also *infra* pp. 302–3.

set up to decide on a criminal charge as such, nor do they trigger other human rights protections. As far as the rights of the defence are concerned, this was explicitly decided by the European Commission on Human Rights in respect of extradition procedures[16] and there is no reason why the conclusion should be any different in respect of mutual assistance procedures.[17]

The thesis that international co-operation cannot be allowed to infringe upon the fundamental rights of the persons concerned is, however, what it is: a thesis. For many years, the individual was looked upon as a mere object of international co-operation in criminal matters that had no standing to assert individual rights. In the *Soering* decision of the European Court of Human Rights it became clear that not every infringement of a human rights provision stands in the way of international co-operation,[18] an outcome which is probably at least in part attributable to the fact that human rights provisions were conceived with respect to internal and not to international procedures.[19] In addition, human rights requirements are also more difficult to apply in international procedures than traditional requirements like double criminality, because domestic courts are often loath to investigate the fairness of judicial procedures in the requesting state. In extradition law, for example, the rule of noninquiry is so firmly embedded in the municipal extradition law of some countries that courts will refuse extradition only in the most shocking circumstances.[20] The precise role of human rights requirements in relation to international co-operation in the field of money laundering will be discussed later.[21] At this stage it is, however, already useful to draw a distinction between direct and indirect control. Indirect control of foreign

---

[16] European Commission on Human Rights, *H. v. Spain*, Decision of 15 December 1983, *Decisions and Reports* (37), p. 93; *E. M. Kirkwood v. UK*, Decision of 12 March 1984, *Decisions and Reports* (37), p. 158; *R. Whitehead v. Italy*, 2 March 1989, *Decisions and Reports* (60), p. 272.

[17] A. Donatsch, 'Konventionsrecht in Verfahren der kleinen Rechtshilfe', *RPS* (1996), 282–283.

[18] European Court of Human Rights, *Soering v. UK*, judgment of 7 July 1989, *Publ. ECHR*, Series A, No.161. See C. Van den Wyngaert, 'Applying the European Convention on Human Rights to Extradition: Opening Pandora's Box', *ICLQ* (1990), 757–779.

[19] C. Van den Wyngaert, 'Rethinking the Law of International Criminal Co-operation: The Restrictive Function of International Human Rights Through Individually-Oriented Bars', in *Principles and Procedures For A Transnational Criminal Law*, A. Eser and O. Lagodny (Freiburg: Max-Planck Institut, 1992), pp. 500–3.

[20] J. Dugard and C. Van den Wyngaert, 'Reconciling Extradition with Human Rights', *Am.J.Int'l. Law* (1998), 189–191. Cf. Swart, 'Human Rights and the Abolition of Traditional Principles', 509. Cf. International Law Association, *Report of the Committee on Extradition and Human Rights*, 1998.   [21] See *infra* pp. 400–7.

procedural acts is fairly commonly accepted: it can take place by the court of the requesting state by excluding evidence which was unlawfully obtained abroad. Direct control is much less accepted as it implies that the person concerned has the right to object to the requested measures in the requested state.[22] At least under the case law of the European Commission and European Court of Human Rights, a state remains responsible for violations of human rights, also when acting to comply with international obligations[23] (e.g. by carrying out a request for assistance) or when acting outside its national territory.[24]

The level of protection of human rights in the context of international co-operation should in principle be the same, irrespective of whether this co-operation takes place through judicial, administrative or police channels. Although administrative and police assistance lack the guarantee of a judicial intervention, the case law of the European Court of Human Rights has made clear that evidence which is transmitted in this way is subject to the same human rights strictures as evidence that was transmitted through the channels of judicial co-operation in criminal matters.[25]

[22] See on this distinction: Vogel, 'Combating International Organized Crime by International Co-operation: The German View', 353 and C. Van den Wyngaert, 'The Transformations of International Criminal Law', 216–18.

[23] European Commission on Human Rights, decision of 9 February 1990, M & Co. v. Germany, 13258/87, Decisions and Reports (64), 138.

[24] European Court of Human Rights, Loizidou v. Turkey (Preliminary Objections), judgment of 23 March 1995, Publications of the European Court of Human Rights, Series A, No.310, paras.61–2. See in general: A. Klip, 'The Decrease of Protection under Human Rights Treaties in International Criminal Law', RIDP (1996), 291–310.

[25] European Court of Human Rights, Funke v. France, 25 February 1993, Publ. ECHR, Series A, No.256–A.

12   The money laundering regime: new modes of international evidence-gathering

International, treaty-based co-operation between judicial authorities was traditionally portrayed as the sole mode of gathering evidence abroad. It will be shown, however, that in the context of the international fight against money laundering (and also outside this particular context), new modes of international evidence-gathering have become increasingly important. On the one hand, administrative and police co-operation are expanding and have partly taken over the functions of judicial mutual assistance. In this respect, the exchange of information between FIUs has obtained a very important role and the conditions under which this type of mutual administrative assistance takes places, merit to be scrutinised. Apart from this evolution, some national authorities have had recourse to unilateral extraterritorial measures instead of using the channels of international judicial co-operation. These new developments in the field of international evidence-gathering make it necessary to investigate the exact position of treaty-based co-operation in criminal matters.

Exchange of information relating to suspicious financial transactions: judicial, administrative or police assistance?

The important role that is played by the FIUs in the combat against money laundering, has already been expounded in Part 2.[1] In order to fulfil their role, these FIUs mutually exchange information. The international co-operation between FIUs takes place almost completely outside the framework of traditional judicial co-operation in criminal matters. By mutually exchanging information, FIUs are often able to clarify the background of suspicious transactions and thus succeed in fitting the pieces of the pro-

---

[1] See *supra* pp. 183–99.

verbial jigsaw puzzle together. This exchange of information can take different forms: on request, spontaneously (i.e., on the initiative of the financial intelligence unit that provides information) or periodically.

The importance of this type of co-operation has been underlined by various international fora,[2] although there is as yet no formal international law basis for it. The hybrid nature of the authorities (i.e., the national FIUs) involved in this exchange of information makes it difficult to categorise this type of assistance. Notwithstanding the fact that the borderlines between judicial, police and administrative assistance have become increasingly blurred, it will be argued that this type of assistance is most akin to administrative assistance, although it undeniably takes place against the background of the criminal fight against money laundering. Precisely because of the repressive goal of this information exchange, the question as to whether this type of administrative assistance could also take place through police or judicial assistance will be studied in some detail.

Shifting borderlines between mutual administrative assistance, police assistance and judicial international co-operation

Whereas international co-operation in criminal matters was traditionally the province of judicial authorities, new forms of mutual assistance have come to light, in particular mutual police assistance and mutual administrative assistance. The borderlines between these various forms of mutual assistance were traditionally delineated in accordance with the powers of the authorities involved. Thus, a request for measures which can only be taken by judicial authorities was normally brought under the heading of mutual legal assistance, that is, co-operation between judicial authorities. Consequently, coercive measures are excluded from the application field of police or administrative assistance for the reason that they can, in principle, be taken only by judicial authorities.[3] This rule is nevertheless subject to exceptions which makes it preferable to draw the borderline between various forms of international co-operation in terms of

---

[2] See, e.g., the *First Commission's report on the implementation of the Money Laundering Directive*, p. 14 and recommendation 6(XXXVIII) of the Commission on Psychotropic Substances of the United Nations of 28 June 1995 and the Recommendation AGN/64/RES/24 of the General Assembly of Interpol (1995).

[3] See D. Heimans, 'Internationale uitwisseling van politieinformatie: over het grensvlak tussen rechtshulp en privacybescherming', *DD* (1994), 135. Cf. G. J. Kriz, 'International Co-operation to Combat Money Laundering: The Nature and Role of Mutual Legal Assistance Treaties', *Commonwealth Law Bulletin* (1992), 727.

purposes rather than in terms of the authorities that initiate or respond to requests for co-operation. Thus the lifting of banking secrecy normally requires the intervention of a judicial authority and is therefore normally granted only in the course of a judicial co-operation. Nevertheless, many FIUs also have the power to lift banking secrecy and can consequently exchange information covered by banking secrecy laws. In the latter case the information will normally be exchanged only for intelligence purposes,[4] so that this co-operation should be classified as administrative assistance.

It is moreover a general trend that the borderlines between various forms of mutual assistance are shifting. As follows, it will be argued that, in spite of the increasing blurring of the demarcations between judicial, police and administrative assistance, the various forms of international co-operation should as much as possible be separated from each other in the context of the fight against money laundering.

Formal borderlines between various forms of assistance disappear at various levels. In domestic legislation, numerous examples can be found of provisions that allow judicial authorities to co-operate with administrative or police authorities and vice versa.[5] This is not surprising in view of the fact that the same functions are exercised by different authorities in different countries. The same evolution is reflected in international legal assistance treaties. The application field of older treaties, such as the European Convention on Mutual Assistance in Criminal Matters (1959),[6] was limited to requests emanating from judicial authorities. Many mutual assistance treaties of more recent vintage, however, have broadened their application field so as to accommodate requests from administrative authorities. This is, for example, the case in the Schengen Convention (1990)[7] and in some bilateral mutual legal assistance treaties (MLATs). In respect of the latter, the United States–Switzerland MLAT (1973) was a precursor in that it also allowed

---

[4] See infra pp. 273–6.
[5] See, e.g., the UK Criminal Justice (International Co-operation) Act 1990, which allows English courts to render assistance before a formal criminal investigation is started. See Harding, 'Treaty-Making in the Field of International Co-operation', p. 241 and Levi, 'Pecunia non olet', 265–6. See in general: J. J. E. Schutte, 'La coopération administrative', in Actes du colloque organisé par l'ARPE à l'Abbaye de Royaumont (Paris: Economica, 1993), pp. 202, 207.   [6] Strasbourg, 20 April 1959, ETS, No. 30.
[7] Convention of 19 June 1990, applying the Schengen Agreement of 14 June 1985 between the Governments of the States of the Benelux Economic Union, the Federal Republic of Germany and the French Republic on the Gradual Abolition of Checks at their Common Borders, ILM (1991), 84.

for requests from administrative authorities (though not in purely administrative matters[8]).

This general trend can also be noted in the particular context of international co-operation in the fight against money laundering in different respects. Thus, both multilateral co-operation conventions in the field of the fight against money laundering contain provisions which attest to this trend. Article 7(1) of the Vienna Convention declares that Parties shall afford one another 'the widest measure of mutual legal assistance in investigations, prosecutions and judicial proceedings in relation to criminal offences established in accordance with article 3, paragraph 1 [i.e. drug trafficking and drug money laundering]'. Article 9 refers to 'other forms of co-operation and training' and demands that states 'co-operate closely with one another . . . with a view to enhancing the effectiveness of law enforcement action to suppress the commission of [these] offences'. Both provisions are so construed as to cover the wide variance between different legal systems as to which forms of assistance can be provided by which authorities.[9] Article 8 of the Money Laundering Convention requires parties to 'afford each other, upon request, the widest possible measure of assistance in the identification and tracing of instrumentalities, proceeds and other property liable to confiscation'. This provision also embraces other proceedings than criminal proceedings, in so far as they are directed towards the confiscation and are related to a criminal activity.[10]

In the following pages, it will further be set out in detail that the above-described trend of shifting borders between administrative, police and judicial co-operation is very clearly discernible in the context of the exchange of information on suspicious financial transactions between FIUs.

---

[8] See Article 1(a) of the MLAT. For comment, see H. Schultz, 'Practical Problems Arising from Treaties on Mutual Legal Assistance Between Continental and Common Law States: The Example of Switzerland and the United States of America', in *Principles and Procedures For A Transnational Criminal Law*, A. Eser and O. Lagodny (Freiburg: Max-Planck Institut, 1992), pp. 313–14; L. Frei and S. Trechsel, 'Origins and Applications of the US–Switzerland Treaty on Mutual Assistance in Criminal Matters', *Harv.Int.LJ* (1990), 83; and Aubert and others, *Le secret bancaire suisse*, p. 547. See also the case law of the Swiss Supreme Court in this respect: ATF 109 Ib 47 and ATF 115Ib 196.

[9] *Report US Delegation*, p. 128.

[10] *Explanatory Report with the Convention on Laundering, Search, Seizure and Confiscation of the Proceeds from Crime*, 23. See also Gilmore, *Dirty Money*, p. 145.

Administrative character of the international exchange of information between FIUs

Administrative assistance (*assistance administrative*, *Amtshilfe*) can generally be defined as international assistance that takes place between administrative government authorities, that is, outside the judicial framework, with a view to the application of or compliance with specific administrative rules.[11] It differs from judicial assistance (*entraide judicaire*, *Rechtshilfe*), both in terms of authorities concerned and of objectives.

The authorities involved in administrative assistance can comprise any kind of government authority except judicial authorities. As far as the objectives are concerned, administrative assistance (and administrative law enforcement in general), differ from judicial assistance (and criminal law enforcement) in that they are not so much geared towards repressing criminality but more at ensuring the correct application of administrative rules. The objective of administrative law enforcement is thus much wider than that of criminal law enforcement. Administrative authorities that find infringements of administrative rules will often try to remedy the situation (*redressement administratif*), rather than transmit the case to the competent law enforcement authorities. Some therefore even define administrative assistance as assistance that takes place outside the context of litigation.[12]

As far as the exchange of information between FIUs is concerned, however, two remarks need to be made on the administrative nature of this type of assistance. First, not all FIUs are administrative authorities. The discussion of the nature of the authorities responsible for combating money laundering in Part 2 revealed that in some states police or even judicial authorities have been charged with collecting and analysing information transmitted by financial institutions.[13] As far as judicial FIUs are concerned, these are excluded from the international exchange of information that takes place between other FIUs. Because of their general duties they cannot guarantee the limited and confidential use of information unless there is a specific statutory provision which allows them to retain confidential information received from foreign FIUs. Police authorities – such as the UK National Crime Intelligence Service – do, however, take part in the international information exchange.[14] However, this does

---

[11] Schutte, 'La coopération administrative', p. 194.
[12] U. Zulauf, 'Rechtshilfe-Amtshilfe', *RSDA* (1995), 51, referring to J. W. Simon, *Amtshilfe. Allgemeine Verpflichtungen, Schranken und Grundsätze* (Chur/Zürich: Reihe Verwaltungsrecht, Bd.12, 1991), p. 35.   [13] See *supra* pp. 185–8.
[14] See approvingly: R. Lamp, 'Financiële informatie de grens over', *DD* (1999), 50.

not necessarily preclude this type of information exchange from being classified as administrative assistance, since police assistance can also be considered as a type of administrative assistance, that is, assistance between non-judicial government authorities.

A second remark pertains to the objectives of administrative assistance between national FIUs. As was already pointed out, this assistance serves a clearly repressive goal, given the important role that FIUs play in the domestic enforcement of anti-money-laundering laws: they mostly act as an intermediary between the financial institutions and judicial authorities. Even though most of the FIUs have no proper law enforcement tasks,[15] their mission is nevertheless clearly geared towards criminal law enforcement. Unlike other administrative agencies, they have no possibilities of administrative law enforcement (e.g. by amicable settlements, administrative fines, etc.) and they have little or no room to implement their own policy.

Nevertheless, the exchange of information between FIUs can be best classified as mutual administrative assistance. In many cases the authorities are not police services and even if police services are involved, the exchange of information takes place outside the mainstream of international police co-operation. Moreover, it will in the following be argued that it would be impracticable and unwise to bring this type of *sui generis* co-operation under the heading of police or judicial co-operation.

International exchange of information between FIUs through the channels of police or judicial assistance: a viable alternative?

In view of the undeniable law enforcement background of the exchange of information between FIUs, it is useful to investigate whether this type of co-operation could not take place through the channels of police assistance, or even via judicial assistance. As far as judicial assistance is concerned, such a movement would be in keeping with the more general trend of blurring borders between all forms of co-operation (administrative, police and judicial) so that judicial co-operation can nowadays also include co-operation with administrative authorities. Nevertheless, several arguments can be invoked against exercising such an option.

The stringent specialty principle to which some of the administrative FIUs are subjected makes it impossible for them to forward information to foreign judicial FIUs as these would not be able to safeguard this specialty principle.

---

[15] See, however, *supra* p. 188.

Apart from this specific obstacle, the procedural context of judicial assistance differs from that of administrative assistance. Whereas the former is concerned with exchanging evidence in the context of a criminal investigation that is often already centred on identified suspects, administrative assistance of this type consists mainly of exchanging of information on suspicious transactions. Although this type of information may obviously also contain information on individuals, these individuals will not (yet) have the status of suspects. In fact a substantial part of the so-called suspicious transactions that are scrutinised by FIUs will eventually turn out not to be related to money laundering operations. The administrative concept of a suspicious transaction, as operated by (administrative and police) FIUs is therefore wider than the judicial concept of a suspicious transaction. This, in turn, also has implications for international co-operation and some states even go so far as to require a *prima facie* case for the purposes of accommodating a request for judicial assistance.[16] It is obvious that such a requirement cannot possibly be met at the preliminary stage during which FIUs exchange information on suspicious transactions. Moreover, it will often not be possible to assess other requirements that are generally posed in the context of judicial co-operation. Thus, it may in practice be impossible to ascertain whether the condition of double criminality is met as it will not be clear from what type of predicate offence (if from an offence at all) the funds are derived.

The use of channels of international police co-operation for exchanging information on suspicious financial transactions also seems an attractive option. There are undeniably significant advantages to the use of police co-operation for exchanging information on suspicious financial transactions. Police services generally have a greater access to databases and to other means of analysing, checking and controlling information than do most administrative FIUs. Exploiting these police information sources on an international level is bound to create synergies of investigation power that can be difficult to attain through administrative assistance.

Some EU Member States, such as Germany, Ireland and Austria are willing to exchange information only at a police level. In the context of the European Union, the use of police channels for exchanging information on suspicious financial transactions is moreover an especially attractive avenue in view of the possible role for Europol. The European Police Office, set up by the Europol Convention of 26 July 1995,[17] only became truly operational on 1 October 1998 (after ratification of the Convention

---

[16] See *infra* pp. 338–9.   [17] *OJ*, No. C316, 27.1.1995, p. 1.

by the 15 EU Member States), has as its mission to improve the effectiveness and co-operation of the competent authorities of the Member States in preventing and combating a number of crimes which are indicated in (the appendix to) the Europol Convention (notably drug offences, trade in nuclear and radioactive substances, illegal immigration and trade in human beings and trade in stolen vehicles).

Setting up a central index reference system at Europol under the wider umbrella of the Europol information system, as has been proposed in some quarters,[18] would open a huge potential for the analysis and processing of information related to suspicious transactions. Europol has access to large databases and analysis files which contain potentially very interesting information for analysing reports on suspicious financial transactions. Another important advantage of the exchange of information on suspicious transactions through Europol is that it would put in place an 'indirect exchange' of money laundering information, whereby information exchange takes place through a central information point (Europol) instead of on a bilateral basis. A type of indirect exchange of information already takes place through the Egmont Secure Web, a secure website of the Egmont Group,[19] which allows members of this group to exchange general information on a multilateral basis and even to ask questions for information on a multilateral basis. This Egmont Secure Web, which was set up in 1997, does not equate to a hypothetical central index reference system at Europol, however, as the latter would not be limited to a centralised exchange of information, but would imply the setting up of a central database. At any rate, indirect, the centralised exchange of information can never completely do away with the need for direct, bilateral exchange of information, for the indirect exchange of information on suspicious transactions would take place via computer links to Europol and would therefore also be limited to certain types of information. More substantial exchange of information (e.g. of documents or dossiers) will always have to take place on a bilateral footing, especially in view of the fact that some national authorities may wish to limit the type of information they put into the centralised index reference system.[20]

The most problematic aspect for a role of Europol in this field is the way in which its competence has been attributed. Article 2(3) of the Convention explicitly states that Europol shall also be competent with

---

[18] See the study carried out by KPMG and commissioned by the Dutch Ministry of Justice during the Dutch EU Presidency: *Feasibility Study for a Potential Computerised System Concerning Money Laundering*, 1998.   [19] On the Egmont Group, see *infra* pp. 269–70.

[20] See also KPMG/Dutch Ministry of Justice, *Feasibility Study*, p. 4.

respect to 'illegal money laundering activities in connection with these forms of crime or specific manifestations thereof', as well as 'related criminal offences'. It is, however, seldom possible to ascertain at an early stage of a police or even judicial investigation from which predicate offences the suspicious funds are derived. Consequently, it is almost impossible for Europol to ascertain at an early stage whether the money laundering activities in question fall under its competence or not. The problem was not properly addressed in the Treaty of Amsterdam which only contains an official acknowledgement of the possibility of joint actions in the field of 'the collection, storage, processing, analysis and exchange of relevant information, including information by law enforcement services on reports on suspicious financial transactions, in particular through Europol, subject to appropriate provisions on the protection of personal data' (Article K.2 of the European Union Treaty (or Article 30 TEU, as amended by the Treaty of Amsterdam)). It is doubtful whether – as is suggested by some sources[21] – this should suffice to make Europol legally competent to store data on suspicious transactions. It is submitted this would require an enlargement of the treaty-based competences of Europol so that they would encompass any illegal money laundering activity, regardless of the nature of the predicate offences from which the funds involved are derived. This is also envisaged by action point 26 of the EU Action Plan to combat organised crime.[22]

The discussion of the difficulties in using Europol for the purpose of exchanging information on suspicious transactions, leads to the more general drawbacks to the use of police channels for these purposes.

Already under the present situation extensive co-operation between national FIUs, both police services and administrative financial intelligence units, is taking place. For the main part, however, this co-operation is situated outside the mainstream of international, multilateral police co-operation – which operates to a large extent through Interpol – but is instead based on bilateral agreements, often in the form of memoranda of understanding, which set out a number of obligations for the receiving (police) authority, such as confidentiality and limited use of information. Apart from this direct international co-operation with police FIUs, administrative FIUs can also communicate with their domestic police services in order to obtain information on suspicious transactions. These domestic police services can in turn contact their foreign counterparts, through the 'classic' (i.e. Interpol) police channels. The use of Interpol police channels

---

[21] KPMG/Dutch Ministry of Justice, *Feasibility Study for a Potential Computerised System Concerning Money Laundering*, 1998, p. 39.   [22] *OJ* No. C 251, 15.08.1997, p. 1.

for the exchange of information on suspicious financial transactions is, however, at best doubtful. In view of the stringent secrecy rules that govern many, especially administrative FIUs, the Interpol channels are not advisable for exchanging this type of information as the Interpol rules do not allow for this type of confidentiality (which often precisely prohibits the disclosure of any substantial information to police forces, domestic or foreign), but are instead based on the principle of wide, mutual exchange of information. As a consequence, the indirect use of the international police channels by administrative FIUs *de facto* boils down to an untenable situation in which foreign police services are asked to provide information, but are never able to obtain information from the requesting FIU.

In general, one might ask oneself whether using police channels for the purpose of exchanging information on suspicious financial transactions is a viable option. This type of information, forwarded by financial institutions (either on their own initiative, or on request) and originally covered by banking secrecy rules, is generally very sensitive so that bankers are very reluctant to hand over this type of information to police services. This is precisely why many legislators choose instead to set up a specific administrative authority to deal with the reports made by financial institutions. Channelling the international exchange of this information through police channels, would in part undermine the 'filtering' function of these administrative FIUs on the international level. It is therefore submitted that the exchange of information on suspicious financial transactions should be allowed to take place through international police co-operation channels only under strict conditions.[23] International police co-operation in the field of suspicious financial transactions should be structured in such a way that the trust of financial institutions in the reporting system is not jeopardised. In particular, the fear of bankers that any information they disclose might be used for many different purposes in foreign jurisdictions needs to be allayed. First, international or supranational criteria for determining what is a 'suspicious transaction', and what type of information can therefore be exchanged through the international police channels, need to be established. At present there is wide divergence in domestic practice as to what FIUs consider to be a 'suspicious' transaction.[24] It is therefore necessary to find international agreement (with the European Union, or in the larger framework of the FATF) on the criteria for delineating the concept of a 'suspicious transaction'. An additional 'security lock' which could be installed to allay the fears of the

[23] See also *Second Commission Report*, p. 15.
[24] Thony, 'Processing Financial Information', 261–2.

financial sector is to impose a specialty principle on the use of information that would be exchanged through international police co-operation channels. In this way the guarantee of the specialty principle which exists in a number of domestic legal systems could also be safeguarded internationally. Under the Europol Convention, this is already possible: the state or body that communicates information to Europol can impose restrictions on the use that may be made of it, which can be overridden, however, by the provisions of domestic law (Article 17(2)). In addition, the use of information from the Europol database, index system or data files is at any rate limited to preventing and combating those crimes that fall within the competence of Europol and to combating other serious forms of crime (Article 17(1)). The need for a specialty principle in the context of exchange of information on suspicious transactions is apparent in other contexts as well. In the field of so-called vertical co-operation between EU Member States and the European Commission, Article 7 of the Second Protocol of the Convention on the protection of the European Communities' financial interests[25] provides for co-operation between Member States and the European Commission in the fight against EC fraud, active and passive corruption and money laundering. The provision encourages the competent authorities in the Member States to exchange information with the Commission, while acknowledging the requirements of investigation secrecy and data protection. It also allows a Member State that supplies information to the Commission to set 'specific conditions covering the use of information, whether by the Commission or by another Member State to which that information may be passed'. In the 1999 Commission proposal for amending the Money Laundering Directive, which contains a similar provision on this exchange of information, there is, however, no reference to a specialty principle, but only to the rules of secrecy.[26] Moreover, the specialty principle is – as will be shown in the following pages – also the quintessential stricture in the field of mutual administrative assistance between FIUs.

---

[25] *OJ*, No. C 221, 19.7.1997, p. 11.

[26] See Article 2 (11) of the *Proposal for a European Parliament and Council Directive amending Council Directive 91/308/EEC of 10 June 1991 on Prevention of the Use of the Financial System for the Purpose of Money Laundering*, Brussels, 14.7.1999, COM(1999) 352 final, 99/152 (COD).

Mutual administrative assistance between FIUs: basis, restrictions and ramifications on criminal proceedings

In the following section, the conditions under which FIUs can mutually exchange, on a bilateral basis, information relating to suspicious or unusual financial transactions, will be examined. This is something of a venture, given the fact that most of this co-operation takes place on the basis of Memoranda of Understanding (MOUs) which are normally not made public and may even have no formal basis at all. Given that both the FATF recommendations and the European Money Laundering Directive are silent on this point, there are moreover no international standards in this field. It is particularly regrettable that the Council of the European Community was not able to lay down the basic conditions for mutual assistance between the authorities responsible for combating money laundering in the Money Laundering Directive as it did, for example, in the Insider Dealing Directive,[27] or in the Second Banking Directive. Apparently, the drafters of the Money Laundering Directive thought that the Community lacked the competence to lay down the conditions for mutual assistance or to provide the basic legal framework for enabling Member States to conclude MOUs in this respect.[28] This difference between the Money Laundering Directive and the Insider Dealing Directive is surprising given that they are both based on Article 100a of the EEC Treaty. Mutual administrative assistance between FIUs within the European Union would undoubtedly have benefited considerably from a European set of rules defining the conditions for the mutual co-operation, as has also – belatedly – been acknowledged by the European Commission itself.[29] It would have made mutual administrative assistance much more transparent[30] and would also have given the conditions governing mutual assistance a justiciable character, for the information exchanged in this way may subsequently be introduced as evidence into criminal proceedings.

Some attempts have been made to streamline this type of administrative assistance under the aegis of the so-called Egmont Group – a group of national FIUs that meet regularly to discuss the problems of international

---

[27] See Article 10 of the Council Directive of 13 November 1989 co-ordinating regulations on insider dealing, *OJ*, No. L 334, 18.11.1989, p. 30.

[28] See Schutte, 'Strafrecht in Europees verband', 15–16 and also *supra* pp. 25–7.

[29] *Second Commission Report*, p. 13.

[30] For a criticism of the lack of transparency of this type of mutual administrative assistance, see V. Mul and C. D. Schaap, 'Internationale informatieuitwisseling omtrent witwassen; mogelijkheden en onmogelijkheden', *Justitiële Verkenningen* (1996, No.9), 45.

co-operation. The group derives its name from the Brussels Egmont Palace, where its first meeting took place at the initiative of the Belgian and American FIUs. The Egmont Group has made substantial and very commendable efforts in the field of international co-operation between FIUs resulting amongst other things in a Model Memorandum of Understanding, which has now been adopted by national FIUs.

In the following, the conditions under which this type of mutual administrative assistance functions will be outlined, not only with respect to their role in the co-operation between FIUs, but also in view of their possible impact on subsequent criminal proceedings, in particular regarding the admissibility of evidence that is introduced into criminal proceedings but came into the possession of the prosecuting authority through mutual administrative assistance between FIUs.

Requirement and justiciability of an MOU

Unless the domestic law of either the state providing the information (hereinafter referred to as: the providing state) or of the state receiving the information (hereinafter referred to as: the receiving state) contains a requirement to the effect that exchange of information with foreign FIUs can take place only on the basis of a formal agreement, mutual administrative assistance of this type can also take place in the absence of an agreement. Even in the absence of such a statutory requirement, many FIUs, however, prefer to co-operate only on the basis of an MOU.

When there is such an MOU, the question may arise as to whether the restrictions it imposes on exchange of information between the FIUs concerned are in any way judicially enforceable. In practice this problem will pose itself only if information that was exchanged is being introduced as evidence into criminal proceedings. The problem is rather novel and no case law on the topic is known. The apparent lack of case law is probably in great part due to the fact that these MOUs are usually not made public. Unlike treaties, MOUs are not concluded between states but between national government authorities, notably between FIUs.

Although some – mainly American – authors suggest[31] these MOUs only

---

[31] See, e.g., M. D. Mann, J. G. Mari and G. Lavdas, 'Internationalisation of Insider Trading Enforcement – a Guide to Regulation and Co-operation', in *European Insider Dealing*, K. Hopt and E. Wymeersch (London: Butterworths, 1991), pp. 354–5; L. M. Ruiz, 'European Community Directive on Insider Dealing: A Model for Effective Enforcement of Prohibitions on Insider Trading in International Markets', *Colum.JTransnat'l L* (1995), 233. See also Zagaris, 'Dollar Diplomacy', 514. Even Swiss authors opine that only fully-fledged treaties can bind Swiss authorities: M. Aubert, *et al.*, *Le secret bancaire suisse*, p. 632.

structure co-operation between the authorities concerned, it is submitted they are normally also binding on the authorities that conclude them. At least most FIUs themselves seem to consider these MOUs to be binding on themselves. This is demonstrated by the fact that many MOUs contain an *ordre public* clause which functions like a 'safety valve' in that it allows FIUs to refuse assistance in case the sovereignty, security, *ordre public*, or other essential interests of the requested state are at stake. Should the FIUs consider the MOUs they enter into as not binding, there would be no need for such a provision, as assistance could *ex hypothesi* be refused anyway. This does not, however, answer the question of whether these MOUs should also be considered as binding on the respective states from which the FIUs emanate and on other, notably judicial, authorities of that state. The answer to this question hinges on the legislation and constitution of the state concerned.

When the legislation of the state concerned enables the FIU to enter into an agreement, that agreement is binding on that state and in principle prevails over the domestic law of that state. In the absence of 'enabling' legislation, however, it cannot be accepted that the agreements entered into by an administrative authority (i.e., an FIU) that is not the constitutionally mandated treaty making power would be binding on the citizens and other authorities of the state concerned, nor that the terms of an agreement would prevail over the domestic law of the state concerned.[32] It follows that any violation of MOUs that have been entered into by FIUs, can be successfully invoked by a defendant and can give rise to exclusion of evidence only when the municipal legislation of the state concerned enabled the FIU to enter into the MOU. Of course, violation of any of the conditions imposed on mutual administrative assistance between FIUs can always give rise to exclusion of evidence or other sanctions if these conditions are laid down in domestic law or in a fully-fledged international treaty (i.e., a treaty entered into and ratified by the constitutionally mandated treaty making power of the state concerned).

Condition of double criminality

Unlike in international judicial co-operation in criminal matters, where the condition of double criminality plays a pivotal role, this condition has

---

[32] L. L. Laudati, *Study of Exchange of Confidential Information Agreements and Treaties between the US and Member States of the EU in areas of Securities, Criminal, Tax and Customs* (Brussels: European Commission (DG IV – Competition) and European University Institute, 1996), p. 6.

no role of importance in mutual administrative assistance.[33] Often administrative authorities have, as a result of their strictly delineated powers, access only to a limited type of information regarding infringements of law (that may possibly also give rise to criminal sanctions), but which they can unlimitedly exchange, that is, irrespective of a link with a request or a certain set of facts or offences. In many cases it will not be clear whether the information can be linked to a criminal offence so that the assistance will not (yet) serve a criminal prosecution goal. It would therefore be illogical to impose a condition of double criminality on mutual administrative assistance which almost invariably takes place at a stage of the procedure at which there is as yet no (formal) suspicion of crime. This would not only be illogical, but also practically impossible in view of the fact that the request for information is not and cannot (yet) be linked to a specific offence. Sometimes the information will not be linked to specific information, but to criminal cash flows or even to general statistics or strategic information (although some states refuse to exchange information other than on a case-to-case basis).[34] This is especially true in respect of money laundering, where it may often take a long time before it can be ascertained from which predicate offences the funds involved in the money laundering operation are derived. It is therefore very likely that an exchange of information will also take place in respect of money laundering acts that are not liable to criminal sanctions in the receiving and/or providing state. In respect of some types of mutual administrative assistance, the condition of double criminality has even been explicitly ruled out. Thus Article 10(1) of the Insider Dealing Directive obliges the national administrative authorities that are charged with supervising the insider dealing prohibition to exchange information, including information related to actions that are prohibited only in the requesting state.[35]

Specialty principle

The fact that the exchange of information between FIUs is not subject to the fulfilment of a condition of double criminality, does not mean that there is no limitation on this type of mutual administrative assistance.

---

[33] Laudati, *Study of Exchange of Confidential Information Agreements*, p. 16. See, however, in respect of MLATs, *infra* p. 288.

[34] KPMG/Dutch Ministry of Justice, *Feasibility Study*, pp. 33–6.

[35] See, however, critically as to the practical implementation: A. Hirsch, 'International Enforcement and International Assistance in Insider Trading', in *European Insider Dealing*, K. Hopt and E. Wymeersch (London: Butterworths, 1991), pp. 379–80.

The main stricture, however, becomes operative after the exchange of information has already taken place through the imposition of a specialty principle which limits the use that can be made of information received from a foreign FIU. By subjecting the use of this information in the receiving state to a specialty principle, it can be ensured that the use of this information is subjected to the same limitations as in the providing state. Limiting the evidential consequences of mutual administrative assistance rather than limiting mutual assistance itself is logical in view of the fact that the possible criminal uses of the information are not yet clear at that stage.

A specialty principle can be grounded in various bases. First, an FIU that is subject to a domestic specialty principle will in principle have to abide by it, both in general and when receiving information from a foreign counterpart. In principle, no greater use can be made of information received from abroad than from internally received information. Second, the applicable MOU can stipulate limitations on the use of information exchanged. Thus, all MOUs entered into by the Belgian FIU for example, contain a provision which limits the use of information provided by the Belgian FIU in the same way as under Belgian domestic law.[36]

In view of the secret nature of most MOUs it is difficult to assess the way in which provisions on the specialty principle have been formulated. In general, it seems that MOUs depart from the principle of free exchange of information for intelligence purposes (analysing and processing information by the receiving FIU), but require a prior consent from the providing FIU for use for evidentiary purposes or, more generally, for use by any other authority than the receiving FIU. This is the general outline of the Model MOU of the Egmont Group, for example, which has been adopted by the Dutch financial intelligence unit.[37] The requirement of a prior consent should, however, essentially be seen against the backdrop of the divide between administrative and judicial co-operation.

Limitations flowing from the administrative nature of mutual assistance: relation to judicial assistance

The task of most FIUs, though clearly linked to the repressive combating of money laundering, is essentially an administrative one in that they are set up as an intermediary between financial institutions and judicial authorities. Although some may have been vested with limited investigatory powers, their task is not so much to investigate money laundering

---

[36] See on this *supra* pp. 195–6.   [37] Lamp, 'Financiële informatie de grens over', 45–6.

operations and to gather evidence, rather to filter the relevant reports from non-relevant ones.

This limitation of the task of the FIUs to the preliminary stage of a criminal investigation also has ramifications at the international level of co-operation. Mutual assistance between FIUs should in principle be geared towards the function of FIUs, that is filtering relevant from non-relevant reports (a clearing-house function). The exchange of information between FIUs should therefore be limited to intelligence purposes and should not go beyond this by exchanging evidence rather than information. This limitation also has as a consequence which is that, in principle, an FIU should not request (additional) information regarding a certain (set of) transaction(s) once a criminal investigation has commenced. It is therefore a matter of some surprise that the EU *Draft Report of the Informal Money Laundering Experts Group*[38] recommends that it should always be possible for an FIU to obtain additional information to supplement a disclosure without requiring a rogatory letter. Although this may be desirable from an efficiency point of view, it seems to take no notice of the principal divide between administrative and judicial assistance.

In order to safeguard the concern that mutual administrative assistance should not substitute for judicial co-operation, co-operation agreements (MOUs) or domestic legislation may stipulate that assistance will be refused if the requesting state has already started a judicial investigation/proceeding concerning the facts at issue. Such a provision is contained in the Model MOU of the Egmont Group. Analogous provisions can be found in the context of mutual administrative assistance in tax matters[39] and in insider dealing.[40]

Notwithstanding the principal divide between mutual administrative assistance and judicial co-operation, it is possible that information that has been lawfully obtained through channels of mutual administrative assistance will prove to be useful as evidence in criminal proceedings. To require that a request for judicial co-operation be issued to obtain the same information would amount to unnecessary and overzealous formalism. A far more efficient solution, and one which protects the rights of the providing state equally well, is one that requires the authorities of the pro-

---

[38] p. 32.

[39] The Convention for Mutual Administrative Assistance in Tax Matters (drafted under the aegis of the OECD and opened for signature on 25 January 1988) excludes mutual administrative assistance once the tax file has been transmitted to the penal authorities: see *Explanatory Report on the Convention on Mutual Administrative Assistance in Tax Matters* (Strasbourg: 1989), pp. 19–20.

[40] Article 10(2)(b) of the Insider Dealing Directive.

viding state to give their consent for the use of information as evidence in criminal proceedings. This solution has already gained acceptance in other fields of mutual administrative assistance,[41] and it is submitted that it should also be adopted in the context of information that is exchanged between FIUs. Such a requirement is also stipulated in the Model MOU drawn up by the Egmont Group.

It effectively allows the avoidance of using mutual administrative assistance to circumvent the – generally more stringent – requirements of judicial co-operation in criminal matters.[42] Moreover, requiring the agreement of the providing authority also gives that authority the option of controlling the further use that is made of the information it has provided to a foreign authority for initially purely administrative purposes (in the case of information exchanges between FIUs, for the purpose of separating relevant from non-relevant reports). This 'control principle' also gives the providing FIU an opportunity to ensure that no broader use is made of the information than could have been made of it in the providing state. Thus, for example, when a use immunity has been granted by the providing state to the person who initially forwarded the information concerned, then the providing FIU can in this way ensure that this use immunity is also respected abroad. Some providing FIUs will, as a rule, give their consent for the use of information only for law enforcement purposes if – on an internal level – they are able to transmit the information to the law enforcement authorities in their country. This is the case in the Netherlands, for example.[43] In Belgium, it is an established practice not to exchange any information on an international level if that information has not yet been transmitted to competent prosecution authorities in Belgium. In general, this type of requirement allows the providing FIU to ensure that the same limitations which are deemed essential at a domestic level are also safeguarded on an international level. In this sense the requirement of prior consent before use of information as evidence also safeguards the 'workability' of domestic reporting systems and of FIUs in general. Some authors,[44] however, criticise this condition because it is more stringent than that which is required in the framework of judicial co-operation, where at least some states provide

---

[41] See Article 4 of the Convention for Mutual Administrative Assistance in Tax Matters. See also Article 23sexies of the Swiss Banking Act regarding information provided by the Swiss Banking Commission.

[42] Zulauf, 'Rechtshilfe–Amtshilfe', 58 and Schutte, 'La coopération administrative', 203.

[43] Lamp, 'Financiële informatie de grens over', 46–7.

[44] See Lamp, 'Financiële informatie de grens over', 52.

assistance without ascertaining that there is indeed a reasonable suspicion of a criminal offence.[45]

In some instances, still another purpose is served by requiring the consent of the providing state, namely the protection of individual rights. One of the reasons why judicial co-operation is generally looked upon as providing more guarantees to the individual(s) concerned than mutual administrative assistance is that in the former case the evidence is provided by a judicial authority. In some cases, information provided by administrative or police authorities can be used as evidence in criminal proceedings only if the judicial authorities of the requesting state have given their agreement. This requirement, which is imposed by Article 39(2) of the Schengen Agreement for the use of information provided by the police, for example, gives the judicial authorities an opportunity to assess whether the information is fit for use as evidence of a criminal offence (e.g., whether it was lawfully gathered). In the context of information exchanges between FIUs, it is for the providing state to decide which authority should give its agreement for the use of information as evidence of a criminal offence. In most cases the providing FIU is probably better placed to assess whether the information – which it gathered itself – may be used as evidence or not, but there may be countries where a judicial authority of the providing country attests that the information may be used for law enforcement purposes. As far as the protection of individual rights is concerned, an agreement by the FIU does not necessarily offer fewer guarantees than an agreement by a judicial authority. This is all the more true when one bears in mind that some FIUs are composed of magistrates, as is the Belgian *Cellule pour le traitement des informations financières\Cel voor financiële informatieverwerking*, for example.

Do internal limitations of competences limit the use of information obtained from foreign FIUs?

An important question in the field of mutual administrative assistance between FIUs is whether an FIU can request that a foreign FIU obtain additional information, if necessary by exercising its investigatory powers. This possibility has explicitly been acknowledged by international instruments in the field of mutual administrative assistance in tax matters, for example.[46] However, whether this is also possible in the context of assis-

---

[45] See, however, *infra* pp. 336–41 on the prohibition of fishing expeditions.

[46] See Article 2(2) of Council Directive 77/799/EEC of 19 December 1977 concerning mutual assistance by the competent authorities of the Member States in the field of direct taxation, which allows for this possibility. Article 5(2) of the Convention for Mutual Administrative Assistance in Tax Matters even turns this into an obligation.

tance between FIUs, and under which conditions, always depends on the domestic law of the requested state and on the text of the MOU. The powers of an FIU, as are those of any government authority, are always determined by the domestic legislation on which it is based. It follows that an FIU can use only those powers that are granted by the enabling legislation. If the enabling legislation of the FIU of whom information is requested does not provide for powers to take investigatory measures on behalf of a foreign FIU, then the former can only exchange information that it already has in its files.[47] In those cases (e.g. Belgium) the investigatory powers can be exercised only if there is an independent ground for action on the basis of the domestic law of the state concerned (i.e. the requested state).

Under no circumstances can the FIU of whom information is requested take measures that it is not allowed to take under its own domestic law. Moreover, on the basis of the principle of reciprocity, a requested FIU can refuse to take measures that the requesting financial intelligence unit would not be able to take under its own domestic law. This application of the principle of reciprocity, which is intended to exclude co-operation in cases in which the requesting state would not be able to comply with an analogous request, is also posed in other fields of mutual administrative assistance[48] and in the context of judicial co-operation in criminal matters.[49] Of course, nothing prevents states and their domestic authorities from entering into agreements which derogate from the principle of reciprocity.

The most difficult question, however, concerns information obtained by the providing FIU through powers which are not available to the receiving FIU. The question may arise whether this type of information may be exchanged or may eventually be introduced as evidence in the receiving state. One might refer to international rules in the context of judicial international co-operation in criminal matters[50] which allow refusal of co-operation in such circumstances or to established practices in the field of mutual administrative assistance in tax matters[51] under which such evidence is not used. It is, however, submitted that no such limitations exist, or indeed should exist, in the context of co-operation between FIUs.

---

[47] This often also the case in the context of mutual assistance between customs authorities: Laudati, *Study of Exchange of Confidential Information Agreements*, p. 10.

[48] Laudati, *Study of Exchange of Confidential Information Agreements*, p. 13. See e.g. Article 8(3) of Council Directive 77/799/EEC of 19 December 1977 concerning mutual assistance by the competent authorities of the Member States in the field of direct taxation and Article 21(2) of the Convention for Mutual Administrative Assistance in Tax Matters.

[49] See, e.g., Article 8(1) of the Swiss Mutual Assistance Act. See *infra* p. 305.

[50] See, e.g., Article 18(3) of the Money Laundering Convention.

[51] H.-R. Depret and L. Deklerck, *Le Secret bancaire* (Brussels: Jurifi, 1991), p. 64.

Confidentiality requirements

Most FIUs are subjected to a statutory confidentiality provision which limits the possibility of exchanging information with other services, both domestic and foreign. Though most confidentiality provisions make room for the possibility of exchanging information with foreign FIUs, they often also require that the receiving FIU be subjected to an (equally stringent) confidentiality provision.[52] The domestic confidentiality provisions of the receiving state will almost invariably apply to the information received from abroad. In addition, a confidentiality requirement is often also laid down in MOUs.[53]

Unilateral extra-territorial measures

Apart from administrative assistance, another new trend in international evidence gathering is the use, in particular by US law enforcement authorities, of unilateral measures which purport to give an extraterritorial reach in order to obtain evidence. Although this trend has been most notable in respect of evidence gathering, there are also examples of extra-territorial seizures or even extra-territorial confiscations of assets. These are measures which are taken unilaterally by the authorities of one state and therefore essentially differ from measures taken in the course of international co-operation in criminal matters which by definition involve the authorities of at least two states. The use of unilateral measures in the context of the international fight against money laundering will be discussed later, but at this stage it is appropriate to chart the territory by clarifying the general circumstances and motives which have given rise to the use of unilateral extraterritorial measures. Three factors merit investigation: the differences in perspective between criminal justice and international co-operation in criminal matters, the role of prosecutors and the power position of states.

Different visions of criminal justice and of international co-operation in criminal matters

One can discern two fundamentally different visions on international co-operation in criminal matters, which stem from differences between

---

[52] See, e.g., Article 17 (2) of the Belgian Money Laundering Act of 11 January 1993 and Article 26-2 of the Luxembourg Code of Criminal Procedure.

[53] Laudati, *Study of Exchange of Confidential Information Agreements*, p. 14.

common law and civil law regarding the role of parties in criminal proceedings, especially during the pre-trial stage. The continental, inquisito-
rial investigation model departs from a vertical perspective in which the
investigation is directed by a judicial authority who investigates both *à
charge* and *à décharge*, whereas the accusatorial investigation model
departs from a horizontal perspective in which each party must carry out
its own investigation.[54] The continental model emphasises the role of judicial (and police) authorities in carrying out an impartial investigation,
contrary to the common law model which leaves more room for investigations by the suspect, who is seen as the adversary of the prosecuting party
and hence as requiring the same investigatory powers as the prosecuting
party. Consequently, in common law systems, and especially in the United
States, suspects have powers that in continental systems can only be exercised by police or judicial authorities. Common law systems consider
investigating as an essentially private activity and not as an exclusive right
of police or judicial authorities. On the contrary, it is in principle the
responsibility of the defendant to gather and adduce evidence *à décharge*.
Only when coercive measures are needed, as when a (third) party refuses
to hand over (documentary) evidence, will a judge intervene in the investigatory process in the common law by, for example, ordering discovery.
The greater leeway which is provided to parties is also demonstrated by
the much wider possibilities for plea bargaining that exist under common
law. Under the continental investigation model the exclusive responsibility for gathering evidence rests with the competent authority, in some
cases a judicial authority.[55] Even at the trial stage, the judge may intervene
if additional evidence is deemed necessary.

Though this distinction primarily relates to the way in which domestic
criminal justice systems function, it also has important consequences in
evidence-gathering activities in an international context. Given the (perceivedly) private nature of evidence-gathering activities in a common law
perspective, these can in principle take place without a requirement of

---

[54] On these differences, see B. De Smet, 'De inquisitoire onderzoeksmethode op de
beklaagdenbank', *Panopticon* (1995), 341–4 and *De hervorming van het strafrechtelijk
vooronderzoek in België. Moet het gerechtelijk vooronderzoek in zijn huidige vorm behouden
blijven?* (Antwerp: Intersentia, 1996), pp. 236–8.

[55] C. Markees, 'The Difference in Concept Between Civil and Common Law Countries as to
Judicial Assistance and Co-operation in Criminal Matters', in *A Treatise on International
Criminal Law*, Volume II, Jurisdiction and Co-operation, ed. M. C. Bassiouni and V. P.
Nanda (Springfield: Charles C. Thomas, 1973), pp. 172–5 and D. D. Spinellis, 'Securing
Evidence Abroad – A European Perspective', in *International Criminal Law*, Volume II,
Procedure, ed. M. C. Bassiouni (New York: Transnational Publishers, Inc., 1986), p. 355.

judicial authorisation, not only in a domestic situation but also in an international context, that is, in the territory of a foreign state. From a common law viewpoint, the concept of legal assistance is therefore in principle confined to the intervention of a foreign judge in order to aid a (private) party in its evidence-gathering activities. In continental European law, however evidence gathering is an exclusively governmental function: a law enforcement authority which seeks to obtain evidence located abroad, must hence request that the competent judicial authorities of the state where the evidence is located take all the necessary measures. When a judicial authority of a continental law jurisdiction intervenes in the course of an international co-operation procedure, it does so in a neutral capacity and not in aid of one of the parties to the criminal investigation.[56] In the American perspective, a judicial authority needs to intervene only in case a party runs into difficulties in gathering evidence. This gives the term 'legal assistance' a distinctly different meaning from 'judicial assistance'.

These different concepts of international co-operation also allow to explain why US authorities consider treaty co-operation mechanisms as merely one of a number of alternative means of obtaining evidence located abroad. In principle, private parties can carry out investigations in the territory of another state as foreign parties are, in principle, allowed to conduct their investigations in American territory.[57] This type of 'private investigation' is an anathema in most continental countries, where the power to gather evidence is exclusively vested in the authorities of that state.

This distinction is not merely a matter of domestic law, but has also a distinct feature in international law. Thus, the investigations that have been launched by some (in particular American) law enforcement authorities on the territory of foreign states without the permission of those states, are clearly in breach of international law. Article 2(3) of the Vienna Convention even explicitly states that parties 'shall not undertake in the territory of another Party the exercise of jurisdiction and performance of functions which are exclusively reserved for the authorities of that other Party by its domestic law'. In general, any investigation *iure imperii*, that is an exercise of government functions, outside the boundaries of the national territory must be considered violative of international law, given

---

[56] Markees, 'The Difference in Concept Between Civil and Common Law Countries', p. 175; and A. Eser, 'Common Goals and Different Ways in International Criminal Law: Reflections from a European Perspective', *Harv.Int'l IJ* (1990), 120–1.

[57] A. Klip, *Buitenlandse getuigen in strafzaken* (Arnhem: Gouda Quint, 1994), pp. 243–4.

the strictly territorial character of enforcement jurisdiction.[58] As will be seen, however, the thrust of the problem often lies in determining what measures amount to extraterritorial enforcement.[59] This prohibition on extra-territorial investigations is self-evident in case of coercive measures which are the hallmark of the exercise of sovereign power of a state,[60] but can, arguably, also be deemed to extend to non-coercive, peaceful investigations.[61] The allergy to foreign evidence-gathering, whether it be by private parties or foreign government authorities, has in some continental legal systems even spawned statutory provisions that criminalise the disclosure of information to foreign parties (see e.g. Article 273 of the Swiss Criminal Code, laying down the *délit de renseignements à l'étranger*).[62]

Role of prosecutors in various systems

Some of the differences in approach to international evidence gathering between the common law and the continental systems also stem from the different roles that are played by prosecutors in different criminal justice systems. Heymann even distinguishes between what he calls the 'prosecutorial model', under which co-operation takes place in an informal manner without treaty basis, and the 'international law model', in which co-operation is based on mutual legal assistance treaties.[63] It is respectfully submitted that Heymann's analysis is flawed in some respects as, for example, when he suggests that, whereas the prosecutorial model in principle takes place between friendly nations with similar interests, the international law model is based on a carefully designed set of rules that could potentially apply between any two states. The fact is, however, that the most detailed co-operation treaties have been drafted under the aegis of the Council of Europe, which is precisely composed of states that have a high degree of trust in each other's legal systems which are relatively homogeneous. The undeniable merit of Heymann's analysis is, however, to have pointed out that international co-operation in the United States is

---

[58] See *supra* pp. 212–13.   [59] See *infra* pp. 321–7.

[60] Jennings and Watts, *Oppenheim's International Law*, pp. 383–4; Ch. Rousseau, 'Principes de droit international public', *Rec.Cours.* (1958), I, p. 406; and Rigaux, *Droit public et droit privé dans les relations internationales*, (Paris: Ed. A. Pedone, 1977), pp. 313–19.

[61] Mann, 'The Doctrine of Jurisdiction', 138–9. Contra Rigaux, *Droit public et droit privé dans les relations internationales*, p. 321.

[62] On this provision see Aubert *et al.*, *Le secret bancaire suisse*, pp. 117–18 and 657–60; Trechsel, *Schweizerisches Strafrecht. Kurzkommentar*, pp. 720–26; and from an American point of view: Nadelmann, *Cops Across Borders*, p. 331.

[63] Heymann, 'Two Models of National Attitudes', 102–5.

much more controlled and directed by prosecutorial authorities than in continental Europe. American prosecutors are, to a much larger degree than their European counterparts, acquainted with informal negotiation procedures in order to resolve charges and it is only logical that they apply these techniques also in cases having international features. Continental lawyers, including prosecutors, tend to think along more Cartesian, rigorous lines of reasoning which allow less room for bargaining techniques. On an international plane, this way of thinking results in an almost exclusive emphasis on the use of the framework of international judicial assistance and a diffidence towards procedural techniques that circumvent this traditional framework.[64] This reluctance in continental countries to use bargaining techniques is, however, gradually withering away and it will be shown that this may also have international implications for the field of evidence gathering or seizing and confiscating assets.[65]

Relative power position of states

Another important, but non-legal, factor which also helps to explain the recourse of (especially) US authorities to unilateral extraterritorial measures is the undeniable power of the position of the United States on the international scene. Powerful states have in general less interest in international, treaty-based co-operation, but will often be inclined to take unilateral measures which purport to have an extra-territorial reach. Often they will only enter into MLATs when their unilateral measures fail to have the expected result. Thus, the enhanced willingness of the United States since the 1980s to negotiate MLATs is in important part the result of the international tensions that were engendered by the use of unilateral extra-territorial measures by the United States.[66] Smaller, less powerful states, which are more open to foreign pressures, have in general a more outspoken interest in carefully drafted treaty obligations, than bigger, more powerful states.[67]

---

[64] Heymann, 'Two Models of National Attitudes', 105–6.   [65] See *infra* pp. 384–5.

[66] See Nadelmann, *Cops Across Borders*, pp. 315 and 341–84; E. A. Nadelmann, 'Negotiations in Criminal Law Assistance Treaties', *Am.J.Comp.L.* (1985), 467; and B. Zagaris, 'Developments in International Judicial Assistance and Related Matters', *Denv.J.Int'l L.& Pol'y* (1990), 352.

[67] Heymann, 'Two Models of National Attitudes', 106–7.

On the relative importance of treaty-based co-operation in criminal matters

It has been shown that international co-operation in criminal matters is viewed by American authorities as merely one means of seeking to obtain evidence abroad (or more broadly, seeking to have measures executed abroad). This view has been explicitly espoused by American case law[68] and is also enshrined in paragraph 442(1)(c) of the Restatement (Third) of the American Law Institute, which cites the availability of treaty co-operation mechanisms as one of the factors that need to be taken into account by an American court when ordering disclosure of information located abroad.[69] This position clearly flies in the face of the continental view of international co-operation mechanisms as an exclusive means of having measures executed on the territory of a foreign state.[70] In some instances the United States has even contrived to insert a provision in MLATs to the effect that the use of other national and international procedures is allowed.[71] On some occasions, however, as for example in the context of attempts to obtain information covered by foreign banking secrecy, the resort to unilateral extra-territorial measures by American authorities in defiance of existing treaty mechanisms has led to international tensions and even conflicts. In relation to the 1973 American–Swiss MLAT,[72] these tensions eventually resulted in a Memorandum of Understanding Between the United States of America and the Government of Switzerland on Mutual Assistance in Criminal Matters and Ancillary Administrative Proceedings (1987),[73] which acknowledges the

---

[68] *United States v. Vetco Inc.*, 691 F.2d 1281 (9th Cir.), *cert.denied*, 454 US 1098 (1981); *In re Grand Jury Proceedings, United States v. The Bank of Nova Scotia*, 691 F.2d 1384 (11th Cir.1982), *cert.denied*, 462 US 1119 (1983) [*Nova Scotia I*]; *In re Sealed Case*, 832 F.2d 1268 (DC Cir.1987).

[69] See P. J. Bschorr and M. H. Mullin, 'Court-ordered Waivers of Foreign Banking Secrecy Rights: an Evaluation of the American Position', in *Beiträge zum Schweizerischen Bankenrecht*, R. Von Grafenfried (Bern: Verlag Stämpfli, 1989), p. 201; Gane and Mackarel, 'The Admissibility of Evidence Obtained from Abroad', 103–95; and H. G. Maier, 'Extra-territoriality: Compelling Foreign Judicial Assistance in the Production of Documents and Evidence', *Am.Soc'y Int'l L.Proc.* (1985), 4.

[70] On this difference see Lagodny, 'Grundkonstellationen des internationalen Strafrechts', *RPS* (1989), 994–5; and M.-C. Krafft, 'Secret bancaire et conflits de juridiction. Le point de vue d'un internationaliste', in *Beiträge zum Schweizerischen Bankenrecht*, R. Von Grafenfried (Berne: Verlag Stämpfli, 1989), p. 217.

[71] See e.g. Article 38(1) of the American–Swiss MLAT; Article 18(1) of the American–Dutch MLAT (ILM, 1982, 916) and Article 3(1) of the American–Canadian MLAT (*ILM*, 1985, 1002). See also Gane and Mackarel, 'The Admissibility of Evidence Obtained from Abroad', 103–4.   [72] See on this MLAT *infra* pp. 332–3.

[73] Washington, 10 November 1987, *ILM*, 1988, 480.

priority (but not the exclusiveness) of co-operation mechanisms. It is important to emphasise that the wish of the United States to be able to resort to other means of evidence gathering than the co-operation mechanisms provided for by the treaty is not (merely) an expression of the American power position, but is in fact an element of American legal culture so deeply ingrained that organisations such as the National Association of Criminal Defence Lawyers, the Criminal Justice Section of the American Bar Association and the American Civil Liberties Union have voiced their concerns about the exclusion of other mechanisms to gather evidence abroad.[74]

In spite of the exclusiveness that is sometimes bestowed upon treaty-based co-operation mechanisms, the contention of the author is that treaty-based co-operation has no exclusive claim to international evidence-gathering, but that, bar some exceptions, international evidence-gathering measures (and certainly international measures that encroach upon proprietary rights (e.g. seizure and enforcement of confiscation) have to be taken by the territorially competent authorities on the request of another state. International law does not stand in the way of loose forms of co-operation without a treaty basis but is far more critical of unilateral extra-territorial measures. Various arguments lead to this conclusion.

First, the administrative and police authorities of many countries, including those having a continental law system, co-operate intensely – sometimes on a day-to-day basis – without a treaty basis. The importance of this type of co-operation in the international fight against money laundering has already been underscored.[75] Second, judicial co-operation in criminal matters also takes place without a treaty basis in many continental countries[76] (e.g. in Belgium,[77] The Netherlands[78] and Switzerland.[79]) There is indeed no reason why judicial assistance should not be granted in the absence of a treaty (as was done by Switzerland, for example, in the investi-

---

[74] See M. Abell, 'Department of Justice Renews Assault on Defendant's Right to Use Treaties on Mutual Legal Assistance in Criminal Matters to Obtain Evidence from Abroad in Criminal Cases', International Enforcement Law Reporter (1998), 54.

[75] See supra p. 258 et seq.

[76] See in general: C. Markees, 'Aktuelle Fragen aus dem Gebiete der internationalen Rechtshilfe', RPS (1973), 232.

[77] Stessens, De nationale en internationale bestrijding van het witwassen, p. 441.

[78] Article 552k of the Dutch Code of Criminal Procedure; cf. A. H. J. Swart, annotation with the judgment of the Dutch Supreme Court of 14 September 1987, NJ (1988), No.301, 1236.

[79] Article 1(3) of the Swiss Mutual Legal Assistance Act and the judgment of the Swiss Supreme Court of 25 May 1977, JT (suisse), IV (1979), 16.

gation into misappropriated funds of the Marcos family[80]), provided there is a legal basis under the municipal law of the requested state for carrying out the requested measures. However, in some instances the domestic mutual assistance legislation of the requested state requires that the requesting state has entered into a treaty with the requested state before a request for co-operation can be complied with. This is often the case in the field of extradition, for example, but also in respect of the seizure of assets and enforcement of foreign confiscations.[81] However, when this requirement is not part of the domestic law of the requested state, there is no reason why more far-reaching co-operation than that provided for by the otherwise applicable treaty should not be possible. Thus, on the basis of its domestic law,[82] Switzerland can take provisional measures on the request of the United States before a formal request for confiscation has been made, even though neither the American–Swiss MLAT nor US legislation provides for this possibility.[83] Moreover, under certain circumstances, European continental courts have accepted that evidence which was gathered by police forces on foreign territory may be introduced into criminal proceedings. For example, the Dutch Supreme Court has allowed evidence gathered by Dutch police authorities on the territory of a foreign state in that no rule of international law was violated.[84]

In the light of the proposition that treaty-based co-operation is not the only means of obtaining evidence located abroad, or, more generally, of taking investigatory or provisional measures on the territory of another state, the question then arises as to the position of treaty-based co-operation mechanisms. In this respect, it is submitted that the use of other techniques and procedures than treaty-based co-operation mechanisms should never be allowed to result in a lower level of human rights protection than the one catered for in the relevant treaty.[85] However, it is doubtful whether this is always the case in practice. For one thing, this requires that the relevant treaty provisions should have direct effect in the

[80] ATF 113 Ib, *La Semaine judiciaire* (1987), 609.   [81] See *infra* p. 367.

[82] See Article 8 of the Loi fédérale relative au traité conclu avec les Etats-Unis d'Amérique sur l'entraide judiciaire en matière pénale (3 October 1975).

[83] Frei and Trechsel, 'Origins and Applications of the US-Switzerland Treaty', 91. See also L. Frei, 'Beschlagnahme und Einziehung als Rechtshilfemassnahmen', *RPS* (1988), 314 and M. D. Mann, J. G. Mari and G. Lavdas, *Developments in International Securities Law Enforcement and Regulation*, Securities and Exchange Commission, 1994, p. 2.

[84] See the judgments of the Dutch Supreme Court of 7 June 1988, *NJ* (1988), No.987 and of 26 April 1988, *NJ* (1988), No.186.

[85] See also the annotation of A. H. J. Swart with the judgment of the Dutch Supreme Court of 14 September 1987, *NJ* (1988), No.301 and the judgment of 25 May 1993, *NJ* (1993), No.784.

domestic law system of the defendant's country so that he can avail himself of it before a domestic court. Yet, as will be expounded more in detail at another place in this book, some MLATs explicitly stipulate that a defendant cannot invoke the provisions of the treaty.[86]

---

[86] See *infra* pp. 345–6.

13   Some of the conditions, principles and exceptions of mutual judicial assistance in criminal matters revisited

In the following, three pivotal features of international co-operation in criminal matters will be critically analysed: the condition of double criminality, the political and fiscal offence exception and the *locus regit actum* principle. All three aspects play an essential role in the international fight against money laundering and their position will be vetted, not only in the context of mutual judicial assistance, but also in the context of new forms of (primary) co-operation in criminal matters. The crucial question in this respect is whether the chauvinistic rationales that underpin these basic rules of international co-operation can still be reconciled with the internationalist approach that was advocated earlier.[1]

The condition of double criminality

Double criminality as a condition to co-operation, that is as a requirement for taking measures on a foreign request, needs to be distinguished from double criminality as a condition to jurisdiction, that is as a requirement for punishing conduct that took place abroad.[2] After an overview of the role and legal basis of the condition of double criminality, in particular in the context of co-operation against money laundering, it will be argued that, save in the particular case where a confiscation procedure is started upon a foreign request, the condition of double criminality is not rooted in the legality principle. Hence the thesis that the condition of double criminality can be abolished without lowering the level of (human) rights protection will be defended.

---

[1] See *supra* p. 254.   [2] See *supra* pp. 229–30.

The condition of double criminality in international co-operation in criminal matters

Mutual judicial assistance has long been subjected to the same conditions as extradition, and hence also to the condition of double criminality. Nevertheless, there is a clear tendency towards relaxing the requirement of double criminality in the context of mutual assistance. This evolution began with the European Mutual Assistance Convention of 1959 which did not impose any requirement on providing mutual assistance, given the fact that, in principle, it did not, unlike extradition, entail any coercion.[3] Only in respect of two measures that implied the use of coercion, as did extradition, namely search and seizure, does the convention allow parties – most of whom have already effectively used this possibility – to make a declaration according to which requests for search or seizure are subject to certain requirements, such as the condition of double criminality (Article 5(1)), for example. In the same vein, the text of the UN Model Treaty on Mutual Assistance in Criminal Matters makes no mention of the condition, but nevertheless leaves room for it in its commentary as an optional ground for refusal.[4]

Some bilateral co-operation conventions do not contain a condition of double criminality but subject the execution of the requested procedural measures to the condition of conformity to the domestic legislation of the requested state. If the requested state's legislation requires double criminality, the condition of double criminality is thus imported into the co-operation scheme. Whereas in some MLATs,[5] the United States has succeeded in foisting the abolishment of the condition of double criminality on their treaty partners, they have failed with other MLAT partners to do away with the condition of double criminality. In some instances, double criminality is even cumulated with a requirement that the offence be mentioned in an appendix of the MLAT,[6] or with the requirement of a minimum penalty.[7]

---

[3] See F. Thomas, *De Europese rechtshulpverdragen in strafzaken. Ontstaan en evolutie van een Europees strafrechtsbeleid van uitlevering tot overdracht van strafvervolging* (Ghent, 1980), p. 286.

[4] *International Legal Materials* (1991), 1421. The text of the UN Model Treaty is also reproduced at C. Van den Wyngaert and G. Stessens, *International Criminal Law. A Collection of International and European Instruments* (The Hague: Kluwer Law International, 1996), p. 319.

[5] See e.g. Article 1(3) of the American–Canadian MLAT and Article 1(3) of the American–Italian MLAT

[6] See Article 4(2) of the American–Swiss MLAT. On the cumulative nature of these requirements, see the judgment of the Swiss Supreme Court of 26 January 1983, *La Semaine judiciaire* (1984), 273 and A. Ellis and R. L. Pisani, 'The United States Treaties on Mutual Assistance in Criminal Matters', in *International Criminal Law*, vol. II, Procedure, M. C. Bassiouni (New York: Transnational Publishers, 1986), p. 151.

[7] See, e.g., Article 5(1) of the American–Dutch MLAT.

The tendency in favour of a (partial) abolishment of the condition of double criminality appears to be limited to the field of mutual assistance and does not (or barely) extend to other forms of co-operation in criminal matters. As far as primary forms of national co-operation in criminal matters such as transfer of enforcement of sentences are concerned, the condition of double criminality is almost invariably imposed, which is probably due to their more far-reaching nature.[8]

Double criminality in the context of the fight against money laundering

In the context of money laundering, the condition of double criminality is especially prone to pose problems in respect of the predicate offence. As far as the money laundering conduct itself is concerned, most states have criminalised the different types of money laundering acts that are laid down in the relevant international instruments. The result is that the condition of double criminality is almost always fulfilled in this respect, as was also envisaged by the drafters of the Vienna Convention, the Money Laundering Convention and even the European Money Laundering Directive, which originally also aimed to incriminate money laundering.[9] In practice, however, there may still be circumstances in which the illegal money laundering activities that took place in the requesting state are not criminalised in the requested state. When, for example, the requested state has not criminalised negligent money laundering, this lack of double criminality *in abstracto* may be a ground for refusal of co-operation.

In the context of the international fight against money laundering the condition of double criminality is, however, more likely to pose problems in respect of the predicate offence. One of the most important consequences of the extension of the range of predicate offences in many domestic legislations is therefore to be sought in the ramifications arising from international co-operation.[10] It is logical that the Vienna Convention does not mention the condition of double criminality as such: every Party is obliged to criminalise the offences laid down in Article 3(1) of the Convention. The position is different, however, in respect of more broadly based anti-money laundering incriminations rules: Article 18(4) of the Money Laundering Convention allows a requested state to refuse co-operation when 'the offence to which the request relates would not be an offence under the law of the requested Party if committed within its

---

[8] D. J. M. W. Paridaens, *De overdracht van tenuitvoerlegging van strafvonissen* (Ijsselstein: Drukkerij Casparie, 1994), pp. 295–6.

[9] B. J. Drijber, 'EEG-richtlijn inzake het witwassen van geld vastgesteld', *TVVS* (1991), 294.

[10] *Second Commission Report*, p. 8.

jurisdiction'. Double criminality is thus not a mandatory condition, but only an optional ground for refusal which is moreover limited to requests for coercive measures. Whereas it suffices for investigatory measures that the condition of double criminality is fulfilled *in abstracto*, in relation to confiscation orders it ought to be applied *in concreto*.[11] In the former case it is only required that the relevant conduct be incriminated in both states, but in the latter case, one also needs to ensure that, taking into account possible grounds of exclusion of criminal liability, the perpetrator of the (alleged) offence would effectively have been liable to punishment in the requested state, had the offences taken place there.[12] It is of course incumbent upon the requested state to judge whether there is double criminality *in concreto*, but this should not lead to a new investigation of the facts.[13] Double criminality *in concreto* does not mean that the *nomen iuris* of the offences should be identical in the requesting and requested state; it generally suffices that the elements of an offence are also known under the legal system of the requested state so that the facts would be hypothetically punishable. This comparative technique is often referred to as *Sinngemässe Umstellung des Tatbestandes*.[14]

The difference in application of the condition of double criminality between the investigatory stage and the confiscation stage is attributable to the fact that the first stage involves only mutual assistance, that is, secondary assistance, whereas the confiscation stage involves forms of primary co-operation, which are almost invariably subjected to double criminality *in concreto*.[15] As long as an (alleged) offence is still being inves-

---

[11] *Explanatory Report with the Convention on Laundering, Search, Seizure and Confiscation of the Proceeds from Crime*, pp. 37–8.

[12] For a more detailed account of the different applications of the condition of double criminality, see S. Gafner d'Aumerie, *Le principe de la double incrimination. En particulier dans les rapports d'entraide judiciaire internationale en matière pénale entre la Suisse et les Etats-Unis* (Basle: Helbing & Lichtenhahn, 1992), pp. 35–8.

[13] Paridaens, *De overdracht van tenuitvoerlegging van strafvonnissen*, pp. 310–13 and 316 and *Explanatory Report with the Convention on Laundering, Search, Seizure and Confiscation of the Proceeds from Crime*, p. 38.

[14] On this concept, see F. Thomas, cited by G. Stessens, 'Compte-rendu des débats. Questions et réponses', in *La lutte contre la fraude-CEE dans la pratique*, ed. L. Huybrechts, Th. Marchandise and F. Tulkens (Antwerp: Maklu, 1994), p. 234 and M. Plachta, 'The Role of Double Criminality in International Co-operation in Criminal Matters', in *Double Criminality. Studies in International Criminal Law*, ed. N. Jareborg (Uppsala: Iustus Förlag, 1989), p. 110. Cf. Blakesley and Lagodny, 'Finding Harmony', 54–8.

[15] This is also the case, e.g., under the European Convention on the International Validity of Criminal Judgments (The Hague, 20 May 1970, *ETS*, No. 70) and the European Convention on the Transfer of Proceedings in Criminal Matters (Strasborg, 15 May 1972, *ETS*, No. 73). See Resolution II(1b) of the 9th Congress of the AIDP (*Association Internationale de Droit Pénal*), The Hague, 1964, *Zeitschrift für die gesammte*

tigated, it will moreover often be difficult to assess whether the condition of double criminality is fulfilled *in concreto*. Nevertheless, the requesting state will in principle be obliged to specify the predicate offence in its request for assistance, a specification which is not always required in a domestic prosecution.[16] This also explains why, in respect of provisional measures, the Explanatory Report to the Money Laundering Convention distinguishes between requests for provisional measures that are made at a moment when the requesting party has instituted confiscation proceedings, or after a request for a confiscation has been made by the requesting party. Only in the latter case, the condition of double criminality needs to be fulfilled *in concreto*.[17] In that case, the provisional measures cannot be said to be taken in the course of an investigation, but are clearly linked to the enforcement of a foreign sanction and should therefore be subjected to the same 'double criminality regime' as the proper enforcement of foreign sanctions.

A specific problem related to double criminality concerns corporate criminal liability. In the context of extra-territorial jurisdiction, it has already been argued that the lack of 'double corporate criminal liability' should not constitute a bar to the exercise of extra-territorial jurisdiction.[18] This argument *a fortiori* holds water in the context of international co-operation, where double criminality is merely a condition for taking certain procedural measures on request of a foreign state.

In case of assistance rendered on the basis of the Money Laundering Convention, any lack of corporate criminal liability in the requested state should not give rise to problems, given the text of Article 18(8)(a): 'Without prejudice to the ground for refusal provided for in paragraph 1.a of this article: (a) the fact that the person under investigation or subjected to a confiscation order by the authorities of the requesting Party is a legal person shall not be invoked by the requested Party as an obstacle to affording any co-operation under this chapter'. Because of its reference to the 'fundamental principles of the legal system of the requested Party' (Article 18(1)(a)), this provision cannot, however, be read as implying an obligation for contracting parties to introduce corporate criminal liability. In many jurisdictions, the lack of corporate criminal liability is precisely linked to fundamental legal principles. Although it may in practice be very difficult

Strafrechtswissenschaften (1965), p. 685. See also Paridaens, *De overdracht van tenuitvoerlegging van strafvonissen*, p. 315 and Y. G. M. Baaijens-van Geloven, *Overdracht en overname van strafvervolging* (Arnhem: Gouda Quint, 1996), pp. 157–8.

[16] See *supra* p. 231.

[17] *Explanatory Report with the Convention on Laundering, Search, Seizure and Confiscation of the Proceeds from Crime*, p. 37.   [18] See *supra* pp. 235–7.

to investigate the whereabouts, the origin and the (beneficial) ownership of proceeds nominally held by corporations,[19] the lack of corporate criminal liability as such is unlikely to constitute a legal impediment to international co-operation at the investigatory stage, but rather when provisional measures are taken and confiscation sanctions are enforced.[20]

The condition of double criminality in international co-operation in criminal matters and the legality principle

It is widely accepted that the condition of double criminality is not a principle of international law and does not flow from human rights conventions as such.[21] Its existence and scope therefore depend on the relevant treaty or applicable domestic law. The condition of double criminality is nevertheless often linked to the legality principle, a human rights requirement.[22]

It is the purpose of the following paragraphs to demonstrate that this link cannot be made as far as mutual judicial assistance is concerned and that to comply with a request for mutual legal assistance (e.g. by executing a search of premises) in the absence of double criminality is not violative of the legality principle as enshrined in Article 7 of the European Convention on Human Rights and Article 15 of the International Covenant on Civil and Political Rights. Already in the context of jurisdiction it has been argued that the condition of double criminality does not safeguard the legality principle (but is only intended to avoid conflicts of law).[23] A fortiori, no link can be made between double criminality and the legality principle, in the context of mutual assistance, where double criminality is not a condition for penalising those who have been accused, but merely for carrying out certain investigatory or provisional measures. Furthermore, the fact that at least some domestic case law[24] assesses the

---

[19] See supra pp. 37–8.
[20] P. Bernasconi, 'Achtung Briefkastenfirmen! Warnzeichen für Unternehmer, Treuhänder und Revisoren sowie für Staatsanwälte und Steuerfahnder', RPS (1996), 294–303.
[21] Swart, 'Human Rights and the Abolition of Traditional Principles', pp. 520–1; Lagodny 'Grundkonstellationen', 998–9 and S. A. Williams, 'The Double Criminality Rule Revisited', Israel Law Review (1993), 298. Contra Plachta, 'The Role of Double Criminality', pp. 111–12. See also, in the context of extradition, the decisions of the American Supreme Court (Factor v. Laubenheimer 290 US 276 (1923)) and the Canadian Supreme Court (United States v. Charles McVey II [1992] 3 SCR 475).
[22] See, e.g., Plachta, 'The Role of Double Criminality', pp. 107–8; Williams, 'The Double Criminality Rule Revisited', 298 and Van den Wyngaert, 'Rethinking the Law of International Criminal Co-operation', pp. 492–3.   [23] See supra p. 236.
[24] See the judgments of the Dutch Supreme Court of 16 January 1973 (NJ, 1973, No.280) and of 28 June 1977 (NJ, 1978, No.438).

condition of double criminality at the moment of the decision on the admissibility of the request and not on the moment the offence was committed (which is normally the crucial point in time for the assessment of the legality principle), militates against the view that the condition of double criminality is grounded in the legality principle.

The foregoing does not mean that investigatory or provisional measures taken on request of another state should not have a legal basis. In fact, many investigatory and provisional measures constitute interferences with the freedoms protected by international human rights provisions, for which these provisions require that the measures be 'prescribed by law' (see e.g. Articles 8(2) of the ECHR and Article 17 of the ICCPR in respect of the right to privacy). A domestic law, or even a national treaty making allowance for this possibility, however, will be sufficient for this purpose.[25] The European Court of Human Rights has even recognised common law as a sufficient basis for interferences with human rights.[26] The requirement of a legal basis for investigatory or provisional measures does not mean that the offences in respect of which these measures are taken should also exist under the domestic law of the requested state. In this respect, a distinction should be made between the substantive legality principle, that is, the *nullum crimen, nulla poena sine lege* principle, and the formal legality principle, that is, the requirement that every government act that implies an infringement of individual rights or liberties should have a legal basis. Although the case law of the European Court of Human Rights equates the concept of 'prescribed by law' of Article 8(2) with the concept of 'law' in Article 7 of the European Convention on Human Rights, this only pertains to the fact that the legal basis required for interfering with the right to privacy should meet the same qualitative requirements as the one implied in the concept 'law' of Article 7, notably those of accessibility and foreseeability.[27] The fact that the same qualitative requirements are posed in both instances, does not mean that the formal legality principle, that is, the requirement that every government act that implies an infringement of individual rights or liberties should have a legal basis can be equated with the substantive legality principle. The

---

[25] See the judgment of the Belgian Supreme Court of 26 September 1978, *Pasicrisie* (1979), I, 128.

[26] European Court of Human Rights, *Sunday Times v. United Kingdom*, judgment of 24 April 1979, *Publ.ECHR*, Series A, No.30, para. 47; *Tolstoy Miloslavsky v. United Kingdom*, judgment of 13 July 1995, *Publ.ECHR*, Series A, No.316–B, para. 37.

[27] European Court of Human Rights, *S.W. v. United Kingdom*, judgment of 22 November 1995, *Publ.ECHR*, Series A, No.335–B, para. 35; *C.R. v. United Kingdom*, judgment of 22 November 1995, *Publ.ECHR*, Series A, No.335–C, para. 33.

condition of double criminality is only linked with the formal legality principle, not with the substantive legality principle.[28] The latter principle is concerned with making sure that (alleged) criminals can be held liable and punished only in respect of acts which the law clearly lays down as punishable, whereas the former principle protects every citizen against unauthorised government interferences. The two principles, the substantive and the formal legality principle, are not only theoretically but also practically distinct. Often, investigatory or provisional measures will be taken in respect of third parties who are not suspected of having committed criminal offences; they are not protected by the substantive legality principle, but are shielded from unauthorised government protection by the formal legality principle. Moreover, in general, an investigatory measure implies no guilt on behalf of the individual in respect of whom the measure is taken, and this also applies in the context of a purely internal investigation.

It could be argued that, in respect of primary forms of international co-operation in criminal matters, there is more reason to link the condition of double criminality to the substantive legality principle. This probably also explains why the condition of double criminality is always judged *in concreto* in respect of primary forms of co-operation. If a requested state enforces a foreign confiscation or starts a new confiscation procedure at foreign request, it undeniably punishes an individual, for which a legal basis is required. This does not, however, automatically mean that the legal basis should be found in the law of the requested state. In case of enforcement of foreign sanctions (e.g. confiscations), the individual will have been judged and found guilty according to the criminal law of the requesting state so that the argument that the enforcement of a foreign confiscation in the absence of double criminality violates the legality principle, fails. In the context of the enforcement of foreign sanctions, the respect for the legality principle as well as for the presumption of innocence should be judged by reference to the law and judicial proceedings of the requesting state, not of the requested state.

It is different, however, for the transfer of criminal proceedings. If a state takes over criminal proceedings, or, in the context of money laundering, starts a new confiscation proceeding on the request of a foreign state, the legality principle requires that the offence involved be punishable under the law of the requested state. Under this form of international co-

---

[28] Contra P. O. Träskman, 'Should We Take The Condition of Double Criminality Seriously?', in *Double Criminality. Studies in International Criminal Law*, ed. N. Jareborg (Uppsala: Iustus Förlag, 1989), pp. 150–1.

operation in criminal matters – and only under this form, it might be stressed – it is therefore the law of the requested state according to which criminal liability is assessed and sanctions are imposed. Consequently, it is only in respect of this form of international co-operation in criminal matters that the condition of double criminality can be linked with the substantive legality principle.

The condition of double criminality: an obsolete obstacle to efficient international co-operation

In respect of all other forms of international co-operation in criminal matters, the imposition of the condition of double criminality is a 'political' choice which cannot be defended on the ground that it cogently flows from the substantive legality principle. In view of the divergent domestic legislations in respect of predicate offences, it is obvious that the condition of double criminality may seriously hamper international co-operation in the fight against money laundering.[29] In the following it will be argued that the condition of double criminality is rooted in a chauvinistic, even parochial, attitude which runs counter to the importance of the goals of international co-operation, namely the collection of evidence and the seizure and confiscation of criminally derived assets and that, in view of the unconvincing rationales that are advanced to underpin it, it should be abolished.

A first series of rationales that is sometimes cited to support the condition of double criminality relates to national sovereignty. The most prominent of these rationales is that the requirement of double criminality ensures reciprocity.[30] This rationale has rightly been criticised;[31] it in no way relates to the attainment of the goals of international co-operation.

Sometimes it is also argued that the condition of double criminality purports to allow a requesting state to refuse co-operation in respect of conduct which it considers not blameworthy, or not sufficiently blameworthy to incriminate.[32] A requested state which refuses to co-operate for this reason, however, focuses exclusively on its own domestic law to

---

[29] FATF-II, p. 36

[30] Gafner d'Aumerie, *Le principe de la double incrimination*, pp. 23–8; P. Gully-Hart, 'Loss of Time Through Formal and Procedural Requirements in International Co-operation', in *Principles and Procedures For A Transnational Criminal Law*, A. Eser and O. Lagodny (Freiburg: Max-Planck Institut, 1992), p. 261; and Plachta, 'The Role of Double Criminality', p. 107.

[31] Swart, 'Human Rights and the Abolition of Traditional Principles', p. 521.

[32] Plachta, 'The Role of Double Criminality', p. 122.

determine whether conduct is 'blameworthy' enough to co-operate, irrespective of where the conduct took place. Building on the idea that the condition of double criminality is intended to safeguard the idea of justice, one could even tentatively argue, then, that every foreign incrimination which does not figure in the criminal law of the requested state is unjust.[33] Such a stance is surely unacceptable and detrimental to the efficacy of international co-operation in criminal matters. Specifically with regard to the 'comparative patchwork' of predicate offences, the application of the condition of double criminality risks reducing international co-operation to the lowest common denominator of national legislations.

It is highly debatable whether a state, which for internal purposes has limited the application field of its anti-money laundering legislation to a number of predicate offences, should refuse to comply with requests for assistance for the reason that the money laundering offence concerned involves proceeds from a predicate offence that falls outside the application field of its domestic money laundering incrimination. The reasons which have induced domestic legislators to limit the application field of the anti-money laundering legislation to certain predicate offences will often be of a pragmatic nature. The limitation of the application field of a country's domestic anti-money laundering legislation is rarely based on fundamental objections against the 'blameworthiness' of those offences, as these have often been criminalised anyway. If the predicate offence is not criminalised in the requested state, this may be for more fundamental reasons, but it is far from certain whether these reasons should be allowed to block international co-operation.

A second set of reasons that is sometimes advanced to justify the condition of double criminality relates to the protection of the individual rights and freedoms that may be at stake. Thus a request may concern facts which were (partially) carried out on the territory of the requested state and are not criminalised under the legislation of the requested state. Although this does not formally involve a violation of the legality principle as the person involved will be tried under the law of the requesting state, it is submitted that in these circumstances the requested state is nevertheless justified if it wishes to refuse co-operation. The individual concerned is entitled to rely on the locally applicable law to encourage him to believe that his acts were lawful and, concomitantly, is entitled to expect that the requested state will not take any investigatory measures

---

[33] In this respect, see the incisive remarks by C. Markees, 'Suisse', *RIDP* (1968), 750.

to establish the punishability of conduct that is considered perfectly lawful under the law of that state. Moreover, in this type of conflict of laws, priority should always be given to the territorially applicable law.[34] To refuse co-operation under such conditions does not, however, necessitate a recourse to the condition of double criminality. It will be sufficient – and corresponds better to the reality – to invoke the fundamental legal principles of the requested state in this respect. Thus Article 18(1) of the Money Laundering Convention, which allows the requested state to refuse co-operation if '(a) the action sought would be contrary to the fundamental principles of the legal system of the requested Party; or (b) the execution of the request is likely to prejudice the sovereignty, security, ordre public or other essential interests of the requested Party', is perfectly suited to refuse co-operation in the above-described circumstances.[35] The same ground for refusal can also be invoked in the rare cases where the law on which the request is based is contrary to fundamental human rights.[36] Whenever human rights are jeopardised, a request for co-operation should be turned down,[37] but this does not require the condition of double criminality.

The case for the abolition of the condition of double criminality

The foregoing sufficiently demonstrates that the condition of double criminality can be abolished without jeopardising the protection of individual human rights. Except for the enforcement of foreign (confiscation) procedures, the condition cannot be based on the substantive legality principle. Most of the arguments advanced in favour of double criminality are in fact rooted in chauvinistic concepts of justice. In the few circumstances where the condition safeguards individual rights, this role can be better fulfilled by other provisions (such as the inclusion of a human rights clause) in co-operation treaties or legislation. Although it is

---

[34] See *supra* p. 236. See also Mann, 'The Doctrine of Jurisdiction', 90 and Träskman, 'Should We Take The Condition of Double Criminality Seriously?', 151.

[35] See *Explanatory Report with the Convention on Laundering, Search, Seizure and Confiscation of the Proceeds from Crime*, p. 35.

[36] See for examples of such incriminations: European Court of Human Rights, *Norris v. Ireland*, judgment of 26 October 1988, Publ. ECHR, Series A, No.142; *Modinos v. Cyprus*, judgment of 22 April 1993, *Publ. ECHR*, Series A, No.259 (both relating to the incrimination of homosexual acts) and *Kokkinakis v. Greece*, judgment of 23 May 1993, *Publ.ECHR*, Series A, No.260–A (relating to the criminalisation of proselytism).

[37] Dugard and Van den Wyngaert, 'Reconciling Extradition with Human Rights', 191–5; Swart, 'Human Rights and the Abolition of Traditional Principles', pp. 523–4 and Van den Wyngaert, 'The Transformations of International Criminal Law', pp. 212 *et seq.*

admittedly true that to refuse co-operation by invoking human rights and *ordre public* clauses is much more delicate and sensitive than to do so on the ground that the condition of double criminality is not fulfilled, this is essentially a political or diplomatic, and not a legal argument. There is an undeniable element of hypocrisy in providing for human rights and *ordre public* clauses in domestic legislation and co-operation agreements but, for political motives, refraining from applying them.

The combination of the condition of double criminality and the limited nature of the domestic money laundering legislation of a state can turn that state into a safe haven for proceeds that have elsewhere been criminally obtained and this should be avoided in the light of the international fight against money laundering. It can be assumed with reasonable certainty that a number of states have deliberately limited their domestic money laundering legislation (or even abstained from incriminating money laundering at all) with the object of providing a safe haven for foreign funds that have been obtained in violation of the (criminal) laws of other countries. This in effect boils down to the 'selling' of sovereignty, certainly in the case of a number of small, or micro, states for whom foreign capital is one of the only sources of income. This limited scope of some domestic money laundering legislations was discussed in Part 1.[38] While it was acknowledged that the sovereignty of every state gives it the right to define its own money laundering legislation as it wishes, it was also emphasised that the concept of sovereignty may be read as implying a duty upon states not to frustrate the laws of other states. The condition of double criminality exemplifies how the concept of sovereignty can be used to block international co-operation in the fight against money laundering. The abolishment of the condition of double criminality would have the advantage of leaving intact the sovereignty of states to define their domestic criminal legislation as they choose, while at the same time facilitating international co-operation in the fight against money laundering. Of course, an objection from the international law point of view is that, regardless of double criminality, a state can never be coerced into co-operating with other states. While this is undeniably true, double criminality, which has sometimes been elevated into a sacrosanct principle, gives states an ideal legal pretext for veiling their obstinate refusal to co-operate in the international fight against money laundering. It is submitted that this pretext should be removed.

[38] See *supra* pp. 94–5.

The fiscal and political offence exception

Article 18(1)(d) of the Money Laundering Convention allows states to refuse to co-operate because of the political or fiscal nature of the offence concerned. Article 3(10) of the Vienna Convention, on the other hand, stipulates that, for the purpose of co-operation under the convention, drug trafficking or the laundering of the proceeds from drug trafficking shall not be considered as fiscal or political offences, 'without prejudice to the constitutional limitations and the fundamental domestic law of Parties'.

The exception for fiscal offences stems from a traditional concept of sovereignty by which states are seen as competitors whose economic interests collide. The concept of protectionism and the legislation that has sometimes been created to enforce this economic ideology also flow from the same, obsolete notion of sovereignty.[39] The fiscal offence exception allowed states to decline to prosecute offences if doing so might compromise their competitive position. Often fiscal offences pertained to the taxes and excise duties levied on imports in order to protect the state's economy. The exception of fiscal offences encapsulated the refusal of states to co-operate in respect of this type of prosecution, which sometimes (indirectly) targeted the economic interests of (nationals of) the requested state, whereby the interest of international criminal justice was placed second to the economic interests of states. The fiscal offence exception in this sense amounts to a legal device which allows some states to protect the economic interests of their finacial sector.

Even in the context of money laundering, states were able to abolish the fiscal offence exception only for proceeds from drug trafficking, but not in general. The maintenance of the fiscal offence exception can theoretically be justified by referring to the mutual administrative assistance in tax matters, which should allow tax administrations to recover outstanding tax debts in other countries (so-called *assistance au recouvrement*). Although this is theoretically correct, it is nevertheless deplorable that co-operation can be excluded in the case of fiscal offences. If some infringements of tax law are deemed so serious that they are criminalised, there is no reason why states should not collaborate in the fight against the laundering of the proceeds from these fiscal offences. In an increasingly globalised community of states, the majority of which accept the principle of free trade, it is difficult to see what other interests are served by this

---

[39] Markees, 'The Difference in Concept Between Civil and Common Law Countries', pp. 176–8.

exception than the interests of jurisdictions that are willing to be used as tax havens in which citizens of other countries can stash away income that they have not declared to their tax authorities. As with double criminality, this is also an example of a legal device – rooted in the concept of sovereignty – used by states which allows citizens of other states to avoid compliance with the laws of those states.

Unlike the fiscal offence exception, the political offence exception, which originated in the law of extradition, is intended to protect individual rights.[40] It protects persons who have committed an offence against the political institutions of a state and are who therefore deemed not to stand a chance of receiving a fair trial in that country. It has sometimes been argued that it would be contradictory to refuse to extradite for political offences, but to allow seizure and confiscation of assets upon request of a foreign state in respect of a political offence.[41] There is, however, an important difference between the two forms of international co-operation. Although the latter is a form of primary assistance, it has the distinct advantage over the former type of assistance that a requested state can vet the procedure which has resulted in the confiscation. In respect of extradition, on the other hand, a state is in most cases asked to co-operate – by handing over the requested person – at a stage at which there has as yet been no judgment. In view of the possibility that states may refuse to enforce a foreign confiscation order if it is established that the procedure in which the confiscation order was imposed did not offer the fundamental fair trial rights,[42] it would seem acceptable to do away with the political offence exception in the context of the international fight against money laundering. States have already done so in an *ad hoc* way in respect of drug trafficking (Article 3(10) of the Vienna Convention) and of corruption (Article 17 of the Inter-American Convention against Corruption), for example.[43] In respect of proceeds from terrorist offences, Article 8(1) of the European Terrorism Convention also excludes the exception for political offences,[44] but it should be pointed out that this 'neutralisation' of the

---

[40] See C. Van den Wyngaert, *The Political Offence Exception to Extradition. The Delicate Problem of Balancing the Rights of the Individual and the International Public Order* (Deventer: Kluwer, 1980), especially pp. 191–229.

[41] See G. Van Hecke, 'Confiscation, expropriation and the conflict of laws', *The International Law Quarterly*, (1951), reproduced in *Miscellanea Georges Van Hecke* (Antwerp: Kluwer, 1985), p. 242.   [42] See *infra* pp. 403–7.

[43] Caracas, 29 March 1996, *International Legal Materials* (1996), 724; reproduced at Van den Wyngaert and Stessens, *International Criminal Law. A Collection of International and European Instruments*, p. 159.

[44] European Convention on the Suppression of Terrorism, Strasbourg, 27 January 1977, *ETS*, No.90.

political offence exception only relates to proceeds from offences defined by Articles 1 and 2 of this convention and in no way encompasses funds held by terrorist groups in general. In addition, Article 8(2) of the European Terrorism Convention rightly reserves the right for a state to refuse co-operation if it 'has substantial grounds for believing that the request for mutual assistance in respect of an offence mentioned in Article 1 or 2 has been made for the purpose of prosecuting or punishing a person on account of his race, religion, nationality or political opinion or that person's position may be prejudiced for any of these reasons'. The same is also accepted in relation to drug trafficking.[45]

This reticence to abolish the political offence exception in general, as reflected in Article 18(1)(d) of the Money Laundering Convention, is understandable given the protective background of this exception and the fact that it is formulated in a broad way, encompassing all forms of co-operation in the fight against money laundering (including investigatory and provisional measures to be taken at a stage where there is no judgment yet).

The locus regit actum principle

International co-operation in criminal matters takes place almost invariably on the basis of the *locus regit actum* principle, according to which the requested state applies its own (procedural) law in carrying out requests for co-operation. This principle is laid down in mutual assistance treaties,[46] as well as in the municipal law of many states.[47]

Klip distinguishes between what he calls the 'substantive' and the 'formal' locus rule. Under the substantive locus rule, a request for assistance is carried out under the same procedural rules that also apply in domestic investigations. Some jurisdictions, however, have elaborated specific rules for carrying out foreign requests for assistance. In that case, it will still be the law of the requested state that applies, but not the same substantive rules as the ones which apply in purely domestic investigations: this is the formal locus rule.[48]

---

[45] *Report US delegation*, pp. 107–8.

[46] See, e.g., Article 3(1) of the European Convention on Mutual Assistance in Criminal Matters (1959), Article 6 of the UN Model Treaty on Mutual Assistance in Criminal Matters (1990), Article 7(12) of the Vienna Convention and Article 9 of the Money Laundering Convention.

[47] See, e.g., the judgment of the Belgian Supreme Court of 26 September 1966, *Pasicrisie* (1967), I, 89 and Articles 12 and 64 of the Swiss Mutual Assistance Act.

[48] See Klip, *Buitenlandse getuigen in strafzaken*, pp. 246–7.

The advantages and the drawbacks of the *locus regit actum* principle will now be discussed. Although a successful international fight against money laundering may require some deviations from or attenuations of the *locus regit actum* principle, the author's contention is that the principle is well founded and should in no way be jettisoned. It will also be demonstrated that this principle plays an essential role in safeguarding of individual rights against the extra-territorial measures to which some authorities have occasionally resorted in order to penetrate foreign banking secrecy regulations.

The rationales and advantages of the locus regit actum principle

The *locus regit actum* principle, which is also deeply ingrained in private international law, is both theoretically and practically well founded.

The principle is rooted in the sovereignty of the requested state. Carrying out investigatory measures is essentially a government task, certainly when doing so implies the use of coercion. This is all the more so for provisional and enforcement measures. Only from a common law, and particularly from an American, viewpoint is gathering evidence looked on as a primarily private activity and hence one in which the *lex loci* is not automatically applicable. Foreign parties are in principle free to gather evidence in the United States in accordance with the law of their own state. The *forum regit actum* principle, which is adhered to in the United States, can only be applied, however, if no coercive measures are required. The use of coercive measures always requires the intervention of the local authorities in accordance with the locally applicable law.

On a practical level, the *locus regit actum* principle offers the advantage of allowing the authorities of the requested state to apply their own law to which they are accustomed. However, this principle functions not only to the advantage of the authorities of the requested state but also of the individuals who are the subject of the request. The *locus regit actum* principle guarantees that they will be confronted only with measures that can be taken under the law of the requested state and not with the unknown measures of a foreign legal system which they do not know and which is, in principle, not binding on them. This more arcane effect of the *locus regit actum* principle is not deliberately intended, but merely a side-effect of the concept of sovereignty.[49] It was highlighted in a case before the Canadian Supreme Court which centred on the question of whether the Canadian

---

[49] Cf. Klip, *Buitenlandse getuigen in strafzaken*, p. 256.

standard for the issuance of a search warrant needed to be satisfied before Canada could submit a letter of request to foreign (in this case, Swiss) authorities to search and seize the defendant's banking documents and records. Lamer CJ correctly pointed out that a Canadian residing in a foreign country should expect his privacy to be governed by the laws of that country. He shrewdly remarked that it may be fairly safely assumed that a person who decides to conduct financial affairs and keep records in a foreign state has made an informed choice about where to conduct business and thereby to create banking records. Banking secrecy rules are in fact among the important considerations a bank customer will take into account when deciding where to conduct his affairs.[50] Consequently, the Canadian Supreme Court declined to apply the Canadian standard to the issuing of a request for mutual assistance to Switzerland.

Under many legal systems, the *locus regit actum* principle also determines the assessment of the legality of foreign evidence. Various domestic courts have accepted that evidence gathered abroad should be checked against the law of the country where it was collected to establish its legality.[51] In accordance with the *locus regit actum* principle, these courts have thus preferred to apply foreign law, rather than applying the *lex fori* principle. This adherence to the *locus regit actum* principle is not universal, though. In the often-cited *Chinoy* case, the Queen's Bench Division refused to exclude evidence which was collected in breach of the locally applicable law.[52] Although the decision in this case can be criticised on the ground that it does not defer sufficiently to foreign legal systems,[53] it does not treat foreign evidence differently from evidence collected in England and Wales. Also in purely domestic affairs, an English court is under no obligation to exclude illegally obtained evidence.[54] A similar conclusion was arrived at in *R v. Cook* by the Canadian Supreme Court, which, although applying the Canadian Charter of Rights and Freedoms to the actions of Canadian police officers on foreign territory, did not exclude the evidence obtained in breach of the Charter as the breach was not considered so

---

[50] *Canada (Attorney General) v. Schreiber* [1998] 1 SCR 841, para. 23.

[51] See e.g. the judgments of the Belgian Supreme Court of 26 January 1993 (*RDP* (1993), 768), of 12 October 1993 (*Arr.Cass.* (1993), No.404), as well as the judgment of the Dutch Supreme Court of 25 May 1993 (*NJ* (1993), No.784). See also the judgment of the English Court of Appeal, *R. v. Konscol*, 18 May 1993.

[52] *R v. Governor of Pentonville Prison*, ex parte Chinoy [1992] 1 All ER 317, 330–2. In its decision of 4 September 1991 (*Chinoy v. United Kingdom* (15199/89)), the European Commission of Human Rights did not find any violation of human rights.

[53] Gane and Mackarel, 'The Admissibility of Evidence Obtained from Abroad', 119.

[54] *R v. Sang* [1979] 2 All ER, 1222, 1230. See now section 78(1) Police and Criminal Evidence Act 1984.

serious as to impair the defendant's right to a fair trial. In that sense, this English and Canadian case law should not be amalgamated with the infamous judgment of the American Supreme Court, which, in *Verdugo-Urquidez*, declared the Fourth Amendment to the US constitution not to be extra-territorially applicable, thus providing *carte blanche* to American police agents operating abroad.[55]

The drawbacks of the locus regit actum principle

It should be acknowledged that the *locus regit actum* principle has definite drawbacks. Often the requesting state will require that the evidence be gathered in accordance with certain procedures if it is to be introduced as evidence in criminal proceedings in its own state.[56] It will not always be possible to accommodate such requests without departing from the principle that the requested state applies its own law. Many mutual assistance treaties, therefore, expressly take this factor into account and provide for the possibility of deviating from the *locus regit actum* principle. Thus, Article 9 of the Money Laundering Convention demands that requests 'be carried out as permitted by and in accordance with the domestic law of the requested Party and, to the extent not incompatible with such law, in accordance with the procedures specified in the request'. Obviously, such complaisance has its limits. It can in no way be expected that a requested state would carry out a measure that is not provided for under its own legal system as to do so would violate the formal legality principle.

In the context of the fight against money laundering, this consequence of the *locus regit actum* principle is particularly likely to pose problems in respect of measures designed to lift banking secrecy, or in general to obtain documentary evidence – which is crucial in any financial investigation. Thus, in many continental European legal systems, neither private litigants nor public prosecuting authorities nor the police have access to the same range of disclosure orders and production orders that are available in most common law countries. Production orders are of common law origins, and, though also known in German law, are largely unknown in continental European law jurisdictions based on the French legal system which favour seizure as a means of obtaining (documentary) evi-

[55] *US v. Verdugo-Urquidez*, 110 S.Ct. 1056 (1990). Cf. Gane and Mackarel, 'The Admissibility of Evidence Obtained from Abroad', 111–12.

[56] See Klip, *Buitenlandse getuigen in strafzaken*, pp. 258–60 and Heymann, 'Two Models of National Attitudes', 99.

dence.[57] Some civil law countries use production orders, but their scope is often confined to the boundaries of private litigation (see e.g. Belgium[58]), although they also exist in the field of criminal law in some civil law countries (e.g. The Netherlands[59]). The problem of the existence of divergent national procedural measures for lifting banking secrecy was acknowledged by the drafters of the Money Laundering Convention, who have attempted to attain a modicum of harmonisation in this respect. Article 4 of the Convention not only obliges parties to abolish banking secrecy rules as an obstacle to investigations or provisional or confiscation measures, it also requests that parties consider the introduction of 'special investigative techniques facilitating the identification and tracing of proceeds and the gathering of evidence related thereto', amongst which are access to computer systems and orders to produce specific documents.

Under the present system of international co-operation in criminal matters, however, the law of the requested state remains decisive as to which measures can be taken. This is also demonstrated by the optional ground for refusal to co-operate which is contained in the Money Laundering Convention and which allows a requested state to refuse coercive investigatory measures as well as provisional measures 'if the measures sought could not be taken under the domestic law of the requested Party for the purposes of investigations or proceedings, had it been a similar domestic case' (Article 18(2)). A similar ground for refusal is provided for in Article 7(15)(c) of the Vienna Convention.

A request for assistance can moreover always be turned down via the classic exemptions of international co-operation in criminal matters, namely by referring to the *ordre public* and the fundamental principles of the requested state's own legal system (Article 18(2)) or 'if the measures sought or any other measures having similar effects would not be permitted under the law of the requesting Party' (Article 18(3) of the Money Laundering Convention).

In the context of the international co-operation in fighting money laundering, the most important inroads into the *locus regit actum* principle have, however, been made at the stages of provisional measures and enforcement of confiscations, where, as will be seen,[60] treaty mechanisms have been set up that oblige parties to take certain measures that they do not apply for internal purposes.

---

[57] G. Arzt, 'Zur Beweisbeschaffungspflicht der Bank im Strafverfahren', in *Beiträge zum Schweizerischen Bankenrecht*, ed. R. Grafenfried (Bern: Verlag Stämpfli, 1989), p. 326.

[58] See Stessens, *De nationale en internationale bestrijding van het witwassen*, pp. 281–2.

[59] See Article 126a(1) of the Dutch Code of Criminal Procedure.

[60] See *infra* pp. 373 and 396.

Apart from being motivated by a desire to ensure a successful co-operation, requested states sometimes also deviate from the *locus regit actum* principle with a view to another goal, namely to accommodate the rights of the defence. To this end, the presence of defendants' counsel at the execution of letters rogatory has on occasion been allowed. In this respect a number of mutual assistance treaties contain explicit provisions. Thus Article 4 of the European Convention on Mutual Assistance (1959) explicitly allows 'officials and interested persons (i.e., the counsel of suspects)' to be present at the execution of letters rogatory, if the requested Party consents. Such a possibility is obviously likely to improve the execution of letters rogatory: the judicial authorities of the requesting state will be able to assist the authorities of the requested state with their in-depth knowledge of the case and to point out the requirements of the law of evidence of the requesting state that may apply.[61] Their contribution can be especially valuable in money laundering investigations, and in financial investigations in general, which are often highly complex. In money laundering cases, the theoretical possibility for the defence to attend the execution of letters rogatory will, however, almost always be excluded. Given the need to conduct an investigation into the whereabouts of the proceeds from crime discreetly, without alerting those who have access to these proceeds, interested parties will never be apprised, either of a domestic investigatory measure, or of an investigatory measure that was requested. In fact, financial investigations will usually be kept secret as long as possible while in any event, in many countries banks (and other third parties) often have a legal confidentiality obligation which forbids them from disclosing to their clients that their accounts have been investigated.[62] In their zeal to protect banking secrecy, the Swiss negotiators of the American–Swiss MLAT of 1973,[63] even expressly excluded the presence of representatives of an American authority if this 'would result in providing to the United States facts which in Switzerland a bank is required to keep secret, or facts which are manufacturing or business secrets therein', unless very stringent conditions are met (see Article 12(3)(d)). It follows from Article 65a(3) of the Swiss Mutual Assistance Act as well as from the case law of the Swiss Supreme Court[64] that foreign authorities are generally not allowed to be made aware of facts covered by banking secrecy before a judgment has

---

[61] See H. Grützner, 'International Judicial Assistance and Co-operation in Criminal Matters', in *Treatise of International Criminal Law*, ed. M. C. Bassiouni and V. P. Nanda (Springfield: Charles C. Thomas, 1973), pp. 243–4.   [62] See *infra* pp. 347–8.
[63] On this MLAT, see *infra* pp. 332–3.   [64] ATF 117 Ib 51.

been made on the admissibility of the request for assistance and on the extent of such assistance.

Locus regit actum and the extra-territorial application of secrecy duties

The *locus regit actum* principle is also very important in answering a question that has arisen in the context of many transnational money laundering investigations that involved the lifting of foreign banking secrecy: is a banker, or in general anyone bound by a duty of secrecy, also obliged to honour that duty outside the state that has imposed the secrecy duty? Or, to put the question differently: can someone who is bound by a duty of secrecy be punished for extra-territorial violations of that duty?

It follows from the *locus regit actum* principle that persons who are concerned by a request for assistance (e.g. because they are interrogated) have the same procedural rights and obligations as they have in a purely domestic investigation. Persons who are bound by a (professional) privilege, retain that privilege when they are interrogated in the course of the execution of letters rogatory. Thus, attorneys who cannot be obliged to disclose privileged information (or may even be prohibited from doing so) in the context of a domestic procedure cannot be obliged to do so in the course of an international co-operation procedure. This reveals the protective nature of the *locus regit actum* principle: the persons concerned, both individuals and corporate bodies, in principle retain the same rights in an international procedure as they have under a domestic procedure.[65] When, in the requested state, they have a right or obligation to decline to give evidence in a domestic procedure, they can also avail themselves of this right when the judicial authorities of that state take certain measures on request of another state. This normally flows automatically from the *locus regit actum* principle, but is sometimes even explicitly stipulated in the domestic law of the requested state.[66]

Some mutual assistance treaties go beyond this and offer additional protection in that they also allow persons concerned to invoke the privileges they have under the law of the requesting state. This is the case under the American–Swiss MLAT (Articles 10 and 25), for example, and has

---

[65] See also the report by the Dutch scientific commission: *Commissie tot bestudering van de positie van verdachten en andere belangstellenden in de internationale strafrechtelijke samenwerking, Individu en Rechtshulp in strafzaken*, pp. 9 and 13. Cf. Klip, *Buitenlandse getuigen in strafzaken*, p. 317.

[66] See, e.g., Articles 9 and 12 of the Swiss Mutual Assistance Act, which allow persons concerned to invoke any professional privilege they may have, either under Swiss federal law or under cantonal law.

been provided for under the UN Model Treaty on Mutual Assistance in Criminal Matters (1990) (Article 12). This 'double' protection is not generally recognised, but depends on an explicit provision in the relevant mutual assistance treaties. In most treaties, such as for example the European Convention on Mutual Assistance (1959), as well as the Vienna Convention and the Money Laundering Convention, for example, such a provision is lacking. Both multilateral money laundering conventions moreover explicitly exclude banking secrecy as a possible ground for refusal.[67]

The *locus regit actum* principle and the protection of privileged information that follows from it, is, however, intrinsically linked to co-operation mechanisms, that is, the execution by the authorities of the requested state of investigatory or provisional measures on the territory of the requested state. It is a quite different matter where the state interested in the (privileged) information abstains from asking for co-operation, but rather chooses to make orders against persons over whom it has adjudicative jurisdiction (e.g., because they are present on its territory) in order to obtain the information. The question as to the extent to which information that would be privileged from disclosure in the requested state is then still protected is a vexed one. From a procedural point of view, the person concerned will normally be able to rely only on such privileges as are recognised by the law of the state which exercises jurisdiction to adjudicate. The problem therefore has to be studied, not so much from a procedural angle, but from a substantive law point of view.

In practice, tensions have arisen where bankers have been obliged to give evidence in a foreign state. Where banking secrecy is considered a purely contractual obligation to secrecy, a violation of that civil duty can in principle give rise to sanctions irrespective of where the violation was committed. If a banker is legally obliged, under threat of sanction, to disclose privileged information, he will, however, in most cases be able to avail himself of a ground of excuse for doing so.

Where banking secrecy is enshrined in criminal law and violations are punishable by criminal sanctions, the question that arises is one of extraterritorial jurisdiction. Does the state which criminalises violations of banking secrecy have jurisdiction over offences that have been committed abroad?

This question has been cogently posed in respect of Swiss banking secrecy. It follows from the text of Article 47(4) of the Swiss Banking Act[68]

---

[67] See *infra* p. 333.
[68] 'Sont réservées les dispositions de la législation fédérale et cantonale statuant l'obligation de renseigner l'autorité et de témoigner en justice'.

that a banker can be relieved from his duty to secrecy only by Swiss stat-utory provisions, which, for example, allow a Swiss court of law – acting either in the context of a Swiss internal investigation or on request of a foreign state – to lift banking secrecy. When a Swiss banker discloses priv-ileged information in a foreign court, he can consequently be held in vio-lation of Swiss banking secrecy law. This, however, presupposes that Swiss courts have jurisdiction over the violation that took place outside Swiss territory. Although Swiss courts can refer to the nationality principle in order to claim jurisdiction over extra-territorial violations of Swiss banking secrecy by Swiss bankers, this possibility is restrained by the requirement of double criminality, which means that their conduct must also be punishable under the *lex loci delicti* principle (see Article 6 of the Swiss Criminal Code). This condition will rarely be met as violations of banking secrecy are seldom criminalised.

Extra-territorial claims over violations of Swiss banking secrecy laws have sometimes also been defended on the ground that these extra-territorial violations provoke results in Switzerland as they pertain to information which is privileged under the Swiss Banking Act. In this respect, Article 7 of the Swiss Criminal Code, which refers to the result of an offence as one of the criteria to localise an offence on Swiss territory, has sometimes been invoked.[69] In view of the case law of the Swiss Supreme Court, which narrowed this application of this provision to result offences (i.e., offences for which the result of the criminalised conduct is also a constituent element),[70] extra-territorial violations of Swiss banking secrecy laws can no longer be based on Article 7 of the Swiss Criminal Code, as these violations are regarded as a conduct offence and not as a result offence.

Some authors nevertheless continue to advocate an extra-territorial application of the offence of violating Swiss banking secrecy, albeit on an unclear legal basis.[71] They argue that to limit the spatial application field of Article 47 of the Swiss Banking Act to Swiss territory would result in a drastic decrease in the level of protection for Swiss banks and their per-sonnel, which would thus be exposed to pressure from foreign authorities to disclose privileged information. In particular, it is feared that limiting the application field of the incrimination of violation of Swiss banking secrecy to conduct which took place on Swiss territory will cause some foreign authorities acting outside Switzerland to try to force individuals

---

[69] M. Aubert, 'Quelques aspects de la portée du secret bancaire en droit pénal interne et dans l'entraide judiciaire internationale', *RPS* (1984), 169.   [70] ATF 105 IV 326.

[71] Aubert, 'Quelques aspects de la portée du secret bancaire', 170–171 and Aubert and others, *Le secret bancaire suisse*, pp. 101–2.

bound by Swiss banking secrecy laws to disclose information in such a way that Swiss courts would not be able to hold those individuals liable for violating Swiss secrecy laws. The lack of adequate legal 'retaliation powers' to the unilateral measures that have been taken by foreign, especially American, authorities to lift foreign banking secrecy also explains the strong, diplomatic objections to them from the Swiss and other (e.g. the German) governments who consider these measures tantamount to a violation of the sovereignty of the state under whose laws the information concerned is privileged.[72] These measures will be discussed in the following chapter in respect of lifting of foreign banking secrecy.

[72] See Krafft, 'Secret bancaire et conflits de juridiction', pp. 209 and 214–15 and Aubert, 'Quelques aspects de la portée du secret bancaire', 170.

14   Lifting banking secrecy in an international context

Law enforcement authorities investigating money laundering offences, or any other type of profitable offence, are often confronted with the type of situation in which, although an offence has in part taken place on their territory, the fruits of the crime have been siphoned away to a secrecy jurisdiction, where information relating to the proceeds is protected by stringent banking secrecy rules. Where financial transactions were part of the criminal scheme, the information thus shielded from the prying eyes of law enforcement authorities will not only relate to the proceeds from the offence, but to the *actus reus* itself. An international report on offshore jurisdictions – commissioned by the United Nations – correctly points out that offshore financial systems offer not only an excellent conduit for money laundering, but also a 'tool kit' for the perpetration of certain types of financial crime.[1] In the efforts of law enforcement authorities to penetrate foreign (banking) secrecy rules, two main strands of international evidence gathering can be recognised. On the one hand, a number of co-operative mechanisms have been created to allow access to information and evidence which is located abroad and shielded by a secrecy duty. Alternatively, and at least as important, certain unilateral measures have been adopted by some, notably American, authorities to obtain this information. It is interesting that the diplomatic tensions that have been created by American measures of this type almost exclusively concern attempts to penetrate foreign banking secrecy rules rather than the obstacles posed by foreign professional secrecy duties of, for example, lawyers. It seems therefore that US authorities have greater respect for foreign professional privileges than for foreign banking secrecy rules.[2] Although

---

[1] United Nations Office for Drug Control and Crime Prevention, *Financial Havens, Banking Secrecy and Money Laundering*, p. 26.

[2] Bschorr and Mullin, 'Court-ordered Waivers of Foreign Banking Secrecy Rights', p. 199.

American law enforcement authorities have been the most ardent in their unilateral attempts to lift foreign banking secrecy, authorities from other countries, especially those with common law jurisdictions, have also issued orders of this kind.

It is therefore proposed that we examine in the first instance the background of this approach which is at odds with the continental European, civil law approach of seeking co-operation from the territorially competent authorities to lift banking secrecy. Next, the extra-territorial disclosure orders that have been made in order to lift foreign banking secrecy will be analysed. Finally, having demonstrated the intricate legal situations to which these measures may lead, the need for international co-operation in the lifting of foreign banking secrecy will be set out and the co-operative mechanisms that have been created to this end will be analysed.

Background of the American approach to extra-territorial disclosure orders

Various factors account for the robust attitude that American law enforcement agencies, backed up by American court orders, have often taken with regard to the disclosure of information protected by foreign banking secrecy rules. Some are more general and pertain to general differences in legal culture, whereas others are specific to the context of lifting banking secrecy.

Differing legal attitudes to international co-operation

A first, obvious, factor that explains the use of unilateral procedures to obtain evidence located abroad is the absence, in many cases, of treaty mechanisms and the harrowing slowness and deceiving efficacy of letters rogatory.[3] As in the case of treaty-based co-operation, then, the slowness of international co-operation mechanisms has been a major source of frustration for requesting authorities. This is particularly the case in the context of international co-operation for lifting foreign banking secrecy, where there is, as it was cogently put in the EU *Draft Report of the Informal Money Laundering Experts Group*, a 'difference in speed between on the one hand the international transfer of money and on the other hand the exe-

---

[3] See Nadelmann, *Cops Across Borders*, pp. 318–24 and C. Todd Jones, 'Compulsion Over Comity: The United States' Assault on Foreign Bank Secrecy', *Nw.JInt'l.L. & Bus.* (1992), 471–3.

cution of a letter of request for information or any other legal action'.[4] It therefore comes as little surprise that it is precisely the time delay that results from the cumbersome procedures for lifting foreign banking secrecy that has been identified as the most problematic aspect of banking secrecy.[5] The elaborate procedures for lifting banking secrecy and the multiple remedies that are available to those who are accused of not providing information, and to any party concerned – especially in offshore jurisdictions and large financial centres – have become strongly resented by some requesting authorities. Thus the numerous foreign complaints about the long procedures necessary under the Swiss Mutual Assistance Act for lifting banking secrecy[6] nudged Switzerland in 1996 to trim its appeal procedures under this.[7] Also on an international level, action is being undertaken to streamline international co-operation in this field. It is one of the main concerns behind the EU Joint Action of 3 December 1998 concerning the arrangements for co-operation between Member States in respect of the identification, tracing, freezing or seizing and confiscation of instrumentalities and the proceeds from crime. The concern for swift and effective co-operation was also taken into account by the drafters of the Vienna Convention (Article 7(8)) and the Money Laundering Convention (Article 24(1)), both of which allow central authorities to communicate directly with each other. The latter convention moreover allows judicial authorities (including public prosecutors) to communicate with each other directly in respect of non-coercive measures and even in respect of coercive measures that are urgent (Article 24(2) and (5)).

A second, also general, factor relates to the divide between the common law (especially American) legal culture and the continental European legal culture. This difference, as has already been discussed, also has important implications for the concept of international evidence gathering.[8] In the specific context of measures to lift banking secrecy, the different procedural texture of common law and civil law plays an important

---

[4] p. 33.

[5] United Nations Office for Drug Control and Crime Prevention, *Financial Havens, Banking Secrecy and Money Laundering*, 17.

[6] See, e.g., Mann, Mari and Lavdas, *Developments in International Securities Law Enforcement*, p. 47.

[7] This happened by the Act of 4 October 1996, which entered into force on 1 February 1997. See Y. Graf, 'Switzerland Revises its Law in Mutual Assistance in Criminal Matters', *Int'l.Enf.LR* (1997), 98–100; C. M. Baer, 'Revision des Rechtshilfegesetz und des Bundesgesetz zum Rechtshilfevertrag mit den Vereinigten Staaten von Amerika – Wichtigste Aspekte und Zusamenfassung der Vernehmlassungsergebnisse', *RSDA* (1995), 80–2 and V. Jeanneret, 'La nouvelle loi suisse sur l'entraide internationale en matière pénale', *Agon* (1997), No.15, 11–14.   [8] See *supra* pp. 278–81.

role. In view of the great importance that is attached to discovery as an essential instrument for establishing the truth and for ensuring fair trial for all parties, it should come as no surprise that extensive use has been made, also in an international context, by the US authorities of disclosure orders to lift banking secrecy, mostly by means of grand jury subpoenas but sometimes by summonses issued by administrative authorities such as the Internal Revenue Service (IRS).[9]

Differing visions on banking secrecy

A third, more specific element, which is also very important to understanding the American approach is the attitude that is taken in the United States to banking secrecy, an attitude that is distinctly different from the attitude taken by other countries, for example, civil law countries.

In many quarters nowadays, a great deal of opprobrium is attached to the term 'banking secrecy', as it is seen as a shield which allows drug traffickers, terrorists, kleptocrats and other criminals to stash away the fruits of their crimes. However, banking secrecy is in the first place a duty of secrecy imposed on bankers whose purpose is to guarantee the confidential treatment of information communicated to bankers by their customers. The degree to which different legal systems afford legal protection to this confidential information varies greatly from country to country, reflecting the various degrees of importance that is attached to this type of confidentiality. It is a matter of simple logic that these varying approaches to banking secrecy, not just from a legal viewpoint, but also from a political, economic and social perspective, influence the way in which domestic law enforcement authorities act in attempting to lift (foreign) banking secrecy. Whereas the so-called secrecy jurisdictions attach great importance to banking secrecy for legal reasons, but quite obviously also for economic and political motives, these stringent banking provisions, which often have no equivalent in other countries, receive less esteem abroad.[10] In order to grasp this matter fully, it is useful

---

[9] On the summons authority of the IRS and the US Department of Treasury in the context of the fight against money laundering, see Harmon, 'United States Money Laundering Laws', 6 and 27–8.

[10] See M. Levi, *Consumer Confidentiality, Money-Laundering, and Police Bank Relationships: English Law and Practice in a Global Environment*, (The Police Foundation, 1991), pp. 1–10. Cf. H. S. Erbstein, 'Palm Trees Hide More Than Sunshine: The Extra-territorial Application of Securities Laws in Haven Jurisdictions', *Dick.J.Int'l.L* (1995), 477 and Stultz, *Swiss Bank Secrecy*, 81.

to draw out the legal distinctions that exist, from a comparative point of view, in the design of the rules relating to a banker's duty to keep information secret (i.e. not to disclose it to third parties, including government authorities).

From a comparative point of view, the most stringent type of secrecy duty is undoubtedly that provided for in Article 378 of France's 1810 Napoleonic *Code Pénal*, which criminalised violations of professional secrecy pertaining to confidential information entrusted to certain professionals (attorneys, doctors, pharmacists, etc.). This criminalisation of violations of professional secrecy – which was rooted in the secrecy duty imposed by canonic law on priests[11] – was emulated by many other continental European legal systems (see, e.g. Article 458 of the Belgian and of the Luxembourg Criminal Code, Article 272 of the Dutch Criminal Code and Article 321 of the Swiss Criminal Code). This very stringent protection of confidential information communicated to a limited number of professionals, contrasts with the common law approach which does not criminalise violations of professional secrecy but which privileges the information provided by clients to certain professionals, especially lawyers (legal privilege, also known as attorney-client privilege).[12]

At common law, banking secrecy is based on the contractual relationship between a banker and his client and has no relation whatsoever to legal privilege. It is indicative of the low (legal) esteem in which banking secrecy is held in the United States, that the US Supreme Court has exempted the seizure of bank documents[13] from constitutional protection so that it required a legislative intervention to entrench the right of a customer to ensure that the information he communicates to his banker be kept secret (Right to Financial Privacy Act (1978)).[14]

However, in most European continental legal systems that recognise professional secrecy, banking secrecy is not equated with professional

---

[11] On the history of professional secrecy, see P. Lambert, *Le Secret Professionnel* (Brussels: Nemesis, 1985), pp. 15–24.

[12] See *Archbold: Pleading, Evidence and Practice in Criminal Cases*, ed. S. Mitchell, D. J. Richardson and D. A. Thomas (London: Sweet & Maxwell, 1988), pp. 1111–14 and L. G. Peires, 'Legal Professional Privilege in Commonwealth Law', *ICLQ* (1982), 609–39. For a comparison with continental-law-type of professional secrecy, see J. B. M. Vranken, 'Het Professionele (Functionele) Verschoningsrecht', in *Handelingen Nederlandse Juristenvereniging* (Zwolle: Tjeenk Willink, 1986), pp. 20–38.

[13] *United States v. Miller*, 425 US 435 (1976). See also *supra* pp. 144–5.

[14] On the background of this act, see C. T. Plombeck, 'Confidentiality and Disclosure: The Money Laundering Control Act of 1986 and Banking Secrecy', *Int'l Law*. (1988), 69–70 and 94–5 and Schroth, 'Bank Confidentiality', pp. 286–7.

secrecy. In some countries (e.g., Belgium[15] and The Netherlands[16]), case law has explicitly held that a banker is not bound by a duty of professional secrecy, but merely by a civil duty of secrecy, violation of which can make a banker liable under civil law, but which cannot give rise to criminal sanctions. Only in Luxembourg is the duty of the banker to keep secret information communicated to him by his customers equated with professional secrecy. This *opinio juris* gradually emerged after the Second World War and was for the first time statutorily entrenched in Article 16 of the 1981 Banking Act.[17] The duty to secrecy of the Luxembourg banker is nowadays laid down in Article 41 of the Luxembourg Act of 5 April 1993,[18] which refers to Article 458 of the Criminal Code (the provision on professional secrecy). In Switzerland, which is also (in)famous for its stringent banking secrecy provisions, banking secrecy is not equated with professional secrecy,[19] but is enshrined in a separate statutory provision, Article 47 of the Swiss Banking Act 1934, which makes disclosure of confidential information communicated to a banker a criminal offence, punishable by a fine of up to 50,000 Swiss francs and/or up to six months imprisonment. This criminal law protection obviously supersedes the protection offered by the private law basis of banking secrecy.[20]

These very divergent legal concepts of banking secrecy offer great scope for conflict between legal systems when the authorities of one state try to penetrate the banking secrecy of another. This is further highlighted by

---

[15] See the judgment of the Belgian Supreme Court of 25 October 1978, *Journal des Tribunaux* (1979), 371 with annotation by A. Bruyneel, 'Le secret bancaire en Belgique après l'arrêt rendu par la Cour de cassation le 25 octobre 1978'. Cf. J. Spreutels, 'Secret bancaire et droit pénal', *RDP* (1979), 433–44 and G. Du Bois, 'Het bankgeheim', *TPR* (1986), 436–8.

[16] See the judgment of the Dutch Supreme Court of 28 March 1938, *NJ* (1939), 122 and of the Court of Appeal of Amsterdam, of 18 December 1974, *NJ* (1975), 441. See also M. S. Groenhuijsen and F. Molenaar, 'Bank Confidentiality and Governmental Control of Exchange Operations and Their Unlawful Effects – The Netherlands', in *Blanchiment d'argent et secret bancaire*, Rapport général du XIVe Congrès international de droit comparé, P. Bernasconi (The Hague: Kluwer Law International, 1996), pp. 179–82.

[17] Loi du 23 avril 1981 transposant en droit national la première directive bancaire CEE visant la coordination des dispositions législatives, réglementaires et administratives concernant l'accès à l'activité des établissements de crédit et son exercice.

[18] On this evolution see G. Harles, 'Luxembourg', in *International Bank Secrecy*, D. Campbell (London: Sweet & Maxwell, 1992), p. 472; J. Kaufmann, 'Le secret bancaire en droit luxembourgeois', *DPCI* (1990), 75–8 and 'Le secret bancaire en droit luxembourgeois – aspects actuels et perspectives', p. 535.

[19] K. Mueller, 'The Swiss Banking Secret From a Legal View', *ICLQ* (1969), 362.

[20] On this contractual basis of banking secrecy, see Aubert *et al.*, *Le secret bancaire suisse*, pp. 48–52; H. Bollmann, 'Switzerland', in *International Bank Secrecy*, D. Campbell (London: Sweet & Maxwell, 1992), pp. 665–6; Giovanoli, 'Switzerland', 185–6 and Stultz, 'Swiss Bank Secrecy', 67–9.

the remarkable fact that a number of the so-called secrecy jurisdictions have enacted laws criminalising banking secrecy violations following the attempts of foreign authorities to exercise pressure on customers or on bank officials, to obtain information covered by banking secrecy in that jurisdiction. Thus, the enactment of Swiss legislation criminalising violations of banking secrecy is said to be prompted by German Nazi legislation which obliged all German citizens, under threat of the death penalty, to apprise the German authorities of all funds held abroad.[21] A similar analysis can even be made in respect of a secrecy jurisdiction as exotic as that of the Cayman Islands.[22] Again, it has sometimes been asserted in relation to Luxembourg that the statutory entrenchment of the applicability of the criminalisation of violations of professional secrecy to banking secrecy was inspired by a decision of the Belgian Supreme Court – the case law of which is typically adhered to in Luxembourg as well – to the effect that a banker is not entitled to invoke professional secrecy if he wishes to avoid disclosing confidential information.[23]

These similar backgrounds to the enactment of criminal law provisions punishing violations of banking secrecy suggest that the primary reason for criminalising violations of a (banker's) secrecy duty lies in deterring foreign authorities from exercising pressure on bankers to obtain information protected by banking secrecy rules. Thus the criminal law fence that is erected around banking secrecy in some countries is not so much designed to give stronger protection to banking confidentiality for domestic purposes – for it in no way precludes that banking secrecy is lifted for the purposes of a criminal investigation – but rather aims to provide a legal means for deterring and sanctioning foreign encroachments of banking secrecy. This rationale is moreover not limited to the criminalisation of violations of banking secrecy but extends to other types of secrecy, notably in the economic sphere, the most important function of which is often to erect a legal wall against external threats to the national economy.[24] In this sense the background of some banking secrecy laws –

[21] See M. Aubert, 'Quelques aspects de la portée du secret bancaire', 167–8; Mueller, 'The Swiss Banking Secret', 362; Stultz, 'Swiss Bank Secrecy', 70–2 and Todd Jones, 'Compulsion Over Comity', 455. Cf. Bollmann, 'Switzerland', p. 663.

[22] On the background to the enactment of the Confidential Relationships (Preservation) Law 1976, see I. Paget-Brown, 'A Cayman Perspective', in *International Tracing of Assets*, ed. M. Ashe and B. Rider (London: FT Law and Tax, 1997), p. S2/8.

[23] F. Entringer, 'Le secret bancaire remis en question', in *Stromates*, ed. F. Entringer (Luxembourg, 1997), p. 128.

[24] Cf. *Conseil de l'Europe, Secret et transparence: l'individu, l'entreprise et l'administration. Actes du colloque du dix-septième Colloque de droit européen* (Strasbourg: 1988, Editions du Conseil de l'Europe), p. 25.

which have in principle a general application field and are not specifically directed against foreign authorities – is similar to that of so-called blocking laws which explicitly aim to prevent the disclosure of information to foreign authorities. Blocking laws have been defined as laws that aim 'to prohibit the disclosure, copying, inspection or removal of documents located in the host country in compliance with orders of foreign authorities'.[25] This analysis also reveals the extent to which domestic banking secrecy provisions express the economic and political interests of the states concerned. It is a truism that conflicting political and economic interests of states can hamper the efficacy of international co-operation and of international evidence gathering in general.[26] The conflicts that have arisen over attempts to pierce foreign banking secrecy only serve to illustrate this.

Extra-territorial disclosure orders

Law enforcement authorities conducting an investigation into (alleged) money laundering offences will often be confronted with the impediment of foreign banking secrecy which forbids the disclosure of information relevant to their investigation. US authorities have in particular tried to pierce foreign banking secrecy by issuing extra-territorial disclosure orders, that is, disclosure orders in respect of information held abroad. These disclosure orders are made in varying contexts, often in the course of private litigation, where the person or institution who was defrauded seeks to recover his funds and to that end seeks disclosure orders in relation to assets held abroad. Many of the cases referred to hereinafter are not money laundering cases, or even criminal cases, but the issues they raise are material to international money laundering investigations. In the following it is proposed to examine the techniques and legal bases common law courts have used to issue this type of order. Thereafter, the compatibility of the various techniques with international law will be scrutinised.

---

[25] Restatement (Third), § 442 (reporter's note 4). See Todd Jones, 'Compulsion Over Comity', 463–4 and A. Lowe, *Extraterritorial Jurisdiction* (Cambridge: Grotius Publications, 1983), xviii.

[26] Heymann, 'Two Models of National Attitudes', 100–1 and E. A. Nadelmann, 'The Role of the United States in the International Enforcement of Criminal Law', *Harv.Int'l IJ* (1990), 43.

Legal arguments invoked for making extra-territorial disclosure orders

One of the most important factors which has stimulated the use of extra-territorial disclosure orders is the fact that an 'international bank' is usually a unitary global corporation, composed of one head office and various branches in different parts of the world. The reason for not setting up separately incorporated subsidiaries, as is often done in the context of multinational corporations, is that banks need to have access to their global resources for the purposes of lending.[27] Thus an international bank will not only hold relevant information in a secrecy jurisdiction but will also have a branch in the state where the investigation is taking place, especially if the latter state is an economically powerful country such as the United States or the United Kingdom.

Typically, US and UK courts have issued disclosure orders to banks located within their jurisdiction, but pertaining to information held at foreign branches of that bank. Apart from *subpoenas duces tecum*, which require banks to produce documents, American law enforcement authorities – often after review by the US Department of Justice – have also served *subpoenas ad testificandum* on bankers or bank officers who happened to be present within US territory (often by accident, e.g. on holiday), obliging them to testify in respect of (alleged) money laundering operations.[28] In some instances, subpoenas have even been served on agents of the banks acting within the United States such as law firms representing a foreign bank, for example.[29] Another type of measure is the so-called 'Ghidoni waiver',[30] whereby customers are required to give a written consent directive, ordering their bank abroad to provide the relevant documents. In case of refusal to make such a consent directive, the individual can be held in contempt.[31] In *Doe v. US* the US Supreme Court declined to consider such consent directive as violative of the privilege against self-incrimination, because the person

[27] See D. E. Alford, 'Basle Committee Minimum Standards: International Regulatory Response to the Failure of BCCI', *Geo.Wash.J.Int'l L.& Econ.* (1992), 280–1.
[28] *United States v. Field*, 532 F.2d 404 (5th Circ.1976).
[29] *United States v. Bowe*, 694 F.2d 1256 (11th Circ.1982).
[30] *United States v. Ghidoni*, 732 F.2d 814 (11th Cir.1984), cert.denied, 469 US 932 (1984). See Nadelmann, *Cops Across Borders*, pp. 363–4 and Stratenwerth, 'Der behördlich erzwungene Verzicht auf das Bankgeheimnis', p. 238.
[31] J. T. Bergin, 'Piercing the Secret Bank Account For Criminal Prosecutions: An Evaluation of United States' Extra-territorial Discovery Techniques and the Mutual Assistance Treaty', *Ariz.JInt'l & Comp.L* (1990), 334–5.

concerned did not identify the documents sought, nor confirm their existence.[32]

The common feature of all these cases is that the authorities who have issued these extra-territorial disclosure orders have based themselves on an *in personam* jurisdiction, that is, adjudicative jurisdiction over the person against whom these orders are issued in order to regulate the conduct of these (juridical) persons abroad. Whether this amounts to an unacceptable usurpation of enforcement jurisdiction will be discussed hereinafter. In the course of one particular high-water litigation, the action undertaken by the US authorities may, in the absence of an *in personam* jurisdiction, even be looked upon as amounting to a claim of enforcement jurisdiction. The litigation concerned a criminal investigation into alleged tax frauds committed on a massive scale by an American crude oil trading company, Marc Rich International SA, which was the wholly owned subsidiary of a Swiss company, Marc Rich SA. The proceeds from the alleged tax frauds had been channelled via the New York branch of Marc Rich International SA to the Swiss mother company, which itself had no branches or activities in the United States. Nevertheless, a subpoena was issued to the Swiss mother company, obliging it to produce documents in Switzerland[33] and Marc Rich SA was even held in contempt for not complying with the subpoena and fined US$50,000 for each day it failed to produce the documents. The basis on which the Court of Appeal of the Second Circuit claimed jurisdiction to issue an extra-territorial subpoena was remarkable: the protection principle and the territoriality principle. Although enforcement jurisdiction can of course be founded in the territoriality principle, it is clear from the facts of the Marc Rich case that enforcement was not purported to take place in the United States, but in Switzerland. As far as the protection principle is concerned, this is commonly accepted for prescriptive jurisdiction, but here the court invoked it with a view to ground enforce-

---

[32] *Doe v. US*, 487 US 201. Cf. Bergin, 'Piercing the Secret Bank Account', 334–7. On the relation between the production of documents and the privilege against self-incrimination, see in general G. Stessens, 'The Obligation to Produce Documents Versus the Privilege Against Self-incrimination: Human Rights Protection Extended Too Far?', *ELR*, Human Rights Survey (1997), 45–62.

[33] *In re Grand Jury Subpoena Directed to Marc Rich & Co.*, aff'd sub nom. *In re Grand Jury Subpoena Directed to Marc Rich & Co., Marc Rich & Co. v. United States*, 707 F.2d 663 (2nd Cir. 1983). On this case see 'Note to, "The Marc Rich Case: Extension of Grand Jury Subpoena Power to Nonresident Alien Corporations",' *Geo.Wash.JInt'l. L & Econ.* (1984), 97; Krafft, 'Secret bancaire et conflits de juridiction', pp. 212–13 and 220–1; Mann, 'The Doctrine of International Jurisdiction Revisited', pp. 53–5 and Nadelmann, *Cops Across Borders*, 338.

ment jurisdiction.[34] This judicial reasoning is therefore clearly at variance with international law.

Compatibility of extra-territorial disclosure orders with international law

These extra-territorial disclosure orders have often provoked fierce reactions because they have been considered as violating the sovereignty of
other states in that they purport to obtain information or even documents
covered by foreign banking secrecy. These reactions have not been merely
academic but have also been political and judicial as well, as was, for
example, demonstrated in the context of the above-mentioned Marc Rich
case. In that case the Swiss government intervened by seizing the documents to which the disclosure order against Marc Rich SA pertained,
thereby effectively precluding their production.[35] In another case related
to the Marc Rich saga, a grand jury subpoena was issued to Citibank New
York relating to documents held by the London branch of Citibank in its
capacity of bankers for the Swiss mother company. Marc Rich SA subsequently successfully moved for an injunction in London against Citibank
restraining it from disclosing confidential information held in its capacity as banker.[36]

In assessing the compatibility of this type of extra-territorial disclosure
order with international law, the crux of the matter lies in the answer to
the question as to whether these measures amount to a form of extra-
territorial enforcement of jurisdiction. Enforcement jurisdiction is certainly limited in a strictly territorial manner, as was already underlined
by the Permanent Court of International Justice.[37]

The incompatibility of extra-territorial investigations with international law is beyond discussion and has already been discussed above.[38] In
case of so-called extra-territorial disclosure orders, the question of their
compatibility with international law is more difficult. It is useful to distinguish between various forms of extra-territorial disclosure orders in
order to determine whether they amount to a form of enforcement jurisdiction which a state is not allowed to exercise outside its territory. The

---

[34] Cf. Harmon, 'United States Money Laundering Laws', 39.

[35] See P. Bernasconi, 'Flux internationaux de capitaux d'origine illicite. La Suisse face aux
nouvelles stratégies', in *Nuovi strumenti giudiziari contro la criminalità economica
internazionale* (Naples: Edizioni Città del sole, 1995), pp. 167–8.

[36] *XAG. v. A.Bank*, [1983] 2 All ER 465. For comment see C. McLachlan, 'The Jurisdictional
Limits of Disclosure Orders in Transnational Fraud Litigation', *ICLQ* (1998), 36.

[37] Permanent Court of International Justice, *Lotus SS, France v. Turkey, Publ. CPIJ* (1927), Series
A., No.10, pp. 18–19. See *supra*, p. 213.   [38] See *supra* pp. 280–1.

most obvious form of extra-territorial enforcement jurisdiction is where the disclosure order is actually served abroad. The service of documents in another state by officials (e.g. consuls) or other agents employed by the enforcing state should be considered illegal under international law in the absence of treaty or an *ad hoc* permission,[39] notwithstanding case law of the US Supreme Court to the contrary.[40] In respect of service of documents by post, a distinction should be made between documents containing a command as opposed to documents containing a mere notification. The act of service of a document which contains a command such as a subpoena constitutes an exercise of sovereign power. In the absence of treaty arrangements, service of a document containing a command should therefore be considered as violative of international law.[41] This is also apparent from the fact that some mutual legal assistance instruments explicitly provide for the possibility to serve orders on the territory of another party.[42] When, in addition – as is very likely to be the case when disclosure orders are made with respect to information covered by banking secrecy – the service of a document collides with rules of the *lex situs* (e.g. banking secrecy or blocking laws) prohibiting the enforcement of the command contained therein, there is a conflict of enforcement jurisdiction. It is submitted that, as a matter of international law, no state is in principle entitled to require the commission of an illegality or a criminal offence within the territory of another state.[43]

The question is more vexed when the disclosure order, though served on a person present within the territory of the enforcing state, pertains to information held abroad, as did the American cases discussed above. Do such extra-territorial disclosure orders amount to an intolerable exercise of extra-territorial enforcement jurisdiction?

As a matter of principle it may be accepted that such disclosure orders

---

[39] Mann, 'The Doctrine of Jurisdiction', p. 132. For a general overview of American law on service of process abroad, see G. B. Born and D. Westin, *International Civil Litigation in United States Courts* (Deventer: Kluwer Law and Taxation Publishers, 1992), pp. 153–220.

[40] *Blackmer v. US* 284 US 421 (1932). This case law was, however, superseded by *US v. Lansky*, 496 F.2d 1063 (1974).

[41] See the judgment by the DC Court of Appeals, in *Federal Trade Commission v. Compagnie de Saint-Gobain-Pont-à-Mousson* (636 F.2d 1300 (DC1980)). See also Mann, 'The Doctrine of Jurisdiction', pp. 133–5 and 'The Doctrine of International Jurisdiction Revisited', pp. 39–41 and B. Straüli, 'Territorialité de l'enquête pénale et garantie d'une activité irréprochable', in *Journée 1995 de droit bancaire et financier*, L. Thévenoz (Bern: Stämpfli, 1995), p. 126.

[42] See, e.g., Article 15 of the American–Italian MLAT (*ILM*, 1985, 1535) and Article 52 of the Schengen Convention.

[43] Mann, 'The Doctrine of International Jurisdiction Revisited', p. 45.

need not necessarily infringe international law. When, in the course of private litigation, the court of a state which has adjudicative jurisdiction, orders discovery against (one of) the parties in respect of information or documents held abroad, it may be accepted that this extra-territorial disclosure order is not violative of any rule of international law – even where the discovery would be illegal according to the *lex situs*[44] – because the parties have agreed to play the game by the local rules.

The type of situation concerned here is fundamentally different, however, as it does not pertain to private litigation but to litigation for the enforcement of public or prerogative rights, *in casu* the right to punish. The importance of this distinction lies in the fact that, whereas judgments enforcing a private right are internationally valid and can in principle also be enforced abroad, a judgment enforcing a public right is in principle not internationally valid and cannot be enforced abroad in the absence of explicit treaty arrangements to that effect.[45] Although the rule of non-enforcement of foreign public law may need to be relaxed in some respects,[46] any conflict of enforcement jurisdiction should be resolved in favour of the state having territorial jurisdiction. The situation is different in another respect as well, in that financial institutions against which these (extra-territorial) disclosure orders are made are not party to the litigation but are merely involved as third parties.

A distinction needs to be made between two types of situation. In the first, the head office of an international bank is located within the territory of the enforcing state, but the documents sought after are held abroad in a foreign branch. Given that the head office in principle has control over the foreign branch – the bank being a unitary corporation – the head office cannot resist the production order on the ground that the documents are located abroad. Provided that the enforcing state has prescriptive jurisdiction over the matter investigated, it is also entitled to require compliance from its nationals in respect of conduct abroad. When the bank is merely involved as a third party, as will often be the case in money laundering investigations, the enforcing state will be entitled to order the disclosure of documents held abroad only if it has prescriptive jurisdiction over the person who is being investigated.[47]

---

[44] Mann, 'The Doctrine of Jurisdiction', pp. 156–7 and 'The Doctrine of International Jurisdiction Revisited', p. 49 and C. McLachlan, 'Extra-territorial Orders Affecting Bank Deposits', in *Extraterritorial Jurisdiction in Theory and Practice*, ed. K. Meessen (London: Kluwer Law International, 1996), pp. 44–7 and 'The Jurisdictional Limits of Disclosure Orders', 46–7.   [45] Mann, 'The Doctrine of Jurisdiction', pp. 147–8.

[46] See *infra* pp. 365–7.

[47] Mann, 'The Doctrine of International Jurisdiction Revisited', pp. 49–50.

More important is that the enforcing state cannot order a foreign branch of a bank to produce documents if that production would amount to an illegality or a criminal offence under the *lex situs*. This follows from the principle that has already been propounded, namely that, as a matter of international law, no state is in principle entitled to require the commission of an illegality or a criminal offence within the territory of another state.[48] This principle also incorporates the non-intervention principle.[49]

In the past, American courts have occasionally upheld this rule. In *First National City Bank v. Internal Revenue Service*, a subpoena issued to the American head office of a bank regarding documents held in its Panamian branch was upheld in view of the fact that Panamian law did not prohibit discovery.[50] In *Société Internationale v. Rogers* (1958), the US Supreme Court accepted that a Swiss defendant who could not produce all documents without violating Swiss banking secrecy had acted in good faith and should not be sanctioned for not fully complying with the production order.[51] This case, which was moreover concerned with private litigation in which a Swiss company was the plaintiff, embodied a deference to the *lex situs* that has since been gradually abandoned in American case law. Drawing on the subsequent Restatements of the Foreign Relations Law of The United States by the American Law Institute, US courts now regularly embark on an interest-balancing process in the context of extra-territorial discovery. The outcome of this process has almost invariably been in favour of the interests of the United States, even where the extra-territorial disclosure order may expose the person concerned to sanctions under the *lex situs*.[52] This has rightly led some commentators to consider this interest-balancing process as a thinly veiled form of American legal chauvinism.[53] The underlying attitude of American courts often seems to have

---

[48] Mann, 'The Doctrine of International Jurisdiction Revisited', pp. 45, 50.

[49] Cf. 'UN Declaration on Friendly Relations and Co-operation among States of 24 October 1970', ILM (1970), 1292. See Krafft, 'Secret bancaire et conflits de juridiction', p. 214.

[50] 271 F.2d 616 (1959), cert.denied, 361 US 948 (1960) (Citibank I). Cf. *Ings v. Ferguson*, 282 F.2d 149 (1960); *In re Chase Manhattan Bank*, 297 F.2d 611 (1962).

[51] *Société Internationale v. Rogers* (1958) 357 US 197, 208–9 and 211–12. Cf. Erbstein, 'Palm Trees Hide More Than Sunshine', 470–1.

[52] On this interest-balancing process see Born and Westin, *International Civil Litigation*, p. 384 et seq.; P. Kinsch, *Le fait du prince étranger* (Paris: Librairie générale de droit et de jurisprudence, 1994), pp. 97–116; McLachlan, 'The Jurisdictional Limits of Disclosure Orders', 35 and Todd Jones, 'Compulsion Over Comity', 488–99.

[53] Mann, 'The Doctrine of International Jurisdiction Revisited', pp. 23 and 45. Cf. H. G. Maier, 'Extra-territorial Jurisdiction at the Crossroads: An Intersection Between Public and Private International Law', *AJIL* (1982), 280 and 'Interest Balancing and Extraterritorial Jurisdiction', *AJIL* (1983), 589.

been that foreign companies that operate within the United States have to accept concomitant obligations, including the process of (grand jury) subpoenas. As it was cogently put by Milton Pollack J in a well-known case of insider trading: 'It would be a travesty of justice to permit a foreign company to invade American markets, violate American laws if they were indeed violated, withdraw profits and resist accountability for itself and its principals for the illegality by claiming their anonymity under foreign law'.[54]

Fortunately, the courts of other countries have been more considerate to the *lex situs* when faced with (applications for) extra-territorial disclosure orders.[55] Thus, in *Mackinnon v. Donaldson, Lufkin & Jenrette Securities Corporation,* Hoffman J (as he then was) approvingly referred to F. Mann to set out the principle that the fact that courts of a state have personal (i.e. judicial) jurisdiction over a person does not permit them to regulate by orders the conduct of those persons abroad.[56] This is only possible 'if the state of the forum also has substantive jurisdiction to regulate the conduct in the manner defined in the order'.[57]

The problem is even more serious in a second type of situation where, as US authorities have often done, the extra-territorial disclosure order is served on one branch of a bank and relates to documents held at another. Here, the state clearly lacks enforcement jurisdiction in respect of the documents held abroad. It may have prescriptive jurisdiction over the subject matter and enforcement jurisdiction over the (juridical) person present within its territory but this does not give it enforcement jurisdiction over information held at a foreign branch over which the domestic branch has no control. This illegality under international law is only compounded by the fact that the production is often illegal according to the *lex situs*. It is matter of regret that US courts have failed to pay due consideration to this. Apparently only the District of Columbia Circuit Court refuses to uphold subpoenas issued to American branches of foreign banks in respect of documents held abroad.[58] Other American courts have

---

54 *Securities and Exchange Commission v. Banca della Svizzera Italiana*, (1981) 92 F.2d 119. For comment, see Erbstein, 'Palm Trees Hide More Than Sunshine', 469–72 and M. D. Mann, J. G. Mari and G. Lavdas, *Developments in International Securities Law Enforcement and Regulation*, pp. 31–3.

55 See in general Kinsch, *Le fait du prince étranger*, pp. 93–7.

56 [1986] 1 All ER 653, 658. See also *R v. Grossman* (1981) 73 *Crim.App.R* 302 (CA). See, however, *London and County Securities v. Caplan* (26 May 1986), cited by McClean, *International Judicial Assistance*, p. 274.

57 Mann, 'The Doctrine of Jurisdiction', p. 146.

58 See *In re Sealed Case*, 825 F.2d 494 (D. C. Cir), *cert.denied*, 108 S.Ct. 451 (1987) (regarding an investigation of alleged violations of the Bank Secrecy Act).

explicitly refused to set great store by the fact that the production of these documents would render the bank guilty of violation of the banking secrecy laws of those countries. In *Nova Scotia I*, involving a grand jury investigation into money laundering practices, a subpoena was served on the Miami branch of the Canadian Bank of Nova Scotia relating to documents held at branches in the Bahamas.[59] The US Court of Appeals of the Eleventh Circuit confirmed this subpoena, holding that the bank had not made a good faith effort to comply with the subpoena. In the same vein, in *Nova Scotia II*, the same court again refused to allow the defence that the production of documents was illegal according to the *lex situs*. In both cases the court expressly referred to a prior judgment in *Field*, pointing out that the bank itself had chosen to set up branches in different jurisdictions and had thereby subjected itself to the risk of conflicting court orders: 'In a world where commercial transactions are international in scope, conflicts are inevitable. Courts and legislatures should take every reasonable precaution to avoid placing individuals in the situation [the bank] finds [it]self. Yet this court simply cannot acquiesce in the proposition that United States investigations must be thwarted whenever there is a conflict with the interests of other states'.[60]

Everything that up until now has been said on the compatibility of extra-territorial disclosure orders with international law also applies to the production of documents. Of course the question of discovery against witnesses may also arise. What is the position under international law if a banker is forced to testify and the questions posed to him relate to information covered by foreign banking secrecy? Should he be able to avail himself of foreign secrecy laws in order to refuse to answer the questions? It is submitted that such a defence should not be allowed. If a state has proper personal jurisdiction over an individual, it is entitled to require from that person that he complies with its procedural laws and answers the questions posed to him. It is difficult to see how this could amount to an unacceptable exercise of extra-territorial enforcement jurisdiction. As

---

[59] *United States v. Bank of Nova Scotia*, 691 F.2d 1384 (11th Circ. 1982), *cert.denied*, 462 US 1119 (1983) (Nova Scotia I). For comment see Bergin, 'Piercing the Secret Bank Account', 330–2; J. I. Horowitz, 'Piercing Offshore Banking Secrecy Laws Used to Launder Illegal Narcotics Profits: the Cayman Islands Example', *Tex.Int'l LJ* (1985), 156–8; Mann, 'The Doctrine of International Jurisdiction Revisited', p. 52 and Nadelmann, *Cops Across Borders*, p. 358.

[60] *United States v. Field*, 532 F.2d 404, 410 (5th Circ.1976); cited in *United States v. Bank of Nova Scotia*, 691 F.2d 1384, 1391 (11th Circ. 1982), *cert.denied*, 462 US 1119 (1983) (Nova Scotia I). *United States v. Bank of Nova Scotia*, 740 F.2d 817, 828 (11th Circ. 1984), *cert.denied*, 469 US 1106 (1985), (Nova Scotia II). For comment, see Horowitz, 'Piercing Offshore Banking Secrecy Laws', 160–1.

was shown earlier, whether a person has the right to decline to give evidence is in principle determined by the law of the state where the witness is questioned (*locus regit actum*).[61] To allow a defence based on foreign secrecy laws would frustrate the administration of justice, as was correctly pointed out by La Forest J. in *Spencer v. The Queen*.[62] In that case, the Canadian Supreme Court rejected the contention from the appellant, who was the manager of the Bahamas branch of a Canadian bank, that he could not be compelled to testify to the Crown in a prosecution under the Canadian Income Tax Act against a client of that bank because to do so would make him liable for prosecution under Bahamian law. Where a state invokes its domestic secrecy legislation in order to object to a subject giving evidence abroad, it is the objecting state that is attempting to enforce its laws extra-territorially. It is reiterated that an extra-territorial application of an incrimination of violation of banking secrecy can in principle only be allowed where this conduct is also criminal according to the *lex loci delicti*.[63] If states refrain from the application of their secrecy laws in this manner, the potential for conflicting legal obligations is dramatically reduced.

Privilege against self-incrimination v. extra-territorial disclosure orders

Another line of defence which has sometimes been taken by parties,[64] confronted with an extra-territorial disclosure order, compliance with which would make them criminally liable under the *lex situs*, relies on the privilege against self-incrimination. It is beyond discussion that a defendant can always rely on this privilege in order to refuse to answer questions, and under some, limited, circumstances even to refuse the production of documents,[65] but it has sometimes been argued that to invoke this privilege in the case of compliance with a disclosure order would make the party liable to prosecution.[66] If the privilege against self-incrimination allows a person to refuse to give evidence if this would incriminate him with respect to an offence he may have committed in the past, it is reasoned, it will surely also allow him to decline to give evidence if the giving of the evidence itself will make him liable for a criminal offence. It is, however, submitted that such a claim should not be allowed to stand in these circumstances as the legal policy considerations underpinning the

---

[61] See *supra* pp. 307–8.   [62] [1985] 2 SCR 278, 281.   [63] See *supra* p. 309.
[64] *Brannigan and others v. Davison* (1997) 2 BHRC 395 (PC).
[65] See Stessens, 'The Obligation to Produce Documents', 45–62.
[66] Straüli, 'Territorialité de l'enquête pénale', pp. 130–31.

privilege against self-incrimination do not apply. The privilege against self-incrimination gives an accused the right to decline to give self-incriminating evidence. In an international context, the crucial question is whether the privilege against self-incrimination also allows a defendant to refuse to give evidence where he fears that his testimony will be used against him by a foreign authority. From a comparative perspective, there is no unanimous answer to this question. Under English law, there is scant and contradicting authority on this point,[67] while the American Supreme Court has excluded concern with foreign prosecution from the purview of the Self-Incrimination Clause of the Fifth Amendment.[68] It is to be emphasised that it is in principle the content of the evidence sought which determines whether a person should be allowed to invoke the privilege.[69] In the case of extra-territorial disclosure orders that infringe the criminal provisions of the *lex situs*, it is not the content of the evidence which is incriminating but the rendering of evidence itself. The state which criminalises the disclosure of evidence covered by banking secrecy is not interested in the content of evidence, but on the contrary seeks to prevent any information from being made public. The interest of a foreign state in such circumstances is completely the reverse of that which applies in self-incrimination cases, where the (foreign) authority is interested in obtaining evidence.[70] It is a matter of some regret that in some cases this distinction has not been made and that courts have nevertheless engaged in investigating whether the defendants could avail themselves of the privilege against self-incrimination. In what came to be known as the *Winebox* inquiry, a New Zealand Commission of Inquiry set up to investigate allegations of fraudulent misuse by New Zealand Companies of tax credit issued by the Cook Islands government, had to grapple with the claim by witnesses in New Zealand that to comply with the disclosure orders would make them liable for criminal prosecution in the Cook Islands. The case went on appeal to the Privy Council, which rejected the claim based on the privilege against self-incrimination, but only on the

---

[67] *The King of the Two Sicilies v. Willcox* (1851) 1 Sim NS 301 and *USA v. McRae* (1867) LR 4 Eq 327, both cited in *Brannigan and others v. Davison* (1997) 2 BHRC 395 (PC). On this point see also Kinsch, *Le fait du prince étranger*, pp. 89–92.

[68] *United States v. Balsys*, 524 US 666 (1998). See D. M. Amann, 'A Whipsaw Cuts Both Ways: The Privilege Against Self-Incrimination in an International Context', *UCLA Law Review* (1998) 1201–95.

[69] European Court of Human Rights, *Serves v. France*, judgment of 20 October 1997, *Reports of Judgments and Decisions* (1997–IV), 2159, para. 48.

[70] See Kinsch, *Le fait du prince étranger*, pp. 87–92 and McLachlan, 'The Jurisdictional Limits of Disclosure Orders', 44–5.

ground that the common law privilege against self-incrimination should not be extended to criminal sanctions under foreign law.[71] This decision has rightly been criticised for conflating the problem of conflicting obligations in the context of disclosure orders with the privilege against self-incrimination.[72]

International co-operation in lifting foreign banking secrecy

Many of the unilateral measures that have been taken to penetrate foreign banking secrecy laws do not pass muster at international law. Moreover, they often result in a drastic decrease of protection of rights under the *lex situs* of the persons concerned, financial institutions and their customers alike. Unilateral disclosure orders are taken on the basis of the law of the foreign, investigating, states which is, in principle, not binding upon the persons concerned. For example, a person who holds a bank account at a bank in Country X is entitled to trust that his bank account will be governed by the laws of Country X, including its rules on confidentiality and banking secrecy. As was said by the Hong Kong Court of Appeal, '[t]here is no reason for him to suspect that the extent of such confidentiality might vary from bank to bank depending on where its head office is located'.[73]

International co-operation, on the other hand, accommodates these justified expectations of defendants and third parties because it takes place on the basis of the *locus regit actum* principle. Hence defendants and third parties are able to rely on any privileges they may have under the *lex situs*. Some international co-operation agreements even allow the defendant to invoke the privileges he might have under the law of the requesting state.[74] International co-operation in criminal matters thus not only eschews the international law objections to extra-territorial disclosure orders, but also ensures that the level of the protection of the rights of the person is not adversely affected as a consequence of the international ramifications of a (money laundering) investigation. This also confirms the argument that was propounded earlier,[75] namely, that the *locus regit actum* principle is an essential feature of the rights of the defence and of third parties in an international procedure because, in principle, it gives them the same rights as they would have had in a domestic action.

---

[71] *Brannigan and others v. Davison* (1997) 2 BHRC 395 (PC). For a comment see McLachlan, 'The Jurisdictional Limits of Disclosure Orders', in particular 42–5.

[72] McLachlan, 'The Jurisdictional Limits of Disclosure Orders', 44.

[73] *FDCCo. v. Chase Manhattan Bank* [1990] 1 *HKLR* 277, 286.   [74] See *supra* pp. 307–8.

[75] See *supra* pp. 302–3.

The problems generated by extra-territorial disclosure orders can in general be solved only by co-operative mechanisms which take account of the sovereignty of the state where the information sought is located, but which at the same time serve the general interest of crime fighting by lifting banking secrecy. In most countries, banking secrecy and other secrecy duties (of, e.g., lawyers and doctors) can be lifted only by way of judicial intervention. Countries are at any rate urged by the international instruments on money laundering to allow this to happen. Article 4 of the Money Laundering Convention requires parties to 'adopt such legislative and other measures as may be necessary to empower its courts or other competent authorities to order that bank, financial or commercial records be made available or be seized in order to carry out the actions referred to in Articles 2 and 3. A Party shall not decline to act under the provisions of this article on grounds of bank secrecy'. The same requirements flow from Article 5(3) of the Vienna Convention and were, moreover, already contained in FATF recommendation 37. It is only logical therefore that co-operation designed to lift banking secrecy should take place between judicial authorities.

The road of international co-operation in criminal matters is, however, not an easy one, strewn as it is with impediments when it comes to lifting foreign banking secrecy. Although most states are now in principle willing to lift foreign banking secrecy laws on the request of a foreign state for the purpose of a foreign money laundering investigation, this willingness is not unqualified but is subject to a number of legal conditions and exceptions. Apart from two features that have already been discussed earlier, namely the condition of double criminality and the exception for fiscal offences,[76] there are a number of legal requirements that are incorporated in many co-operation mechanisms which may substantially affect the possibility of smooth co-operation in the lifting of foreign banking secrecy rules. After examining the principal possibility of lifting banking secrecy in the course of international co-operation in the fight against money laundering, the main focus will then be placed on the three legal conditions of international co-operation that are very material to the lifting of banking secrecy: the prohibition of fishing expeditions, the specialty principle and the confidentiality requirements.

---

[76] See *supra* pp. 286–301.

Principal possibility of lifting banking secrecy at the request of a foreign state

As banking secrecy could in most countries – even in some financial secrecy jurisdictions[77] – be lifted for the purpose of internal investigation, it was never retained as an express ground for refusal in co-operation treaties. Nevertheless, in the past, countries sometimes refused co-operation in respect of requests pertaining to information covered by banking secrecy and, to this end, invoked the *ordre public* clause, which figures in most co-operation treaties (e.g. Article 2(b) of the European Mutual Assistance Convention). The vague character of this type of exception, which relates to the sovereignty, security and *ordre public* of the requested state, allows a requested state to invoke this exception in order to refuse to lift banking secrecy.[78] Countries have exceptionally also allowed that the private interests of companies can coincide with the public interest of the requested state and thus justify a refusal of co-operation. Scarce examples of this can be found in domestic case law[79] and in statutory provisions such as the former Article 10(2) of the Swiss Mutual Assistance Act, which allowed Swiss authorities to refuse to comply with a request for assistance, even in the case of a treaty obligation to the contrary:[80] 'La révélation d'un secret de fabrication ou d'affaires, au sens de l'article 273 du code pénal, ou d'un fait qu'une banque est habituellement tenue de garder secret est inadmissible lorsqu'elle permet de craindre que l'économie suisse n'en subisse un grave préjudice et que celui-ci paraît insupportable, au vu de l'importance de l'infraction.' (The disclosure of a commercial secret in the sense of Article 273 of the Penal Code or of a fact which a bank is normally required to keep secret, cannot be allowed if there are grounds to fear that the Swiss economy would sustain serious damage and if this seems unacceptable in view of the importance of the offence.)

This provision, which is now abridged, was something of an anomaly, given the fact that banking secrecy was never a proper ground in Switzerland for refusal to provide information.[81] The Swiss Supreme

---

[77] See, e.g., W. S. Walker, 'The Cayman Islands', in *International Bank Secrecy*, ed. D. Campbell, (London: Sweet & Maxwell, 1992), pp. 148–51; M. L. Paton, 'The Bahamas', in *International Bank Secrecy*, pp. 67–71 and D. Penn, 'British Virgin Islands', in *International Bank Secrecy*, pp. 104–5.

[78] See, e.g., Thomas, *De Europese rechtshulpverdragen in strafzaken*, pp. 298–9.

[79] See, e.g., the judgment of the Dutch Council of State of 20 December 1976, *Administratiefrechtelijke beslissingen* (1979) 70.

[80] Aubert and others, *Le secret bancaire suisse*, pp. 519–20.

[81] See, e.g., ATF 115 Ib 83 E.4 b and ATF 120 Ib 251 E.5c. Cf. P. Bernasconi, 'Bankbeziehungen und internationale Rechtshilfe in Strafsachen: Neuere Entwicklungen', *RSDA* (1995), 63.

Court moreover expressly rejected the argument that the *ordre public* clause of the Swiss Mutual Assistance Act could be invoked to refuse to lift banking secrecy: 'La législation sur l'entraide et les accords internationaux y relatifs doivent contribuer à ce que la Suisse perde la réputation de pays où, grâce à la protection du secret bancaire, peuvent être mis à l'abri des biens patrimoniaux acquis de manière illicite.' (The mutual assistance legislation and the international agreements to this respect should contribute to the fact that Switzerland loses its reputation as a country where, due to banking secrecy, illegally derived proceeds can be sheltered.)[82]

The first mutual legal assistance treaty that was explicitly drafted with a view to allowing foreign banking secrecy to be lifted was the 1973 American–Swiss MLAT. The United States has since signed MLATs with more than twenty other countries, but chose Switzerland as the first country with which to enter into an MLAT in view of the difficulties American law enforcement authorities had run into when confronted with Swiss banking secrecy in the course of judicial and tax investigations. Although Switzerland was considered the 'hardest nut to crack' by the American negotiators, Switzerland did already allow for the lifting of banking secrecy in the context of internal investigations – unlike a number of other financial secrecy jurisdictions.[83] Both the legal differences between the common law system of the United States and the Swiss civil law system and the diverging political and economic opinions contributed to the length of the negotiations, which eventually resulted in the convention being signed on 23 May 1973 (although it only entered into force on 23 January 1977). Its importance flows both from the fact that is the first MLAT to have benefited from bridging both a common law and a civil law jurisdiction, as well as from its extensive use.[84]

It may be a matter of some surprise that the MLAT does not expressly provide that banking secrecy cannot be invoked as an exception to mutual assistance. The fact that both states are obliged to comply with requests for lifting of banking secrecy follows from the general provision which obliges parties to render assistance in criminal investigations (Article 1) and is also implicitly confirmed by the fact that the MLAT provides for an

---

[82] Judgment of the Swiss Supreme Court of 28 November 1984, cited by Bernasconi, 'Flux internationaux', p. 166.

[83] See Nadelmann, 'Negotiations in Criminal Law Assistance Treaties', 471 and *Cops Across Borders*, pp. 324–7 and Frei and Trechsel, 'Origins and Applications of the US–Switzerland Treaty', p. 78.

[84] In 1983 the American–Swiss MLAT had served as a basis for 202 requests which were said to have contributed to 145 convictions: Nadelmann, *Cops Across Borders*, pp. 340–1.

explicit protection for information which is covered by banking or commercial secrecy and which concerns non-implicated third parties (Article
10(2)).[85]

The US followed up its MLAT with Switzerland by entering into other
MLATs which also contain no explicit provision to the effect that banking
secrecy cannot be invoked as an exception.[86] This type of co-operation
mechanism of course guarantees success in the lifting of banking secrecy
only to the extent that the requested state does not rely on the *ordre public*
exception which is typically contained in these MLATs. Thus, it has been
suggested that the Bahamas, which entered into an MLAT with the United
States in 1987, may still claim the right to refuse co-operation in respect
of information that is covered by banking secrecy.[87]

The first fully-fledged prohibition at international law to invoke
banking secrecy as a ground for refusal was Article 7(5) of the 1988 Vienna
Convention, which firmly stipulates that: 'A Party shall not decline to
render mutual legal assistance under this article on the grounds of bank
secrecy'. Although this provision presupposes that the requested state's
legislation provides for procedures to lift banking secrecy, Article 7 –
which has sometimes been called a mini mutual legal assistance treaty[88]
– it is, certainly in the United States, considered to be self-executing and
thus does not require specific implementation legislation.[89]

Article 18(7) of the Money Laundering Convention, which poses the
same principle in the wider context of money laundering investigations
in general (not restricted to drug proceeds), is somewhat more elaborate:
'A Party shall not invoke bank secrecy as a ground to refuse any co-operation under this chapter. Where its domestic law so requires, a Party may
require that a request for co-operation which would involve the lifting of
bank secrecy be authorised by either a judge or another judicial authority, including public prosecutors, any of these authorities acting in relation to criminal offences'.

---

[85] See *infra* p. 349.
[86] See Nadelmann, 'Negotiations in Criminal Law Assistance Treaties', 481–504. See also
M. C. Bassiouni and D. S. Gualtieri, 'International and National Responses to the
Globalization of Money Laundering', in *Responding to Money Laundering. International
Perspectives*, ed. E. Savona (Amsterdam: Harwood Academic Publishers, 1997), pp. 116–200.
[87] Erbstein, 'Palm Trees Hide More Than Sunshine', 455–7.
[88] Report US Delegation, 127; D. W. Sproule and P. St.-Denis, 'The UN Drug Trafficking
Convention: An Ambitious Step', in *The Canadian Yearbook of International Law* (Vancouver:
University of British Columbia Press, 1989), p. 285 and W. C. Gilmore, 'Going After The
Money: Money Laundering, The Confiscation of The Assets of Crime and International
Co-operation', in *Working Paper Series 'A System of European Police Co-operation after 1992'*
(Edinburgh: 1991), p. 9.   [89] *Report US Delegation*, 129.

Of course this prohibition of the refusal to co-operate on the ground of banking secrecy is only applicable insofar as the requested state has ratified the treaty concerned. The provisions concerned may, however, also have an exemplary role in that analogous provisions may be inserted in future international agreements, as has, for example, already happened in a number of international agreements on corruption.[90]

An important feature of international judicial co-operation in criminal matters in general and of international co-operation mechanisms that allow a requested state to lift foreign banking secrecy rules in particular is that co-operation is only possible at the express request of another state. Some states (e.g. Switzerland[91]) strictly adhere to this principle and refuse to give more information than has been requested: *nec ultra petita*. When, for example, different bank accounts which all have been used in the same or connected money laundering schemes are held at the same bank, and the request only relates to one account, then only information pertaining to that account will be forwarded. There are different ways of circumventing this problem, the best of which is a careful drafting of the request for judicial assistance.[92] If the first request embraces all possible accounts and other financial relationships that may have been established to launder money, then requesting authorities should in principle seldom be faced with an incomplete reply. The proposal to draft a uniform international model of request for information on funds held at or passed through financial institutions[93] should therefore meet with approval. Such an internationally accepted uniform request model would benefit judges, public prosecutors, law enforcement agents and financial institutions

---

[90] See, e.g., Article 16 of the Inter-American Convention against Corruption (1996), Article 9 of the OECD Convention on Combating Bribery of Foreign Public Officials in International Business Transactions (Paris, 17 December 1997) and Article 26 of the Council of Europe Criminal Law Convention on Corruption (Strasbourg, 27 January 1999, *ETS*, No. 173).

[91] P. Bernasconi, 'Le marché financier suisse: entre contrôle étatique et autorégulation', in *L'éthique des marchés financiers*, ed. J.-V. Louis and D. Devos (Brussels: Editions de l'Université de Bruxelles, 1991), p. 110 and 'Modèle international d'ordonnance judiciaire de saisie et de production des documents. Un nouvel instrument de l'enquête internationale concernant le blanchiment de l'argent', in *Bulletin de la Société internationale de défense sociale, Cahiers de défense sociale* (1990/91), 171–2.

[92] See P. Bernasconi, 'New Legal Instruments for the Seizure of Proceeds from Drug Trafficking', in *Nuovi strumenti giudiziari contro la criminalità economica internazionale* (Naples: Edizioni Città del sole, 1995), pp. 193–201 and 'Modèle international', pp. 178–181.

[93] Bernasconi, 'Modèle international', p. 184. See also Secretary-General of the United Nations, *Note: Strengthening Existing International Co-operation in Crime Prevention and Criminal Justice*, pp. 18–19.

alike, as all would then have to work with only one type of request. Such a uniform request model would not only be beneficial to the intentional exchange of information, but also in respect of provisional measures to be taken at the request of another state. It would effectively prevent assets not covered by a first co-operation request from being moved before the second, more broadly termed, request is formulated.

But even when the requesting state takes the necessary care to draft its request, the requested state may be in a position where it has access to information which might be interesting for the requesting state, but which falls outside the object of the request; or where it has information which it deems useful for a foreign state, but for which that state has not issued a request. Article 10 of the Money Laundering Convention was drafted to deal with this type of situation. This provision allows states to communicate information spontaneously, that is, without a prior request, 'when it considers that the disclosure of such information might assist the receiving Party in initiating or carrying out investigations or proceedings or might lead to a request by that Party'. Even outside the context of the Money Laundering Convention, some states have exchanged information covered by banking secrecy without a formal treaty-based (judicial) request for assistance. This is, for example, possible under English law[94] and Hong Kong law.[95]

Another way of circumventing the problems relating to the requirement of an official request for information was demonstrated in the context of the intense level of co-operation achieved by Italian and Swiss magistrates when the former were leading large-scale bribery investigations at the beginning of the 1990s (*mani pulite*). In order to circumvent the lengthy appeal procedures which stayed the transmittal of the requested information, Swiss magistrates sometimes initiated judicial proceedings themselves and then made a 'fake request' to the Italian authorities, which often contained most of the information which the Italian authorities had requested. This technique of so-called *commissions rogatoires croisées*[96] was clearly at variance with the law of international co-operation in criminal matters and was, unsurprisingly, condemned by the Swiss

---

[94] R v. Crown Court at Southwark, ex p. Customs and Excise Commissioners and R v. Crown Court at Southwark, ex p. Bank of Credit and Commerce International [1989] 3 WLR 1054. See K. D. Magliveras, 'The Regulation of Money Laundering in the UK', JBus.L (1991), 532–3.
[95] FATF, Evaluation of Laws and Systems in FATF Members, p. 9.
[96] See Bernasconi, 'Bankbeziehungen und internationale Rechtshilfe', 69–70 and A. Vogelweith and M. Vaudano, Mains propres, Mains liées. France-Italie: la leçon des affaires (Paris: Austral, 1995), pp. 191–2.

judicial authorities.[97] It may be a matter of disappointment to some that Switzerland, which has ratified the Money Laundering Convention, has excluded the application of Article 10 of the Convention to evidence covered by banking secrecy. Information (not evidence) can be disclosed to a foreign authority only if this information will allow the authority to make a request to the Swiss authorities.[98] This can only be regarded as logical, however, if one takes into account the larger framework which governs the exchange of information that is covered by banking secrecy (e.g. the prohibition of fishing expeditions and the specialty principle). Many of the restrictions imposed in that respect would be difficult to enforce if information could also be exchanged spontaneously. The fact that Swiss law excludes the spontaneous exchange of evidence only in respect of banking secrecy indicates that, at least under Swiss law, these restrictions, which in principle apply to any exchange of evidence, are especially designed to facilitate the lifting of banking secrecy.

The prohibition of fishing expeditions

One of the limitations which is liable to cause problems in international co-operation[99] is the prohibition of fishing expeditions. English courts have defined them as 'a roving inquiry designed to elicit information which might lead to the obtaining of evidence'.[100] A distinction was made between 'discovery of indirect material on the one hand, and proof or direct material on the other hand'.[101] It will be argued hereinafter that the prohibition of fishing expeditions is not a general principle of international co-operation in criminal matters, but rather flows from the domestic law of some states and that it should be applied in a restrictive manner.

The prohibition of fishing expeditions should not be seen as embodying a basic principle of international law, but merely as a technique which allows requested states to guarantee some deeply cherished national rules. This is demonstrated by the origin of the prohibition of fishing expeditions in English law, which is linked to American letters rogatory in civil

---

[97] Judgment of the Swiss Supreme Court of 7 November 1996, *La Semaine judiciaire* (1997), 199.

[98] See Article 67(4)(5) of the Swiss Mutual Assistance Act, as amended by the Act of 4 October 1996.   [99] FATF, *Evaluation of Laws and Systems in FATF Members*, p. 9.

[100] *Re State of Norway's Applications (Nos 1 and 2)* [1989] 1 All ER 745, 749 per Lord Goff.

[101] *Radio Corporation of America v. Rauland Corporation* [1956] 1 All ER 549, 550–4 per Devlin J. See also the judgment of the House of Lords in *RTZ v. Westinghouse* [1978] 1 All ER 434, 442 per Lord Wilberforce.

matters. For long, English courts excluded pre-trial discovery against third parties on the ground that discovery is possible during trial by examining witnesses or producing documents.[102] Requests from the United States, where the possibility of pre-trial third party discovery is an essential part of civil litigation, were consequently declared inadmissible.[103] In view of the frictions caused by American requests of this type, Article 23 of the Hague Evidence Convention[104] even explicitly allows states to eschew this type of fishing expedition by making a reservation to the effect that they will not engage in pre-trial discovery of documents.[105]

Also in criminal matters, the American case law is less strict; thus the Supreme Court has held that the government is not required to show the relevance of the requested documents to a grand jury investigation,[106] again reflecting the great store that is set by discovery and the relatively low importance that is attached to (banking) secrecy. It was therefore only under Swiss pressure that an anti-fishing expedition clause was inserted into the American–Swiss MLAT: Article 1(2) requires that there be a reasonable suspicion in the requesting state that acts have been committed which constitute the elements of an offence. At the request of other states, a similar clause was inserted in a number of other MLATs into which the United States entered.[107] This Swiss move for an anti-fishing expedition clause is understandable in view of the Swiss case law on fishing expeditions (*enquêtes exploratoires, Beweisausforschungen*), which are defined as general and unspecified requests for evidence. Requests for co-operation which are intended merely to confirm ungrounded

---

[102] Cf. *Norwich Pharmacal Co. v. Customs and Excise Comsr* [1973] 2 All ER 943, 947 per Lord Reid. This rule against third party discovery was subsequently relaxed in civil fraud cases: *Arab Monetary Fund v. Hashim and others (No. 5)* [1992] 2 All ER 911, 913–14 per Hoffmann J.

[103] *Radio Corporation of America v. Rauland Corporation* [1956] 1 All ER 549 and *RTZ v. Westinghouse* [1978] 1 All ER 434. On the difference between English and American law in this respect, see also J. Fellas, 'Give Me Your Documents: Discovery of Material in the US', *NLJ* (1996), 27–8.

[104] Hague Convention on the Taking of Evidence Abroad in Civil or Commercial Matters, 18 March 1970, 847 UNTS 231.

[105] P. Nobel, 'Die Rechtshilfe in Zivilsachen im Lichte der Ratifikation der Haager Konvention von 1970 über die Beweisaufnahme im Ausland in *Zivil- und Handelssachen*', *RSDA* (1995), 78. On the American reaction to these reservations, see S. F. Black, 'United States Transnational Discovery: The Rise and Fall of the Hague Evidence Convention', *ICLQ* (1991), 903.   [106] *United States v. Dionisio* 410 US 17 (1973).

[107] See the MLAT with the Bahamas and with the Cayman Islands (Article 3(2)(c); *ILM*, 1987, 536). See Nadelmann *Cops Across Borders*, pp. 364, 373.

suspicions are not allowed. This embargo on fishing expeditions, both in the context of internal investigations[108] and of international co-operation,[109] is to a large extent an application of the proportionality principle which is one the main principles governing Swiss law of international co-operation in criminal matters.[110] Under this principle, the requested authority must balance the importance of the offence investigated abroad against the likely impact of the execution of the request in Switzerland. Especially in the case of coercive measures touching on banking secrecy, this balancing exercise assumes a critical importance. According to the case law of the Swiss Supreme Court, the requesting authority should indicate the concrete facts on which it surmises the presence of evidence within one or more given banks.[111] Hence it is forbidden to make a random request to all banks with whom a suspect may have a bank account or to require the production of all bank statements pertaining to a certain customer.[112] The same limitations flow from English case law which, albeit in a civil context, has clearly established that a request for the production of documents can be allowed only if it relates to specified particular documents of whose existence it is certain and which are likely to be in the possession of the person concerned.[113] Regarding international co-operation in criminal matters, the powers of search and seizure are available under the UK's Police and Criminal Evidence Act 1984 only when they are 'likely to be of substantial value' and the United Kingdom therefore typically requires a reasonable explanation of how the requested information would be materially relevant to the investigation in question.

It seems to be a common feature of at least English and Swiss law that the prohibition of fishing expeditions primarily pertains to requests for

---

[108] See, e.g., ATF 102 Ia 529; ATF 103 Ia 624; ATF 106 IV 413 and Arzt, 'Zur Beweisbeschaffungspflicht der Bank', pp. 324–325; Aubert and others, Le secret bancaire suisse, pp. 146, 155 and Bernasconi, 'Droits et devoirs de la banque', pp. 399–400.

[109] See, e.g., the judgments of the Swiss Supreme Court of 1 July 1987, La Semaine judiciaire (1987), 609; of 26 March 1990, JT (suisse) (1993, IV), 22 and of 21 December 1992, La Semaine judiciaire (1993), 337. Cf. Aubert and others, Le secret bancaire suisse, p. 473.

[110] Aubert and others, Le secret bancaire suisse, pp. 471–3 and Bernasconi, 'Droits et devoirs de la banque', pp. 396–7.

[111] Bernasconi, 'Droits et devoirs de la banque', p. 400. Cf. Aubert and others, Le secret bancaire suisse, p. 472.

[112] Bernasconi, 'Geldwäscherei und organisierte Kriminalität', pp. 121–2. See also ATF 118 Ib 111.

[113] See the decision of the House of Lords in Re Asbestos Insurance Coverage Cases [1985] 1 All ER 717, 721 per Lord Fraser of Tullybelton. See also s.2(4) Evidence (Procedure in other Jurisdictions) Act 1975.

the production of documents and not to the interrogation of witnesses.[114] An interrogation of a witness may moreover be necessary to establish the prima facie case that is required for the lifting of bank secrecy, that is, to make a specified request for the production of documents. Such prima facie case may of course also be established by information forwarded by financial institutions on the basis of their proactive reporting duties.[115]

Swiss law, however, differs from English law, in that, whereas the latter requires that an offence has been committed, or is reasonably suspected of having been committed, in the requesting state and either that proceedings have been instituted, or that an investigation is taking place in the requesting state,[116] no such requirements exist under Swiss law.[117] Irrespective of the differences in the precise requirements that are posed by various domestic legal systems in this respect, it may be safely assumed that very few, or indeed no, jurisdictions would allow unqualified access by law enforcement officers to information held by financial institutions.[118]

Various reasons suggest a cautious application of the prohibition on fishing expeditions. First, as was repeatedly acknowledged by the Swiss Supreme Court,[119] the requirement of a prima facie case should not be applied too stringently in view of the fact that the investigating authority will, at an early stage of investigation, often not yet have much detailed information on the precise nature of the offence.[120] Second, future legal developments in the context of the fight against money laundering may make the prohibition of fishing expeditions more difficult to apply. Already, the law of some states (e.g., Australia, Hong Kong and New Zealand[121]) allows (foreign) law enforcement authorities to apply for a monitoring order in relation to drug trafficking and money laundering

---

[114] Arzt, 'Zur Beweisbeschaffungspflicht der Bank', pp. 325 and 332; *RTZ v. Westinghouse* ([1978] 1 All ER 434, 478) per Lord Keith. Cf. *Re Asbestos Insurance Coverage Cases* [1985] 1 All ER 717, 722–3.   [115] See Levi, 'Consumer Confidentiality', *Money Laundering*, p. 11.

[116] Sections 3(1) and 4(1)(2) Criminal Justice (International Co-operation) Act 1990.

[117] See, e.g., the seizure of assets of former President Marcos of the Philippines: judgment of the Swiss Supreme Court of 1 July 1987, *La Semaine judiciaire* (1987), 609.

[118] United Nations Office for Drug Control and Crime Prevention, *Financial Havens, Banking Secrecy and Money Laundering*, pp. 17–18.

[119] See the judgments of the Swiss Supreme Court of 31 October 1984, *La Semaine judiciaire* (1985), 372; of 1 July 1987, *La Semaine judiciaire* (1987), 609; of 26 March 1990, *JT (suisse)* (1993, IV), 22 and of 18 July 1994, *La Semaine judiciaire* (1995), 13.

[120] See, in this respect, the critical remarks by M. D. Mann, 'Extra-territoriality: Compelling Foreign Judicial Assistance in Production of Documents and Evidence', in *Am.Soc'y Int'l L.Proc.* (1985), 7–8.

[121] FATF, *Evaluation of Laws and Systems in FATF Members*, p. 9.

offences. Such an order allows them to obtain current and future documents and information in relation to drug trafficking and money laundering. It is self-evident that the requirement to give precise information about the offences investigated can then not always be complied with as the information sought mostly relates to offences that are going to take place in the future. Third, in keeping with the internationalist approach that was advocated earlier,[122] it is submitted that requested states should, as far as possible, not foist their domestic legal culture on other, requesting, states. Certainly in English law, the prohibition of fishing expeditions originated as a reaction against perceivedly broad requests from foreign (mostly American) requests for assistance. In the same vein, the prohibition of fishing expeditions may in part also be seen as a counter-reaction to the refusal of some states to apply some (human rights) requirements to requests for mutual legal assistance. Thus, when under the domestic law of the requesting state the prosecution is normally required to demonstrate *ex ante* a 'reasonable suspicion' before search and seizure can take place, this requirement will not necessarily hold when a request for mutual assistance is issued. The Canadian Supreme Court has ruled in this sense,[123] but there is American law which nevertheless imposes the American (Fourth Amendment) standards on requests for assistance.[124] Although it is thus solely incumbent on the authorities of the requested state to guarantee that the right to privacy under its domestic law is not violated, the evidence thus gathered may of course still be excluded *post facto*.[125]

It is submitted that there are, however, no cogent reasons which make it necessary to insert the prohibition on fishing expeditions or the required 'reasonable suspicion' of a criminal offence in international co-operation instruments as a condition to the granting of assistance. It is therefore a matter of some regret that the EU Joint Action of 3 December 1998 concerning arrangements for co-operation between Member States in respect of identification, tracing, freezing or seizing and confiscation of instrumentalities and the proceeds from crime refers to such condition (Article 1(3)). The optional ground for refusal that is contained in the Money Laundering Convention and which allows states to refuse co-operation if 'the measures sought could not be taken under the domestic

---

[122] See *supra*, pp. 252–4.
[123] See *Schreiber v. Canada* [1998] 1 SCR 841. See *supra* pp. 302–3. For a critical attitude in this respect, see Bassiouni and Gualtieri, 'International and National Responses', pp. 144–5.
[124] *Colello et al. v. United States Securities and Exchange Commission et al.*, 908 F. Supp. 738 (CD Cal. 1995), cited by Zagaris, 'U.S. International Co-operation against Transnational Organised Crime' *RIDP* (1999), 532.   [125] See also *supra* p. 303.

law of the requested Party for the purposes of investigations or proceedings, had it been a similar domestic case' (Article 18(2)),[126] should in principle suffice for requested states to ensure compliance with the domestic requirements (e.g., those relating to the right to privacy). The treaty requirements that oblige the requesting state to specify in detail the information it is requesting moreover allow the requested state to assess whether it is confronted with a fishing expedition and to turn down the request if it deems it necessary to do so.[127]

The specialty principle

One of the main concerns of states – especially those that set great store by banking secrecy – which explains their reticence in lifting banking secrecy, is their fear that the information covered by banking secrecy which they are asked to disclose for the purpose of an investigation into a serious (money laundering) offence will subsequently also be used for other purposes, especially for fiscal purposes. Information covered by banking secrecy is likely to contain not only information which relates to the offences for which banking secrecy was lifted, but also to other criminal and fiscal wrongdoings. It is not difficult to see that international co-operation mechanisms that have been designed to combat money laundering can also be used for tax purposes.[128] As was astutely noted by Nadelmann: 'Indeed, one of the most important consequences of current efforts in detecting drug money laundering is the impetus which those efforts provide to law enforcement efforts in other areas'.[129]

This fear of states explains the importance that they attach to the specialty principle, that is, the principle that the information which is disclosed to the requesting state can be used only for limited purposes. Though the application field of this principle is normally not confined to information covered by banking secrecy, it is so treated here because it is in this context that the principle assumes most of its importance. In order to assess the expediency of the specialty principle, it is proposed, as a first point of attention, to look into the legal background of the specialty

---

[126] See also Article 7(15)(c) of the Vienna Convention.

[127] See, e.g., Articles 27(1)(c) and (e)(ii) of the Money Laundering Convention and Article 7(10)(c) of the Vienna Convention. Cf. *Explanatory Report with the Convention on Laundering, Search, Seizure and Confiscation of the Proceeds from Crime*, p. 22.

[128] Bernasconi, 'Droit pénal européen', 487–8.

[129] Nadelmann, 'Unlaundering Dirty Money', 72–3. Cf. M. De Feo, 'Depriving International Narcotics Traffickers and Other Organised Criminals of Illegal Proceeds and Combatting Money Laundering', *Denv. J Int'l L & Pol'y* (1990), 413.

principle. Subsequently, the various treaty formulations of the principle, and the possible sanctions for the violation of the specialty principle, will be discussed.

The specialty principle has its roots in the law of extradition, where it was originally aimed at preventing an extradited person from standing trial for political crimes for which he could not have been extradited.[130] It has correctly been called the 'coping-stone' of extradition law: it makes little sense to subject extradition to a number of limiting clauses when the extradited person could afterwards nevertheless face trial for other offences than the one(s) for which extradition was granted.[131]

This, in origin limited, concept of specialty principle has now also been adopted in the law of mutual assistance in criminal matters where it limits the use of information or of evidence transmitted. Unlike in extradition law, the specialty principle in the context of mutual assistance in criminal matters does not *per se* limit the 'action possibilities' of the requesting state to the offences for which assistance was granted. Often mutual assistance treaties limit the use of information to offences for which assistance was requested or to offences for which assistance could have been granted.[132]

In the field of mutual assistance in criminal matters, the specialty principle was adopted much later and does not have the same general character as in extradition law, where it is considered as a principle of international law which consequently does not need to be laid down expressly in the applicable extradition treaty.[133] In the context of mutual assistance the specialty principle is only applicable if and in the form laid down in the treaty. Whereas older multilateral mutual assistance conventions, such as the 1959 European Mutual Assistance Convention, do not provide for the specialty principle,[134] more recent multilateral instruments in the field of mutual assistance such as the 1990 Schengen Convention (Article 50(3)), for example, do. The principle is also laid down in the UN Model Treaty on Mutual Assistance in Criminal Matters (1990)

---

[130] Bernasconi, 'Droit pénal européen', pp. 480–1; D. Poncet and P. Gully-Hart, 'Le principe de la spécialité en matière d'extradition', *RIDP* (1991), 201–2 and A. H. J. Swart with K. Helder, *Nederlands uitleveringsrecht* (Zwolle: Tjeenk Willink, 1986), p. 339.

[131] Swart with K. Helder, *Nederlands uitleveringsrecht*, p. 339.

[132] See, e.g., Article 67,(1) and (2) of the Swiss Mutual Assistance Act. See also Article 8 of the UN Model Treaty on Mutual Assistance in Criminal Matters.

[133] Swart with K. Helder, *Nederlands uitleveringsrecht*, p. 339 and J. Remmelink, *Uitlevering* (Arnhem: Gouda Quint, 1990), p. 96.

[134] See the judgment of the Swiss Supreme Court of 31 October 1984, *La Semaine judiciaire* (1985), 372.

(Article 8) and the Commonwealth Scheme on Mutual Assistance in Criminal Matters (§ 11).

As with the prohibition on fishing expeditions, the specialty principle seems more rooted in the domestic law of some requested states – in particular of some secrecy jurisdictions – than in the international law of co-operation in criminal matters. It should come as no surprise that the principle is especially well developed in Swiss law; some even venture to speak about a *spécialité suisse*.[135] Switzerland traditionally puts great emphasis on the specialty principle in order to prevent the information or evidence it transmits in the context of co-operation in criminal matters subsequently being used for fiscal purposes. It is well known that Switzerland refuses to co-operate with requests for information relating to fiscal fraud, save in the case of so-called fiscal swindling (*escroquerie fiscale* – Article 3(3) of the Swiss Mutual Assistance Act 1981), a concept which seems to be interpreted fairly loosely.[136]

Swiss law generally operates two concepts of the specialty principle: an absolute and a relative concept. The former prohibits the use of information in a penal or administrative procedure for fiscal or similar (e.g. customs) purposes (save for fiscal swindling cases), including the indirect use of information.[137] The latter concept forbids any use in a judicial pro-ceeding for the prosecution of offences other than the one for which co-operation was requested and granted, but allows the possibility of other uses in case of prior consent by the Swiss Federal Police Department.[138] The relative concept of the specialty principle is laid down in Article 67 of the Swiss Mutual Assistance Act as well as in most of the reservations and declarations Switzerland has made in treaties such as the Money Laundering Convention. The Swiss position has, understandably, some-times collided with that of other states. During the negotiations that resulted in the 1973 American–Swiss MLAT, the American view that any information that was adduced as evidence in a trial was public information which could be used for any purpose fell foul of the Swiss

---

[135] Bernasconi, 'Droit pénal européen', pp. 480–1.

[136] Aubert, 'Quelques aspects de la portée du secret bancaire', 178. See the judgment of the Swiss Supreme Court of 27 November 1987, *La Semaine judiciaire* (1986), 266.

[137] See the judgments of the Swiss Supreme Court of 9 October 1981, *JDF* (1982), 354–5 with annotations by J. Malherbe and of 6 December 1989, *JT (suisse)* (1991, IV), 151. Cf. Aubert and others, *Le secret bancaire suisse*, p. 478.

[138] See on this distinction Bernasconi, 'Droits et devoirs de la banque', pp. 361–2 and 'Internationale strafrechtliche Bankuntersuchungen', in *Aspects juridiques de l'organisation économique actuelle. Journées des Avocats Suisses*, ed. P. Bernasconi (Lugano: Banca del Gottardo, 1989), p. 49.

position. Eventually a compromise was reached, under which it was agreed that evidence 'shall not be used for investigative purposes nor be introduced in evidence in the requesting State in any proceedings relating to an offense other than the offense for which assistance has been granted', but some limited exceptions were nevertheless allowed (Article 5 of the American–Swiss MLAT).

It is submitted that, in the context of mutual assistance in criminal matters, the specialty principle is mainly a 'political' principle, which stems from the sovereignty of the requested state, rather than from human rights considerations. The extension of this principle outside the boundaries of extradition law, where it has indeed a human rights rationale, cannot therefore be met with unanimous approval as it unduly restricts the possibilities of international co-operation in the fight against money laundering.[139]

In the context of mutual assistance in criminal matters, a request is usually made at an early stage of the investigation at which the investigating authority will lack a complete overview of the offences that may have been committed. The restrictions imposed by the specialty principle are therefore a matter of some regret, especially in relation to organised crime where all the offences forming part of an organised crime scheme may not immediately be apparent. The fact that information or evidence which was lawfully transmitted for the purpose of investigating crime X is subsequently also used in the investigation of or in the trial relating to crime Y, does not retroactively void the lawfulness of the co-operation. It is therefore submitted that the specialty principle should be given as limited an application field as possible, namely in those circumstances where states are not willing to co-operate unless satisfied that the information they provide will not be used for other purposes than those agreed on. There is no reason, however, to elevate the specialty principle to the level of a general principle of (international) law, as in the field of extradition. In this perspective, the formulation of the specialty principle in the Money Laundering Convention merits attention as a model because it does not make the specialty principle into a general rule (as does Article 7(13) of the Vienna Convention, for example), while at the same time acknowledging the political reality that some states will co-operate only if they receive the assurances the specialty principle provides. The provision runs as follows:

---

[139] See also F. Rouchereau, 'La Convention des Nations Unies contre le trafic illicite de stupéfiants et de substances psychotropes', in *Annuaire français de droit international* (Paris: Editions du CNRS, 1988), p. 608.

1   The requested Party may make the execution of a request dependent on the condition that the information or evidence obtained will not, without its prior consent, be used or transmitted by the authorities of the requesting Party for investigations or proceedings other than those specified in the request.

2   Each Party may, at the time of signature or when depositing its instrument of ratification, acceptance, approval or accession, by declaration addressed to the Secretary General of the Council of Europe, declare that, without its prior consent, information or evidence provided by it under this chapter may not be used or transmitted by the authorities of the requesting Party in investigations or proceedings other than those specified in the request.

A last point regarding the specialty principle pertains to sanctions for violations of the specialty principle. Before discussing the range of possible sanctions, a preliminary question merits attention, namely the primacy and justiciability of international treaties. As the specialty principle is usually laid down in an international treaty, this question assumes some importance in this respect, at least in countries adhering to the 'monist' system. This is the system under which domestic and international law are seen as being part of one system, in contrast to 'dualism', which considers them as two separate systems under which the provisions of an international treaty can have effect in the domestic system only when incorporated into a country's domestic law.[140] But even under the monist system a treaty provision can be applied by a judge directly only if it is self-sufficient, that is, sufficiently clearly and unconditionally drafted that a judge can apply it. When the treaty's provision of the specialty principle is self-sufficient and all the internal, as well as the international, conditions for entry into force are satisfied, then the judge should apply it directly, even in the face of contrary domestic law (e.g. when domestic legal provisions oblige the authorities of the requesting state to prosecute all offences).[141]

In many of the MLATs that it has concluded, however, the United States has contrived to insert a clause stating that private persons have no

---

[140]   On this distinction, see the excellent comparative overview in F. G. Jacobs and S. Roberts, *The Effect of Treaties in Domestic Law* (London: Sweet & Maxwell, 1987), p. 288. See also I. Brownlie, *Principles of Public International Law* (Oxford: Clarendon, 1990) pp. 32–4; Jennings and Watts, *Oppenheim's International Law*, pp. 53–70; M. Shaw, *International Law* (Cambridge: Cambridge University Press, 1997), pp. 104–28 and Nguyen Quoc Dinh, P. Daillier and A. Pellet, *Droit international public* (Paris: Librairie générale de droit et de jurisprudence, 1980), pp. 98–103.

[141]   Cf. Swiss Supreme Court, judgment of 31 October 1984, *La Semaine Judiciaire* (1985), 372 and Bernasconi, 'Droits et devoirs de la banque', p. 363.

capacity to invoke a violation of the treaty.[142] For example, under Article 37(1) of the American–Swiss MLAT, no person has the right 'to take any action in the United States to suppress or exclude any evidence or to obtain judicial relief in connection with requests under this Treaty, except . . .' The result of this provision, among others, is that possible violations of the specialty principle laid down in Article 5 of the Treaty cannot be invoked in a US court[143] so that the only possible action – in the absence of an unlikely *ex officio* sanction by a US court – is a complaint to the Swiss Federal Police Office, which might result in diplomatic action being taken.[144]

In any event, the sanction for a violation of the specialty principle is always determined by the requesting state and not by the requested state, whereas it is the latter's interests that are protected by the specialty principle. At least in some countries, case law has excluded evidence which has been used in violation of an applicable treaty provision.[145] In extradition law, violations of the specialty principle are often sanctioned by declaring the prosecution inadmissible.[146] Such a sanction would clearly be inapposite in the context of mutual assistance, where the specialty principle normally operates *in rem* (i.e., in respect of the information transmitted) and not *in personam* (i.e., in respect of the extradited person).

Other than through diplomatic action, the only way in which the requesting state can voice its discontent with violations of the specialty

---

[142] See e.g. Article II(4) of the American–Canadian MLAT and Article 1(3) of the American–British MLAT regarding the Cayman Islands and Article 1(5) of the American–Mexican MLAT (*ILM*, 1988, 443). Compare Article 18(2) of the American–Dutch MLAT. See Gane and Mackarel, 'The Admissibility of Evidence Obtained from Abroad', 105–7.

[143] *US v. Johnpoll*, 739 F.2d 702, 714 (2nd.Cir.), *cert.denied*, 469 US 1075 (1984); *US v. Davis*, 767 F.2d 1025, 1029 (2nd.Cir. 1985). See Gane and Mackarel, 'The Admissibility of Evidence Obtained from Abroad', 105–6, 117.

[144] Cf. the letter of Mr Shelby Cullom Davis, Ambassador of the United States of America to Dr A. Weitnauer, Ambassador of Switzerland and the reply to it by Dr A. Weitnauer (*ILM* (1973), 962–5).

[145] See, e.g., the judgments of the Dutch Supreme Court of 26 April 1988, *NJ* (1989), No.186, 7 June 1988, *NJ* (1988), No.987 and of 25 May 1993, *NJ* (1993), No.784

[146] See in general, and in particular in respect of Switzerland: Poncet and Gully-Hart, 'Le principe de la spécialité', 204–8. For Belgium, see: Belgian Supreme Court, judgment of 15 June 1992, *RW* (1982–3), 1497; for The Netherlands: Dutch Supreme Court, judgment of 27 September 1983, *NJ*, 1984, No.96; for the United States, see *United States v. Rauscher* 119 US 407 (1886) and M. C. Bassiouni, *International Extradition: United States Law and Practice* (New York: Oceana, 1996), pp. 434 *et seq.* For Austria, see Austrian Supreme Court, judgment of 17 December 1975, *Österreichische Zeitschrift für Rechtsvergleichung* (1976), 221; and for France: French Supreme Court, judgment of 2 April 1979, *Dalloz Sirey* (1979), 549, cited by Remmelink, *Uitlevering*, p. 96.

principle by the requesting state is to refuse future co-operation. This is, however, a very strong sanction to apply, in view of the fact that international co-operation, certainly where it is based on a treaty, normally presupposes mutual trust in the legal system of the other state.[147]

Confidentiality requirements with respect to lifting foreign banking secrecy

As a condition of lifting foreign banking secrecy, two types of confidentiality requirements may be imposed, the first of which is dictated by the necessities of an effective investigation while the second seems more inspired by the political and economic motives of some of the requested states. These requirements were not included in the 1959 European Mutual Assistance Convention, but have been provided for in later co-operation treaties, a trend which in part reflects a growing sensitivity towards privacy issues. Thus, these requirements can be found in the Money Laundering Convention (Article 33) and also in the Vienna Convention, as far as the first type of confidentiality requirement is concerned (Article 7(14)). Additionally, both the UN Model Treaty on Mutual Assistance in Criminal Matters (Article 9) and the Commonwealth Scheme on Mutual Assistance in Criminal Matters (§ 10) provide for both types of confidentiality requirement.

The first confidentiality requirement relates to the necessities of an ongoing (international) investigation. Additionally, in the context of domestic measures aimed at lifting banking secrecy, there is also a great need to ensure that customers are not made aware of such measures, especially in view of ensuring the effectiveness of any provisional measures (particularly freezing bank accounts) that may subsequently be taken. Both FATF recommendation 17 and Article 8 of the European Money Laundering Directive prohibit financial institutions from communicating to their customer (or to other third persons) the fact that information relating to them is being transmitted to the authorities responsible for money laundering. The wording of these provisions, as well as those of many implementation legislations, seem to limit the ambit of this prohibition to the reports that are made in the context of the proactive or reactive reporting duties of the authorities responsible for combating money laundering.[148] The need for confidentiality is of course at least as pressing

---

[147] Aubert and others, *Le secret bancaire suisse*, p. 479 and Bernasconi, 'Droits et devoirs de la banque', 362–5.

[148] See, e.g., Article 10(3) of the Swiss Money Laundering Act of 10 October 1997 and Article 40(4) of the Luxembourg Act of 5 April 1993.

in the context of a criminal investigation, especially in view of the fact that in some countries financial institutions generally have a right,[149] or even a duty,[150] to warn their customers of any measure that is taken in respect of their bank account(s). The criminalisation of tipping-off, which is, for example, provided for in English law (s.53 DTA 1994 and s.93D CJA 1988) and in Dutch law (Article 189 Dutch Criminal Code) therefore merits close attention as a possible way forward. In the absence of a general provision prohibiting the disclosure of the fact that investigatory or provisional measures have been taken, the magistrate leading the investigation will have to issue orders on an *ad hoc* basis enjoining financial institutions to disclose information to their customers. But even then a legal basis for this action is normally required, though this is not always the case as, for example in Switzerland.[151]

Such a legal basis is also required if countries are to comply with the requirements that nowadays are laid down in many co-operation treaties which demand that the request for co-operation is not made public except to the extent necessary to the execution of the request.[152]

A second type of confidentiality requirement relates to the evidence and information that is provided by the requested party. As with the former confidentiality requirement, the application field of this requirement, which is laid down in a number of co-operation treaties, is not limited to information covered by banking secrecy, but it does assume a particular importance in this context.

The rationale of this confidentiality requirement recognises the specialty principle: because of the great store that is set by the protection of banking secrecy, some countries want as far as possible to limit public access to evidence and information originally covered by banking secrecy rules. Though the speciality principle does not coincide with the confiden-

---

[149] *Barclays Bank plc v. Taylor; Trustee Savings Bank of Wales and Border Counties v. Taylor* [1989] 3 All ER 563. See, however, the decision of the Privy Council in *Robertson v. Canadian Imperial Bank of Commerce* [1995] 1 All ER 824, which suggests a duty to warn the customer. For comment, see C. Passmore, 'Banks and subpoenas', *NLJ* (1995), 89–90.

[150] See, e.g., in Belgium: Du Bois, 'Het bankgeheim', 451 and A. Bruyneel, 'Le secret bancaire en Belgique après l'arrêt rendu par la Cour de cassation le 25 octobre 1978', *JT* (1979), 375, annotation with the judgement of the Belgian Supreme Court of 25 October 1978.

[151] See Aubert and others, *Le secret bancaire suisse*, pp. 162–3; Bernasconi, 'Droits et devoirs de la banque', 378–9 and 'Internationale strafrechtliche Bankuntersuchungen', 38–42. But see also Article 10(3) of the Swiss Money Laundering Act of 10 October 1997.

[152] *Explanatory Report with the Convention on Laundering*, p. 47. Cf. Bernasconi, 'Il nuovo diritto europeo sul sequestro e le indagini riguardanti il provento di reati transnazionali', p. 393.

tiality requirement, the latter is essential to the well functioning of the former: without a confidentiality requirement, it is difficult to ensure that information provided by the requested party will not be used for other purposes than agreed, although publication of information transmitted as such has been considered as not violative of the specialty principle.[153] It is only logical therefore that Switzerland, which puts great emphasis on the specialty principle, should also pose very stringent requirements with regard to confidentiality.

The Swiss concern regarding confidentiality has centred particularly on the protection of so-called non-implicated third parties (*tiers non impliqués*). On a request to Switzerland, Article 10(2) of the American–Swiss MLAT provides that the Swiss Central Authority (i.e., the Federal Police Department) shall only give 'evidence or information which would disclose facts which a bank is required to keep secret or are manufacturing or business secrets, and which affect a person, who, according to the request, appears not to be connected in any way with the offense which is the basis of the request' under a number of stringent conditions, which are meant to embody the proportionality principle. These treaty conditions (seriousness of the offence, importance of the evidence for the investigation and subsidiarity) suggest that the disclosure of banking, manufacturing or business secrets requires more stringent conditions in the context of an international than in a national procedure.[154] It is submitted that this is an unwarranted requirement for, as in national procedures, any type of investigatory measure infringing on the privacy of individuals needs to be proportionate. This follows explicitly from the case law of the European Court of Human Rights with respect to Article 8(2) of the Convention on Human Rights.[155] To make a distinction at the investigatory stage between suspects and third parties is moreover very questionable from a human rights perspective. As a matter of principle, everyone is to the same extent entitled to the enjoyment of his fundamental rights (amongst which is the right to privacy) so that to give less protection to the privacy of suspects seems to verge on an infringement of the presumption of innocence. As with the specialty principle, this confidentiality requirement seems more inspired by an overzealous wish to protect

---

[153] In this respect, see the case law of the Swiss Supreme Court discussed by Bernasconi, 'Droits et devoirs de la banque', p. 363.

[154] Markees, 'The Difference in Concept Between Civil and Common Law', 182.

[155] See, in particular, with respect to international investigations: European Court of Human Rights, judgment of 25 February 1993, *Publications of the European Court of Human Rights*, Series A, No.256–A, para.56.

the interests of Swiss banks and their customers than by a proper consideration of human rights.

Irrespective of the expediency of such a special protection regime for non-implicated third parties, such protection seems at any rate very difficult to enforce in practice. The time-honoured Swiss practice of making the names of non-implicated third parties on bank documents that are disclosed unreadable (so-called *caviarder*)[156] was difficult to reconcile with the requirements of American judicial proceedings, in particular the requirement of a public trial dictated by the Sixth Amendment to the US Constitution.[157] A half-hearted compromise was therefore reached, according to which evidence or information relating to a non-implicated third party should 'be kept from disclosure to the fullest extent compatible with the constitutional requirements in the requesting state' if the requested state is of the opinion that 'its importance so requires and an application to that effect is made' (Article 15 of the American–Swiss MLAT).

That such a solution is hardly workable became subsequently clear in the larger context of the Swiss Mutual Assistance Act 1981, which provided for a similar protection for non-implicated third parties. Because of the very wide interpretation of who is an implicated third party, the concept of a non-implicated third party was practically emptied of its meaning[158] so that the Swiss legislator abolished this provision (Article 10(1)) when revising the Swiss Mutual Assistance Act in 1996.

The concern to protect third parties who are not implicated in the offence concerned from disclosure of their identity and financial details is understandable, especially in a continental vision of privacy[159] and of banking secrecy in particular. For the reasons set out above, this concern should not, however, be allowed to influence the way in which assistance is provided. This assistance is provided at the investigatory stage of the proceeding, where it may be very difficult to determine exactly who is a 'non-implicated third party'. It is therefore submitted that this confidentiality requirement should be allowed to play a role only at the trial stage, that is, when it has been decided who will be prosecuted and who will not.

---

[156] On this practice, see Bernasconi, 'Droits et devoirs de la banque', pp. 386–7.

[157] See the letter of Mr Shelby Cullom Davis, Ambassador of the United States of America to Dr A. Weitnauer, Ambassador of Switzerland (*ILM* (1973), 973–5). Cf. Nadelmann, *Cops Across Borders*, pp. 328–9.

[158] See Bernasconi, 'Droits et devoirs de la banque', pp. 365–7; Aubert and others, *Le secret bancaire suisse*, pp. 489–91 and Frei and Trechsel, 'Origins and Applications of the US–Switzerland Treaty', 87–8.

[159] On the difference with the concept of common law vision of privacy, see *supra* pp. 144–5.

At that stage it may be advisable, insofar as it is possible, not to disclose the identity of non-implicated third parties. But whether this is, or is not, possible, however, ultimately depends on the law of the requesting party's country as is acknowledged by Article 33(2) of the Money Laundering Convention: '[t]he requesting Party shall, if not contrary to basic principles of its national law and if so requested, keep confidential any evidence and information provided by the requested Party, except to the extent that its disclosure is necessary for the investigation or proceedings described in the request'. The same requirement may be imposed with respect to spontaneously communicated information (Article 33(3)).

15   Provisional measures for preserving alleged proceeds of crime in an international context

The term 'provisional measure' is used here to denote the large range of measures that exist under municipal law, such as seizure, freezing, restraint orders, sequestrations, etc., that are designed to enable the preservation of alleged proceeds of crime, or of legitimate assets which may be used for executing a (value) confiscation order. This relatively new type of seizure should be distinguished from the more traditional type of seizure with which most criminal justice systems are familiar and which is intended to preserve elements of proof. Whereas the latter type of seizure belongs to the realm of investigatory measures, the former is a provisional measure. Of course, there are also completely different types of provisional measure, namely those that are designed to ensure that the suspect will not abscond such as provisional arrest. Hereinafter the term 'provisional measures', however, will exclusively refer to measures that are taken to ensure that assets are preserved with a view to the enforcement of a possible confiscation.

Both the Vienna Convention (Article 5(2)) and the Money Laundering Convention (Article 7(2)) require parties to adapt their domestic legislation in order to introduce provisional measures. The availability of this type of provisional measure that allows the prevention of the dissipation of assets during the investigation or pending trial is indeed a prerequisite for any attempt at an effective fight against money laundering and acquisitive crime in general. In order to act effectively, it is obviously necessary to do so without warning the person concerned, which explains why provisional measures in the context of a criminal investigation are taken *ex parte*, or, in continental European law systems, unilaterally by an investigating magistrate or public prosecutor. For provisional measures to fulfil their function, it is equally necessary that they be taken swiftly, as is also the case with international provisional measures.[1] When the assets which the investigating or prosecuting authority wants to seize are located outside the national territory, there is an obvious problem of enforcement jurisdiction, the possible solutions to which will be discussed hereinafter. First, the attempts of national authorities to give their own provisional measures an extra-territorial reach and the problems to which these have given rise, will be scrutinised. Next, it is proposed to look into the arguments that necessitate the use of international co-operation mechanisms for international provisional measures. Finally, these co-operation mechanisms will be discussed in detail.

Domestic provisional measures with an extra-territorial reach

In view of the strictly territorial character of enforcement jurisdiction, it could be expected that provisional measures, which by definition imply the use of coercion, have a strictly territorial scope. It is indicative of the self-evident character of the strictly territorial nature of seizure in continental European law systems that the possibility of giving them an extra-territorial reach seems to have been barely discussed in doctrine. As it was cogently put in the context of attachment: '. . . le tribunal saisi doit constater son défaut de juridiction quand la mesure sollicitée implique un acte de coercition localisé hors du territoire de l'Etat du for ou comporte une injonction adressée à des autorités étrangères' (the tribunal needs to find itself without jurisdiction when the requested measure implies an act of coercion outside the forum state or an injunction to foreign authorities).[2] With some exceptions,[3] this position seems to be accepted in most civil law countries, although the opposite view has sometimes been advocated.[4] This not only holds true for civil remedies of attachment, but also for provisional measures in the context of criminal investigations. It is only logical therefore that the order of a Swiss investigating magistrate restraining assets held at a foreign branch of a Swiss bank was rescinded by the Geneva Chamber of Indictment.[5]

Nevertheless, some national authorities have attempted to prevent the dissipation of assets located outside the national territory, thereby giving

---

[1] See FATF-Recommendation 38.

[2] Rigaux and Fallon, *Droit international privé, Tome II. Droit positif Belge*, p. 205.

[3] See, e.g., the judgment of the French Supreme Court of 30 May 1985, *Rev.Crit.DIP* (1986), 328 annotated by H. Battifol.

[4] McLachlan, 'Extra-territorial Orders Affecting Bank Deposits', p. 40.

[5] Geneva Chamber of Indictment, judgment of 17 January 1995, annotated by Sträuli, 'Territorialité de l'enquête pénale', p. 123 *et seq.*

their domestic provisional measures an extra-territorial reach. As with extra-territorial disclosure orders, these practices have especially been practised by common law authorities, often in civil fraud cases. Disclosure orders have, in fact, often been issued as ancillary orders to injunctive orders.[6] First, the basis for these extra-territorial provisional measures will be examined; the problems to which these extra-territorial provisional measures have given rise will then be highlighted.

Basis for extra-territorial reach of provisional measures

Common law courts have long since accepted that they could refer to an adjudicative jurisdiction over a defendant in order to issue an injunction relating to the acts of the defendant abroad, given the fact that an injunction operates *in personam*.[7] A prominent example of this was given by the US Court of Appeals for the Ninth Circuit, when, at the request of the Philippine government which was seeking to recover some of the funds defrauded by (the family of) former President Marcos, it issued an injunction enjoining Mr and Mrs Marcos to part with their assets:

> The injunction is directed against individuals, not against property; it enjoins the Marcoses and their associates from transferring certain assets wherever they are located. Because the injunction operates *in personam*, not *in rem*, there is no reason to be concerned about its territorial reach . . . A court has the power to prevent a defendant from dissipating assets in order to preserve the possibility of equitable remedies . . . The injunction here enjoins the defendants from secreting those assets necessary to preserve the possibility of equitable relief.[8]

The same principle lies at the heart of the judicial development of worldwide *Mareva* injunctions in England. This type of pre-trial injunction – developed in two leading cases decided by the Court of Appeal in 1975[9] – allows a defendant to be prevented from removing his assets from the relevant jurisdiction or from dissipating them, which was not possible before in England. The injunction is addressed to the defendant and creates an obligation for him to comply with its terms. Non-observance of

---

[6] Cf. McLachlan, 'The Jurisdictional Limits of Disclosure Orders', 6–7.

[7] L. Collins, 'Provisional and Protective Measures', pp. 108–9.

[8] *Republic of the Philippines v. Marcos*, 862 F.2d 1355, 1363–4 (9th Cir.), cert.den. 490 US 1035 (1988).

[9] *Nippon Yusen Kaisha v. Karageorgis* [1975] 1 WLR 1093 (CA); *Mareva Compania Naviera SA v. International Bulkcarriers SA* [1975] 2 Lloyd's Rep. 509 (CA). Other Commonwealth countries such as Canada, Australia and New Zealand have likewise developed *Mareva* injunctions. See L. Collins (ed.), *Dicey and Morris on The Conflict of Laws* (London: Sweet & Maxwell, 1993), p. 189.

this obligation can be punished as contempt of court. However, third parties, including banks, under notice of the order, are also potentially liable to contempt proceedings if they aid in its breach or do not take the necessary steps to prevent its breach.

The originally strictly territorial character[10] of *Mareva* injunctions was broadened in 1988 in a series of cases involving allegations of massive fraud conducted through the international banking system in which the Court of Appeal accepted that, given their *in personam* character, *Mareva* injunctions could be issued in respect of property held abroad.[11] The far-reaching character of this change was demonstrated in the context of the litigation that took place between the new government of the Republic of Haiti and its ousted president 'Baby Doc' Duvalier.[12] When the latter was sued by the Republic of Haiti in France where he had taken refuge, the English Court of Appeal, having *in personam* jurisdiction over the English firm of solicitors employed by and thus the agents of the Duvalier family, granted a worldwide *Mareva* injunction against the Duvalier family in support of the French proceedings on the basis of Article 24 of the Brussels Convention.[13] The family was restrained from dissipating its assets and – at least as important – was ordered to disclose their worldwide assets via their English firm of solicitors.[14]

Mareva injunctions relate to private litigation, but similar techniques have been applied in the context of criminal investigations. In *Securities and Investments Board (SIB) v. Pantell*,[15] which concerned an international swindling scheme, SIB, an English prudential authority, obtained a *Mareva* injunction in respect of deposits held at bank accounts in England and in Guernsey, part of the Channel Islands (a separate jurisdiction). It is equally interesting to note that in respect of the restraint orders that can be made in the context of money laundering and confiscation of proceeds

---

[10] *Ashtiani v. Kashi* [1987] QB 888 (CA).

[11] *Babanaft International Co. SA v. Bassatne* [1989] WLR 232, 257; *Derby & Co.Ltd. and others v. Weldon and others* [1990] Ch 48 (CA) (Nos.3 & 4) [1990] Ch 65 (CA); *Derby & Co.Ltd. and others v. Weldon and others* (No.6) [1990] 1 WLR 1139 (CA). See Collins, 'Provisional and Protective Measures', pp. 116–17 and 'The Territorial Reach of *Mareva* Injunctions', *LQR* (1989), 262.

[12] On the responsibility of former heads of state for acts of fraudulent enrichment, see in general N. Kofele-Kale, *International Law of Responsibility for Economic Crimes. Holding Heads of State and Other High Ranking State Officials Individually Liable for Acts of Fraudulent Enrichment* (The Hague: Kluwer Law International, 1996), p. 369 and also J.-L. Van Boxstael, 'Le juge et les "biens mal acquis"', *JT* (1998), 96–101.

[13] Convention on jurisdiction and the enforcement of judgments in civil and commercial matters. For a recent version, see *OJ* No. C 189, 13.08.1990.

[14] *Republic of Haiti v. Duvalier* [1990] 1 QB 202 (CA). For comment see Collins, 'Provisional and Protective Measures', pp. 155–6 and McLachlan, 'The Jurisdictional Limits of Disclosure Orders', 14–15.   [15] [1989] 2 All ER 673.

from crime, there is no statutory limitation as to where the property is located, whether it be in England and Wales or elsewhere, although these restraint orders cannot be served outside England and Wales.[16]

Legal arguments against the extra-territorial reach of provisional measures: status quaestionis

Although it has sometimes been argued that worldwide *Mareva* injunctions are in reality not extra-territorial orders,[17] it will be shown that in many cases these orders do have far-reaching extra-territorial implications, which run into objections, not only from a public international law, but also from a private international law perspective. Before discussing these objections in detail, the dire consequences this type of international provisional measure may have, especially on third parties (financial institutions), will be demonstrated by discussing a highly interesting international insider trading case: *Securities and Exchange Commission v. Wang & Lee.*[18]

On 27 June 1988 the American Securities and Exchange Commission (SEC) commenced proceedings against Messrs Wang and Lee in the US District Court for the Southern District of New York for alleged violations of the Securities Exchange Act 1934 by virtue of insider trading. On the same day, the District Court issued a number of *ex parte* orders, including a temporary restraining order and an order freezing assets.

Lee, a Taiwan national and resident of Hong Kong, was suspected of having traded securities on the basis of non-public information which Wang had obtained in his capacity as financial analyst with a firm of investment bankers, Morgan Stanley & Co. Wang eventually agreed to an out-of-court settlement with SEC and pleaded guilty to the charge of having given non-public information to Lee. The latter, who got away with the lion's share of the profits (US$19,417,740), was not prepared to give up his illegal profits, however. Although initially admitting to having com-

---

[16] Section 62(2) DTA 1994 and s.102(3) CJA 1988. See M. Levi and L. K. Osofsky, 'The End of the Money Trail: Confiscating the Proceeds of Crime', in *Butterworths International Guide to Money Laundering Law and Practice*, R. Parlour (London: Butterworths, 1995), p. 309.

[17] McLachlan, 'Extraterritorial Orders Affecting Bank Deposits', pp. 40 *et seq.*

[18] *Nanus Asia Co. Inc. v. Standard Chartered Bank* [1990] 1 *HKLR* 396. See Collins, 'Provisional and Protective Measures', pp. 125, 132–8; M. Levi, *Consumer Confidentiality, Money-Laundering, and Police Bank Relationships: English Law and Practice in a Global Environment*, pp. 57–9; M. D. Holmes, '*SEC v. Wang*: A Warning Signal to International Banks of Potential Double Liability', *Tex.Int'l LJ* (1991), 159–87 and M. D. Mann, J. G. Mari and G. Lavdas, *Developments in International Securities Law Enforcement and Regulation*, pp. 37–9.

mitted insider trading, he then transferred almost US$5million via the New York branch of Standard Chartered Bank, an English bank, to accounts held by two companies – which he controlled – at a branch of Standard Chartered Bank in Hong Kong. When, on 1 August 1988, Lee, through his Hong Kong lawyers, demanded payment of accounts maintained at the Hong Kong branch of Standard Chartered Bank, the bank, relying on the restraint order issued by the New York District Court, refused to honour his demand. The two corporations subsequently sued the bank in Hong Kong, demanding payment of the funds held in the account. The SEC subsequently obtained a new order from the District Court in New York, directing the New York branch of Standard Chartered Bank to pay into the court registry all assets controlled by Lee. Under protest, the bank deposited US$12.5 million, ensuring, however, that it obtained a declaration from the New York District Court that it was absolved from all legal obligations to the two corporations. Given the fact that the companies controlled by Lee were consequently unable to obtain payment in New York, their only hope was to be paid out in Hong Kong.

The SEC had, however, also obtained an *ex parte* anti-suit injunction against Lee, enjoining him from commencing a suit relating to the restraining order anywhere other than in the US District Court for the Southern District of New York. The Hong Kong court refused to recognise the order of the New York District Court, stating that it had no direct or indirect effect in Hong Kong and also recognised that to enforce it would contravene the rule that foreign public law could not be enforced in Hong Kong.[19] As the contract between Standard Chartered Bank and the two corporations was governed by Hong Kong law, the New York court order was not a valid defence. Nevertheless, the application by the companies controlled by Lee was not successful. The Hong Kong court held that, in view of the fact that the bank was given notice by the SEC that the funds it held could be proceeds from insider trading, it was subject to a constructive trust in favour of allegedly defrauded investors as beneficiaries. Because the bank was deemed to be aware of the constructive trust, the Hong Kong court held that its contractual duty to comply with its customers' instructions was void. The New York District Court then entered final judgment against Lee. It ordered that the exact amounts of profits from the insider trading be determined and then disgorged into the registry and that they should be administered through a constructive trust for the benefit of the defrauded investors. Standard Chartered Bank

---

[19] *Nanus Asia Co. Inc. v. Standard Chartered Bank* [1990] 1 *HKLR* 396, 411–16. On this rule, see *infra* pp. 362–8.

appealed against this decision, but the case was settled before a decision was handed down.

The arguments against unilateral extra-territorial measures and the case for co-operation mechanisms

The quagmire of procedures in the *SEC v. Wang & Lee* saga amply illustrates that provisional measures with an extra-territorial reach may create conflicting obligations for third parties caught in the middle. These risks are inherent to any type of extra-territorial measure issued in one state that seeks to freeze or confiscate assets located in another state(s). The nub of the problem is that these measures are not recognised in other states, as a consequence of which banks (and other third parties) eventually run the risk that they will have to pay twice; once to the customer in a country where the confiscation order is not recognised and again to the state which issued the confiscation order.[20] In this sense, the increasing risks that attach to having stewardship over other persons' finances are considerably exacerbated in an international context.

The problems surrounding the extra-territorial reach of provisional measures only to a certain extent foreshadow the problems that arise when national authorities give an extra-territorial reach to confiscation orders, as these are generally not recognised or enforceable in other countries. Giving provisional measures or confiscations an international reach can function only if these measures are internationally recognised and enforced, for they will otherwise put third parties in jeopardy. It will be shown hereinafter that, for various legal reasons, the recognition of unilateral provisional measures is hard to conceive. The author will argue that provisional measures aimed at preventing the dissipation of assets that are (potentially) liable to confiscation should be taken by the state in which the assets are located. International provisional measures therefore presuppose international co-operation mechanisms, mostly, though not necessarily, based on explicit treaty arrangements.

The potential for conflict of enforcement jurisdiction

A first argument against international unilateral provisional measures is the lack of enforcement jurisdiction and especially the potential conflicts of enforcement jurisdiction that may ensue in the context of this type of

[20] See P. Adriaanse, *Confiscation in Private International Law* (The Hague: Martinus Nijhoff, 1956), p. 55.

measure: problems which have already been discussed in the context of extra-territorial disclosure orders.[21]

As far as worldwide *Mareva* injunctions are concerned, the English courts are in most cases probably entitled under international law to issue orders regulating the conduct of defendants abroad as these are issued in the context of private litigation and the plaintiff is usually required to show that he has a cause for action in England.[22] The most controversial feature of worldwide *Mareva* injunctions from an international law perspective is their effect on third parties, including banks, especially where those third parties are faced with conflicting legal obligations from different legal systems. It is useful to underline that, as far as third parties are concerned, the question is one of pure enforcement jurisdiction, as the court will typically have no adjudicative jurisdiction over the third party. English courts have endeavoured to come to terms with this potential conflict with foreign law by subjecting worldwide *Mareva* injunctions to provisos (originally called Babanaft provisos[23]), the modern form of which are now drafted as follows:

> *Effect of this Order outside England and Wales*
> The terms of this order do not affect or concern anyone outside the jurisdiction of this court until it is declared enforceable or is enforced by a Court in the relevant Country and they are to affect him only to the extent they have been declared enforceable or have been enforced unless such person is:
> (a) a person to whom this Order is addressed or an officer or an agent appointed by power of attorney of such person; or
> (b) a person who is subject to the jurisdiction of this Court and (i) has been given written notice of this Order at his residence or place of business within the jurisdiction of this Court, and (ii) is able to prevent acts or omissions outside the jurisdiction of this Court which constitute or assist in a breach of terms of this Order.[24]

Although this proviso is reassuring to banks that act wholly outside English territory, it does not resolve the situation – which frequently arises – in which an international bank has a branch in England, but the assets of the defendant are held by that bank abroad. Under point (b)(ii) of the above proviso, these banks are still required to obey the order in as far as they are able to do so abroad. It is unclear what should be understood

---

[21] See *supra* pp. 321–7.

[22] See McLachlan, 'Extra-territorial Orders Affecting Bank Deposits', pp. 44–7.

[23] *Babanaft International Co. S.A. v. Bassatne* [1989] 1 All ER 433. Cf. *Derby & Co.Ltd. v. Weldon (No.2)* [1989] 1 All ER 1002, 1015).

[24] *Ex p. Mareva Injunctions and Anton Piller Orders* 28 July 1994 (*The Times*, 2 August 1994).

by the stricture 'able to prevent acts or omissions outside the jurisdiction of this Court'. It is submitted that, notwithstanding the penumbras of international law in this respect, it should be clear that a third party, including an international bank, should never be required to do something that is illegal according to the *lex situs* of the assets.[25] In some countries the local law criminalises the restraint of assets on account of a foreign authority (see, e.g., Article 271 of the Swiss Penal Code). In these circumstances, provisional measures that are to have an effect on assets located in that state can be taken only by the relevant authorities of that state.

It has sometimes been suggested that the stricture in the proviso 'able to prevent acts or omissions outside the jurisdiction of this Court' should be understood as envisaging what third parties can lawfully do abroad, that is, with respect for the locally applicable law.[26] It has correctly been pointed out that, irrespective of possible sanctions stipulated by the local law, it is difficult to imagine a legal system which would not require a bank to act on its customer's instructions in the absence of a local court order or law to the contrary.[27] This brings us to the private international law arguments underpinning the thesis that provisional measures should be taken by the authorities of the state where the assets concerned are located.

Private international law objections

From a private international law point of view, proprietary rights are in principle determined by the *lex situs* of the property. In order to determine the proper law governing a bank account (i.e., the contract law), it is necessary to determine its *situs*. Since a bank account is in effect a contract between a bank and its customer, the funds held in a bank account are its debts; under most legal systems, a bank customer does not 'own' money in the bank, he has a personal, and not a real, right to it. The proper law governing a bank account is, unless otherwise stipulated, the law of the place where the bank account is kept.

When a person's bank account (i.e. a debt) is seized or subjected to another type of provisional measure, the material question then is whether those provisional measures also bite on bank accounts (i.e. debts)

---

[25] See also *supra* p. 324 in the context of extra-territorial disclosure orders.

[26] A. Malek and C. Lewis, 'Worldwide Mareva injunctions: the position of international banks', *Lloyd's Mar.& Com.LQ* (1990), 94.

[27] McLachlan, 'Extraterritorial Orders Affecting Bank Deposits', p. 49.

held by that customer at other, foreign, branches of the same bank. The answer should in principle be in the negative. As debts are governed by the law of the place where they are held, bank accounts held at the foreign branch are in principle governed by the law of that country. It is a generally accepted rule of private international law that performance of a contract is excused only if it has become illegal by the law of the contract (*lex contractus*) or if it necessarily involves the commission of an act which is deemed unlawful by the jurisdiction in which the act is committed. Hence, provisional measures constitute a valid exception to the performance of a contract (*in casu* the bank's promise to repay) only when they are taken under the proper law of contract.[28]

This will generally not be the case with extra-territorial measures, as is demonstrated in the two following cases.

The first case centred on an American Presidential Order by which all Libyan assets under US control were frozen, including those at overseas branches of US banks. Libyan Arab Foreign Bank, a Libyan corporation wholly owned by the Central Bank of Libya, had two US dollar accounts with Bankers Trust, an American bank, namely a demand account at its New York head office and an interest-bearing call account at its London branch. In spite of the American freezing order, Libyan Arab Foreign Bank demanded payment at the London branch of Bankers Trust. After having determined that the proper law of contract governing the London bank account was English law, Staughton J (as he then was) held that Libyan Arab Foreign Bank was entitled to payment of its debt, that is, the credit of the London bank account.[29]

A similar line of reasoning was applied in the context of the litigation between SEC and Wang and Lee, when the Hong Kong Court refused to recognise the provisional orders issued by the US District Court as a valid exception to the performance of the contract between the corporations of Lee and Standard Chartered Bank.[30] In addition, the court based its reasoning on the separate entity rule, under which every branch of an international bank is treated as a separate entity. This rule, adhered to in the banking law of various countries, is essential to the feasibility of international banking in that it guarantees that a customer can in principle

---

[28] See O. Lando, 'Contracts', in *International Encyclopedia of Comparative Law, Volume III: Private International Law*, Ch.24, 1976, Nos.14–24, pp. 8–13.

[29] *Libyan Arab Foreign Bank v. Bankers Trust Co* [1989] 3 All ER 252. For comment, see C. McLachlan, 'Splitting the Proper Law in Private International Law', in *British Yearbook of International Law 1990* (Oxford: Clarendon, 1990), pp. 331–4.

[30] *Nanus Asia Co. Inc. v. Standard Chartered Bank* [1990] 1 *HKLR* 396, 410–11. See *supra* pp. 356–7.

demand payment only at the branch where he holds his account so that branches do not have to check whether payment has already been made at another foreign branch of the same bank.[31] The rule was developed in English case law at the beginning of the twentieth century[32] and is also known in the federal banking law of the United States.[33] Lord Denning also invoked this rule to enunciate the principle that branches of international banks are in principle only subjected to court orders emanating from the courts of the country where they are located.[34] The conclusion, then, is clear: provisional measures should always be taken by the authorities of the jurisdiction where the assets are located.

Refusal to enforce foreign public law

Apart from the conflict of enforcement jurisdiction and the private international law objections to which they have given rise, attempts to give an extra-territorial reach to provisional measures have often also foundered on a deeply ingrained legal aversion to enforcing foreign public law. The recognition and enforcement of foreign judicial decisions was traditionally confined to civil and commercial matters. It is 'a well-established and almost universal principle that the courts of one country will not enforce the penal and revenue laws of another country'.[35] This principle extends to public law in general, as public law is, much more than private law, an expression of the sovereignty of the state. Although the rule has particularly been invoked with respect to

---

[31] *Cronan v. Schilling*, 100 NYS2d 474 (1950), cited by Holmes, '*SEC v. Wang*: A Warning Signal', 174–5.   [32] *Richardson v. Richardson* [1927] All ER 92.

[33] *Chrzanowsky v. Corn Exchange Bank*, 173 A. D. 285, 291, 159 NYS 385, 388 (1916) and *Pan-American Bank & Trust Co. v. National City Bank*, 6 F.2d 762, 767 (2d Cir.), *cert.denied*, 269 US 554 (1925), both cases cited by Holmes, '*SEC v. Wang*: A Warning Signal', 174.

[34] *Power Curber International Ltd. v. National Bank of Kuwait SAK* [1981] 3 All ER 607, per Denning LJ.

[35] Collins, *Dicey and Morris*, p. 97. Cf. G. Van Hecke, 'Droit public et conflits de lois', *Travaux.Com.fr.dr.int.privé* (1983–84), 225. This rule is indeed also adhered to in many countries; see in general R. B. Chapman, 'Tax Compliance and the Revenue Rule in Prosecutions for Wire and Mail Fraud', *ICLQ* (1999), 437–8. For the United States, see *Banco Nacional de Cuba v. Sabbatino* 376 US 398 (1964); Cardozo, 'Congress versus *Sabbatino*: Constitutional Consideration', *Colum.JTransnat'l L* (1966), 297; L. Henkin, 'The Foreign Affairs Power of the Federal Courts: *Sabbatino*', *Col.LRev.* (1964), 805; F. Mann, 'The Legal Consequences of *Sabbatino*', *Va.LRev.* (1965), 604. For Belgium see: G. Van Hecke and K. Lenaerts, *Internationaal Privaatrecht*, APR (Ghent: Story-Sciëntia, 1989), p. 96; for Switzerland see: A. F. Schnitzer, *Handbuch des internationalen Privatrecht* (Basle: Verlag für Recht und Gesellschaft, 1950), pp. 541, 544. For The Netherlands see: J. Kosters and C. W. Dubbink, *Algemeen deel van het Nederlands internationaal privaatrecht* (Erven F. Bohn: Haarlem, 1962), pp. 388–90.

attempts to enforce extra-territorial confiscations, it is equally material with respect to extra-territorial provisional measures and it is therefore useful to discuss it at this stage.

Extra-territorial confiscations and provisional measures can be precisely distinguished from purely territorial provisional measures or confiscations by the need for the assistance of a foreign state for their enforcement. If a state cannot seize the assets itself, but needs the active or passive assistance of another state, the confiscation or provisional measure must be classified as extra-territorial.[36]

This principle only prohibits the enforcement of foreign public law, not the recognition of foreign public law. One is confronted with an attempt to enforce foreign public law when the state where the assets are located is asked to enforce a foreign title based on public law. As was demonstrated, this will always be the case in respect of extra-territorial provisional measures and confiscations, which *per se* imply the assistance of a foreign state. Such assistance was traditionally refused.[37]

Purely territorial provisional measures or confiscations, on the other hand, can be recognised by another state. In such cases the state that issued these measures does not demand the enforcement of its title based on public law, but merely its recognition. Especially in respect of confiscation, a person whose assets have been seized or confiscated will sometimes attempt to regain control over these assets through judicial procedures commenced before the courts of another state. The confiscating state which physically controls the assets and has sometimes transported them abroad as a defendant will in such instances demand recognition of its title, which is in principle allowed.[38]

This delicate distinction between the enforcement and recognition of foreign public law was crystallised in *Attorney-General of New Zealand v. Ortiz*,[39] a case involving a valuable historic Maori carving, the export of which was prohibited under the New Zealand Historic Articles Act 1962, save the prior permission of the New Zealand Home Minister. In the case of an unauthorised export of a historic article, s.12(2) of the Act stated that 'it shall be forfeited to Her Majesty'. When the Maori carving was illegally exported and subsequently put up for sale at an auction in London, the Attorney-General of New Zealand commenced proceedings before the Commercial Court of the Queen's Bench Division in London, demanding

---

[36] Adriaanse, *Confiscation*, p. 54.

[37] For a rich, if somewhat dated, account of comparative law, see Adriaanse, *Confiscation*, pp. 78–96 and Van Hecke, 'Confiscation, Expropriation and the Conflict of Laws', 240–1.

[38] Adriaanse, *Confiscation*, pp. 57–77.   [39] [1982] 3 All ER 451.

that the court prohibit the sale and restore the carving to New Zealand. The Attorney-General claimed that, by the illegal export itself, the carving was forfeited to the New Zealand government. After having determined that the New Zealand law did not provide for automatic forfeiture, the court was left with the question of whether the provisions of the New Zealand law could be enforced in England. The UK Court of Appeal answered the question in the negative. Lord Ackner, however, indicated that, had the court been faced with a mere recognition of the New Zealand Historic Articles Act 1962, there would have been no problem: '. . . if the carving had been seized and condemned in New Zealand, thereby being reduced into the possession of the New Zealand government, then that government would have been entitled to enforce its proprietary title in this country by reference to the Historic Articles Act'.[40] In casu, the Attorney-General did not demand the enforcement of a proprietary title, but of a foreign law.

In the same vein, courts have, for example, accommodated requests of foreign national museums which demanded the restitution of stolen works of art, although these decisions may also be seen as merely the recognition of the title of a bona fide purchaser.[41] What is decisive is thus not the fact that a foreign state institutes proceedings, but the nature of the claim the state makes. Lord Ackner emphasised that, in determining the legal nature of a provision of law, what matters is not so much the formal denomination of that provision, but its content and purpose.[42] The purpose of criminal law is the vindication of justice. If a sanction is attributed to the state or to someone representing the state, then, one is confronted with a criminal sanction.

Though the principle of the non-enforcement of foreign public law is generally accepted both in common law and civil law countries, its theoretical foundation is the matter of some controversy.[43] Unlike private law, public law is in principle exclusively concerned with the benefit of the state. Hence it has been propounded that the courts of a state should be used only to the benefit of that state, not to the benefit of another state.[44]

---

[40] [1982] 3 All ER 451, 465.
[41] See, e.g., Kunstsammlungen zu Weimar v. Elicofon 678 F.2d 1150 (2nd.Cir.1982). See also J. P. Verheul ('Foreign Export Prohibitions: Cultural Treasures and Minerals', NILR, 1984, 419–27), who criticises the decision in Ortiz.
[42] Attorney-General of New Zealand v. Ortiz [1982] 3 All ER 451, 465. Cf. F. A. Mann, 'Conflicts of Law and Public Law', in Rec.Cours (1971), I, p. 176.
[43] Cf. Re State of Norway's Applications (Nos 1 and 2) [1989] 1 All ER 745, per Lord Goff, LJ.
[44] Mann, 'Conflicts of Law and Public Law', pp. 166–70 and F. Rigaux, Droit public et droit privé dans les relations internationales, pp. 171–3.

The use of the judicial administration and machinery of State B with a view to enforce the public laws of State A, rests on the wrong presumption that State A is entitled to enforce its public laws in State B, that is, to assert its sovereignty in the territory of another state.[45] It is therefore said that every attempt to enforce the 'prerogative rights' of a state through foreign courts is tantamount to an unacceptable excess of international jurisdiction.[46]

It is submitted that the need for an effective international co-operation in the fight against international crime makes it necessary to relax this principle. The proposition that the judicial administration and machinery of one state should not be used for the benefit of another state is obsolescent as far as international co-operation in criminal matters is concerned. The thesis that international co-operation in criminal matters, particularly in the context of combating money laundering, should be governed by the general interest of crime fighting, rather than by the individual interests of states, was expounded earlier.[47] In keeping with this thesis, states should be willing to use their own courts for the enforcement of penalties and sentences handed down in another state. In an admittedly different context, the point was correctly made that the extra-territorial enforcement of foreign laws protecting common interests should not be refused on the sole ground of their foreign public law nature.[48]

The arguments that were traditionally put forward against the enforcement of foreign public law often seemed rooted in the strongly political character of the claims foreign states were attempting to enforce extra-territorially. Thus, foreign confiscations (often amounting to nationalisations of private property) were traditionally denied any extra-territorial effect because they were seen as the assertion of a foreign state's prerogative right.[49] These confiscations, or rather nationalisations, were moreover often acts of the national legislature or executive, rather than the result judicial decisions. Their extra-territorial effect was often denied because of the political character of these laws or for reasons of public policy.[50] In

---

[45] See Keith LJ in *Government of India Ministry of Finance (Revenue Division) v. Taylor* [1955] 1 All ER 292, 299 and Mann, 'Conflicts of Law and Public Law', p. 168.

[46] Mann, 'The International Doctrine of Jurisdiction', p. 142 and 'The Doctrine of International Jurisdiction Revisited', pp. 42–4 and J. Dehaussy, 'Le statut de l'Etat étranger demandeur sur le for français: Droit international coutumier et droit interne', *JDI* (1991), 116.   [47] See *supra* p. 254.   [48] Verheul, 'Foreign Export Prohibitions', 423.

[49] See, e.g., Mann, 'Conflicts of Law and Public Law', p. 177 and Van Hecke, 'Confiscation, Expropriation', p. 242.

[50] F. Münch, 'Les effets d'une nationalisation à l'étranger', *Rec.Cours*, 1959, III, pp. 442–5 and 451–3.

the context of money laundering, confiscations and provisional measures are, in principle, not issued on political grounds but with a view to ferreting out forms of crime that adversely affect the state concerned and other states as well.

The absurdity of an orthodox adherence to the rule of non-enforcement of foreign public law is demonstrated by the fact that this would even exclude a conviction for money laundering if the proceeds have been derived from a foreign crime. For example, in a case involving the smuggling of tobacco from the United States to Canada, the US Court of Appeals of the First Circuit refused to uphold a conviction for conspiracy to defraud Canada of duties and taxes because this 'would amount functionally to penal enforcement of Canadian customs and tax laws'.[51] In the context of money laundering, such an overzealous application of the 'revenue rule' (i.e., the rule that courts refuse to enforce the revenue and penal laws of a foreign state), would greatly frustrate the efficacy of the fight against international money laundering.

As it has been shown,[52] states are willing to apply their own money laundering statutes to the laundering of proceeds that have been obtained through violation of foreign criminal law. This in no way amounts to the enforcement of foreign public law. Although the state that has criminalised money laundering in these circumstances does admittedly take account of the violation of a foreign criminal law (i.e. the predicate offence), this is not even tantamount to indirect enforcement of foreign public law (in which foreign public law is but a mere *datum*, a legal fact which determines the answer to a preliminary situation, rather than the *lex causae*, that is, the law governing the legal relationship).[53] There is only indirect enforcement of public law when a foreign state or its agent seeks a remedy which, though not based on a foreign public law rule, is designed to give it an extra-territorial reach; or when a private party (not a representative of a state) raises a defence based on foreign public law in order to vindicate the right of the foreign state.[54] This is obviously not the case with a conviction for the laundering of proceeds from a foreign offence.

---

[51] *United States v. Boots*, 80 F.3d 580, 587 (1st. Cir. 1996). This decision conflicts with a decision of the Court of Appeals for the Second Circuit on very similar facts: *United States v. Trapilo* 130 F.3d 547 (2d Cir. 1997). See Chapman, 'Tax Compliance and the Revenue Rule', 437–47.   [52] See *supra* pp. 216–17 and 227.

[53] For the definition of a datum, see H. W. Baade, 'Chapter 12: Operation of Foreign Public Law', in *International Encyclopedia of Comparative Law, Volume III: Private International Law* (Tübingen: J. C. B. Moher (Paul Siebeck), 1991), pp. 16–22.

[54] Collins, *Dicey and Morris*, pp. 98–9.

If states are, rightly, willing to apply their money laundering incrimina-tions to the laundering of proceeds that have been obtained through the violation of foreign criminal law, there is in principle no reason why they should refuse to co-operate in the enforcement of foreign confiscations of proceeds from crime, including the taking of provisional measures at the request of foreign authorities. The only requirement flowing from the rule of non-enforcement of foreign public law that should be reckoned with is that foreign states or their representatives should not be allowed to com-mence proceedings before the courts of a foreign state. This makes it nec-essary to institute co-operative proceedings whereby states can ask foreign states to take provisional measures or to enforce confiscations.

It has on occasion been asserted that the enforcement of foreign public law almost always presupposes a treaty and legislation, for this is the only way to ensure reciprocity of treatment.[55] Although it may be accepted that the enforcement of foreign public law requires the permission of the sove-reign, and hence can only take place on the basis of a statutory provision allowing judges to take provisional measures at the request of foreign authorities or to enforce foreign penalties, it is submitted that foreign public law can also be enforced in the absence of a treaty. The requirement of reciprocity has for too long been looked on as a sacrosanct requirement of international co-operation in criminal matters. There is no absolute requirement under international law that international co-operation in criminal matters should take place on the basis of a treaty,[56] although many states have incorporated this requirement into their domestic law. This unduly restrains the capacity of those countries to co-operate with other countries and, as far as the international co-operation in the fight against money laundering is concerned, effectively turns them into a 'safe haven' for criminal proceeds emanating from countries with which they have not entered into treaty arrangements. The argument that the treaty requirement allows countries to confine international co-operation in criminal matters to those countries in whose legal system they have suffi-cient trust loses force once countries enter into multilateral agreements, such as the 1988 Vienna Convention, which are in principle open to any state. While the treaty requirement may, admittedly, also play a humani-tarian role in that it excludes extradition to countries that have not been

---

[55] See Mann, 'Conflicts of Law and Public Law', p. 168; Dehaussy, 'Le statut de l'Etat étranger demandeur', 117. See also *Attorney-General of New Zealand v. Ortiz* [1982] 3 All ER 451, 460 per Denning LJ; the judgment of the French Supreme Court of 20 May 1990, *JDI* (1991), 137 and *United States v. Boots*, 80 F.3d 580, 588 (1st. Cir. 1996).

[56] See *supra* pp. 283–6.

deemed 'worthy' of entering into an extradition treaty (because of the poor humanitarian record of that country), at the same time it undermines the humanitarian dimension of international co-operation in criminal matters in the context of transfer of enforcement of imprisonment sanctions, where it has the effect of denying the benefit of serving an imprisonment sanction in their own country precisely to those who are imprisoned in countries with a poor humanitarian record.[57] At any rate, such humanitarian considerations do not come into play in the context of the transfer or enforcement of confiscation orders and provisional measures taken in that context. It is to be noted, moreover, that the drafters of the Vienna Convention did not consider a treaty basis as a *conditio sine qua non* for taking provisional measures or enforcing confiscations on request of another state.[58]

The case for co-operative mechanisms for provisional measures

It might be argued that a number of the objections that have been discussed could be removed simply by recognising the provisional measures (and confiscations) that have been issued by the authorities of another state, through judicial proceedings in the state where the assets are located. It will be shown, however, that this form of co-operation is not suited for the type of unilateral provisional measures that are typically taken in the context of a criminal investigation. At the same time, it will be demonstrated that the case for using co-operation mechanisms to take provisional measures not only rests on the aforementioned objections against the extra-territorial nature of unilateral provisional measures, but equally on arguments in favour of the taking of provisional measures by the authorities of the state where the assets are located.

In civil matters, foreign provisional measures can in principle be recognised and enforced through judicial proceedings in the state where the recognition and enforcement of the provisional measures are envisaged, usually the state where the assets to which the measures will pertain are located. Under the Brussels Convention, which is applicable only in civil and commercial, not in criminal, matters, recognition of foreign judg-

---

[57] See H. Van der Wilt, 'De WOTS jubileert; maar valt er eigenlijk wel wat te vieren?', *Delikt & Delinkwent* (1998), 237–40.

[58] This follows a contrario from the text of Article 5(4)(f) of the Vienna Convention: '*If* a Party elects to make the taking of measures . . . conditional on the existence of a relevant treaty, that Party shall consider this Convention as the necessary and sufficient treaty basis' (italics added).

ments in principle takes place automatically, that is, without the necessity for judicial proceedings to achieve recognition. Nevertheless, there are a few exceptions to this rule. One of them relates to provisional measures. Although in two cases involving French provisional measures relating to property in Germany, the Court of Justice acknowledged the possibility of recognising and enforcing extra-territorial foreign provisional measures,[59] this possibility is limited to provisional measures that have been rendered in partes.[60]

Ex parte provisional measures, which have been rendered without affording the party concerned a hearing and an opportunity to present its arguments, can in principle not be enforced without a judicial recognition procedure in which the party concerned has the right to present its arguments. It is clear that, in the context of criminal investigations, this type of recognition procedure would empty the provisional measures of their meaning as the defendant would be apprised of the authorities' intentions beforehand.

Article 24 of the Brussels Convention (as well as similar provisions in other treaties on the recognition and enforcement of foreign judgments) therefore gives jurisdiction to the state where the assets are located to take ex parte provisional measures, even when that state has no jurisdiction to determine the merits of the case. In Denilauder v. Couchet Frères the Court of Justice rightly pointed out that the courts of the state where the property is located are best placed to assess the need to take provisional measures and to determine the conditions and modalities for these measures.[61] They have in principle access to the most detailed and adequate information about the context in which provisional measures are to take effect (e.g., a change of ownership or of the location of the assets). This is especially important in view of the expeditiousness that is usually required in respect of this type of provisional measure.

An equally important argument in favour of the solution of Article 24

---

[59] Court of Justice, De Cavel v. De Cavel (No.1), judgment of 27 March 1979, ECR [1979] 1055 and Denilauder v. Couchet Frères, judgment of 21 May 1980, ECR [1980] 1553. For comment see Collins, 'Provisional and Protective Measures', 126–7; A. Vandecasteele, 'La reconnaissance et l'exécution des mesures provisoires et conservatoires dans la convention sur la compétence et l'exécution des décisions en matière civile et commerciale du 27 septembre 1968', Journal des Tribunaux (1980) 737–9; E. Mezger, Rev.Crit.DIP (1980), 801–4 and G. Maher and B. J. Rodger, 'Provisional and Protective Remedies: The British Experience of the Brussels Convention', ICLQ (1999) 312 et seq.

[60] Court of Justice, Denilauder v. Couchet Frères, judgment of 21 May 1980, ECR [1980] 1553, 1571.

[61] Court of Justice, Denilauder v. Couchet Frères, judgment of 21 May 1980, ECR [1980] 1553, 1570.

of the Brussels Convention is that it affords better protection to the defendant. Although *ex parte* provisional measures always imply that the defendant is not heard, whether they are taken by the court having jurisdiction on the merits of the case or by the court of the state where the assets are located, the latter court will usually be in a better position to assess the information on the situation of the defendant that is presented to it. Moreover, the defendant or any other person concerned by the provisional measures will in that case at least be able to apply to courts of their 'own' state for variation of the provisional measures, and will not be forced to apply to the courts of the foreign state which took the provisional measures. The thesis in favour of jurisdiction of the state where the assets are located is thus also firmly buttressed by considerations that favour the defendant.[62]

Although these arguments for jurisdiction to take provisional measures in favour of the state where the assets are located are derived from a civil context, they apply with equal force in criminal matters. This solution also avoids the problems that are likely to arise in relation to extra-territorial unilateral provisional measures. There will be no possibility of a conflict of enforcement jurisdiction and third parties will not have to face conflicting obligations. In the following section the treaty arrangements that have been devised to make provisional measures possible in an international context will be discussed.

The treaty mechanisms for taking provisional measures

Innovating character of the Vienna Convention and the Money Laundering Convention

Both the Vienna Convention and the Money Laundering Convention instituted co-operation mechanisms that are designed to allow one state to take provisional measures at the request of another state. The innovating character of these mechanisms should be clear from what has been set out above, but can also be established by studying previous multilateral treaties on co-operation in criminal matters, where this possibility is mostly absent or under-developed.

Thus under Article 5 of the European Mutual Assistance Convention, the possibility of the seizure of property is generally deemed to be limited to seizure of items of evidence, and excluding the seizure of assets for the

---

[62] See the conclusion of Advocate-General Mayras in *Denilauder v. Couchet Frères: ECR* [1980] 1578.

purpose of safeguarding the enforcement of an eventual confiscation,[63] though some domestic courts have ruled differently in this respect.[64] The two conventions of the Council of Europe that did provide for the possibility of provisional measures – albeit in an unsatisfactory way – have received very few ratifications. Article 36 of the European Convention on the International Validity of Criminal Judgments (1970) provides for the possibility of provisional seizure of property, but only at the moment of a request for the enforcement of a confiscation order. This is of little avail in the context of money laundering investigations, where provisional measures often need to be taken at an early stage of the investigation, when there will obviously be no confiscation order as yet. Although the European Convention on the Transfer of Proceedings in Criminal Matters (1972) contains a section on provisional measures in the requested state, the provisions contained therein (Articles 27 to 29) are almost exclusively concerned with remand in custody (although Article 28 also refers to seizure of property).[65] One of the only multilateral conventions that did expressly provide for the possibility of provisional seizure of property, the Benelux Convention on the enforcement of judicial decisions (1968), has never come into force.[66]

The Vienna Convention and the Money Laundering Convention were thus the first multilateral conventions that properly addressed the issue of provisional measures to be taken in view of the enforcement of confiscation sanctions. They both allow provisional measures to be taken at the request of another party before a request for (the enforcement of) a confiscation is made.

In the following, some of the features of the international co-operation mechanisms under these conventions that are instrumental to the taking of provisional measures on request of a foreign authority will be

---

[63] See the *Explanatory Report with the European Convention on Mutual Assistance in Criminal Matters* (reprinted in ed. E. Müller-Rappard and M. C. Bassiouni, *European Inter-State Co-operation in Criminal Matters. The Council of Europe's Legal Instruments* (Dordrecht: Martinus Nijhoff, 1993), I, p. 26); *Explanatory Report with the Convention on Laundering*, p. 7 and Nilsson, 'The Council of Europe Laundering Convention', p. 462.

[64] See the judgment of the Dutch Supreme Court of 12 June 1984, NJ (1985), No.173, with the contrary opinion of Advocate-General Leijten. See also the judgment of the Swiss Supreme Court: ATF 112 Ib, 576.

[65] See also the *Explanatory Report on the European Convention on the Transfer of Proceedings in Criminal Matters* (reprinted in Müller-Rappard and Bassiouni (eds.), *European Inter-State Co-operation in Criminal Matters*, pp. 881–2).

[66] See Articles 33–5 of the Beneluxverdrag inzake de tenuitvoerlegging van rechterlijke beslissingen, Brussels, 26 September 1968, *Belgisch Staatsblad/Moniteur belge*, 24 October 1967.

highlighted. Not all conditions and grounds for refusal in respect to the co-operation mechanisms will be discussed, however, as some have already been studied[67] while others will be analysed in Chapter 16.[68] Through a discussion of the main features of international co-operation mechanisms for taking provisional measures, it will be endeavoured to show that, while imposing a duty to co-operate, the co-operation mechanisms at the same time allow states to limit provisional measures to what they deem acceptable encroachments on proprietary rights with regard to property located on their territory. Thus, the right of every state to decide on provisional measures affecting property located on its territory, which is the main reason for setting up co-operation mechanisms, is maintained; there is no unqualified duty for parties to take provisional measures at the request of another party. First, it is proposed to discuss the types of measure that can be taken. Some of the conditions and exceptions relating to the taking of provisional measures at request of a foreign state will then be analysed. Thirdly, the possibility of lifting provisional measures that have been taken on a foreign request will be looked into. Finally, the question of possible liability for wrongful provisional measures will be considered.

Types of measures to be taken

Under the co-operation mechanisms a great variety of provisional measures can be taken. The Money Laundering Convention deliberately refers not to a specific type of provisional measure, but speaks generally about 'necessary provisional measures, such as freezing or seizing, to prevent any dealing in, transfer or disposal of property which, at a later stage, may be the subject of a request for confiscation or which might be such as to satisfy the request' (Article 11). A similar wording can be found in the Optional Protocol to the UN Model Treaty on Mutual Assistance in Criminal Matters concerning the Proceeds of Crime (1990).[69] Although Article 5(4)(b) of the Vienna Convention refers to 'measures to identify, trace and freeze or seize proceeds, property, instrumentalities . . . for the purpose of eventual confiscation', the requested state can undoubtedly also take other types of provisional measures, such as a restraint order or a sequester. The type of provisional measure that can be taken is normally

---

[67] See *supra* pp. 287–301 on the fiscal and political offence exception and the condition of double criminality.   [68] See *infra* pp. 397–407.

[69] *ILM* (1991), 1432. The text is also reprinted at Van den Wyngaert and Stessens, *International Criminal Law*, p. 327.

determined by the *lex situs*, that is the law of the requested state, rather than the text of the treaty itself.[70] Both Article 5(4)(b) of the Vienna Convention and Article 12(1) of the Money Laundering Convention stipulate that the execution of provisional measures is governed by the law of the requested state.

One aspect on which the domestic laws on provisional measures may vary significantly relates to the difference between object and value confiscation. States that only recognise object confiscation will typically not be able to take provisional measures with regard to legitimately acquired property that later may be used to satisfy a value confiscation; while conversely, a state that is familiar only with value confiscation may not have the legal means at its disposal to seize the objects that constitute the alleged proceeds from crime. The Vienna Convention does not reckon with this difference, which may give rise to intricate co-operation difficulties. The Money Laundering Convention on the other hand, which obliges states to co-operate in the enforcement of both object and value confiscation, does take this difference into account. It follows from the wording of Article 11 of the Money Laundering Convention that provisional measures have to be taken with regard to both systems of confiscation. It may, however, be accepted that a state will take provisional measures with respect to legally acquired property only if this is explicitly requested by the requesting state.[71]

Another particularity of the domestic confiscation law of some states that may cause co-operation difficulties, even at the stage of provisional measures, is the possibility of *in rem* confiscation procedures. As will be set out more in detail later,[72] co-operation in respect of confiscations issued in this type of procedure – which is especially popular in the United States[73] – can be refused on the basis of the Money Laundering Convention. Hence states are also allowed to refuse to take provisional measures with a view to the ulterior enforcement of a confiscation issued on an *in rem* procedure, although some states have nevertheless done so.[74]

Grounds for refusing to take provisional measures

A first ground for refusal which allows states to limit their obligation to take provisional measures at the request of another party is double

---

[70] See in a civil context: L. Gaillard, 'Les mesures provisionnelles en droit privé international', *La Semaine Judiciaire* (1993), 157.

[71] *Explanatory Report with the Convention on Laundering*, p. 24.

[72] See *infra* p. 398.   [73] See *supra* pp. 39–42.   [74] *Re S-L* [1995] 4 All ER 159

criminality. At this point it is useful to refer to our contention that the condition of double criminality does not serve a human rights interests purpose but is merely intended to safeguard the sovereignty interests of the requested state.[75] In the context of international co-operation with a view to provisional measures, this ground for refusal allows a state to refuse co-operation if it would not be able to do so with regard to the same type of conduct in an internal situation. If the provisional measures are requested at the same time that, or after, a request regarding confiscation has been made, then the double criminality may even be judged *in concreto.*[76]

It is submitted that there is no need for the double criminality requirement, as the rights of defendants and of other interested parties are sufficiently protected by the fact that the provisional measures will be taken under the law of the requested party, that is, the *lex situs*, and that the requested state in principle retains full sway over the decision as to which measures will be taken in respect to which property. In this sense, it is a remarkable fact that the Money Laundering Convention expressly excludes the possibility of making declarations in respect of the obligation to institute provisional measures under domestic law (Article 3). Although states are able to limit the scope of confiscation of proceeds from crime to certain offences, they cannot do so in respect of provisional measures, which means that parties to the Money Laundering Convention should in principle not be able to refuse to take provisional measures on the pretext that provisional measures are not allowed under their domestic law in respect of the offence for which co-operation is requested.[77]

Because of their invasive character, provisional measures are subject to a number of restrictions in many legal systems. The power to order provisional measures is mostly restricted to judicial authorities (sometimes including public prosecutors). A requirement that is often posed – also in a domestic context – is that there is a reasonably good chance that a confiscation order will eventually be made. Besides a requirement of probability, there is sometimes also a need to show a risk of dissipation.[78]

This type of requirement may fulfil an important human rights protection in that it can ensure that provisional measures are proportional to the eventual confiscation in view of which they are taken. Provisional

---

[75] See *supra* pp. 292–5.

[76] *Explanatory Report with the Convention on Laundering,* pp. 37–8. See *supra* pp. 290–1.

[77] *Explanatory Report with the Convention on Laundering,* p. 18.

[78] See also FATF, *Evaluation of Laws and Systems in FATF Members Dealing with Asset Confiscation and Provisional Measures,* p. 6.

measures by definition imply an infringement of the right of every man to the peaceful enjoyment of his possessions, as guaranteed by Article 1 of the First Protocol to the European Convention on Human Rights (1952). They are therefore, as was explicitly acknowledged by the European Court of Human Rights,[79] subject to the proportionality principle, which limits any lawful infringements of this right.[80]

In the United States, provisional measures are limited through the requirement of 'probable cause', which a law enforcement agency requesting the seizure of property is normally required to show. This is certainly logical in the context of civil *in rem* confiscation procedures, where the onus of proof falls on the defendant after seizure.[81] Notwithstanding legislative intervention to the contrary,[82] this requirement is also posed in the context of *in personam* confiscation procedures, if the prosecution issues a request for a pre-indictment restraining order. In the period before an indictment has been made, such an order will be issued only if the court finds that there is a substantial probability that the government will prevail on the issue of forfeiture, that there is a risk that the property will be made unavailable for forfeiture and that the need to preserve the availability of property outweighs the hardship on any party against whom the order is to be granted. The probability requirement can also be satisfied by the filing of an indictment.[83]

In England and Wales, an *ex parte* application to the High Court by the police for restraint orders under s.26 DTA 1994 or s.77 CJA 1988 will be successful only if the police can establish a *prima facie* case. It is required that proceedings have been instituted against the defendant for the relevant offence which have not yet been concluded and that 'it appears to the court that there are reasonable grounds for thinking that a confiscation order may be made' (s.76(1)(c) CJA 1988; cf. s.25(1)(c) DTA 1994). The same

---

[79] European Court of Human Rights, *Raimondo v. Italy*, judgment of 23 February 1994, *Publications of the European Court of Human Rights*, Series A, No.281–A, para. 27.

[80] On the proportionality principle under this provision in general see: European Court of Human Rights, *Sporrong and Lönnroth v. Sweden*, judgment of 23 September 1982, *Publications of the European Court of Human Rights*, Series A, No.52, para. 69; European Court of Human Rights, *James and others v. United Kingdom*, judgment of 21 February 1986, *Publications of the European Court of Human Rights*, Series A, No.98, para. 69. See also Frowein, 'The Protection of Property', 524–6 and Van Dijk and Van Hoof, *Theory and Practice of the European Convention on Human Rights*, pp. 461, 465.

[81] Gordon, 'Prosecutors Who Seize too Much', 753–4 and Stahl, 'Asset Forfeiture', 279–81.

[82] See Spaulding, '"Hit Them Where It Hurts"', 269–79.

[83] 18 USC section 1963(d)(1) (RICO statute) and 21 USC section 853(e)(1) (narcotics statute). See L. K. Osofsky, 'Comparing the US Law of "Forfeiture" with the Law of "Confiscation" in England and Wales', *JIBL* (1994), 300.

prima facie case requirement is posed by Swiss case law, which demands that there be a link between the offence that is being investigated and the seizure of property. As it was concisely expounded by the Swiss Supreme Court: 'Une saisie indistincte de tous les biens patrimoniaux de la personne poursuivie, sans que, prima facie, une relation puisse être faite avec une infraction, serait dès lors inadmissible.' (A general seizure of all property belonging to the defendant, without a *prima facie* case that is established with an offence, would be inadmissible.)[84] The *prima facie* case requirement thus purports to limit provisional measures to what can be reasonably required with a view to an ulterior confiscation.[85] In some countries such as the Netherlands, for example, the possibility of provisional measures is even limited to the most serious offences.[86]

It is only logical that the same type of limitation is imposed at the international level of co-operation. Otherwise international co-operation would take place to the detriment of the rights of the individual concerned. Although the *prima facie* requirement is not inserted as such in the Vienna Convention or the Money Laundering Convention, both conventions provide for mechanisms that allow the exclusion of requests that do not meet this requirement. A first limitation which may allow the requested state to refuse a request for 'random' provisional measures is the requirement that criminal proceedings or proceedings for the purpose of confiscation have been instituted (Article 11 of the Money Laundering Convention), a requirement that is also expressly posed by English law, for example (s.76(1)(a) CJA 1988 and s.25(1)(a) DTA 1994). More importantly, a request for provisional measures that does not meet the *prima facie* requirement can also be refused on the basis of other safety valves, namely 'if the measures sought could not be taken under the domestic law of the requested Party for the purposes of investigations or proceedings, had it been a similar domestic case'[87] or 'if the importance of the case to which the request relates does not justify the taking of the action sought'.[88]

---

[84] Judgment of the Swiss Supreme Court of 23 January 1996, *La Semaine Judiciaire* (1996), 357.   [85] Cf. K. Rees, 'Confiscating the Proceeds of Crime', *NLJ* (1996), 1271.

[86] See Article 94a of the Dutch Code of Criminal Procedure. See Cleiren and Nijboer, *Strafvordering*, p. 193.

[87] Article 18(2) of the Money Laundering Convention. Cf. Article 15(c) of the Vienna Convention.

[88] Article 18(1)(c)) of the Money Laundering Convention. On this ground for refusal see more *in extenso infra* p. 399.

Lifting provisional measures in the context of international co-operation

Almost any country whose legislation allows for provisional measures also foresees procedures for lifting these provisional measures. It is submitted that indefinite provisional measures, that is, those without an automatic periodical control of their legality and expediency or a right to apply for variation of the measures by the individuals concerned,[89] are contrary to the right of every man to the peaceful enjoyment of his possessions, as guaranteed by Article 1 of the First Protocol to the European Convention on Human Rights. Although this provision allows that measures are taken to enforce such laws as the state 'deems necessary to control the use of property in accordance with the general interest', these measures need to be proportionate to the purpose for which they are taken.[90] Measures that may have been proportionate at the moment they were decided on may cease to be so after a while. An example of this – which has been condemned by the European Court of Human Rights – is those provisional measures that continue to be in existence after the acquittal of the defendant.[91] To guarantee respect for the proportionality principle, it is therefore necessary that there be a legal procedure which allows for a periodical control and for the possibility of lifting provisional measures. This is all the more necessary when one takes into account that third parties may also be subjected to provisional measures. In countries where third parties' property can be subjected to provisional measures, whether it be in the context of a domestic or of an international investigation, they should be provided with a right to apply for variation or discharge of those measures.[92] The procedure for variation or discharge of provisional measures can in principle be the same in the context of an international co-operation procedure as in a domestic procedure (as is e.g. the case in The Netherlands).[93]

Neither the Vienna Convention nor the Money Laundering Convention contain any provision on the right of the individuals concerned to apply for variation of provisional measures. Such a right, if it is recognised, is

---

[89] See, e.g., s.77(7) CJA 1988 and s.26(6) DTA 1994.

[90] On Article 1 of the First Protocol, see *supra* pp. 62–4.

[91] European Court of Human Rights, *Raimondo v. Italy*, judgment of 23 February 1994, *Publications of the European Court of Human Rights*, Series A, No.281–A, para. 36 and *Manlio Venditelli v. Italy*, judgment of 18 July 1994, *Publications of the European Court of Human Rights*, Series A, No.293–A, paras. 38–40. For comment, see R. Danovi 'Le délai raisonnable de la procédure et le droit au respect des biens, en Italie', *RTDH* (1995), 447–53.   [92] See, e.g., s.6(6) DTA 1994 and s.77(7) CJA 1988.

[93] See Article 552a of the Code of Criminal Procedure.

necessarily governed by the law of the requested state, that is, the state which has taken the provisional measures. This also flows from Article 12(2) of the Money Laundering Convention, which demands that the requested party, before lifting any provisional measure taken upon request of another party, shall give that party 'an opportunity to present its reasons in favour of continuing the measure'. This could be done through an intervention *amicus curiae* or via a notification through official channels,[94] a possibility which has been further elaborated in some bilateral treaties.[95] If the requesting state has not been given such an opportunity, provisional measures may not be lifted, save for special reasons.[96] Such a special reason may, for example, be a statutory provision which automatically lifts the provisional measures after a lapse of time, as is the case under various Swiss cantonal laws. In general, however, provisional measures that have been taken in Switzerland at the request of a foreign authority can be maintained only if the formal request is received within a certain period of time (Article 18(2) of the Swiss Mutual Assistance Act).[97]

This type of consultation procedure is very important in view of the fact that the state that has requested the provisional measures may have a different view, and also different information, than the state that took the provisional measures. Judicial authorities may be more inclined to lift provisional measures when these have been taken at the request of a foreign authority than in the context of a purely domestic investigation as, in the former context, they will not be concerned with the final outcome of the investigation. Defendants will moreover often try to obtain the discharge of provisional measures taken abroad so as to nudge the requesting authority to commence the trial at a moment when the investigation is still running. If the requesting authorities surmise that the provisional measures might be lifted in the near future, they may institute proceedings even though they may not yet have gathered all the evidence. Consultation procedures, like that catered for by Article 12 of the Money Laundering Convention, may prevent provisional measures

[94] *Explanatory Report with the Convention on Laundering*, p. 26.

[95] See e.g. Article V of the Agreement between the Government of the Kingdom of The Netherlands and the Government of the United States of America regarding mutual co-operation in the tracing, freezing, seizure and forfeiture of proceeds and instrumentalities of crime and sharing of forfeited assets, Washington, 20 November 1992, *Tractatenblad der Nederlanden* (1993), No.5.

[96] *Explanatory Report with the Convention on Laundering*, p. 26.

[97] See L. Frei, 'Beschlagnahme und Einziehung als Rechtshilfemassnahmen', *RPS* (1988), 322; and, in the context of the American–Swiss MLAT see also: Kohler, 'The Confiscation of Criminal Assets', 33.

from being lifted where this might have strongly disadvantageous consequences for the criminal procedures in the requesting state. It is therefore a matter of some regret that the Vienna Convention has not provided for this type of consultation procedure.

Liability for wrongful provisional measures in the context of an international co-operation procedure

In the case of provisional measures that have been taken in respect of property which eventually proved not to be liable to confiscation, the owner may decide to sue the state for damages. An important question of private international law in this respect is which state should be held liable for wrongful provisional measures that were taken by State A at the request of State B. The answer to this question seems to differ from state to state. In some, the liability is determined on the basis of an 'organic' criterion: the state whose (judicial) organs took the provisional measures, that is, the requested state, is liable for eventual wrongful provisional measures, regardless of whether these were taken for domestic purposes or for the purpose of a foreign investigation (often as a consequence of the necessity to comply with international obligations).[98] A similar line of reasoning has explicitly been espoused by the European Commission on Human Rights in respect of the question regarding the responsibility for human rights violations.[99] Other legal systems tend to underline the fact that provisional measures were taken at the behest of a foreign state, for the purpose of an investigation that is conducted in that state, and put the liability at the door of the requesting state.[100] Whereas the former rule will, in most cases, be more suitable for the person concerned, who may sue in the country where he suffered damages, the outcome of the latter rule may correspond better to the true responsibility, as the wrongful character of provisional measures taken upon request of a foreign state will often flow from wrongful information it acted on and which was provided by the requesting state.

It is therefore submitted that it would be desirable to elaborate a treaty provision according to which the requested state would be able to recover

---

[98] See e.g. Article 8 of the Swiss statute on co-operation with the United States: Loi fédérale relative au traité conclu avec les Etats-Unis d'Amérique sur l'entraide judiciaire en matière pénale (3 October 1975).

[99] European Commission on Human Rights, *M & Co. v. the Federal Republic of Germany*, decision of 9 February 1990, *Decisions and Reports* 64, 138.

[100] See, e.g., in Germany: M. Grotz, 'Die internationale Zusammenarbeit bei der Abschöpfung von Gewinnen aus Straftaten', *JR* (1991), 184.

from the requesting state any damages it was obliged to pay for wrongful provisional measures that it took on request of the latter state. Similar provisions have, for example, been laid down in the Schengen Convention (Article 116) and the Europol Convention (Article 38) regarding damages caused by the use of wrongful information which was transmitted by another party. It is a matter of some regret that a similar type of provision has not been inserted into the Money Laundering Convention, or in the Vienna Convention. This type of provision may prove to be not only a good solution to the private international law question as to which state should be held liable for wrongful provisional measures taken in the course of international co-operation, it may also be beneficial to the efficacy of co-operation between states generally. Authorities that are faced with foreign requests for provisional measures will often be somewhat reluctant to take these measures, not least because of their financial implications. Requested authorities will be even more reticent because they are less familiar with the precise details of the investigation which is conducted in a foreign state. If the requested authorities were assured that any liability which might flow from provisional measures they might take upon request of a foreign authority will revert to the requesting state, this reticence would strongly diminish.

16 International enforcement of confiscation orders

The enforcement of confiscation orders in an international context can give rise to legal problems as the state that wants to enforce a confiscation order may lack enforcement jurisdiction because the property on which it wants to enforce the confiscation order is situated abroad. This problem is most likely to arise with object confiscation, when the property specified in the confiscation order is located abroad, but can also present itself in case of value confiscation, when the convicted person refuses to pay his confiscation order and has no or not enough property on the territory of the state concerned.

Two scenarios can be posited to deal with this lack of enforcement jurisdiction. First, the state wishing to enforce its confiscation order on property located abroad can issue unilateral measures to this end. Second, the state which lacks enforcement jurisdiction can request co-operation from a state that has enforcement jurisdiction, that is, a state on whose territory property is located on which the confiscation order may be enforced. This co-operation will mostly take place on the basis of the co-operation mechanisms such as those provided for by the Vienna Convention and the Money Laundering Convention. Co-operation should not be excluded in the absence of a treaty basis, however, a proposition which has been set out more in detail elsewhere in this book.[1] It is proposed first to analyse the unilateral measures to enforce confiscation orders. The co-operation mechanisms for enforcing confiscation orders will then be studied, as will the practice of international asset sharing.

Unilateral confiscation measures

The nub of the question that arises here is whether a state has jurisdiction to confiscate property located outside its territory. In discussing this

[1] See *supra* pp. 283–5.

question, it is necessary to distinguish between extra-territorial confiscation orders on the one hand, and attempts to enforce extra-territorial confiscation orders on the other. In view of the strictly territorial character of enforcement jurisdiction, the enforcement of a confiscation order on the territory of another state is clearly at variance with international law. This does not necessarily imply that the making of a confiscation order relating to property located outside the national territory should also be regarded as incompatible with international law. Whereas the former question relates to enforcement jurisdiction, the latter comes under the heading of adjudicatory jurisdiction. The pivotal question is in respect of which conduct a state (whether it be in its legislative or judicial capacity) has the right to apply its criminal laws and to sanction violation of these laws by ordering the confiscation of the proceeds or instrumentalities of crime. The question of adjudicatory jurisdiction to order a confiscation order can in principle only arise in the context of property confiscation (when the property specified in the order is located abroad) and not with a value confiscation order, which never specifies the property on which the confiscation order needs to be enforced.

When a domestic court orders the confiscation of proceeds from crime or of the instrumentalities of an offence, the adjudicatory jurisdiction of the court is determined by the offence. The jurisdiction of criminal courts is by no means limited to offences committed on the national territory, but may, under certain conditions, also extend to offences carried out abroad (e.g., by nationals). Under public international law, there is no general limitation of the right of states to extend the application field of their criminal legislation to acts carried out outside the boundaries of their national territories.[2] It is submitted that, as far as the geographical *situs* of the property is concerned, there are consequently no limitations under international law as to when a state can order a confiscation. In some cases, a domestic court ordering the confiscation of an asset, may not even be aware of the location of these assets.

This proposition is confirmed by the domestic practice of a number of states. In a case involving the confiscation of funds held at a French bank account and real estate in the United States, the Swiss Supreme Court acknowledged the capacity of the Swiss courts to order the confiscation of property located abroad.[3] The same capacity has been expressly provided for by the Belgian legislator in Article 43ter of the Belgian Criminal Code.

---

[2] See *supra* p. 213 (*Lotus*).
[3] Judgment of the Swiss Supreme Court of 31 January 1986, *La Semaine Judicaire* (1986), 520.

Also in England and Wales, legislation has given the courts the capacity to order the confiscation of property located abroad (s.102(3) CJA 1988 and s.62(2) DTA 1994). The same goes for the United States: under the Anti-Money Laundering Act 1992 this is possible even in the case of civil forfeitures for which the presence of the 'suspect' assets on American territory was traditionally a *sine qua non* condition. The jurisdiction of federal courts to order civil forfeitures is normally determined by the place where any of the acts or omissions giving rise to forfeiture occurred, or where the property is found, but for assets located outside the United States, the US District Court for the District of Columbia has jurisdiction.[4] The Supreme Court clearly posits the requirement that the court before which an *in rem* procedure is commenced has control over the property (*res*) involved.[5] American courts have construed this requirement in a broad manner by accepting constructive control over assets that have been seized by foreign authorities on American request so that the enforceability of a confiscation order is satisfied as is the case with assets over which the American courts have (territorial) jurisdiction.[6] This line of reasoning is circular, however, in that foreign courts are requested to seize assets with a view to an American confiscation order, which American courts can make only once the assets are seized abroad.[7]

Confiscation orders that pertain to property located on the territory of another state can be enforced only with the help of the authorities of that state. They are in this sense truly extra-territorial: their enforcement is dependent on the co-operation of another state. From a private international law point of view, it is unanimously accepted that extra-territorial confiscations cannot be enforced on the territory of another state other than the state ordering the confiscation.[8] This proposition essentially supports the point of view of the state on whose territory the property involved is located: its courts will typically refuse to recognise and enforce the foreign confiscation, often on account of the principle that courts do

---

[4] 28 USC 1355(b)(1) and (2) and 28 USC 1395. For comment, see L. Smith, '*In Rem* Forfeiture Proceedings and Extra-territorial Jurisdiction', *ICLQ* (1996), 907.

[5] *Republic National Bank of Miami v. US* 113 SCt. 554 (1992).

[6] *US v. All Funds on Deposit in Any Accounts Maintained in the Names of Meza de Castro or de Castro*, 63 F.3d 148 (1995), *cert.den.*, 116 SCt. 1541 (1996), cited by Smith, '*In Rem* Forfeiture Proceedings', 907–8 and W. J. Snider, 'International Co-operation in the Forfeiture of Illegal Drug Proceeds', *Criminal Law Forum* (1995), 380. Cf. B. Zagaris, 'U.S. International Co-operation against Transnational Organised Crime', 524–5.

[7] See Smith, '*In Rem* Forfeiture Proceedings', 908–9.

[8] See Adriaanse, *Confiscation*, pp. 78–96 and Van Hecke, 'Confiscation, Expropriation and the Conflict of Laws', 240–1.

not enforce the penal laws of another country.[9] The judicial authorities of that state will thus protect the property that is located on its territory, the status of which, according to a unanimously recognised rule of private international law, is governed by the *lex situs*.[10] A foreign confiscation order can also for that reason not be enforced: it was not taken on the basis of the *lex situs*, but on the basis of the law of a foreign state ordering the confiscation.

American authorities have sometimes had recourse to a number of unilateral measures to circumvent this traditional refusal to enforce foreign confiscations. On occasions, American courts have ordered defendants to transfer their proprietary rights vested in the property to the American government.[11] Refusal to comply with such orders can make defendants liable to contempt of court, a sanction which is, however, not really a deterrent for defendants who face considerable imprisonment sanctions anyway. Sometimes banks are ordered to transfer funds held at foreign branches to the United States, occasionally even under the threat of a money laundering prosecution.[12] The United States thus purports to obtain enforcement jurisdiction over these funds. In the same vein, defendants in the United Kingdom can be ordered to co-operate with the receiver in liquidating the assets the confiscation of which has been ordered.[13]

This type of measure is clearly at variance with international law as it will often involve a violation of the *lex situs*: it has already been argued in the context of extra-territorial disclosure orders that no state should use its public law to force a private person to commit an illegality under the law of another state.[14]

International law, however, does not necessarily militate against the use of extra-judicial methods to gain control of the proceeds of crime located abroad. The use of out-of-court settlements to obtain proceeds of crime, and the policy objections that can be adduced against it, were set out

---

[9] On this principle see *supra* pp. 362–4 and Adriaanse, *Confiscation*, pp. 85–6 and 155–9.

[10] Adriaanse, *Confiscation*, p. 158; Baade, 'Chapter 12: Operation of Foreign Public Law', 26–8; McClean, *International Judicial Assistance*, p. 216; Rigaux and Fallon, *Droit international privé. Tome II*, pp. 445–6 and Van Hecke, 'Confiscation, Expropriation and the Conflict of Laws', 345–57.   [11] Kohler, 'The Confiscation of Criminal Assets', 27.

[12] *U.S. v. $433,461,255.64, and Bank of New York, Republic National Bank, American Express Bank, Banco Commerciale Italiana, Bankamarica International, Citibank, Extebank, Bank of Credit and Commerce, Bancamerica Casa Bancaria et al.*, 89 Civ.2091 (SDNY 1989) (civil forfeiture); *US v Escobar Gaviria* (money laundering); both cited by Harmon, 'United States Money Laundering Laws', 17. See also Ackermann, *Geldwäscherei*, p. 344 and Candler, 'Tracing and Recovering', 17.   [13] Candler, 'Tracing and Recovering', 16.   [14] See *supra* p. 234.

above.[15] Various types of out-of-court settlement can also be used in an international context: co-operating witnesses or plea-bargaining defendants may, for example, agree to transfer funds from abroad to the United States so that the United States obtains enforcement jurisdiction over the property. Defendants may also consent to waive their property rights in favour of the US government, which may then, in its capacity as owner of the property, sell the property abroad or transfer it from abroad to the United States.[16] The possibility of an international application of out-of-court settlements undoubtedly also exists under other domestic law systems and has, for example, explicitly been acknowledged in respect of Dutch law.[17] This practice will normally be able to pass muster at international law: no extra-territorial enforcement of public law takes place if it is an enforcement of a proprietary title.

International co-operation mechanisms for the enforcement of confiscations

Two forms of co-operation

International co-operation for effecting an extra-territorial confiscation order can take two forms: either the foreign confiscation is recognised and enforced in the state where the property is situated or that state institutes new proceedings itself and enforces the confiscation order that is made in those proceedings. The former type of co-operation can be brought under the heading of enforcement of foreign judgments in criminal matters, whereas the latter type is a form of transfer of proceedings in criminal matters. Both forms of co-operation take a foreign confiscation order as a starting point and imply a recognition of it as *res judicata*. In case of a new confiscation procedure in the requested state, the foreign order will serve

[15] See *supra* pp. 58–60.
[16] See Kohler, 'The Confiscation of Criminal Assets', 26–7; Zagaris, 'US International Co-operation', 524 and J. Antenen, 'Problématique nouvelle relative à la poursuite pénale du blanchissage d'argent, à la confiscation et au sort des avoirs confisqués', RPS (1996), 53. See, e.g., the 1993 case involving the *Banque Leu (Luxembourg) SA*, which pleaded guilty in California to a charge of money laundering and agreed to forfeit over US$1,000,000 which had been provisionally seized in Luxembourg: see K. W. Munroe, 'The Extra-territorial Reach of the United States Anti-Money Laundering Laws', in *Money Laundering Control*, ed. B. Rider and M. Ashe (Dublin: Round Hall Sweet & Maxwell, 1996), pp. 300–2.
[17] See Handelingen Tweede Kamer, 1989–90, 21 504, No.3, 50; N. J. M. Ruyters, 'Internationale ontneming', in *Ontneming Crimineel Vermogen in het buitenland* (Congresbundel Zuthpen 4 September 1996, Bureau Ontnemingswetgeving Openbaar Ministerie, Bureau Internationale Rechtshulp van het Ministerie van Justitie), p. 14.

as a starting point for that procedure. The enforcement of a foreign confiscation order is the most direct form of recognising the *res judicata* effect of a foreign confiscation order and implies the recognition of the extraterritorial character of the foreign confiscation order.[18]

Both the Vienna Convention and the Money Laundering Convention cater for both modes of international co-operation, but parties fulfil their treaty obligation if they provide for either mode of co-operation under their domestic law. Notwithstanding the long-standing aversion of recognition of foreign penal law, many states seem to have a preference for the enforcement of foreign confiscation orders.

It is normally the requesting state (i.e. the state that has ordered the confiscation) that will decide whether it will file a request for enforcement of the confiscation or a new confiscation procedure. Ultimately, it depends upon whether the domestic law of the requested state (i.e., the state where the property is located) will be able to accommodate the request. When a state receives a request for the enforcement of a foreign confiscation order, it may still opt to start a new confiscation procedure.[19] In some cases this may even be necessary as, for example, when the requested state receives a request for the enforcement of a confiscation order issued against a corporation but the requested state's legislation does not provide for criminal corporate liability. In that case, the requested state will have to start a new procedure in order to determine in respect of which natural persons' property this confiscation order needs to be made. Exceptionally, the requesting or the requested state might even opt to use a combination of both modes of co-operation. The request for enforcement of a confiscation order might relate to the property representing primary proceeds from crime, whereas a new confiscation procedure might be commenced in respect of secondary proceeds (e.g., interest gained on criminally derived funds held at a bank), or proceeds intermingled with legitimate property, or properties in respect to which third parties have rights. The transfer of proceedings as a consequence of which a confiscation procedure will be commenced in the requested state can be especially apposite in those cases where a defendant has moved most of his property abroad to the requested state, so that the latter will be in a better position to assess the scope of the criminally derived assets, and to order their confiscation, than the state in which the predicate offence took place.

---

[18] Schutte, *Ter vergroting van de afpakkans*, p. 29 and Paridaens, *De overdracht van tenuitvoerlegging van strafvonissen*, p. 14.
[19] *Explanatory Report with the Convention on Laundering*, p. 28.

Both modes of co-operation will hereinafter be discussed, after which it is proposed to analyse some of the common features of both. As with provisional measures, it will be demonstrated that, while putting in place co-operation mechanisms which allow states to enforce confiscation orders on property located in another state than the one in which the criminal proceedings were conducted, these treaty mechanisms still allow the requested state to safeguard its basic concepts of (public) law. The question of whether the conditions and exceptions of these modes of international co-operation can be reconciled with the internationalist approach which was advocated earlier on[20] will be investigated.

Transfer of the enforcement of confiscation orders

The transfer of the enforcement of criminal judgments was introduced in the 1960s and 1970s as a means of attaining a better result in the rehabilitation of international offenders. A number of the treaties that were concluded were primarily aimed at either allowing the transfer of the enforcement of criminal sanctions or at the transfer of prisoners to the state where the offender was domiciled,[21] though some also allowed – albeit in a subordinated manner – for the enforcement of foreign pecuniary criminal sanctions.[22] In the context of the international fight against money laundering, this form of international co-operation, which was originally grounded in social considerations, now serves exclusively repressive goals. This transformation is undoubtedly characteristic of a larger wider neo-classicism movement in criminal law which is gaining ground.

From a legal point of view, the transfer of the enforcement of confiscation orders that is made possible by the Vienna Convention and the Money Laundering Convention constitutes a major innovation. The deeply ingrained character of the rule according to which courts refused to enforce foreign penal law has already been emphasised.[23] Before, the conventions on the transfer of the enforcement of (imprisonment) sanctions

---

[20] See *supra* p. 254.

[21] For an overview of these treaties, see C. Van den Wyngaert and G. Stessens, 'Mutual legal assistance in criminal matters in the European Union', in *Changes in Society, Crime and Criminal Justice in Europe*. Volume II. *International Organised and Corporate Crime*, ed. C. Fijnaut, J. Goethals, T. Peters and L. Walgrave (Antwerp: Kluwer, 1995), pp. 145–67 and Paridaens, *De overdracht van tenuitvoerlegging van strafvonissen*, pp. 62–125.

[22] See the Benelux Convention on the enforcement of judicial decisions (1968) (Articles 42 to 48) and the European Convention on the International Validity of Criminal Judgments (1970) (Article 2).   [23] See *supra* pp. 362–4.

were one of the few examples of treaties that deviated from this well-established rule of (private) international law. Apart from treaties for co-operation in criminal matters, a number of conventions have also been drafted for the purpose of recovering tax debt (*assistance au recouvrement*).[24] Nevertheless, this radical innovation in international co-operation in criminal matters did not come out of the blue, but was foreshadowed by a doctrinal movement. Already in 1964 the Fourth Section of the Ninth Congress of the *Association internationale de droit pénal* had starkly stated that the recognition of foreign criminal judgments was not irreconcilable with the concept of sovereignty.[25] In the same vein, the *Institut de droit international* acknowledged a trend towards increased co-operation and mutual assistance in the enforcement of public law claims.[26] In its resolution, the *Institut de droit international* nevertheless excluded public law claims before foreign courts if the subject-matter of such claims was related to the exercise of governmental power. By way of exception, the resolution allowed such claims if the state of the forum thought this was necessary in view of the subject-matter of the claim, the requirements of international solidarity or the coinciding interests of the states involved.[27]

This mode of co-operation of course requires a procedure for the recognition of foreign confiscation orders (*procédure d'exequatur*), which allows the enforcement of a foreign confiscation order as if it were a confiscation ordered by a domestic court. Unlike with provisional measures, there are no principal objections to such an adversarial procedure as the defendant will already be aware of the confiscation order. In most cases a request for the enforcement of a confiscation order will have been preceded by, or will coincide with, as the case may be, a request for provisional measures. The requested state is in principle bound by 'the findings as to the facts insofar as they are stated in a conviction or judicial decision of the requesting Party or insofar as such conviction or judicial decision is implicitly based on them'.[28] This rule epitomises the larger principle that a request for co-

---

[24] Baade, 'Chapter 12: Operation of Foreign Public Law', 42. See e.g. the Model Convention for Administrative Assistance in the Recovery of Tax Claims of the OECD 1981 (Paris) and the Convention on Mutual Administrative Assistance in Tax Matters, 25 January 1988 (*ILM* (1988), 1160) and the *Explanatory Report on the Convention on Mutual Administrative Assistance in Tax Matters* (Strasbourg, 1989). Cf. J. P. Springer, 'An Overview of International Evidence and Asset Gathering in Civil and Criminal Tax Cases', *Geo.Wash.JInt'l L & Econ.* (1988–89), 300–2.

[25] Resolution I.1: Entschliessungen des IX. Internationalen Strafrechtskongresses in Den Haag, *Z.St.W.* (1965), 685.   [26] *Ann.Inst.dr.int.* (1977, II), 329.

[27] Parts I(a) and (b), II of the Resolution 'Public Law Claims Instituted by a Foreign Authority or a Foreign Public Body', *Ann.Inst.dr.int.* (1977, II), 329–31.

[28] Article 14(2) of the Money Laundering Convention. See also the analogous provision of

operation is deemed to be made in good faith (*principe de confiance, vertrou-wensbeginsel*), a principle which is adhered to in The Netherlands[29] and Switzerland, amongst other countries.[30] The effect of this rule may be clarified by the following example: a defendant who has been convicted for importing 15 kilograms of cocaine cannot dispute this fact by contending it was in fact hash of a lower retail value. Parties may, however, limit the scope of Article 14 of the Money Laundering Convention in accordance with their country's constitutional principles and the basic concepts of its legal system (Article 14(3) of the Money Laundering Convention). Moveover, the fact that the requested state is bound by the facts stated in the judicial decision of the requesting state does not prevent the former from taking into account facts which only came to light, or which occurred, after the original decision was rendered (*factum superveniens*).[31] At any rate, the facts can be given a new qualification by the requested state: thus a ground for non-confiscation that was rejected in the requesting state may still be accepted in the requested state.[32]

Requirement of an enforceable judicial decision

The Money Laundering Convention gives courts exclusive competence to order confiscations (see Article 1(d)) so that the recognition of confiscations is restricted to orders made by courts. Other conventions, such as the Vienna Convention (Article 1(f)), for example, are less restrictive and also allow confiscation, and consequently recognition, of foreign confiscation orders made by non-judicial, administrative authorities.[33] Article 5(4)(c) of the Vienna Convention, however, stipulates that co-operation shall take place 'in accordance with and subject to the provisions' of the requested state. If the latter state's legislation requires that the confiscation order was made by a judicial authority – as is often the case – co-operation is excluded in the case of administrative confiscations.

The judicial decision should be enforceable and definite. This requirement is grounded in considerations relating both to legal security and to

---

Article 42 of the European Convention on the International Validity of Criminal Judgments (1970).

[29] B. Swart, 'Extradition', in *International Criminal Law in the Netherlands*, B. Swart and A. Klip (Freiburg: Max-Planck Institut, 1997), p. 95.

[30] Bernasconi, 'Droits et devoirs de la banque', p. 362.

[31] *Explanatory Report with the Convention on Laundering*, p. 31.

[32] *Explanatory Report with the Convention on Laundering*, p. 32.

[33] See also Article 1(b) of the European Convention on the International Validity of Criminal Judgments (1970).

the rights of the defence. In a purely internal context, a judicial decision will normally be enforceable only after it has obtained the status of *res judicata*. It is only logical that the same requirement be made effective at the international level. Although the fact that a decision has obtained *res judicata* status does not necessarily guarantee that the rights of the defence have been fully respected, this is nevertheless an essential condition to the respect for the rights of the defence. Article 18(4)(e) of the Money Laundering Convention allows a requested state to refuse co-operation when the 'confiscation is either not enforceable in the requesting Party, or it is still subject to ordinary means of appeal'. It is a matter of surprise that this only an optional ground for refusal, whereas Article 27(3)(ii) obliges the requesting party to provide the requested state with an attestation of the fact 'that the confiscation order is enforceable and not subject to ordinary means of appeal'. Many legislators (e.g. those of Belgium,[34] The Netherlands,[35] the UK[36] and Switzerland[37]) have turned this optional ground for refusal into a mandatory requirement under their domestic legislation. Because this requirement has often been laid down in domestic legislation, it is also mandatory in respect of co-operation under the Vienna Convention which, although it does not expressly stipulate this requirement, refers to the domestic legislation of the requested state (Article 5(4)(c)).

In absentia judgments

A traditional stumbling block to international co-operation in the enforcement of foreign criminal judgments are judgments rendered *in absentia*. Examples of the hesitance to co-operate in the enforcement of *in absentia* judgments can be found in the resolutions of the Fourth Section of the Ninth Congress of the *Association internationale de droit pénal* (1964), which in principle excluded the enforcement of foreign judgments rendered *in absentia*.[38] The same hesitance can also be found in treaty provisions which

---

[34] See Article 4, 5° of the Belgian Act of 20 May 1997.
[35] Article 3a of the Dutch Act of 10 September 1986 on the Transfer of Enforcement of Criminal Judgments.
[36] See s.40(1)(a) DTA 1994 and s.97(1)(a) CJA 1988. See McClean, *International Judicial Assistance*, 246. Cf. Article 10(2)(a)(b) of the United Kingdom Model Agreement Concerning Mutual Assistance in Relation to Drug Trafficking (May 1990), reprinted in Mitchell, Hinton and Taylor, *Confiscation*, p. 300.
[37] See Article 94(1) of the Swiss Mutual Assistance Act.
[38] See Resolution II, 1(a). Only in respect of minor offences an exception was made: Entschliessungen des IX. Internationalen Strafrechtskongresses in Den Haag, *Z.St.W.* (1965), 685

allow states to refuse to co-operate in respect of judgments rendered *in absentia*, as, for example, in Article 20 of the European Convention on the International Validity of Criminal Judgments (1970) and Article 3 of the Second Additional Protocol to the European Extradition Convention (1978).[39] A similar ground for refusal is contained in Article 18(4)(f) of the Money Laundering Convention which allows a requested state to refuse co-operation if 'the request relates to a confiscation order resulting from a decision rendered *in absentia* of the person against whom the order was issued and, in the opinion of the requested Party, the proceedings conducted by the requesting Party leading to such decision did not satisfy the minimum rights of defence recognised as due to everyone against whom a criminal charge is made'.

This reluctance of states to co-operate in respect of *in absentia* judgments can be explained by their justifiable wish to safeguard the rights of the defence. The European Court of Human Rights has held that, although Article 6(1) of the European Convention on Human Rights as such does not prohibit *in absentia* procedures – which under certain circumstances may be necessary – a defendant should never be completely deprived of his right to be present at his trial.[40] Particularly in common law systems, the anxiety to respect the rights of the defendant is such that *in absentia* judgments are excluded altogether. This concern to safeguard the rights of the defence should, however, be balanced against the need for effective international co-operation in criminal matters. In the context of money laundering, it may be pointed out that a confiscation order rendered *in absentia* may sometimes be the only manner to deprive an absconded offender of the fruits of his wrongdoing.

In order to avoid a complete breakdown of international co-operation in criminal matters in respect of *in absentia* judgments, the Committee of Ministers of the Council of Europe drafted a Resolution on the criteria governing proceedings held in the absence of the accused (1975).[41] The recommendations contained therein, amongst others, aim at ensuring that defendants are properly summonsed so as to avoid *in absentia* judgments as much possible and to provide persons who have been convicted *in*

---

[39] Strasbourg, 17 March 1978, *ETS*, No. 98.

[40] See *European Court of Human Rights, Colozza v. Italy*, judgment of 12 February 1985, *Publ. ECHR*, Series A, No.89; *Poitrimol v. France*, judgment of 23 November 1993, *Publ.ECHR*, Series A, No.277–A; *Lala v. The Netherlands*, judgment of 22 September 1994, *Publ.ECHR*, Series A, No.297–A and *Pelladoah v. The Netherlands*, judgment of 22 September 1994, *Publ. ECHR*, Series A, No.297–B.

[41] 21 May 1975; reprinted in Müller-Rappard and Bassiouni (eds.), *European Inter-State Co-operation in Criminal Matters*, p. 429.

absentia with the option of lodging an appeal. Many conventions therefore, while allowing states to refuse co-operation in respect of *in absentia*
judgments, at the same time limit the circumstances in which this
ground for refusal can be invoked. Thus Article 18(5) of the Money
Laundering Convention says that a decision shall not be considered to
have been rendered *in absentia* if '(a) it has been confirmed or pronounced
after opposition by the person concerned; or (b) it has been rendered on
appeal, provided that the appeal was lodged by the person concerned'.[42]
In considering whether the minimum rights of defence of a person tried
in his absence have been satisfied, the requested state is also asked to take
into account 'the fact that the person concerned has deliberately sought
to evade justice or the fact that person, having had the possibility of
lodging a legal remedy against the decision made *in absentia*, elected not
to do so' or that 'the person concerned, having been duly served with the
summons to appear, elected not to do so nor to ask for adjournment'. Thus
the drafters of the Money Laundering Convention have taken great care to
ensure that a ground for refusal which was designed to safeguard the
rights of the defence is not used to frustrate co-operation. The only point
of disappointment is that, in respect of requests for the enforcement
of confiscation orders rendered *in absentia*, the Money Laundering
Convention does not provide for a duty for the requested state to take
action to cause the person sentenced to be personally notified of the decision rendered in the requesting state. Such an obligation is, for example,
laid down in Article 23 of the European Convention on the International
Validity of Criminal Judgments (1970).

Transfer of confiscation proceedings

The transfer of proceedings in criminal matters was originally devised as
a co-operation instrument which allowed states to transfer criminal proceedings to the state deemed to be in the best position to try a case: often
the state in which the defendant was residing. This new form of co-
operation in criminal matters was portrayed as an attractive alternative to
extradition, both because of its potential efficacy and because of its advantages for the defendant (who could be tried in his country of residence).
This instrument embodied an international concept of proper administration of justice and gave shape to the idea of an international division of

---

[42] Although the *Explanatory Report with the Convention on Laundering* is silent on this point,
this provision seems to be inspired by Article 21(3) of the European Convention on the
International Validity of Criminal Judgments (1970).

labour as a sinew of international co-operation in criminal matters.[43] The conventions that were drafted with a view to transfer of proceedings received a disappointingly low rate of ratifications, however.[44]

However, under the influence of the new profits-oriented criminal justice policy, this form of co-operation in criminal matters has, like transfer of enforcement of criminal judgments, been given a new dimension and has evolved into a primarily repressive instrument designed to deprive the (alleged) offender of the fruits of his crime.

Both under the Money Laundering Convention and under the Vienna Convention, transfer of proceedings is conceived as an obligation for the requested party to submit the request to its competent authorities (e.g., the prosecuting authorities) for the purpose of obtaining and enforcing a confiscation order. When there is a *prima facie* ground for refusal, the requested state is not, however, obliged to submit a request to its authorities.[45] In the context of the enforcement of confiscation orders, this type of co-operation therefore presupposes that the requesting state has a separate confiscation procedure under its domestic law (independent of the trial of the offender), a procedure that some countries have also created for internal purposes.[46] The requirement of a separate confiscation procedure flows from several factors, the first being that a new procedure which deals exclusively with the question of the confiscation is both more efficient for the state and less burdensome for the defence than a new criminal procedure *in toto*. Moveover, some states are reluctant to conduct entire criminal proceedings in the absence of the defendant: a procedure which is concerned only with the determination of the confiscation may overcome this diffidence. Third, the lack of prescriptive jurisdiction over offences which have taken place abroad may prohibit states from conducting proper criminal proceedings. It has already been argued that this type of co-operation does not necessarily require that the requested state has prescriptive jurisdiction over the offences which gave rise to the confiscation procedure.[47] Moreover, this type of co-operation may also offer the advantage that it allows states to cling on to their traditional refusal to enforce foreign public law.[48]

If the requested state's legislation does not allow for a separate confis-

[43] On these concepts see B. Swart, 'General Observations', in *International Criminal Law in The Netherlands*, ed. B. Swart and A. Klip (Freiburg: Max-Planck Institut, 1997), pp. 17–19.
[44] See Van den Wyngaert and Stessens, 'Mutual Legal Assistance', pp. 161–5 and 177–8.
[45] *Explanatory Report with the Convention on Laundering*, p. 28.
[46] See *supra* pp. 42–3.   [47] See *supra* pp. 247–8.
[48] Schutte, *Ter vergroting van de afpakkans*, p. 29.

cation procedure, this type of co-operation is virtually excluded. The only possibility left, then, is for the requested state to take over criminal proceedings in their entirety for the sole purpose of making a new confiscation order, a very burdensome way of co-operating. Such a complete transfer of criminal proceedings is not provided for by the Vienna Convention or the Money Laundering Convention, but has to take place outside the framework of these two conventions.

The requesting state should provide the requested state with a statement of the facts sufficient to enable the latter to seek the order under its domestic law.[49] The requested state is not bound by this statement, however. Only where the requesting state has made a request for the enforcement of a confiscation order, but the requested state has preferred to institute a new confiscation procedure, will the requested state be bound by the facts, as they were contained in a judicial decision. If the facts of a case have already been tried by the competent authorities of the requesting state, they should not be tried anew by the authorities of the requested state.[50] This rule seems underpinned by (partly) the same rationales as the *non bis in idem* principle, namely that the outcome of judicial proceedings should be accepted (*res judicata pro veritate habetur*) and that a person should not be burdened with being charged with the same offence more than once (*nemo debet bis vexare pro una et eadem causa*).[51]

The locus regit actum principle and its exceptions in the context of enforcing confiscations on foreign request

The importance of the *locus regit actum* principle for international co-operation in criminal matters has already been emphasised.[52] At this point, the consequences of this principle for international co-operation in respect of the enforcement of confiscation orders will be analysed as will the exceptions to this principle that have been inserted in the Money Laundering Convention. It has explicitly been stipulated in the Money Laundering Convention that the law of the requested state (i.e., the *lex fori*) governs matters of procedure and mode of confiscation proceedings as well as matters relating to evidence.[53]

Although simple at first sight, this principle may have particularly intri-

---

[49] Article 5(4)(d)(ii) of the Vienna Convention and Article 27(3)(b) of the Money Laundering Convention.   [50] *Explanatory Report with the Convention on Laundering*, p. 31.

[51] See on these (and other) rationales of the *non bis in idem* principle: Van den Wyngaert and Stessens, 'The *non bis in idem* principle', 784–6.   [52] See *supra* pp. 301–7.

[53] Article 14(1); *Explanatory Report with the Convention on Laundering*, pp. 29–30.

cate ramifications, as is evidenced by the consequences of the principle regarding limitation of actions. This may come into play both in relation to the trial of the original offence and the imposition of a confiscation as well as in relation to the enforcement of a confiscation order. When the imposition or the enforcement of a confiscation order is statute-barred under the law of the requested state, it cannot be enforced even though it may not be barred under the law of the requesting state. Insofar as transfer of confiscation procedures is concerned, this automatically follows from the law of the requested state, irrespective of any treaty provision; a state cannot commence a confiscation procedure if it is statute-barred from doing so under its own law. Concerning the transfer of the enforcement of confiscation procedures, an explicit treaty provision is normally required to justify a refusal of co-operation. Such a ground for refusal is provided by Article 18(4)(c) of the Money Laundering Convention, which allows parties to refuse co-operation if 'under the law of the requested Party confiscation may no longer be imposed or enforced because of the lapse of time'. This optional ground for refusal has been turned into a mandatory requirement under some domestic legislation (e.g., that of Belgium,[54] The Netherlands[55] and Switzerland).[56] Under the Vienna Convention, parties may rely on the broader ground of refusal which allows requested states to refuse measures which, under their domestic law, they would be prohibited from taking in the course of an internal investigation (Article 7(15)(c)).

In the case of the enforcement of a confiscation order that is statute-barred under the law of the requesting state but not under the law of the requested state, Article 18(4)(e) of the Money Laundering Convention still allows the requested state to refuse the enforcement: a confiscation should in principle be enforceable. The requesting party should even inform the requested party of any development by reason of which the confiscation order ceases to be wholly or even partially enforceable.[57] This optional ground for refusal – which has no reciprocal provision in the Vienna Convention – is confined to transfer of enforcement of confiscation orders, however. In the case of the transfer of confiscation proceedings, the question of limitations will not arise in terms of the enforceability of a confiscation order, but in the terms of the possibility of instituting confiscation procedures. If the requesting state is barred from

---

[54] Article 4, 6° of the Belgian Act of 20 May 1997.
[55] Article 6(1) of the Dutch Act of 10 September 1986 on the Transfer of Enforcement of Criminal Judgments.   [56] Article 95(1)(a) of the Swiss Mutual Assistance Act.
[57] Article 31(2)(a) of the Money Laundering Convention. See *Explanatory Report with the Convention on Laundering*, p. 30.

instituting confiscation procedures by lapse of time but the requested state is not, there is nothing in the Money Laundering Convention or the Vienna Convention which obliges the requested state to refuse co-operation. Here, the only possible avenue of action for the person concerned might be an application to a judicial authority in the requesting state for a judicial review of the decision through which a request for co-operation was made, notwithstanding the fact that the requesting state was barred from instituting confiscation proceedings.

Under the Money Laundering Convention there is one main exception to the *locus regit actum* principle which relates to the distinction between object and value confiscation. States whose legislation only provides for one model of confiscation can, on account of the *locus regit actum* principle, comply only with requests made under that model of confiscation. This may give rise to insoluble problems under the Vienna Convention. For example, when State A requests the enforcement of a value confiscation order to State B which is only familiar with object confiscation, State B will not be able to comply with State A's request. With a view to achieving effective international co-operation, Article 7(2)(a) of the Money Laundering Convention therefore requires states to operate both models of confiscation for the purposes of international co-operation. The EU Joint Action of 3 December 1998 concerning arrangments for co-operation between Member States in respect of the identification, tracing, freezing or seizing and confiscation of instrumentalities and the proceeds from crime contains the same requirement. This has, for example, been made possible in Belgian,[58] Dutch[59] and English[60] law. Article 13(3) of the Money Laundering Convention obliges parties to allow requests for value confiscation, including cases where the requested state does not operate this model of confiscation for internal purposes: if payment is not voluntarily made, the requested party should enforce the claim on any property available for that purpose. This may also include property owned by third persons (e.g., ostensible persons) or in cases where some type of revocatory action might be invoked under domestic law.[61] A request for the confiscation of a specific item of property (object confiscation) will be enforced on this item of property, unless, however, parties 'agree that the requested Party may enforce the confiscation in the form of a requirement to pay a sum of money corresponding to the value of the property' (Article 13(4)).

---

[58] Article 5 of the Belgian Act of 20 May 1997.
[59] Article 31a(2) of the Dutch Act of 10 September 1986 on the Transfer of Enforcement of Criminal Judgments.   [60] S.96(2) CJA 1988 and s.39(2) DTA 1994.
[61] *Explanatory Report with the Convention on Laundering,* p. 29.

Condition of double criminality and double 'confiscability'

In circumstances where a confiscation cannot be obtained in a domestic context, several provisions of the Money Laundering Convention allow a requested state to refuse co-operation in the enforcement of confiscation orders. Co-operation is thus governed by, and effectively limited to, the domestic concepts of confiscation of the requested state.

The most obvious optional ground for refusal under the Money Laundering Convention is double criminality, which has been fiercely criticised elsewhere in this book[62] and which has been made into a mandatory condition in many domestic legal systems (see, e.g., Belgian,[63] Dutch,[64] English[65] and Swiss[66] legislation) in the context of co-operation for the purpose of (making and) enforcing confiscation orders.

Co-operation may, moreover, also be refused if, under the national legislation of the requested state, confiscation is not provided for in respect of the offence for which assistance was requested (Article 18(4)(a) of the Money Laundering Convention). Some parties to the Money Laundering Convention have made a declaration under Article 2 of the convention limiting the scope of confiscation to certain specified offences. The Netherlands, for example, has excluded confiscation in relation to offences punishable under legislation on taxation or customs and excise. In respect of the offences for which confiscation is not provided, they may therefore refuse co-operation, even when the condition of double criminality is fulfilled.

Co-operation in the field of confiscation can also be refused if this 'would be contrary to the principles of the domestic laws of the requested Party concerning the limits of confiscation in respect of the relationship between an offence and (i) an economic advantage that might be qualified as its proceeds; or (ii) property that might be qualified as its instrumentalities' (Article 18(4)(b) of the Money Laundering Convention). The stricture indicated by the wording 'an economic advantage that might be qualified as its proceeds', however, does not allow a requested state to refuse co-operation for the reason that the request relates to value confiscation, the enforcement of which might involve property that has no relation to the offence. Article 13(3) of the Convention obliges states to co-operate in respect of the enforcement of value confiscations. Article

---

[62] See *supra* pp. 295–8.   [63] See Article 4, 2° of the Belgian Act of 20 May 1997.

[64] Article 3 of the Dutch Act of 10 September 1986 on the Transfer of Enforcement of Criminal Judgments.   [65] See s.96(2) CJA 1988.

[66] See Article 94(1)(b) of the Swiss Mutual Assistance Act.

18(4)(b) refers only to the assessment stage and allows the requested state to refuse co-operation when, for example, the relationship between the proceeds and the offence is too remote to qualify for confiscation under the domestic law of the requested state.[67] An example would be a request for the confiscation of legitimate assets which, under the domestic law of the requesting state, have become liable to confiscation by the mere fact that they have been intermingled with the proceeds of crime.

Requirement of a judicial decision

A request for confiscation which does not relate to 'a previous conviction, or a decision of a judicial nature or a statement in such a decision that an offence or several offences have been committed, on the basis of which the confiscation has been ordered or is sought' can also be refused. This ground for refusal (Article 18(4)(d) of the Money Laundering Convention) was particularly designed in view of the possibility which exists under some domestic legislations of obtaining a confiscation order without a conviction of the (alleged) offender or on the basis of a conviction which relates only to one (or a few) of the larger group of offences, the proceeds of which have been taken into account to make a confiscation order. The latter possibility exists under both Dutch and English law, for example.[68] The mere fact that such possibility does not exist under the law of the requested state does not justify a refusal of co-operation, however. Article 18(4)(d) only allows a requested state to refuse co-operation with respect to this type of conviction if no judicial decision exists in which it has been ascertained that these offences have been committed. Thus, co-operation may, for example, be refused in respect of American civil *in rem* forfeitures which are ordered without any criminal proceedings. Some states, such as the United Kingdom, for example, have nevertheless agreed to co-operate in respect of confiscations that are issued in *in rem* procedures, even if outside the treaty framework of the Money Laundering Convention.[69]

Purely administrative confiscations are likewise excluded from the scope of co-operation.[70] A requested state may, moreover, refuse co-operation if it thinks that the rights of the defence or the presumption of

---

[67] *Explanatory Report with the Convention on Laundering*, p. 40.   [68] See *supra* pp. 71–4.

[69] *Re: F Crown Office*, judgment of 15 November 1996, (http//www.fear.org). Cf. *Re S-L* ([1995] 4 All ER 159) and *Re JL Drug Trafficking Offences Act 1986*, *The Times*, 4 May 1989 (QBD), cited Smith, 'In Rem Forfeiture Proceedings', 906.

[70] *Explanatory Report with the Convention on Laundering*, p. 41.

innocence have not been respected in the procedure which led to the imposition of the confiscation order.[71]

Co-operation can also be refused when the requested state is of the opinion that 'the importance of the case to which the request relates, does not justify the taking of the action sought'. Although this ground for refusal in Article 18(1)(c) of the Money Laundering Convention applies to all stages of international co-operation, it will be especially important at the stage of enforcement of confiscation orders. According to the Explanatory Report, this ground for refusal is intended to cover three different types of situation. First, there may be an imbalance between the action sought and the offence to which it relates as, for example, when the confiscation of a large sum of money is sought for a relatively minor offence, or when the costs involved in enforcing (or obtaining) a confiscation order outweigh the expected law enforcement benefit. Second, the sum may as such be too small to justify the use of international co-operation mechanisms: the maxim *de minimis non curat praetor* also holds true on an international level. Third, co-operation should also be avoided where the offence itself is inherently minor.

Unlike the previously discussed grounds for refusal, this exception is not linked to the legal system of the requested system, nor is it designed to safeguard the main legal principles of the latter. The disproportionality exception may, for example, also be invoked when the possibility of making confiscation orders is not limited by any proportionality requirement under the domestic law of the requested state. Nevertheless, the requested state which invokes this ground for refusal will often do so on the basis of concepts with which it is familiar under its own legal system.

Excluded exceptions

Lastly, it is also necessary to mention a number of exceptions that have explicitly been excluded: parties can under no circumstances invoke these factors to refuse co-operation. Article 18(7) of the Money Laundering Convention excludes banking secrecy as an exception, not only at the investigation or provisional measures stages, but also at the stage of the enforcement of confiscation orders. Article 5(3) of the Vienna Convention offers the same guarantees.

Article 18(8) of the Money Laundering Convention, moreover, forbids parties from refusing to co-operate on the ground that: either the person

---

[71] On this ground for refusal see *in extenso infra* pp. 400–7.

subjected to a confiscation order by the authorities of the requesting party is a legal person; or that the natural person against whom an order of confiscation of proceeds has been issued has subsequently died, or that a legal person against whom an order of confiscation of proceeds has been issued has subsequently been dissolved. Under some circumstances the obligation to co-operate in the making and enforcement of a confiscation order against a natural person who has died may be contrary to Article 6 of the European Convention on Human Rights. As explained earlier, the European Court of Human Rights has held that a criminal sanction cannot be ordered after the person to whose conduct it relates has died.[72] It is submitted that, under these circumstances, co-operation should be refused on the ground that co-operation would be contrary to the fundamental principles of the legal system of the requested party. The possibility of invoking this independent ground for refusal, which will be discussed shortly, is expressly safeguarded by Article 18(8) of the Money Laundering Convention. It is to be feared that the same safety break will also be used by some states to refuse to enforce confiscation orders against juristic persons in defiance of the text of Article 18(8)(a).

Ordre public, fundamental legal principles and human rights

The thesis that the willingness of states to co-operate in the international fight against money laundering, and in particular against the enforcement of confiscation orders, is restricted by that which is acceptable according to the legal concepts of the requested state, is nowhere more clearly epitomised than in the grounds for refusal which tend to safeguard the *ordre public* and the fundamental legal principles of the requested state.

The *ordre public* exception in international co-operation in criminal matters, a classic ground for refusal, is contained in many mutual assistance treaties[73] and in domestic legal systems[74] as well, which acts as a safety valve: it allows the state to refuse co-operation when its essential

---

[72] *European Court of Human Rights, AP, MP and TP v. Switzerland*, judgment of 29 August 1997, *Reports of Judgments and Decisions* (1997–V), 1447. See *supra* pp. 55 and 68.

[73] This exception is, for example, also contained in the European Mutual Assistance Convention (Article 2(b)), the UN Model Treaty on Mutual Assistance in Criminal Matters (Article 4(1)(a)) and the Commonwealth Scheme Relating to Mutual Assistance in Criminal Matters (Article 7(2)(a)).

[74] See, e.g., Article 3(1)1° of the Belgian Act of 20 May 1997; and Article 1a of the Swiss Mutual Assistance Act.

interests are at risk. Because it is worded in broad terms, it can be invoked in a wide variety of situations. Article 18(1)(b) of the Money Laundering Convention and Article 7(15)(b) of the Vienna Convention allow a requested state to refuse the execution of a request which is likely to prejudice the 'sovereignty, security, *ordre public* or other essential interests' of the requested state. The Money Laundering Convention, moreover, contains a reference to 'the fundamental principles of the legal system of the requested Party'. If the action sought would be contrary to the law of the requested party, it may refuse co-operation (Article 18(1)(a)). This type of ground for refusal was also inserted in earlier conventions of the Council of Europe regarding primary assistance.[75] The Vienna Convention lacks a similar provision, but stipulates that the procedures specified in the request for co-operation will be executed only to the extent that they are compatible with the domestic law of the requested state.

The distinction between this and the *ordre public* exception is not always clear-cut and the two exceptions may to a certain extent overlap, although there are of course a number of situations which might justify a recourse to the *ordre public* exception, but which would not involve a violation of the fundamental legal principles of the requested state. It seems clear therefore that the *ordre public* exception is designed to function in the context of secondary assistance,[76] whereas reference to the fundamental legal principles of the requested state is more apt in the context of primary assistance, where it would be inconceivable for the requested state to take over (enforcement) proceedings in defiance of the fundamental principles of its legal system.

It is submitted that the function of this type of exception should be moderated in the context of the enforcement of foreign confiscation orders, in that a foreign decision, made in accordance with foreign law, already exists so that its influence on the domestic law system of the requested state is therefore likely to be minimal. In the context of private international law, it is likewise accepted that the *ordre public* exception should, to a great extent, be less invoked to refuse the recognition and enforcement of foreign judgments than to reject the application of

---

[75] See the European Convention on the Transfer of Proceedings in Criminal Matters (1972) (Article 11(j)) and the European Convention on the International Validity of Criminal Judgments (1970) (Article 6(a)).

[76] See, however, Resolution II.3. of the Fourth Section of the Ninth Congress of the Association Internationale de Droit Pénal in 1964: Entschliessungen des IX. Internationalen Strafrechtskongresses in Den Haag, *Z.St.W.* (1965), 686.

foreign law by a domestic court (a type of situation which is in principle excluded in criminal proceedings).[77] The *ordre public* exception may play a much stronger role in the application of foreign evidence, both in criminal[78] and civil[79] proceedings, where it may be used to exclude evidence which was gathered in a way that is irreconcilable with the *ordre public* or the fundamental legal principles of the requested state. This type of *ordre public* exception should, however, be sharply distinguished from the type of *ordre public* exception that is used in the context of international co-operation. In the context of international co-operation, the exception functions as a shield to protect states from foreign requests for co-operation, whereas in the context of foreign evidence it is used to exclude the use of foreign evidence in a domestic procedure, because of the quirky evidence-gathering methods that may have been used by the requesting state. This latter type of *ordre public* exception is applied by the courts (as is done in the context of private international law), whereas the former exception is often applied by an administrative authority (e.g. a department of Justice) which is responsible for controlling the (*prima facie*) admissibility of foreign requests for co-operation.

Whether the *ordre public* exception or the 'fundamental legal principles' exception needs to be invoked, will always depends on the concrete circumstances of the request. Nevertheless, a number of typical examples can be enumerated. Thus the domestic law of the requested state may forbid it to confiscate certain types of property (e.g. because a minimum of income is guaranteed to every person or because it is statutorily or even constitutionally forbidden to confiscate a person's entire estate). Exorbitant jurisdiction claims made by the requesting party may likewise justify a refusal of co-operation founded in reference to the 'fundamental legal principles' of the requested state. Another case in point would be where the interests of the requested state's own nationals could be jeopardised as, for example, when a request for enforcement of a confiscation order concerns property which is already subject to a restraint order for a privileged creditor.[80]

---

[77] See B. Audit, *Droit international privé* (Paris: Economica, 1995), p. 263; Rigaux, *Droit international privé, Tome I. Théorie générale*, p. 344 and J. Kropholler, *Internationales Privatrecht* (Tübingen: J. C. B. Mohr (Paul Siebeck), 1994), p. 223. See also the decision of the French Supreme Court of 17 April 1953, *Rev.Crit.DIP* (1953), 412 with annotation by H. Battifol.

[78] As is the case, for example, in the case law of the Belgian Supreme Court: see, e.g., the judgments of 19 February 1985, *Arr.Cass.* (1984–85), No.370; of 26 January 1993, *RDP* (1993), 768; of 12 October 1993, *Arr.Cass.* (1993), No.404 and 30 May 1995, *R.Cass.* (1996), 151.

[79] See Dalloz, *Répertoire de droit internationale*, T. II, v° *Preuve*, Nos.28, 57–9 and 61.

[80] See on these examples: *Explanatory Report with the Convention on Laundering*, pp. 35–6.

These exceptions should not be invoked in a general way to refuse any request for co-operation that deviates from the national law of the requested country. This thesis is also accepted in private international law, where a distinction is made between the internal *ordre public* and the international *ordre public*, the latter concept being much more restricted than the former.[81] The ground for refusal of Article 18(1)(a) of the Money Laundering Convention is rightly restricted to the fundamental principles of the legal system of the requested party. Among the most fundamental legal principles are undoubtedly human rights, which, although internationally recognised, may also have national aspects. By inserting the ground for refusal contained in Article 18(1)(a), the drafters of the Money Laundering Convention have ensured that the obligation to co-operate under this convention cannot conflict with other international obligations under human rights treaties. Such a conflict is possible under extradition treaties, for example, into which this type of ground for refusal is typically not inserted. Thus, a state can refuse to enforce a foreign confiscation order that has been made pursuant to a reversal of the burden of proof which it considers contrary to the presumption of innocence enshrined in Article 6(2) of the European Convention on Human Rights. It would, however, not be acceptable to refuse co-operation because of a reversal of the burden of proof, if such a burden of proof was also accepted under the domestic law of the requested state, albeit in respect of a different type of offence.[82]

This type of ground for refusal is typically optional and its operation is in any event determined by the requested state. The question may arise, therefore, as to whether there are circumstances in which, from a human rights viewpoint, a requested state is obliged to refuse co-operation and whether it may engage its human rights responsibility by not doing so. The question is especially likely to arise in the context of the enforcement of foreign confiscation orders when the confiscation order was made in the course of a procedure which did not meet the Convention's fundamental human rights requirements.

Thus, a requested state may be confronted with a situation where a foreign confiscation order is based on evidence which was gathered through what the requested state considers to be a violation of human rights. Such evidence would undoubtedly be excluded in a domestic

---

[81] See the judgment of the Belgian Supreme Court of 4 May 1950, *Pasicrisie* (1950, I), 642. See Rigaux, *Droit international privé, Tome I: Théorie générale*, p. 347 and Van Hecke and Lenaerts, *Internationaal Privaatrecht*, pp. 82 and 169.

[82] *Explanatory Report with the Convention on Laundering*, p. 35.

procedure in the requested state by force of the *ordre public* exception, but it is not certain whether a state should always refuse co-operation for that reason. In the context of the transfer of the enforcement of criminal judgments, including confiscation orders, the (human rights) responsibility of states is not the same. A foreign confiscation order or judicial decision is in the first place the responsibility of the requesting state in which that order or decision was made. It is submitted that the human rights responsibility of the requested state is less acute in the context of the transfer of the enforcement of criminal sanctions than in the context of other, secondary co-operation mechanisms since criminal proceedings, in which the defendant will have had the right to complain of possible infringements of his human rights, will already have taken place. This is not to say that the question of the human rights responsibility of the requested state can be ignored altogether. It seems that, in delineating the responsibility of the requested state, the principle of mutual trust can play an important role. The requested state is in principle entitled to assume that the criminal judgment or the confiscation order was rendered in accordance with a human rights requirement, certainly when the requesting state is party to an international human rights convention. But even if the requesting state is not party to an international human rights convention, the requested state should not be burdened with a duty to investigate whether any human rights infringements have taken place in the requesting state. It is submitted that the responsibility of the requested state for human rights violations that occurred in the requesting state should be limited to cases where states agree to co-operate in the face of flagrant violations of human rights in the requesting state. This also follows from the decision of the European Court of Human Rights in *Drozd and Janousek v. France and Spain.*[83] Drozd and Janousek were sentenced in Andorra to a term of imprisonment of fourteen years, which they could choose to serve either in France or in Spain. After having chosen to serve their sentence in France and having been transferred to France, they filed a complaint with the European Commission of Human Rights for violation of Article 6 of the European Convention on Human Rights by France and Spain (Andorra, where the trial and the alleged violation of Article 6 had taken place, could not be the subject of a complaint as it was not a party to the Convention) and Article 5 by France. The Court did not find that either Article had been violated:

---

[83] European Court of Human Rights, judgment of 26 June 1992, *Publications of the European Court of Human Rights*, Series A, No.240.

As the Convention does not require the Contracting Parties to impose its standards on third territories, France was not obliged to verify whether the proceedings which resulted in the conviction were compatible with all the requirements of Article 6 of the Convention. To require such a review of the manner in which a court not bound by the Convention has applied the principles enshrined in Article 6 would also thwart the current trend towards strengthening international co-operation in the administration of justice, a trend which is in principle in the interest of the persons concerned. The Contracting States are, however, obliged to refuse their co-operation if it emerges that the conviction is the result of a flagrant denial of justice.[84]

It seems that this limitation of the requested state's responsibility to 'flagrant denials of justice' is justified on several grounds. It would indeed be risky to attempt to restrain international co-operation in an undue manner. Some states, such as those who apply different procedural standards, for example, might *de facto* be prevented from international co-operation. Other states who may be party to an international human rights convention might be reluctant to engage in international co-operation in view of the risk of being held internationally responsible for human rights violations, should such violations eventually be found to have taken place. Another point which merits attention is that to accept a charge of a human rights violation entails much graver consequences in this than in a purely domestic context, for in the former context it will automatically result in a refusal to enforce a foreign confiscation order.

Whether a conviction or a confiscation order is the result of a flagrant denial of justice, is of course impossible to sum up in a formula, but examples would be where a defendant was denied the right to assistance by counsel, or was not given the opportunity to have sufficient time and facilities to prepare his defence.[85]

It is, moreover, important to point out that the limited possibility of establishing a requested state's responsibility for violations of human rights under Article 6 was only accepted under the 'umbrella' of Article 5 of the Convention, that is, via the requirement of lawful detention by the state to which the enforcement of an imprisonment sanction was transferred. The case law of the European Court of Human Rights and the

---

[84] European Court of Human Rights, judgment of 26 June 1992, *Publications of the European Court of Human Rights*, Series A, No.240, para. 110. This line of case law was confirmed in *Iribarne Pérez v. France*, judgment of 24 October 1995, *Publications of the European Court of Human Rights*, Series A, No.325–C, para. 29.

[85] See S. Trechsel, 'The Role of International Organs controlling Human Rights in the Field of International Co-operation', in *Principles and Procedures for a New Transnational Criminal Law*, ed. A. Eser and O. Lagodny (Freiburg: Max-Planck Institut, 1992), pp. 658–9.

European Commission of Human Rights itself, is predicated on an 'organic' criterion of allocating human rights responsibility in an international (criminal law) context: the question of which state is responsible for human rights violations is determined by which state's organs have so acted.[86] Thus, as the criminal proceedings in *Drozd and Janousek* were not conducted before organs of the French state, France could not directly be held responsible for alleged violations of Article 6.[87]

In the context of transfer of enforcement of confiscation orders, a strict adherence to this criterion would exclude any possible human rights responsibility for alleged violations of Article 6 on the part of the requested state: direct responsibility is excluded if its organs have not interfered in any way in the procedure that led to the imposition of the confiscation order, and indirect responsibility under the heading of Article 5 is obviously also excluded in the context of pecuniary sanctions. It is submitted that such an absolute thesis cannot be accepted. In *Soering v. the United Kingdom*, the European Court of Human Rights accepted, as a matter of principle, that a requested state may refuse extradition in order to avoid a flagrant violation of Article 6 in the requesting state.[88] Even though that case concerned a future violation of human rights in the course of an ongoing procedure, the same line of reasoning should *a fortiori* be adhered to if the flagrant violation has already taken place. This allows the European Convention on Human Rights, and any other human rights instrument, to have the effect it was intended to have namely, to attain a higher protection of human rights (*effet utile*). It may moreover be pointed out that, whereas the exclusion of human rights responsibility of the state that enforces a sanction may be justified on humanitarian grounds in the context of transfer of imprisonment sanctions (namely to allow the convicted person to serve his sentence in his 'home' state), such humanitarian considerations are completely lacking in the context of the enforcement of confiscation orders.

With respect to the second form of co-operation, it is extremely unlikely that a state which commences confiscation proceedings at the request of

---

[86] European Court of Human Rights, *Loizidou v. Turkey*, judgment of 23 March 1995, *Publications of the European Court of Human Rights*, Series A, No.310, paras.61–2. See on this topic: Klip, 'The Decrease of Protection under Human Rights Treaties', 304–9.

[87] See European Court of Human Rights, judgment of 26 June 1992, *Publications of the European Court of Human Rights*, Series A, No.240, paras. 84–97.

[88] European Court of Human Rights, judgment of 7 July 1989, *Publications of the European Court of Human Rights*, Series A, No.161. For comment, see C. Van den Wyngaert, 'Applying the European Convention on Human Rights to Extradition: Opening Pandora's Box', *ICLQ* (1990), 757–79.

a foreign state will be obliged to live by its human rights obligations. What if the requested state is, however, provided with a judicial decision rendered in proceedings which clearly did not meet the human rights requirements of Article 6? It is submitted that in such circumstances the requested state should equally refuse to lend its assistance to the enforcement of a foreign judicial decision which was the result of a flagrant denial of justice, even though this assistance may have been rendered through the commencement of a confiscation procedure. To suggest otherwise would imply that a state which is confronted with a request for the enforcement of a foreign confiscation order which was the result of a flagrant denial of justice, could avoid its human rights responsibility by starting new confiscation proceedings, circumstances which cannot be described as acceptable.

International non bis in idem

One of the most forceful arguments against the unilateral enforcement of extra-territorial confiscations is that they may give rise to double payment obligations for third parties, such as financial institutions, for example, which may therefore end up paying twice: once to the state which made the confiscation order and once to the customer in the country where the confiscation was not recognised. The double jeopardy problem with which we are concerned here is of a different nature: *non bis in idem* protection relates to the defendant. The problems of avoiding 'double confiscation' at a national level[89] are compounded when transferred to the international level, where more than one state may wish to order confiscation. This can only be avoided through the effective operation of an international *non bis in idem* principle.

Such an international *non bis in idem* principle can function in three different contexts. The outcome of foreign procedures can be taken into account first, when prosecuting a person for a crime committed on the territory of the state concerned; second, when prosecuting a person for a crime committed on the territory of another state (i.e. when exercising extra-territorial jurisdiction); and, third, when taking part in international co-operation in criminal matters. Only in respect of the third function, have specific provisions been created, albeit only in the Money Laundering Convention (the Vienna Convention is silent on the subject). In the following, it will be argued that the specificity of the international

---

[89] See *supra* pp. 79–81.

fight against money laundering calls for a specific international *non bis in idem* protection.

The lack of an effective international *non bis in idem* protection under international human rights law is well known. Notwithstanding the fact that the first and most important rationale of the *non bis in idem* principle, the protection of the individual, seems as valid on an international as on a domestic plane, the relevant human right provisions offer no protection in this respect. Article 4 of the Seventh Additional Protocol to the European Convention on Human Rights explicitly stipulates that it offers protection only as far as proceedings in the same state are concerned, and the Human Rights Committee has held the same in respect of Article 14, para. 7 of the International Covenant on Civil and Political Rights.[90] Many continental courts, in contrast to their common law counterparts, have consistently refused to recognise foreign criminal judgments as *res judicata*, certainly in the case of territorial offences, that is offences committed on the territory of the state that institutes new proceedings.[91]

The reason for this reluctance of many states to recognise foreign criminal judgments as *res judicata* is in part rooted in sovereignty-related motives, but may also stem from a concern for the effective punishment of crimes. The first international *non bis in idem* rules drafted under the aegis of the Council of Europe (Articles 53–5 of the 1970 European Convention on the International Validity of Criminal Judgements and Articles 35–7 of the 1972 European Convention on the Transfer of Proceedings in Criminal Matters) as well as Article 54 of the Schengen Convention, recognise the *non bis in idem* effect of a foreign sentence only insofar as it has been served or is currently being served or can no longer be carried out under the sentencing laws of the other state involved. In keeping with these provisions, it is submitted that the *non bis in idem* effect of foreign confiscation orders should under no circumstances be recognised if the order has not yet been enforced. Another exception contained in these treaties is less expedient: the *non bis in idem* effect of foreign judgments is 'excluded in respect of offences that took place on the territory of the requested state'. International *non bis in idem* is thus guaranteed only in the second context (prosecuting of extra-territorial offences), but not in the first context as there is no bar to new prosecutions for territo-

---

[90] Decision of 16 July 1986 in the case of *AP v. Italy* (Communication No.204/1986, CCPR/C/31/D/204/1986, para. 7.3.). Cf. M. J. Bossuyt, *Guide to the 'Travaux Préparatoires' of the International Covenant on Civil and Political Rights* (Dordrecht: Martinus Nijhoff, 1987), p. 316.

[91] See *in extenso* Van den Wyngaert and Stessens, 'The International *Non Bis In Idem*', 786–8.

rial offences. This may effectively empty the international *non bis in idem* rule from its content in respect of money laundering offences, which may often be located very easily in the territory of the requested state.[92]

Another point of criticism concerns the way the international *non bis in idem* is conceived, namely, as a bar to prosecutions for 'the same offence'. It has already been pointed out, in the context of the national *non bis in idem* protection, that, in order to afford protection against 'double confiscation', previously imposed payment obligations in respect of the same proceeds derived from the same facts should be imputed to the new confiscation sanction (*Anrechnungsprinzip*). This should also be done in an international context, where foreign, enforced, confiscation orders (or otherwise fulfilled payment obligations) should be imputed to the new confiscation order.

In the third context, that of the enforcement of foreign criminal judgments including confiscation orders, an international *non bis in idem* principle can have various functions.

A first function which is generally attributed to the principle is to exclude co-operation when the requested state or a third state has already undertaken action with respect to the same offence. Article 18(1)(e) of the Money Laundering Convention allows a requested state to refuse co-operation if it 'considers that compliance with the action sought would be contrary to the principle of *ne bis in idem*'. This goes much less far than the relevant provisions of the 1970 European Convention on the International Validity of Criminal Judgements and of the 1972 European Convention on the Transfer of Proceedings in Criminal Matters, however. As the Money Laundering Convention does not define *non bis in idem* in any way, this provision will be construed in accordance with the domestic law of the requested state so that it does not provide any additional protection other than that flowing from the national law of the requested state (except for having inserted the possibility of invoking this ground of refusal in the context of co-operation based on the convention). Given the restricted nature of many domestic international *non bis in idem* provisions, it is to be feared that co-operation will be refused only where the requested state has itself already taken action in respect of the foreign offence, and not where the offence has already been tried in a third state. In the latter circumstances, co-operation will be refused only if the domestic law of the requested state expressly so stipulates (see e.g. Article 5 of the Swiss Mutual Assistance Act).

---

[92] See *supra* pp. 217–25.

The second function of the international *non bis in idem* principle in the context of international co-operation is that it prohibits the requested state from taking any further action after it has agreed to co-operate. Where new confiscation proceedings have been commenced, this function is normally automatically guaranteed by the *res judicata* effect of the confiscation order that, pursuant to the request for co-operation, will have been made under the law of the requested state. In the case of the recognition of a foreign confiscation order, this order will have the same *res judicata* effect as a domestic confiscation order.

Lastly, the *non bis in idem* principle in international co-operation should also ensure that the requesting state is barred from attempting to enforce a confiscation order after it has transferred its enforcement to another state, or from commencing confiscation proceedings after it has transferred confiscation proceedings to another state. In the past, this function did not receive much attention, as *non bis in idem* was conceived as a bar to new prosecutions rather than as a bar to new enforcement actions (or new confiscation proceedings). It should nevertheless be considered as an essential part of a well-functioning international *non bis in idem* rule.[93] The provisions contained in the Money Laundering Convention in this respect are wholly unsatisfactory. Article 16 of the Convention stipulates that:

1 A request for confiscation made under Article 13 does not affect the right of the requesting Party to enforce itself the confiscation order.
2 Nothing in this Convention shall be so interpreted as to permit the total value of the confiscation to exceed the amount of the sum of money specified in the confiscation order. If a Party finds that this might occur, the Parties concerned shall enter into consultations to avoid such an effect.

According to the Explanatory Report,[94] this provision is inspired by Article 11 of the 1970 European Convention on the International Validity of Criminal Judgements, according to which the sentencing state may no longer itself begin enforcement of a sanction which it has requested another state to enforce. This is, however, not the effect of Article 16 of the Money Laundering Convention, which, to the contrary, expressly preserves the right of the requesting state itself to enforce the confiscation order. This possibility can hardly be dismissed as a merely theoretically danger. Via the technique of value confiscation – which allows the

---

[93] See in this respect also Article 5 of the Resolution of the Institut de droit international, accepted at the Bath Session (1950) (*Annuaire de l'Institut de droit international* (1950, II) pp. 313–14.   [94] *Explanatory Report with the Convention on Laundering*, p. 33.

requested state to enforce a confiscation order on legitimate property – a person against whom a confiscation order was made still stands a substantial risk of being subjected to the enforcement of such an order, even though its enforcement has been transferred to another state (where it may already have been enforced). Paragraph 2 of Article 16 calls on parties to enter into consultations to prevent the total value of property confiscated from exceeding the sum of money specified in the confiscation order, but this does not provide the individual concerned with an enforceable right. To this end, it would have been preferable to have inserted a self-executing provision which would have forbidden states to enforce a confiscation order after it had already been enforced by another state.

Rights of third parties

The need for and the difficulties in protecting the rights of *bona fide* third parties have already been underlined in Part 1.[95] It was shown that the international requirements regarding the protection of the rights of third parties are limited to procedural requirements, that is, the obligation for states to make available to third parties all the necessary recourse to their (proprietary) rights. Such an obligation can obviously be truly effective in an international context only if the obligation to notify third parties extends to third parties living outside the state that takes the measures that may affect their rights. This requires extra-territorial notification[96] which is made possible (though not obligated) by Article 21 of the Money Laundering Convention.

But even when foreign third parties are duly notified, it may prove difficult to guarantee effective protection of the rights of third parties, as the property on which those rights have to be enforced is often located in another country. In an international context, the state that has instituted criminal proceedings against a defendant and has made a judgment in favour of third parties is typically not the state in which the property is located. In the following, the various techniques for international cooperation that allow these difficulties to be overcome will be discussed. Different hypotheses will be identified, according to whether third parties wish to claim their rights in the requesting state (i.e. the state in which the criminal proceedings took place) or in the requested state (i.e. the state in which the property that is liable to confiscation is located). The state in

---

[95] See *supra* pp. 76–9.
[96] On the possible international law ramifications of extra-territorial notifications, see *supra* pp. 321–7.

which third parties choose to avail themselves of their rights may depend on a wide variety of factors, but the domicile of the third parties is likely to be one of the most important.

It is proposed to examine first two modalities of international co-operation that tend to safeguard the rights of third parties in the requesting state, namely, the recognition of judgments regarding third parties' rights taken in the requesting state and the transfer of property to another state with a view to its restitution to third parties. As a third point, the possibility of obtaining a decision on the rights of third parties in the requested state will be investigated.

If a decision regarding the rights of third parties has already been taken in the requesting state, that is, the state which has ordered the confiscation (or at an earlier stage, the state which has taken provisional measures), the question arises as to what is the value of such a decision in the requested state. According to Article 22 of the Money Laundering Convention, such decisions need in principle to be recognised by the requested state, but provision is made in respect of a number of important exceptions to this rule:

1   When dealing with a request for co-operation under Section 3 and 4, the requested Party shall recognise any judicial decision taken in the requesting Party regarding rights claimed by third parties.
2   Recognition may be refused if:
   (a)   third parties did not have adequate opportunity to assert their rights; or
   (b)   the decision is incompatible with a decision already taken in the requested Party on the same matter; or
   (c)   it is incompatible with the *ordre public* of the requested Party; or
   (d)   the decision was taken contrary to provisions on exclusive jurisdiction provided for by the law of the requested Party.

These exceptions are inspired by the Brussels Convention on jurisdiction and enforcement of judgments of 1968 which enumerates the circumstances in which a court of one state has exclusive competence (Article 16) and in which foreign judgments are consequently excluded from recognition and enforcement (Article 27).[97] This provision is self-sufficient so that it can in principle be applied directly in the requested state.

Older conventions sometimes provide for another instrument that makes it possible to safeguard the rights of third parties in the requesting state, namely, the transfer of property from the requested state to the

[97] Tweede Kamer, 1990–91, 22083, No.3, 20.

requesting state (which can, then, restore the property to its lawful owner). It may be a matter of some surprise that this instrument is often found in extradition treaties (e.g. in the treaty between Belgium and Switzerland),[98] but is absent in the multilateral money laundering conventions as well as in many mutual legal assistance treaties. Thus, transfer of property to the requesting state is not possible under the American–Swiss MLAT, whilst it is provided for in the American–Swiss Extradition Treaty.[99] Under the American–Swiss MLAT, the return of assets is possible only if the assets belong to the requesting state. It seems, however, that the United States cannot rely on this doctrine to demand the return of proceeds from crime to which it is entitled under the relation-back doctrine. Article 14 of the American–Italian MLAT is one of the few international provisions in international mutual legal assistance treaties to provide for the return of confiscated assets to the requesting country. There may be different explanations for the absence of this capacity in the multilateral money laundering conventions. A first factor relates to the spirit in which these treaties were drafted. The money laundering conventions have been drafted in the context of proceeds-oriented criminal justice, which is primarily focused on crimes without a victim, and at any rate tends to place greater weight on depriving offenders of the fruits of their offences than on restoring property to its lawful owner. In connection with this, it is noteworthy that a confiscation that takes place in the requested state is very advantageous to the requesting state in that the confiscated assets in principle accrue to the Treasury of that state (subject to the possibility of asset sharing).[100] Another possible explanation is related to the nature of the international co-operation in criminal matters. Whereas extradition is a form of secondary assistance whereby the requested state is assisted in its domestic procedure, the enforcement of foreign confiscation orders or of transfer of confiscation proceedings, are forms of primary assistance which result in the requested state taking over the procedures of the requesting state. Within the framework of primary assistance, it is far less logical to transfer assets to the requesting state as that state has abdicated its procedural responsibilities in favour of the requested state.

Even in cases where the applicable international convention does not

[98] See Article 7 of the Convention pour l'extradition des malfaiteurs entre la Belgique et la Confédération suisse, Berne 13 May 1874, *Moniteur Belge*, 8 July 1874.

[99] See Article XII of the Extradition Treaty between the United States and Switzerland, 14 May 1900 and *Grosby c. Ministère public fédéral* (2 June 1971) 97 ATF I, 372–86, 382 cited by Kohler, 'The Confiscation of Criminal Assets', 31–2.   [100] See *infra* pp. 416–19.

provide for it, the return of property may still be possible if the law of the requested state permits it. Thus Switzerland is able to offer more far-reaching assistance than that provided for in the American–Swiss MLAT on the basis of Article 74a of the Swiss Mutual Assistance Act. This enables the Swiss authorities to hand over property to the requesting state with a view to its confiscation or restitution to its lawful owner.[101] The provision makes an obvious allowance for any rights third parties (including possible victims) in Switzerland may have on the property. Although Article 74a in principle requires that there be a definite and enforceable foreign judgment before the transfer of property is ordered, in exceptional cases this may also be allowed even before such a judgment has been entered. This was, for example, what happened in the context of the litigation concerning funds of former President Marcos of the Philippines and his relatives in Swiss bank accounts, where the Swiss Supreme Court did not find any obstacles to allowing the transfer of these funds to an escrow account at the Philippines National Bank, provided that the Philippines state guaranteed that the restitution or confiscation proceedings would meet the requirements of the International Covenant on Civil and Political Rights (1966).[102] This case at the same time exemplifies the major weakness of this type of co-operation: handing over property to another state so that it can be subjected to confiscation or restitution procedures in that state presupposes a considerable deal of trust in that state and in its judicial system, especially if no definite judgment yet exists. Even if a foreign judgment exists, it is obvious that handing over the property to a foreign state requires a higher degree of trust from the requested state than the enforcement of a foreign confiscation order. The latter technique gives the requested state more power to control the confiscation process in relation to its compatibility with human rights demands, amongst others.[103] It is nevertheless clear that the restitution of alleged proceeds to a requesting state is potentially a very valuable co-operation technique, especially in view of preserving any rights third parties may have in the requesting state.

Although this capacity to return property connected to the offence to the requesting state was originally conceived in the context of extradition – it is sometimes referred to as *extradition matérielle (Sachauslieferung)* –

---

[101] See in general on this possibility: Frei, 'Beschlagnahme und Einziehung', 328–9, Harari, 'Corruption à l'étranger', 8–10 and Ackermann, *Geldwäscherei*, pp. 343–4.
[102] Judgment of the Swiss Supreme Court of 10 December 1997, ATF 123 II 595.
[103] See *supra* pp. 402–4.

there is no reason why it should not be applied in the wider context of international co-operation in criminal matters in general.[104]

If no decision has been taken yet in respect of the rights of third parties in the requesting state at the time it requests co-operation in the enforcement of a confiscation, third parties may try to safeguard their rights by instituting proceedings in the requested state. This demands no international co-operation, but the court will in that case often be faced with questions of private international law as the rights on which third parties rely will often have originated under the law of another state.

This may result in the application of foreign law. If the third party claims damages as a consequence of the offence for which the confiscation was imposed, the court will often have to apply the *lex loci delicti commissi*, although some legal systems (e.g. the United Kingdom's) refer to the *lex fori*, and others (e.g. Germany's) to the law of the country where the result of the offence occurred.[105] In the case of claims based on a contract, the law governing the contract (*lex contractus*) will be applied. When a third party seeks to reclaim property that was unlawfully taken from it and that property is located in the territory of the requested state, one might argue that the court will have to apply the *lex situs* (i.e. its own relevant law). Nevertheless, the proprietary rights that are, under the law of a foreign state, lawfully vested in property before it is transferred to another state, will have to be recognised. Thus, Greece succeeded in claiming back valuable ancient Greek coins which it owned under Greek law and which had been illegally exported by a Greek citizen to Germany.[106] If, however, after the transfer of the property to another state, other third parties have vested real rights in it under the *lex situs*, these rights will be upheld and, in case of conflict, will have precedence over the rights that were vested in it in another country.[107] It is to be emphasised that norms of foreign law will in any event only have to be applied to determine the existence of real rights; the right to restitution and its modalities will always be determined by the *lex fori*.

---

[104] See in this respect also the remarks made by the Swiss Supreme Court in its judgment of 10 December 1997, ATF 123 II 595, 602.

[105] See H. Van Houtte, 'Internationale forumshopping bij onrechtmatige daad', in Mélanges Roger.-O. Dalcq. *Responsabilité et assurances* (Brussels: Larcier, 1994), pp. 579–583 and J. Erauw, *De onrechtmatige daad in het internationaal privaatrecht* (Antwerp: Maklu, 1982), pp. 141–5.

[106] Oberlandesgericht Schleswig, judgment of 10 February 1989, NJW (1989), 3105.

[107] On this conflit mobile see: Rigaux and Fallon, *Droit international privé, Tome II: Droit positif belge*, pp. 455–6 and Van Hecke and K. Lenaerts, *Internationaal Privaatrecht*, pp. 156–7.

International asset sharing

Both the Vienna Convention (Article 5(5)(a)) and the Money Laundering Convention (Article 15) embody the principle that the destination of confiscated property is regulated solely by the law of the state which enforces the confiscation, that is, the requested state. In most cases this boils down to the fact that the confiscated assets accrue to the national Treasury of the requested state. From a moral viewpoint, it may seem unjust that the countries where criminals stash away their fruits of crime will ultimately benefit when those funds are eventually confiscated. From a strictly legal point of view, this is no more than the logical consequence of the *locus regit actum* principle, and is ultimately derived from the concept of national sovereignty. Of course the state disposing of the property may decide to use it for special purposes, perhaps for law enforcement activities, for example, as is the case in the United States. The state which has enforced the confiscation order may also decide to contribute (part of) the value of the confiscated property to the inter-governmental bodies that specialise in fighting crime or assistance to victims. This possibility, which is explicitly provided for in various international instruments (Article 5(5)(b) of the Vienna Convention, Article 7 of the CICAD Model Regulations and Recommendation 9 of the Report of the Caribbean Drug Money Laundering Conference),[108] has up until now scarcely been used. Thus, in 1998, the United Nations International Drug Control Programme (UNDCP), had received confiscated drug proceeds from only one country, Luxembourg, which has set up a special fund for confiscated drug trafficking proceeds (as have seven other FATF members).[109] Notwithstanding this sobering result, calls are increasingly made – at the Twentieth Special Session of the United Nations General Assembly in June 1998, for example – for the establishment of a world fund for the fight against drug criminality, which would be fuelled with money obtained from the confiscations of criminally derived proceeds.[110] Certainly in the context of the global drug trafficking phenomenon, these calls have an undeniably geographical quality and tend to emphasise the perceived need to come to a (more) equal sharing of the costs and the profits of the global fight against

---

[108] See also FATF Interpretative Note with Recommendation 38 (FATF-III, p. 39).
[109] Fonds de lutte contre le trafic des stupéfiants. See Spielmann, 'La confiscation en droit luxembourgeois', 223–4 and A. Brausch and H. Beythan, 'Luxembourg', in *Butterworths International Guide to Money Laundering Law and Practice*, R. Parlour (London: Butterworths, 1995), p. 121. See also FATF, *Evaluation of Laws and Systems*, p. 12.
[110] See UN Press Release GA/9413, 8 June 1998.

drugs between, on the one hand, the drug producing countries (the 'South') and, on the other hand, the drug consuming countries (the 'North').

Although the linkage of the funding of the fight against drugs with the North–South problem has sometimes been criticised,[111] it is a political reality which cannot be denied. For example, it is also notable in connection with a second exception to the rule that confiscated assets are deposited into the national treasury of the requested state, namely international asset sharing. Under this practice, states which have co-operated in the proceedings that ultimately lead to the confiscation of the assets share the confiscated assets. This practice, explicitly made possible by the Vienna Convention and the Money Laundering Convention and encouraged by Recommendations 38 and 39 of the FATF, is clearly inspired by the international dimension of the drug problem.[112] International asset sharing has sometimes also been portrayed as a necessary instrument for ensuring the co-operation of law enforcement agencies in Latin-American countries that are otherwise prone to fall victim to corruption.[113]

Given the fact that international asset sharing is – at least in legal terms – an exception to the rule that confiscated assets accrue exclusively to the national treasury of the requested state, this practice is dependent on the existence of (mostly bilateral) treaties and of national legislation of the requested state. Some might argue there is no need for such specific regulation and that asset sharing should take place on an *ad hoc* basis whenever the specific circumstances of a case require it. As a rule, the requested state both bears the costs of complying with a request and reaps the eventual benefits from it. At least as far as the costs are concerned, Article 34 of the Money Laundering Convention provides that in respect of costs of a substantial or extraordinary nature 'Parties shall consult in order to agree the conditions on which the request is to be executed and how the costs shall be borne'. It may be possible to limit asset sharing to the same kind of exceptional circumstances.

It should indeed be avoided that the financial return of international co-operation in criminal matters becomes an end in itself, as was the case in the past, for example, as when the Venetian Republic volunteered to take over the enforcement of imprisonment sanctions so as to provision

---

[111] See Wilkitzki, 'Development of an Effective International Crime and Justice Programme – A European View', p. 279.   [112] See, e.g., *US Delegation Report*, pp. 117–18.

[113] See B. Zagaris and E. Kingma, 'Asset Forfeiture Under International and Foreign Law: An Emerging Regime', *Emory Int'l LRev.* (1991), 506 and Zagaris, 'US Co-operation against Transnational Organised Crime', 522–4.

itself with galley-slaves.[114] It is, however, submitted that the mechanism of asset sharing should be considered as a correction to this profit-driven way of international co-operation rather than as the apogee of proceeds-oriented criminal justice in an international perspective. Without asset sharing, the confiscated assets accrue to the treasury of the state in which they are located, which is often not the state where the predicate offence took place. States should therefore endeavour to equip themselves with the necessary legislative instruments and to negotiate the international agreements necessary to enable them to share assets with other states. The financial considerations of states, and specifically expectations of shared assets, play an important role in international co-operation, as much for the requesting state, which may feel entitled to a share of the confiscated funds, as for the requested state(s) that lend their assistance – especially at the stage of seizure and confiscation – which may feel they are also entitled to a financial reward. The willingness of states to engage in international co-operation may be critically affected if they are deprived of what they feel is their entitlement and may well decide to opt instead for unilateral extra-territorial measures rather than international co-operation.[115] Ideally, asset sharing should also be possible, outside the framework of international co-operation, every time proceeds (e.g. as a result of a prosecution for money laundering) that derive from an offence committed in another state are confiscated.[116] Unfortunately, those countries whose legal systems have provided for the possibility of asset sharing have done so only in respect of international co-operation procedures.

So far, only a few countries seem to have introduced specific legislation that allows for international asset sharing, although an FATF report reveals that sixteen FATF members are able to share confiscated assets.[117] The United States has played a leading role in this field. One of the most prominent examples of asset sharing is the proceedings against the *Banco de Occidente*,[118] which eventually resulted in a plea agreement in which the

---

[114] D. Oehler, 'Recognition of Foreign Penal Judgments. The European System', in *International Criminal Law, Volume II*: Procedure, ed. M. C. Bassiouni (New York: Transnational Publishers, 1986), p. 200.

[115] Antenen, 'Problématique nouvelle relative à la poursuite pénale du blanchissage d'argent', 55.   [116] Harari, 'Corruption à l'étranger', 23.

[117] *Evaluation of Laws and Systems*, p. 13, para. 37.

[118] *United States v. Escobar-Gaviria*, No.CR89–086–A (*NDGa*); *United States v. Ramirez*, No.CR89–091A (*NDGa*), cited by Zagaris and McDonald, 'Financial Fraud and Technology', 98 and Munroe, 'The Extra-territorial Reach', pp. 299–300. See also, 344; and P. Gasser, 'Von der vermuteten Unschuld des Geldes-Die Einziehung von Vermögenswerten krimineller Herkunft', in *Bekämpfung der Geldwäscherei. Modellfall Schweiz?*, ed. M. Pieth (Basle: Helbing & Lichtenhahn, 1992), 161.

bank agreed to forfeit US$5 million to the United States. In exchange, the provisional measures that had been taken with respect to the bank accounts of the Banco de Occidente in several countries were lifted. Switzerland and Canada both received US$1 million for their co-operation in the investigation.

Together with Australia and Canada,[119] the United States is one of the few countries to have elaborated legislation in this field. Under 18 USC § 981(i)(1) the Attorney-General or the Secretary of Treasury may, under certain conditions, transfer forfeited property or the proceeds of any such property to any foreign country which participated directly or indirectly in the seizure or forfeiture of the property. Section 1616a(c)(2) gives the same powers to the Secretary of Treasury in respect of property seized by a US Customs Service officer and 21 USC § 881(e)(1)(E) authorises the Attorney-General to transfer forfeited property to a foreign country that has participated directly or indirectly in the seizure or forfeiture of drug-related property. All three provisions require the same conditions: approval by the Secretary of State; authorisation for such a transfer in an international agreement between the United States and the foreign country; and, if applicable, certification of the foreign country in question under 22 USC § 2291(h). The decision to share assets can be taken *proprio motu* by the United States, but also on request of a foreign state. A number of treaties and executive agreements explicitly provide for this possibility.[120]

In most states, the sharing of confiscated assets is possible only pursuant to a treaty-based request; some countries, such as the United Kingdom, for example,[121] have actively sought to negotiate bilateral assistance treaties that allow for the sharing of confiscated assets.

---

[119] See G. Leclerc and M. Ducquette, 'Canada', in *Butterworths International Guide to Money Laundering Law and Practice*, R. Parlour (London: Butterworths, 1995), p. 49 and D. P. Murphy, 'Canadian Perspective on Forfeiture Cooperation and Asset Sharing', in VI *International Anti-Corruption Conference. 1993 Cancun, Mexico Proceedings* (Mexico: 1994), II, p. 555.

[120] See the Switzerland–United States Memorandum of Understanding on Mutual Assistance in Criminal Matters and Ancillary Administrative Proceedings, 10 November 1987, *ILM* (1988), 480; the United States Memorandum of Understanding with Canada on Drug Enforcement, 2 February 1988, *ILM* (1988), 403 and the Mexico–United States Treaty on Mutual Legal Assistance, 9 December 1987, *ILM* (1988), 443.

[121] See Harding, 'Treaty-Making in the Field of International Co-operation' p. 239.

Epilogue: The Fight Against Money Laundering, Goals and Effectiveness

At the end of this book on the international fight against money laundering, it seems appropriate to assess the effectiveness of the fight. But before attempting to assess the effectiveness of the international anti-money laundering regime, it is, of course, necessary to spell out its goals. These are, however, not clearly delineated. Though the various purposes that are served by the fight against money laundering were discussed in Chapter 1, it is far from clear which of these purposes are pursued by policy-makers either on an international or on a domestic level. Nevertheless, it is above all necessary to distinguish between the ultimate goals and the intermediate purposes[1] that are served by the fight against money laundering. A number of the goals that have been set by various national and international authorities in the context of combating money laundering are in fact only means to an end, intermediate goals that it is necessary to reach before attaining an ultimate, final goal. Sometimes, those involved in the fight against money laundering have lost sight of this essential distinction. Thus, it seems that American law enforcement authorities are sometimes tempted to consider the seizure and forfeiture of assets as the primary goal of the fight against money laundering, in the attainment of which any means is justified,[2] whereas it is only an intermediate goal subsidiary to reaching the ultimate goal of reducing crime. In the same vein, compliance by financial institutions with anti-money laundering rules has sometimes been looked on as an end in itself, whereas it is in fact no more than a means of providing law enforcement authorities with useful information and protecting the financial industry from criminal influence.

---

[1] See M. Levi, 'Evaluating the "New Policing": Attacking the Money Trail of Organized Crime', *The Australian and New Zealand Journal of Criminology* (1997) 3.
[2] For a critique, see *supra* pp. 56–8.

Some intermediate goals may serve more than one of the final goals of the anti-money laundering regime. The goal of deterring money launderers serves both the 'repressive' goal of reducing crime and the 'preventive' policy of protecting the economy from criminal influence.

In view of the background (drugs, organised crime) against which the fight against money laundering developed, there is no denying that one of the ultimate goals of the fight against money laundering is the reduction of crime. The (perceived) failure of traditional criminal law instruments to bring about a significant reduction of this form of crime eventually resulted in the fight against money laundering assuming an international dimension. By virtue of the philosophy that no offender should benefit from his crime (the prevention of unjust enrichment) and on the basis of the economic belief that depriving criminals and criminal organisations of the proceeds of their crimes will reduce their influence (the incapacitation approach), the criminal law of many countries has been extended by the introduction of two new instruments: the confiscation of the proceeds of crime and the criminalisation of money laundering. These adaptations were made necessary by the nature of the forms of criminality with which contemporary society is faced, and notably by the absence of a single victim able to take procedural steps to safeguard his pecuniary interests. There are two aspects to this fundamental idea. First, many forms of acquisitive crime – notably the offences in the context of which the fight against money laundering originated – are nowadays crimes without a victim. Second, because of the ease with which (criminally derived) funds (under whatever form) can now be moved internationally, the victims of these forms of crime are often powerless to recover their losses or to act in any way against the (alleged) perpetrators of the crimes of which they are the victims.[3] This fundamental fact of the absence of a victim able to institute recovery claims against the alleged perpetrators of a crime has had a number of far-reaching effects on how the fight against money laundering has been shaped. For instance, it has provided a better understanding of a number of the far-reaching changes that have been wrought in respect of the confiscation of the proceeds from crime. This type of confiscation has often been branded by some legislators (and courts) as a reparative sanction intended to justify some of the exceptions to the general rules of criminal law and criminal procedure such as the reversal of the burden of proof in respect of the criminal origin of the proceeds, the imposition of confiscation sanctions after an offender

---

[3] See, however, M. S. Kenney and E. S. Becker, 'About Serious Fraud – Recovering the *Fructus Sceleris*', September 1996.

has died, *in rem* procedures, the relation-back doctrine and the use of the civil standard of proof.[4]

The fundamental idea of the absence of a victim also required the creation of a new offence of money laundering, as the traditional offences of handling stolen goods applied only to property obtained directly from victims, and not to property into which stolen goods have been changed, nor to the proceeds of victimless crime. Another consequence of the absence of a single victim motivated to obtain recovery is the need to institute reporting obligations on financial institutions and other economic operators in order to obtain information on the ocurrence of the offence of money laundering. For not only are many of the predicate offences which generate proceeds victimless crimes, but the crime of money laundering is itself also victimless.

However, in practice, this seems to have had the consequence that the burden of administering preventive anti-money laundering measures falls largely on the private sector, unlike the cost of judicial (confiscation) investigations which is carried by the state. The relatively low resources that governments have allocated to confiscation investigations have sometimes resulted in an apparent distortion between on the one hand the efforts of the private sector, both in terms of dedicated resources and the output of reports, and on the other hand the way in which law enforcement authorities have effectively acted on this information. This distortion again makes it clear that it is necessary to keep in mind the primary goals of anti-money laundering measures. This is not only necessary in order to be able to assess the true effectiveness of these measures, but also in order to sustain the effectiveness of the global community's anti-money laundering defences. If one is confronted with a situation whereby an intermediate goal of the fight against money laundering is apparently attained, namely the triggering of a number of suspicion-based reports by the private sector, but where this does not seem to result in a significant reduction of the crime level, then this may in the long term also impair the attainment of the intermediate, as well as the ultimate, goal, since financial institutions may begin to question the purpose and the usefulness of the efforts they are required to make.

There are various possible explanations for this distortion. A first explanation concerns what often happens at the operational level in terms of insufficient manpower and expertise in confiscation and money laundering investigations, for example. The EU Multidisciplinary Group on

---

[4] See *supra* pp. 50–6.

Organised Crime made a number of recommendations in its *Draft Report of the informal Money Laundering Experts Group* to deal with this problem.[5] Apart from a lack of police or judicial follow-up of the reports that have been made, deceptively poor results of the fight against money laundering in terms of assets effectively taken from criminals and the reduction of (organised) crime may, however, also be attributable to the inherent limitations of confiscation as an instrument for combating organised crime. Organised criminals, or any kind of sophisticated criminals for that matter, will always be motivated to organise themselves so as to protect their assets from confiscation.

The apparently low effectiveness in terms of confiscation and conviction rates may also be seen as an indicator of the low effectiveness of banks in detecting sophisticated money laundering operations.[6] It must, however, also be acknowledged that there are limits to what banks (and economic operators in general) can be expected to do, as is demonstrated by the fact that banks themselves, quite regularly, also fall victim to fraud.[7] It is, however, no coincidence that it is precisely those underdeveloped banking systems that are not sufficiently guarded against money laundering, that are the ones that are also more prone to become victims of fraud. On a more general level, the effectiveness of an increasing burden of anti-laundering measures may be questioned, especially when considering the growing complexity of money laundering operations and the resulting difficulty for financial intelligence units, and other authorities engaged in the combat against money laundering, to differentiate between legal and illegal financial transactions.[8]

The extent to which reports result in effective convictions and deprivations of criminal proceeds, let alone their general influence on the crime level, is admittedly extremely difficult to assess given the statistical black hole that exists in this respect.[9] Whilst the implementation of preventive anti-money laundering measures is reasonably well documented in terms of statistics (mostly by the financial intelligence units), such basic data is missing in respect of law enforcement implementation. Little data is

---

[5] See, e.g., recommendations 4, 6 and 7 of the report.
[6] See e.g. M. Levi, 'Money Laundering and Regulatory Policies', in *Responding to Money Laundering. International Perspectives*, ed. E. Savona (Amsterdam: Harwood Academic Publishers, 1997), pp. 266–73.
[7] Cf. Levi, 'Money Laundering and Regulatory Policies', p. 279.
[8] United Nations Office for Drug Control and Crime Prevention, *Financial Havens, Banking Secrecy and Money Laundering*, 14.
[9] See, in this respect, Recommendation 1 of the *Draft Report of the informal Money Laundering Experts Group* (p. 29), aimed at generating more and better statistical data.

available on how many investigations, prosecutions and convictions have been made as a result of reports filed by financial institutions and/or in the context of money laundering. Even if figures on the volume of assets the confiscation of which is ordered are sometimes available, it is seldom known what proportion of these orders has actually been enforced.

The effectiveness of the fight against money laundering, that is, the impact on crime (both predicate crimes and the crime of money laundering) is moreover difficult to measure as the extent of the existing crime is a matter of speculation.[10] In addition, in assessing the impact of money laundering reporting systems on police and judicial activities, it is necessary to distinguish between new investigations that are triggered by reports and the additional information that is provided to ongoing investigations by such reports.[11]

Another goal of the international anti-money laundering regime has of course been the protection of (parts of) the economy – especially the financial sector – against corruption by crime, and in particular organised crime. Although this goal is sometimes portrayed as an intermediate goal, its importance justifies its consideration as another of anti-money laundering legislation's ultimate goals, the attainment of which has an 'intrinsic' value, not dependent on the attainment of another, 'higher' goal. Some even pinpoint it as the most important motive behind the world-wide action against money laundering.[12] Irrespective of the reduction of the crime level that is sought, it is important to ensure that economic institutions are not taken over by, or act as accomplices to, criminals.

While it cannot be denied that there is little evidence that the fight against money laundering is having a significant effect on the levels of crime, the available data seem to suggest a reasonably high level of compliance in the private sector with the anti-money laundering measures. The 'carrot and stick' approach which has been practised towards banks, which consists of combining the threat of criminal sanctions with the capacity for banks to obtain exonerations by co-operating with the government,[13] seems to work.

One way in which the international community has purported to assess the effectiveness of domestic anti-money laundering measures is by setting up international monitoring mechanisms. The core of these monitoring mechanisms that have been developed by the FATF – and which are

---

[10] See *supra* pp. 87–9.   [11] Levi, 'Evaluating the "New Policing"', 4.
[12] M. Pieth, 'The Prevention of Money Laundering: A Comparative Analysis', *Eur.JCr., Cr.L & Cr.J* (1998), 161.   [13] See *supra* pp. 171–8.

now being implemented by other international organisations as well – consists of mutual evaluation rounds. First, member countries of the FATF were asked to respond to self-evaluation questionnaires regarding the implementation of the forty FATF Recommendations. This self-evaluation was later supplemented by rounds of mutual evaluation, in which evaluation teams consisting of representatives of FATF members conducted inquiries into the compliance levels achieved by FATF members. Such a mutual evaluation procedure essentially comprises two steps: first, all the relevant information is assembled, and, second, this information is analysed and assessed. The information gained is both quantitative and qualitative information and covers legal as well as financial aspects of members' activities. It will normally be gathered through extensive questionnaires, to which the member country should provide detailed answers, and through interviews carried out by the evaluation team during one or more on-the-spot visits. The evaluation team then drafts a report, which is submitted in its draft form to the country concerned in order to give it an opportunity to present its reactions to the report. The finalised version of the report is then disclosed to the other FATF members.[14] Summaries of these reports are published in the FATF's annual reports. Apart from a general evaluation of the success with which FATF members implemented the FATF's recommendations, the FATF has also conducted a number of cross-country evaluations on specific topics such as the confiscation of assets and customer identification.

This type of mutual evaluation procedure can, however, also be seen as a means of assessing the effectiveness of anti-laundering measures in that it does not stop at evaluating the adaptation of anti-money laundering measures by countries, but also encourages them to improve existing counter-measures. The idea underlying these monitoring mechanisms is to exert public and peer pressure: by mutually evaluating each other and by publishing the reports that are drawn up pursuant to these evaluation rounds, it is hoped that countries will adapt their legislation along the lines suggested in these reports. These monitoring mechanisms therefore also have an undeniable political element.

The relative success of these monitoring mechanisms is illustrated by the fact that similar monitoring mechanisms are now also used by other international organisations. This is not only true for other organisations active in the field of anti-money laundering measures (the Select Committee of the Council of Europe (PC-R-EV), which conducts self- and

---

[14] For more detail on the mechanism of self and mutual evaluation see: FATF-III, 9–10.

mutual evaluation exercises in the twenty-two Council of Europe countries that are not members of the FATF, the Caribbean Financial Action Task Force, the Gulf Co-operation Council, the Asia/Pacific Group on Money Laundering and the Offshore Group of Banking Supervisors[15]), but also for other international organisations. The European Union, for example, has established mutual evaluation rounds pursuant to the Joint Action of 5 December 1997, establishing a mechanism for evaluating the application and implementation at a national level of international undertakings in the fight against organised crime.[16] This joint action provides for evaluation methods in respect of the legislation and practice of Member States in this field, modelled on the mutual evaluation rounds devised by the FATF, except that the final reports drawn up pursuant to the evaluation rounds are confidential, although the EU Member State concerned may publish its own report on its own behalf (Article 9). Another example is the monitoring of the implementation which is provided for by the Revised draft United Nations Convention Against Transnational Organised Crime.[17] Article 28 of this draft convention foresees the establishment of a Committee of States Parties to conduct an evaluation of the implementation of the measures provided for by the convention to combat organised crime. The envisaged evaluation mechanism also consists of the adaptation of periodic reports and of visits by evaluation teams. In concurrence with the monitoring mechanism, state parties will also be required to submit periodic reports to the UN Commission on crime prevention and criminal justice.

It is, however, doubtful, whether these mutual evaluation rounds can make a significant contribution to an increase in the effectiveness of the measures that these international instruments seek to promote. Even in the context of an international law enforcement model, the implementation and effectiveness of crime-fighting or crime-preventing measures remain in the first place the responsibility of national authorities. It is only on a subsidiary level that mutual evaluation mechanisms can provide an impetus to an effective implementation of these measures by national authorities. As these mutual evaluation mechanisms are contingent on mutual trust and equality between the states concerned, it is moreover questionable whether they can also function in a global context (as does the United Nations), where there is arguably more equivocation on the type of measures that should be taken. However, the most funda-

---

[15] FATF-VIII, pp. 20, 21, 23 and FATF-IX, pp. 31–2 and FATF-X, p. 37. See also the Caribbean Financial Action Task Force, *Annual Report 1996–97*, pp. 9–10, 25.

[16] *OJ* No. L 344, 15.12.1997, p. 7.   [17] UN General Assembly, A/AC.254/L/1/Add.2.

mental weakness of mutual evaluation mechanisms as a means of heightening the effective implementation of international measures against money laundering is that these self- and mutual evaluation rounds result more in procedural than in substantive compliance.[18] It seems that these mutual evaluation rounds are at any rate more aimed at attaining a harmonisation of legislation than at gauging the effectiveness of the anti-money laundering measures that have been put in place. This was also recognised, albeit only implicitly, by the EU Multidisciplinary Group on Organised Crime when, in its *Draft Report of the informal Money Laundering Experts Group*,[19] it praised on the one hand the accomplishments of the Member States in complying with the international anti-money laundering instruments, but on the other hand made a number of detailed recommendations for enhancing the perceivedly low effectiveness of the anti-money laundering measures already in place. It should therefore come as no surprise that a reading of the reports issued by the FATF pursuant to the mutual evaluation rounds shows that the emphasis lies on compliance with the FATF recommendations, although it must be acknowledged that, at least in some respects, these reports also purport to gauge the actual effectiveness of existing domestic anti-money laundering measures.

From a cynical point of view, it may be argued that any success that anti-money laundering legislation manages to achieve is at best illusionary: that it has only succeeded in driving up the price of the co-operation of the remaining few economic institutions that wish to lend their assistance to money laundering and has also resulted in a shift of the phenomenon to other sectors of the economy, or to other geographical regions. It is submitted this cynical view springs from an over-ambitious, idealistic position, in which the fight against money laundering is considered a failure as long as money laundering practices continue to exist.

A more realistic view is that different economic sectors, and especially different countries, have different priorities and different views of the need and the means to control money laundering and that the money laundering phenomenon cannot be curbed overnight. The cynical view moreover confuses the two ultimate goals that are served by the anti-money laundering regime: the fact that the money laundering phenomenon is shifted to other geographical regions and economic sectors does not mean that the goal of insulating an economic sector from economic crime cannot be attained. To take the opposite view therefore amounts to

---

[18] *Cf.* United Nations Office for Drug Control and Crime Prevention, *Financial Havens, Banking Secrecy and Money Laundering*, pp. 47–8.   [19] p. 28.

denying that the second ultimate goal (i.e. insulating economic sectors from crime) exists in its own right.

This brings us to an essential point for consideration when regarding the implementation and the future perspectives of the international fight against money laundering. Because of the flexibility and adaptability of the money laundering phenomenon, any type of anti-money laundering measure is likely to result in a shift of the phenomenon to other economic sectors as well as to other geographical regions. It is therefore crucial to understand that the extension of the anti-money laundering regime, in terms of the predicate offences, economic sectors and geographical regions to which it applies, is part of the very nature of this regime.

As far as the predicate offences are concerned, an effective clamp-down on a particular form of acquisitive crime and the money laundering practices that relate to it, may very well result in a shift to other forms of crime, especially in the context of organised crime groups. This also explains the importance of having broadly based anti-money laundering legislation.[20] It may therefore safely be assumed that those national jurisdictions which still restrict their money laundering offence to proceeds from drug trafficking, or to a limited number of offences, will be forced to extend their legislation in the future.

In terms of the economic institutions that are subjected to anti-money laundering measures, an expansion in the range of those measures can equally be expected in the light of the findings that the relatively high level of compliance in the financial sector has caused a shift in the money laundering phenomenon to other sectors of the economy. The 1999 proposal of the European Commission to amend the money laundering directive in order to subject other categories of institutions and professions to anti-money laundering regimes bears witness to the trend towards extending the anti-money laundering regime to other sectors.

The expansion of the anti-money laundering regime on which the effectiveness of the fight against money laundering is most contingent, however, is the geographical expansion. As far as geographical shifts of the money laundering phenomenon are concerned, the role of regional anti-money laundering regimes in spreading the anti-money laundering measures to various parts of the world has been demonstrated.[21] A particularly thorny issue in this respect is the position of countries that do not co-operate in the international fight against money laundering. These countries can be divided into two categories.[22]

---

[20] See *supra* p. 117 et seq.   [21] See *supra* pp. 19–24.
[22] See Savona, 'International Money Laundering Trends', p. 65.

The first comprises those countries that do not have the technical, logistical or legal means required to co-operate in the fight against money laundering. Countries which lack the know-how and legislation to deal effectively with money laundering can be helped by other countries. In this respect considerable efforts have been made by the FATF. On a par with the sustained process of self- and mutual evaluation, the FATF has consistently pursued a goal of extending the reach of the FATF recommendations to third countries. The FATF has endeavoured to establish a worldwide anti-money laundering network through the development of contacts with third countries and international and regional organisations such as the United Nations International Drug Control Programme (UNIDCP), the Council of Europe, the International Monetary Fund (IMF), the World Bank, Interpol and the Customs Co-operation Council. In this respect, the FATF has developed or participated in a number of anti-money laundering activities of 'FATF-style', regional and other bodies, such as the Caribbean Financial Action Task Force (CFATF) and the American Commission Against Narcotic Drug Abuse (CICAD), aimed at curbing money laundering in regions not represented within the membership of FATF. Although the strategy of the FATF is in general more geared towards the promotion of the FATF recommendations to jurisdictions that are not members of the FATF than towards the provision of training and technical assistance to those jurisdictions, this latter type of assistance has also been provided.[23] As from 1999 onwards, the FATF has also adopted a strategy of expanding its membership to include a limited number of additional, but strategically important, countries. To this end, the FATF drew up a list of *sine qua non* criteria for admission.[24]

More difficult are those countries in the first category which, though externally sovereign, are internally not sovereign (i.e. which do not effectively control their territory or the persons living in it) and simply do not have the means to combat criminality, let alone (sophisticated) money laundering operations, effectively.

The most problematic countries, however, are those that fall into the second category, namely, those countries that are unwilling to co-operate in the fight against money laundering. The problem of lack of co-operation from offshore havens can partly be dealt with by constructing the international legal co-operation regime in such a way that traditional legal stumbling blocks, such as the condition of double criminality, the fiscal exception and the lack of treaty-based co-operation mechanisms,

---

[23] FATF-VIII, pp. 18–19.   [24] See FATF-X, p. 34.

cannot hamper international co-operation. Several proposals have been made to that end in this book, especially in the fourth part.

This approach, however valuable, can provide only part of the response to the problem posed by offshore havens. In order to prevent offshore havens from continuing to frustrate the efforts of other countries to curb the international money laundering phenomenon, it is required that, on an international political level, economic measures should be taken against these unco-operative jurisdictions. In the future, punitive taxes and especially the prospect of exclusion from the global financial community may be able to persuade these jurisdictions to accept the fundamentals of the international anti-money laundering regime.[25] However, for the time being, though, these proposals have not yet been put into practice.

An international 'stick' that is already being used to ensure compliance with international anti-money laundering regimes are the measures taken by the FATF towards non-co-operative countries. Although the FATF has declined to draw up a 'black list' of countries that do not co-operate in the fight against money laundering, it has nevertheless taken measures to exercise peer and public pressure on those countries, both inside and outside the FATF, that are seen as not sufficiently active in the implementation of anti-money laundering measures.

As far as non-complying FATF members are concerned, the FATF in 1996 adopted a policy, according to which a graduated approach would be followed aimed at enhancing peer pressure.[26] The only FATF member in respect of which all steps contained in this policy (i.e. a letter by the President of the FATF to the member country concerned, the sending of a high-level mission and the issuance of a public statement expressing concern about the lack of compliance[27]) were taken, is Austria, for its continuing refusal to abolish anonymous passbooks. This refusal also aroused the ire of the European Commission, which brought an action against Austria before the Court of Justice of the European Communities for not fulfilling its obligations under the EC Treaty and the Money Laundering Directive.[28]

The FATF has, however, also exerted public pressure on non-members that are unwilling to co-operate in the global fight against money laundering, the most blatant example being the condemnation of the Seychelles bill on immunity for launderers.[29] Although the action undertaken in this

---

[25] See *supra* pp. 94–5.   [26] See FATF-VII, p. 24, FATF-IX, pp. 24–5.
[27] FATF News Release of 11 February 1999: 'FATF Issues a Warning about Austrian Anonymous Savings Passbooks'.
[28] Case C-290/98, Notice 98/C299/29, *OJ* No. C299, 26.08.1998, p. 18.   [29] See *supra* p. 92.

one case resulted in the withdrawal of the tabled bill, it is however doubtful whether this type of political pressure will in all cases have effect. The
stubborn refusal of Austria to abolish its regulation on anonymous passbooks illustrates the limits of this type of peer pressure. If anonymous
passbooks are eventually abolished, it will be consequent to a decision of
the Court of Justice of the European Communities. In cases where such
supranational or international judicial review is absent, however, it is to
be feared that some jurisdictions that are unwilling to implement anti-
money laundering measures will only be forced to do so through strong
economic measures such as punitive taxes or the prospect of being
expelled from the international financial payments system. For the 'soft'
diplomatic measures, such as mutual evaluations and public condemna-
tions which have been used hitherto will by themselves not suffice to
make the global fight against money laundering effective. It seems that
this realisation is dawning on the European Union too: recommendation
5 of the *Draft Report of the informal Money Laundering Experts Group* of the
Multidisciplinary Group on Organized Crime and the FATF *Report on Non-
Cooperative Countries and Territories* also foresee the hitherto excluded possibility of black-listing an offshore centre which does not sufficiently
apply the 40 FATF Recommendations.

Bibliography

Literature

Abell, M., 'Department of Justice Renews Assault on Defendant's Right to Use Treaties on Mutual Legal Assistance in Criminal Matters to Obtain Evidence from Abroad in Criminal Cases', *International Enforcement Law Reporter* (1998), 53–8.

Abi-Saab, G., 'Eloge du "droit assourdi". Quelques réflexions sur le rôle de la *soft law* en droit international contemporain', in *Nouveaux itinéraires en droit. Hommage à François Rigaux*, Brussels: Bruylant, 1993, pp. 59–68.

Ackermann, J.-B., *Geldwäscherei – Money Laundering. Eine vergleichende Darstellung des Rechts und der Erscheinungsformen in den USA und der Schweiz*, Zurich: Schultess Polygraphischer Verlag AG, 1992.

Adams, W., 'Effective Strategies for Banks in Avoiding Criminal, Civil, and Forfeiture Liability in Money Laundering Cases', *Ala.LRev.* (1993), 669–701.

Adriaanse, P., *Confiscation in Private International Law*, The Hague: Martinus Nijhoff, 1956.

Albrecht, H.-J., 'The Money Trail, Developments in Criminal Law, and Research Needs: An Introduction', *Eur.JCr, Cr.L & Cr.J* (1997), 193–5.

Alford, D. E., 'Basle Committee Minimum Standards: International Regulatory Response to the Failure of BCCI', *Geo.Wash.JInt'l L & Econ.* (1992), 241–91.

Amann, D. M., 'A Whipsaw Cuts Both Ways: The Privilege Against Self-Incrimination in an International Context', *UCLA Law Review* (1998), 1201–95.

Antenen, J., 'Problématique nouvelle relative à la poursuite pénale du blanchissage d'argent, à la confiscation et au sort des avoirs confisqués', *RPS* (1996), 42–59.

Arzt, G., 'Zur Beweisbeschaffungspflicht der Bank im Strafverfahren', in *Beiträge zum Schweizerischen Bankenrecht*, Von Grafenfried, R., Berne: Verlag Stämpfli, 1989, pp. 321–41.

'Das schweizerischen Geldwäschereiverbot im Lichte amerikanische Erfahrungen', *RPS* (1989), 160–201.

Aubert, M., 'Quelques aspects de la portée du secret bancaire en droit pénal interne et dans l'entraide judiciaire internationale', *RPS* (1984), 167–84.

Aubert, M., Beguin, P.-A., Bernasconi, P., Graziano-Von Burg, J., Schwob, R. and Treuillaud, R., *Le secret bancaire suisse. Droit privé, pénal, administratif, fiscal, procédure, entraide et conventions internationales*, Berne: Ed. Staempfli & Cie, 1995.

Audit, B., *Droit international privé*, Paris: Economica, 1995.

Baade, H. W., 'Chapter 12: Operation of Foreign Public Law', in *International Encyclopedia of Comparative Law, Volume III: Private International Law*, Tübingen: J. C. B. Mohr (Paul Siebeck), 1991, pp. 1–54.

Baaijens-Van Geloven, Y. G. M., *Overdracht en overname van strafvervolgingen*, Arnhem: Gouda Quint, 1996.

Baer, C. M., 'Revision des Rechtshilfegesetz und des Bundesgesetz zum Rechtshilfevertrag mit den Vereinigten Staaten von Amerika – Wichtigste Aspekte und Zusamenfassung der Vernehmlassungsergebnisse', *RSDA* (1995), 80–4.

Bassiouni, M. C., 'Critical Reflections on International and National Control of Drugs', *Denv.JInt'l L & Pol'y* (1990), 311–7.

International Extradition: United States Law and Practice, New York: Oceana, 1996.

Bassiouni, M. C. and Gualtieri, D. S., 'International and National Responses to the Globalization of Money Laundering', in *Responding to Money Laundering. International Perspectives*, Savona, E., Amsterdam: Harwood Academic Publishers, 1997, pp. 107–88.

Bekaert, H., *La manifestation de la vérité dans le procès pénal*, Brussels, Bruylant, 1972.

Bergin, J. T., 'Piercing the Secret Bank Account For Criminal Prosecutions: An Evaluation of United States's Extra-territorial Discovery Techniques and the Mutual Assistance Treaty', *Ariz.JInt'l & Comp.L* (1990), 325–50.

Bernard, F., 'Les banques contre le blanchiment de l'argent', *Eurépargne* (1990, No.49), 17–23.

Bernasconi, P., 'Geldwäscherei und organisierte Kriminalität', in *Finanzunterwelt. Gegen Wirtschaftskriminalität und organisiertes Verbrechen.*, Bernasconi, P., Zürich: Verlag Orell-Füssli, 1988.

'Internationale strafrechtliche Bankuntersuchungen', in *Aspects juridiques de l'organisation économique actuelle, Journées des Avocats Suisses* (Lugano, 1989), Bernasconi, P., Banca del Gottardo, 1989, pp. 19–47.

'Droits et devoirs de la banque et de ses clients dans la procédure d'entraide judiciaire internationale en matière pénale', in *Beiträge zum Schweizerischen Bankenrecht*, Von Grafenfried, R., Berne: Verlag Stämpfli, 1989, pp. 343–410.

'The Fight against Money Laundering in the Prevention of the Drug Supply', in *Toward Scientifically Based Prevention.*, Bruno, F., Andreotti, M. E. and Brunetti, M., Rome: UNICRI, 1990, pp. 129–41.

'Blanchiment d'argent. Les nouvelles solutions légales suisses', *RSC* (1990), 646–50.

'Modèle internationale d'ordonnance judiciaire de saisie et de production des

documents. Un nouvel instrument de l'enquête internationale concernant
le blanchiment de l'argent', in *Bulletin de la Societé internationale de défense
sociale, Cahiers de défense sociale* (1990/91), 167–93.

'Le marché financier suisse: entre controle étatique et autorégulation', in
L'éthique des marchés financiers, Louis, J.-V. and Devos, D., Brussels: Editions de
l'Université de Bruxelles, 1991, pp. 103–19.

'Droit pénal européen et droit de l'entraide suisse face au droit pénal fiscal
européen', in *Aktuelle Probleme der Kriminalitätsbekämpfung, Festschrift zum
50jahrigen bestehen der Schweizerischen Kriminalistischen Gesellschaft*, Gauthier, J.,
Marty, D. F. and Schmid, N., Berne: Verlag Stämpfli, 1992, pp. 473–93.

'La criminalité organisée et d'affaires internationale', in *Changes in Society,
Crime and Criminal Justice in Europe: A Challenge for Criminological Education and
Research, Volume II. International Organised and Corporate Crime*, Fijnaut, C.,
Goethals, J., Peters, T. and Walgrave, L., Antwerp: Kluwer, 1995, pp. 1–16.

'New Legal Instruments for the Seizure of Proceeds from Drug Trafficking', in
Nuovi strumenti giudiziari contro la criminalità economica internazionale, Naples:
Edizioni Città del sole, 1995, pp. 185–214.

'Il nuovo diritto europeo sul sequestro e le indagini riguardanti il provento di
reati transnazionali', in *Nuovi strumenti giudiziari contro la criminalità
economica internazionale*, Naples: Edizioni Città del sole, 1995, pp. 349–404.

'Flux internationaux de capitaux d'origine illicite. La Suisse face aux nouvelles
stratégies', in *Nuovi strumenti giudiziari contro la criminalità economica
internazionale*, Naples: Edizioni Città del sole, 1995, pp. 89–132.

'Bankbeziehungen und internationale Rechtshilfe in Strafsachen: Neuere
Entwicklungen', *RSDA* (1995), 63–71.

'Rapport général', in *Blanchiment d'argent et secret bancaire*, Rapport général du
XIVe Congrès international de droit comparé, Bernasconi, P., The Hague:
Kluwer Law International, 1996, pp. 3–27.

'Achtung Briefkastenfirmen! Warnzeichen für Unternehmer, Treuhänder und
Revisoren sowie für Staatsanwälte und Steuerfahnder', *RPS* (1996), 289–312.

'Obstacles in Controlling Money Laundering Crimes', in *Responding to Money
Laundering. International Perspectives*, Savona, E., Amsterdam: Harwood
Academic Publishers, 1997, pp. 249–58.

Black, S. F., 'United States Transnational Discovery: The Rise and Fall of the
Hague Evidence Convention', *ICLQ* (1991), 901–6.

Blakesley, C. L., 'Extra-territorial Jurisdiction', in *International Criminal Law, Volume
II: Procedure*, Bassiouni, M. C., New York: Transnational Publishers, Inc., 1986,
pp. 1–53.

*Terrorism, Drugs, International Law, and the Protection of Human Liberty. A
Comparative Study in International Law, Its Nature, Role, and Impact in Matters of
Terrorism, Drug Trafficking, War, and Extradition*, New York: Transnational
Publishers, Inc., 1992.

Blakesley, C. and Lagodny, O., 'Finding Harmony Amidst Disagreement Over

Extradition, Jurisdiction, The Role of Human Rights, and Issues of Extra-territoriality Under International Criminal Law', *Vand. J.Transnat'l L.* (1991), 1–73.

Blumenson, E. and Nilsen, E., 'Policing for Profit: The Drug War's Hidden Economic Agenda', *University of Chicago Law Review* (1998), 35–114.

Bollmann, H., 'Switzerland', in *International Bank Secrecy*, Campbell, D., London: Sweet & Maxwell, 1992, pp. 661–99.

Born, G. and Westin, D., *International Civil Litigation in the United States Courts*, Deventer: Kluwer Law and Taxation Publishers, 1992.

Bos, J. T. K., 'Plukze-wet', *AA* (1993), 816–22.

Bosly, H.-D., 'Du droit pénal des affaires', in *Punir mon beau souci*, Brussels: Ed. de l'Université de Bruxelles, 1984, pp. 186–207.

Brausch, A. and Beythan, H., 'Luxemburg', in *Butterworths International Guide to Money Laundering Law and Practice*, Parlour, R., London: Butterworths, 1995, pp. 115–21.

Bribosia, H., 'Liberté, sécurité et justice: l'imbroglio d'un nouvel espace', *RMC* (1998), 27–54.

Brown, A., 'Money Laundering: A European and U.K. Perspective', *JIBL* (1997), 307–10.

Brownlie, I., *Principles of Public International Law*, Oxford, Clarendon, 1990.

Bruyneel, A., 'Le secret bancaire en Belgique après l'arrêt rendu par la Cour de cassation le 25 octobre 1978', *JT* (1979), 371.

Bschorr, P. J. and Mullin, M. H., 'Court-ordered Waivers of Foreign Banking Secrecy Rights: an Evaluation of the American Position', in *Beiträge zum Schweizerischen Bankenrecht*, Von Grafenfried, R., Berne: Verlag Stämpfli, 1989, pp. 181–205.

Bucy, P. H., 'Epilogue: The Fight Against Money Laundering: A New Jurisprudential Direction', *Ala.LRev.* (1993), 839–69.

Buyle, J. P., 'Le blanchiment: status quaestionis', in *Financieel recht tussen oud en nieuw*, Wymeersch, E., Antwerp: Maklu, 1996, pp. 467–89.

Byrne, J. J., 'The Bank Secrecy Act: Do Reporting Requirements Really Assist the Government?', *Ala.LRev.* (1993), 801–38.

Candler, L. J., 'Tracing and Recovering Proceeds of Crime in Fraud Cases: A Comparison of US and UK Legislation', *The International Lawyer* (1997), 3–40.

Cardozo, H., 'Congress versus *Sabbatino*: Constitutional Consideration', *Colum.JTransnat'l L* (1966), 297.

Castillo de la Torre, F., annotation with Court of Justice, 23 February 1995, *Bordessa*, *CMLR* (1995), 1025, annotation with Court of Justice, 14 December 1995, *LE Sanz de Lera e.a.*, *CMLR* (1996), 1065.

Chaikin, D. A., 'Money Laundering as a Supra-national Crime: An Investigatory Perspective', in *Principles and Procedures For A Transnational Criminal Law*, Eser, A. and Lagodny, O., Freiburg: Max-Planck Institut, 1992, pp. 415–55.

Chang, E. and Herscowitz, A. M., 'Money Laundering', *Am.JCr.L* (1995), 449–523.

Chapman, R. B., 'Tax Compliance and the Revenue Rule in Prosecutions for Wire and Mail Fraud', *ICLQ* (1999), 437–47.

Chapuis, J.-P., 'Le droit de communication du financier', *RPS* (1995), 257–72.

Charney, J., 'The Need for Constitutional Protections for Defendants in Civil Penalty Cases', *Cornell L Rev.* (1974), 487–517.

Clarotti, P., 'Un pas décisif vers le marché commun des banques', *RMC* (1989), 453–64.

Cleiren, C. P. M. and Nijboer, J. F. (eds.), *Strafvordering. Tekst & Commentaar*, Deventer: Kluwer, 1995.

Collins, L., 'The Territorial Reach of *Mareva* Injunctions', *LQR* (1989), 263–82.
  'Provisional and Protective Measures in International Litigation', in *Rec.Cours* (1992), III, 9–238.
  (ed.), *Dicey and Morris on The Conflict of Laws*, London: Sweet & Maxwell, 1993.

Corboz, B., 'Le secret professionnel de l'avocat selon l'article 321 CP.', *La Semaine judiciaire* (1993), 77–108.

Cornils, K., 'The Use of Foreign Law in Domestic Adjudication', in *Double Criminality. Studies in International Criminal Law*, Jareborg, N., Uppsala, Iustus Förlag, 1989, pp. 70–83.

Craig, P., 'Directives: Direct Effect, Indirect Effect and the Construction of National Legislation', *ELR* (1997), 519–38.

Credot, F. J., 'Le principe de non-ingérence et le devoir de vigilance', *Banque et Droit-Numéro spécial* (1990), 17–22.

Cullen, P. J., 'Money Laundering: The European Community Directive', in *Money Laundering*, The David Hume Institute, Edinburgh University Press, 1993, pp. 34–49.

Dale, R., 'Reflections on the BCCI Affair: A United Kingdom Perspective', *Int'l Law* (1991), 949–62.

Danovi, R., 'Le delai raisonnable de la procédure et le droit au respect des biens, en Italie', *RTDH* (1995), 447–53, noot onder EHRM, 18 July 1994, *Manlio Venditelli v. Italy*, *RTDH* (1995), 443.

Dassesse, M., 'Les rapports entre la proposition de directive blanchiment et la seconde directive bancaire de décembre 1989. Incohérences et contradictoires', *Banque et Droit-Numéro spécial* (1990), 13–16.
  'La lutte contre le blanchiment et la fraude fiscale ne donne pas aux autorités tous les droits', noot onder *H.v.J.*, 23 February 1995, *JDF* (1995), 245–9.

De Boer, J., 'Art.8 EVRM Algemeen', in *Handelingen der Nederlandse juristenvereniging*, (1990), Zwolle: Tjeenk Willink, 1–64.

De Feo, M., 'Depriving International Narcotics Traffickers and Other Organised Criminals of Illegal Proceeds and Combating Money Laundering', *Denv.JInt'l L& Pol'y* (1990), 405–15.

De Groot, F. C. V., 'De ontneming van wederrechtelijk verkregen voordeel', in *Maatregelen tegen witwassen in het koninkrijk*, Corstens, G. J. M., Joubert, E. J., Kortmann, S. C. J. J., Arnhem: Gouda Quint, 1995, pp. 67–82.

Dehaussy, J., 'Le statut de l'Etat étranger demandeur sur le for français: Droit international coutumier et droit interne', *JDI* (1991), 109–29.

Delmas-Marty, M., 'La "matière pénale" au sens de la Convention européenne des droits de l'homme, flou du droit pénal', *Rev.sc.crim. et dr.pén.comp.* (1987), 819–62.

'Personnes morales étangères et françaises', *Revue des Sociétés* (1993), 255–60.

De Nauw, A., *Les métamorphoses administratives du droit pénal de l'entreprise*, Ghent: Mys & Breesch, 1994.

'De verschillende luiken van het wettelijk systeem tot bestraffing en tot voorkoming van het witwassen van gelden en de fiscale fraude', in *Fiscaal strafrecht en strafprocesrecht*, Rozie, M., Ghent: Mys & Breesch, 1996, 219–46.

Depret, H.-R. and Deklerck, L., *Le Secret bancaire*, Brussels: Jurifi, 1991.

De Smet, B., 'De versnelling van de strafrechtspleging met instemming van de verdachte. Is de invoering van een 'guilty plea' naar Angelsaksisch model wenselijk?', *Pan.* (1994), 420–44.

'De inquisitoire onderzoeksmethode op de beklaagdenbank', *Pan.* (1995), 341–4.

De hervorming van het strafrechtelijk vooronderzoek in België. Moet het gerechtelijk vooronderzoek in zijn huidige vorm behouden blijven?, Antwerp: Intersentia, 1996.

De Swaef, M., 'De bijzondere verbeurdverklaring van de vermogensvoordelen uit misdrijven', *RW* (1990–91), 491–3.

Dickson, A., 'Taking Dealers to the Cleaners', *NLJ* (1991), 1068–9 and 1120–2.

Dietzi, H., 'Der Bankangestellte als eidgenössisch konzessionierter Sherlock Holmes? Der Kampf gegen die Geldwäscherei aus der Optik des Ersten Rechtskonsulenten einer Grossbank', in *Bekämpfung der Geldwäscherei. Modellfall Schweiz?*, Pieth, M., Balse: Helbing & Lichtenhahn, 1992, pp. 67–96.

Dini, L., 'The Problem and its Diverse Dimensions', in *Responding to Money Laundering. International Perspectives*, Savona, E., Amsterdam: Harwood Academic Publishers, 1997, pp. 3–8.

Dirix, E., 'De verbeurdverklaring met toewijzing aan de benadeelde', in *Om deze redenen. Liber Amicorum Armand Vandeplas*, Ghent: Mys & Breesch, 1994, pp. 185–99.

Donatsch, A., 'Konventionsrecht in Verfahren der kleinen Rechtshilfe', *RPS* (1996), 277–88.

Doorenbos, D. R., 'Money Laundering. De rol van de financiële sector', *DD* (1993), 764–79.

'Bestrijding van witwassen door vrije beroepsbeoefenaars', in *Maatregelen tegen witwassen in het koninkrijk*, Corstens, G. J. M., Joubert, E. J., Kortmann, S. C. J. J., Arnhem: Gouda Quint, 1995, pp. 117–45.

'Witwassen en (misbruik) van verschoningsrecht', *Advocatenblad* (1996), 111–15.

Over witwassen en voordeelsontneming, Deventer: Tjeenk Willink, 1997.

Dorresteijn, A. F. M., 'Aansprakelijkheid van banken bij weigering of melding van ongebruikelijke transacties', in *Misdaadgeld*, Van Duyne, P. C., Reijntjes, J. M. en Schaap, C. D., Arnhem: Gouda Quint, 1993, pp. 161–74.

Drage, J., 'Countering Money Laundering: The Response of the Financial Sector', in *Money Laundering*, The David Hume Institute, Edinburgh University Press, 1993, pp. 60–72.

Drijber, B. J., 'EEG-richtlijn inzake het witwassen van geld vastgesteld', *TVVS* (1991), 294–5.

Du Bois, G., 'Het bankgeheim', *TPR* (1986), 433–69.

Dugard, J. and Van den Wyngaert, C., 'Reconciling Extradition with Human Rights', *Am.JInt'l.Law* (1998), 187–212.

Dupuy, P.-M., *Droit international publique*, Paris: Dalloz, 1995.

Ellis, A. and Pisani, R. L., 'The United States Treaties on Mutual Assistance in Criminal Matters', in *International Criminal Law, Volume II, Procedure*, Bassiouni, M. C., New York: Transnational Publishers, 1986, pp. 151–79.

Elvinger, M., 'Libres propos sur l'utilité d'un code de bonne conduite en matière bancaire', in *Droit bancaire et financier au Grand-Duché de Luxembourg*, 10e anniversaire de l'association luxembourgeoise des juristes de banque, Brussels: Larcier, 1994, pp. 589–615.

Entringer, F., 'Le secret bancaire remis en question', in *Stromates*, Entringer, F., Luxembourg, 1997.

Erauw, J., *De onrechtmatige daad in het internationaal privaatrecht*, Antwerp: Maklu, 1982.

Erbstein, H. S., 'Palm Trees Hide More Than Sunshine: The Extra-territorial Application of Securities Laws in Haven Jurisdictions', *Dick.JInt'l L* (1995), 443–78.

Eser, A., 'Common Goals and Different Ways in International Criminal Law: Reflections from a European Perspective', *Harv.Int'l LJ* (1990), 117–28.

Ewing, A., 'The Draft EEC Money Laundering Directive: An Overview', *JIBL* (1991), 139–44.

Fawcett, J. E. S., 'General Course on Public International Law', in *Rec.Cours* (1971), I, 363–558.

Fedders, J. M., 'Policing Internationalised US Capital Markets: Methods to Obtain Evidence Abroad', *Int'l Law* (1984), 89–108.

Fellas, J., 'Give Me Your Documents: Discovery of Material in the US', *NLJ* (1996), 27–8.

Flore, D., 'Quelle répression pour le blanchiment des bénéfices tirés des fraudes?- Le droit international et comparé', in *De juridische bescherming van de financiële belangen van de Europese gemeenschappen*, Tulkens, F., Van Den Wyngaert, C. and Verougstraete, Y., Antwerp: Maklu, 1992, pp. 163–71.

Fortson, R., 'Annotations with the Criminal Justice Act 1993', *Current Law* (1993), c.36.

  'Annotations with the Drug Trafficking Act 1994', *Current Law* (1994), c.37.

Francescakis, Ph. (ed.), *Dalloz. Répertoire de droit international*, Paris: Dalloz, 1969.

Franken, A. A. and Van Der Landen, D., 'Het zwarte gat van de MOT', *NJB* (1997), 59–63.

Frei, L., 'Beschlagnahme und Einziehung als Rechtshilfemassnahmen', *RPS* (1988), 312–35.

Frei, L. and Trechsel, S., 'Origins and Applications of the US–Switzerland Treaty on Mutual Assistance in Criminal Matters', *Harv.Int.LJ* (1990), 77–97.

Freiberg, A., 'Confiscating the Literary Proceeds of Crime', *Crim.LR* (1992), 96–106.

Fried, D. J., 'Rationalising Criminal Forfeiture', *JCr.L& Crim.* (1988), 328–436.

Friedli, G., 'Die gebotene Sorgfalt nach Art. 305ter Strafgesetzbuch für Banken, Anwälte und Notäre', in *Bekämpfung der Geldwäscherei. Modellfall Schweiz?*, Pieth, M., Basle: Helbing & Lichtenhahn, 1992, pp. 123–56.

Froomkin, S. M., 'The Reluctant Policemen', in *The Regulation of Financial and Capital Markets*, 1992, pp. 84–93.

Frowein, J. A., 'The Protection of Property', in *The European System for the Protection of Human Rights*, Macdonald, R.St.J., Matscher, T. and H. Petrold, Dordrecht: Martinus Nijhoff Publishers, 1993, pp. 515–30.

Gafner d'Aumeries, S., *Le principe de la double incrimination. En particulier dans les rapports d'entraide judiciaire internationale en matière pénale entre la Suisse et les Etats-Unis*, Basle: Helbing & Lichtenhahn, 1992.

Gaillard, L., 'Les mesures provisionnelles en droit privé international', *La Semaine Judiciaire* (1993), 141–64.

Galli, S. J. and Wexton, J. L., 'Anti-Money Laundering Initiatives and Compliance – US Perspective', in *Money Laundering Control*, Rider, B. and Ashe, M., Dublin: Round Hall Sweet & Maxwell, 1996, pp. 316–82.

Gane, C. and Mackarel, M., 'The Admissibility of Evidence Obtained from Abroad into Criminal Proceedings – The Interpretation of Mutual Legal Assistance Treaties and Use of Evidence Irregularly Obtained', *Eur.JCr., Cr.L & Cr.J* (1996), 98–121.

Gardocki, L., 'The Principle of Universality', in *Double Criminality. Studies in International Criminal Law*, Jareborg, N., Uppsala: Iustus Förlag, 1989, pp. 57–69.

Gasser, P., 'Von der vermuteten Unschuld des Geldes-Die Einziehung von Vermögenswerten krimineller Herkunft', in *Bekämpfung der Geldwäscherei. Modellfall Schweiz?*, Pieth, M., Basle: Helbing & Lichtenhahn, 1992, pp. 123–56.

Gauthier, J., 'Quelques aspects de la confiscation selon l'article 58 du Code pénal suisse', in Walder, H. and Trechsel, S., *Lebendiges Strafrecht. Festgabe zum 65. Geburtstag Hans Schultz*, Berne: Revue Pénal Suisse/Verlag Stämpfli, 1977, pp. 364–76.

Gilmore, W. C., 'Going After The Money: Money Laundering, The Confiscation of The Assets of Crime and International Co-operation', in *Working Paper Series 'A System of European Police Co-operation after 1992'*, Edinburgh, 1991.

'Money Laundering: The International Aspect', in *Money Laundering*, The David Hume Institute, Edinburgh University Press, 1993, pp. 1–11.

'International Initiatives', in *Butterworths International Guide to Money Laundering Law and Practice*, Parlour, R., London: Butterworths, 1995, pp. 15–28.

Dirty Money. The Evolution of Money Laundering Counter-Measures, Strasbourg: The Council of Europe Press, 1995.

'International and Regional Initiatives', in *International Tracing of Assets*, M. Ashe and B. Rider (eds.) London: FT Law & Tax, 1997, Vol.1, pp. R1.

(ed.), *International Efforts To Combat Money Laundering*, Cambridge: Grotius Publications Limited, 1992.

Giovanoli, M., 'Switzerland. Some Recent Developments in Banking Law', in Cranston, R. (ed.), *European Banking Law: The Banker – Customer Relationship*, London: LLP, 1993, pp. 183–226.

Glaser, S., *Droit pénal international conventionnel*, Brussels: Bruylant, 1970.

Gleason, S., 'The Involuntary Launderer: The Banker's Liability for Deposits of the Proceeds of Crime', in *Laundering and Tracing*, Birks, P., Oxford: Clarendon Press, 1995, pp. 115–34.

Gordon, J. E., 'Prosecutors Who Seize too Much and the Theories They Love: Money Laundering, Faciliation, and Forfeiture', *Duke LJ* (1995), 744–76.

Graber, C. K., *Geldwäscherei. Ein Kommentar zu Art.305bis und 305ter StGB*, Berne: Verlag Stämpfli, 1990.

'Zum verhaltnis der Sorgfaltsplichtvereinbarung der Banken zu Art.305ter Abs1 StGB', *RSDA* (1995), 161–8.

Graf, Y., 'Switzerland Revises its Law on Mutual Assistance in Criminal Matters', *Int'l.Enf.LRep.* (1997), 98–102.

Grant, T. D., 'Towards a Swiss Solution for an American Problem: An Alternative Approach for Banks in the War on Drugs', *Ann.Rev.Bank.L* (1995), 225–68.

Groenhuijsen, M. S., 'Legaliteit als probleem', *NJB* (1982), 277–87.

Groenhuijsen, M. S. and Molenaar, F., 'Bank Confidentiality and Governmental Control of Exchange Operations and Their Unlawful Effects – The Netherlands', in *Blanchiment d'argent et secret bancaire*, Rapport général du XIVe Congrès international de droit comparé, Bernasconi, P., The Hague: Kluwer Law International, 1996, pp. 177–206.

Groenhuijsen, M. S. and Van Der Landen, D., 'De financiële aanpak van de georganiseerde criminaliteit', *NJB* (1995), 613–21.

Grosjean, F., 'Le blanchiment de l'argent: l'esprit des loi à l'épreuve du quotidien', *Journ.Proc.* (1996, No.300), 22–3; (1996, No.301), 14–19 and (1996, No.302), 20–3.

Grotz, M., 'Die internationale Zusammenarbeit bei der Abschopfung von Gewinnen aus Straftaten', *JR* (1991), 182–4.

Grützner, H., 'International Judicial Assistance and Co-operation in Criminal Matters' in *Treatise of International Criminal Law*, Bassiouni, M. C. and Nanda, V. P., Springfield: Charles C. Thomas, 1973, pp. 189–247.

Guill, J., 'Législation internationale et luxembourgeoise sur le blanchiment d'argent', in *Droit bancaire et financier au Grand-Duché de Luxembourg*, 10e anniversaire de l'association luxembourgeoise des juristes de banque, Brussels: Larcier, 1994, pp. 551–88.

Guldenmund, R., Harding, C. and Sherlock, A., 'The European Community and

Criminal Law', in *Criminal Justice in Europe: A Comparative Study*, Harding, C., Fennel, P., Jörg, N. and Swart, B., Oxford: Clarendon, 1995, pp. 107–26.

Gully-Hart, P., 'Loss of Time Through Formal and Procedural Requirements in International Co-operation', in *Principles and Procedures For A Transnational Criminal Law*, Eser, A. and Lagodny, O., Freiburg: Max-Planck Institut, 1992, pp. 245–66.

Gurule, J., 'The Money Laundering Control Act of 1986: Creating a New Federal Offence or Merely Affording Federal Prosecutors an Alternative Means of Punishing Specified Unlawful Activity?', *Am.Cr.LR* (1995), 823–54.

Harari, M., 'Corruption à l'étranger: quel sort réserver aux fonds saisis en Suisse', *RPS* (1998), 1–25.

Harding, A., 'Treaty-Making in the Field of International Co-operation', in *Principles and Procedures For A Transnational Criminal Law*, Eser, A. and Lagodny, O., Freiburg: Max-Planck Institut, 1992, pp. 235–43.

Harles, G., 'Luxembourg', in *International Bank Secrecy*, Campbell, D., London: Sweet & Maxwell, 1992, pp. 469–80.

Harmon, J. D., 'United States Money Laundering Laws: International Implications', *NYUJInt'l L& Comp.L* (1988), 1–45.

Haynes, A., 'Money Laundering and Changes in International Banking Regulation', *JIBL* (1993), 454–60.

'Recent Developments in Money Laundering Legislation in the United Kingdom', *JIBL* (1994), 58–63.

Heijder, A., 'Nullum crimen sine lege', in *Non sine causa. Opstellen aangeboden aan Prof. Mr. G. J. Scholten ter gelegenheid van zijn afscheid als hoogleraar aan de Universiteit van Amsterdam*, Zwolle: Tjeenk Willink, 1979, pp. 135–53.

Heimans, D., 'Internationale uitwissing van politieinformatie: over het grensvlak tussen rechtshulp en privacybescherming', *DD* (1994), 125–42.

Henkin, L., 'The Foreign Affairs Power of the Federal Courts: *Sabbatino*', *Col.LRev.* (1964), 805.

Hermans, R. M., 'Het ontmantelen van verhaalsconstructies. Enkele civielrechtelijke problemen bij de toepassing van de "plukze-wet"', *NJB* (1995), 772–82.

Heymann, Ph.B., 'Two Models of National Attitudes Toward International Co-operation in Law Enforcement', *Harv.Int'l LJ* (1990), 99–107.

Hirsch, A., 'International Enforcement and International Assistance in Insider Trading', in *European Insider Dealing*, Hopt, K. and Wymeersch, E., London: Butterworths, 1991, pp. 377–80.

'"Dirty Money" and Swiss Banking Regulations', *JComp.Bus.& Cap.Market L* (1986), 373–80.

Holmes, M. D., '*SEC v. Wang*: A Warning Signal to International Banks of Potential Double Liability', *Tex.Int'l LJ* (1991), 159–87.

Horowitz, J. I., 'Piercing Offshore Banking Secrecy Laws Used to Launder Illegal Narcotics Profits: the Cayman Islands Example', *Tex.Int'l LJ* (1985), 133–64.

Hulsman, L. H. C., 'Transmision des poursuites pénales à l'état de séjour et exécution des décisions pénales étrangères', in *Le droit pénal international. Receuil d'études en hommage à Jacob van Bemmelen*, Leiden: E. J. Brill, 1965, pp. 108–36.

Ivsan, J. V., 'Informational Liability and International Law: A Post-*Ratzlaf* Comparative Analysis of the Effect of Treasury Reporting Requirements on International Funds Transfers', *Ohio Northern University LR* (1994), 263–95.

Jacobs, F. G. and Roberts, S., *The Effect of Treaties in Domestic Law*, London: Sweet & Maxwell, 1987.

Jakhian, G., 'L'infraction de blanchiment et la peine de confiscation en droit belge', *RDP* (1991), 765–88.

Jason-Lloyd, L., 'Money Laundering – The Complete Guide', *NLJ* (1995), 149–50; 183–5; 219 and 278–80.

Jeanneret, V., 'La nouvelle loi suisse sur l'entraide internationale en matière pénale', *Agon* (1997, No.15), 11–14.

Jennings, R., 'Extra-territorial Jurisdiction and the United States Antitrust Laws', *British Yearbook of International Law* (1959), 146–74.

Jennings, R. and Watts, A., *Oppenheim's International Law*, London: Longman, 1992.

Jonckheere, A., Capus-Leclerc, M., Willems, V. and Spielmann, D., *Le blanchiment du produit des infractions en Belgique et au Grand-Duché de Luxembourg*, Brussels: Larcier, 1995.

Junod, C.-A., 'La garantie d'une activité irréprochable. De la surveillance à la tutelle des banques?', in *Beiträge zum Schweizerischen Bankenrecht*, Von Grafenfried, R., Berne: Verlag Stämpfli, 1989, pp. 91–131.

Kauffman, J., 'Le secret bancaire en droit luxembourgeois – aspects actuels et perspectives', in *Droit bancaire et financier au Grand-Duché de Luxembourg*, 10e anniversaire de l'association luxembourgeoise des juristes de banque, Brussels: Larcier, 1994, pp. 521–50.

'Le secret bancaire en droit Luxembourgeois', *DPCI* (1990), 73–105.

Keohane, R. O. and Nye, J., *Transnational Relations and World Politics*, Harvard University Press, 1972.

Power and Interdependence: World Politics in Transition, Boston: Little, Brown & Co., 1977.

After Hegemony: Co-operation and Discord in the World Political Economy, 1984, Princeton NJ, 290.

Keulen, B. F., 'MOT met de strafrechter', *TVVS* (1993), 281–5.

Keyser-Ringnalda, F., 'De "Pluk ze-wetgeving" in het licht van de rechtsbeginselen', *DD* (1991), 1078–98.

'European Integration with regard to the Confiscation of the Proceeds of Crime', *European Law Review* (1992), 499–515.

'De buitgerichte benadering van de Pluk ze-wetgeving', *NJB* (1993), 335–9.

Keyser-Ringnalda, L. F., *Boef en buit. De ontneming van wederrechtelijk verkregen vermogen*, Arnhem: Gouda Quint, 1994.

Kinsch, P., *Le fait du prince étranger*, Paris: Librairie générale de droit et de jurisprudence, 1994.

Kistler, M., *La vigiliance requise en matière d'opérations financières. Etude de l'article 305ter du Code pénal suisse*, Zürich: 1994.

Klip, A., *Buitenlandse getuigen in strafzaken*, Arnhem: Gouda Quint, 1994.

Klip, P., 'The Decrease of the Protection under Human Rights Treaties in International Law' *Revue internationale de droit pénal* (1996), 291–310.

Knecht, 'Extra-territorial Jurisdiction and the Federal Money Laundering Offense', *Stan.JInt'l L* (1986), 189–240.

Kofele-Kale, N., *International Law of Responsibility for Economic Crimes. Holding Heads of State and Other High Ranking State Officials Individually Liable for Acts of Fraudulent Enrichment*, The Hague: Kluwer Law International, 1996.

Kohler, N., 'The Confiscation of Criminal Assets in the United States and Switzerland', *Houston J. I. L.* (1990–91), 1–38.

Kortmann, C. A. J. M., *Constitutioneel recht*, Deventer: Kluwer, 1990.

Kortmann, S. C. J. J., 'De (ontwerp) landsverordeningen MOT; civielrechtelijke aspecten', in *Maatregelen tegen witwassen in het koninkrijk*, Corstens, G. J. M., Joubert, E. J., Kortmann, S. C. J. J., Arnhem: Gouda Quint, 1995, pp. 159–70.

Kosters, J., and Dubbink, C. W., *Algemeen deel van het Nederlands internationaal privaatrecht*, Haarlem: Erven F. Bohn, 1962.

Krafft, M.-C., 'Secret bancaire et conflits de juridiction. Le point de vue d'un internationaliste', in *Beiträge zum Schweizerischen Bankenrecht*, Von Grafenfried, R., Berne: Verlag Stämpfli, 1989, pp. 207–25.

Krauskopf, L., 'Geldwäscherei und organisiertes Verbrechen als europäische Herausforderung', *RPS* (1991), 385–94.

Kriz, G. J., 'International Co-operation to Combat Money Laundering: The Nature and Role of Mutual Legal Assistance Treaties', *Commonwealth Law Bulletin* (1992), 723–34.

Kropholler, J., *Internationales Privatrecht*, Tübingen: J. C. B. Mohr (Paul Siebeck), 1994.

Kuus, A. H. J., 'De Wet melding ongebruikelijke transacties en de privacy van klanten van banken', *Computerrecht* (1994), 163–7.

Lagodny, O., 'Grundkonstellationen des internationalen Strafrechts', *RPS* (1989), 987–1011.

Lagodny, O. and Schomburg, W., 'International Cooperation in Criminal Matters and Rights of the Individual from a German Perspective', *Eur.JCr., Cr.L & Cr.J* (1994), 379–405.

Lambert, P., *Le Secret Professionnel*, Brussels: Nemesis, 1985.

Règles et usages de la profession d'avocat du barreau de Bruxelles, Brussels: Bruylant, 1994.

Lamp, R., 'Financiële informatie de grens over', *DD* (1999), 41–53.

Lando, O., 'Chapter 24: Contracts', in *International Encyclopedia of Comparative Law, Volume III: Private International Law*, Tübingen, J. C. B. Mohr (Paul Siebeck), 1986.

Larguier, J., 'Chronique de jurisprudence. Droit pénal général', *RSC* (1983), 463–6.

Larose, L., '*Austin v. United States*; Applicability of the Eight Amendment to Civil *In Rem* Forfeitures', *New. Eng. L Rev.* (1995), 729–61.

Leclerc, G., Ducquette, M., 'Canada', in *Butterworths International Guide to Money Laundering Law and Practice*, Parlour, R., London: Butterworths, 1995, pp. 47–61.

Levi, M., *Consumer Confidentiality, Money Laundering, and Police Bank Relationships: English Law and Practice in a Global Environment*, The Police Foundation, 1991.

'Regulating Money Laundering. The Death of Bank Secrecy in the UK', *Br.JCr.* (1991), 109–25.

'*Pecunia non olet*: Cleansing the Money Launderers from the Temple', *Crime, Law and Social Change* (1991), 217–302.

'Incriminating Disclosures: An Evaluation of Money Laundering Regulation in England and Wales', *Eur.JCr., Cr.L & Cr.J* (1995), 202–18.

'Réglementation sur le blanchiment de l'argent au Royaume-Uni: une évaluation', *Deviance et société* (1995), 379–85.

'Taking Financial Services to the Cleaners', *NLJ* (1995), 26–7.

'Evaluating the "New Policing": Attacking the Money Trail of Organised Crime', *The Australian and New Zealand Journal of Criminology* (1997), 2–25.

'Money Laundering and Regulatory Policies', in *Responding to Money Laundering. International Perspectives*, Savona, E., Amsterdam: Harwood Academic Publishers, 1997, pp. 259–82.

'Taking the Profit Out of Crime: The UK Experience', *Eur.JCr, Cr.L & Cr.J* (1997), 228–39.

Levi, M. and Osofsky, L. K., 'The End of the Money Trail: Confiscating the Proceeds of Crime', in *Butterworths International Guide to Money Laundering Law and Practice*, Parlour, R. , London: Butterworths, 1995, pp. 301–16.

Lombois, C., *Droit pénal international*, Paris: 1979.

Lutgen, A., 'Les moyens de lutte internationaux contre le blanchiment de l'argent et la protection du budget des Communautés européennes', *Agon* (May 1994), 11–12.

Magliveras, K. D., 'The Regulation of Money Laundering in the UK', *JBus.L* (1991), 525–35.

'Defeating the Money Launderers – the International and European Framework', *JBus.L* (1992), 161–77.

Maher, G. and Rodger, B. J., 'Provisional and Protective Remedies: The British Experience of the Brussels Convention', *ICLQ* (1999) 302–39.

Maier, H. G., 'Extra-territorial Jurisdiction at the Crossroads: an Intersection between Public and Private International Law', *AJIL* (1982), 280–320.

Malek, C. and Lewis, C., 'Worldwide *Mareva* Injunctions: The Position of International Banks', *Lloyd's Mar.& Com.LQ* (1990), 88–98.

Mann, F., 'The Legal Consequences of *Sabbatino*', *Va.LRev.* (1965), 604.

Mann, F. A., 'The Doctrine of Jurisdiction in International Law', in *Rec.Cours* (1964), I, 1–162.

'Conflicts of Law and Public Law', in *Rec.Cours* (1971), I, 107–96.

'The Doctrine of International Jurisdiction Revisited After Twenty Years', in *Rec.Cours* (1984), III, 9–116.

Mann, M. D., 'Extra-territoriality: Compelling Foreign Judicial Assistance in the Production of Documents and Evidence', in *Am.Soc'y Int'l L.Proc.* (1985), 6–8.

Mann, M. D., Mari, J. G. and Lavdas, G., 'Internationalisation of Insider Trading Enforcement – a Guide to Regulation and Co-operation', in *European Insider Dealing*, Hopt, K. and Wymeersch, E., London: Butterworths, 1991, pp. 339–76.

Developments in International Securities Law Enforcement and Regulation, New York: Securities and Exchange Commission, 1994.

Markees, C., 'Suisse', *RIDP* (1968), 742–57.

'Aktuelle Fragen aus dem Gebiete der internationalen Rechtshilfe', *RPS* (1973), 230–71.

'The Difference in Concept Between Civil and Common Law Countries as to Judicial Assistance and Co-operation in Criminal Matters', in *A Treatise on International Criminal Law, Volume II: Jurisdiction and Co-operation*, Bassiouni, M. C. and Nanda, V. P., Springfield: Charles C. Thomas, 1973, pp. 171–88.

McClean, D., *International Judicial Assistance*, Oxford: Clarendon Press, 1992.

McLachlan, C., 'Splitting the Proper Law in Private International Law', in *British Yearbook of International Law 1990*, Oxford: Clarendon, 1990, 311–37.

'Extra-territorial Orders Affecting Bank Deposits', in *Extra-territorial Jurisdiction in Theory and Practice*, Meessen, K., London: Kluwer Law International, 1996, pp. 39–51.

'The Jurisdictional Limits of Disclosure Orders', *ICLQ* (1998), 3–49.

Messerli, B., 'Die Geldwäscherei de lege lata et ferenda', *RPS* (1989), 418–33.

Meyer, J., 'The Vicarious Administration of Justice: An Overlooked Basis of Jurisdiction', *Harv.Int'l LJ* (1990), 108–16.

Mitchell, A. R., Hinton, M. G. and Taylor, S. M. E., *Confiscation*, London: Sweet & Maxwell, 1992.

Mok, M. R. and Duk, R. A. A., 'Toepassing van het Nederlandse strafrecht op buiten Nederland begane delicten', in *Handelingen der Nederlandse Juristenvereniging* (1980), Zwolle: Tjeenk-Willink, 3–149.

Mueller, K., 'The Swiss Banking Secret From a Legal View', *ICLQ* (1969), 361–77.

Mul, V., 'Vrijwaringsbepalingen: vrijheid of gebondenheid?', in *Financiële integriteit. Normafwijkend gedrag en (zelf)regulering binnen het financiële stelsel*, Hoogenboom, A. B., Mul, V. and Wielinga, A., Arnhem: Gouda Quint, 1995, pp. 103–17.

Mul, V. and Schaap, C. D., 'Internationale informatieuitwisseling omtrent witwassen; mogelijkheden en onmogelijkheden', *Justitiële Verkenningen* (1996, No.9), 36–45

Müller-Rappard, E. and Bassiouni, M. C. (eds.), *European Inter-State Co-operation in Criminal Matters. The Council of Europe's Legal Instruments*, Dordrecht, Martinus Nijhoff, 1993.

Münch, F., 'Les effets d'une nationalisation à l'étranger', *Rec.Cours* (1959), III, 411–504.

Munroe, K. W., 'The Extra-territorial Reach of the United States Anti-Money

Laundering Laws' in *Money Laundering Control*, Rider, B. A. K. and Ashe, M., Dublin: Round Hall Sweet & Maxwell, 1995, pp. 290–303.

Murphy, D. P., 'Canadian Perspective on Forfeiture Co-operation and Asset Sharing', in *VI International Anti-Corruption Conference. 1993 Cancun, Mexico Proceedings*, Mexico: 1994, II, pp. 551–5.

Nadelmann, E. A., 'Negotiations in Criminal Law Assistance Treaties', *Am.J.Comp.L.* (1985), 467–504.

'Unlaundering Dirty Money Abroad: US Foreign Policy and Financial Secrecy Jurisdictions', *Inter-American LR* (1986), 33–81.

'The Role of the United States in the International Enforcement of Criminal Law', *Harv.Int'l LJ* (1990), 37–76.

Cops Across Borders. The Internationalisation of US Criminal Law Enforcement, Pennsylvania: The Pennsylvania State University Press, 1993.

Nardell, G., 'Presumed Innocence, Proportionality and the Privy Council', *LQR* (1994), 223–8.

Natterer, J., 'Money Laundering and Forfeiture Legislation in Switzerland', *Eur. J Crime, Cr.L and Cr.J* (1997), 220–7.

Nguyen Quoc Dinh, Daillier, P. and Pellet, A., *Droit international public*, Paris: Librairie générale de droit et de jurisprudence, 1980.

Nicgorski, A., 'The Continuing Saga of Civil Forfeiture, the "War on Drugs", and the Constitution: Determining the Constitutional Excessiveness of Civil Forfeitures', *Nw.ULRev.* (1996), 374–412.

Nilsson, H. G., 'The Council of Europe Laundering Convention: A Recent Example of a Developing International Criminal Law', in *Principles and Procedures For A Transnational Criminal Law*, Eser, A. and Lagodny, O., Freiburg: Max-Planck Institut, 1992, pp. 457–78.

Nobel, P., 'Die neuen Standesregeln zur Sorgfaltspflicht der Banken', *Wirtschaft und Recht* (1987), 149–66.

'Die Rechtshilfe in Zivilsachen im Lichte der Ratifikation der Haager Konvention von 1970 über die Beweisaufnahme im Ausland in Zivil- und Handelssachen', *RSDA* (1995), 72–9.

'Bankgeschäft und Ethik – Freiheit und Strafrecht', *RSDA* (1996), 97–105.

Nogueira, M.-J. and Raimundo, M., 'Blanchiment des capitaux. Une première approche au Portugal', *Agon* (1994, April), 8–9.

Note: 'The Marc Rich Case: Extension of Grand Jury Subpoena Power to Non-resident Alien Corporations', *Geo.Wash.JInt'l. L & Econ.* (1984), 97.

Oehler, D., *Internationales strafrecht: Geltungsbereich des Strafrechts, internationales Rechtshilferecht, Recht der Gemeinschaften, Völkerstrafrecht*, Cologne: Carl Heymann Verlag, 1983.

'Recognition of Foreign Penal Judgments. The European System', in *International Criminal Law, Volume II: Procedure*, Bassiouni, M. C., New York: Transnational Publishers, 1986, pp. 199–217.

Osofsky, L. K., 'Fighting Money Laundering, American Style', *JIBL* (1993), 359–64.

'Comparing the US Law of "Forfeiture" with the Law of "Confiscation" in England and Wales', *JIBL* (1994), 298–304.

Oswald, K., 'Money-Laundering Legislation in Germany: Selected Results from a Recent Research Project', *Eur. J Cr., Cr.L & Cr.J* (1997), 196–202.

Paget-Brown, I., 'A Cayman Perspective', in *International Tracing of Assets*, Ashe, M. and Rider, B., London: FT Law & Tax, 1997, pp. 52.1–52.33.

Paoli, L., 'The Banco Ambrosiano case: An Investigation into the Underestimation of the Relations Between Organized and Economic Crime', *Crime, Law & Social Change* (1995), 345–65.

Pardon, J., 'Le blanchiment de l'argent et la lutte contre la criminalité axée sur le profit', *RDP* (1992), 741–57.

Paridaens, D. J. M. W., *De overdracht van tenuitvoerlegging van strafvonnissen*, Ijsselstein: Drukkerij Casparie, 1994.

Passmore, C., 'Banks and subpoenas', *NLJ* (1995), 89–90.

Paton, M. L., 'The Bahamas', in *International Bank Secrecy*, Campbell, D., London: Sweet & Maxwell, 1992, pp. 59–75.

Paust, J. J., Bassiouni, M. C., Williams, S. A., Scharf, M., Gurule, J. and Zagaris, B., *International Criminal Law*, Durham, North Carolina: Carolina Academic Press, 1996.

Peeman, T., 'Het MOT-meldpunt: een (te) moeizaam compromis?', in *Financiële integriteit. Normafwijkend gedrag en (zelf)regulering binnen het financiële stelsel*, Hoogenboom, A. B., Mul, V. and Wielinga, A., Arnhem: Gouda Quint, 1995, pp. 95–102.

Peires, L. G., 'Legal Professional Privilege in Commonwealth Law', *ICLQ* (1982), 609–39.

Penn, D., 'British Virgin Islands', in *International Bank Secrecy*, Campbell, D., London: Sweet & Maxwell, 1992, pp. 101–14.

Persoon, R., 'Geplukt of aangeslagen? De fiscaalrechtelijke implicaties van de strafrechtelijke maatregel ter ontneming van wederrechtelijk verkregen voordeel', *DD* (1996), 747–70.

Peters, R. G., 'Money Laundering and its Current Status in Switzerland: New Disincentives for Financial Tourism', *Nw.J Int'l L & Bus.* (1990), 104–39.

Peukert, W., 'Die Rechtsprechung des EGMR zur Verhältnismässigkeit einer Eigentumsentziehung nach zollrechtlichen Vorschriften', *EuGRZ* (1988), 509–13.

Picca, G., 'Le 'blanchiment' des produits du crime: vers de nouvelles stratégies internationales?', *Rev.int.de crim.et de pol.techn.* (1992), 483–5.

Pickholz, M. G., *Securities Crimes*, New York: CBC, 1997.

Pieth, M., 'Zur Einfuhrung: Geldwäscherei und ihre Bekämpfung in der Schweiz', in *Bekämpfung der Geldwäscherei. Modellfall Schweiz?*, Pieth, M., Basle: Helbing & Lichtenhahn, 1992, pp. 1–27.

'"Das zweite Paket gegen das Organisierte Verbrechen", die Überlegungen des Gesetzgebers', *RPS* (1995), 225–39.

'The Prevention of Money Laundering: A Comparative Analysis', *Eur. J Cr., Cr.L & Cr.J* (1998), 159–68.

Plachta, M., 'The Role of Double Criminality in International Co-operation in Criminal Matters', in *Double Criminality. Studies in International Criminal Law*, Jareborg, N., Uppsala: Iustus Förlag, 1989, pp. 84–134.

Plombeck, C. T., 'Confidentiality and Disclosure: The Money Laundering Control Act of 1986 and Banking Secrecy', *Int'l Law.* (1988), 69–98.

Poncet, D. and Gully-Hart, P., 'Le principe de la spécialité en matière d'extradition', *RIDP* (1991), 199–229.

Raphael, Monty, 'Money Laundering and the Legal Profession', *NLJ* (1995), 1377–8.

Rees, K., 'Confiscating the Proceeds of Crime', *NLJ* (1996), 1270–2, 1345–6 and 1519–20.

Remmelink, J., *Uitlevering*, Arnhem: Gouda Quint, 1990.

Reynolds, R. M., Sicilian, J. and Wellman, Ph.S., 'The Extra-territorial Application of the US Antitrust Laws to Criminal Conspiracies', *ECLR* (1998), 151–5.

Rider, B. A. K, 'Cosmetics or Surgery – Fraud in the City', *Co.L* (1992), 162.
'Launderers and Whistle-Blowers', *Co.L* (1992), 202.
'Taking The Profit out of Crime' in *Money Laundering Control*, Rider, B. A. K. and Ashe, M., Dublin: Round Hall Sweet & Maxwell, 1995, pp. 1–26.

Rigaux, F., *Droit public et droit privé dans les relations internationales*, Paris: Ed. A. Pedone, 1977.
Droit international privé, Tome I: Théorie générale, Brussels: Larcier, 1987.

Rigaux, F. and Fallon, M., *Droit international privé, Tome II: Droit positif belge*, Brussels: Larcier, 1993.

Robert, Ph. and Faugeron, Cl., *Les forces cachées de la justice. La crise de la justice pénale*, Paris: Le Centurion, 1980.

Roth, R., 'Territorialité et extra-territorialité en droit pénal international', *RPS* (1995), 1–25.

Rouchereau, F., 'La Convention des Nations Unies contre le traffic illicite de stupéfiants et de substances psychotropes', in *Annuaire Français de droit international*, Paris: Editions du CNRS, 1988, pp. 601–17.

Rousseau, Ch., 'Principes de droit international public', *Rec.Cours* (1958), I, 369–549.

Ruiz, L. M., 'European Community Directive on Insider Dealing: A Model for Effective Enforcement of Prohibitions on Insider Trading in International Markets', *Colum.JTransnat'l L* (1995), 217–47.

Ruyters, N. J. M., 'Internationale ontneming', in *Ontneming Crimineel Vermogen in het buitenland*, Congresbundel Zuthpen 4 September 1996, Bureau Ontnemingswetgeving Openbaar Ministerie, Bureau Internationale Rechtshulp van het Ministerie van Justitie.

Sallon, C. and Bedingfield, D., 'Drugs, Money and the Law', *Crim.LR* (1993), 165–7.

Sarkar, L., 'The Proper Law of Crime in International Law', *ICLQ* (1962), 446–70.

Sauloy, M. and Le Bonniec, Y., *A qui profite la cocaïne*, Paris: Calman-Lévy, 1992.

Savona, E. and De Feo, M. A., 'International Money Laundering Trends and Prevention/Control Policies', in *Responding to Money Laundering. International Perspectives*, Savona, E., Amsterdam: Harwood Academic Publishers, 1997, pp. 9–70.

Schaap, C. D., 'Witwassen als verschijnsel', in *Maatregelen tegen witwassen in het koninkrijk*, Corstens, G. J. M., Joubert, E. J., Kortmann, S. C. J. J., Arnhem: Gouda Quint, 1995, pp. 7–43.

Schalken, T. M., 'Rechtshandhaving en het nieuwe premiejagen', *DD* (1992), 543–6.

Schmid, N., 'Das neue Einziehungsrecht nach StGB Art.58ff.', *RPS* (1995), 321–68.

Schnitzer, A. F., *Handbuch des internationalen Privatrecht*, Basle: Verlag für Recht und Gesellschaft, 1950.

Schroth, P. W., 'Bank Confidentiality and the War on Money Laundering in the United States', in *Blanchiment d'argent et secret bancaire*, Rapport général du XIVe Congrès international de droit comparé, Bernasconi, P., The Hague: Kluwer Law International, 1996, pp. 283–308.

Schultz, H., 'Remarques sur l'élément moral dans l'Avant-projet de Code pénal', *Ann.Dr.Louv.* (1986), 131–45.

'Practical Problems arising from Treaties on Mutual Legal Assistance between Continental and Common Law States: The Example of Switzerland and the United States of America', in *Principles and Procedures For A Transnational Criminal Law*, Eser, A. and Lagodny, O., Freiburg: Max-Planck Institut, 1992, pp. 311–16.

Schutte, J., *Ter vergroting van de afpakkans, een inleiding op de ontwikkeling van de interstatelijke samenwerking gericht op het ontnemen van wederrechtelijk verkregen voordeel*, Arnhem: Gouda Quint, 1990.

Schutte, J. J. E., 'Het wetsvoorstel inzake ontneming van wederrechtelijk verkregen voordeel', in *Hercodificatie Wetboek van Strafvordering.*, Doorenbos, D. R. and Verweij, R. J., Nijmegen: Ars Aequi Libri, 1991, 162–73.

'Strafrecht in Europees verband', *Justitiële Verkenningen* (1990, No.9), 8–17.

'La coopération administrative', in *Actes du colloque organisé par l'ARPE à l'Abbaye de Royaumont*, Economica, 1993, 194–210.

Seidl-Hohenfeldern, I., *Völkerrecht*, Keulen, Carl Heymanns Verlag, 1975.

Shaw, J., 'The Use of Information in Competition Proceedings', *ELR* (1993), 154–9.

Shaw, M., *International Law*, Cambridge University Press, 1997.

Sherman, T., 'International Efforts to Combat Money Laundering: the Role of the Financial Action Task Force', in *Money Laundering*, The David Hume Institute, Edinburgh University Press, 1993, pp. 12–33.

Smid, A. C. H., 'Ervaringen vanuit politie en justitie met het meldpunt MOT', in *Maatregelen tegen witwassen in het koninkrijk*, Corstens, G. J. M., Joubert, E. J., Kortmann, S. C. J. J., Arnhem: Gouda Quint, 1995, pp. 185–200.

Smith, G. W., 'Competition in the European Financial Services Industry: The Free

Movement of Capital versus the Regulation of Money Laundering',
    UPa.JInt.Bus.L (1992), 101–40.
Smith, L., '*In Rem* Forfeiture Proceedings and Extra-territorial Jurisdiction', *ICLQ*
    (1996), 902–9.
Snider, W. J., 'International Co-operation in the Forfeiture of Illegal Drug
    Proceeds', *Criminal Law Forum* (1995), 377–89.
Spaulding, K. R., '"Hit Them Where It Hurts": RICO Criminal Forfeitures and
    White Collar Crime', *JCr.L& Crim.* (1989), 197–292.
Spielmann, D., 'La confiscation en droit luxembourgeois à l'aube de la réforme
    du Code pénal', *Ann.Dr.Louv.* (1995), 201–25.
Spinellis, D. D., 'Securing Evidence Abroad – A European Perspective', in
    International Criminal Law, Volume 2: Procedure, Bassiouni, M. C., New York:
    Transnational Publishers, 1986, pp. 351–71.
Spreutels, J. P., 'Secret bancaire et droit pénal', *RDP* (1979), 433–49.
Springer, J. P., 'An Overview of International Evidence and Asset Gathering in
    Civil and Criminal Tax Cases', *Geo.Wash.J Int'l L & Econ.* (1988–89), 277–330.
Sproule, D. W. and St.-Denis, P., 'The UN Drug Trafficking Convention: An
    Ambitious Step', in *The Canadian Yearbook of International Law*, Vancouver,
    University of British Columbia Press, 1989, pp. 263–93.
Stahl, M. B., 'Asset Forfeiture, Burdens of Proof and the War on Drugs', *JCr.& Cr.L*
    (1992), 274–337.
Stessens, G., 'Compte-rendu des débats. Questions et reponses', in *La lutte contre la
    fraude-C.E.E. dans la pratique*, Huybrechts, L., Marchandise, Th. and Tulkens, F.,
    Antwerp: Maklu, 1994, pp. 227–34.
    'Corporate Criminal Liability: a Comparative Perspective', *ICLQ* (1994), 493–520.
    'La négligence et les infractions du droit pénal économique: un mal
    nécessaire?', intervention in 'Le défaut de prévoyance à l'épreuve des faits et
    du droit. Droit belge et comparé', *RDP* (1994), 537–40.
    *De nationale en internationale bestrijding van het witwassen. Onderzoek naar een meer
    effectieve bestrijding van de profijtgerichte criminaliteit*, Antwerp: Intersentia,
    1997.
    'Beroepsgeheim versus (economisch-financieel) strafrecht', in *CBR Jaarboek
    1996-97*, Antwerp: Maklu, 1997, pp. 442–4.
    'The Obligation to Produce Documents Versus the Privilege Against Self-
    incrimination: Human Rights Protection Extended Too Far?', *ELR*, Human
    Rights Survey (1997), 47–54.
Stewart, P., 'Internationalising The War on Drugs: The UN Convention Against
    Illicit Traffic in Narcotic Drugs and Psychotropic Substances', *Denv.JInt'l L&
    Pol'y* (1990), 387–404.
Stratenwerth, G., 'Der behördlich erzwungene Verzicht auf das Bankgeheimnis',
    in *Beiträge zum Schweizerischen Bankenrecht*, Von Grafenfried, R., Berne: Verlag
    Stämpfli, 1989, pp. 227–43.
    'Geldwäscherei – ein Lehrstuck der Gesetzgebung', in *Bekämpfung der*

Geldwäscherei. Modellfall Schweiz?, Pieth, M., Basle: Helbing & Lichtenhahn, 1992, pp. 97–122.

Straüli, B., 'Territorialité de l'enquête pénale et garantie d'une activité irréprochable', in *Journée 1995 de droit bancaire et financier*, Thevenoz, L., Berne: Stämpfli + Cie, 1995, pp. 123–37.

Strijards, G. A. M., *Internationaal strafrecht, strafmachtsrecht. Algemeen deel*, Arnhem: Gouda Quint, 1984.

Stultz, E. A., 'Swiss Bank Secrecy and United States Efforts To Obtain Information From Swiss Banks', *Vand.JTransnat.L* (1988), 63–125.

Swart, A. H. J., 'Human Rights and the Abolition of Traditional Principles', in *Principles and Procedures For A Transnational Criminal Law*, Eser, A. and Lagodny, O., Freiburg: Max-Planck Institut, 1992, pp. 505–34.

Swart, A. H. J. and Helder, K., *Nederlands Uitleveringsrecht*, Zwolle: Tjeenk Willink, 1986.

Swart, B., 'Extradition', in *International Criminal Law in The Netherlands*, Swart, B. and Klip, A., Freiburg: Max-Planck Institut, 1997, pp. 85–122.

'General Observations', in *International Criminal Law in the Netherlands*, Swart, B. and Klip, A., Freiburg: Max-Planck Institut, 1997, pp. 1–20.

Taisch, F., 'Swiss Statutes Concerning Money Laundering', *Int'l Law.* (1992), 695–714.

Taymans, A. and Nihoul, P., 'Money Laundering: An Analysis of European and International Legal Instruments', *Bank.Fin.* (1992), 57–66.

Thomas, F., *De Europese rechtshulpverdragen in strafzaken. Ontstaan en evolutie van een Europees strafrechtsbeleid van uitlevering tot overdracht van strafvervolging*, Ghent: 1980.

Thony, J. F., 'Processing Financial Information in Money Laundering Matters: The Financial Intelligence Units', *Eur.JCr., Cr.L & Cr.J* (1996), 257–82.

Todd Jones, C., 'Compulsion Over Comity: The United States' Assault on Foreign Bank Secrecy', *Nw.Jof Int'l Law & Bus.* (1992), 455–507.

Träskman, P. O., 'Should We Take The Condition of Double Criminality Seriously?', in *Double Criminality. Studies in International Criminal Law*, Jareborg, N., Uppsala: Iustus Förlag, 1989, pp. 135–55.

Trechsel, S., *Schweizerisches Strafrecht. Kurzkommentar.*, Zürich: Schulthess Polygraphisher Verlag, 1989.

'The Role of International Organs Controlling Human Rights in the Field of International Co-operation', in *Principles and Procedures for a New Transnational Criminal Law*, Eser, A. and Lagodny, O., Freiburg: Max-Planck Institut, 1992, pp. 633–65.

Van Boxstael, J.-L., 'Le juge et les "biens mal acquis"', *JT* (1998), 96–101.

Vandecasteele, A., 'La reconnaissance et l'exécution des mesures provisoires et conservatoires dans la conservation sur la compétence et l'exécution des décisions en matière civile et commerciale du 27 septembre 1968', *Journal des Tribunaux* (1980), 737–9.

Van den Wyngaert, C., *The Political Offence Exception to Extradition. The Delicate Problem of Balancing the Rights of the Individual and the International Public Order*, Deventer: Kluwer, 1980.

'De toepassing van de strafwet in de ruimte. Enkele beschouwingen' in *Liber Amicorum Frédéric Dumon*, Antwerp: Kluwer Rechtswetenschappen.

'Double Criminality as a Requirement to Jurisdiction', in *Double Criminality. Studies in International Criminal Law*, Jareborg, N., Uppsala: Iustus Förlag, 1989, pp. 43–56.

'Applying the European Convention on Human Rights to Extradition: Opening Pandora's Box', *ICLQ* (1990), 757–79.

'Rethinking the Law of International Criminal Co-operation: The Restrictive Function of International Human Rights Through Individual-Oriented Bars', in *Principles and Procedures for a Transnational Criminal Law*, Eser, A. and Lagodny, O., Freiburg: Max-Planck Institut, 1992, pp. 489–503.

Van den Wyngaert, C. and Stessens, G., 'Mutual Legal Assistance in Criminal Matters in the European Union', in *Changes in Society, Crime and Criminal Justice in Europe, Volume 2: International Organised and Corporate Crime*, Fijnaut, C., Goethals, J., Peters, T. and Walgrave, L., Antwerp: Kluwer, 1995, pp. 137–79.

International Criminal Law. A Collection of International and European Instruments, The Hague: Kluwer Law International, 1996.

Vandeplas, A., 'De verbeurdverkaring van vermogensvoordelen', in *Liber Amicorum Marc Châtel*, 383–406, Antwerp: Kluwer, 1991.

Van der Wilt, H., 'De WOTS jubileert; maar valt er eigenlijk wel wat te vieren?', *DD* (1998), 234–47.

Van Dijk, P., and Van Hoof, G. J. H., *Theory and Practice of the European Convention on Human Rights*, Deventer-Boston: Kluwer, 1990.

Van Duyne, P. C., 'Geld witwassen: omvangschattingen in nevelslierten', in *Misdaadgeld*, Van Duyne, P. C., Reijntjes, J. M. and Schaap, C. D., Arnhem: Gouda Quint, 1993, pp. 13–32.

'Money-Laundering: Pavlov's Dog and Beyond', *The Howard Journal of Criminal Justice* (1998), 359–74.

Van Gerven, W., 'La deuxième directive bancaire et la jurisprudence de la Cour de Justice', *Bank.Fin.* (1991), 39–46.

Van Hecke, G., 'Droit public et conflits de lois', *Travaux.Com.fr.dr.Int.privé* (1983–84), 225–41.

'Confiscation, Expropriation and the Conflict of Laws', *The International Law Quarterly*, 1951, 345–57, reproduced in *Miscellanea Georges Van Hecke*, Antwerp: Kluwer, 1985, pp. 240–1.

Van Hecke, G. and Lenaerts, K., *Internationaal Privaatrecht*, in *APR*, Ghent: Story-Sciëntia, 1989.

Van Houtte, H., 'Internationale forumshopping bij onrechtmatige daad', in *Mélanges Roger.-O. Dalcq. Responabilité et assurances*, Brussels: Larcier, 1994, pp. 575–90.

Van Koppen, P. J., 'Financieel rechercheren in de opsporing', *Justitiële Verkenningen* (1996, No.9), 57–69.

Van Outrive, L., 'De intergouvernementele en communautaire behandeling van drughandel en georganiseerde misdaad in de Europese Gemeenschap', *Pan.* (1992), 590–602.

'La lutte contre le blanchiment de l'argent: un emplâtre sur une jambe de bois?', *Deviance et société* (1995), 371–7.

Van Soest, J. P., 'Europees witwassen', in *Misdaadgeld*, Van Duyne, P. C., Reijntjes, J. M. and Schaap, C. D., Arnhem: Gouda Quint, 1993, pp. 147–57.

Van Strien, A. L. J., 'De rechtsmacht van Nederland ten aanzien van rechtspersonen', in *Grensoverschrijdend strafrecht*, Arnhem: Gouda Quint, 1990, pp. 65–83.

Vasseur, M., 'La loi du 12 juillet 1990 relative à la participation des organismes financiers à la lutte contre le blanchiment de capitaux provenant du trafic des stupéfiants', *Banque et Droit-Numéro spécial* (1990), 23–40.

Velthuyse, H. E. M., 'Money Laundering in The Netherlands', *JIBL* (1994), 370–7.

Verbruggen, F., 'Proceeds-Oriented Criminal Justice in Belgium: Backbone or Wishbone of a Modern Approach to Organised Crime', *Eur. J Cr., Cr.L & Cr.J* (1997), 314–41.

Verhaegen, J., 'L'erreur non invincible de fait et ses effets en droit pénal belge', *RDP* (1989), 17–27.

Verheul, J. P., 'Foreign Export Prohibitions: Cultural Treasures and Minerals', *NILR* (1984), 419–27.

Verstraeten, R. and Dewandeleer, D., 'Witwassen na de Wet van 7 april 1995: kan het nog witter?', *RW* (1995–96), 689–702.

Vervaele, J. A. E., 'La saisie et la confiscation à la suite d'atteintes punissables au droit aux Etats-Unis', *RDP* (1998), 947–1003.

'Les sanctions de confiscation en droit pénal: un intrus issu du droit civil? Une analyse de la jurisprudence de la CEDH et de la signification qu'elle revêt pour le droit (procédural) pénal néerlandais', *Rev.sc.crim.*, (1998), 39–56.

Vlas, P., *Rechtspersonen in het internationaal privaatrecht*, Deventer: Kluwer, 1982.

Vogel, J., 'Geldwäsche – ein europaweit harmonisierter Straftatbestand?', *Z.St.W.* (1997), 342–7.

Vogelweith, A. and Vaudano, M., *Mains propres, Mains liées. France-Italie: la leçon des affaires*, Paris: Austral, 1995.

Vranken, J. B. M., 'Het professionele (functionele) verschoningsrecht', in *Handelingen Nederlandse Juristenvereniging* (1986), Zwolle: Tjeenk Willink, 1–133.

Wedgwood, R., 'International Decisions. US v. Verdugo-Urquidez', *AJIL* (1990), 747–54.

Wilkitzki, P., 'Development of an Effective International Crime and Justice Programme – A European View', in *Principles and Procedures For A Transnational Criminal Law*, Eser, A. and Lagodny, O., Freiburg: Max-Planck Institut, 1992, pp. 267–91.

Williams, S. A., 'The Double Criminality Rule Revisited', *Israel Law Review* (1993), 297–309.

Wolswijk, H. D., *Locus delicti en rechtsmacht*, Deventer: Gouda Quint, 1998.

Wöretshofer, J., ' "Pluk ze" – Nieuwe mogelijkheden tot ontneming van crimineel vermogen', in *Misdaadgeld*, Van Duyne, P. C., Reijntjes, J. M. and Schaap, C. D., Arnhem: Gouda Quint, 1993, pp. 33–62.

X., 'IBA Adopts Anti-Laundering Resolution', *Int'l Enf. LR* (1996), 45–6.

X., 'Two US Interior Designers Convicted of Laundering for Cali Cartel Member', *Int'l. Enf. LR* (1998), 93–4.

X., 'OAS Strengthens Anti-Money Laundering Efforts', *Int'l. L Enf. R* (1998), 260–4.

X., 'Identificatieplicht', *NJB* (1987), 836–7.

Young, O. R., 'International Regimes: Problems of Concept Formation', *World Politics* (1980), pp. 331–56.

Zagaris, B., 'Dollar Diplomacy: International Enforcement of Money Movement and Related Matters – a United States Perspective', *Geo.Wash.JInt'l L & Econ.* (1988–89), 465–552.

'Developments in International Judicial Assistance and Related Matters', *Denv.JInt'l L& Pol'y* (1990), 339–86.

'US Enacts Anti-Money Laundering Act', *International Enforcement Law Reporter* (1998), 485–87.

'Proposed US Know Your Customer Rule Will Formalise Internal Control Procedures', *International Enforcement Law Reporter* (1998), 488–91.

Zagaris, B. and McDonald, S. B., 'Financial Fraud and Technology: the Perils of an Instantaneous Economy', *Geo.Wash.JInt'l L & Ec.* (1992), 61–107.

Zagaris, B. and Kingma, E., 'Asset Forfeiture Under International and Foreign Law: An Emerging Regime', *Emory Int'l L.Rev.* (1991), 445–513.

Ziegler, J., *La suisse lave plus blanc*, Paris: Ed. Du Seuil, 1990.

Zuberbühler, D., 'Banken als Hilfspolizisten zur Verhinderung der Geldwäscherei? Sicht eines Bankaufsehers', in *Bekämpfung der Geldwäscherei. Modellfall Schweiz?*, Pieth, M., Basle: Helbing & Lichtenhahn, 1992, pp. 29–66.

Zuberbühler, P., 'Das Verhaltnis zwischen der Bankenaufsicht, insbesondere der Überwachung der einwandfreien Geschäftätigkeit und der neuen Sorgfaltspflichtvereinbarung der Banken', *Wirtschaft und Recht* (1987), 167–97.

Zulauf, U., 'Rechtshilfe – Amtshilfe', *RSDA* (1995), 50–61.

Official reports

European Union

First Commission's report on the implementation of the Money Laundering Directive (91/308/91/EEC) to be submitted to the European Parliament and to the Council, Luxembourg: Office for Official Publications of the European Communities, 1998, COM(1995) 54 final.

Second Commission's report to the European Parliament and to the Council on the implementation of the Money Laundering Directive, Luxembourg: Office for Official Publications of the European Communities, 1998, COM(1998) 401 final.

European Commission, *Proposal for a European Parliament and council Directive amending Council Directive 91/308/EEC of 10 June 1991 on the Prevention of the use of the financial system for the Purpose of Money Laundering*, Brussels, 14.7.1999, COM(1999) 352 final, 99/152 (COD).

European Committee on Crime Problems, *The European conventions on mutual assistance in criminal matters seen as an instrument of a common criminal policy*, Strasbourg, 1971.

European Committee on Crime Problems, *Extra-territorial criminal jurisdiction*, Strasbourg, 1990.

European Parliament, Resolution of 9 March 1999 on the 'Second Commission Report to the European Parliament and the Council on the implementation of the Money Laundering Directive'.

Action plan to combat organised crime, OJ No. C 251, 15.08.1997, p. 1.

Draft Report of the informal Money Laundering Experts Group, 12706/98, CRIMORG 173, Brussels, 6 November 1998.

EFTA Surveillance Authority, *Report of the EFTA Surveillance Authority on the Implementation of the Money Laundering Directive by Iceland, Liechtenstein and Norway*, Brussels, 4 November 1998.

Financial Action Task Force (FATF): http://www.oecd.int/fatf/

First Report of the Financial Action Task Force on Money Laundering, containing 40 recommendations (1990) (FATF-I).

Second Report of the Financial Action Task Force on Money Laundering (1991) (FATF-II).

Third Report of the Financial Action Task Force on Money Laundering (1992) (FATF-III).

Fourth Report of the Financial Action Task Force on Money Laundering (1993) (FATF-IV).

Fifth Report of the Financial Action Task Force on Money Laundering (1994) (FATF-V).

Sixth Report of the Financial Action Task Force on Money Laundering (1995) (FATF-VI).

Seventh Report of the Financial Action Task Force on Money Laundering (1996) (FATF-VII).

Eighth Report of the Financial Action Task Force on Money Laundering (1997) (FATF-VIII).

Ninth Report of the Financial Action Task Force on Money Laundering (1998) (FATF-IX).

Tenth Report of the Financial Action Task Force on Money Laundering (1999) (FATF-IX).

Other reports

Beare, M. E. and Schneider, S., *Tracing illicit funds: money laundering in Canada*, Ottawa, Solicitor General Canada, 1990.

Cel voor financiële informatieverwerking:
Activiteitenverslag 1993/1994, Brussels.

2e Activiteitenverslag 1994/1995, Brussels.

3e Activiteitenverslag 1995/1996, Brussels.

4e Activiteitenverslag 1996/1997, Brussels.

5e Activiteitenverslag 1997/1998, Brussels.

Centrale Dienst ter bestrijding van de georganiseerde financiële en economische delinquentie, *2e Activiteitenverslag Jaren 1994–96*, Brussels, 1997.

KPMG, Dutch Ministry of Justice, *Feasibility study for a potential computerised system concerning money laundering*, 1998.

Laudati, L. L., *Study of exchange of confidential information agreements and treaties between the US and member states of the EU in areas of securities, criminal, tax and customs*, Brussels: European Commission (DG IV Competition) and European University Institute, 1996.

President's Commission on Organised Crime, *The cash connection: organized crime, financial institutions and money laundering*, Washington, DC, 1985.

Quirk, P. J., *Macroeconomic implications of money laundering*, IMF Working Paper No. 96/66.

Report drawn up by the Committee of Enquiry on the spread of organised crime linked to drugs trafficking in the Member States of the European Community. Rapporteur: Mr Patrick Cooney, A3–0358/91.

Report of the Caribbean Drug Money Laundering Conference, 1990 reprinted at Gilmore, W. C., *International Efforts to Combat Money Laundering*, Cambridge: Grotius Publications Ltd., 1992, p. 27.

Tanzi, V., *Money laundering and the international financial system*, IMF Working Paper No. 96/55.

Terlouw, G. J. and Aron, U., *Twee jaar MOT. Een evaluatie van de uitvoering van de Wet melding ongebruikelijke transacties*, WODC, Gouda Quint, 1996.

United Nations, *1987 United Nations International Conference on Drug Abuse and Illicit Trafficking: Comprehensive Outline of Future Activities in Drug Abuse Control*, reprinted at Gilmore, W., *International Efforts To Combat Money Laundering*, Cambridge: Grotius Publications Limited, 1992, p. 57.

United Nations, *Official Records of the United Nations Conference for the Adoption of a Convention against Illicit Traffic in Narcotic Drugs and Psychotropic Substances*, Volume II, E/CONF.82/16/Add.1.

United Nations Economic and Social Council, Commission on Crime Prevention and Criminal Justice, *Review of Priority Themes, Control of Proceeds of Crime–Report of the Secretary-General*, Vienna: 13–23 April 1993, E/CN.15/1993.

United Nations Office for Drug Control and Crime Prevention, *Financial Havens, Banking Secrecy and Money Laundering* (New York: United Nations, 1998).

United Nations Political Declaration and Action Plan against Money Laundering, adopted at the Twentieth Special Session of the United Nations General Assembly devoted to 'countering the world drug problem together', New York, 10 June 1998.

US General Accounting Office, *Money Laundering. A Framework for Understanding US*

Efforts Overseas, Report to the Ranking Minority Member, Committee on Banking and Financial Services, House of Representatives, GAO/GGD-96-106, Washington D.C., 1996.

US General Accounting Office, *Money Laundering. Regulatory Oversight of Offshore Private Banking Activities*, Report to the Chairman, Sub-committee on General Oversight and Investigations, Committee on Banking and Financial Services, House of Representatives, GAO/GGD-98-154, Washington DC, June 1998.

US Delegation, *Report of the United States Delegation to the United Nations Conference for the adoption of a Convention Against Illicit Traffic in Narcotic Drugs and Psychotropic Substances*, reproduced in Gilmore, W. C., *International Efforts to Combat Money Laundering*, Cambridge: Grotius Publications Ltd., 1992, pp. 98–138.

Index

5227083R00291

Printed in Germany
by Amazon Distribution
GmbH, Leipzig